For Sylvia

Contents

Acknowledgements

While writing this book I have been generously assisted by institutions, friends, and colleagues.

By electing me to a two-year Research Readership, which relieved me of teaching, the British Academy made the initial research on the Wittgenstein manuscripts easier and more efficient than it would otherwise have been. I am grateful to my college, St John's, for the many facilities it offers to its Fellows. Its support for research and the pursuit of scholarship is heart-warming. I am indebted to the Bodleian Library, in particular to the staff of the Western Manuscript Department, for many services. The publishing team at Basil Blackwell Ltd, especially Mr S. Chambers and Mr A. McNeillie, have been most helpful in planning and executing this difficult publishing project. As in the past, so too now, it has been a pleasure to work with them in close cooperation. I am most grateful to Miss Jean van Altena for the excellence of her copy-editing.

Professor N. Malcolm, Dr S. Mulhall, Professor H. Philipse, Professor J. Raz, Mr B. Rundle, Professor S. Shanker, Mr T. Spitzley, and Professor T. Taylor kindly read and commented on various drafts of essays or exegesis. Their criticisms, queries, and suggestions were of great assistance. I am especially indebted to Dr H. J. Glock and to Dr J. Hyman, whose comments on essays and exegesis alike were invaluable. Dr Glock and Mr Spitzley kindly checked my German transcriptions and translations. Participants in the university seminars which I have given together with Dr G. P. Baker over the past three years have contributed greatly to the clarification of my thoughts. Their questions were challenging and a stimulus to further efforts. I am most grateful to them all, but especially to Dr O. Hanfling, who both curbed some of my excesses and spurred me on to improve my arguments.

For various reasons it was not feasible for Dr Baker to join me in writing this third volume of Analytical Commentary. However, despite occasional disagreement in interpretation and deeper disagreement over nuance (and it is the chiaroscuro that finally makes the sketch), he read the whole manuscript and joined me in giving the university seminars. His painstaking and helpful criticisms as well as his constructive suggestions saved me from error again and again.

Finally, I am, as before, indebted to the Wittgenstein executors for permission to quote from the unpublished *Nachlass*. Professor G. H. von Wright has, as always, been unstintingly generous in putting at my disposal the results of his extensive bibliographical research on the *Nachlass*.

P.M.S.H.
St John's College, Oxford
1989

Thoughts reduced to paper are generally nothing
more than the footprints of a man walking in
the sand. It is true that we see the path he
has taken; but to know what he saw on the way,
we must use our own eyes.

Schopenhauer

Preface

The first volume of this Analytical Commentary was begun in 1976. Little did I then dream that a decade later I should still be struggling through the thousands of pages of the *Nachlass,* attempting to piece together a surveyable representation of the most fascinating array of philosophical arguments of the twentieth century. The task proved far more difficult and controversial, and certainly involved much greater labour, than originally envisaged. With hindsight, this is hardly surprising. For on every major issue about which he wrote, Wittgenstein undermined the fundamental presuppositions of the debate. The landscape he traversed is familiar; but the routes he took were always new, and his footsteps are not easy to follow. New solutions to received questions are difficult enough to come to terms with. New questions regarding well-worn subjects are difficult to put into fruitful perspective. But a challenge to the very presuppositions of the questions, old and new, which characterize philosophical reflection is far harder to understand and accommodate. There is no short-cut to Wittgenstein's viewpoint: one must follow his trail and look afresh at each landmark. The *Philosophical Investigations* does not aim to add a fresh theory—about meaning and understanding, about necessity or the nature of the mind—to the array of established ones. Nor is its purpose to examine opposing positions in centuries-old debates—such as realism versus nominalism, mentalism versus behavioursim, or Platonism versus formalism—in order to side with those supported by superior arguments. Its goal is to dissolve the questions themselves by showing that they rest upon illegitimate presuppositions and misguided expectations. What is legitimate about philosophical questions can be resolved by a careful description of the uses of words; the rest is illusion. As Wittgenstein observed in one of his more startling remarks, 'In philosophy, all that isn't gas is grammar' (LWL 112).

Wittgenstein: Understanding and Meaning (Volume 1 of this Analytical Commentary) laid the groundwork for understanding the trajectory of his thought. It gave due prominence to the Augustinian picture of language as an *Urbild* informing a multitude of philosophical theories about the nature of language, all of which Wittgenstein aimed to undermine. Misconceptions about the essential nature of words as names and of sentences as descriptions stand in the way of an unprejudiced view of the manifold techniques of using words and of the diverse functions of sentences in the stream of life. These misconceptions give rise to philosophical mythologies about 'the name-relation', logically proper names, sentence-radicals and semantic-mood operators, determinacy of sense, and 'the general propositional form'. They generate misguided pictures of the relationship between language and reality, and of ostensive definition as forging a connection between the two. This in turn contributes to the pervasive illusion that grammar is answerable to reality or that it reflects, and must reflect, the essential structure of the world. Against the background of Wittgenstein's demythologizing, his radical conception of philosopy was displayed. He held philosopy to be therapeutic, not theoretical. It destroys idols, but does not replace them. It is a quest for a surview of grammar, not for an armchair preview of future science. Achievement in philosophy consists in dissolution of philosophical questions, not in acquisition of new information that provides answers to them. Understanding is indeed attained; but it consists in arriving at a clear vision of what is known and familiar, rather than in grasping the articulations of a new theory about the nature of things. Theory construction lies within the province of science, and philosopy—in its questions, methods, and results—is wholly distinct from science.

Once this had been clarified, it was possible to put Wittgenstein's discussion of understanding in the right perspective. Meaning, explanation of what something means, and understanding constitute a triad of key concepts in philosophical investigations into language and the nature of linguistic representation. Reversing the direction of fit between these concepts that is presupposed by the prevailing philosophical tradition, Wittgenstein elaborated the consequences of the grammatical propositions that meaning is what is given by an explanation of meaning, and that it is what is understood when the meaning of an utterance is understood. Understanding (which is akin to an ability rather than a mental state) and the criteria of understanding assume a dominant role in his descriptions of the network of grammar in this domain. Clarification of the internal relations between meaning, understanding, and explanation also illuminates their complex connections with truth, evidence, justification, definition, rules of use, grammatical proposition, and so forth.

Wittgenstein: Rules, Grammar and Necessity, Volume 2 of the Analytical Commentary, constituted an alteration to the original plans. The complexities of §§185–242 of the *Investigations* needed very detailed analysis, the extensive controversies over the interpretation of Wittgenstein's intentions required the presentation of much background material from the *Nachlass,* and the generally ill-understood consequences of his account of grammar and rule-following demanded at least a fragmentary investigation of his philosophy of logic and mathematics. Hence the whole of Volume 2 was dedicated to the clarification of Wittgenstein's discussion of rules, acting in accord with a rule, and following a rule. This led to an examination of his discussion of the autonomy of grammar and of his remarks on the nature of necessity in the domains of logic, mathematics, and metaphysics.

The present volume, *Wittgenstein: Meaning and Mind,* takes the Analytical Commentary forward from §243 to §427. These sections are no less controversial than the preceding ones. To be sure, the rocky ground already traversed should have taught one much. But as one plunges into the tropical undergrowth of the great private language arguments, it is all too easy to lose one's bearings. The path is overgrown with prevalent misinterpretations, and dark distorting shadows are cast across it by our disposition to extract theories from Wittgenstein's descriptions. The position of these arguments in the overall structure of the book needs to be clarified. Why, at this particular point, is the question of whether a private language is possible raised? To what extent are the previous remarks presupposed? Is Wittgenstein simply moving on to yet another of the 'great questions of philosophy', or is there a natural progression from the preceding argument? Why is the discussion of a private language followed by an investigation of thinking and imagining—and why is there no discussion of remembering and other faculties of the mind?

Not only is the rationale of the locus of these sections in the grand strategy controversial, but the very subject of debate in §§243ff. is disputed. What is a 'private' language? And why should anyone be interested in whether there could be a language which, unlike ordinary languages, only its speaker can, logically, understand? What is Wittgenstein's purpose? Is he trying to demonstrate the essential *social* nature of language, to show that it is an *a priori* truth that only a social creature can speak or use symbols? Is he aiming to refute a *recherché* form of scepticism about knowing what one means by one's words? Or is his target quite different?

If the subject is disputed, so too is the conclusion. Is he arguing that there can be no such thing as a 'private' ostensive definition, or rather that such a mode of assigning meaning to an expression is possible only within the context of mastery of a shared, public, language? How can a philosopher who repudiates theses and proofs in philosophy go on to try to *prove* that there cannot be a private language? Or was he not trying to prove this at all?

The tactical moves are equally subject to divergent interpretation. Does Wittgenstein implicitly rely on a verification principle? Is his denial of the possibility of a private language dependent on worries about the reliability of memory? And if there is such a philosophical, as opposed to practical, worry, how could it possibly disappear in company? It is evident that he denies that sensations are 'inner objects', but does he contend instead that they are nothing at all? He explicitly denied that he was propounding any form of behaviourism, but many have argued that his philosophy of psychology is a version of logical behaviourism. This too needs elucidation.

If the path through this terrain is shrouded in gloom, its direction is no less difficult to discern. It is clear that Wittgenstein thought that the matter of a private language bears directly on solipsism and idealism. But why is this never explicitly shown? Is the argument meant to be an implicit refutation of idealism? But is the issue not too important for such cursory treatment? Or are these venerable philosophical doctrines merely ancient idols in the jungle which are briefly illuminated as he passes by, intent upon an altogether different goal? Was Wittgenstein trying to re-orient completely our picture of the mind, so that *everything* would appear in a new light? Certainly the relation between the 'inner' and the 'outer' is as philosophically problematic, especially when viewed from the perspective of the Augustinian picture of language, as the relation between proof and truth in mathematics. Wittgenstein's treatment of the latter theme involved a radical break with all traditional approaches. It is not unreasonable to expect his discussion of the former to involve an equally startling repudiation of the very presuppositions of the debates between idealism and realism, dualism and monism, mentalism and behaviourism. Surely we should take seriously his avowal that he was destroying 'houses of cards' and 'clearing up the ground of language on which they stand' (PI §118).

The thirteen essays in this volume survey the central issues in §§243 – 427. As in Volume 1, each essay is as self-contained as possible. This goal could be achieved only at the cost of some repetition. As Wittgenstein travels 'over a wide field of thought criss-cross in every direction' (Preface, p. ix), the same landmarks are re-encountered, but always from a different direction. Each essay in this volume endeavours to represent a part of the web of the grammar of psychological concepts as he saw it. The same nodes often recur in different essays, but in each case their links with different strands are in view. The order of the essays has been determined by the sequence of remarks in the text. However the essay on criteria found no natural location, since there is no extended discussion of the subject in the *Investigations*. It has been placed, *faute de mieux,* at the end of the book, and redeems the promissory note issued in Volume 1.

The exegesis follows the pattern established by the previous volumes. Again, there is a deliberate, limited degree of overlap between exegesis and essays. This Analytical Commentary is not designed to be read through at successive sittings. It has been assumed that those who wish to study Wittgenstein's text with the aid of the exegesis will not wish to be paging back and forth between exegetical material and essays. This consideration weighed all the more in view of the fact that the forthcoming paperback edition, which will be economically accessible to students, will be published in two separate volumes, one of essays, one of exegesis (as with Volume 1). Occasional essential cross-reference, however, has been unavoidable (for example, between the discussion of private ownership of experience in 'Privacy', §2, and Exg. §253). In general the exegesis aims to elucidate Wittgenstein's individual remarks and their role in his progressive argument, and the complementary essays aim to give a surveyable representation of his ideas on a given subject. Since many of the remarks in this part of the *Investigations* have been the source of heated interpretative controversy, extensive material from the *Nachlass* has sometimes been presented. Although a particular reading has typically been favoured, it seemed desirable, in cases where substantially different interpretations are reasonable, to display all the relevant evidence.

The arguments of §§243 – 427 do not constitute the 'foundations' of, let alone the whole of, Wittgenstein's philosophy of mind. But they provide essential methodical guidelines and fundamental insights. They are the route to 'the correct logical point of view'—but to achieve it, one must follow the arduous trail he blazed. In the following pages I have tried to plot it as best I could. Doubtless I have erred in places, but I hope that I have captured the direction of his thought. If he is right, then the mainstream of philosophical psychology, past and present, is misguided—flowing from misconceived questions to quagmires of confused pseudo-theories. Of course, his ideas run counter to the spirit of the age, and today the will to illusion is stronger than ever. Only when philosophers wish to be cured of the sicknesses of the understanding that beset them, will they be in a position to take up the legacy of Wittgenstein.

Abbreviations

1. *Published works*

The following abbreviations are used to refer to Wittgenstein's published works, listed in chronological order (where possible; some works straddle many years). The list includes derivative primary sources and lecture notes taken by others.

NB   *Notebooks 1914–16,* ed. G. H. von Wright and G. E. M. Anscombe, tr. G. E. M. Anscombe (Blackwell, Oxford, 1961).

TLP   *Tractatus Logico-Philosophicus,* tr. D. F. Pears and B. F. McGuinness (Routledge and Kegan Paul, London, 1961).

RLF   'Some Remarks on Logical Form', *Proceedings of the Aristotelian Society,* suppl. vol. ix (1929), pp. 162–71.

WWK   *Ludwig Wittgenstein und der Wiener Kreis,* shorthand notes recorded by F. Waismann, ed. B. F. McGuinness (Blackwell, Oxford, 1967). The English translation, *Wittgenstein and the Vienna Circle* (Blackwell, Oxford, 1979), matches the pagination of the original edition.

PR   *Philosophical Remarks,* ed. R. Rhees, tr. R. Hargreaves and R. White (Blackwell, Oxford, 1975).

M   'Wittgenstein's Lectures in 1930–33', in G. E. Moore, *Philosophical Papers* (Allen and Unwin, London, 1959).

LWL   *Wittgenstein's Lectures, Cambridge 1930–32, from the notes of John King and Desmond Lee,* ed. Desmond Lee (Blackwell, Oxford, 1980).

PG   *Philosophical Grammar,* ed. R. Rhees, tr. A. J. P. Kenny (Blackwell, Oxford, 1974).

GB   'Remarks on Frazer's "Golden Bough" ', tr. J. Beversluis, repr. in C. G. Luckhardt (ed.), *Wittgenstein: Sources and Perspectives* (Cornell University Press, Ithaca, 1979), pp. 61–81.

AWL   *Wittgenstein's Lectures, Cambridge 1932–35, from the notes of Alice Ambrose and Margaret MacDonald,* ed. Alice Ambrose (Blackwell, Oxford, 1979).

BB   *The Blue and Brown Books* (Blackwell, Oxford, 1958).

LPE 'Wittgenstein's Notes for Lectures on "Private Experience" and "Sense Data" ', ed. R. Rhees, *Philosophical Review*, 77 (1968), pp. 275–320.

LSD 'The Language of Sense Data and Private Experience' (Notes taken by R. Rhees of Wittgenstein's lectures, 1936), *Philosophical Investigations*, 7 (1984), pp. 1–45, 101–40.

RFM *Remarks on the Foundations of Mathematics,* ed. G. H. von Wright, R. Rhees, G. E. M. Anscombe, revised edition (Blackwell, Oxford, 1978).

LA *Lectures and Conversations on Aesthetics, Psychology and Religious Beliefs,* ed. C. Barrett (Blackwell, Oxford, 1970).

LFM *Wittgenstein's Lectures on the Foundations of Mathematics, Cambridge 1939,* ed. C. Diamond (Harvester Press, Sussex, 1976).

PI *Philosophical Investigations,* ed. G. E. M. Anscombe and R. Rhees, tr. G. E. M. Anscombe, 2nd edition (Blackwell, Oxford, 1958).

Z *Zettel,* ed. G. E. M. Anscombe and G. H. von Wright, tr. G. E. M. Anscombe (Blackwell, Oxford, 1967).

RPP I *Remarks on the Philosophy of Psychology*, Volume I, ed. G. E. M. Anscombe and G. H. von Wright, tr. G. E. M. Anscombe (Blackwell, Oxford, 1980).

RPP II *Remarks on the Philosophy of Psychology*, Volume II, ed. G. H. von Wright and H. Nyman, tr. C. G. Luckhardt and M. A. E. Aue (Blackwell, Oxford, 1980).

LPP *Wittgenstein's Lectures on Philosophy of Psychology 1946–7*, notes by P. T. Geach, K. J. Shah, A. C. Jackson, ed. P. T. Geach (Harvester·Wheatsheaf, Hemel Hempstead, 1988).

LW *Last Writings on the Philosophy of Psychology*, Volume I, ed. G. H. von Wright and H. Nyman, tr. C. G. Luckhardt and M. A. E. Aue (Blackwell, Oxford, 1982).

C *On Certainty,* ed. G. E. M. Anscombe and G. H. von Wright, tr. D. Paul and G. E. M. Anscombe (Blackwell, Oxford, 1969).

CV *Culture and Value*, ed. G. H. von Wright in collaboration with H. Nyman, tr. P. Winch (Blackwell, Oxford, 1980).

PLP *The Principles of Linguistic Philosophy*, F. Waismann, ed. R. Harré (Macmillan and St Martin's Press, London and New York, 1965).

R *Ludwig Wittgenstein: Letters to Russell, Keynes and Moore*, ed. G. H. von Wright (Blackwell, Oxford, 1974).

Reference style: all references to *Philosophical Investigations,* Part I are to sections (e.g. PI §1), except those to notes below the line on various pages. References to Part II are to pages (e.g. PI p. 202). References to other printed works are either to numbered remarks (TLP) or to sections signified '§' (Z, RPP, LW); in all other cases references are to pages (e.g. LFM 21 = LFM page 21), or to numbered letters (R).

2. *Nachlass*

All references to unpublished material cited in the von Wright catalogue (G. H. von Wright, *Wittgenstein* (Blackwell, Oxford, 1982), pp. 35ff.) are by MS. or TS. number followed by page number. Wherever possible, the pagination entered in the original document has been used. The Cornell xeroxes in the Bodleian are defective; sometimes a dozen or more pages have been omitted. Consequently, where access to the originals or to complete xeroxes has not been possible, some errors of page reference will unavoidably have occurred. For memorability, the following special abbreviations are used.

Manuscripts
Vol. I   refer to the eighteen large manuscript volumes (= MSS. 105–22)
Vol. II written between 2 February 1929 and 1944. The reference style
etc.   Vol. VI, 241 is to Volume VI, page 241.

Typescripts
BT   The 'Big Typescript' (TS. 213): a rearrangement, with modifications, written additions and deletions, of TS. 211, 1933, vi pp. table of contents, 768 pp. All references are to page numbers. Where the page number is followed by 'v.', this indicates a handwritten addition on the reverse side of the TS. page.
PPI   'Proto-Philosophical Investigations'[1] (TS. 220): a typescript of the first half of the pre-war version of the *Philosophical Investigations* (up to §189 of the final version, but with many differences); 1937 or 1938, 137 pp. The shortened title form 'Proto-Investigations' is used freely. All references are to sections (§).
PPI (I) The so-called Intermediate Version, reconstructed by von Wright; it consists of 300 numbered remarks; 1945, 195 pp. All references are to sections (§).

3. *Abbreviations for works by Frege*

FA   *The Foundations of Arithmetic*, tr. J. L. Austin, 2nd edition (Blackwell, Oxford, 1959).

---

[1]This is not Wittgenstein's title

GA   *Grundgesetze der Arithmetik, begriffsschriftlich abgeleitet*, Band I,
       (Hermann Pohle, Jena, 1893).
PW   *Posthumous Writings*, ed. H. Hermes, F. Kambartel, F. Kaulbach,
       tr. P. Long, R. White (Blackwell, Oxford, 1979).

4. *Abbreviations for works by Russell*

AM   *The Analysis of Mind* (George Allen and Unwin, London, 1921).
LK   *Logic and Knowledge, Essays 1901–1950*, ed. R. C. Marsh (Allen
       and Unwin, London, 1956).

5. *References to previous volumes of this Analytical Commentary*

References to Volume 1 are flagged 'Volume 1' with a page number
referring to the hardback edition. Where necessary the abbreviation MU
(with a page number) is used, referring to the paperback volume of
essays entitled *Wittgenstein: Meaning and Understanding* (Blackwell,
Oxford, 1983). References to Volume 2, *Wittgenstein: Rules, Grammar and
Necessity*, are flagged 'Volume 2'.

Analytical
Commentary

CHAPTER 1

The private language arguments
(§§243 – 315)

INTRODUCTION

§§243 – 315 constitute the eighth 'chapter' of the book. Its point of
departure is a natural query with respect to the conclusion of the
immediately preceding argument, viz. that for a language to be a means
of communication, there must be agreement not only in definitions but
also in judgements. Could there not be a language which was wholly
independent of such interpersonal agreement or even any possibility of
such agreement? Can we not imagine a language the words of which
cannot be explained to other people, although the speaker of such a
language knows perfectly well what they mean? Indeed, on certain
natural philosophical assumptions, is the language each person uses to
talk about his inner experiences not, in some deep and important sense,
such a private language?

Part A (§§243 – 55) opens by clarifying what a 'private' language is
supposed to be — not a contingently private language which no one else
happens to understand, but an essentially private language which it is
logically impossible for another to understand. What the words of such a
language refer to are the speaker's immediate private sensations and
experiences, which only he can know. §244 clarifies what it is for a word
to refer to or name a sensation such as pain. 'S' names a sensation of pain
if the first-person use of 'S' in an utterance replaces the natural behavioural expression of the sensation. This verbal expression of a sensation,
however, is not a description of the behaviour it replaces or of the
sensation itself; for it is incoherent to suppose that one might even want
to insert language (in this case, a description) between pain and its
expression (§245). §§246 – 8 subject the supposition of epistemic privacy
to critical scrutiny. 'Only I can know whether I am in pain' is in one
sense simply wrong, in another nonsense. The only truth here is that it
makes no sense for me to doubt whether I am in pain. The epistemic
privacy of sensations is a grammatical proposition dressed up in the guise

of an epistemic truth. §§249 – 50 can be connected to §246 in as much as they exemplify cases where doubts about the experiences of others based on the possibility of pretence are excluded. They can also be viewed as raising an objection to the argument of §244: if verbal expressions of pain are learnt as replacements for natural pain-behaviour, might the infant's natural pain-behaviour not be mere pretence? The possibility of pretence would cast a cloud of scepticism over judgements of others' experiences, just as the possibility of illusion enshrouds in doubt our knowledge of objects. But one's scruples are groundless. §§251 – 2 pick up the theme of §248, viz. that 'sensations are private' is a grammatical proposition in metaphysical guise — one cannot imagine the opposite, but not because of limitations on one's powers of imagination — rather because there is here nothing to imagine. For the negation of a grammatical proposition is not a description of an impossibility, any more than a grammatical proposition is a description of a (necessary) actuality. §§253 – 5 examine the idea that another person cannot have my pain, but only a similar one. What looks like a metaphysical limitation on sharing or transferring mental objects merely conceals a grammatical confusion. For different people can have the same pain. It appears otherwise only because we misguidedly project the grammar of 'same object' onto 'same pain', and hence misconstrue the criteria of identity for pain. §255 closes this set of remarks with a methodological observation on the therapeutic character of philosophical investigation.

The structure of Part A:

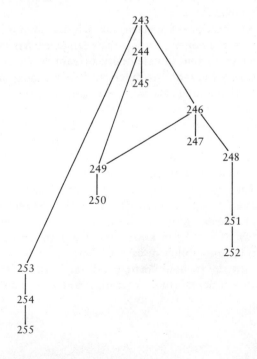

Part B (§§256 – 71) reverts to §243: having clarified 'private owner-ship' and epistemic privacy, W. examines the hypothesis that a 'private' language as envisaged in §243 is intelligible to its alleged speaker. The words for sensations cannot be tied up with the natural expression of sensation, for then the language would not be 'private'. So the speaker must be conceived to *associate* names with sensations and to use them in descriptions (§256). The intelligibility of this conception is the subject of Part B. That such a name of an unexpressed sensation could not be taught is brushed aside as irrelevant, for W. concentrates on the question of what it is to *name* a sensation (§257). Naming, as argued (§§26 – 37), presupposes stage-setting. The moot question is whether the mind can supply the appropriate stage, and whether its furniture can constitute a serviceable set. The example of a private diary (§258) is introduced to demonstrate the unintelligibility of private ostensive definition. For here there would be no distinction between remembering correctly the connection between the sign 'S' and the sensation that defines it, and seeming to remember it. But the rules of a private language cannot be merely impressions of rules, for one cannot determine whether one has what is to be called 'S' by reference to an *apparent* rule relative to which there is no distinction between being right and seeming right (§259). Falling back on the pious hope that one may *believe* that one has reidentified S correctly is useless, since nothing has been fixed to determine what *counts* as S — that was what was intended to be effected by the private ostensive definition (§260).

§261 is a pivotal remark: an ostensive definition, e.g. of 'red', presupposes the grammar of the definiendum, viz. that it is a colour word. Hence a 'private' ostensive definition of 'pain' must presuppose that it is the name of a *sensation*. But 'sensation' is a word in our common (public) language, and sensations have perceptible expression in behav-iour. Hence the private ostensive definition of the word 'S' in the private language cannot be identified as a definition of a sensation-word by invoking the grammar of 'sensation' in the public language to determine the grammatical post at which 'S' is to stand (cf. §257). Nor does it help to reduce one's commitments by saying that 'S' names *something* the private linguist *has*. For these expressions too have a fixed (public) grammar. §§262 – 4 examine the futility of the supposition that one can invent the technique of using 'S' (i.e. what corresponds in the private language to the technique of using sensation-words in our public language) merely by concentrating on one's private experience and undertaking to call it 'S' in the future. The myth behind this misguided thought is the Augustinian picture of language.

§§265 – 9 introduce a mental table (a kind of dictionary that suppos-edly exists only in the mind) that is intended to function as a subjective justification for the use of the words of a private language. This is unintelligible, for it provides no independent justification for the use of a

word, hence no distinction between correct application and an application that only seems correct. §§266 – 8 give three co-ordinate examples
of similarly futile manoeuvres. §269 rounds off this subset of remarks by
reminding us of the criteria for understanding, not understanding, and
thinking one understands an expression. §§270 – 1 introduce a genuine
use for 'S' as a sensation-name in a diary entry, making it clear that the
supposition of the possibility of misidentification of a sensation, which
must arise in a private language, is vacuous in a public one. The 'private
object' is only a free-wheeling cog in the mechanism of a genuine
language.

The structure of Part B:

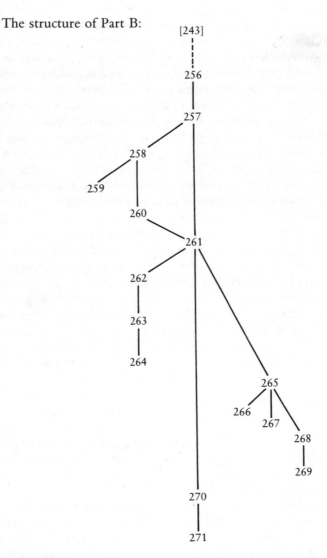

Part C (§§272 – 80) switches from the concept of pain to that of the colour red. When mesmerized by the ideas involved in a 'private' language, philosophers construe the grammar of 'pain' as analogous to the grammar of colour-words such as 'red' — only 'in private'. But it is only natural that they should then construe the grammar of colour-words on the model of the grammar of 'pain' thus misconstrued. The immediate consequence (§272) is that the assumption of an 'inverted spectrum' becomes intelligible, for no one has 'access' to another person's 'private' samples. That in turn suggests, absurdly, that colour-words are ambiguous, signifying now something publicly perceptible, now something private to each perceiver (§273). We are inclined to say that 'red' *refers to* something 'private': this does not clarify matters, but is importantly symptomatic of the confusion under which one labours here (§274), a confusion that besets us only when language 'goes on holiday' (§275). The following two sections focus on a feature of the phenomenology of these philosophical confusions (§§276 – 7), and the next remarks stress the vacuity of one's insistence in this context that one *knows* how a certain colour looks to one (§§278 – 9). The concluding remark (§280) makes it clear that it is an illusion to think that when one imagines something, one's mental image clarifies to oneself, in a unique way inaccessible to others, precisely what one imagines. Similarly, the mental image one might have when one imagines something red cannot serve to inform oneself what one means by 'red'.

The structure of Part C:

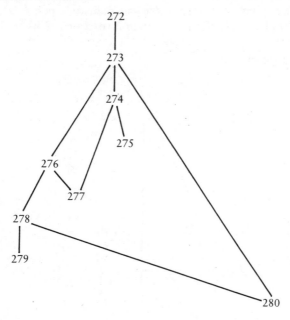

Part D (§§281 – 7) examines the restriction of experiential predicates to human beings and to what behaves like them. W. is not insisting, as a behaviourist might, that there is no pain without pain-behaviour, but rather that it only makes sense to attribute pain to something that can manifest it in behaviour (§281). It is no objection that in fairy-tales inanimate things are said to have pains, for this is essentially a secondary use of 'pain' (§282). One is inclined to think that one acquires the concept of pain by concentrating on one's own pains (i.e. something 'mental' and wholly 'private'), and that one then transfers the idea of pain to external objects (i.e. other living creatures) — although not to stones, etc. The pain then is surely attributed either to the body or to the mind associated with it! §§283 – 7 undermine this thought by focusing on the supposition that it is logically possible that I might turn to stone yet my pain continue, i.e. that 'for me', my pain is independent of my body and my behaviour. It makes no sense to attribute pain to a stone, and it is of no avail to suppose that it is the soul or mind, which the stone has if I turn to stone, that has the pain. For that too makes no sense, because it is senseless to suppose that a stone might 'have' a soul or mind. Grammar restricts the attribution of psychological predicates to what *behaves* in appropriate ways. It is not the body *or* the soul which the body 'has' that is the bearer of pain, but the *living human being* who has a soul. Only of what behaves like a human being can one say that it *has* pains. §§284 – 5 examine the absurdity of attributing pain to the inanimate or dead. The living move, behave, and that is a categorial difference — a case of the transition 'from quantity to quality'. §§286 – 7 argue that it is grammar, not the facts, which precludes ascribing pain to a person's body. But grammar here has facts about our natural reactions as its background.

The structure of Part D:

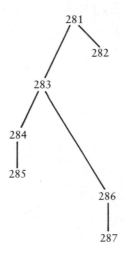

Part E (§§288 – 92) picks up the petrification example of §283 in order to examine afresh avowals (*Äusserungen*) of pain. Following §246, W. repeats that doubt or error about whether one has a pain is senseless; the expression of doubt would be a criterion for not knowing what the word 'pain' means. An avowal of pain is a criterion for the speaker's being in pain, but he avows pain without any criteria. However, if one cuts out the behavioural expression of pain, if one assumes the abrogation of the normal language-game (as in the petrification case), then, *per absurdum*, a criterion of identity for the 'sensation' would be necessary in one's own case, and the possibility of error would exist. §§289 – 90 emphasize the absence of justifying grounds for saying 'I am in pain', clarifying the fact that this is no epistemic *defect*. One is misled here by the assumption that all sentences serve to describe, and also by an unwarranted assumption of the grammatical uniformity of descriptions (§§291 – 2).

The structure of Part E:

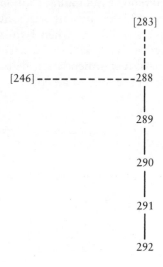

Part F (§§293 – 303) picks up the supposition of §283 that one knows what the word 'pain' means only from one's own case. If so, one must say something similar of others. The example of the beetle in the private box is invoked to show that *if* one construes the grammar of the expression of sensation on the model of name and object (e.g. 'beetle' and the insect named), then the 'object' *would* drop out of consideration as irrelevant to the shared language-game. (But the actual grammar of 'pain' is the grammar of a sensation-word, the characteristic first-person present-tense use of which is a manifestation (*Äusserung*) of a sensation.) §294 explores the claim that the 'private object' cannot even be said to be a something (cf. §261), for 'something' holds a place for a determinate category, which, in the private linguist's case, has not been determined. §295 reverts to the confused claim in §293 that one knows what 'pain' means only from one's own case. This is neither an empirical proposition nor a grammatical one, but one might view it as an allegorical picture. §296 introduces a similarly uninformative proposition, viz. that there is *something* accompanying one's cry of pain. This too could be said to be a pictorial representation of our grammar. §297 gives an analogy for the misconceived 'something' that is held to accompany pain (cf. §§294, 296): the pain one has does not play the role in the language-game that one is inclined to attribute to it, viz. the role of a paradigm or 'picture' of pain. §§298 – 9 emphasize the vacuity of the claim that there is *something* accompanying the cry of pain. §§300 – 302 make clear that the language-game with 'pain' involves no inner paradigm of pain, that to imagine pain is not to conjure up a 'private sample' of pain. One can, of course, imagine someone else's pain, but not on the model of a putative 'private language', for that would require imagining pain one does *not feel* on the model of pain one *does feel*. §303 rounds off the discussion by reverting to the supposition (cf. §246) that I *know* when I am in pain but can only surmise whether another is. This looks like a claim about epistemic possibilities, but is in fact a recommendation that we adopt a different grammar — and we have no reason to accept it.

The structure of part F:

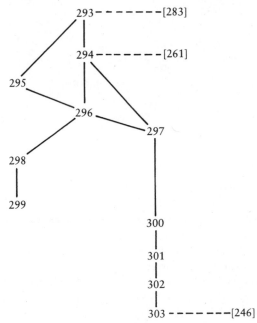

Part G (§§304 – 15) clarifies why W.'s grammatical elucidations do not commit him to a form of behaviourism. Indeed, to the extent that they might appear to do so, to that extent one has misunderstood his remarks. The interlocutor insists on the difference between pain-behaviour without pain and pain-behaviour with pain. W. concedes that there could be no greater difference. But, reverting to §294 and §261, it seems that W. is arguing that the pain is a nothing. But this is an illusion; pain is neither a something nor a nothing. That appears paradoxical only as long as one conceives of the grammar of the expression of pain on the pattern of object and name (cf. §293). One must break with the Augustinian picture of language according to which language has the uniform function of conveying thoughts concerning how things are (§304). The interlocutor insists that inner processes take place, e.g., when remembering. W. replies that he denies nothing other than the misleading picture we associate with the expression 'inner process' (§§305 – 6). It seems that W. is a behaviourist, that he is arguing that everything apart from behaviour is a fiction. But this misconstrues his argument: it is the *grammatical* fiction about 'inner processes' that he denies (§§307 – 8). And his aim is not to deny *facts*, but to show the fly the way out of the (grammatical) fly-bottle (§309).

The interlocutor reverts to his (correct) point that there is a difference between pain-behaviour with and without pain: do not our attitudes to the sufferer *show* that in the former cases we *believe* that there is something behind the manifestations of pain (§310)? No; our attitudes prove that we commiserate with the sufferer's suffering, believe that he is in pain — not that we believe a misguided philosophical thesis according to which pain is a 'private object' hidden behind pain-behaviour. The final remarks (§§311 – 15) demolish a last objection: is not the difference between pain-behaviour with pain and pain-behaviour without pain precisely one which a person can privately exhibit to himself? This too is an illusion. One can imagine pain, but to imagine pain is not to give oneself a private exhibition of pain (§§311 – 12). One can exhibit pain, but not 'privately' (§313). It is a misunderstanding to believe that the philosophical problems concerning psychological concepts can be clarified by concentrating upon one's experiences (§314), and a confusion to think that a person cannot master the use of a psychological concept, e.g. pain, unless he has experienced pain (§315).

The structure of Part G:

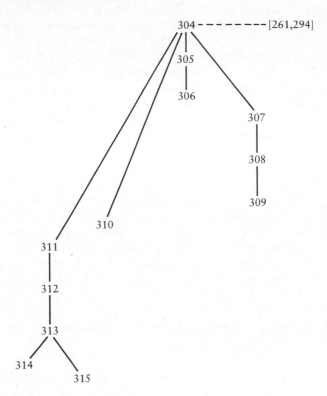

Correlations

The early version of the *Investigations*, which, as in previous volumes is referred to as the 'Proto-Philosophical Investigations' (PPI), is TS. 220, compiled in 1937 or 1938 on the basis of the now lost MS. 142. It corresponds roughly to §§1 – 188 of the final version, and was continued in TS. 221 into a version of Part I of the *Remarks on the Foundations of Mathematics*. In 1944 and early 1945, Wittgenstein compiled the so-called Intermediate Version (*Mittelversion*) of the *Investigations* (PPI(I)), which has been reconstructed by von Wright. This modified and extended the early version. It consists of 300 numbered remarks, the last of which corresponds to *Investigations* §421. Pages 1 – 143 of the Intermediate Version are identical with the pages of the final typescript, save for MS. modifications. Pages 144 – 91 (where the Intermediate Version ends) are derived from a preliminary typescript (TS. 241) compiled in 1944 or early 1945. The immediate MS. source of these remarks is the first 89 pages of MS. 129, begun 17 August 1944.

From Easter 1945 Wittgenstein worked on yet a further revision of his material. He compiled the typescript known as *Bemerkungen I*, consisting of 698 remarks derived primarily from Manuscript Volumes X – XII (MSS. 114 – 16) and MSS. 129 – 30. Four hundred of these remarks were selected for inclusion in the final typescript, some dovetailed into the Intermediate Version, and the majority contributing to its extension from §422 – §691.

The following list correlates remarks on the *Investigations* with, in the first instance, the numbered remarks of the Intermediate Version (PPI(I)). The 'gaps' in the column indicate remarks inserted (largely) from *Bemerkungen I* in the course of reworking PPI(I). The next column gives the immediate MS. source of PPI(I), viz. MS. 129. The remaining columns give more remote MS. sources that were copied into MS. 129, as well as MS. sources, immediate and remote, of remarks in *Bemerkungen I* which do not occur in PPI(I).

PI§	PPI(I)§	MS. 129	MS. 124	MS. 165	Vol. XII	Others
243	213	36 – 7	213 – 14[1] 222[2]			MS. 180(a), 13 – 14[1], 20 – 1[2]
244	214	38	222 – 4			MS. 180(a), 21 – 2
245			270			
246	215	39 – 40	224 – 5			MS. 180(a), 22 – 4
247		152				MS. 128, 16
248					179	Vol. XVI, 241
249					336[3]	Vol. XV, 84[4]
250		111	269	66		
251					75	Vol. X, 121 – 2
252					78	
253	216	40 – 1				
254	217	41 – 2				
255					323	
256	218(a)	42 – 3	225 – 6			MS. 180(a), 24 – 5
257						Vol. XI, 91; BT 209v.
258	218(b)	43 – 4	226			MS. 180(a), 25 – 7; MS. 179, 47; Vol. XV, 256 – 9
259	218.1[5]	24				MS. 163, 136
260	219[6]	44 – 5	227[7]	225[8]		
261	220	45 – 6	227	230, 42[9]		
262					338	
263					251	
264					118	
265					249 – 50	Vol. XVI, 125 – 6, 148 – 9
266					337	
267					250 – 1	Vol. XVI, 150
268					251 – 2	
269						MS. 130, 15
270	221	46 – 7	282 – 3	145 – 8 226 – 30		
271	222	48	271			MS. 179, 36
272	224	51	291	179 – 80		
273	225	50 – 1	290 – 1	178 – 9		
274	226	52 – 3	291 – 2	43 – 4, 180 – 1		
275	227	51 – 2	292	181 – 2		

PI§	PPI(I)§	MS. 129	MS. 124	MS. 165	Vol. XII	Others
276	228	22				MS. 163, 129
277	229	1		183 – 6		
278	230	23				
279					339	
280	231	23 – 4				
281	232	53 – 4	238			
282	233	54 – 5	239	95^{10} $188 – 9^{11}$		
283	234	19 – 20	284 – 5	152 – 6		MS. 179, 68 – 9
284	235	55 – 6	242 – 4			
285	236	56	244			
286	237	20 – 1				MS. 179, 69 – 71
287	238	1 – 2		188		
288	239	56 – 8	245 – 7	140 – 4		
289	239.1^{12}	49^{13} 89^{14}	132^{14} 272^{13}			
290	240	67	286	160 – 1		
291	241	22				MS. 163, 129 – 30
292		155 – 6				MS. 180(b), 47 – 8
293	242	58 – 60	256 – 7			
294					209 – 10	
295	243	60 – 1	258 – 9			
296	244	61	259			
297					207	Vol. XVI, 56 – 7
298	245	61 – 2	259 – 60			
299					316	
300						MS, 162(b), 66 – 8
301						MS, 130, 33
302	246	18				MS. 179, 66
303	247	62 – 3	269^{15}			MS. 179, 32 – 3
304	248	63 – 4		163		
305					252	
306					246	
307		114	5 – 6			MS. 161, 80 – 1
308					335	
309						Vol. XIII, 92; Vol. XIV, 142 – 3
310	249	64 – 5	288	170 – 2		
311	250	65 – 6	288 – 9	173 – 4		
312	251	66 – 7	289 – 90	175 – 7		
313	252	67	290	178		
314	253	68	271			
315	254	67 – 8	286	162		

[1] PI §243(a) only.
[2] PI §243(b) only.
[3] PI §249(a) only.
[4] The first sentence corresponds roughly to PI §249(b).
[5] Transposed from p. 160 of this typescript.
[6] PI §260(a)–(b) only.
[7] PI §260(a) only.
[8] PI §260(b) only.
[9] MS. 165, p. 230, continues onto p. 42.
[10] A variant of PI §282(a) (see also MS. 165, 126 – 7).
[11] PI §282(c) only.
[12] Transposed from p. 165 of the typescript, where it was the sequel to PPI(I) §223.

[13] PI §289(a) only.
[14] PI §289(b) only.
[15] PI §303(a) only.

THE PRIVATE LANGUAGE ARGUMENTS

1. *Preliminaries*

§§243 – 315 of the *Philosophical Investigations* are commonly referred to as 'the private language argument'. The name is not Wittgenstein's, although in his notebooks he did allude to 'the discussion of a private language' (MS. 165, 101), which language no one but its speaker can understand. There is indeed such a discussion, but the received name is misleading, for these sections incorporate not one argument but many. It would be futile by now to advocate abandoning this name, but if it must be retained, it would be preferable to pluralize it and to refer to this part of the book as 'the private language arguments'. Many different but closely interwoven themes are investigated, and a wide variety of grammatical clarifications emerge. They are indeed all connected more or less directly with the *prima facie* curious idea of a language which cannot logically be understood by anyone other than its speaker. But their global purpose is to reveal the incoherence of a comprehensive picture of human nature, of the mind and of the relation between behaviour and the mental, of self-knowledge and of knowledge of other people's experience, of language and its foundations, that has dominated philosophy since Descartes. Indeed, despite the fact that we all happily avow that we are anti-Cartesians now, and are prone to view Cartesian dualism as a kind of infantile disease of philosophy which we have all outgrown, that picture, in subtle and insidious ways, still dominates contemporary thought. Central state materialism, functionalism in all its forms, and so-called 'cognitive science', despite their superficial sophistication, are as beset with the confusions which Wittgenstein diagnosed, as were rationalist, empiricist, and Kantian metaphysics of the heroic age of philosophy and behaviourism and phenomenalism earlier this century. This is not merely because contemporary philosophy still trails clouds of Cartesianism and classical empiricism in its wake. Rather the conception of the mental that informs the philosophical tradition is one to which we naturally cleave. Philosophers and non-philosophers alike, when reflecting upon the nature of the mind, on experience, or on mental states and processes, are disposed to move along these deceptively smooth tracks. We are naturally inclined to represent things to ourselves thus. Deceived by similarities of grammatical forms and oblivious to differences of use, we project characteristics of one language-game onto another. Philosophical theories give articulate form to this 'natural disposition of reason'.

The resultant picture of the mind might be dubbed 'the inner/outer conception of the mental'.[1] It stands to the philosophy of psychology somewhat as the Platonist conception of number stands to the philosophy of mathematics. Indeed, it is no coincidence that Wittgenstein hesitated as to whether to continue the early draft of *Investigations* §§1 – 189 (i.e. PPI) with his reflections on the philosophy of mathematics (RFM, Part I) or with his examination of the contour lines of the grammar of the mental (cf. Volume 2, 'Two fruits upon one tree'). For both the inner/outer picture of the mind and the Platonist conception of number, as well as their dialectical contraries, behaviourism and formalism, are rooted in the Augustinian picture of language. (Which is not to say that the philosophical theories that grow from these roots are not fed by numerous different streams.) These are informed by misconceptions about words, misunderstandings of what it is to be the name of a sensation (or experience) or to be the name of a number — the former being conceived to signify a private, mental object, the latter an abstract object. They are moulded by the illicit assumption that sentences uniformly or fundamentally serve to describe — first-person psychological sentences in the present tense being conceived to be descriptions of one's own mental states, mathematical sentences to be descriptions of relations between abstract objects.

Closely associated with — indeed perhaps indissociable from — that picture of the mental is an equally erroneous conception of language. The source of all our knowledge, empiricists argued, and of the 'materials' of thought and reasoning, is *experience*. Experience constitutes 'the given', the data of sense and introspection. According to this classical conception, the foundations of knowledge are constituted by 'ideas' given by (or derived by abstraction from) inner and outer sense. The fundamental indefinables of a language were accordingly conceived to be names of simple ideas. So language was envisaged as having its foundations in mental or subjective objects, the names of which link language to reality. (A more modern view conceives of the fundamental rules of a language as given, antecedently to experience — because innate. And the form in which they are given is imagined to be 'mental representations'.) Accordingly, the roots of language are essentially subjective or mental.

The question of whether Wittgenstein himself ever succumbed to any of these illusions is of considerable historical interest. A comprehensive case for or against such an indictment would require detailed exami-

---

[1] But how the nature of the 'inner' is conceived varies from one philosophical doctrine to another: e.g., a mental substance thinking thoughts (Descartes), subjectless impressions and ideas (Hume), images and sense-data (phenomenalists), brain states (central state materialists), and functional states with neural realization (contemporary functionalists). In all these cases an otherwise harmless, and by no means silly, metaphor is grotesquely reflected in the distorted mirror of philosophical theory.

nation of the *Notebooks 1914 – 16*, the *Tractatus*, and the writings ('Remarks on Logical Form', *Philosophical Remarks*, and the manuscript notebooks), lectures (Lee's and Moore's lecture notes), and dictations (to Schlick and Waismann) between 1929 and 1932. This would be out of place here. Nevertheless, a few schematic suggestions may be ventured. Some of the Schopenhauerian ideas in the *Notebooks*, traces of which are visible in the obscure remarks on solipsism in the *Tractatus*, can arguably be interpreted as a transcendental form of solipsism. If so, then there would appear to be in these writings elements of the general picture that Wittgenstein later strove to destroy.[2] Similarly, the preoccupation with the logical analysis of the *visual field*, evident in the *Notebooks* and prominent in the 1929 manuscript volumes and 'Remarks on Logical Form', strongly suggest a subjective, though idiosyncratic, notion of 'the given'.[3] Be that as it may, the conception of naming as effecting a connection between words and world, and of the proposition as essentially a picture or description of a state of affairs, arguably leaves no room in the framework of the *Tractatus* for any *other* account of names of sensation or experiences and of first-person experiential sentences.

That is controversial. But this much is clear: both Wittgenstein's remarks in 1929/30 about what he *used* to think concerning 'the primary', and his writings and lectures during this transitional phase involve an unambiguous commitment to numerous distortions of experiential concepts. He held that the only 'genuine propositions' were descriptions of *immediate experience*, that such propositions get compared with reality for verification and can thereby be conclusively verified and so known to be true (or false). The verification of first-person present-tense experiential propositions was conceived to be radically unlike the verification of third-person ones, and hence to differ categorially in sense, the latter being not genuine propositions, but hypotheses. His account was in effect a version of methodological solipsism[4], a conception which he would subsequently reject as incoherent.

The change came during the academic year 1932/33 when he repudiated the idea that first-person experiential utterances are 'the genuine

---

[2] This is a controversial claim which cannot be defended here. It is briefly touched on again in 'Behaviour and behaviourism', §2, 'I and my self', §1, and 'The world of consciousness', §1. Further confirmation for it can be found in a letter of Russell's and in a coded passage in the pre-*Tractatus* notebooks (see B. F. McGuinness, *Wittgenstein, A Life: Young Ludwig (1889–1921)* (Duckworth; London, 1988), pp. 106, 225). See also Frege's letter to Wittgenstein, dated 3 April, 1920.

[3] It does not follow, on such an interpretation, that the 'objects' of the *Tractatus* are sense-data. For while a coloured patch in my visual field can be considered a *phenomenal complex*, the simple objects of which it is composed, e.g. points in the visual field specified by co-ordinates (as in RLF) and unanalysable shades of colour, can be viewed as indestructible sempiternalia, beyond existence and inexistence.

[4] The terminology is Carnap's, not Wittgenstein's. Their respective positions differ, but the label is convenient provided it does not mislead.

propositions', denied that they get compared with reality at all or have a verification. Further advances in his thinking are evident in the *Blue and Brown Books* discussion of experience, mental states and processes, idealism and solipsism (1933 – 5). In the 'Notes for Lectures on "Private Experience" and "Sense Data" ' (1935 – 6), the notion of a private language makes its first appearance (see also Rhees's lecture notes from 1936 entitled 'The Language of Sense Data and Private Experience' and the 'Lecture on Privacy' (MS. 166)). By this time most of the issues which are to be found in *Investigations* §§243 – 315 were already taking shape. His ideas were further refined and developed, principally in 1937 – 9 (Vols. XV – XVII, MSS. 158, 160, 162(b)) when the skeleton of the arguments is created, and then in 1944 – 5 (Vol. XII, MSS. 124, 129, 165, 179, 180(a)) when they were completed and polished. What we see in the condensed sixteen pages of the *Investigations* §§243 – 315 is the precipitate (cf. PI, Preface) from many hundreds of pages of notes in which Wittgenstein struggled with awesome tenacity to clarify the concepts of experience and to destroy the philosophical illusions and mythologies that surround these crucial but mundane (non-theoretical) expressions that inform our lives and thought.

In Volume 2 it was argued that the suggestion that 'the real private language argument' is completed by §202 is a mistake (Volume 2, pp. 169 – 79 and Exg. §202). Wittgenstein's discussion of following rules was not meant to show that it only makes sense to talk of someone's behaviour as constituting an instance of following a rule in the context of a community of rule-followers. Rather, it was designed to show that it only makes sense to talk of following a rule in the context of a practice — a behavioural regularity — informed by normative activities (e.g. using the formulation of a rule as a standard of correctness, rectifying mistakes, justifying action by reference to a rule). Such practices, with us, are typically shared, although they need not always be, and are typically learnt in a social context, though some may be invented in solitude for one's private use. But, as Wittgenstein's numerous discussions of Robinson Crusoe, solitary cavemen, etc. demonstrate, there is no conceptual incoherence in imagining a person following a rule in an asocial context. That a language is learnt from other speakers is an important fact about the genesis of a linguistic ability, but it does not enter into the grammatical (logical) characterization of the ability (cf. PG 188; BB 12, 97; PI §495). For an ability is characterized by what it is an ability to do. The criteria for speaking a language do not require the production of a school or even a parental certificate. We would determine whether a solitary caveman or desert islander could speak or use signs quite independently of determining how he learnt to do so (cf. Exg. §243).

Had the discussion up to *Investigations* §202 been intended to prove that following a rule, like trade and barter, is only conceivable in a social group, it would not have shown that a public language in a social group is not a congruence of 'private' languages built on private ostensive definitions — as Locke explicitly, and most other empiricists implicitly, had supposed. Were Wittgenstein's conclusion at §202 merely that it is impossible to follow a rule privately (as opposed to 'privately', cf. Exg. §202), then the application of that argument to the language of sensations would not have required the association of sensation-names with, or the introduction of private ostensive definitions by reference to, 'private objects' which no one else can have or be acquainted with. For the point to be established would be that one person alone, independently of a social setting and antecedent training in a social group, could not talk about his own sensations or experiences *no matter how these concepts are defined*. The misconceived claims that different people cannot have the identical sensation and that sensations are epistemically private would be strictly irrelevant to the argument. For, even if sensations are not thus conceived, it would be impossible for a person in solitude to use a language to talk about his sensations unless he had acquired his language in a social setting. The claim that a language concerned with sensations is impossible unless shared by a community would not differ in principle from the claim that a language about physical objects is impossible unless shared by a community. In fact, Wittgenstein's concern in this strand in the web of arguments is not whether one person alone could or could not talk of his experiences in an unshared language, but whether all of us, in our normal social setting, can be conceived to be following rules constituted by mere association of a word and a mental 'object' or by private ostensive definitions. And private ostensive definitions are not ostensive definitions which other people do not happen to know about, but putative definitions (rules) which cannot be communicated to other people. It is such rules which were presupposed as the foundations of our common public languages by the mainstream of philosophy. And it is by showing that there can be no such rules, that representational idealism (and contemporary 'cognitive representationalism'), classical British idealism, phenomenalism, and solipsism can be shown to be philosophical chimeras.

Far from §§243 – 315 constituting simply an application of the account of following rules to a special problem about sensation-language, the discussion of the possibility of a 'private' language is concerned, as Wittgenstein wrote (MS. 165, 102), with idealism and solipsism, in particular with the sources of these intellectual diseases. Its global target is a misconstrual of our concepts of experience, of the nature of the mental and its relation to behaviour, that is pervasive in philosophy. These misconceptions inform philosophical, psychological, and theoretical linguistic accounts of the nature of a language, of the foundations of language in 'private' experience and 'private' rules (and so-called mental representations of rules), and of the putative foundations of knowledge.

Not only is this task not essentially completed by §202; it has barely begun.

It would, of course, be wrong to think that §§243 – 315 are independent of the preceding arguments of the book. They presuppose the antecedent clarifications of following rules, techniques of application, ostensive definitions, samples, meaning, understanding, and explanation. The crucial question which has not yet been broached is whether there can be private analogues of these, i.e. analogues within the 'private' confines of the mind. It makes sense to speak of a person's following a rule only in the context of a regularity of action involving normative activities (cf. Volume 2, p. 47) manifesting a technique of application (cf. Volume 2, pp. 161 – 5). The pertinent question in relation to a private language is not whether there can (logically) be such a thing in solitude, in an extra-social context independently of antecedent training in a social group, for Wittgenstein has shown that to be perfectly intelligible. It is rather whether there can be an analogue of following a rule[5] if, despite the person's living in a community, the putative rule which he purports to be following could not logically be followed by, or even communicated to, anyone else. For this is what would be the case were sensation-names (or, more generally, names of 'experiences') defined by private ostensive definition — and here 'private' does not mean contingently private. If anything deserves the name '*the* private language argument', it is the discussion of this crucial issue in the *Investigations* §§243 – 315, but fewer than a third of these sections are directly concerned with it, and much else is brought into view.

Ostensive definition has previously been clarified as one legitimate form of explaining the meaning of a word. It gives a rule for the use of a word, and typically introduces a sample to function as a standard of correct application. The crucial question for the idealist and representational idealist traditions is not whether one can give a private ostensive

---

[5] Wer uns die Sprache eines Volkes beschreibt, beschreibt eine Gleichformigkeit ihres Benehmens. Und wer eine Sprache beschreibt, die Einer mit sich allein spricht, der beschreibt eine Gleichformigkeit seines Benehmens und nicht etwas, was sich *ein*mal zugetragen hat.

Aber 'eine Sprache sprechen' werde ich nur ein Verhalten nennen, das unserm, wenn wir unsere Sprache sprechen, analog ist. (MS. 124, 279)

(Someone who describes the language of a people, describes a regularity of their behaviour. And someone who describes a language which a person speaks to himself alone, describes a regularity of his behaviour, and not something that has happened only *once*.

But I shall only call behaviour 'speaking a language' if it is analogous to ours, when we speak our language.)

This remark occurs in the MS. after a draft of PI §206(c). It is the regular behaviour (including normative activities) of a person which constitutes the criteria for saying of him (even if he speaks only to himself) that he has mastered the technique of speaking a language.

definition of a word by reference to a sample one keeps secret (i.e. does not show to anyone else), but whether one can give such a definition by reference to a 'private' sample (i.e. one which it is logically impossible to show anyone else). If not, then there can be no intelligible distinction in a 'private' language between correct and incorrect uses of signs, and hence no use of language at all.

Similarly, it has been argued earlier that the meaning of a word is not an object of any kind, but rather is given by an explanation of meaning, and an explanation is a rule for the use of a word. Understanding a word — knowing what it means — is manifest in correct use, i.e. use in accord with an appropriate explanation. It is also exhibited in correctly explaining what a word means. (If a speaker understands what he says, he must be able to say what he means, and what he means and what it means typically converge). The moot question for a private language is not so much whether one can explain to others what one means by a word, but whether one can even explain it to oneself. Hence also, not so much whether others can understand, but whether one understands oneself — indeed whether there is anything to understand at all. One could also put it thus: is the idea of an expression which it is logically impossible to explain to others and which it is logically impossible for others to understand not incoherent? If it is logically impossible for anyone else to understand, must it not also be logically impossible for oneself to understand? For does it not then follow that there actually is nothing to understand?

What Wittgenstein aimed to show is not that sensation-language, like the rest of language, is essentially shared, but that it is essentially sharable. That requirement is not met by the received accounts in the dominant philosophical tradition (or in psychology and linguistic theory). The refutation of the supposition of the possibility of a private language is, in a loose sense, a *reductio ad absurdum* of an array of deep presuppositions. For here there are and can be no rules, *a fortiori* no ostensive definitions, no samples and no techniques of application, no distinction between correctly and incorrectly following a rule, but only a *Schein-praxis* — an illusion of meaning.

This is one dominant theme in the private language arguments of §§243 – 315, but there are many others tightly interwoven in a fine tapestry of exceptional richness and subtlety of design.

2. *From grammatical truth to metaphysical theory*

Each person has 'experiences', in a generous sense of the term. He enjoys or endures sensations, perceptual experiences, emotions, and moods. People believe, imagine, and think. Just as there are physical states, events, and processes, so too there are mental ones. The experiences that a person has are, tautologically, his experiences. These are often exhibited in his behaviour. The experiences a person manifests in his behaviour are, again tautologically, *his* experiences. There is no such thing, for example, as one person manifesting the suffering of another.

Numerous psychological expressions are names of experiences which a person enjoys or endures. The word 'pain' is the name of a kind of sensation, the expressions 'seeing red' or 'having a mental image of A' are names of different kinds of experiences. If a person knows what such a psychological predicate means, he knows what it stands for. To know what the word 'pain' means is to know that it stands for a certain kind of sensation — viz. pain.

A person who has mastered a language can say what experiences he is having. His ability to do so is (typically) independent of his observation of his own behaviour, and what he says does not rest on the evidence of what he does. He cannot *doubt* whether, for example, he is in pain, wants a drink, feels dizzy, etc. Though self-deception is sometimes possible, mistake is not. When a person says how things are with him, what sensations and perceptual experiences he has, then (at least in paradigmatic cases) what he says has privileged status. There is such a thing as describing one's states of mind — an activity at which Proust, for example, excelled.

Judgements about other people's sensations, perceptions, and emotions rest on observations of what they do and say. They may say or otherwise reveal how things are with them, or they may keep things to themselves. But there is also such a thing as pretence or dissimulation, which complicates matters.

These truisms are not empirical generalizations obvious to all, but for the most part grammatical propositions partly constitutive of the constituent concepts. Philosophers, hungry for theories about the nature of the mind, typically stray from such narrow and familiar paths into the minefields of metaphysics. It is but a short step from grammatical platitudes to metaphysical theses, and from there to perdition. The following sketch indicates some of the routes.

(A) The mental realm

(i) Parallel to the public physical world, each of us enjoys access to a private realm of the mind. The mental world consists of objects (e.g. pains, images, sense-impressions, perhaps also ideas, thoughts, and beliefs), processes (imagining, remembering, thinking), and states (believing, understanding, knowing) which are logically just like physical objects, processes, and states — only mental. These are doubtless mysterious; we talk about them, but with due caution leave their nature undecided — future investigations and theories will dispel our current ignorance (PI §308).

(ii) To have an experience, for example a sensation (such as pain) or an emotion (like fear), is to stand in a certain relationship to such an object, process, or state. 'A has a pain' and 'A has a penny' (as well as 'I have a pain' and 'I have a penny') have the same logical form, the latter signifying a relation to a physical object, the former to a mental object. The nature of the mental being undecided, these objects, processes, and states may be (a) *sui generis* — essentially distinct from and irreducible to the physical; (b) neural, the experience of the subject consisting in modifications of the brain as apprehended 'from the inside'; (c) functional objects, processes, and states with a neural 'realization'.

(iii) One person cannot have the identical experience which another has, but only a similar one. I cannot have your pain, but only one just like it. So experiences are inalienable 'private property'.

(B) Names of the mental

(i) One knows what the name of a (simple) mental entity means if one knows what it stands for; e.g. one knows what 'pain' means if one knows that it stands for the sensation of pain. One can only know what such an expression means if one is acquainted with what it stands for, i.e. if one has or has had a pain. For if the meaning of a word is the thing for which it stands, to know its meaning *is* to know, i.e. be acquainted with, that thing. Alternatively, if the meaning of a word is denied to be what the word stands for, it is still plausible to argue that a word which cannot be defined by an analytical definition must be explained by an ostensive definition — and an ostensive definition of, e.g., 'pain' requires that one *have* a pain. That knowing the meaning of such words presupposes acquaintance with what they signify seems confirmed by the thought that the blind do not really know what colour–words mean because they are not acquainted with colours, i.e. lack the sensory experiences of seeing colours.

(ii) A child learns what names of experiences mean by first having the experience, and then (a) being brought to *associate* the name with his experience; or (b) being brought to give himself a mental ostensive definition by *concentrating* on the experience. Concentrating is conceived to be a mental analogue of physically pointing at an object.

(iii) Once meaning has been assigned to such a name, subsequent uses of the word can be explained (a) by causal theorists, as a matter of 'habit memory', or (b) by normative theorists, as a matter of calling up an exemplar stored in the memory. On the latter view, we link names of experiences with copies, representatives, or exemplars of the experience in question which are deposited in our 'storehouse of ideas'.

(C) Knowledge of the subjective realm

(i) Since I cannot doubt whether I am, for example, experiencing pain when I am so doing, cannot wonder whether I have a pain or not, cannot think I have a pain when I do not, therefore (a) if I have an experience, I know that I do; (b) my knowledge of my own experiences is certain; (c) my knowledge of my experiences is incorrigible.

(ii) Since having experiences is standing in a relation to mental objects, states, processes, etc., and since that relation yields knowledge, there must be an inner analogue of the corresponding relation with respect to 'outer objects', viz. perception. This analogue is *inner sense, introspection, consciousness,* or *awareness* (variously conceived and often assimilated). For, (a) when I have an experience I am conscious or aware of it — an experience of which I were not conscious would, as Kant put it, 'be as nothing to me'. I cannot have a pain, for example, and not be aware of it. 'I had a terrible pain, but I was not aware of it' is nonsense. (b) I can think about, reflect on, my current experiences — hold them, as it were, in view — and say precisely what they are like. I thus observe *in foro interno* the stream of experiences I enjoy.

(iii) Hence, one's mind is transparent to oneself. The objects, events, and processes in it are immediately known by introspection, and what is believed to be in the mind is in it. An alternative tack is to deny certainty and incorrigibility and to insist that introspection is as fallible as perception. Far from being transparent, much of the mind is opaque, and the mental states and processes in it must often be hypothesized — by psychoanalysts, theoretical linguists, and, in the fullness of time, by super-neurologists.

(iv) First-person psychological utterances are essentially descriptions of what is revealed to introspective scrutiny. What I observe, privately, *in foro interno*, I can report, for the benefit of others, *in foro externo*.

(v) Since I can describe my experiences without reference to my own behaviour, first-person psychological propositions are logically independent of behaviour. Mental states, etc. are causes of behaviour.

(D) Knowledge of others' mental states

(i) One cannot know of other people's experiences and mental states as one knows one's own, viz. by introspection. Rather, one observes their behaviour, and one infers from this what mental states or experiences are causally responsible for their behaviour.

(ii) The experiences and mental states of others are hidden, inaccessible to direct observation. For even if others tell us what they are experiencing, this is just words — and anyway, they may be lying. Similarly, even if they behave in such-and-such characteristic ways, this is just behaviour, not the experience itself — and they may be dissimulating.

(iii) The behaviour of other people consists of bare movements and the emission of sounds. The body that behaves is a physical organism subject to the causal laws that determine the movements of all physical bodies.

(iv) Since a mental state can obtain or an experience be enjoyed without any corresponding behaviour occurring, and behaviour may occur without the appropriate mental state or experience, behaviour is not logically connected with the mental.

(v) Since the experiences and mental states of others are known by inference from behavioural externalities, and since the connection between behaviour and the mental is external, the inference cannot be logical. Given the impossibility of any non-inductive identification of the inner states of others, our inferences cannot be inductive either, since inductive correlation presupposes non-inductive identification. Hence it must be either analogical or hypothetical (an inference to the best explanation).

(vi) We cannot achieve genuine knowledge of others' mental states, as we can of our own. Hence we can, at best, only *believe* that things are thus-and-so with them.

This picture has seemed to many philosophers and psychologists to be persuasive, even unavoidable. Indeed, it is obtained by seemingly minor modifications to the array of grammatical truisms previously sketched. And if the latter are not viewed as grammatical propositions, but rather as empirical platitudes, it may well seem that the theses (A)–(D) which make up this picture are merely an enrichment or further elaboration of the elementary truisms. But in fact, while the truisms are grammatical, the theses are a subtle weave of metaphysical nonsense with the occasional plain falsehood. One has only to take a few further steps from the highroad of grammar for the nonsense to explode, as it were, before one.

(a) *Scepticism about other minds*: The picture sketched out above leads convincingly to the view that we can at best attain true beliefs about other people's experiences or mental states. But the tough-minded will rightly push on. Can we even attain justified *beliefs*? If all that is available as evidence is mere behaviour (bodily movements), is any inference really licit? The analogy between ourselves and others is shaky — after all, why should I assume that the causal connections that I am aware of in my case also obtain in theirs? Maybe where I see red, for example, others see green but *call* it 'red', and so forth. An inference to the best explanation is useless if its confirmation transcends any possible experience. And is it not consistent with anything that I could experience that others are mere automatons? This, surely, we can never prove or disprove!

(b) *Scepticism about communication*: If two people cannot have the very same experience, and if the words of their languages are defined by reference to their experiences, then the supposition of mutual intelligibility is distinctly shaky. It rests wholly on hope. For although one cannot in principle know what experiences others have, one hopefully assumes that what others call 'pain' or 'red' is what one calls thus oneself; or at least, that it is very similar. And here too, it seems, nothing could definitely show that to be so.

(c)   *The impossibility of communication*: A moment's further reflection shows that such hopes must be futile. For it seems *logically* impossible for another person to have what I have when I have a pain, and if I define 'pain' by reference to what *I* have then, given the assumptions about meaning which are in play, it is logically impossible for another person to know what I mean by the word 'pain'. My language must, it seems, be a radically private one, viz. unintelligible to others. For it does not even make sense to suppose that what others have when they say 'I have a pain' is similar to what I have when I have a pain. This can only be supposed if there is some operational criterion of similarity. But although I surely have one in my own case, viz. a mental *sample*, it is logically impossible for there to be one for the interpersonal case.

(d)   *Collapse into solipsism*: If what I *call* 'experience' is defined in my language ('the only language I understand') by reference to what *I* have and no one else can have, then there is no longer a question of whether, for all I know, others may not be automatons. Rather, it becomes obvious that it can make no sense for there to *be* any other owners of (what I call) experience. For the supposition that there are other subjects of experience seems to be tantamount to the supposition that someone else could have *this*, which I now have. But *I* uniquely have it. So *my* experience *is* experience: there can be no other. 'I am the vessel of life' (BB 65).

Of course, no one has ever believed this. That, however, does not diminish its philosophical importance. For arguably the only reason it has not been embraced is that philosophers have found it incredible.[6] And equally, the presuppositions of their metaphysical and linguistic theories lead ineluctably to solipsism. So it must not be dismissed as ridiculous, but must be closely examined to see how we were led to this monstrosity.

---

[6] They were wrong. It is not *incredible,* but either nonsense or, alternatively, a confused recommendation to adopt a new form of representation.

3. *Deviations and dialectic*

The above picture is a simple paradigm or range of connected paradigms, an Ideal Type rather than a set of theses any one philosopher has embraced in precisely this form. The history of modern philosophy since Descartes displays many deviations from it, as well as a variety of manoeuvres to try to avoid its unwelcome consequences. Cartesianism provided the parameters for a pernicious dialectic. Successive philosophical antitheses were adumbrated, each repudiating an element in previous accounts, yet retaining cancerous components that contributed to inevitable self-destruction. For what were rejected were never the deepest origins of the incoherence. 'One keeps forgetting to go right down to the foundations,' Wittgenstein observed, 'One doesn't put the question marks *deep* enough down' (CV 62). Consequently, although metastases were excised, their source was not located, and it continued to throw off fresh malignant growths.

Descartes' dualism involved two substances in causal interaction. The Occasionalists accepted the duality, but rejected the interaction. The Idealists repudiated the Cartesian conception of body, but retained an important part of the conception of mind either with (in the case of Berkeley) or without (in the case of Hume) the attendant idea of a mental substance. For their notion of inner sense and of self-knowledge was *au fond* Cartesian, and they conceived of the relation between the mental and behaviour as external, even though these were now construed as distinct sets of *ideas* which were externally related. Materialists and, later, behaviourists repudiated the Cartesian conception of the mind, but inherited distorted concepts of behaviour and of the human body. More recently, central state materialists reverted to a form of dualism, but identified the mental with the neural, replacing mind/body dualism with brain/body dualism, and conceiving of mental properties as properties of the brain that are causally responsible for behaviour. Currently functionalists repudiate the central state materialists' type-identity thesis in favour of a token–identity thesis in which 'mental states' are held to be functional states of a human organism that are, in some way or other, neurologically 'realized'. But the fundamental *philosophical* (theoretical) picture of the 'inner' and the 'outer' is retained. The dialectic continues, but the grammar of the mental is not laid bare, precisely because the questions do not go 'deep enough down'. Instead, metaphysical doctrines and pseudo-scientific theories are advocated which are no more than manifestations of grammatical confusions about our psychological and behavioural concepts and of methodological confusions about the nature of philosophical (conceptual) investigations. The acme of absurdity is to dream of a scientific millennium in which our psychological concepts would be jettisoned in favour of 'better' or 'more correct' concepts — as if it were our *language* that is at fault!

This pernicious dialectic is also visible more locally. So, for example, 'ownership' of experience is wrongly conceived as a relation of entities, and the debate turns on *what* entities stand in this relation: are they the 'self' (a mental substance) and 'experiences' (mental objects, events, states, and processes), or the body (a physical substance) and experiences (forms of behaviour and behavioural disposition), or the brain and experiences (neural states causally responsible for behaviour). The first-person pronoun is held to be a referring expression, and the disputable question is whether it refers to the 'self', the person speaking, the body, or the brain, or whether it merely signifies a logical construction. The moot point, however, is whether its role is that of a typical referring expression at all, and whether the subject of experience can coherently be conceived to be anything other than the living human being.

Psychological expressions are held to be names of inner objects (or properties), states, events, or processes which are logically akin to names of outer ones. So the debate turns on the nature of what these expressions name, whether their nominata are mental and *sui generis* or neural; or alternatively whether they signify behavioural dispositions and their actualization or just fictions. But what goes unexamined is the distinctive use of these expressions and the conditions under which they have a use. The question that needs to be addressed, however, is whether the grammar of 'is the name of an experience' is isomorphic with that of 'is the name of an object', and whether the concepts of mental state, event, process, etc. are as similar to the concepts of physical state, event, process, etc. as their grammatical appearance suggests (viz. that the former are, as it were, 'just like' the latter, only *mental*).

It is generally agreed that first-person present-tense psychological utterances are descriptions, and the question which is typically investigated is what it is that they describe, whether and how they are known to be true. The Cartesian conception of incorrigible knowledge is rejected by many philosophers in favour of corrigible knowledge. Infallible knowledge based on introspection is displaced by the metaphor of a corrigible self-scanning device causally linked to behaviour. But the moot question is how cognitive verbs are used in the context of first-person present-tense psychological sentences. Is 'I know I have a pain' or 'I know what I think' really a cognitive claim at all? And what is it, in the practice of speaking our language, that we actually call 'self-knowledge'? Granted that there is such a thing as describing one's own state of mind, is it obvious that 'I believe what you say', 'I think he will come', 'I have a toothache', 'I want a drink' are such descriptions? The grammar of 'description' and of 'state of mind' must be clarified, and likewise the question of whether genuine descriptions of one's own state of mind are grammatically akin to descriptions of states of the room, the garden, or the economy, etc. must be answered.

The inner/outer picture of the relationship between the mental and behaviour is generally accepted, or, in the characteristic pernicious dialectic, the inner is *reduced* to the outer. What is questioned in that move is *one* half of a distorted dichotomy, but it is rarely noticed that *both* halves misrepresent our concepts. Debate turns on the character of inferences from the 'outer' to the 'inner', but what counts as 'outer' is typically taken for granted, as is the characterization of the inference as being from the observed to the unobserved. But the behaviour of a human being is not the movement of a bodily machine, and experiences are not hidden *behind* anything. Moreover, our very descriptions of the 'outer' depend upon our terminology of the 'inner'.

Wittgenstein aimed to show how we can put an end to this wearisome dialectic, not by proposing an ultimate synthesis, but by attaining clarity, so that the philosophical problems will completely disappear (PI §133). To clear the ground of misguided theories, he had to dig right down to the grammatical roots of error. In relation to the philosophical tradition, the results of his labours are as radical as his parallel investigations in the philosophy of mathematics. The presuppositions of the centuries-old debate are laid bare and rejected. Clarifications are proposed: a private language is impossible; inner states stand in need of outer criteria; avowals are not descriptions of experience; 'I know I have a pain' is not an epistemic claim; different people can have the same experience; and so on. But these are not theses, set up in competition with previous philosophical theses. They are grammatical elucidations arrived at by painstaking examination of the uses of expressions. They are not philosophical propositions asserted to be true, but epitomes of grammatical surviews. If anyone challenges them, he should be answered not by defending a thesis, but by examining how the challenger uses psychological and behavioural expressions in practice. 'The problems are solved, not by giving new information, but by arranging what we have always known' (PI §109).

The net of Wittgenstein's arguments is densely woven. He moves from strand to strand as he follows each thread until arriving at a knot. To unravel that typically requires going off in another direction before returning to pick up the thread and follow it — until the next knot is encountered. The different strands in the weave can be separated. In subsequent essays the themes of privacy, avowals and descriptions, private ostensive definition, criteria, the 'inner' and the 'outer', minds and machines, behaviour and behaviourism, are tackled separately. The price is twofold. First, one may generate the impression that the various issues are mutually independent. But the argument against the possibility of a private language is not independent of the repudiation of the

traditional picture of self-knowledge. The account of first-person utterances is not independent of the insight that behaviour is a *criterion* of the
mental, and that in turn hangs on a transformed conception of behaviour. This involves rejecting behaviourism and examining afresh the
conception of inference from the 'outer' to the 'inner'. All these
grammatical insights cannot be severed from the dramatic focal shift in
the representation of the concepts of the 'inner' and the 'outer'. Secondly,
by separating the interwoven strands of Wittgenstein's discussion, one's
account gains in local *Übersichtlichkeit* at the cost of increasing the
difficulty of obtaining a global surview. For each confusion in the history
of the philosophical debate derives support from misconceptions *elsewhere* in the complex structure of psychological and behavioural concepts. (Hence removing *one* buttress, as it were, leaves the overall
structure intact.) The great difficulty lies in holding all in mind simultaneously, for as light is shed upon one aspect, the others sink into
shadow. The only remedy is to examine the structure from each angle
again and again, to work on oneself until one can grasp the whole.
Surveying the concepts we use in talking about and giving expression to
our inner life is no less difficult than surveying our inner life.

EXEGESIS §§243-5

SECTION 243

1   The long trek of clarifying the concept of following a rule concluded with the claim that if language is to be a means of communication there must be agreement not only in definitions but also in judgements. At this point one is inclined to insist that the concept of *a language* is not thus bound up with agreement. Is it not possible for a person to have a language which he employs only to communicate *with himself*, to tell himself things? Here, it seems, neither agreement nor even the possibility of agreement with others is requisite.

§243(a) opens with the truism that there is a multitude of reflexive speech-acts and speech-related activities. We can even imagine people *all* of whose uses of language are thus reflexive, i.e. they speak *only* to themselves. (Note that W. does *not* claim that such reflexive speech-acts are parasitic on non-reflexive ones.) Does this not show that the concepts of language and of agreement are *not* internally related? No, for the necessity is for *possible* agreement. In order to communicate, people must actually agree in definitions and judgements. For communication to be possible, it must be intelligible that people should agree. For activity to count as the use of a language, it must be possible that another person should come to understand the signs employed. This requirement *is* secured in the case of the imaginary monologuists. They accompany their activities by talking to themselves, and there is sufficient regularity in their behaviour in given circumstances, i.e. between the sounds they emit and what they do or experience, for an explorer to translate their language into ours. 'The common behaviour of mankind is the system of reference by means of which we interpret an unknown language' (PI §206). But this means precisely that the explorer *can* come into accord with the monologuists' judgements, can achieve the requisite 'constancy in results of measurement' (PI §242). For the possibility of interpreting (translating) an unknown language presupposes a large measure of consensus in judgement (expressed in the monologuists' 'units of measurement', which need not coincide in any simple way with the explorer's). This is further emphasized by the parenthetical remark that the explorer would be able to *predict* the monologuists' actions from their expressions of intention. As has been noted previously, understanding rule-governed techniques (in this case, reflexive speech-acts) provides foundations for predictions (Volume 2, pp. 46, 162), *a fortiori* interpreting correctly their expressions of decisions and intentions does so.

(b) clarifies what supposition would undermine the claim that there is an internal relation between the concept of a language and the possibility of agreement. This would be the supposition of the conceivability of a language which, unlike the monologuists', is used to register or voice for oneself features of one's inner life. W.'s interlocutor retorts correctly that one can do just this in our ordinary language. But this is not what W. has in mind. Rather, the supposed language, a *private language*, must be conceived of as consisting exclusively of words which refer to what can be known only to the speaker. On one widespread (mis)conception of sensations (or, more generally, 'inner experiences — feelings, moods, and the rest'), these are indeed known only to their owner. If this were so, and if the supposition of such a private language made sense, then no one else could understand the language. It would be essentially private, unlike the language of a solitary monologuist, cavemen, or Robinson Crusoe. For in this case, unlike the others, the explorer could not attain 'agreement in results of measurement', for neither what measures nor what is measured would be accessible to him. If this makes sense, then agreement (or rather even the mere possibility of agreement) in definitions and judgements is not internally related to the very concept of a language.

1.1   (i) 'by talking to themselves': (cf. PI §260) speaking when no one else is present ('Is anyone here?'; 'Blow, winds and crack your cheeks!') is not necessarily talking to oneself, and one can talk to oneself even in company.

(ii) 'für den eigenen Gebrauch': 'for his own use'.

(iii) 'aufschreiben, oder aussprechen': 'give vocal expression' is too close to 'Äusserung', so better 'write down or voice'. The introduction of *writing* things down for oneself prepares the way for the 'private diary' example (§258). It also strengthens the putative counter-example. It is not obvious that saying to oneself 'I have a pain' is a case of telling oneself something (communicating something to oneself), although saying to oneself 'I have a toothache, so I had better skip lunch and ring up the dentist' might be said to be. But writing 'I have a pain' in one's diary can obviously be recording one's experiences for one's subsequent use, and might be called 'communicating with oneself'.

(v) 'wovon nur der Sprechende wissen kann': 'to what can be known only to the speaker'. This idea is examined in PI §§246f.

(v) 'are to refer to': cf. §244 and, more critically, §§273f. One *can* say that 'pain' is the name of a sensation or even that it refers to a sensation, but in a philosophical discussion this is likely to incorporate the wrong picture, namely that of 'object and name' (cf. §293).

(vi) 'So another person cannot understand the language': if meaning is a matter of correlating words with things which are their meanings (or defining samples), and if immediate private sensations can be known only to their subject, then a language the words of which refer to private experiences cannot be understood by anyone other than the speaker. But, these premises are incoherent, and the concept of privacy is here abused.

2   The ideas embodied in this remark had somewhat different roles in earlier manuscripts. Their initial emergence seems to have been in 1936 reflections (Vol. XII, 117) on *contingently* private uses of signs and a corresponding contrast between objective and subjective understanding of signs. A language, in so far as it is only subjectively understood, is not a means of communicating with others, but rather a set of tools for one's own private use. Should such utterances of sounds, writing of signs, still be called 'a language' or 'tools'? Only if one plays language-games with them. But this one surely can do! Just think of Robinson Crusoe, who employs a language (signs) for his private use. You see him (without his knowing it) in a multiplicity of circumstances making marks on wood or emitting sounds. If you can discern a certain kind of regularity here, you would rightly say that this is a use of signs. But if we detect *no* regularity, should we conclude that he is speaking a purely private language, in which the same sounds are always associated with the same mental image?

Subsequently (Vol. XII, 138) we find W.'s first observations on self-addressed speech-acts that are the ancestry of PI §243(a). One can engage in such activities, as indeed one can play chess against oneself or win money from oneself.[1] 'One can' in such cases means, W. remarks, 'one does such-and-such, and does one not call that thus-and-so?' What then is communicating with oneself, talking to oneself ? Not looking at a piece of paper and saying 'This paper is white', or coming into an empty room in which one expected to meet someone and saying 'I am alone'; for in such cases one does not use this sentence to tell oneself something (*Mitteilung*), but rather as an exclamation. But if I come in and look around in surprise, saying 'It is empty. I can do what I like here,' and proceed to do this or that, then we have here a case of telling oneself something (Vol. XV, 201).

MS. 165, 88–124 explores adjacent territory at length, and the criss-cross route illuminates the web of remarks in *Philosophical Investigations*. Beginning from the puzzle of PI §198(a), viz. how can a rule which can be variously interpreted show me what I have to do at a given point, the discussion moves (MS. 165, 90) to PI §217(a)–(b): how I can follow a rule is explained by either causes or reasons; if causes are not in question, then one is concerned with justifications; but justifications come to an

---

[1] It is less than obvious what would be called 'winning money from oneself' (cf. PI§268); but it is noteworthy that Pepys, amusingly, used to promise himself not to frequent the theatre too often, and to threaten himself with a fine; when he broke his promise, as he often did, he fined himself and paid the fine into the poorbox!

end in the practice of following the rule; acting thus is what is called 'following this rule'. But that presupposes agreement (PI §206(a) ≃ MS. 165, 92); following a rule is akin to obeying orders: lack of agreement over what counts as accord with a rule would be akin to lack of agreement over the meaning of orders. There would in such cases be a 'confusion of tongues'. An explorer coming to an unknown country identifies the people's utterances as orders, questions, answers, etc. by reference to their behaviour in the given circumstances (MS. 165, 97; PI §206(b)). Yet are not these behavioural 'externalities' necessary only for *others* to *recognize* that, say, an order has been given? He who issues the order knows what he means even if the others do not! (Here lies the connection between PI §206 and PI §243.) No; this conception of mere 'externalities' is misleading, for there is an imperative form in a language only in the context of a family of modes of *action*. Orders can sometimes be disobeyed, but not always. One can mean what one says as an order, but only against the background of a practice of using words thus and of responding to this use appropriately. Then follows the core of the idea of a private language:

Und hier sind wir im Rande einer Diskussion über die Sprache in der Einer nur zu sich, nur für ihn selber verständlich, über seine privaten Erlebnisse spricht. In diese Diskussion, die zu den Problemen des Idealismus und Solipsismus gehört, werde ich an dieser Stelle hier nicht eintreten. Nur soviel will ich sagen, dass hier keine Sprache beschrieben wurde, obwohl es so scheint. Es verbürgt uns nicht, dass ein Wort dieser Sprache zweimal in gleicher Bedeutung verwendet wird. Denn, sagst Du, die Gegenstände sind hier gleich, wenn sie dir gleich scheinen, so frage ich: 'Wenn sie Dir *wie* scheinen?' 'Gleich' is ja ein Wort der *allgemeine* Sprache. (MS. 165, 101ff.)

   (And here we are on the brink of a discussion about the language in which someone speaks to himself about his own private experiences and is intelligible only to himself. This discussion, which belongs to the problems of idealism and solipsism, will not be broached here. I want to say only this much, that here no language is actually described, even though it appears to be. There is no warrant here that a word of such a language is used twice with the same meaning. For if you say, the objects here are the same when they appear the same to you, then I ask: 'When they appear *how* to you?' 'The same' is surely a word of *common* language.)

In another sense, W. continues, there is, of course, such a thing as a private language, e.g. the one which a Crusoe uses to talk to himself, although to be sure talking to oneself does not mean: being alone and talking (MS. 165, 103 ≃ PI §260(c)). One need not be alone, and just talking is not enough. Then follows an early draft of PI §243(a): we can imagine a person who encourages himself, asks himself questions and answers them, reproaches himself, etc. We would call such a pheno-menon 'a language' if the modes of action of such a person resembled corresponding human actions embedded in normal human contexts and if we could understand his gestures and mien as expressions of sadness, joy, reluctance, etc. After all, we can imagine someone living alone who draws pictures of objects on the wall of his cave, and such a picture-language would be readily understood. On the other hand, mastery of a language one speaks only to oneself no more implies mastery of a language one speaks to others than mastery of patience implies mastery of bridge. Then follows the remark that languages are first and foremost the languages spoken by the peoples of the world; i.e. English, Russian, Chinese, etc. are languages, and we call other things 'languages' because of their similarity to these (cf. PG 190). Thus ordering is a technique of our language, and it is none too difficult for an explorer to realize that he is being given an order even though he does not understand the alien tongue. It would be more difficult, however, to recognize a Crusoe's self-addressed orders.

The theme of the explorer (PI §206) is pursued further, as is the possibility of a solitary caveman who speaks only to himself (cf. Volume 2, pp. 174ff.). It is possible to imagine this, and we could come to understand his reflexive speech-acts if he used only simple signs. What is more problematic, however, is the idea of a language which one speaks to oneself only in the imagination. For though we can speak to ourselves *in foro interno*, is it intelligible that such a phenomenon obtain *independently* of the patterns of *behaviour* into which speech is woven? Note that W.'s point is not epistemological. The issue does not concern the conditions under which we can come to *know* whether someone speaks to himself in his imagination, but rather the conditions and presuppositions under which something *counts* as so doing (whether we know that a person is doing so is a further question). Even one's silent and unrevealed talk must be interwoven in complex ways with one's actions and reactions. To describe the language of a people is to describe a regularity of their behaviour; and to describe a language which someone speaks only to himself is to describe a regularity of his behaviour, not something which happens only once (cf. RFM 334f.; MS. 124, 279). Something constitutes speaking a language only in so far as it is analogous to what we do when we speak our language.

It is noteworthy that much earlier in MS. 165 a further thread was spun that connects with these reflections:

Aber is es nicht das//unser//*Meinen*, das dem Satz Sinn gibt? (Und dazu gehört natürlich: sinnlose Wortreihen kann man nicht meinen.) Und das Meinen ist etwas im Reich der Seele.//im seelischen Bereich.// Aber es ist auch etwas Privates! Es ist das *ungreifbare* Etwas; vergleichbar nur dem Bewusstsein selbst.

Man könnte es einen Traum unserer Sprache nennen . . . (MS. 165, 5)

(But isn't it the //our// *meaning it* that gives sense to the sentence? (And along with this, of course, goes: one cannot mean senseless strings of words.) And meaning it is something in the realm of the mind //mental domain.// But it is also something private! It is the ungraspable something comparable only to consciousness itself.

One could call this a dream of our language . . .)

MS. 124, 213ff. develops these ideas further. Following a draft of PI §241, W. wrote:

Wäre es denn aber nicht denkbar, dass jeder Mensch nur für sich selbst dächte, nur zu sich selbst redete? (In diesem Fall könnte dann auch jeder seine eigene Sprache haben.)

Es gibt Fälle, in welchen wir sagen, Einer//jemand//ermahne sich selbst; befehle, gehorche, bestrafe, tadle, frage und antworte sich selber. Dann kann es also Menschen geben, die nur die Sprachspiele kennen, die jeder mit sich selbst spielt. Ja, es wäre denkbar, dass solche Menschen ein reiches Vokabular hätten. Wir können uns denken, dass ein Forscher in ihr Land käme und beobachtete wie jeder von ihnen seine Tätigkeiten mit artikulierte Laute begleitet, sich aber dabei nicht an Andere wendet. Der Forscher kommt irgendwie auf den Gedanken, dass diese Leute Selbstgespräche führen, belauscht sie bei ihren Tätigkeiten und es gelingt ihm eine w̲a̲h̲r̲s̲c̲h̲e̲i̲n̲l̲i̲c̲h̲e̲ Übersetzung ihrer Reden in unsere Sprache. Er ist durch das Lernen ihrer Sprache auch in den Stand gesetzt Handlungen vorauszusagen welche die Leute später ausführen, denn manches was sie sagen ist der Ausdruck von Entschlüssen oder Vorsätzen. (Wie diese Leute ihre Sprache haben lernen können ist hier gleichgultig.)

Aber wenn nun so ein Mensch sich selbst befiehlt auf diesen Baum zu klettern und wenn anderseits ich es mir befehle, der diesen Befehl nicht nur sich//mir//selbst, sondern auch einem//dem/Andern geben kann: ist *der Gedanke* dieses Befehls in beiden Fällen der gleiche?

Das kannst Du beantworten, wie Du willst. Stell Dir nur nicht vor, dass der Gedanke eine Begleitung des Sprechens ist.

(Is it not imaginable, that each human being should think only for himself, speak only to himself? (In this case each person could even have his own language.)

There are cases in which we say, someone has admonished himself, ordered, obeyed, punished, blamed, asked, and answered himself. So then there can be human beings who are acquainted only with language-games which one plays by oneself. Indeed, it is imaginable that these human beings should have a rich vocabulary. We could imagine that an explorer came to this country and observed how each one of them accompanied his activities with articulate sounds, but did not address others. Somehow the explorer gets the idea that these people are talking to themselves, listens to them in the course of their activities, and succeeds in producing a p̲r̲o̲b̲a̲b̲l̲e̲ translation of their talk into our language. By learning their language, he reaches the position in which he can predict actions which the people subsequently perform, for some of their utterances are expressions of decisions or plans. (How these people were able to learn their language is here irrelevant.)

But now, when such a person orders himself to climb up this tree and when, on the other hand, I, who can give this order not only to myself but also to the others, order myself to climb up the tree, is *the thought* of this order the same in both cases?

You may answer that as you please. Only don't imagine that the thought is an accompaniment of the speaking.)

It is important to note here the following features: (i) The explicitly stated irrelevance of the genesis of linguistic abilities to their identification and to the intelligibility of the tale. (ii) That the imagined human beings are not conceived of as having *previously* spoken a shared language. On the contrary: (a) they are *acquainted* only with language-games one plays alone; and (b) one could even imagine each of them speaking a different language. (iii) The question of whether their self-addressed orders mean the same as our corresponding self-addressed orders would not even arise if their language was being conceived to be a degenerate fragment of an ordinary shared language (e.g. like the language of a monastic community sworn not to talk to each other, but where each monk has learnt to speak the language in an ordinary social setting before joining the order).

W. then pursues the issue of the relation of thought to utterance, and returns to our theme only on page 221:

Die Private Sprache, die ich oben beschrieben habe ist eine solche, wie sie etwa Robinson auf seiner Insel hätte mit sich selbst sprechen können. Hätte ihn jemand belauscht und beobachtet, er hätte diese Sprache Robinsons lernen können. Denn die Bedeutungen der Worte zeigten sich im <u>Verhalten Robinsons</u>.

Wäre aber nicht eine Sprache denkbar in der Einer für seinen eigenen Gebrauch seine privaten Empfindungen, seine inneren Erlebnisse ausspricht oder aufschreibt? Diese Sprache wäre dann natürlich nur für ihn selbst verständlich, denn niemand als er könnte je wissen worauf sich die Worte, Zeichen, der Sprache beziehen.

(The Private Language which I have described above is like the one Robinson had on his desert island in which he was able to talk to himself. Had someone heard and observed him, he would have been able to learn Robinson's language. For the meanings of the words are apparent in <u>Robinson's behaviour</u>.

But couldn't we imagine a language in which a person could voice or write down his private sensations, his inner experiences, for his own use. Of course, this language would then be intelligible only to himself, for no one else could ever know to what the words, signs, of the language refer.)

From this remark we can extract the further points: (iv) The monologuists' languages are not, in respect of the present concern, essentially different from Crusoe's. Hence (a) the fact that Crusoe learnt English in London, whereas the manner of the monologuists' language acquisition is irrelevant, is here unimportant; and (b) the fact that Crusoe was acquainted with language-games with two or more people, whereas the monologuists were not, is here likewise unimportant. What *is* crucial is (v) the fact that a language is being spoken is manifest in *behaviour* — how that behaviour pattern was acquired is *not* relevant to determining whether a language is in use. And (vi) that the contrast W. is concerned with is not between a shared language which can be employed in solitude (on a desert island) and an unshared, non-social language (which is nevertheless translatable), but rather between a sharable, translatable language on the one hand and an unsharable, untranslatable one on the other.

It is perspicuous from this discussion that W. is not concerned here with claims about the social genesis of a language or of an individual's linguistic abilities. Nor is his argument aimed at establishing that an unshared language is conceivable only in so far as it is derived, by accident (the last Mohican), degeneration (monks who speak only to themselves), or invention (Esperanto before it was taught to others), from a shared one. He is not claiming that reflexive speech-acts are essentially parasitic on non-reflexive, communicative ones. Consequently he is not trying to show that the phenomenon of language is essentially, logically, social — like trade and barter. Rather, his target is the idea of an unsharable language, one which cannot, in principle, be made intelligible to anyone other than its speaker. For the idea that such a language is not merely possible but actual is an unnoticed presupposition tacit in the reasoning underlying idealism (both problematic and dogmatic) and solipsism. It has also, unwittingly, dominated philosophical and theoretical linguistic reflections on language and communication for centuries.

MS. 180(a), 13ff. is derived from MS. 124 with further variations; the final MS. draft is MS. 129, 36ff., where PI §243 occurs after the following sequence: PI §§211, 217, 212 – 13, 209(a)–(b), 208(g), RFM 417(b)–(c), PI §§208(f), 208(e).

Section 244

1   Of course, we do talk about our sensations and use sensation-words to refer to them. (Whether the sensations thus named are known only to the speaker is deferred until §246; what is potentially misleading about talking of *referring* here is discussed in §§273f., 293.) But the crucial question to be clarified (cf. PI §51) is what it means for a word to correspond to, be the name of, a sensation *in the practice of speaking a language*. One cannot hang a name-plate on the sensation (MS. 124, 122), so how is the connection between name and sensation established? How is the practice of employing 'pain' as a sensation-word set up? To answer this, we must look to how the technique of its use is learnt,[2] how we teach or train a person to use such words correctly — for there we shall see what it is that one who has learnt to use the word has thereby learnt to *do*. W. canvasses what he here calls 'one possibility', viz. that sensation-words are taught as substitutes for natural expressive behaviour. It is natural for children to cry when they fall and hit their knee, when they touch something hot and burn themselves. Their parents

---

[2] This is perfectly consistent with the principle that what a conceptual capacity is, what technique has been mastered in acquiring it, is independent of its genesis (cf. 'Explanation', Volume 1, pp. 70ff.; MU pp. 30ff.)

teach them to exclaim 'Ow!', later 'Hurts, hurts!' and then 'I have hurt myself', 'I have a pain'. These utterances are new pain-*behaviour*, grafted onto and partially replacing the natural pain-behaviour in circumstances of injuring oneself. But this is not to say that they do not *also* have other uses, subsequently learnt, e.g. in reporting one's pains to the doctor.

The initial question was: how are sensation-words connected with the sensations they name? In the case of pain, W.'s reply is that it is connected, *qua* replacement, with natural expressive behaviour. This seems to imply that 'pain' means not pain, but pain-*behaviour* — for it is connected thus to the *behaviour*, not to the sensation which that behaviour manifests. Hence the interlocutor's question in §244(b). But the apparent implication does not hold. 'Pain' does not mean crying; it means pain. The fact that 'I have a pain' is a learnt replacement for moaning or crying is *not* comparable to the fact the word 'bachelor' is a substitute for the phrase 'unmarried man' and means an unmarried man. The word 'pain' does not mean the same as the *word* 'moan'; rather, groaning 'It hurts' or 'I am in pain' replaces moaning and crying out in pain. To moan is not to say 'I moan', and saying, 'I am in pain' is not a learnt substitute for *saying* 'I moan', but for *moaning* (cf. LSD 11). 'I have a toothache' (unlike 'I am holding my cheek') is not a description of behaviour.

1.1 (i) 'und benennen sie': 'and name them', i.e. refer to them by name; assigning them a name (giving them a name) is not in question in this sentence.

(ii) 'This question is the same as . . . ': what of the case, which W. countenances (PG 188; BB 12, 97; PI §495), of a being born with an innate mastery of a natural language? Here there would be no question of how the connection between the name and the thing named is *set up*, and that connection could not be clarified by describing how one *learns* the meaning of names of sensation. Nevertheless, this kind of case does not conflict with W.'s argument. For here too the articulate avowal of pain is a substitute for an inarticulate groan of pain; it is a piece of linguistic pain-*behaviour*, and, like inarticulate pain-behaviour, it constitutes a criterion for third-person ascriptions of pain.

(iii) 'Here is one possibility': i.e. one way in which a human being learns the meaning of names of sensation, such as the word 'pain'. The possibility here canvassed is by way of training a child to replace its primitive, natural expressive pain-behaviour first with exclamations and later with sentences such as 'I have a toothache'. Are there other possibilities? Yes, indeed. §288 introduces one: if we have grounds for thinking that an adult does not know what the English word 'pain' means, we should explain it to him, perhaps by gestures, or by pricking him with a pin and saying 'See, that's what pain is!' Here we have a case not of training, but of explaining, and — as with any other explanation — it may be understood rightly, wrongly, or not at all. One might likewise point at someone who is manifestly in pain and say, 'There, that is what it is to be in pain', or even 'That is pain' (cf. LPP 238 – 40, see 2.1(vi)(b) below). Whether these different possibilities for teaching the use of the word 'pain' have been successful in a particular case will be evident in how the learner goes on to use the word.

Are all sensation-names thus bound up with primitive expressive behaviour? After all, there are many cases in which there is no distinctive natural mode of expressive behaviour which is pre-linguistic, e.g. sensations of pressure, of tingling, and throbbing sensations. So the expression 'a throbbing sensation' cannot be viewed simply as a learnt replacement for natural expressive behaviour. This may be granted; but in all these cases the concept of *sensation* is invoked; and *that* concept is bound up with the natural manifestations of sensation, such as groaning with pain, scratching itches, laughing or wriggling when tickled, etc. (cf. 2.1(vi)(a) below).

(iv) 'the primitive, the natural, expression': not symbols but expressive behaviour, as laughter is an expression of amusement.

2   The picture of the relation between experience and its first-person linguistic expression that W. strove to displace is immensely powerful, and his suggestion that we view typical verbal expressions of sensation as learnt forms of sensation-behaviour is still pregnant with a multitude of possible misunderstandings stemming from the classical picture. Some of these are:

(i) LSD 41f.: one is inclined to object that whereas 'I have a pain' is articulate and says something definite, moaning with pain is not. He who moans does not *say* that he is in pain. So how can the avowal of pain be said to resemble a groan of pain? ('Resemble', not 'be the same as'; cf. LSD 11.) The objection is misleading, for a groan is as direct and clear an expression of pain as there is, i.e. the avowal 'I have a pain' is *no closer* to the pain than the groan (cf. PI §245). A person's inarticulate moans manifest his suffering no less than his groaning 'It hurts' or 'I have a pain'.

(ii) LSD 42: We are inclined to say that 'pain' in 'I have a pain' *refers* to a certain phenomenon. This is not incorrect, but it can mislead in this context; for we are inclined to construe it on the model of '"chair" in "I have a chair" refers to something'. But in the former case one cannot *point* to the pain to explain to what the word refers; and in so far as we wish to talk of the 'phenomenon' of pain, then what we call 'pointing to the phenomenon of pain' is to point at a sufferer's groaning. But that does not mean that 'pain' signifies groaning; rather, that 'pain is a certain phenomenon' is philosophically misleading here, for it looks analogous to 'lightning is a certain phenomenon' (viz. this ↗), but is not.

(iii) RPP I §146 elaborates the classical picture. We are inclined to think that a child learns to use the word 'pain' correctly in as much as in such-and-such circumstances it acts thus-and-so, and we think it feels what we too feel in similar circumstances. We teach it to say 'I have a pain', and if our supposition is correct, it learns to associate 'pain' with its feeling and uses it when that feeling recurs. Rather than attacking this associative picture, W. milks what he can from it. What kinds of errors does it correctly exclude? That the word 'pain' is not the name of the pain-behaviour or the circumstance of injury; also that 'pain' is not used now for this feeling, now for another quite different one. These platitudes W. does *not* deny; but he repudiates the associative picture that here accompanies them.

(iv) RPP I §§304ff. emphasizes that what is called 'expression of pain' is *spontaneous* behaviour in certain circumstances. One is not taught to use 'I have a pain' by guessing which of the inner processes connected with falling and scraping one's knees is called 'pain'. Rather, one learns to use it as a manifestation of pain, i.e. as a piece of expressive pain-behaviour. Otherwise it would make sense to wonder on account of *which* sensation one cries out when one falls and hurts oneself (*this* one or *that* one). The question of how one knows whether the sensation one has is one called 'pain' does not arise; but it would if (*per absurdum*) there were no natural spontaneous expression of pain. We are inclined to think that mastering the use of 'pain' in the first person is a matter of attaching the word to the sensation, and *hence* that the child's pain-behaviour is just an occasion for the adult to get the child to attach the name to its sensation. But is there any such thing as attaching a name to a sensation *within oneself*? What are the consequences of this hypothesized act? W. draws an ironic analogy: if one shuts a door in one's mind, is it then shut? What are the consequences? That in one's mind no one can get in?

The argument intimated is that to shut a door in one's mind, if it means anything, is to imagine shutting a door, not to shut an imaginary door (*that* is what Marcel Marceau does on the stage, not in his mind!). The consequences of shutting a door in one's mind are not causal. One can imagine attaching a name-plate to a door, but what follows? That it does not fall off, fade, disappear? Well, one might say, it's your story! But can one attach a name to a sensation *in one's mind*? It is altogether opaque what this means. What is it to attach a name to a sensation *without* the mind? One cannot hang a name-plate on a sensation, hence one cannot imagine doing so either. The grammar of 'attaching a word to a sensation', W. argues, is not that of 'attaching a word to a physical object'. What is it then? 'Pain' is attached to the sensation of pain to the extent that exclaiming 'I have a pain' is an expression (*Äusserung*) of the sensation, and hence too a criterion for someone else to assert 'He has a pain'. If so, then there is indeed no such thing as attaching a name to a sensation *in the mind*. For to say to oneself (in one's imagination) 'I have a pain' is precisely *not* to manifest or give expression to one's pain.

PI §244 emphasizes the primitiveness of the sufferer's pain-behaviour. In other contexts it is no less important to remember the elemental character of our *reactions* to the pain of *others* (Z §545).

2.1   (i) 'How do words refer to sensations?': this seems but a special case of 'How do words refer?', and one is inclined to think that there is a global answer (e.g. by having a sense which determines a referent; or by standing to their referent in the name-relation; or by calling up an idea of their referent in one's mind). This is precisely what W. combats: Z §434 compares the shift from the language-game with physical objects (i.e.

with expressions that name or refer to physical objects) to the language-game with sensations with the shift from talking of transferring posses-sions to talking of transferring joy or pride in possessions. There is something new here in each case, and it requires fresh investigations.

(ii) 'don't we talk about sensations every day': MS. 124, 222 adds 'for example, all kinds of pain, sadness, joy, etc.' As W. later pointed out (Z §§483ff.), it is incorrect to call sadness or joy 'sensations' or 'sense-impressions' (although 'Empfindung' has a wider range than its English counterpart); but it is clear already in §243 that W.'s target is larger than the domain of sensations.

(iii) 'und benennen sie': W. does not deny that 'pain' is the name of a sensation, but rather denies that the grammar of '"pain" is the name of a sensation' is akin to ' "chair" is the name of an article of furniture' or ' "Red" is the name of a colour'. So different are they that 'The word "pain" is the name of a sensation' is equivalent to ' "I've got a pain" is a manifestation of sensation (*Empfindungsäusserung*)' (RPP I §313). To that extent it is potentially misleading to talk of *naming* sensations, and MS. 179, 25 remarks: 'Frage nicht so sehr, "Wie kann man Empfindungen benennen?" als "Wie kann man die Namen der Empfindungen anwen-den?" ' ('Do not ask so much "How can we name sensations?" as "How can one apply the names of sensations?" ')

(iv) 'primitive': Z §541 (RPP I §916), the behaviour is *pre-linguistic*; it is the prototype of a way of thinking, not the result of thought. The language-game is based *on it*.

(v) 'adults talk to him and teach him exclamations': MS. 124, 223 adds 'first, perhaps, baby-language, then the language of adults'. Even the most elementary *verbal* expressions of pain are learnt (in England children say 'Ow', elsewhere 'Owa' or 'Aya'), and onto this adults graft further stages of the modes of verbal expression of pain, e.g. 'Has Johnny got an Ow in his knee?' ('Hast Du ein Weh-weh?') and only later 'Have you hurt yourself?' (cf. Vol. XVI, 220).

(vi) 'Here is one possibility': (a) MS. 124, 224 adds at the end of a draft of PI §244(b), 'Und so sind alle sprachlichen Äusserungen der Empfin-dungen mit den ursprünglichen Empfindungsäusserungen verknüpft worden'. ('And all linguistic manifestations of sensations have been bound up in this way with the primitive manifestations of sensation.') This obviously does not imply that all linguistic expressions of sensation are learnt as substitutes for natural behaviour (for throbbing or tingling sensations have no natural expression), but only that they are linked, directly or indirectly, via the concept of sensation, with primitive expressive behaviour, and are used, in the first-person present tense, as forms of expressive behaviour. Of course, they also have other uses, e.g. as reports.

(b) LPP 238 – 40 argues that one can give an ostensive definition of rage by pointing at a man in a fury and saying 'There, that is rage'. This then is a further possibility of teaching the name of a feeling (emotion), which could be extrapolated to teaching an adult what the English word 'pain' means. To be sure, it does not introduce a private sample, or indeed a public one, by reference to which one can justify one's avowals of pain (or rage). It can be called 'ostensive definition', since, as W. emphasizes, ostensive definitions are ostensive to a degree (LPP 239). Neither pain nor rage are kinds of behaviour, and whether the distinctive uses of 'pain' or 'rage' are successfully conveyed by such an ostensive explanation will be seen in what the learner does with these words. It is obviously wrong to say that one cannot acquire the concept of rage unless one has been enraged and learnt the use of 'I'm furious' as a substitute for a roar of fury. But the learner must realize that the utterance 'I'm furious' is an expression of rage and a criterion for saying of a person that he is enraged.

SECTION 245

1   How can one even want to use language to get between pain and its behavioural expression? What is it, or rather, what does it seem to be, to insert language between experience and its manifestation? And why is it that one is tempted to do this?

§244 argued that avowals of pain replace natural pain-expressions. To the blinkered eye, this seems unjustly to assimilate the avowal 'I have a pain' to *mere* pain-behaviour;[3] but pain-behaviour can occur without pain. And, it seems, when another manifests pain-behaviour, I can never be sure, but only believe, that he is in pain (cf. PI §§246, 303). But in my own case, one is inclined to think, I *know* I am. So my saying 'I am in pain', unlike emitting a groan, is a *true description* of how things are with me, and not mere behaviour, let alone a description of my behaviour (§244(b)). In my case I can apprehend directly, virtually perceive 'clearly and distinctly', the difference between pain plus pain-behaviour and mere pain-behaviour unaccompanied by pain. And 'I am in pain', at any rate *for me*, describes the inner experience.

That is how one wants to insert language between pain and its expression, i.e. that is how one is tempted into this position. But why is this called 'inserting language between pain and its expression'? On this conception, 'I have a pain' is thought to be closer to the pain (i.e. to what it depicts) than is expressive pain-behaviour (which is conceived to a *mere consequence* of what 'I have a pain' depicts). For surely it is as close to it as a

---

[3] But note W.'s remark: 'Of course "toothache" is not *only* a substitute for moaning — but it is *also* a substitute for moaning: and to say this shows how utterly different it is from a word like "Watson" ' (LSD 11).

proposition is to the fact that makes it true (and what could be closer than that — they are even closer than a picture and what it is a picture of! (cf. Exg. §194)). But if so, then the meaning of 'pain' must be independent of the expression of pain (and so, indeed, it seems to be — for do I not know that I am in pain without waiting to see whether I groan?!) It is in this sense that we are tempted to insert language between pain and its expression, and we do not see that 'I have a pain' *is* an expression of pain (*Schmerzäusserung*) and not a picture (*Bild*) of pain.

It is, of course, true that when I groan, I can, if I wish, tell someone whether I am in pain or just groaning. It is also true that when I am in pain, I can say to myself 'I am in pain'. But these truisms do not force upon us the fallacious picture sketched above. In that picture a number of ramifying confusions reinforce each other, giving it a compelling force: (a) I know that I am in pain whenever I am (cf. PI §246); hence 'I know I am in pain' must make sense as a claim to empirical knowledge; (b) I can only believe, not know, that others are in pain (cf. PI §§246, 303); (c) 'I am in pain' is a description (cf. PI §§290f.); (d) behaviour, the outward sign of the inner, can always lie (cf. PI §§249f.; LPE 293). All these confusions are later assailed in the indicated remarks, but, of course, without denying the above truisms.

What are the immediate consequences of thus inserting language between pain and its expression? It would make sense to ask, 'How do you know that what you have is called "pain"?' Since the word 'pain' would not be connected with pain in the manner described in §244, we would be driven to suppose that it is attached to the sensation by mental ostensive definition — a supposition that will be shown to be incoherent (PI §§258ff.). Since the concept of pain would not be essentially connected with the natural spontaneous expressions of pain, the question of what makes *this* behaviour an expression of *pain* would, absurdly, be opened. For one could then properly ask what connection between pain (defined independently of behaviour) and action makes such-and-such action an expression of pain rather than of something else.

1.1   'Wie kann ich . . . treten wollen': 'How can I even want to . . . '

2   MS. 124, 270 introduces this remark in the context of PI §303(b): 'Just try — in a real case[4] — to doubt someone else's fear or pain'. It makes it clear that the classical conception of first-person psychological utterances as true descriptions, known for certain by the subject, is committed to wanting, absurdly, to insert language between pain and its expression. Pretence is possible, the MS. elaborates, but only in special contexts. A dog cannot pretend to be joyful, but not because it is too honest (PI

---

[4] Of someone screaming in pain after severe burns, for example.

§250). We are inclined to say (PI §303(a)) that one can only *believe* that another is in pain, whereas one *knows* in one's own case. This seems the more appropriate expression when philosophizing here; but what we are inclined thus to say, what seems appropriate, is of importance only in so far as it makes clearer the temptations that beset us. One might say to a philosopher, 'I assure you I am not just behaving as if I had pain, I really feel it; I know exactly what "pain" means.' But why should he not reply; 'This too is just pain-behaviour'? Then follows PI §245, succeeded by PI §§314, 271.

RPP I §§305ff. elaborates: if one could learn what pain means independently of one's spontaneous expressions of pain, how could one learn *what* is an expression of *pain*? (cf. Exg. §244, 2 (iv)).

PRIVACY

1. *The traditional picture*

When we reflect upon the nature of our experience and its objects, it is easy to become captivated by a misleading picture of a fundamental ontological duality which we characterize as the physical and the mental. The physical world consists of objects that exist in an objective spatio-temporal framework, that are made of matter of one kind or another, and that interact with each other in physical processes and events. But, as Frege remarked, 'even an unphilosophical man soon finds it necessary to recognize an inner world distinct from the outer world, a world of sense-impressions, of creatures of his imagination, of sensations, of feelings and moods, a world of inclinations, wishes and decisions.'[1] If we succumb to this philosophical picture of the mental as *a world*, we will be prone to populate it with objects, states, events, and processes which we conceive to be, as it were, just like physical objects, states, events, and processes, only immaterial or ethereal (BB 47).

Corresponding to this distinction, a further, metaphysical, duality is characteristically introduced. Objects in the physical world are independent existences. They belong to the public domain, can be perceived by all who are appropriately situated, can often be owned, shared among several owners, or exist unowned. But objects in the 'inner world' are *essentially* owned: 'It seems absurd to us that a pain, a mood, a wish should go around the world without an owner independently. A sensation is impossible without a sentient being. The inner world presupposes somebody whose inner world it is.'[2] Not only are these inner objects essentially owned, they are also essentially untransferable and unshareable. Each person's inner world is metaphysically private property (LPE 277).

To someone who thinks thus, yet another duality, this time an epistemological one, will seem fitting. If the inner world is private property, it is natural to suppose that its owner has privileged access to it. It seems that he can know in a unique way what objects, states, or processes are in it. For while anyone can perceive the public objects in the physical world by means of his senses, only the owner of an inner world can apprehend its occupants by means of introspection. 'Internal sense'[3] or 'inner-sense'[4] is the source of our knowledge of the subjective objects

---

[1] G. Frege, 'Thoughts', repr. in B. McGuinness *Collected Papers on Mathematics, Logic, and Philosophy*, ed. B. McGuinness (Blackwell, Oxford and New York, 1984), p. 360.
[2] Ibid.
[3] Locke, *An Essay Concerning Human Understanding*, Bk II, Ch. i, Sect. 4.
[4] Kant, *Critique of Pure Reason*, A22/B37.

in our private inner world, and it gives us an *immediate, non-inferential, acquaintance* with them, which contrasts with the inferential, perception-mediated knowledge that we strive to attain of objects in the public domain.

> When I see the sun, I am often aware of my seeing the sun; thus 'my seeing the sun' is an object with which I have acquaintance. When I desire food, I may be aware of my desire for food; thus 'my desiring food' is an object with which I am acquainted. Similarly, we may be aware of our feeling pleasure or pain, and generally of the events which happen in our minds. This kind of acquaintance, which may be called self-consciousness, is the source of all our knowledge of mental things. It is obvious that it is only what goes on in our minds that can be thus known immediately.[5]

Not only is our knowledge of the inner immediate, according to this venerable picture, it is also certain. Descartes argued that as long as we restrain ourselves from imputing the character of our current experiences to anything 'outside the mind', then our sensations and thoughts (*cogitationes*) are 'clearly and distinctly perceived',[6] and hence *indubitable*. Unlike the physical world, the inner world is *transparent* to its owner:

> Since all actions and sensations of the mind are known to us by consciousness, they must necessarily appear in every particular what they are, and be what they appear. Everything that enters the mind, being in reality a perception, 'tis impossible anything should to *feeling* appear different. This were to suppose that even where we are most intimately conscious, we might be mistaken.[7]

To the dualities of the physical and mental worlds, and of the public and private, there correspond epistemological dualities of the dubitable and indubitable, the corrigible and incorrigible. 'I cannot doubt that I have a visual impression of green, but it is not so certain that I see a limeleaf. So . . . we find certainty in the inner world, while doubt never leaves us in our excursions into the external world.'[8] It seems therefore that the private is better known than the public. It is a striking, if somewhat paradoxical, feature of philosophers of the post-Cartesian, materialist era to have argued persistently that mind is better known than matter.

Wittgenstein subjected this traditional philosophical picture to critical scrutiny. In every respect he found it a distortion of grammar in the flawed mirror of metaphysics. His resolution of the tangle of philosophical problems in this domain is not a version of 'logical behaviourism' or a form of 'verificationism'. Indeed, it does not lie on the traditional map of possibilities at all. Rather, he aimed to undermine the whole range of

[5] B. Russell, *The Problems of Philosophy* (Oxford University Press, London, 1967), pp. 26f.
[6] Descartes, *The Principles of Philosophy*, Pt I, Sect. 68.
[7] Hume, *A Treatise on Human Nature*, Bk. I, Pt iv, Sect. 2, ed. L. A. Selby-Bigge, rev. P. H. Nidditch (Clarendon Press, Oxford, 1978), p. 190.
[8] Frege, 'Thoughts', p. 367.

received options, leaving behind, as it were, 'only bits of stone and rubble' (PI §118).[9]

2. *Private ownership*

One source of the misconceptions of the classical picture lies in the idea that another person cannot have my experiences: you cannot have my toothache or feel my anger; nor can you have my mental images, for they lie before my mind's eye — they are inner objects in my subjective world. This claim seems to say something about the nature of experience — not something physiological or psychological — but rather something metapsychological or metaphysical. It seems to pinpoint the essence of personal experience that is antecedent to its causal connections with other phenomena (LPE 277). Two people can jointly own the same house; or one can own it first and then sell it to another. Two people can *have* the same room in college, can share it, occupy it simultaneously or successively. But 'Nobody else has my pain. Someone may have sympathy with me, but still my pain belongs to me and his sympathy to him. He has not got my pain, and I have not got his feeling of sympathy.'[10]

Of course, we do say that two people can have the same pain, e.g. a throbbing headache in the temples. But, the philosopher will add, this means that the pains are exactly alike, not that they are identical. 'It would be a contradiction to speak of the feelings of two different people as being numerically the same; it is logically impossible that one person should literally feel another's pain.'[11] This seems plausible, for surely if A and B each have a headache, there are *two* headaches, not one! After all, two people cannot *share* a headache as they can share a room or an umbrella, or as two households can share a telephone line or a garden! Another man's headache is, *ex vi termini*, another headache (cf. FA §27). Their respective sensations are qualitatively identical but numerically distinct.

We are tempted to think thus in as much as we project the grammar of names of physical objects onto expressions signifying experiences. If we think of each person's experiences as objects in a particular inner, subjective world, we will also think that an object in one inner world can no more migrate to another inner world than it can enter the public world of physical objects. Not only can you not have my pain while I

---

[9] This essay is concerned only with two common presuppositions underlying the traditional conception, viz. the privacy of 'ownership' and epistemic privacy. Others are discussed in later essays. The discussion of private 'ownership' of experience rectifies a mistake in Volume 2, pp. 270f. and 279 (amended in the 2nd impression of the paperback edition). Cf. also Exg. §253.

[10] Frege, 'Thoughts', p. 361.

[11] A. J. Ayer, *The Problem of Knowledge* (Penguin, Harmondsworth, 1956), p. 202.

have it, since pains are unshareable, but you cannot even have my pain after I no longer have it. If I do not have the pain that previously belonged to me, then that pain has passed, it no longer exists. It cannot enter the inner world of another person, for there is, as it were, no point of contact between distinct subjective worlds. It is part of the nature of experiences to belong to a subject. For the very identity of these inner objects is bound up with the inner world to which they belong.

> States or experiences, one might say, *owe* their identity as particulars to the identity of the person whose states or experiences they are. From this it follows immediately that if they can be identified as particular states or experiences at all, they must be possessed or ascribable . . . in such a way that it is logically impossible that a particular state or experience in fact possessed by someone should have been possessed by anyone else. The requirements of identity rule out logical transferability of ownership. [12]

The inclination to think thus may be strengthened by the unreflective assumption that the location of a sensation is a criterion for who has it. A's pains, one wants to say, are the pains in A's body. If there is a pain in A's knee, it is A's pain. B may have a similar pain in his own knee, but since B's knee cannot be in the same place as A's knee, his pain cannot be in the same place either. So their respective pains are qualitatively identical, but numerically distinct.

In response to this, Wittgenstein invites us to 'consider what makes it possible in the case of physical objects to speak of "two exactly the same", for example, to say "This chair is not the one you saw here yesterday, but exactly the same as it" ' (PI §253). Evidently we draw such a distinction by reference to spatial location: one chair cannot be in two places at the same time, and two chairs cannot simultaneously occupy the same location. Is it not the same with pains? Since A's pain is in *his* body and B's pain in his distinct body, they are, by parity of reasoning, numerically distinct.

The reasoning is confused, for two different language-games are being crossed. There are many different uses of 'in' ('in the afternoon', 'in the army', 'in the story', 'in heaven', 'in the mind', 'in a sentence', etc.), and among them different senses of location (BB 8) — in the drawer, in the book, in the crowd, in the picture. The expression 'a pain in the leg' has a quite different grammar from 'a pin in the leg', even though both determine locations, and we generate confusion by construing the former on the model of the latter. If an object is in X (as a penny may be in my pocket), it can be taken out of X. It must be smaller than X, otherwise it will not fit and will, at best, be half in, half out. It can be perceived to be in X by, for example, opening X. But while it is true that you cannot perceive the pain in my leg, as indeed you cannot see the pin

---

[12] P. F Strawson, *Individuals* (Methuen, London, 1959), pp. 97f.

in the closed pin-box, the pain is not *in* my leg in the same sense. Even if you open up my leg, you will not find my pain inside it. It cannot be extracted or removed (any more than can a cut in my leg), and although it can be made to go away by an analgesic, when it goes away, it does not go elsewhere. A pain in my finger is neither larger nor smaller than my finger, although it may be the whole of my finger that throbs painfully or only the middle joint. If I have a pain in my foot and my foot is in my shoe, I do not have a pain in my shoe (and the same applies to having a cut in my foot), whereas if I have some money in my purse and my purse is in my pocket, I do have some money in my pocket. In short, 'pain in my leg' does not determine a location in the same way as 'penny in my pocket' does. Hence we should be suspicious of the claim that since A's pain is in his foot and B's pain is in *his* foot, therefore their pains are in different places.

It is noteworthy that it is not quite right to claim that if A has a pain, it *must* be 'in' his body, for this is liable to be misconstrued. An amputee will commonly locate a phantom pain where the amputated limb would have been had it not been removed; but it manifests confusion to suggest that in these anomalous cases the person who has the pain is mistaken about where his pain is. For it would be incoherent to argue that his pain is actually located elsewhere, in a part of his body which does *not* hurt, e.g. the stump of the amputated limb! Where it hurts is not necessarily where the injury or infection is, as is evident also from the case of reflected pains. The criteria for the location of a person's pain are where he points to or where he says it is. These normally coincide, i.e. if he says that his leg hurts, then he also points at his leg to indicate where it hurts. So too, the pain is located in the place he assuages, in the limb he limps on or nurses and so on (PI §302). Phantom pains are anomalous, for there is no such thing here as assuaging the place to which the amputee points. Similarly, he may say that his foot hurts, even though he has no foot, and he points not at his foot but at the place where his foot would have been. But although this exception could not become the rule, it does not stretch the concept of pain-location to the breaking-point, since the person did have a limb where he points. We may say that he is wrong in saying that his foot hurts, but right in saying that he has a pain 'there ↗', where his foot would have been. This degree of conflict of criteria can be accommodated. It is a rule of grammar that a person's pain is where he indicates, avows, etc., not a truth of metaphysics that pains are *in* bodies. But the behavioural regularities which give point to our grammatical convention that a person's identification of the location of his pain is authoritative, i.e. a criterion for the location of his pain, consist in the fact that he assuages his injured limb, clutches the part of his body that hurts, and so forth. If a person were systematically to insist that his pains were outside his body, we would not understand him, not because he was *mistaken*, but because the concept of pain-location would be stretched beyond the breaking-point.

The concept of pain-location is parasitic upon the concept of the sufferer from pain, for the location of a pain is where the sufferer says it is. The person who has a pain is he who *manifests* or expresses the pain (or would do so but for such-and-such reasons). Hence it can be misleading to say that A's pains are the pains in A's body, for that may wrongly suggest that the location of a pain determines the possession of a pain, as if 'Where is it?' were prior to 'Whose is it?' or 'Who is hurt?' But, on the contrary, we can only ask *where* a pain is if we can say *who* is suffering. If two people have a pain in their left thumb, we say that they have a pain in the same place. The fact that their thumbs are in different places no more implies that their pains are in different places than the fact that they are sucking their swollen thumbs implies that they have a pain in their mouths. Consequently, it is wrong to say that two people *cannot* (metaphysically!) have a pain in the same place, and mistaken to infer that two people cannot have the same pain *because* their pains must be in different places. (For a discussion of the Siamese twins' pain at the point of juncture, see Exg. §253).

The source of confusion lies in the superficial similarities between the grammar of expressions signifying, roughly speaking, experiences and the grammar of names of objects. Unmasking further differences should dispel the temptation to think that the foregoing arguments are indecisive. We speak of sensations, sense-impressions, feelings, and moods (but not so much emotions) as *things that we have*. In philosophical discourse we talk of the 'owner' of experiences, and insist, as Frege did, that while ownership of objects is contingent and transferable, possession of experiences is essential and inalienable (i.e. the experiences only 'exist' in as much as they belong to someone). If a person owns a car, a certain relationship obtains between two objects. Is it not the same when a person has a headache? Of course, in the first case, the related objects are independent existences in that the same car may be owned by someone else or by no one at all. Whereas 'subjective objects', as Frege called them, are dependent existences. But that is precisely the difference between objects in the physical world and objects in the inner world! Since my pain is an object in my inner world, no one else can *have* my pain — and does that not mean that I stand to this pain in a relation which no one else can have to it? So, despite the previous clarifications, does it not follow that since you manifestly cannot have my pain, your pain cannot be identical with mine, but only exactly similar?

We are deceived here by the *form* of our language, and need to be reminded of the wide range of different logical categories that are represented in the grammatical form of ownership. We speak of having a car, and here there is a relation between a person and a chattel. The car I have belongs to me, but I might sell it to someone else. Indeed, I might have — be in possession of — a car which belongs to my friend, for he may have lent it to me. We also speak of having a wife or a son, and although this signifies a relationship between two particulars, it is not one of ownership at all, but of being married to or being the parent of a person. We also speak of having a duty or an obligation, and this too may signify a relationship, not a relationship between a person and an object called 'a duty' or 'an obligation', but rather a relationship (e.g.) to a person to whom the duty is owed or to whom a promise was made. Similarly, we talk of having a cold, a sharp tongue, or a sense of humour, and in these cases no relationship between a person and an object of any kind is signified. There is no such thing as having a cold and wondering whether it belongs to one — though one might wonder from whom one caught it. Finally, we talk of *having* a relationship to something or someone, and here it is perspicuous that we are employing the form of ownership bereft of any content at all. For to have a relation to something is not to be related to a relation. If we say that the pen has or stands in the relation of *being to the left of* to the ruler, we do not mean that the pen has two relations, one to the ruler and the other to the relation of being to the left of.

Is having a pain a matter of standing in a relationship to an object (an identifiable particular)? And if so, what relationship is masked here by the form of ownership? An obvious answer is suggested by the grammar of 'pain', for do we not speak of *feeling* pain, as we speak of feeling a pin or feeling the warmth of the fire? And is feeling something not standing in a certain relation to an object, viz. a perceptual relation? Grammar is deceptive here. Feeling a pain is not a form of perception. One can feel a pin in the sofa only if there is a pin to be felt; but if there is no pin there, it may *seem* to one that one feels a pin. Furthermore, there may be a pin, and one may feel *for* it with one's fingertips and yet *fail* to detect it. But to feel a pain *is* to have a pain — one cannot feel it and not have it, nor can one have a pain and not feel it. Nor can it *seem* to one as if one has a pain although one has none. Although 'having' here is replaceable by 'feeling', neither expression signifies a relation any more than 'pain' signifies a relatum. To have a pain is to be in pain, to suffer. It is not to *own* anything. It makes no sense to wonder whether the pain I have belongs to me or to someone else. Neither 'It belongs to me' nor 'It does not belong to me' has any sense when what I have is a headache. Two people with migraine may suffer in exactly the same way, viz. both have a splitting headache. And then we say that they have the same pain. Is it then numerically the same? No — it is neither numerically the same nor qualitatively the same. That distinction belongs to the domain of objects and has no application here. The question 'Whose pain?' is answered by identifying the person who manifests pain. The question 'What pain?' is answered by specifying the intensity, phenomenal characteristics, and location of the pain as indicated by the sufferer. And two people who suffer from the same illness may indeed have the same pain, just as two chairs may have the same colour.

A final objection may be raised. Pains, after all, are not like colours. If an abstract painting consists of two red squares on a blue ground, one could call it 'A study in two colours' but not 'A study in three colours'. But if I have a pain in my foot and a similar pain in my hand, surely I have two pains, not one! We may grant this; for in so far as we count pains, difference of location in the subject's body implies *another* pain, and to that extent we do have a thin analogue of the numerical/ qualitative identity as applied to objects. But it does not follow that if you have a headache and I have a headache, then there are two headaches or even one headache (as opposed to two aching heads) in the room, since headaches are not *in the room* at all. Rather, there are two people in the room suffering from headache — which may be the same or different. To the extent that pains are countable, countability is limited to each person.

The grammatical form of ownership characterizes not only our discourse about sensations, sense-impressions, and feelings, but also about ideas, opinions, beliefs, and thoughts. Labouring under the illusion that two people cannot have identical pains, sense-impressions, or feelings, but only exactly similar ones, we may, like Frege, hasten to ensure that two people *can* have, think, or entertain the *identical* thought. For, we may argue, if discourse is to be intelligible, surely what A thinks must be communicable to B; it must be possible for B to grasp the very same thought that A entertains. Indeed, if logic is to govern our discourse, then if A thinks and says that *p* and B says that not-*p*, they must be contradicting each other — which will only be the case if one and the same thought, viz. that *p*, is in question, affirmed by A and denied by B. Hence it is tempting to insist, as Frege did, that thoughts are like experiences in not being perceptible objects in the physical world, but unlike them in not being subjective objects in the inner world that is private to each subject of experience. Like objects in the physical world, thoughts do not need an owner. They are objective, independent existences, like substances, only not spatio-temporal. And one may even go so far as to postulate a 'third realm' for them to exist in, together with numbers and other abstract objects. This seems to ensure that it is intelligible that two people may grasp the very same thought.

This Platonizing myth-making is both incoherent and redundant. It is incoherent in as much as it would only make sense to talk of different people thinking the numerically identical thought if it made sense to talk of them thinking qualitatively identical, but numerically distinct, thoughts. But it does not; for that distinction, which applies to the domain of objects, no more has application to thoughts than it does to experiences. It is redundant, since the apparent difficulty this manoeuvre was designed to meet is itself illusory. Frege was right to deny the psychologicians' thesis that different people's thoughts can at best be qualitatively identical, but misguided to think that the only alternative is to reify thoughts in order to ensure the possibility of the numerical identity of different people's thoughts. (For further critical analysis of 'private ownership' of experience, see Exg. §253.)

3. *Epistemic privacy*

The idea that since no one else can have the very same experience as I have, then no one else can really know what it is like is robbed of part of its force by Wittgenstein's clarification of the concept of having an experience and having the same experience. Nevertheless, the supposition that when I have, say, a pain, I know that I do, and moreover know this with certainty, is still firmly entrenched. After all, I am *aware* of the pains I have, I *feel* them, and if I sincerely say that I am in pain (have such-and-such a visual impression, want this, or intend that), no one can gainsay me. The mainstream of philosophy has insisted upon this fundamental principle — indeed typically taking it as an inexplicable datum of experience:

> When a man is conscious of pain, he is certain of its existence; when he is conscious that he doubts or believes, he is certain of the existence of those operations.
>
> But the irresistible conviction he has of the reality of those operations is not the effect of reasoning; it is immediate and intuitive. The existence therefore of those passions and operations of our minds, of which we are conscious, is a first principle, which nature requires us to believe upon her authority.
>
> If I am asked to prove that I cannot be deceived by consciousness — to prove that it is not a fallacious sense — I can find no proof. I cannot find any antecedent truth from which it is deduced, or upon which its evidence depends. It seems to disdain any such derived authority, and to claim my assent in its own right.[13]

This infallibilist conception of 'inner sense' did not go unchallenged. If 'inner sense' is a form of self-observation yielding knowledge, if awareness of, for example, pain is akin to awareness or consciousness of objects by means of a perceptual faculty, then it is, as Reid admitted, a mystery that it is infallible. As long as the putative infallibility was viewed as a fact of nature, it was bound to be challenged. Comte argued that 'this pretended direct contemplation of the mind by itself is pure illusion', on the ground that 'The same organ' (viz. the mind) cannot simultaneously perceive, feel, or think, and observe itself so doing: 'The thinker cannot

---

[13] T. Reid, *On the Intellectual Powers of Man*, Essay VI, ch. V. in Sir William Hamilton (ed.), *The Works of Thomas Reid*, 6th edition (Edinburgh, 1863), Vol. I, p. 442.

divide himself into two, of whom one reasons whilst the other observes him reason. The organ observed and the organ observing being in this case identical, how could observation take place?'[14] Mill responded by insisting

that a fact may be studied through the medium of memory, not at the very moment of our perceiving it, but the moment after: and this is really the mode in which our best knowledge of our intellectual acts is generally acquired. We reflect on what we have been doing when the act is past, but when its impression in the memory is still fresh. Unless in one of these ways, we could not have acquired the knowledge which nobody denies us to have, of what passes in our minds.[15]

James agreed with Comte that 'No subjective state, whilst present, is its own object; its object is always something else'.[16] and with Mill that in practice, memory may always be legitimately invoked. But, he stressed, memory is fallible. To be in a mental state is not sufficient for knowledge, otherwise babies would be infallible psychologists. One must not only *have* one's mental states, one must also 'report them and write about them, name them, classify and compare them and trace their relations to other things. . . . And as in the naming, classing, and knowing of things in general we are notoriously fallible, why not also here?' He concluded that 'introspection is difficult and fallible; and that the difficulty is simply that of all observation of whatever kind.'[17]

The arguments were reasonable, given the incoherent premises that saying what one feels or thinks, reporting one's mental states, etc. rest on observation of some kind, and that awareness of one's sensations or emotions is of the same category as awareness of objects. Seeing and hearing are ways of acquiring knowledge about one's environment. But having a pain, feeling cheerful, thinking something are not ways of acquiring knowledge about one's pains, feelings, or thoughts. To be aware or conscious of a pain, a mood, or of thinking does not belong to the category of perceptual awareness, let alone to 'inner perception', but to the categories of capacity, in particular of capacity to say how things are with one, of receptive attention, and (in certain cases) of realization.[18]

---

[14] Auguste Comte, *Cours de Philosophie Positive*, Vol. I, pp. 34–8; quoted in W. James, *The Principles of Psychology* (Dover, New York, 1950), Vol. I, p. 188.

[15] J. S. Mill, *Auguste Comte and Positivism*, 3rd edition (1882), p. 64.

[16] James, *Principles of Psychology*, Vol. I, p. 190.

[17] Ibid, pp. 189f.

[18] Recent writers have recapitulated the confusions of the nineteenth century in challenging the classical thesis of the infallibility of introspection as *factually false*. One example, commonly adduced, demonstrates the muddle: a man being tortured expects another searing pain; his torturers place a piece of ice on his back, and he screams. Did he not believe, falsely, that he had a pain? We might ask the victim why he screamed. He could answer in two ways: (a) because it hurt frightfully — in which case we have discovered that in these circumstances a piece of ice can cause as much pain as a red-hot iron; (b) because he thought it was going to hurt, and screamed in alarm and anticipation. Could he not venture

Wittgenstein's response to the traditional picture of self-knowledge was radical, indeed revolutionary. He denied that we *know* about our current experiences. Contrary to the empiricist, rationalist, and even Kantian conceptions of the 'inner', he insisted that it is wrong, even *nonsense*, to say 'I know I have a pain' (PI §246, pp. 221f.). Such an utterance can be a grammatical assertion, or merely an emphatic affirmation, but not, as philosophers typically take it to be, an epistemic claim. And if it is philosophers' nonsense to claim that I know that I am having such-and-such an experience, it is *a fortiori* absurd to say that in inner sense we have paradigms of propositions that are known with certainty, let alone that they exemplify incorrigible knowledge. Wittgenstein repudiated the very idea of 'inner sense' as an analogue of perception, and denied that an avowal (*Äusserung*) of experience is a report of one's observations or a description of what has been observed *in foro interno*. Our talk of 'introspection', of 'inner vision', is merely a metaphor (Vol. XVI, 61), and the idea of privileged access, viz. that I can 'see' within me, where no one else can, is an absurdity. And even the more modest claim that I must be in a better position than anyone else to say what I am experiencing is brought into question (LPE 279). Consequently, in so far as there is such a thing as self-knowledge, it does not consist in knowing the truth of an array of first-person present-tense experiential propositions, such as 'I have a toothache', 'I have a visual impression of red', or 'I intend to go soon'.

Wittgenstein's arguments, if correct, overturn centuries of consensus. It should, however, be borne in mind that, faithful to his methodological principles, he was not propounding new theories in opposition to antiquated ones. He did not contend that we are ignorant about our own states of mind, or that our 'introspective investigations' are in fact subject to doubt. In denying that we have privileged access to our own mental states, he was not suggesting that we have unprivileged, indirect access. In each case a proposition of traditional philosophy is rejected, not because it is *false* and its denial true, but because it is nonsense — or does not mean what philosophers typically take it to mean. In all cases his manoeuvre is to draw our attention to rules of grammar and to show

---

a different answer, viz. that he thought he was in agony, but was mistaken? No — for this would invite the question 'How did you find out that you were wrong?' Did the sensation change after a few seconds? — in which case he *was* initially in agony, but it then subsided. Or was the sensation the same? — in which case, he initially misidentified it. But that would make sense only if there were available to him criteria of identity for pain in his own case, which he applied incorrectly, private criteria which determine for himself alone whether what he 'has' is a pain or not. That, however, makes no sense (see 'Private ostensive definition'). There is no room in our grammar for a sensation's *seeming* to its owner to be a pain but not really being one. Did it *feel* like a pain, even though it was not one? This is patent nonsense, for there is no 'seeming' here at all. There is no room in our grammar for thinking, rightly or wrongly, that one is in pain; and if we try to make room for this grammatical articulation, the language-game collapses into incoherence.

how we mistakenly construe a grammatical connection or exclusion for an empirical or 'super-empirical' one about the essential nature of the mental.

It makes sense to say of a person that he knows that such-and-such is the case only if it also makes *sense* to deny that he does. For 'A knows that *p*' is meant to be an empirical epistemic proposition, and hence to exclude an alternative. But if there is no such thing as A's being ignorant of *p*, i.e. if it is unintelligible that *p* should be the case, yet A does *not* know it, then 'A knows that *p*' says nothing about A's knowledge. So if the form of words 'A was in pain but he did not know it' is ruled out, i.e. if it does not describe a specifiable possibility, then 'A was in pain and he knew it' is likewise excluded. So too, 'I know I am in pain' can only be conceived as an epistemic utterance if 'I do not know whether I am in pain' is held to be intelligible. But there is no such thing as being ignorant of whether one is in pain; someone who said 'Maybe I am in agony but I do not know whether I am' would not be understood. There is room for indeterminancy ('I am not sure whether the sensation I have is to be called "a pain" or just "a dull ache" '), and, in appropriate cases, e.g. one's thoughts, for indecision ('I don't really know what I think about X'), but not for ignorance.

It might be urged that there is a difference between being in pain and knowing that one is in pain, for in the latter case, over and above the pain, one must recognize that what one has *is* a pain. And, one might add, that is why we do not say of animals that they *know* they are in pain for they are not 'self-conscious' creatures as we are. This is doubly wrong. First, it makes sense to talk of recognizing only if it also *makes sense* to talk of not recognizing or misrecognizing (LSD 111f.). But it does not make sense to say 'I had a pain, but I did not recognize it', let alone to say 'I had a pain, but I thought it was a pleasant sensation'. If someone were to manifest normal pain-behaviour and later say 'I had a pain, but I did not recognize it', we would not know what he was trying to tell us. Secondly, while it is true that we do not say of animals that they know they are in pain, we do not say that they do not know whether they are in pain either. And when our pet is manifestly suffering, we do not console ourselves with the thought that although it is in pain it mercifully does not know it. The simple truth is that animals do not *say* they are in pain, whereas human beings do. The fact that they do not say so does not show that they are ignorant, and the fact that we do does not show that we are better informed. What it shows is that we have learnt to manifest our pain in ways unavailable to animals, whose behavioural repertoire is limited to pre-linguistic behaviour.

The verb 'to know' belongs together with a large group of related epistemic verbs. It makes sense to talk of knowing that *p* where it makes sense to talk of finding out, coming to know, or learning that *p*. But when I have a pain, I do not find out. If one knows that p, one can answer the question 'How do you know?' by citing grounds, e.g. evidence for p or saying that one perceived that p. But when I have a toothache, there is no such thing as my inferring this from evidence, nor is there any such thing as my perceiving my toothache. If it makes sense to talk of knowing that p, it also makes sense to talk of guessing, surmising, and conjecturing that p, and hence too of confirming or disconfirming one's guess or conjecture. But these too make no sense in the case of 'I am in pain' or 'I intend to go'.

Misled by metaphors (e.g. 'the mind's eye') and by homonyms (e.g. '*feeling* pain'), the prevailing tradition in epistemology has confused the *grammatical exclusion* of ignorance with the presence of knowledge. But the exclusion of ignorance, viz. the senselessness of 'I do not know whether I am in pain' also excludes knowledge. 'I know I am in pain' is not an epistemic statement; 'I feel a pain' is not a perceptual claim; and 'I am aware of a pain' is not a cognitive judgement.

Hence too the venerable thesis of the transparency of the mind is confused. It makes sense to say that something appears thus-and-so to a person and that it is as it appears, only if it also makes sense for it to be other than it appears. But it does not make sense to say 'It seems to me that I have a pain, but actually I don't have one', or 'You think you have a pain, but you don't really have one'. So one cannot argue that it is a peculiarity of the mental that things are as they appear and appear exactly as they are, and that *therefore* we know, without a doubt, how things are in the 'inner world' that belongs to us alone. For if there are no 'appearances' in the domain of the mental (from the subject's point of view), then appearances are no guide to knowledge, let alone an infallible guide. So much the better, one might think; for if there is no gap between appearance and reality, then believing that things are thus-and-so with me is a sufficient condition for knowing that they are. But that is mistaken; for it only makes sense to believe that things are empirically thus-and-so if it makes sense for one's belief to be false. Believing truly is inseparable from the possibility of believing falsely. But there is no such thing here as believing falsely; 'He believes he is in pain, but he is wrong' is nonsense. Hence there is no such thing as *believing* that one is in pain.

A similar confusion occurs in the case of certainty and incorrigibility. It is true that I cannot doubt whether I am in pain, but that is not because whenever I am in pain I am certain that I am. It is not that I am *unable*, however hard I try, to doubt whether I am in pain. Rather, nothing counts as *doubting* that one is in pain. Doubt is excluded by grammar, not refuted by grounds for certainty. It makes no sense to say 'I may be in pain or I may not, I am not sure'. Of course, I may be uncertain as to whether the sensation I have qualifies as a pain or is just a rather unpleasant feeling, but *that* doubt does not stem from ignorance, and it is not to be resolved by gathering further information. The apparent incorrigibility of avowals of pain is a distorted reflection of the grammatical exclusion of error. 'I thought I was in pain, but I was mistaken' is nonsense (although 'I screamed because I thought it was going to hurt' is perfectly in order). It is true, as Reid put it, that 'I cannot be deceived by consciousness' in the matter of my sensations; but that it is not because I am so perceptive or because that of which I am conscious is so easy to recognize, but rather because there is no such thing as deception of this kind in this particular language-game. 'I cannot make a mistake' here is like 'I cannot be beaten at patience'. (But *self-deception* is, of course, common when it comes to such 'inner states' as emotions and attitudes – whereon hangs another tale.)

Locke argued that it is 'impossible for anyone to perceive without *perceiving* that he does perceive. When we see, hear, smell, taste, feel, meditate, or will anything, we know that we do so'.[19] That is misconceived: I may see that A sees something, hear what he is manifestly listening to, apprehend what he is thinking, and find out what he wants. But I cannot see that I see something or perceive that I hear a noise – there is no such thing. James observed glibly that 'The word introspection need hardly be defined — it means, of course, the looking into one's own mind and reporting what we there discover. *Everyone agrees that we there discover states of consciousness.*'[20] But I can no more *look into* my mind than I can look into another's, and we often have more insight into the mind of another than into our own. The perceptual metaphor bound up etymologically with the word 'introspection' is profoundly misleading in philosophy and psychology. We confuse the ability to say how things are with us, what we are feeling or perceiving, what we think or want, with the ability to *see* — with the mind's eye, of course — and *therefore*, we think, we can say what is 'within' us.

This picture of our capacity to give verbal expression to our experiences, desires, thoughts, and intentions is distorted by the perceptual model of introspection. For to be able to say that one has a pain when one has one is not to have access to anything, let alone *privileged* access, and an avowal of pain is not the report of an observation. Of course, one can report one's pains, as when one tells the doctor that one's pain this morning is not so severe as yesterday and that the throbbing has subsided. But the cry 'Ow, I've hurt my finger' is not such a report. Similarly, there is such a thing as observation in this domain, as when I record the course of my pains in a diary for medical purposes; but it can be misleading to characterize this as 'observation', since it is not based on *observing* anything (RPP II §177). To say to another 'I'm furious with

---

[19] Locke, *Essay Concerning Human Understanding*, Bk II, Ch. xxvii, Sect. 11.
[20] James, *Principles of Psychology*, Vol. I, p. 185.

you' is typically to express my anger, not to describe something accessible to me alone by introspection, just as to say 'I love you' is to avow one's affections, not to describe oneself or one's emotion. Hence too it is not necessarily the case that I am in a better position than others to say what I see, feel, or think. If I am semi–delirious and in severe pain, I may be unable to do more than groan inchoately, but the doctor, familiar with the disease, may be able to describe my pains in detail. If I am in a fit of rage or ecstasy of delight, words may fail me, and my ability to express my feelings in words, as opposed to deeds, may be less than that of a bystander. And when I have difficulty in expressing my thoughts, someone else may articulate them much better than I could, and I may say 'Yes, that's exactly what I meant'.

What *is* true, but wholly distorted by the traditional picture of self–knowledge and self–awareness, is that *my word* has a privileged *status*. This is not because I have access to a private peep-show and so can describe what I see in it, whereas others cannot. Rather, it is because what I say is an expression or manifestation of my experience, whereas what others say of me is not. 'I have a headache' is typically a manifestation of pain, and comparable to a groan; 'I've decided — I'll go' is an expression of intention, and 'I think that such-and-such' is not a *description* of anything 'inner' but typically (in an appropriate context) an expression of opinion. The privileged status of my utterances is *grammatical*, not epistemic, and it is constituted by the fact that my utterances are *criteria* for how things are with me. They are not statements or reports of what I know, but expressions of what I think, manifestations of my will and purpose, and avowals of what I feel or perceive. (But one must not forget that we have here a whole spectrum of cases, which Wittgenstein described in detail; see 'Avowals and descriptions', §4.) There is indeed such a thing as self–knowledge and self–consciousness; but it does not consist of an array of reports and descriptions of one's sensations, perceptions, thoughts, and feelings. We say of a person that he is highly self–conscious if he has a heightened awareness of his own emotional life, reflects deeply on the character of his reactions, the pattern of his desires, and the subtle nuances of his motives. To attain authentic self–knowledge is typically far more difficult, not easier, than to achieve knowledge of the character, motivation, and personality of others.

Is there *no* use at all for 'I know . . .' in this domain? Does Wittgenstein's contention not fly in the face of linguistic usage? He anticipated this objection: 'If you bring up against me the case of people's saying "But I must know if I am in pain!", "Only you can know what you feel", and similar things, you should consider the occasion and purpose of these phrases. "War is war" is not an example of the law of identity, either' (PI p. 221). One may say 'I know I am in pain' as an emphatic assertion that I *am* in pain (PI §246), as one may say 'I know I intend to go to London' as an exasperated concession to someone who is nagging. Or one may use such expressions as grammatical statements to emphasize that doubt or uncertainty is senseless (PI §247). Of course, we also say such things as 'I don't know what I want (think, intend)'; but this is not an expression of ignorance to be resolved by more careful introspection. Rather, it is an expression of the uncertainty of indecision, and what is requisite is not information about my desires (thoughts, intentions), but resolution. We also say 'I know what I want (think, intend), but I'm not going to tell you'; but that is just to say that I do indeed want (think, intend) something but I am not going to say what it is, or to declare that my mind is made up but that I am going to keep my decision to myself. Wittgenstein was not legislating about linguistic usage, but rather pointing out that these expressions do not belong to the language-game to which they superficially appear to belong:

If I say 'This statement has no sense', I could just point out statements with which we are inclined to mix it up, and point out the difference. This is all that is meant. — If I say 'It seems to convey something and doesn't', this comes to 'it seems to be of this kind, and isn't'. This statement becomes senseless only if you try to compare it with what you can't compare it with. What is wrong is to overlook the difference. (LSD 130)

If we take 'I know I am in pain', 'I know what I see', or 'I know what I want' as epistemic statements, as are 'I know he is in pain', 'I know what he sees', or 'I know what he wants', then we cross language-games and produce philosophers' nonsense (cf. PI p. 221). One should remember that it does not follow from the fact that one is playing a game on a chessboard and has a queen on the board that one is playing chess.

Objections come from various quarters. Surely, one may respond, one can lie about one's plans. But to lie is to know that *p* and to assert that not-*p* with intent to deceive. Does this not show that it *must* make sense to know that one has a pain? Equally, one remembers that one was in pain; but to remember is to know what one previously knew and not to have forgotten it. Does it not follow that if one can remember being in pain, one must have known that one was in pain? If I know that you know such-and-such, then surely I too know it, for are we not eyes and ears to each other? So if I know that you know that I am in pain, do I not therefore know that I am in pain? Surely, if there are nine other people in the room, I may know that no one in the room is in pain (if, e.g., we are all making merry). Does that not imply that I know that I am not in pain?

And finally, one might question the claim that I have no grounds for saying that I am in pain. For, after all, I have the best justification for saying so, namely that I feel the pain!

Wittgenstein anticipated these objections, or at least showed how they may be rebutted. To insist that one can lie about one's pain yet cannot know that one is in pain seems to imply that one can lie about something of which one is ignorant, which is absurd. But the complement of the grammatical observation that there is no such thing as knowing that one is in pain is that there is equally no such thing as not knowing (being ignorant of the fact) that one is in pain. To lie about one's pain is to be in pain and to say that one is not, or not to be in pain and to say that one is (LPE 280). Similarly, to remember that one was in pain is to have been in pain and not to have forgotten it, to know now that one was in pain – not to know now something one knew before. Only dogmatic adherence to a form of analysis (explanation) forces one to construe the recollection of pain as a retention of acquired knowledge. So too, I may, of course, realize that you know that I am in pain; but I neither need nor can use your authority to assure me that it is indeed true that I am in pain, since there is no such thing as my being sure that, or unsure whether, I am in pain. Your knowledge is authoritative for me only if it makes sense for me not to know what you know; but 'I don't know whether I am in pain or not, please tell me' is nonsense.

Although my sincere avowal of pain is authoritative, i.e. constitutes a criterion for others to say of me 'He is in pain', that is not because I have a special epistemic authority with respect to my pains, but because my avowal of pain is an expression of pain, just like a groan. Again, from the fact that I know that no one in the room is in pain, it does not follow that I *know* that I am not in pain, but only that *I* am not in pain and that I know that the other nine people are not either (cf. Exg. §§408f.). Finally, one may insist that one said one had a toothache because one felt it, not because one was acting — i.e. in order to draw that contrast (LPE 315, 319). But feeling a toothache is not a justification for saying one has a toothache as feeling a penny in one's pocket is a justification for saying that there is a penny in one's pocket. For to feel a toothache *is* to have a toothache. One may justify an utterance by citing evidence, but that I have a pain is not evidence for my having a pain. One may also justify an utterance, e.g. 'The curtains are ultramarine', by reference to a sample. But the only sample that could, as it were, justify saying 'I have a pain' would be a 'private' one, and there is no such thing (LPE 293; cf. 'Private ostensive definition', §3). It is, of course, true that I do not say that I have a toothache on the grounds of observing my behaviour (as others do), but it does not follow that I say it on any other grounds. I say it without justification, and rightly so (PI §289; MS. 166, 25f., 44f.).

4. Only a first step

The suggestion that first-person psychological utterances of the kind under consideration are not expressions of knowledge goes against the grain of centuries of philosophical reflection. To accept it involves as dramatic a re-orientation of philosophical thought as does Wittgenstein's parallel argument that propositions of mathematics are not descriptions of a realm of abstract entities, but rather rules of representation, and that accordingly 'knowing', 'believing', 'being certain', etc. in the domain of mathematics have a quite different grammar from that of knowledge, belief, and certainty in the empirical domain (cf. Volume 2, 'Grammar and necessity', §4). That we possess knowledge of our own subjective experience, that we know with absolute certainty how things are with us, has been the common ground of agreement between sceptics and their opponents ever since philosophical debates about the extent and possibility of human knowledge began.[21] It could be challenged, philosophers thought, only in a fit of madness, for here at least our knowledge is secure; we cannot err about our current sensations and feelings, about our sensory experiences, i.e. about how things sensibly seem to us to be. And the debate raged for centuries over how, if at all, we can infer from this solid foundation any knowledge about the 'external' world or about the states of mind of other people.

It was altogether characteristic of Wittgenstein to seek to disentangle the knots in our philosophical understanding by questioning precisely what seemed unquestionable, what was taken for granted virtually before debate began. It seems to have been an almost instinctive maxim of his that where philosophical debate has polarized between a pair of alternatives that seem exhaustive, the appropriate method to follow is not just to examine the conflicting arguments on each side and then opt for the seemingly stronger ones. Rather we should find out what was *agreed* by all participants in the centuries-old debate and reject that.[22]

Of course, rejecting the cognitive conception of first-person present-tense psychological utterances does not mean accepting the view that we do not know but merely believe that things are thus-and-so with us. Indubitable knowledge is not repudiated in favour of dubitable knowledge or mere belief, for, as we have seen, *both* are ruled out. To insist that avowals are made without any grammatical justification is not to insist that they stand in need of justification. Rather, we must come to see that justification in this domain makes no sense, and to view such utterances as none the worse for that. We must learn to see these

---

[21] James, *Principles of Psychology*, Vol. I, p. 185.
[22] Cf. F. P. Ramsey, *The Foundations of Mathematics* (Kegan Paul, Trench, Trubner and Co. Ltd, London, 1931), pp.115f.

language-games from a different perspective, just as in the philosophy of mathematics we must view mathematical propositions from a different perspective than the customary one.

The clarification of the confusions of private ownership of experience and of epistemic privacy with its attendant conceptions of introspection and the subjective transparency of the mind is only a first step. The classical pictures of the mind and their contemporary dialectical anti- theses are held in place, as has been suggested, by numerous further misconceptions. Hence subsequent investigations will explore the inco- herence of private ostensive definition as a means of assigning sense to psychological predicates. The picture of the relation between behaviour and mental state as a relation of 'outer' to 'inner' must be shown to rest on misunderstandings of metaphors and misconstruals of grammar. The distinctive uses of psychological expressions must be brought to light in order to clarify how different they are from the superficially similar uses of names of physical objects and their properties. Only when these further steps have been taken can one break the spell of the mythology of the mind that bewitches us.

EXEGESIS §§246 – 55

Section 246

1   The private language introduced in §243 consists of words which refer
to the speaker's 'immediate private sensations'. Having explored the
connection of the word 'pain' to the sensation, W. now examines one
sense in which sensations are said to be 'private', viz. *epistemic* privacy:
we are inclined to think (a) that only the subject of experience knows
whether he is really experiencing pain, seeing red, feeling joyful, etc.,
and (b) that others merely surmise it. Taken one way, both these
thoughts are false; taken another, both are nonsense. (Cf. 'Privacy', §3.)

It is false that *only I* know whether I am in pain; for others can and
often do know whether I am in pain. And it is false that others always
merely *surmise* that I am in pain: if someone is hit by a motor car and lies
writhing on the ground, could one say 'I surmise that he is in pain'? Does
one need more evidence to go beyond a surmise? What would justify a
knowledge-claim if not this? There are, of course, cases when one
guesses that another is in pain, but a surmise is only intelligible where it
makes *sense* for one to know that which one surmises. If it were
(logically) impossible for another to know that I am in pain, it would be
equally impossible (unintelligible) for another to surmise it.

A philosopher might concede that in the ordinary use of 'know' we do
say that we know that others are in pain, but nevertheless not with the
certainty that the subject has of his own pain. Hence, he might claim,
there is a special sense of 'know' in which I know whether I am in pain
and in which others cannot really know this. This move reveals the
nonsense underlying the two limbs of this conception of epistemic
privacy.

(i) It cannot be said of me at all that I *know* that I am in pain. For this
form of words to fulfil the role the classical epistemologist (e.g. the
Cartesian, empiricist, or Kantian) allocates it, it would have to make
sense for me to guess or surmise that I am in pain and to find out, learn,
and confirm that I am (or am not). It would have to be intelligible that I
be in pain and not know it, but only wonder whether I am. But none of
this makes any sense; we have no genuine use for these forms of words.
Pari passu it makes no sense to say that I am certain that I am in pain
(whereas others cannot have that kind of certainty). For it only makes
sense to be certain where it makes sense not to be certain, to doubt, to
think but not be sure. 'I *know* I am in pain' may be used as an emphatic
way of saying that I *am* in pain. It may be used as a joke ('He wonders

whether I am in pain', I might say with a wry grin, 'I know!') or as a grammatical remark drawing attention to the senselessness of doubt in one's own case.

(ii) It is similarly nonsense to say that others learn of my sensations *only* from my behaviour. For that implies that there is some better way of learning of my sensations, inaccessible to others but available to me. Here we are inclined to think that others know of my sensations only *indirectly*, whereas I know *directly*. But this is nonsense, since I cannot be said either to know or not to know. To know that a person is in pain by observing his behaviour is not a defective, derivative way of finding out; it is what is called 'seeing that another is in pain'. It could even be called 'knowing directly that another is in pain' — if, for example, we called finding out by hearsay that someone is in pain 'knowing indirectly' that he is. There is no 'more direct' way of coming to know that a person is in pain; in particular, *having the pain* is not a direct way of knowing that someone (namely oneself) is in pain, since to have a pain is not to ascertain or come to know that one has a pain.

§246 (c) extracts the meagre grammatical truth from the misconception of epistemic privacy, which is given further emphasis in PI §247.

1.1   'in einer Weise falsch': 'In one way this is false'.

2   Various grammatical points are being invoked here that are made explicit elsewhere. (a) LSD 13 (and elsewhere) emphasizes that it makes no sense to say 'I know that I see' if it makes no sense to say 'I don't know that I see'. Such a proposition and its negation constitute a logical space: the sense of one stands or falls with the other.[5] (b) Contrasting concepts such as 'direct/indirect', 'concealed/revealed', 'immediate/mediate' only make literal sense when we are concerned with *signs of one category* (LPE 280). To say '*His* pains (the 'inner') are hidden from me' is like saying 'These sounds are hidden from my eyes' (LW §885), not like 'The view is hidden by the fog'. (c) Families of concepts *together* surround the same logical space. If it makes sense to know that *p*, it must also make sense to learn, find out, investigate whether, confirm that *p*; and if it makes sense to be certain that *p*, it must make sense to doubt, conjecture, wonder, think but be unsure that *p* and to be right or mistaken (MS. 159, 21; Z §549; LPE 278). Note that these three points are not compromised by conceding that 'I know I have a pain' does have a use, viz. as an emphatic way of saying 'I am in pain' or as a joke. For these emphatic or jocular uses are not *epistemic claims*.

[5] But there are exceptions to the (grammatical) principle of contrast, which reveal the non-uniformity of the concept of a proposition: viz. the whole domain of *a priori* propositions (itself non-uniform) and propositions that are the subject of *On Certainty* (which are equally diverse). Each case must be judged on its own merits.

Vol. XVI, 13ff. examines the retort 'Surely I *must* know whether I have a pain'. Does this mean that I must know that what I have is *called* 'pain'? One is inclined to deny that and say it means that I must know that it *is* pain. But compare this with 'I must know that this is a chair', where one may know various things: that one can sit on it, that this contraption opens out into a chair, etc. What one really means is 'I must surely know what I have' — but what then does one *have*? For one can answer only with words or gestures. The only correct point here is that it is senseless to ask 'Are you sure you have a pain?' — but not because the bearer is obviously certain. One does employ the form of words 'Surely I must know . . .' (and this is a source of the philosophical confusion); but reflect on the circumstances in which it is used, e.g. when the doctor says 'But it doesn't hurt that much!' One might also retort 'Now don't tell me what I feel' (LSD 13). These, one might say, are not epistemic responses but grammatical ones.

MS. 159, 21 examines the notion of 'immediate awareness': propositions of which philosophers say we have 'immediate knowledge' seem certain and unquestionable. (They are 'clear and distinct', 'self-presenting', or 'evident'.) And we are prone to think that that is because they rest securely on something — viz. on the experience one has (and, some philosophers have argued, one *perceives* the experience infallibly). But this is like saying that the earth rests on something that is firm in itself. These propositions rest on nothing (cf. Exg. §289). The expression 'immediate awareness' here is misleading, for it suggests that one is *right* about something. But there is no right or wrong here at all. No one would say 'I'm sure I'm right that I have a pain'.

LPE 280, 293f. examine a natural objection. I can lie about my experience, see something red and say 'I see green'. But surely lying is *knowing*[6] such-and-such and saying something else which one knows to be false. So lying about my pain is knowing that the proposition 'I am in pain' is *true* and saying 'I am not in pain', which one knows to be false. The objection rests on an unwarranted assumption about the uniformity of the concept of lying. To lie about what colour one sees is, e.g., to see red and say 'I see green'; to lie about one's pain is to have a pain and say 'I have no pain'. In short, 'a lie about inner processes is of a different category from one about outer processes' (MS. 169, 104).

SECTION 247

1   One legitimate use for 'Only you can know . . .' is as a grammatical proposition, part of an explanation of the use of certain psychological

---

[6] Believing would suffice here.

expressions. Thus used, it signifies that the expression of doubt or uncertainty (as opposed to indecision) in one's own case is senseless, and that for another to doubt one's sincere avowal of intent is equally absurd.

1.1   'If you had that intention': the tense is puzzling, since obviously you may have had an intention, told me, and forgotten about it, in which case I know that you intended to ϕ, and may remind you. But maybe what W. had in mind is 'Only you can know if just *this* was what you meant to do', as one might say, 'Only you can know whether by ". . . ." you meant such-and-such'. These are grammatical statements drawing attention to the special evidential status of an agent's avowal. (But note that the German uses neither emphasis nor a demonstrative pronoun.)

2   RPP I §§564ff. examines 'Only I know whether or what I am thinking, another cannot know it'. What do I know? That what I am doing is thinking? No; there is no comparing what I am doing with a paradigm to ensure that *this*, which I am doing, *is* thinking. But, of course, it is true that typically another does not know what I am thinking unless I tell him. Does this make a thought *essentially* private? After all, if I utter my thought *aloud* and no one hears me speak, no one will know what I think; but is it 'private'? And if I *tell* another what I am thinking, is the thought still 'hidden'? 'My thoughts are known only to myself' means roughly 'I *can* express my thoughts, say what I am thinking, if I wish'. But it is an important feature of the concept of thinking that if I do *not* tell another what I am thinking, he must typically *guess* (whereas if I do not tell another that I am ill, he may *see* that I am). And whether his guess is right is determined *by my word* (and by such-and-such circumstances).[7] Whereas whether I am ill or not is not determined for the doctor by my word. 'I cannot say what he is thinking (unless he tells me)' is not like 'I cannot say whether he is ill (unless I run such-and-such tests)'. Our confusion here stems from crossing different language-games.

    MS. 171, 4: 'Nur ich weiss, was ich denke, heisst eigentlich nichts andres als: nur ich *denke* meine eignen Gedanken.' ('Only I know what I think actually means nothing other than: only I *think* my own thoughts.')

2.1   'And here "know" means . . .': cf. BB 30: 'Of course I know what I wish', unlike 'Of course I know the ABC', does not imply that I surely know something as simple as that. Rather, it signifies that there is no doubt in this case, since it makes no *sense* to talk of doubt. 'In this way the answer "Of course I know what I wish" can be interpreted to be a grammatical statement.'

---

[7] But, of course, one sometimes can say 'I could see what you were thinking written all over your face'!

What of 'unconscious wishes'? Surely it is a cardinal claim of psycho-analytic theory that we are ignorant of our unconscious wishes? This is confused: an unconscious wish does not stand to a wish as an unheard sound stands to a heard one. (Cf. Volume 2, pp.18f.) So a special explanation is called for. My 'ignorance' of my unconscious wishes (beliefs, desires) is wholly unlike my ignorance of your unvoiced wishes (beliefs, desires).

SECTION 248

1   'One plays patience by oneself' is not an empirical proposition about all hitherto observed games of patience. It is a grammatical proposition which explains an aspect of the game: there is no such thing as playing patience against another, just as there is no such thing as fighting a duel without an opponent. So too, 'Sensations are private' is a grammatical proposition which gives, or perhaps intimates, a rule (or rules) for the use of sensation-words. Here it is used to indicate the senselessness of doubt (and hence too of certainty) in the first-person present tense (cf. Exg. §§246f.); in other contexts it might be used to emphasize the possibility of concealment and dissimulation (Vol. XII, 179) or the privileged status of a person's avowal as a criterion for how things are with him.

2   This occurs in Vol. XII, 179, preceded by the remark:

> Do not say 'one cannot', but say instead: 'it doesn't exist in this game'. Not: 'one can't castle in draughts' but — 'there is no castling in draughts'; and instead of 'I can't exhibit my sensation' — 'in the use of the word "sensation", there is no such thing as exhibiting what one has got'; instead of 'one cannot enumerate all the cardinal numbers' — 'there is no such thing here as enumerating all the members'. (Z §134)

Two points are noteworthy. First, what looks like an inability is a logical impossibility, and a logical impossibility is not a possibility which one cannot actualize. It does not signify limitations upon what can be done, but rather earmarks the bounds of sense. Beyond these is not something one cannot do, but only the void of nonsense. Secondly, in this context (Vol. XII, 179) W. appears to take 'Sensations are private' to signify that there is no such thing as exhibiting to public view the sensation one has, *in the sense* in which I can exhibit what colour something I saw was by pointing at a sample. In PI §248 the remark alludes to epistemic privacy, which is an illusion the truth behind which is only the senselessness of doubt in one's own case. Note that below (PI §§311ff.) W. argues that one *can* exhibit pain (only not *privately*), but to exhibit pain is to *behave* in such-and-such a way — it is not to exhibit to another what one has 'got' (and one cannot do that to oneself either).

LPE 283 remarks, 'Does the solipsist also say that only he can play chess?' The solipsist mistakes the bounds of sense for metaphysical, super-physical, constraints, which he then misconstrues. Applied to the game of patience, the solipsist would claim that only he can play patience!

RPP I §570 adds: ' "Thoughts and feelings are private" means roughly the same as "There is pretending", or: "One can hide one's thoughts and feelings; can even lie and dissimulate". And the question is, what is the import of this "There is . . ." and "One can".' That I can hide my thoughts does *not* signify that *thinking* my thoughts is hiding them, and that I can pretend or lie about my thoughts does not imply that I *know* my thoughts. Conversely, what I think to myself silently can only be said to be 'hidden' from another in the sense that he cannot *guess* it; it does not mean that he cannot perceive my thought because it is in my soul! (LW §977).

SECTION 249

1   This can be linked with §246 and perhaps §244. The connection with §246 is simple. There the interlocutor claimed that one cannot know, but only surmise, that another person is in pain. But, W. replied, if we are using the verb 'to know' as it is normally used, then one often does know when someone is in pain. §249 can be seen as an ironic amplification on the certainty of such knowledge in one kind of case. In the case of an infant's manifestations of experience, there can be no room for doubts based on pretence, for the concept of pretence has no grip here (see below).

The link with §244 (if intended) is more complex. §244 argued that 'pain' and the sensation of which it is the 'name' are connected via the primitive, natural expressions of sensation; for the child is taught to use 'pain' or 'I have a pain' instead of merely crying. §249 can be seen as raising a difficulty: might we not be wrong in assuming that this primitive expressive behaviour is not a pretence? On what is our assumption based?

Why is this a difficulty? And what answer are we expected to give? The difficulty is this: if the smile of the unweaned infant were not an expression of contentment, but a dissimulation, if the cry of the infant when he falls were not an expression of pain, but an instance of shamming pain, then it seems that when adults try to teach the infant to use the word 'pain' as a verbal extension of or replacement for this behaviour, he might learn to use 'pain' as a replacement for shamming pain-behaviour rather than for the spontaneous expression of pain. Indeed, if pain and shamming pain were different states of mind which have the same behavioural expression, we might inadvertently be teaching the child to call 'pain' not what we call 'pain', but whatever state of mind constitutes shamming pain (RPP I §§142ff.). But this drags scepticism in its wake. For if 'pain' is directly connected to 'mere' behaviour, which may be an expression of pain *or* of feigning pain, then what precise inner experience it is thereby connected with *in another* is wholly speculative. Worse still, how do *I* know that I've learned to use the word to express what my teachers (parents) wanted me to express? Should I say that I believe (and hope) I have (LPE 296)? The meaning of 'pain' wavers, and the evidence for others' experiences seems worthless. (Just as illusion threatens to engulf our knowledge of the 'external world', so pretence threatens to nullify our knowledge of the experiences of others.)

But we are not over-hasty in taking the infant's smile to express contentment. And this 'assumption' is not based upon an experience, for in the first place we do not assume the infant's smile to express contentment because we have observed numerous infants and noted that usually when they smile thus they are contented. 'I have never seen a new-born child shamming contentment' is like 'I have never seen a new-born child who thought that π is greater than $\sqrt{7}$'. Secondly, it is not an assumption:[8] 'Assuming it is not pretending, the child is content' would be a joke! Why is this?

> When I say that moaning is the expression of toothache, then under certain circumstances the possibility of its being the expression without the feeling behind it mustn't enter my game.
>
> Es ist Unsinn zu sagen: der Ausdruck kann immer lügen. [It is senseless to say: the expression may always lie.]
>
> The language-games with expressions of feelings are based on games with expressions of which we don't say that they may lie. (LPE 293)

The natural, pre-linguistic behaviour in certain circumstances is the hard ground upon which these language-games are played. But might it not turn out to be sand? Could we not be wrong? No; the foundations of our language-games are not assumptions, but forms of response and action.

Pretending, like lying, is a language-game that must be learned, and there are many things one must already be able to do before one can pretend. Feigning, dissimulating, pretending are false moves within a game; but one cannot make a false move in a game before one knows what counts as a correct move. A new-born child cannot be insincere, but neither can he be sincere. To dissimulate, he must first learn to mimic

---

[8] LPE 295 remarks, 'I must assume an expression which is *not* lying', but W. would surely have corrected this later. I no more assume this than I assume that objects do not cease to exist when I do not perceive them.

and to intend to mimic. But to mimic is not to dissimulate; for to dissimulate, he must further intend to deceive, hence to bring it about that others believe that he is content, in pain, etc. even though he is not. To do so he must be able to *think* that. But that thought and that intention presuppose a multitude of skills, which he must first acquire.

How do we know that he does not already have them? Because what we call an exercise of such capacities requires a highly complex background pattern of behaviour, just as what we call 'making a mistake in calculating' does. We do not say of a child that he has miscalculated until we ascribe to him the capacity to calculate.

The picture underlying the objection sketched out in the third paragraph above is therefore misconceived. Shamming pain is not a state of mind (although one who shams pain is in a different *frame of mind* from one who cries out in pain). The behavioural expression of pain is not linked with pain and shamming pain in the same way (MS. 171, 1), any more than money and counterfeit money are linked in the same way with purchasing power. It is no more possible for all behaviour to be pretence (or all perceptual experiences to be illusions) than it is possible for all money to be counterfeit. It is profoundly mistaken to think that the *same* behaviour is just connected with two distinct 'inner' states or experiences, the one pain and the other shamming pain. The behaviour *may* be the same (as a perfectly forged banknote resembles the genuine prototype), but even then the surrounding circumstances differ. Pretence, like forgery, has a model, and there is a skill and artifice in matching the prototype. The behavioural criteria for pretence differ from the criteria for unfeigned behaviour. The connection of behaviour to the 'inner' is conceptual, not causal, and shamming pain is not an expression (*Äusserung*) of an inner experience of the same category as pain.

1.1   'needs to be learned': one does not learn to lie as one learns to ride a bicycle. One may, in certain circumstances, learn to lie *better*; but one does not *learn* to lie as one learns (is taught) skills. It is true, however, that one must already have learned much, be able to do many complex things, before one is able to lie.

2   This theme preoccupied W. from 1936 onwards, especially after 1945. The following is a selection of points bearing directly on the incoherence of neonate pretence and what must be learnt in order to be able to pretend:

(i) Pretending to be in pain is just *one* form of pain-behaviour without pain (PI pp. 229f.). There are many others, e.g. automatism, perhaps induced by drugs (RPP I §137), hypnosis, miming (RPP II §631) or playing charades, acting the role of someone in pain on the stage (LPE 296), acting the role of someone *pretending* to be in pain on the stage

(LW §863). Hence it is a very *specific* psychological process, though not an 'inner' process (RPP II §612).

(ii) Pretending to be in pain is an activity informed by specific motives and intentions. One may pretend to be injured and incapacitated with pain in order to attack someone who comes to help. The same behaviour can occur without these motives and intentions, and it is this which inclines us, rightly, to insist that there is an 'inner' difference between the cases. But 'inner' is a misleading metaphor here. That there is such a difference is manifest in the fact that one can *confess* that one was dissimulating, i.e. confess such-and-such intentions. But an intention is not something 'inner' (RPP I §824).[9]

(iii) Pretence can (logically) occur only within a highly complex tapestry of life, for it is a pattern with infinite variations within the fabric of life (LW §862; MS. 169, 137). And recognizing behaviour as pretence is akin to recognizing a pattern in a weave. Imagine a long strip of tapestry: here I see pattern S, there pattern V; sometimes I don't know which it is for a while, and sometimes I say at the end, 'It was neither of them.' One is taught to recognize these patterns by being shown simple examples and then more complicated ones of both types, rather as one learns to distinguish the musical styles of two composers (MS. 169, 137). So too with pretence; and were pretence *not* such a complicated pattern within life, then it *would* be conceivable that a new-born child might pretend (MS. 171, 1).

The complexity ramifies in various directions. Pretence presupposes sophisticated capacities, even where the behaviour in question appears not to be sophisticated. An adult can pretend (or manifest sincerity) without saying a word, but merely by facial expression or gesture or even inarticulate sounds (LW §944). But for these apparently simple pieces of behaviour to constitute pretence presupposes complex motives, intentions, and conceptual skills, as well as a complicated *play of expressions*. Can one imagine a languageless new-born child with the play of features and gestures of an adult (LW §§945f.)? Not obviously, for the smooth features of a baby lack the multiplicity and possibilities of articulation characteristic of the lined face of an adult. But to the extent that we can, it is as something dissonant, slightly repulsive, since it would be a meaningless play of expression. For a creature to have such complex intentions, motives, beliefs, etc. as are presupposed by pretence, its pretending behaviour must occur against a backcloth of its own complex behavioural repertoire manifesting the capacity for appropriately sophisticated motives, beliefs, and so forth. Finally, note the variety and complexity of the endless contexts in social life in which we pretend,

---

[9] Of course, in a trivial sense it is (LW §959); but the point is that we have a wrong picture of what we call 'the inner'.

contexts which provide motives and reasons for different *kinds* of pretence, dissimulation, hypocrisy, and charlatanry. These forms of simulation, whether good, evil, or morally indifferent, are only possible against complicated backgrounds of human life.

(iv) A child may find that when he is in pain and screams, he gets coddled. Then he may scream in order to get coddled. But this is not pretence, merely one of its roots (LW §867). We may teach him to say 'toothache' instead of screaming with toothache, and likewise he may then say 'toothache' in order to get treated kindly. But this is not yet lying (LPE 295). There is much more to be learnt before one can pretend[10], lie, or be insincere. For a new-born child cannot be malicious, friendly, or thankful; these are possible only within the context of complicated patterns of behaviour which he has not yet mastered (LW §942). A new-born child not only cannot be insincere, he cannot be sincere either.

(v) What then must the child learn? What must he understand and be able to do before we can justly say that he is pretending to be in pain, dissimulating, being sincere or insincere? W. indicated various features. He must learn to imitate pain-behaviour and must be capable of *intending* to imitate (MS. 171, 5f.). (The execution of such intentions, unlike the natural pain-behaviour which is being imitated here, may be *skilful* or clumsy and inept!) There are grades of pretence, of which simple mimicry is a primitive form. To pretend to be in pain, one must know how one who is in pain behaves and target one's behaviour on that model, *intend* to *reproduce* it. Dissimulative pretence is complex, for it involves an intent to deceive, to behave like someone who is in pain with the intention that someone else should believe falsely that one is in pain. This is a far more sophisticated matter. For this the child must understand such propositions as 'He thinks I'm feeling pain but I'm not' (LW §866). Hence the child learns to dissimulate pain only in the course of learning the complicated use of 'having pain'. He must learn not just the use of 'He has a pain', but also of 'I think (believe) he has a pain' and hence 'He thinks I have a pain' (RPP I, §142).

(vi) One can say of a child 'Today he pretended for the first time', but not 'Today he was sincere for the first time' – yet not because children are naturally sincere (LW §§940–2). Indeed, one *cannot* say of the expressive behaviour of the baby that it is sincere. In order to be sincere, the child must, for example, realize that *insincerity* is bad. Mere unrestrained expressive behaviour is no more sincere than uninhibited verbal expression is candid. One *can* say 'The child is already definitely sincere' (but not 'for the first time'), for the realization of the wrongness of insincerity dawns gradually over a totality of behaviour, informing a

---

[10] But note the qualification below, Exg. §250.

multiplicity of actions and not, as it were, illuminating them one by one (cf. Z §469).

(vii) The wordless sincerity or insincerity we see in the face of an adult exists only in a complicated play of expressions (as false moves exist only in a game) (LW §946). This develops cheek by jowl with the child's acquisition of a multitude of patterns of behaviour, reaction, and interaction. As these evolve, one might say, the soul is developing – something 'inner'. But it is noteworthy that from this perspective the 'inner' no longer appears as the prime mover of the 'outer' expression (LW §947). Rather they are fused, as form and matter.

2.1   'Lying is a language-game that needs to be learned': Vol. XV, 84 elaborates. There is said to be a tribe that is too primitive to lie. This seems paradoxical, for one now thinks of a lying-intent as a product of a language-game. So one may think of such people as being good and innocent, and that they are made evil through learning a technique of language. But to say that one learns the specific language-game of lying is not to say that one therewith learns *pretence* for the first time. For a people who are unacquainted with lying-speech can nevertheless *pretend*, be false and deceitful, just as a child can pretend before he can lie.

SECTION 250

1.1   'die richtige Umgebung': 'the right surroundings', i.e. for a creature's behaviour to constitute pretending, it must occur against a background of highly complex behaviour *of that creature*, e.g. behaviour manifesting complex intentions and capacities.

 2   LW §§859–70 clarifies: for behaviour to be an expression of pain, fear, or joy, it must occur in a very specific context. But for behaviour to be the pretence of pain, it requires an even more far-reaching, particular context. Not every creature that can express fear, joy, or pain can feign them. 'A dog can't pretend to be in pain, because his life is too simple for that. It doesn't have the joints necessary for such movements' (LW §862). To be able to pretend *or* be sincere, a complicated pattern of behaviour must be mastered. 'A dog cannot be a hypocrite; but neither is it sincere' (LW §870; PI p. 229).

MS. 169, 134 allows the concept of pretence more elasticity, presumably because we find it altogether natural to say, for example, of a bird which flutters on the ground to draw a predator away from its nest, that it is pretending to have a broken wing. But, of course, this is akin to (although, being innate, even more primitive than) the infant's crying in order to be coddled (and not to the child's crying in order to induce his mother to believe that he has hurt himself). Hence here W. observes that there are many simple forms of pretence: 'Kann ein Idiot zu primitiv sein, um sich zu verstellen? Er könnte sich auf tierische Art verstellen. Und das zeigt, dass es von da an Stufen der Verstellung gibt.' ('Can an idiot be too primitive to pretend? He could pretend in the way an animal does. And that shows that from there on there are grades of pretence.')

The limited applicability of psychological predicates to animals pre-occupied W. (cf. PI §650; Z §§114–20), for it illuminates the character of our concepts. MS. 179, 17 describes human expectant behaviour and observes that a dog can only expect in a much more primitive sense than we do. The next remark is striking and clarifies the idea that the surroundings of behaviour are crucial for the applicability of psycho-logical concepts: I may sit quietly in my room hoping that someone will come, but if *one minute* of this hoping were, as it were, isolated, cut off from its antecedents and sequel, this would no longer be hoping. The hopeful look at the door, the rising pulse, the muttered exclamation, thus isolated, signify nothing (cf. RFM 336). Behaviour and psychological state are what they are only in the rich tapestry of life; a single thread alone cannot provide the modelling and the contours. And the texture of life of an animal is too loosely woven and too simple to make intelligible its expecting its master to come home tomorrow, sincerity or insincer-ity, honesty or dissimulation.

2.1   'Perhaps it is possible . . .': cf. RPP II §631 (= Z §389), 'A clever dog might perhaps be taught to give a kind of whine of pain but it would never get as far as conscious imitation.'

Section 251

1   'Sensations are private' was compared with 'One plays patience by oneself' (§248). These are grammatical propositions. But the former, especially when cast in the form 'Only I can know whether I am in pain', looks like a description of the necessary limits of human knowledge (for others *cannot* know). In this way metaphysics disguises grammar, and expressions of norms of representation are dressed in the garb of what is represented.

Such propositions as 'My images are private' or 'Only I can know whether I am feeling pain' look like empirical propositions of an especially firm kind, scientific truths that no one would gainsay (BB 55). We often defend ourselves against such claims by trying to highlight their non-empirical character. We might ask, ' "Is what you affirm meant to be an empirical proposition? Can you conceive (imagine) its being otherwise?" – Do you mean that substance has never yet been destroyed, or that it is *inconceivable* that it should be destroyed? Do you mean that experience shows that human beings always prefer the pleasant to the unpleasant?' (PG 130). And in the same spirit, when one wants to show the senselessness of such metaphysical turns of phrase (viz. the absence of an intelligible negation; that these sentences do not divide a logical space), one says 'I can't imagine the opposite of this' or 'What would it be like, if it were otherwise?' (cf. PG 129).

However, this defence against the empirical appearance of meta-physical propositions is almost as fraught with potential confusion as what it is meant to guard against. 'I can't imagine the opposite', although it points to the *a priori*, non-empirical character of, e.g., 'My images are private', *looks* like an appeal to the limitations upon one's powers of imagination. If that were so, one might respond that more imaginative exercises are necessary: sensations are private – that is a brute fact about the human conditions, and if you cannot imagine it otherwise, you must get into training! But this is *not* what was meant by 'I can't imagine the opposite'; rather, it is that one cannot even *try* to imagine the opposite (PG 129), one does not know *what* one is supposed to imagine (MS. 176, 9); indeed, there is nothing here *to* imagine – and *that* is what one means.

Why is this so? Because the negation of an *a priori* proposition is not a description of a possible state of affairs; nor is it a description of an impossible state of affairs. For it is not a description at all, but a senseless form of words. Hence too, the *a priori* proposition itself (e.g. 'Sensations are private') is not a description, but a misleading expression of a grammatical rule (cf. 'Grammar and Necessity', Volume 2, pp. 263ff.).

'I can't imagine the opposite', properly understood, draws attention to the fact that the proposition in question is a norm of representation. But if I cannot imagine or even try to imagine the opposite, one might just as well say that I cannot imagine the thing itself (PG 129). And that would not be like 'I can't imagine that Oxford is in England' (because I already *know* it to be so, and one can only imagine that *p* if one does *not* know that *p*), for that restriction limits 'I can imagine' to possibilities one does not know to be actualized. But so-called necessary truths which one acknowledges as such are not actualizations of possibilities, but expres-sions of grammatical rules; and that one cannot imagine things to be so is not a consequence of one's knowing them to be so, but of the fact that such propositions do not describe how things are at all.

Nevertheless, we do *not* say 'I can't imagine the thing itself', but only 'I can't imagine the opposite'. Why? Because we regard the senseless grammatical proposition (e.g. 'Every rod has a length') as a tautology as opposed to a contradiction (PG 129). Tautologies and contradictions alike are senseless, they say nothing; but we are inclined to favour tautologies, to say that they are true, that we know that it is either raining or not raining, that we are certain that it is not both raining and not raining, etc. But this is misleading in so far as it fosters a disposition to construe degenerate propositions on the model of genuine ones. Similarly here, our inclination to say 'I can't imagine the opposite' and not ' I can't imagine the thing itself' reflects our partiality for, e.g., 'This rod has a length' as opposed to 'This rod has no length'. But this is a parallel misunderstanding. It is based on the thought that 'This rod has a length' is verified by the fact that the rod has a length of 4 metres – after all, 4 metres is a length! But '4 metres is a length' is a *grammatical proposition*, a rule for the use of words. 'This rod has a length' is no less senseless than 'This rod has no length' (PG 129).

Our partiality for 'I can't imagine the opposite', rather than 'I can't imagine the thing itself', is not absurd, for it expresses a dim apprehension of the role of grammatical propositions (and that the negation of a grammatical proposition is not a grammatical proposition). 'Every rod has a length' is a grammatical proposition signifying that the expression 'the length of a rod' (unlike 'the length of a sphere') is meaningful (cf. BB 30), that it always makes sense to ask of a rod 'How long is it?' Now surely one can imagine, make a mental image of, every rod's having a length; one simply conjures up an image of a rod! Does this not show that while one cannot imagine a rod without a length, one *can* picture to oneself every rod's having a length? In a sense it does; but this mental image, and hence this imagining, has a quite different role from the image one might conjure up in connection with 'This table has the same length as that one', for in the latter case there is such a thing as a picture of this table's *not* having the same length as the other. A picture attached to a grammatical proposition is not a picture of how things are (let alone of how they *necessarily* are), but a pictorial *sample* that might perhaps show what such-and-such (e.g. 'the length of a rod') is *called*. And there is no such thing as an 'opposite picture'.

1.1   (i) 'Wir wehren uns mit diesen Worten': 'We defend ourselves with these words against . . .'.

(ii) 'Aber warum sage ich': 'But why do I say'.

(iii) 'Ich kann mir, was du sagst, nicht vorstellen': 'I cannot imagine what you say' when you say that my images are private, etc. This refers back to paragraph (a).

(iv) 'I simply imagine a rod. Only this picture . . .': mental images are not a necessary accompaniment of imagining. But when imagining what is picturable, one may have a mental image (*Vorstellungsbild*). Elsewhere (PI §301, cf. Exg.) W. argues that imagining is not having a *picture*, although a picture corresponds to it; i.e. a mental picture or image is not a kind of picture (as drawings and paintings are different kinds of picture). This does not affect the point being made here.

(v) '((Remark about the negation of an *a priori* proposition))': it is unclear to which remark this refers. The argument, however, is clear. The negation of an *a priori* proposition is altogether unlike the negation of an empirical proposition. The latter describes a possible state of affairs, something that is imaginable. The negation of a true *a priori* proposition does not – but then neither does a true *a priori* proposition. The negation of a true arithmetical proposition, e.g. '~ (2 + 2 = 4)' is not a proposition of arithmetic (although '2 + 2 ≠ 5' is). The negation of a tautology is a contradiction, and contradictions are not propositions of logic (which is not to say that they have no role in logic). But both tautologies and contradictions are senseless. The negation of a grammatical proposition (e.g. of 'Nothing can be red and green all over simultaneously') is not a grammatical proposition, for it does not have the role of a norm of representation (cf. 'Grammar and necessity', Volume 2, pp. 276–81).

2   The ancestors of this remark (e.g. Vol. X, 121f.; Vol. XII, 75ff.) associate it with the venerable idea of the imagination's providing a criterion of logical possibility (now relocated at PI §512). This is evident in PG 128–30 (derived from Vol. X): it looks as if word-language enables senseless combinations of words, whereas the language of imagining does not; for when one wants to show the senselessness of metaphysical turns of phrase, one often says 'I can't imagine the opposite of that'. But this is doubly mistaken. First, the language of images, and hence of drawings too, does allow of senseless representations (think of Escher's etchings). A mistaken blueprint can be exactly analogous to a nonsensical pseudo-proposition. Secondly, this misconstrues the significance of 'I can't imagine the opposite' (and here follows a version of PI §251). We say that such-and-such is unimaginable or *inconceivable*, but do not pause to reflect on how strange it is that one should be *able* to say (or think!) this. For *what is it* that we *cannot conceive*? If we (wrongly) regard thought as an accompaniment of words (or 'ideas' and images as the gold backing for linguistic paper currency), then the words specifying what is inconceivable must be unaccompanied. So what sense does such a statement have? It indicates that this form of words is senseless, excluded from our language like some arbitrary noise. But then the reason for thus explicitly excluding it can only be that we are tempted to confuse it with a genuine sentence.

  RFM 89 criticizes Frege's conception of laws of human thinking, e.g. that it is impossible for human beings to recognize an object as different from itself. Frege presented these as psychological, empirical laws about the workings of the human mind (GA, Introduction, pp. xvff.). But that is absurd, for there is no such thing as recognizing an object as different from itself. If there were, one could *try* to do it (as one can try to run a mile in 4 minutes). But if I look at a lamp and say with greatest intensity

'This lamp is different from itself', have I *tried* to think something I cannot manage to think? It is not that I see immediately that the words I utter are false — they are not false — but rather that I can do nothing with this form of words, for it is senseless. Note that Frege sharply distinguished laws of truth from laws of taking-to-be-true (laws of thinking) and did *not* take imaginability to be a criterion of logical possibility. His confusion was to think that there is something to be imagined as the negation of an *a priori* proposition, and also that creatures might *think* in accord with the negation of 'laws of truth' (cf. Volume 2, pp. 317f.). This confusion is a product of his mistaken idea that *a priori* propositions have *sense*.

Z §442 remarks that the opposite of an *a priori* proposition, i.e. of an expression of a norm of representation in the guise of a proposition about objects, really will be 'unthinkable', since what corresponds to it is a form of expression which we have *excluded*.

2.1   'This table has the same length as the one over there': for the relation between 'has the same length as' and 'has a length', see PG 351f. (cf. also PLP 385f.).

3   William James nicely exemplifies confusion about the role of imaginability. Round squares and objects both black and white all over are conceivable, he argued. 'It is a mere accident, as far as conception goes, that [these expressions] happen to stand for things which nature never lets us sensibly perceive.' To be sure, they are not imaginable, but 'How do we know *which* things we cannot imagine unless by first conceiving them, meaning *them* and not other things?'[11]

W. read James carefully, finding in his work a stark illustration of the deep need for philosophical investigation (MS. 165, 150f.). James claimed that psychology is a science, yet discusses hardly any scientific questions. His moves are just so many attempts to free himself from the metaphysical spider's web in which he is caught. 'He cannot yet walk, or fly at all,' W. added in English, 'he only wriggles.'

SECTION 252

1   A coda to §251. Why are we so inclined? We think of 'This body has extension' as being verified by 'This body has a surface area of 4 square metres' and '4 square metres is an extension' (cf. PG 129). But the latter is a grammatical proposition, and the product of an empirical proposi-

[11] William James, *The Principles of Psychology* (Dover, New York, 1950), Vol. I, p. 463 and n.

tion p and a grammatical proposition q is p — for a grammatical proposition is senseless (cf. '$p. (q \vee \sim q) = p$').

SECTION 253

1   The epistemic sense in which sensations are conceived to be private having been exposed, W. now turns to what might be called 'privacy of ownership', viz. 'Another person cannot have my pains.' This too appears to be a statement of super-physical constraints; but it is in fact a nonsense (MS. 129, 40). Failure to apprehend this leads one to think that another person cannot have the same pain as I do. That this is confused becomes evident if one examines what counts as a criterion of identity here. (Cf. 'Privacy', §2).

W. approaches the question by inviting us to consider what makes it possible, in the case of physical objects, to distinguish between being identical (*dasselbe*) and being exactly the same (*das Gleiche*) but not identical. Why? What bearing does this have on the question? We are strongly inclined to project upon pain (or indeed upon anything that is 'inner') the grammar of physical objects. Someone who is disposed to say that another person cannot have my pains will also typically insist that he really means that another cannot have the *identical* pain (*dasselbe, identische*) I have, though of course he can have the same (sort of) pain (cf. Exg. §254). In the case of a chair we can draw this distinction; two chairs of a Chippendale set are exactly alike but not identical. They are located in different places, exist whether observed or unobserved, may belong to the same person, to different people, or to no one. Hence it makes sense to affirm that this is the chair I saw last week, or to say that it is not the same chair but one exactly like it, the other having gone to be repaired. Two people may successively (or even simultaneously) sit on the same chair, or they may sit on distinct chairs that are exactly alike.

If the distinction between being identical and being exactly the same but not identical applies to pain, then one might indeed argue (as Frege, for example, did) that although your pain may be exactly the same as mine, it is nevertheless not identical. And one might go on to argue that it *cannot* be. But does the distinction apply? What is the criterion of identity for pains?

We distinguish with respect to pain: phenomenal characteristics, intensity, and bodily location, rather as we distinguish with respect to colour: hue, saturation, and brightness. Two objects painted in the same hue, saturation, and brightness are the same (not merely similar) colour. And so too, if my headache is a dull throbbing pain in the temples, and yours is also a dull, throbbing pain in the temples, do we not have the same pain?

One might respond by saying that since your headache is in your temples and my headache is in mine, i.e. in different places, they cannot be the same. This is wrong. What we *call* 'having a headache in the same place' *is* having a pain in the same part of the body, you in yours and I in mine. And as we, including doctors diagnosing illnesses, use the expression 'same pain', two people are said to have the same pain if the pain each has tallies in intensity, phenomenal characteristics, and location.

The interlocutor might reply by saying that 'same place' thus used just means 'corresponding place'. The corresponding location, he might insist, is after all not the same location. So two people *cannot* have the very same pain! Rather than challenging this confusion over sameness and difference of pain-location, W. seems willing to allow this distinction to be drawn and meets the interlocutor on his own ground. Even if we grant that a 'corresponding location' is not 'the same location', it does not follow that two people *cannot* have the same pain. For Siamese twins might feel pain at the point of juncture, not just in 'corresponding locations'. The interlocutor must now concede that as far as this point is concerned, it is logically possible for two people to have the same pain.

This argument works as an *ad hominem* strategy. But it is noteworthy that W.'s concession is misleading. If the head of one of the Siamese twins is conjoined with the back of the other, then one has a headache and the other a backache. And a headache is not the same pain as a backache even though the twins point at and assuage the point of juncture. 'Having a pain in the same place' and 'the location of a pain' are not used to refer to a spatial co-ordinate. If I have a splitting headache and so do you, then we both have the same pain in the same place.

One might be inclined to object that even in this case another person cannot have the same pain as I do, for after all, my pain is *mine* and his pain is *his* (BB 54). But this is to make the owner of the pain *a property of the pain* (PR 91), and that is as absurd as claiming that my chair cannot be the same colour as your chair, because the dark brown of my chair has the property of belonging to my chair and the dark brown of your chair has the property of belonging to your chair, so the two chairs cannot have the same colour (BB 55; LSD 4f.). This misrepresents the grammar of 'the same colour' (and of 'belonging'), and so too the claim that my pain is not the same as his because mine is mine and his is his (or, even more confusedly, I feel mine and he feels his) distorts the grammar of 'the same pain'/'different pain'. Of course, this is not to say that the grammar of 'pain' is isomorphic with the grammar of colour-words: we ask what colour something is, but not what pain it is; we ask where A's pain is, but not where the chair's colour is; and so on.

In so far as it makes sense to say that my pain is the same as his, two people can have the same pain (and often do, when they have the same disease). One might add that in so far as it makes sense to say that my pain *differs* from his, it also makes *sense* for my pain to be the same as his. But why the 'in so far as'? Two explanations might be ventured. First, no qualification is intended on its making sense. Rather, given the clarification of §251, W. is now drawing our attention to the fact that the metaphysician is either making a claim or merely issuing a grammatical recommendation. In so far as he is making a claim, however, then what he says makes sense, and so does its negation. Secondly, the qualification may be in place in order to emphasize that the insertion of the possessive pronoun 'my' or 'his' in 'I have [a] pain' is misleading. W. emphasized this point in PR 93: 'What in my experience justifies the "my" in "I feel *my* pain"? Where is the multiplicity in the feeling that justifies this word? And it can only be justified if we could also replace it by another word.' The truth of the matter, W. then argued, is that 'our language employs the phrases "my pain" and "his pain", and also the expressions "I have (or feel) a pain" and "He has (or feels) a pain". An expression "I feel my pain" is nonsense' (PR 94; cf. LWL 18f.). This argument does not occur after 1932/3, perhaps because by then W. realized that there are contexts in which one can intelligibly say, for example, 'I have your headache now'. Nevertheless, there is an important point here.

Having a pain, unlike having a pin, does not signify a form of ownership or possession. I can have a pin which does not belong to me, but there is no such thing as having a pain which does not belong to me. I can borrow a pin and have it in my possession for a while before returning it to its rightful owner. But in the case of sensations such a distinction makes no sense; the requisite multiplicity is missing. 'My pain' does not mean 'the pain that *belongs* to me', but just 'the pain I have'. Someone else can have the same pain, i.e. a pain with just those characteristics. What he cannot have is the pain that belongs to me, but then neither can I!

This may incline one to insist that ' "I feel his pain" is nonsense', but that would be too hasty. We do say 'He has his father's build' or 'She has the Mona Lisa's smile', as well as 'I have caught your cold'. In such cases the sameness of build, smile, or cold is signified, together with a form of connection, genetic, paradigmatic, or causal. There is nothing misleading about such propositions, because the form of connection in the context indicates the known character of the build, smile, or cold. The proposition 'I have his pain', except in a context in which his pain has been described, is anomalous precisely because no characterization of the pain is thereby intimated, since 'being his' is not a feature of the pain. But if we have both been eating the same food, and you complain of severe stomach cramps, and a few minutes later I too feel severe stomach cramps, I might say 'I've got your pains now', i.e. 'I have the same pains as you.'

The metaphysician wants to insist upon the metaphysical unshareability of pain. But he must also insist that it *makes sense* that two people should have the same pain, for otherwise he could not say what it is that is metaphysically prevented from occurring. If he relinquishes the latter claim, the former one collapses into a recommendation that we change the grammar of 'pain' and no longer say of two sufferers from migraine that they have the same pain, but rather that they have different pains that are exactly alike. However, now we have been given no *reason* for this shift of grammar (viz. treating the 'owner' as a property of the pain or treating *feeling* pain as distinct from *having* pain). The 'metaphysical limitation' was a recommendation masquerading as a reason, but it could be stated only in so far as it did not lead to a shift in grammar.

§253(c) highlights the reaction of one who thinks that being *his* is a property of the pain he has. He might be inclined to strike himself on the breast and say 'Another person can't have *this* pain!' But, we should respond, *which* pain? It is no use replying 'The one I feel', for 'the pain I feel' = 'the pain I have', and we should ask again, '*Which* pain is that?' Stressing 'this' while thumping oneself does not define a criterion of identity; it does not specify *what* it is that another allegedly cannot have, any more than *staring* at the colour of the chair and saying to oneself 'Surely another object can't have *that* colour' does. Worse still, the emphasis deludes us into thinking that we are being reminded of the criterion of identity with which we are conversant (as if being felt by me were a criterion of identity of the pain I feel), whereas by merely thumping one's chest and saying '*This* pain', nothing is indicated about the actual criteria of identity, viz. intensity, phenomenal characteristics, and bodily location.

1.1   (i) 'Another person can't have my pains': once the mistaken claim that two people cannot have the same pain is unmasked, the primary interest in this proposition lapses. Nevertheless, one may still wonder whether some grammatical truth does not lurk behind it. One is tempted to concede that another person can have the same pain as I have, but that nevertheless he cannot have my pain. This makes scant sense.[12] The only truths one can squeeze out of this misbegotten proposition are as follows: (a) 'My pain' does not mean 'the pain that *belongs* to me' as 'my penny' means 'the penny that belongs to me', since pains do not in that sense *belong* to sufferers (see above). 'My pain' = 'the pain I have'. This is a trivial tautology, but it makes clear one purpose that might be served by the misleading metaphysical proposition 'Another person can't have my

---

[12] Contrary to what was argued in Volume 2, pp. 270f. and 279. This error has been corrected in the 2nd impression of the paperback edition of *Wittgenstein: Rules, Grammar and Necessity* (Blackwell, Oxford and New York, 1989).

pain'. If I am asked 'How is your pain now?', it would be a joke to reply 'Much worse, but fortunately I don't have it any longer, John does' or 'I don't know, ask John — he has it'. In this sense, if I do not have it, it is not mine. And if John has it, and the pain gets worse, one cannot say that my pain is getting worse. (b) My pain is manifest in my behaviour, for the person who manifests pain is said to be the person who has a pain. My pain-behaviour is a criterion for *my* being in pain, just as my smile is a criterion for *my* amusement, not yours. Another person's manifestation of pain cannot show *me* to be in pain, any more than his smile can be a criterion for my amusement. Of course, another person may have the same pain or be just as amused as I. (c) If I step on your foot and you yelp 'Ow! That hurt', I might, in a moment of philosophical jocularity, reply 'I did not feel a thing'. Why is that a joke? Because it equivocates between 'It did not hurt *me*', i.e. 'I did not feel a pain in my foot' and 'I did not feel a pain (or the pain) in your foot'. Is the latter merely an empirical proposition? (If so, why is it funny?) Or should one say that there is no such thing as feeling a pain in another's body? W. denied this (WWK 49; PR 92; BB 49ff.) on the grounds that if someone were asked to indicate where it hurts, he might (with eyes closed) point at his neighbour's leg. This can be envisaged in the case of a phantom pain. But it is not sufficient to establish a coherent case for having a pain in another person's body. The moot point is where he points when his neighbour moves his leg, leaves the room, or goes to America. Does the victim point in the direction of America and say 'That is where it hurts'? Would we understand him? And would anyone know *where* it hurts him? Who limps when he has a pain in his friend's leg? Who assuages the pain? The example no more establishes the intelligibility of having a pain in someone else's body than the parallel tale in which he points (with eyes closed) at the table leg demonstrates the intelligibility of having a pain in the table. And the suggestion that I might have toothache in another person's tooth, i.e. wince when his tooth is touched, etc. (WWK 49), is equally problematic. For both the concept of pain-location and the concept of a person's body are being shaken to pieces. If so, then 'I can't feel a pain in another person's body' expresses a grammatical proposition, viz. that there is no such thing. In so far as it makes sense for me to have your headache, it will be in my head. (But no one would say 'I feel your headache in my head'; rather, 'I have your headache' or, better, 'I have the same headache as you'.) (d) There is a noteworthy asymmetry between being aware of one's own pains and being aware of another person's pains. 'I was aware of the pain in my leg' means much the same as 'I had a pain in my leg and it occupied me, held my attention, etc.' But 'I was aware of the pain in his leg' does not mean 'I had a pain in his leg, etc.', but rather 'I was cognizant of the pain in his leg' (for someone told me about it) or 'I perceived that he had a pain in his leg, and this caught my attention'. It is doubtless this that motivates the misguided metaphysical remark 'I can't be aware of another person's pain *in the same way* as I am aware of my own pain'. This is confused, for I am not aware of my own pain in *any way*, i.e. there are no ways or methods of becoming aware of my own pains. It is nonsense to say that I am directly aware of my own pains but only indirectly aware of his. What is true is that I do not perceive that I am in pain, whereas I do perceive that he is. I learn, come to know, that he is in pain by perceiving his behaviour, but there is no such thing as my learning or coming to know that I am in pain. In particular, being aware of my own pain is not coming to know that I am in pain; it is just having a pain (and, perhaps, having my attention caught by it).

(ii) 'Welches sind *meine* Schmerzen?': 'Welches', not 'Welche', so better: '*My* pains — what are they supposed to be?' There are not two distinct questions here, one concerning the criterion for being the subject of pain, which is not answered here at all, the other concerning the criterion of identity for pains. The former question is resolved in §302: the subject of pain is he who manifests it. Here W. is concerned only with confusions over the criterion of identity of pain which incline one to think that two people cannot have the same pain.

(iii) 'Die Emphase spiegelt uns vielmehr nur den Fall vor': 'Rather, what the emphasis does is only to mimic that case in which'.

2   BB 54f. elaborates another objection which the interlocutor might bring. Surely two people could not have the same pain, because we might anaesthetize or kill one of them, yet the other would still be in pain! But if it were the *same* pain, and one ceased to have it, the other would surely lose it too. This objection projects the grammar of physical objects onto pains. If A and B jointly own a pin, and A destroys it, B cannot still have it. But if A and B have hair of the same colour, and A's hair goes white, B's hair need not go white; rather they no longer have hair of the same colour. Similarly, if A and B have the same throbbing headache in the temples, and A takes an aspirin which cures his headache, the sameness of the headache does not imply that B's headache is also cured, but only that they not longer both have a headache.

Vol. XVI, 61f. compares 'ownership' of pain with 'seeing' mental images. One is inclined to say that when I conjure up a mental image, I see it in my mind's eye. But someone standing next to me cannot see it – it belongs to me alone! But this 'seeing' is a mere metaphor, involving a simile of mental vision. If another person imagines the very same thing, why should one not say that he has the same thing before him? If one now objects that surely another cannot have the very same pain that I have, one should query why. Is it that he cannot have the same pain at the same time? If so, then when I have finished with it, he *can* have it! Or is it that he can't have it, come what may?

2.1   'emphatic stressing of the word "this" ': MS. 129, 40 added (and then deleted) '(oder durch den Gebrauch des Wortes "identisch" statt des Wortes "gleich")' — ('(or by the use of the word "identical" instead of the word "same")'). This makes clear the connection between PI §253 and §254. The latter follows in MS. 129, 40 (which explains the deletion of the parenthesis).

SECTION 254

1   The substitution of 'identical' for 'the same' is a parallel tactical move to that in §253(c). The interlocutor is inclined to explain that when he insists that another person cannot have his pains, he does not mean that another cannot have the *same* pains (exactly similar), but rather that another cannot have the *identical* pains. (Like 'You can't have the identical chair I have, since I promised never to part with it, but you can have the same chair — I have ordered an exact reproduction.') This makes it appear as if he is drawing our attention to subtle shades of meaning of 'the same pain', but his manoeuvre presupposes that we are familiar with the distinction between 'identical' and 'the same' (exactly alike but not identical) and know how to draw it. But what we are familiar with is: how to draw such a distinction in a *different domain*. That illuminates nothing about the use of 'the same pain', but rather misguidedly projects the grammar of physical objects onto sensations. Philosophical confusions do not stem from failure to discriminate fine shades of meaning (as it were, olive green from Brunswick green), but rather from failure to discern categorial differences (the greenness of the lawn, of youth, and of envy).

This is exemplified by many cases hitherto discussed. We talk of discovering the construction of a pentagon and of discovering the South Pole, and are unaware of the differences in what can be called 'discovering' in the two cases (BB 29; cf. Volume 2, pp. 295ff.); we speak of believing that it will rain tomorrow, believing that $25^2 = 625$, believing that it is wrong to lie, and fail to notice that the one differs from the others not as hitting the table differs from hitting the chair (the same act with different objects) but as hitting the chair differs from hitting treble C when singing an aria. In these and a myriad other cases our philosophical confusions do not result from failure to pin down the right *nuance* of meaning, but rather from blindness to categorial differences in meaning.

Finding the precise words, the exact shade of meaning, is important in philosophy, but as part of the diagnosis of philosophical confusion, not as part of the therapy. For one must capture the exact physiognomy of error (BT 410), its manifold forms and sources, otherwise one will not be able to follow the path from error to truth (GB 61). The fact that we are tempted to say that, e.g., another person cannot have the identical pain I have is the raw material for philosophy, the culture from which the skilled philosopher can extract the bacteria that plague us. The mathematician is tempted to say that 'Mathematical theorems are true or false; their truth or falsity is absolutely independent of our knowledge of them. In *some* sense, mathematical truth is part of objective reality', and he is disposed to think that the mathematical reality lies outside us, and that our function is to discover or observe it, as the geographer observes new mountain ranges and the explorer discovers the routes to the unconquered peaks.[13] The inclination to say such things, to cleave to these pictures, is something for philosophical treatment. These pictures are not in themselves a philosophy of mathematics, although they have stimulated philosophers to construct philosophical *theories* that will apparently vindicate them (e.g. Frege's or Hilbert's philosophy of mathematics). Such remarks are not a mathematician's *testimony* as to how things are in the mathematical domain (cf. PI §§386(b), 594(c)). Nor are they *assumptions* one is forced to adopt by the nature of things (cf. PI §299). But *that* one is inclined to say such things is an important datum, and discerning *why* one is so tempted is a crucial diagnostic insight.

1.1 'a psychologically exact account': i.e. an account which will exactly articulate the confused philosopher's temptation and win from him the acknowledgement: 'Yes, that is what I meant, that is exactly what I meant' (BT 410). (Cf. Exg. §255).

2.1 'What we "are tempted to say" ': BT dwells at length on the character of philosophical temptation. It can be as hard to refrain from using an expression as it is to hold back tears (BT 406). We are enmeshed in grammatical confusions, and the tendency to think in such-and-such confused ways is deeply rooted in us — for we *want* to think thus.

The confusion of what one is 'tempted to say' with testimony is remarked on in Vol. XII, 177:

Wir verwechseln immer wieder Aussagen der Art: 'Ich bin geneigt dies *so* — nicht *so* zu nennen' — mit der Mitteilung, dass etwas sich hier *so*, und nicht *so* verhält!

Alle metaphysichen (unzeitlichen) Aussagen könnte man in der Form machen 'Ich *bin geneigt* . . . .'. 'Ich bin geneigt, eine Aussage über das, was geschehen *wird*, nicht "Sätze" zu nennen', 'ich bin geneigt, Farbe und Grösse und Lage "Gegenstände" zu

[13] G. H. Hardy, 'Mathematical Proof', *Mind*, 38 (1929), pp. 4 and 18.

nennen', 'ich bin geneigt, die Zahl 3 einen objektiven, nicht wirklichen Gegenstand zu nennen'.

(We constantly confound statements of the form: 'I am inclined to call this *this*—not *that*'—with [a piece of] information that something here is *this* and not *that*!

All metaphysical (atemporal) statements could be made in the form '*I am inclined . . .*'. 'I am inclined not to call a statement about what is *going* to happen "a proposition" ', 'I am inclined to call colour, size and location "objects" '. 'I am inclined to call the number 3 an objective, non-actual object'.)

Section 255

1   Philosophical assertions are expressions of misunderstandings, of pictures that hold us captive, but they appear in the guise of information about the nature of things. They take the form of *theses* that are apparently part of a theory. A false thesis, it seems, must be replaced by a true one so that our theory about reality approximate more closely to the truth. But this is an illusion. A conceptual misunderstanding articulated in the form of a thesis cannot be combatted by a counter-thesis or denial, for the expression of a grammatical misunderstanding, taken one way, violates the bounds of sense, and taken another way, is plainly false (cf. PI §246). And the negation of a nonsense is a nonsense (cf. Volume 2, pp. 279f.). A metaphysical proposition such as 'Only the present is real' makes no sense in our system of representation (AWL 27); 'Only I can know whether I am really in pain', as propounded by the metaphysician, is nonsense (PI §246); but one cannot show such metaphysical propositions to be nonsense by propounding or defending their negations. Metaphysical propositions are *at best* disguised expressions of grammatical rules, e.g. 'Nothing can be red and green all over', 'Sensations are private'. But even in these cases, the philosophical task is not to amass argument or evidence in favour of the 'truth' or such propositions; it is rather to remove their disguise.

We are held captive by false analogies, e.g. between the grammar of objects and the grammar of numbers, between the linguistic forms of perception and those of 'introspection', between the grammatical form of first-person psychological sentences and that of third-person ones. But one cannot be liberated from a misleading analogy by denying it. As W. remarked on mathematics: 'Your concept is wrong — However, I cannot illuminate the matter by fighting against your words, but only by trying to turn your attention away from certain expressions, illustrations, images and *towards* the employment of the words' (Z §463). Mesmerized by analogies in *forms* of expressions, we are oblivious to disanalogies in their uses, for these are difficult to survey. Our confusions, however, can only be resolved by examining the way we use words, the circumstances and presuppositions of their employment. Hence W. assembles *reminders* for a particular purpose (PI §127). No new discoveries are involved in resolving philosophical problems, only the arrangement of what we have always known (PI §109).

The analogy between W.'s techniques of eliminating philosophical confusions and treating an illness is important. Philosophical problems and the theses philosophers propound in answering them are misunderstandings, not supra-empirical questions and false answers that must be displaced by true ones. Achievement in philosophy is disentangling the threads that constitute the philosophical problem (a knot in our understanding). Success lies in making the problems disappear (PI §133), as achievement in treating an illness lies in making it disappear. What remains once illness is cured is good health, in which the patient can function optimally; what remains after philosophical therapy is an understanding of grammatical articulations which will prevent those problems from arising. For one will see what misguided analogies in the grammar of the language one has mastered led one astray.

The diseases of philosophy are sicknesses of the understanding (RFM 302), intellectual maladies. But these surround us in the midst of life no less ubiquitously than the dangers of mental disease surround us (cf. RFM, 1st edition, 157). Although these illnesses are intellectual rather than psychological, it is not surprising that the analogy between his own methods and psychoanalytic techniques struck W. forcefully in the 1930s. The only correct method in philosophy consists in abstaining from philosophical assertion and *treating* the philosophical pronouncements of others (WWK 183f.; cf. TLP 6.53) by tabulating the rules, the entanglement of which led to these assertions. As in psychotherapy, it is all important that the therapist should find precisely the right nuance to articulate the philosophical confusion (PI §254). Only when the patient acknowledges what the therapist articulates *as* the right expression for what he himself is inclined irresistibly to say *is* it the right expression (BT 410). Jokes are psychoanalytically revealing, and similarly grammatical jokes are philosophically revealing, for they shed light on the bounds of sense.[14] Just as the psychotherapist helps the patient to articulate emotions, urges, and beliefs that have been repressed since childhood, so too the philosopher of mathematics, for example, should encourage the person baffled by philosophical problems in this domain to articulate repressed doubts and questions. The mathematician has been trained to suppress these, 'he has acquired a revulsion from them as

---

[14] Indeed, W. remarked that one could imagine a book on philosophy which consisted of nothing but jokes (see N. Malcolm, *Ludwig Wittgenstein: a memoir.* 2nd edition (Oxford University Press, Oxford and New York, 1984), p. 28).

infantile . . . I trot out all the problems that a child learning arithmetic, etc. finds difficult, the problems that education represses without solving. I say to those repressed doubts: you are quite correct, go on asking, demand clarification!' (PG 382). In a sense, each person is a special case for treatment, for the precise physiognomy of error varies subtly from one to another, and what holds one person in thrall may not enslave another. Similarly, what liberates one person may not free another, although the interest of specific errors and diagnoses lies in our general, shared susceptibility to similar confusion. One might even claim that dialogue is the proper form for philosophy, for the philosophical therapist, like the psychotherapist, must help each person to work *on himself* (cf. BT 407). As the neurotic patient is disposed to cleave to his neurotic beliefs and to resist attempts to reveal their true character, so too the philosopher *in us* (TS. 219, 11; cf. Exg. §309) sinks into a morass of metaphysics and intellectual myth-making and resists attempts at extrication. The philosophical therapist is up against the *will*, not (or not only) the intellect (MS. 158, 35; BT 407). For these illusions of reason are deeply attractive to us, often *because* they are also repulsive (and here is an analogy between certain philosophical errors and psychoanalytic *theory* (LA 43)).

There is no single philosophical method, although there are methods, just as there are different therapies (PI §133). For there are many different ways of highlighting the disanalogies in use underlying the mesmerizing analogies of form (cf. Volume 1, pp. 487f.; MU pp. 289f.). But rather as in psychoanalysis, so too 'In philosophizing we may not *terminate* a disease of thought. It must run its natural course, and *slow* cure is all important' (Z §382). W. does not explain why; but perhaps the reason is that deep philosophical error is rarely rooted in one analogy and can rarely be rectified by uprooting *one* confusion. Typically, numerous different features give joint support to an overarching thesis, which will therefore *not* collapse through destruction of one of its supporting struts. Again, it is rarely only *one* misguided analogy that bewitches us, but rather a whole range, and as we cast light upon one, long shadows distort others. So one must slowly and patiently survey the structures of intellectual illusion from all sides, for they cannot be taken in at a glance. But in all cases, one's therapeutic endeavour, like the psychotherapist's, is to make *latent* nonsense *patent* nonsense (PI §§464, 524).

Furthermore, as in psychoanalysis, there is no mechanical, easy cure. Philosophical slogans ('Not all words are names' or 'Inner states stand in need of outer criteria') are not like pills that can effect a cure, but only reminders which are of help in conducting careful surveys of grammatical articulations. Again, as in psychoanalysis, what counts as a successful cure is problematic. It is arguably not just the disappearance of this, that, or the other specific problem; for one may readily lapse, and confusion (neurosis) may break out afresh elsewhere. It is rather being *able to fend for oneself* when confronted with fresh problems (PI p. 206).

It should be noted that the therapeutic role thus allocated to philosophy is not in conflict with, but complementary to, the more positive-sounding surview-giving role. A surview provides us with overall guidelines and helps us find our way around.

PRIVATE OSTENSIVE DEFINITION

1. *A 'private' language*

Anyone can keep a diary in which he records his pains and other sensations, perhaps to report to his doctor the course of his illness. He can also register his feelings, emotions, and moods for his own private purposes. The language in which he writes his diary may be English, a language known to many. And if other people read this diary, they will understand it. To forestall this, the diarist might write in code, in which case others will not understand it unless he explains the code to them. But a code is not a language, let alone a private one. There can be languages which only one person in the world speaks, such as the language of the last Mohican. And it is possible to invent a new language, which no one apart from its inventor understands until he teaches it to others, e.g. Esperanto. There is nothing philosophically problematic about the privacy of such languages.

One can even imagine human beings who spoke only in monologue (PI §243), so that their languages were never employed in interpersonal communication at all, but only in talking to themselves. The idea is far-fetched, but not unintelligible. How they might have learnt their private languages is irrelevant to an account of their linguistic capacity (MS. 124, 214). But the languages of such monologuists might come to be understood by a sufficiently patient and ingenious anthropologist (PI §243). Robinson Crusoe, who learnt English at home, spoke his language in isolation, and we can imagine a caveman using a picture language in solitude (MS. 165, 74, 103ff.; MS. 124, 213f., 221f.). One can even imagine beings born with innate knowledge of a language (cf. PG 188; BB 12, 97; PI §495). These imaginary cases are not conceptually awry. One might perhaps have qualms about the intelligibility of a languageless creature's *inventing* a language, on the grammatical ground that 'to invent a language' is only predicable of one who already speaks a language. But no such objection applies to the idea of innate knowledge of a language. All Wittgenstein's imaginary cases exemplify languages which are, in one innocuous sense or another, private. These languages *could* be taught to others and might be translated into our language (cf. Volume 2, pp. 172 – 9, and Exg. §243).

A 'private language' in the sense pertinent to Wittgenstein's discussion in *Investigations* §§243 – 315 is private in a more radical (and, ultimately, incoherent) way. It is a language the subject-matter of which is exclusively the subjective experience of the speaker. The words of the language refer to (PI §243) or are the names of (PI §§244, 256f.) sensations (PI §244), feelings and moods (PI §243), sense-impressions (PI §§272 – 7; LSD 4, 128; LPE 291), or sense-data (LPE 316; LSD 128f.). Of course, this makes it very unlike any natural language, for our languages abound with names of physical objects, public events, obsrevable properties of objects, sounds, smells, and so on. But it is very like what many philosophers have made of our ordinary languages. For, generally speaking, this is how Descartes, Locke and his empiricist successors, and, more recently, the phenomenalists conceived of the underlying nature of our languages. This conception of a language is a philosophical fiction. The task Wittgenstein undertakes is to expose it for what it is – a tangle of conceptual confusions.

What is 'private' about a language thus conceived? In the first place, the nominata seem to be private in two respects. First, they seem to be privately 'owned'; for do we not say 'You can't have my experiences'? Secondly, the items named seem to be epistemically private. For if another person cannot have my experience, but only a similar one, he cannot know what it is really like. It is important to note at the outset that both these forms of privacy are bogus (PI §§246 – 8, 253 – 4). In so far as it is true that sensations are private, it does not follow that you cannot have the same pain as I have. Nor does it follow that you cannot really know whether I am in pain, what my pain is like, or whether I see red when I look at a ripe tomato. However, on these common philo- sophical assumptions of privacy, the consequences for the envisaged language are radical. Not only are its objects private, but the language itself is private in yet a further sense, viz. that no other person could (logically) understand it. Of course, neither the Cartesians nor the empiricists, who argued that 'words in their primary or immediate signification stand for nothing but the ideas in the mind of him that uses them'[1], typically imagined that they were explaining what it is for words to have a meaning in a language unintelligible in principle to anyone but the speaker. They thought they were explaining the nature of our ordinary languages which in general we use successfully to communicate with each other. Equally, non-philosophers who conceive of subjective experience as being 'private' in the specified senses do not suppose that, on their assumptions, what they say about their experiences must be unintelligible to anyone else.

The consequence of incommunicability, however, flows *perspicuously* from the further assumption that names of experiences (in the requisite sense) are given a meaning, i.e. are explained, by reference to the items they name, and from the misleading principle that to understand such

---

[1] Locke, *Essay Concerning Human Understanding*, Bk III, Ch. ii, Sect. 2.

names is to know what they stand for.[2] On the resultant conception, names of subjective experiences are not tied up with the natural behavioural manifestation of the experiences (PI §256), and recognition of these manifestations is irrelevant to knowing what sensation-words mean.

There are different routes to these suppositions, which originate in the Augustinian picture of language. If it is held that the meaning of a word *is* the object it stands for, and if what the words of the envisaged language stand for are experiences conceived as privately 'owned' and epistemically private, and if, finally, the link between a word and its meaning is associative, then indeed no one else can understand the language. This is a straight and relatively naïve route – a direct conse-quence of that very simple *Urbild*. But one might deny that what names of private experiences stand for are their meanings, yet still insist that these names are indeed given a meaning by reference to such 'private experiences', even though experiences are not meanings. A refinement of the Augustinian picture would suggest (a) that the names are given a meaning not by association with objects which are their meaning, but by a kind of ostensive definition, and (b) that the private experience is a defining sample or paradigm for the use of such a name.[3] But since the sample is inaccessible to and unknowable by all save its owner, i.e. not contingently but essentially private, no one else could come to know what the names in such a language mean. If the 'names of simple ideas' or the 'primitive indefinables' of a language are given a meaning by private ostension involving *essentially* private samples or exemplars, then the language is a radically private one. For, 'The essential thing about private experience is really not that each person possess his own exemplar, but that nobody knows whether other people also have *this* or something else' (PI §272).

It might seem that as soon as one has shown that such a language cannot be a means of interpersonal communication, all interest in this philosophical monstrosity should lapse. After all, it might be said, it is obvious – and surely needs no argument – that our ordinary language is typically understood by speakers and hearers, is teachable and learnable. The question of whether there could be a language which is in principle

---

[2] To say that the word 'pain' stands for the sensation of pain is trivially correct, but says nothing at all about what this 'standing for' consists in, i.e. what it means to say '*that in the technique of using the language*' this word corresponds to, or is the name of, that sensation (cf. PI §51).

[3] Something like this is nicely articulated by Locke: 'Such precise, naked appearances in the mind, without considering how, whence, or with what others they came there, the understanding lays up (with names commonly annexed to them) as standards to rank real existences into sorts, as they agree with these patterns, and to denominate them accordingly' (*Essay Concerning Human Understanding*, Bk II, Ch. xi, Sect. 9).

intelligible to no one other than its speaker seems uninteresting and of no relevance to any philosophical concern. Yet Wittgenstein spends hardly any time on the issue of incommunicability, taking that to be perspic-uous, and focuses primarily on the question of the conceivability of a radically private language.

The explanation is straightforward. It is correct to argue:

A radically private language is not a means of interpersonal communi-cation.
The language I speak is a means of interpersonal communication.
∴ The language I speak is not a radically private one.

But this in unhelpful. For there are immense philosophical pressures which make the ideas that together constitute the notion of a private language seem compelling. It is, after all, no accident that those ideas have dominated the mainstream of philosophy during the last few centuries. What could be more plausible than to hold that I know what 'pain', 'fear', or 'cheerful' mean simply by experiencing such feelings and naming them, just as I learn the names of objects in the 'external world' by encountering them. After all, when I say I have a toothache, I do not have to see whether I am clutching my cheek. My use of names of experiences here seems wholly independent of the behavioural mani-festations of my experiences. And surely, when I have a pain, I know that I do – I could not have a toothache and not know it! And someone else cannot know that I have a toothache as I do – for I *feel* it! But no one else can feel my toothache! Although it is primarily philosophers who go further and insist that names of material objects must ultimately be defined in terms of names of subjective experiences, this does not, at first blush, seem too extravagant. For as most good empiricists will insist, objects are not *given* – it is experiences that are given, and objects are inferred! The foundations of language and the foundations of knowledge alike seem to rest upon private experiences.

A philosopher, a psychologist, or a linguist who succumbs to these pressures can equally argue:

The language I speak is private.
Other people do typically understand what I say.
∴ A private language is intelligible to others.

If the first premise seems irresistible and the second a truism, the obvious conclusion to draw is that, after all, there must be something wrong with the incommunicability claim. And this, after all, is what the mainstream of philosophers since Descartes have, explicitly or implic-itly, taken for granted.

Characteristically, Wittgenstein presses home his attack at the point which seems altogether unquestionable. The crucial issue is, can *I* understand 'a language which describes my inner experiences', on the assumptions that my experiences are privately 'owned', epistemically private, and determine the meanings of their names? The thrust of his argument is not that *others* cannot understand a radically private language, hence such a language is of no great use or interest, but rather that *I* could not understand such a putative language. Consequently, there is no such thing, in this sense, as a private language – it is but a phantasmagoria of philosophy.

2. *Names, ostensive definitions, and samples – a reminder*

The arguments that demonstrate that the concept of a private language is incoherent turn on the interrelated notions of names, naming, ostensive definitions, and samples. These were discussed in Volume 1 in detail ('Augustine's picture of language', 'Explanation', 'Ostensive definition and its ramifications'). Here the salient points that bear upon the matter of a private language will be summarized.

The Augustinian *Urbild* conceives of all words as names – of objects, properties, relations, etc. Names are combined to form sentences the essential role of which is to describe how things are. Learning a language consists in learning the names of things, and inventing a language consists in giving names to things. The meaning of a name is thought to be its bearer, and the grammar of a name is conceived to be a consequence of its meaning, i.e. it flows from the nature of the entity named. Once we assign a name to a thing, we can go on to talk about it, to refer to it in speech. What it is to talk about or refer to a thing is determined by the name-relation which is fixed by the mere act of naming.

This, Wittgenstein argued, is wholly misguided. While it is true that with respect to any expression 'N', one can typically find a form of words ' "N" signifies N', this does not reveal the uniformity of 'the name-relation' or of the functions of words. It says that 'N' has a use, but does not say what use it has. It merely demonstrates a constant form under which we can subsume an endless diversity of grammatically distinct types of expression with different functions. What it is for an expression to be a name, to signify or refer to something, depends upon the grammatical category of the expression, and hence on the rules for its use. There is no such thing as *the* name-relation; rather there are as many 'name-relations' as there are grammatically distinct kinds of name. There is no *one thing* called 'talking about' or 'referring to' things; rather what is called 'referring' varies according to the grammatical category of the expression in question and the character of the language-game being played. The bearer of a name is not the meaning of the name, although what a name means is sometimes explained by pointing to its bearer. The grammar of a name does not flow from the character of the object named but consists in the rules for the use of the name. Assigning a name to a thing does not determine the use of the name, but is preparatory to its application in accord with the grammatical rules for its use. Hence naming presupposes stage-setting in the language which fixes the grammatical category of the expression. It is no coincidence that in Vol. XI and the 'Big Typescript', §27(a) of *Investigations* was followed by §257. We do, to be sure, name sensations and talk about them; but that says nothing about what it is for an expression to be the name of a sensation and indicates nothing about the nature of the stage-setting in the language that is presupposed for the very possibility of giving a sensation a name.

A natural outgrowth of the pre-philosophical Augustinian picture of language is the idea that expressions in a language fall (very roughly) into two broad classes; definables and indefinables (or, in more archaic terminology, names of complex ideas and names of simple ideas). In its simplest form this conception represents definitions as intra-linguistic substitution-rules, the paradigm of which is *Merkmal*-definition. The network of definable expressions rests upon an array of indefinables, and it is the latter which are correlated with objects and properties in the world. Indefinables, according to this view, link language with reality.

But definition is only one form of explanation of meaning, and *Merkmal*-definition only one kind of definition. Though philosophers since Plato have been mesmerized by formal definitions, the latter have no explanatory, normative privilege. It is a philosophical confusion to suppose that the meaning of an expression is uniquely given by specification of a formal definition, and that inability to give such a definition betokens lack of understanding or mere 'tacit' understanding – as if inability so to define an expression constitutes an inability to say what it means, so that one's understanding, manifest in correctly using an expression, outstrips one's ability to say what that expression means and what one means by its use. Formal definitions are *one* form of explanation of meaning, but there are many others which are equally legitimate. Explanations by listing examples, by exemplification, paraphrase, or contrastive paraphrase likewise specify how an expression is to be used, and so too does an ostensive definition. Explanations (including formal definitions) are rules, setting standards for the correct use of expressions. An internal relation obtains between the explanation and the application of an expression and is manifest in and constituted by our own use of the explanation as a measure against which to judge the correctness of the application of the expression. Consequently, anything that constitutes an explanation of meaning must be reproduceable; a measure (like a yardstick) that disappears irretrievably as soon as it is canonized is no measure. Equally, for something to constitute a standard of correctness there must obtain a technique of applying it, a method of projection from the expression of the rule onto its extension. Explanations have a role in our linguistic transactions in so far as they are employed in determinate ways to teach, justify, and distinguish correct from incorrect applications of expressions.

It is hardly surprising that Wittgenstein associated ostensive definition with the Augustinian conception of language (BT 25; cf. PLP 94). It is natural to conceive of ostension as the mechanism linking language with reality – as if the intra-grammatical network of definables were connected to things in the world by pointers. Ostension, it seems, correlates words with things, and this bare correlation suffices to establish meaning, for is the thing pointed at not what the word means? If so, it will be natural to assume that the grammar of the word flows from the nature of the object picked out. In this sense ostension seems to lay the foundations of language; it correlates words with things and thereby gives content to the network of definables. If it is to fulfill this august role, the correlation must be unambiguous and infallible. But pointing with one's hand does not satisfy this requirement; it is not unambiguous and it can be misinterpreted. What one *means*, however, when one points is wholly unequivocal for *oneself*. Indeed, pointing is only necessary to explain to others what an expression means. For oneself, meaning *this* is quite enough. So the fundamental form of correlation of words with things is mental ostension. Indeed, this must be the only form of correlation when the expressions thus correlated are names of sensations, feelings, or sense-data.

This conception is a philosophical mythology, an emblematic picture akin to the story of Adam's naming the beasts in the garden of Eden. The competence of ostensive definition is not restricted to so-called indefinables, for many expressions can be explained both by *Merkmal*-definition and by ostension. Objects, properties, relations, and even numbers can correctly be defined by ostension. One can indeed point at an object, its colour, shape, texture, or number. But this is not by way of mysterious mental acts of *meaning* the one rather than the other. That one means the colour when one points at a poppy and says 'That is red' is manifest in what one counts as another person's understanding one's ostensive definition, i.e. what one counts as his going on to apply the word 'red' correctly to other things. An ostensive definition, like any other explanation of meaning, is misinterpretable. It can be clarified by making explicit the grammatical category of the defined expression, e.g. 'This *colour* is red'. This may avert misunderstanding and ensure uptake, provided the concept of colour is understood. An ostensive definition presupposes the grammatical category of the definiendum. In this sense it is merely one rule among others for the use of a word, for the grammatical place of the word in the language-game must be prepared.

The object or feature pointed at is not the meaning of the defined expression and cannot determine its grammar.[4] Indeed, it is a confusion to suppose that ostensive definition links language to reality at all. Like *Merkmal*-definitions, it is a grammatical rule and remains within language. It links a word (in certain cases) with a defining *sample* or *paradigm* – and samples are best considered part of grammar. They belong to the means of representation. This is manifest in the fact that just as a *Merkmal*-definition is a rule licensing substitution of definiens for definiendum, so too the sample, ostensive gesture, and utterance 'This' are substitutable for the definiendum (e.g. 'The curtains are *this*↗ colour', said while pointing at the sample). It is an illusion to suppose that concentrating one's attention (performing an 'act of meaning'!) determines what is being defined, or that it constitutes a kind of subjective pointing. It is the technique of using the explicit ostensive definition as a criterion of correct use that fixes the grammatical category of the expression defined, the way in which the sample is to be employed as a standard or measure of correct application.

That an object pointed at functions as a sample of a colour, shape, texture, etc. is not an intrinsic feature of the object but of its use in our practices of explaining the meanings of words and justifying their application. An object can be used as a sample only in so far as it represents what it is a sample of (thus one cannot use the sky as a sample of green) and can be copied or reproduced. Its primary role is that of an object for comparison, for it must be capable of measuring other things for identity or difference. Hence it must be possible to 'lay a sample alongside reality' for match or mismatch. So a sample must be perceptible, and there must be a method of comparison, a technique of projection, which determines what counts as matching the sample or failing to match it. This will vary from one grammatical category to another.

The contention that a private language is impossible, i.e. that this very concept is incoherent, turns on the claims that merely associating a name with a nominatum does not suffice to endow the sign with a use, that there is no private analogue of public ostensive definition, that there is no such thing as a mental sample, and that there is no such thing as a technique of applying an expression in accord with a rule which is in principle incommunicable to anyone else.

---

[4] It is easy to see why this *Bedeutungskörper* conception is appealing. Unless the word 'red', for example, is used correctly as a colour-word, we will be inclined to say that the speaker has not correlated the word with the right thing, does not know what it stands for. So if he does know what thing it stands for, he will use it correctly. So, it seems, the correct use of the word, its grammar, is determined by the thing it stands for!

3. *The vocabulary of a private language*

Having clarified the confusions underlying the notions of epistemic privacy and private ownership of experience, Wittgenstein reverts in *Investigations* §256 to the putative private language: 'Now, what about the language which describes my inner experiences and which only I myself can understand?' Experiences here (PI §§256 – 7) are conceived to lack any natural manifestation in behaviour, and so the putative names of experiences are not tied up with any expressive behaviour. This picture conforms to the Cartesian and empiricist conceptions of names of ideas, impressions, or sense-data. In the absence of a connection with expressive behaviour (e.g. by way of substitution in the first-person case and by way of criteria in the third-person case), what form of connection between name and sensation is envisaged? Wittgenstein explores various possibilities.

The most commonly supposed nexus is associative: 'I simply associate names with sensations and use these names in descriptions' (PI §256). If I wish to keep a diary about the recurrence of a certain sensation, all I have to do is to associate the sensation with a sign, say 'S', and enter the sign in the diary whenever I have the sensation (PI §258). What justifies my writing 'S'? Well, surely the fact that I have S! I am justified by what is, in fact, the case!

But this is wrong. What is in fact the case is what makes 'I have S' true (or false), not what justifies its assertion.[5] We are concerned here with a *grammatical* justification – and that is given by a *rule* (LPE 293). But associating a sign with a sensation does not give the sign a grammar, for no conventions of use are established by this association (LSD 4). To be sure, saying 'alpha' when one has a particular impression looks like an act of christening; but genuine acts of christening (in a church) or name-giving (when launching a ship) take place in a complex social setting governed by an array of conventions which determine a particular language-game in which the name has a subsequent use (LSD 4; LPE 290). Making a noise while concentrating one's attention on a sensation does not make the noise a name of anything, for it does not normatively determine what to do with this noise on subsequent occasions. It does not lay down a norm of correct use.

In order to establish a name-relation we have to establish a technique of use. And we are misled if we think that it is a peculiar process of christening an object which

[5] That *p* is the case cannot *justify* the assertion that *p*. Evidence for *p* justifies asserting that *p*, and such evidence may be inductive or criterial. Or an ostensive definition, a rule, may be adduced to justify the use of a word. As will become clear, in the case of 'I am in pain', there is *no* justification for its utterance; and if it is an avowal (*Äusserung*) of pain, it makes dubious sense even to talk of it *being made true* by one's being in pain.

makes a word the word for an object. This is a kind of superstition. So it's no use saying that we have a private object before our mind and give it a name. There is a name only where there is a technique of using it. – That technique can be private, but this only means that nobody but I knows about it . . . (MS. 166; cf. Volume 2, p. 178)

To be sure, a definition establishes a technique of use. So can one not enrich the bare idea of association with that of definition? For surely I can give myself a kind of ostensive definition of 'S', not by pointing with my hand, of course, but rather by concentrating my attention on the sensation (meaning the sensation) and as it were pointing *inwardly* (PI §258). This determines what 'S' is to stand for, and 'once you know *what* the word stands for you know its whole use' (PI §264). Moreover, when one thus concentrates on the sensation, one can inwardly undertake to call it 'S' in the future (PI §262).

This is mere charade. Concentrating one's attention is not a kind of pointing. It seems as if it is, because when one speaks to someone else one occasionally looks intently at an object, and one's gaze functions as a kind of pointing for the other person – but not for oneself (Vol. XII, 189; LSD 38). Concentrating one's attention on something (no matter whether it is a sensation or a colour) is not to give an explanation of the meaning of a word. For 'Explanation is something which shows us how to use a word at some other time as well' (LSD 39). But staring or concentrating does not do that, for neither of these determines a rule or fixes a method of comparison. Contrary to appearances, they have no role in any language-game, not even in one which I might play by myself (a private game). This will become evident in what follows.

Furthermore, as already argued, the object for which a word stands is not its meaning. The essence (*Wesen*) of an object is determined by grammar, not by nature (cf. PI §§371, 373). So the use of the word does not follow from the object it names. Finally, concentrating on a sensation does not suffice for undertaking to use the word as the name of *this* sensation in the future (PI §263). For, (a) what is the *this* upon which one concentrates? One no more determines a criterion of identity by concentration than one does by emphatic stressing of the word 'this' (cf. PI §253). (b) To be the name of a *sensation* requires a specific technique of use, quite unlike the technique of use for colour-names for example. It is of no avail to say that one is going to use the word 'in a certain way' in the future, unless one can spell out *which* way (cf. PI §262). Of course, one way of so doing is to display a sample and explain its role. But, (c) can an impression or sensation be used as a sample? This question is *logical*, not epistemological or sociological. What is the technique of use of such a private sample? How is it to be used as a measure – as an object of comparison (LSD 105)? Is it even logically *possible* so to use it?

A philosopher defending the supposition of the intelligibility of private ostensive definition might reply that there is no difficulty at all here. For the grammatical post at which the sign 'S' is to be stationed is given by the concept of *sensation*. If one can disambiguate a public ostensive definition by saying 'This colour is sepia', why can one not articulate the grammar of a private ostensive definition by impressing upon oneself that this *sensation* is S? But 'sensation' is a word of ordinary language, not a word of a private language intelligible only to oneself (PI §261). The private language theorist is not at liberty to help himself to expressions which are linked to behavioural manifestations of the mental, on pain of relinquishing his claims to the privacy of his putative language. And to argue that 'sensation' too is defined by private ostensive definition will not resolve his difficulty, but compound it. Of course, he might be tempted to a more nebulous fall-back position, viz. to claim that 'S' (or 'pain', as be construes it) means or refers to a *certain phenomenon* (LSD 42), a *certain impression* (LPE 290), or a *certain experience* (LSD 108). But these blank cheques can only be used if they can be cashed in the currency of 'Namely *this* ↗' – and that is not possible here (LSD 42, 105). He might be inclined to insist that 'S' or 'pain' means or refers to *something*, which he *has*. But 'have' and 'something' are likewise words of ordinary language with a determinate use (PI §261). To this he may respond indignantly that surely pain is not a *nothing*! Of course not, Wittgenstein replies. Pain is neither a something nor a nothing; the point is rather that a nothing will serve just as well as a something about which nothing can be said (PI §304).

In order to give a name to a sensation or sense-impression in a putative private language, the private language theorist must show how the name is to be defined or explained. For a sign is a name only in so far as it is given a rule-governed use, and the role of a definition is to determine for future occasions how the expression is to be used (LPE 291). In explanations of word-meaning by public ostensive definition, a sample typically plays a crucial normative role in this respect. Having a sensation, say a toothache, seems to provide one with a mental sample which will function as a standard for subsequent applications of the word 'toothache'. One is indeed tempted to say that someone who has never felt pain could not know what the word 'pain' means (PI §315). Can one not imagine someone having a toothache for the first time and exclaiming 'Now I know what "toothache" means!'? This seems to betoken the availability of a sample which defines 'toothache' (LSD 9).

This, Wittgenstein argues, is an illusion. 'The private experience is to serve as a paradigm, and at the same time admittedly it can't be a paradigm' (LPE 314). Why not? A sample must function as a standard of comparison for subsequent applications, must be preservable or reproducible; and it must be possible to lay a sample alongside reality for match or mismatch. Hence it must be possible for there to be a technique of projection manifest in the use of the sample as a standard of correct use. These requirements are not satisfied in the case of sensations or impressions – although they seem to be.

There can be no such thing as preserving a pain for future use. One cannot take a photograph of it, as one can of pain-behaviour (LSD 42). One can preserve a sample of red, ultramarine, or sepia on a colour-chart and consult it on later occasions; but one cannot preserve an impression of a colour for future use (LSD 42). A sample (of colour, for example) is something which persists, can be examined again, looked at for a time and shown to others (LSD 110).

The private language theorist will concede that one cannnot show others a mental sample, but will insist that there are adequate analogues of the preservability or reproducibility of samples. (a) Could one not imagine a *persistent* sensation, such as a constant pain in one's hand? Could that not function as a private sample? (Of course, the theorist will admit, we do not typically have such persistent sensations; but his point, at the moment, is to break the log-jam of objections!) (b) Not all samples are persistent anyway – it suffices that they be *reproducible* (e.g. samples of musical notes are reproducible by means of a tuning-fork). So cannot one reproduce a sensation of pain, say, simply by pinching oneself to remind oneself what the word 'pain' means? (c) Not all expressions in our ordinary language that are *defined* by reference to samples are *applied* with the aid of samples. It suffices that one remember what they mean (e.g. 'red'). So if one defines 'S' by reference to a certain sensation, it is surely possible to remember the sensation and, if doubt arises, to *recall* this defining sample! Can one not, as it were, store it in one's memory and reproduce it as an image which then functions as a private sample? So even though the sensation passes, what persists is its copy in the reproductive imagination (LSD 33ff., 113).

Persistent samples: One can have relatively persistent sensations. But neither ephemeral nor persistent sensations can function as samples. For, first, persistent samples, such as colour-charts or the standard metre-bar (for, remember, it is the *bar*, not its *length*, that is the sample), have independent criteria of identity. One can detemine whether one's colour-chart, left in the sun, has faded or been stained, or whether the standard metre-bar (or one's own metre-rule) has been bent, snipped, or stretched. In such cases, one will cease using that object *as* a sample; far from being at the mercy of samples, we are free to abandon any given object that has been used as a sample and to adopt or make a new one. For whether something is a sample depends on whether we use it as one (see Volume I, 'The standard metre', §4), and that is up to us. But in the case of a sensation, there is no distinction between the sample and the feature which it represents on the model of the distinction between the metre-bar and the length of which it is a defining sample. So there are no analogous criteria for the sameness or difference *of the sample*. But a sample which can change without making any difference makes no difference! Consequently, if a sensation is to function as a sample, it would have to be akin not to a persistent sample (such as a colour-chart or metre-bar) but to a reproducible one (such as a note produced by a tuning-fork). This will be examined below.

It is natural to object that surely a person must notice whether his sensation is the same or not! If that means that one can say whether one's toothache is still acute and stabbing or whether it is no longer so severe, but a dull, throbbing ache, then that is indeed correct. But these are *descriptions*, and they presuppose the concepts they employ. It is a cardinal error to confuse a sample (a standard of measurement) with a description (the result of a measurement) (LPE 320). One can derive a description from a sample; but when we describe our toothache as being still the same or as having changed thus-and-so, we are not describing the sameness or difference of a sample (in contrast with saying that the metre-bar is bent), nor are we deriving our description from *any* sample. What the subject sincerely says, given that he generally manifests mastery of the technique of using the sensation-name, is the sole criterion (for others) for the sameness or difference of his sensation. *He* has no independent means of determining whether his sensation is still the same or not – he just says so. But this means that the thought that he could use his sensation as a persistent private sample is misconceived, for he would have no way to determine whether the sample had changed or not. But there must always be a difference between a sample's being the same and its being believed or asserted to be the same. *That* distinction collapses here, although it seems not to, because, given the concept of, say, toothache, one *can* say whether one's toothache is the same or not.

Techniques of comparison: Suppose I have a persistent sensation in my hand and I want to define the word 'pain' by using it as a sample. So I go through the motions of giving myself a private ostensive definition. Can I then say that I have a pain in my head, and justify this by claiming that what I have in my head *is* what I have in my hand? After all, I can define the word 'red' by pointing at a colour-chart and saying 'This ↗ is red', and I can describe the roses as being *this* ↗ colour, viz. red.

There is no genuine analogue of this in the case of sensations. (a) I cannot (logically) *perceive* my sensations as I can perceive both the sample of red and the roses and see that the roses are that colour. (b) I cannot (logically) point at my sensation as I can point at the colour-sample, either for others or for myself alone. (c) I cannot (logically) compare a sensation in my hand with a sensation in my head (or in my other hand) for match or mismatch as I can compare an object with a sample.[6] When I compare the roses with the colour-chart or when I measure the table with a yardstick, I can make a mistake – i.e. compare rightly or wrongly. I can check my judgement by looking again in better light or measuring a second time, more carefully. I can ask someone else, who may be more skilful than I at fine discrimination. But there is no such thing as judging that I have a pain in my head by comparing what I have in my head with what I have in my hand. There is no method of projection or technique of comparison here. I cannot, as it were, lay my *hand* alongside my head (as I can lay a yardstick alongside the table) in order to judge whether what I have in my head *is* that sensation (as I can judge that the table is that length).

The private language theorist may accept the first two points, (a) and (b), but have qualms about the third, (c). Though having a pain is not perceiving a pain, is it not enough to have a pain in one's hand in order for it to function as a sample for a pain elsewhere? After all, one *can* have a pain in one's hand and the same pain, e.g. a rheumatic one, in one's other hand; and one may *say so*! That is correct. But there is no such thing as saying so *on the basis of comparison with a sample*. For where there is a comparison with a sample, there is a possibility of making a mistake, i.e. it makes *sense* to compare wrongly. But it makes no sense to say 'I thought I had a pain, but I was mistaken', let alone 'I thought what I had in my head was what I have in my hand, but I was wrong' (as one can say 'I thought the curtains were this ↗ colour [pointing at a sample], but I was wrong'). Furthermore, the question of how one can *apprehend* that what one 'has' in one's head is what one 'has' in one's hand is not answered by saying that one can *feel* that they are the same, for feeling a pain *is* just having a pain; nor can it be answered by saying that one *has* it, for having a pain is not a mode of apprehending its identity with or difference from a sample. In short, it means nothing to say that what I have in my hand *is* that certain phenomenon which I have in my head and which I call 'pain', unless that is just a garbled way of saying that I have the same pain in my hand as in my head. The unintelligibility of there being a technique of comparison is a definitive objection to the idea of private ostensive definition.

Reproducible samples: Granted that we do not typically have persistent sensations, nevertheless we can surely *reproduce* sensations, like notes on a tuning-fork. So if one wants to make sure what the word 'pain' means, can one not simply stick a pin in one's hand? – That does not tell one what the word means! Of course, one is tempted to say that it does – that

---

[6] Of course, I can compare today's headache with yesterday's *in saying* that it is not so bad now. But I cannot employ yesterday's headache as a standard by reference to which to judge whether what I now have is to be *called* 'a headache', for there can be no *technique of comparison*.

it reminds one what one calls 'pain'. For does one not *recognize* the sensation? The temptation must be resisted. (a) It only makes sense to talk of recognizing where it also makes sense to talk of not recognizing or misrecognizing. For 'recognize' is a success-verb, and success presupposes the possibility of failure. But it makes no sense to talk of not recognizing or misidentifying a sensation as a pain, as a headache or backache (as opposed to identifying a pain as angina pectoris). (b) If what one is supposed to recognize here is a *sample* of pain, then, as we have seen, it can make no sense to talk of recognizing it as a pain (or as painful). For if it is to determine the concept of pain, it cannot at the same time be said to fall under it, just as the standard metre-bar cannot be said to be a metre long (cf. Exg. §50, and Volume 1, 'The standard metre'). A sample is a measure; something recognized is something measured. Can't one recognize the sample? No, for as argued, there can be no independent criterion for recognizing it correctly here. One cannot put a British Standards Authority stamp on a putative sample of pain, and putting it on the pin with which one pricks oneself is of no avail. For 'pain' does not mean the same as 'Whatever A feels when he pricks himself with a standard pin'! True enough, one might object; but equally 'C-flat' does not mean 'whatever note is produced by striking such-and-such tuning fork'! So is 'pain' not on the same level as the name of a sound defined by reference to such a method of reproducing a sample? Not so; for we can admit that a tuning-fork is defective. As long as the discriminatory abilities of sensitive hearers persist, a defect in the tuning-fork is perceptible. But pains are not perceptibilia, and there is no such thing as being more or less skilful in distinguishing the sameness or difference of a pain. One can reproduce a sound which can function as a sample, precisely because sounds are perceptible, can be compared for sameness and difference, can be recognized or mistakenly misidentified. (c) Admittedly, pricking oneself with a pin typically gives one a pain. But what one needs is the *concept* of pain or a sample of pain that will be associated with a technique of application to constitute a rule for the use of the word 'pain'. And one has not got that here (cf. Z §§548 – 6; for further ramifications, cf. Exg. §288).

Remembering the sample: Why can one not define a sensation-word 'S' by reference to a certain sensation S and simply *remember* the defining sample. When in doubt, all one has to do is to bring to mind an image of S.[7] After all, one can remember the meanings of colour-words and conjure up mental images of, say, sepia or ultramarine when one wants to remind oneself what these names mean. Isn't it the same with

---

[7] It is unhappy, in English, to talk of 'an image' of pain (see Exg. §300). Not so in German; and the argument would not differ in substance if one were talking of mental images of colours allegedly functioning as private mental samples.

sensation-words? Not at all. One can memorize what words mean, e.g. that 'Tisch' means table. One can learn what colour-words mean by studying a colour-chart and impressing upon oneself the connections between words and samples. And when trying to remember what 'sepia' means, one might call to mind a mental image of sepia. But 'if you say he *learns* this, then you distinguish between a correct and a wrong remembering; if not, there is no learning' (LSD 114). One can 'impress upon oneself' the connection between a name and what it names, but that means that this process brings it about that one remembers the connection *correctly* in the future. That in turn presupposes a criterion, i.e. a standard, of correctness (PI §258). One can remember that 'Tisch' means table or think wrongly that it means fish, and one can check which is correct in a dictionary. Can one not, however, have a *mental dictionary*, one which exists only in the reproductive imagination? After all, one can appeal from one memory to another. Someone with an eidetic memory can think that he remembers what a word, e.g. 'Tisch', means, and check his memory against his mental image of the page in the German/English dictionary. That is correct – but only if *there is* a German/English dictionary. The mental image of the page in the dictionary can only confirm one's recollection of the meaning of a word if it itself can be tested for correctness against the actual page. Otherwise one is checking one's memory of the meaning of a word against one's memory of its meaning, which is like buying several copies of the same newspaper to confirm what is written in it (PI §265).

This argument has seemed to some philosophers to be an expression of scepticism about memory. But that is quite wrong; it is rather a demand for the intelligibility of a distinction between remembering correctly and remembering incorrectly what a word means:

> I cannot remind myself in my private language that this was the sensation I called 'red'. There is no question of my memory's playing me a trick – because (in such a case) there can be no criterion for its playing me a trick. If we lay down rules for the use of colour-words in ordinary language, then we can admit that memory plays tricks regarding these rules. (LSD 8)

Wittgenstein's concern is not whether one can *in fact* find out whether one has remembered rightly (after all, one often cannot in ordinary daily life), but rather whether anything could logically *count* as remembering correctly or incorrectly. For, 'Looking up a table in the imagination is no more looking up a table than the image of the result of an imagined experiment is the result of an experiment' (PI §265). But could one not *guess* the right application of 'S', and might it not be a fortunate fact that normally one guesses correctly? No – 'There is nothing to guess at' (MS. 166, 21). For one can only guess if something *counts* as guessing right, and that requires an independent standard of correctness.

The idea that a mental image can function as a sample is compelling, precisely because one *can* have a mental image of a sample, as when one memorizes a colour-chart. And if the colour-chart is then destroyed, that surely does not mean that suddenly one cannot use the words one previously learnt, such as 'sepia', 'indigo', or 'violet'. So why can't one give a name to a sensation and then, as it were, store a copy of the sensation in one's memory? One's image will then function as a sample of S, as does one's image of sepia. For is a mental image not something like a *picture*? And a picture, to be sure, can function as a sample or a paradigm! Of course, a mental image is a private picture – but why should that matter, since its role is that of a private standard for the use of its owner alone?[8]

This is misconceived. (i) 'Memory can be compared with a storehouse only so far as it fulfils the same purpose. Where it doesn't, we couldn't say whether the things stored up constantly change their nature and so couldn't be said to be stored at all' (MS. 166, 33). Again, the point is not the fallibility of human memory and the consequent fear of error, but rather the absence of any criterion for remembering correctly, hence the collapse of any *distinction* between remembering correctly and remembering incorrectly. Hence it is no use supposing that one might *recognize* the image as an image of S (MS. 166, 26) or *believe* that it is the image of S (cf. PI §260). For this recognition and belief presuppose (a) the concept of S – which is precisely what is in question; and (b) the possibility of misrecognition or believing falsely (LSD 110). But if 'whatever is going to seem right to me is right . . . that only means that here we can't talk about "right" ' (PI §258), hence not about recognition or belief either.

(ii) It is true that a picture can function analogously to a sample. One can (and does) explain what the word 'horse' or 'duck-billed platypus' means by pointing at a picture just as well as by pointing at the animal. A coloured picture of a tomato can replace a ripe tomato in an ostensive definition of the word 'red'. But a mental image is not a picture, even though in certain cases a picture can correspond to it (PI §301). One can imagine sepia and paint what one imagines. What one paints can then function as a paradigm (and can also serve to explain what it was that one imagined). But 'The image of pain is not a picture and *this* image is not replaceable in the language-game by anything that we should call a picture' (PI §300 and Exg.). One can imagine pain, but that presupposes, and so cannot explain, the concept of pain. For one cannot explain what 'pain' means by pointing at, let alone painting, a picture or a paradigm of a pain (LSD 39f.), as opposed to one of pain-behaviour (PI §300).

---

[8] Note that even if this move were valid, the private language theorist would still be confronted with the insurmountable objection that there can be no method of comparison here.

The use of sensation-names in the first person resembles the use of colour-words in certain respects. In neither case are the expressions used on the basis of evidence. There are no criteria for saying 'That is red' or for avowing 'I have a pain'. Here, in a certain sense, one says what one says without (evidential) justification (cf. PI §§289, 381). In typical uses of 'red', 'green', or 'blue', one employs no samples at all, and one employs no sample when one says 'I have a toothache'. But the language-games with colour-words are essentially, grammatically, bound up with samples used in teaching, explaining, and justifying (LSD 121). Not so in the case of sensation-words. 'The impression of a "private table" in the game arises through the *absence* of a table, and through the similarity of the game to one that is played with a table' (Z §552).

4. *Idle wheels*

Wittgenstein was well aware that his arguments demonstrating that the sensation of pain does not enter the language-game with the word 'pain' as a sample of sepia, say, enters the language-game with colour-words gives the impression that he is denying the existence of pain. One is inclined to say that one's justification for moaning is having *pain*, and that one can point inwardly at what one has (LPE 312). Surely *this*, one wants to say, is the important thing (PI §298). After all, 'there is *something* there all the same accompanying my cry of pain. And it is on account of that that I utter it. And this something is what is important – and frightful' (PI §296). One wants to object: 'You seem to deny the existence of something; on the other hand you say you don't deny any existence: why should it seem as if you did? You seem to say: "There is only . . .". You deny, it seems, the background of the expression of sensations. Doesn't the expression point to something beyond itself?' (MS. 166, 35f.). Wittgenstein conceded that it looks like this. 'The "private experience" is a degenerate construction of our grammar (comparable in a sense to tautology and contradiction). And this grammatical monster now fools us; when we wish to do away with it, it seems as though we denied the existence of an experience, say, tooth-ache' (LPE 314). How can this false appearance be dispelled?

Of course, Wittgenstein insisted, there is all the difference in the world between pain-behaviour accompanied by pain and pain-behaviour with-out pain; indeed it is precisely the difference between manifesting one's suffering and pretending to suffer (cf. PI §304). But it is misleading in this context to represent that difference as the difference between behaviour plus an accompaniment and behaviour without an accompa-niment. Where a form of behaviour is an *expression* of something, it is misconceived to think of what it expresses as a hidden accompaniment that lies behind the behaviour. For it is not hidden, but manifest; it does not lie 'behind' the behaviour (there is no 'behind' here), but infuses it; and it is no accompaniment, for that concept is appropriate only where the items said to accompany each other are logically independent (MS. 166, 16; PI §296; Vol. XVII, 7ff.). But it is true that people sometimes have a pain and do not show it and that sometimes they pretend to be in pain.

So is Wittgenstein agreeing that when someone who is truthful says that he sees red or has a pain we can take his word for it? Of course; we believe that what he experiences is as he says it is, *according to the method of projection appropriate to the case* (MS. 166, 34f.).[9] But an incommunicable private object plays, and can play, no role in grammar in either case. Moreover, the genuine sensation of pain (or the mental image of red) has no place *in the grammar* of the word 'pain' (or 'red'). We say of another person that he has a pain on the grounds of his behaviour, and *he* says that he has a pain on no grounds at all and without any (grammatical) justification; rather he gives expression to, or manifests, his pain. Of course, here too there are criteria for whether he knows what the word 'pain' means.

In a final effort to shake the grip of the private object that apparently functions as a private sample for the use of a word and as a private justification, Wittgenstein constructs a *reductio ad absurdum* (Vol. XV, 87ff.). Suppose that at birth everyone were given a table of colours which no one else is allowed to look at. We teach these children the use of colour-words as usual, and tell them to enter the colour-names in their private tables. Before they apply colour-words to objects, they always glance at their tables. They come to use colour-words as we all do. Now suppose we find that on their tables they have written 'red' under the green sample, 'green' under the red one, and so on. Further, we find that a child, before he says that the ripe tomatoes are red, looks at his colour-chart and puts his finger on the green sample and then says 'They are red'. And equally, when we ask him to explain what 'red' means, he looks at his chart, puts his finger on the word 'red' beneath the green sample and then points at a ripe tomato and says 'That colour is red'. Clearly, the private table is an idle wheel in the mechanism of his language. Even if we suppose that when we remove his private chart he falls into confusion and can no longer use colour-words correctly, it is still evident that *grammatically* the chart plays no role in his use of language. And now suppose that this chart exists only in his imagination. Does it now make any difference? A free-wheeling cog does not engage with a mechanism by being transposed into the imagination.

[9] What is appropriate for 'red', viz. the use of a public ostensive definition, is inappropriate for 'pain'. And if someone avows severe pain in his foot, but laughs and behaves normally, does not limp or assuage his foot, etc., we would say that he is joking.

A similar argument occurs in *Investigations* §271: ' "Imagine a person whose memory could not retain *what* the word 'pain' meant – so that he constantly called different things by that name – but nevertheless used the word in a way fitting in with the usual symptoms and presuppositions of pain" – in short he uses it as we all do.' (cf. PI p. 207; MS. 166, 18 and 36f.). One is tempted to reply that one *could not* make such a mistake here, that one *could not* misidentify one's sensation (irrespective of the matter of a private sample). That is both right and wrong; it is true that one could not make a mistake, but not because one always, as a matter of fact, identifies one's sensation correctly. Rather, because there is here neither an identification nor a misidentification, neither a recognition nor a misrecognition (cf. PI §270). The supposition of a private object that gets identified correctly and which is then described by saying 'I have a pain' is the absurdity which Wittgenstein is rejecting. An expression of pain (*Schmerzäusserung*) no more involves the antecedent identification of an inner object than the expression of amusement by laughter involves the identification of an inner feeling of amusement which one then expresses!

'I have a pain' is an expression of pain, just as 'I am frightened' is an expression of fear and 'I am tired' an expression of weariness. These utterances are themselves forms of behaviour that constitute criteria for saying of a person that he is in pain, frightened, or tired. They are learnt extensions of natural expressive behaviour and are essentially bound up with those forms of behaviour.[10] In our philosophical reflections on 'self-knowledge' and 'self-awareness' we are prone to confuse the grammatical exclusion of misidentification or misrecognition with the presence of infallible identification or recognition. Similarly, we are impressed by the fact that an avowal of pain does not rest on any public criteria, for in truth we do not look to see whether we are groaning before we say that we have a toothache. So we wrongly suppose that there must be an inner, private justification. The irony is that if, per *impossibile*, there were an inner justification, e.g. a private mental sample justifying the use of the word or a private object *described* by 'I have a pain', then doubts would be intelligible:

if we cut out human behaviour, which is the expression of sensation, it looks as if I might *legitimately* begin to doubt afresh. My temptation to say that one might take a sensation for something other than what it is arises from this: if I assume the

---

[10] That is not to say that all avowals are substitutes for natural expressive behaviour. Some sensations have little if any form of pre-linguistic manifestations, e.g. heartburn or 'butterflies in the stomach'. But 'I have heartburn' and 'I have butterflies in the stomach' are expressions of *sensation* and to that extent bound up, indirectly, with the natural manifestations of sensation. Such avowals are learnt extensions of the verbal expressions of sensations that are partial substitutes for natural expressive behaviour. Fresh branches may grow from a conventional graft. (Cf. Exg. §244, 2.1(vi).)

abrogation of the normal language-game with the expression of a sensation, I need a criterion of identity for the sensation; and then the possibility of error also exists. (PI §288)

Clearly, that is unintelligible in our language-games with sensation-words. If someone were to say 'Oh, I know what "pain" means; what I don't know is whether *this*, that I have now, is pain', we would not know what he was trying to tell us. 'That expression of doubt has no place in the language-game' (PI §288). This is made vivid in Wittgenstein's example of a genuine diary entry of a real sensation-word 'S'. Suppose I discover, by inductive correlation, that whenever I have a certain sensation my blood-pressure, as measured by a manometer, has risen. So I can keep a diary to register the rise and fall of my blood-pressure without reliance on the manometer. Here it *seems quite indifferent* whether I have recognized the sensation rightly or wrongly; for even if I regularly misidentify it, it does not matter. For I predict correctly the rise in my blood-pressure. Does that show that I correlate the rise in blood-pressure with my *believing*, rightly or wrongly, that I have the sensation in question? On the contrary, it shows that any supposition of recognition, error, identification or misidentification in the case of sensations, is mere show. There is no such thing as believing that one has a pain, for then it would make sense to say 'I had a pain, but I did not believe I did' or 'I believed I had a pain, but I was mistaken'. But these make no sense (cf. Exg. §270).

The word 'pain' is not defined by reference to a 'private object'; nor is it defined by reference to a public *object*. And 'I have a pain' is not a description of an inner experience which is *made true* (and justified) by reference to the occurrence of a particular indefinable experience. To achieve a surview of this part of the grammar of psychology, one must jettison altogether the model of explanation appropriate to words for physical objects and perceptual properties, and with it the mythology of experience as private and incommunicable – i.e. of a 'world' of private experience. Only when these dense mists of language are blown away can we hope to see aright the grammar of experience and its expression.

EXEGESIS §§256 – 80

Section 256

1   Having clarified the putative privacy of sensation, W. now returns to the language envisaged in §243(b). Here the sensation-words are not connected with sensations *qua* substitutes for natural expressions of sensations, as are simple sensation-words in our ordinary languages (PI §244). For if they were, the language would not be 'private', i.e. it would not be impossible for anyone other than myself to understand it. It is a crucial feature of a 'private' language not just that no one else understands it (the language of the last Mohican) or that no community consensus on what counts as following its rules obtains, but that it be *logically impossible* that another person should understand it, i.e. that there be no public criteria (or no communicable rule) for correct application. This negative condition is not satisfied by the language of a Robinson Crusoe or a solitary caveman, etc., but only by a putative language in which sensation-names (or, more generally, names of experiences) are severed from the natural expression of sensation (or experience). How are we to try to conceive of them? As endowed with meaning *by association* with sensations. In one's own language, therefore, sensation-names are associated with *one's own sensations*. But then, it seems, that with which a name is associated is 'inaccessible' to another person. So another person cannot in principle know what I mean by 'pain' (just as a blind man cannot know what we mean by 'eau-de-Nil').

1.1   '*associate* names with sensations and use these names in descriptions': (a) Note the adherence of this conception of a 'private' language to the Augustinian picture: words are names which are for use in describing how things are. (b) This conception is committed to the idea that first-person present-tense psychological sentences are *descriptions* of the inner, that what is called 'a description of the state of my mind' is precisely analogous to a description of the state of my room, save that the latter concerns the 'outer' and the former the 'inner' (see 'Avowals and descriptions'). To query this presupposition, shared by rationalists and empiricists alike, is one of W.'s fundamental innovations.

2   MS. 179, 12 notes:

> Private Sprache für private Erlebnisse. Tagebuch über eine Empfindung. Zeichen mit dem natürlichen Ausdruck der Empfindung verkuppelt. Dann ist das Tagebuch

für Alle gleich verständlich. Wie aber wenn es keinen natürlichen Ausdr. der Empf. gibt? Wie weiss ich das ich dieselbe Empf. habe?

(Private language for private experiences. Diary about a sensation. Sign bound up with the natural expression of sensation. Then the diary is equally intelligible to all. But what if there is no natural expression of the sensation? How do I know that I have the same sensation?)

2.1   'I simply associate names with . . .': it is noteworthy that in so far as the *Tractatus* had anything to say about the 'name-relation' that connects a name to an object, the connection seems to be associative. And the association was conceived as effected by a mental act of *meaning* by such-and-such a name THIS object (cf. NB 70).

Section 257

1   This explores the immediate consequences of the supposition of §256 and indicates the trajectory of the sequel. The first and obvious anxiety is raised by the interlocutor: sensation-names would not be teachable. W. brushes this aside, for this is the least of the troubles consequent upon the supposition. We may, for the sake of argument, assume that the child invents a name for the sensation and so does not have to be taught (for the genesis of a capacity is irrelevant to the explanation of what the capacity is). The interlocutor still worries about the possibility of interpersonal communication: given that the clever child invents the words of this language that can be used to describe his inner experiences (PI §§243, 256), still he could not make himself understood by others. This was precisely the conclusion of §243, but it too is not the *punctum saliens*.

What is supposed by the interlocutor's movement of thought is that the child himself understands these sensation-names, and understands the descriptions of his experiences. The difficulties are supposed to emerge only when it comes to communicating his thoughts *to others*. It is this supposition that W. challenges with the question 'So does he understand the name, without being able to explain its meaning to anyone?' And it is this line of attack that is pursued in subsequent sections. Understanding, as has been argued, is akin to a capacity, and among the things which one who understands an expression (knows what it means) is able to do is: explain what it means. Hence giving a correct explanation is a *criterion* of understanding, and inability to give a correct explanation is a mark of lack of understanding. Is the 'private linguist' here supposed to know what the putative sensation-names mean, but *not* be able to say what they mean – to explain them to another? The answer must be 'Yes, that is precisely the supposition – but, of course, he can explain them to himself!' W. pursues that thread in the sequel, but for the moment he turns to a related issue.

The supposition of a 'private' language involves the idea that the speaker of such a language *names* his sensations (or, more generally, his 'inner experiences'). This is a pivotal component of the Augustinian picture of language: 'One thinks that learning language consists in giving names to objects, viz. to human beings, to shapes, to colours, to pains, to moods, to numbers, etc.' (PI §26). But this conceals the diversity in what is called 'naming', and the dependence, in each kind of case, of what counts as naming upon the language-game to which the specific naming is preparatory. Naming a person is preparatory to such activities as calling him, talking to him, announcing him, introducing him, attribut- ing responsibility or liability to him, etc. Naming a colour is preparatory to a very different array of language-games; for we do not address a colour by its name, call it, modify its name into a pet-name or nickname. But we tell people to reproduce *this* ↗ colour by mixing paints, to bring some cloth which is the *same* colour as the carpet; and we describe objects as being red or green, darker or lighter than others, etc. In the grip of the Augustinian picture, we think that naming is merely a matter of *attaching* a name to a thing (be it an object, a shape, a colour or a pain) and that the entire grammar of the name flows from the nature of the thing correlated with it. How is this 'attaching' done? In some cases we can hang a label on a thing, but doubtless the best glue is mental – we *associate* a name with what it names (PI §256)! And thinking thus, we forget that naming is preparatory to a host of *different* language-games, for to name something is to give a certain expression a *use* within a language-game. Something constitutes naming only when it is thus preparatory, just as one can only arrange the chess-pieces *in their positions* as preparatory to a game of chess – i.e. without the rules of the game and the technique of playing it, an alignment of carved pieces of wood on a chequered board is not positioning chess-pieces.

So what counts as naming a particular pain, e.g. a toothache? The conception involved in the supposed private language is explored in §§258ff. Here W. reminds us of the 'stage-setting' in the language that is presupposed if the mere act of naming a sensation is to make sense. That complex stage-setting is crystallized into the grammar of the expression. For if what is named is a *toothache* (and not something else), then we can both have the same one. Equally, to have a toothache is not to perceive what one has, and if I perceive that you have one, I don't thereby have one. So too, if I have what is named a 'toothache', I don't doubt that I have it (but not because I know it), whereas if you have a toothache, I may not know it or I may wonder whether you do, but be unsure. If it is toothache that is named, it must be in a person's tooth and not in his toe, let alone in the foot of his chair. And so on. If this and a multitude of further articulations did not hold true of what is named, then what is named is not toothache at all, for it will not be a kind of *pain, in a tooth*. In this sense the grammar of 'pain' shows the post where the new word is stationed. And if a certain word is not stationed there, then it is not the name of a *pain*!

1.1   (i) 'invents a name': if the child has not yet mastered a language, one might doubt the intelligibility of his *inventing* a name (cf. 'Private ostensive definition', §1).

    (ii) 'dass Einer dem Schmerz einen Namen gibt': 'someone's giving a name to a pain', i.e. picking up 'seinen Schmerz benannt hat'.

    (iii) 'shows the post where the new word is stationed': this echoes §29.

2   This early remark (BT 209v.; cf. Vol. XI, 91) occurs in the context of PI §§25 – 27(a), where the connection with the Augustinian picture is even more prominent than here. The emphasis upon the diversity of what is called 'naming' and its dependence upon what, in the language-game, follows the assignment of a name was a key preoccupation at this stage. PG 71 emphasizes that giving an ostensive definition of a colour-name is not a kind of consecration or mystical formula. Pointing and saying 'That's red' works only as part of a system containing other bits of linguistic behaviour. LPE 290f. applies this to sensation-names. Just as we are inclined to think that naming red requires only that one *see* red and say 'That's red' while pointing at it, so too we think that to name a sensation requires no more than

> pronouncing the name while one has the sensation and possibly concentrating on the sensation, – but what of it? Does this name thereby get magic powers? And why on earth do I call these sounds the name of a sensation? I know what I do with the name of a man or a number, but have I by this act of 'definition' given the name a use?
> 'To give a sensation a name' means nothing unless I know already in what sort of game this name is to be used. (LPE 290f.)

When W. gave the lectures, he developed the idea further. In some cases we name an object by writing a name on it (although this too is very diverse; compare writing a name on a ship's bow, on the title-page of a book, on a medicine bottle, and on a sample). But there is no such thing as writing a name on a toothache. It seems as though each of us names the sensation *in foro interno*, so that no one else knows what is thus named. But this is a muddle. 'If we know what it is to give a name to a physical object, we don't yet know what it means to give a name to a pain. We can give a name to a pain – but we can only do this in cases where the pain is not private – where the word is to be used by all of us' (LSD 33). This point was further emphasized in the 'Notes for a Philosophical Lecture': in order to *establish* a 'name-relation' between a word and a sensation, we do not need a christening ceremony for private objects that lie before the mind's eye, but a *technique of use* for the name (MS. 166, 6).

SECTION 258

1   §256 established that in the 'private' language, words cannot signify sensations in virtue of being tied up with one's natural expressions of sensation, for then the language would not be 'private'. §257 argued that if sensations lacked behavioural expression, one could not teach the use of sensation-names. It might seem that each speaker might invent names for his own sensations, although, of course, no one else would be able to understand them. This further explores whether one could then name one's own sensations and whether one would be able to understand these putative expressions in one's 'private' language. Imagine that one wants to keep a diary about the recurrence of a certain sensation. This is, after all, something one might well want to do, perhaps for the sake of recollection in tranquillity (Vol. XII, 136) or for medical purposes (Vol. XV, 256f.). And it is certainly something we can do. But now suppose that we conceive of doing so *in accordance with the model of the putative 'private' language*. So we think that to do so, one must *associate* the sensation with a sign, say 'S', and then simply write 'S' down in a calendar whenever one has a sensation. To show the incoherence of this conception is the purpose of §§258ff.

      W.'s first move is that a definition, i.e. a *rule* for the correct use of 'S', cannot be formulated. Why not? Because 'S' is supposedly the name of one's own sensation, which another person can neither have nor know of. We naturally think that one can give *oneself* a kind of ostensive definition of 'S', and that this functions as a rule for the correct use of the sign. Admittedly, it is a peculiar ostensive definition in as much as there is no such thing as pointing privately to the sensation itself, any more than one can point at a visual image of red. But it seems as if concentrating one's attention on the sensation is a kind of mental pointing for oneself alone. So is *this* not a satisfactory private mental ostensive definition?

      No, for the function of a definition is to establish the meaning of a sign, to provide a standard for the correctness of its subsequent use. Concentrating on one's sensation while saying or writing 'S' seems to effect just that, for we think of this as a matter of impressing upon oneself the connection between 'S' and the sensation. But this is an illusion; for while one can impress upon oneself, i.e. memorize, the connection between a sign and what is already signifies (e.g. that 'Tisch' means *that* and 'Sessel' *that*' (cf. MS. 180(a), 27f.; MS. 179, 47), in such cases there is a criterion (i.e. a standard or norm) of correctness and hence too a criterion for remembering *correctly*. (If I look at a chair and say to myself 'That, in German, is called "Tisch" ', then I have made a mistake.) But here we are not concerned with memorizing the connection between a sign and what, in accord with its explanation, it signifies in the practice of using the language. Rather we are trying to mimic, *in foro interno*, the procedure of giving it a use by an ostensive definition employing a sample. W. gradually builds up a case that here we have only the semblance of such a procedure. This remark contributes the single point that unlike legitimate cases of impressing upon oneself the connection between a sign and what it signifies, here there can be no criterion of correctness. Why is this?

The point becomes clear if we compare this putative mental ostensive definition with a typical ostensive definition of a colour-word. If I point at a patch of colour and say 'That ↗ (or that ↗ colour) is eau-de-Nil', I may subsequently say of a piece of material 'That ↗ material is eau-de-Nil'. If challenged (or if I am uncertain), I may refer to the sample, compare the colour of the material with the sample, and say 'This material is *that ↗* colour, so it is eau-de-Nil'. Here the 'post at which "eau-de-Nil" is stationed' is already prepared; it is a colour-word, and bringing *this* material is a correct response to 'Bring something coloured eau-de-Nil', whereas bringing that Brunswick-green stuff is not. There is here a method of laying the sample alongside reality, hence a technique of using the defined expression in accord with this rule for its use. Whether I remember correctly the connection between 'eau-de-Nil' and the colour of which it is the name is precisely the question of whether I understand 'eau-de-Nil'. And the criteria for this understanding are whether I use 'eau-de-Nil' correctly, characterize things as eau-de-Nil only if they are the colour of the sample. (Of course, samples are not always *invoked* in applying colour-words, but these expressions only make sense within a language-game in which samples play an *essential* explanatory and justificatory role (LSD 121).)

However, the putative ostensive definition in the private language is crucially different. For here there is no criterion of remembering correctly the connection between 'S' and the sensation. In some sense, one might say, there *is* no connection between 'S' and a sensation save that one had a sensation and initially wrote 'S'. But what followed from that? Did one thereby give 'S' a use? Did one fix a rule for the correct use of 'S'? One is, of course, inclined to think that one did. For surely if one has it again, one should write down 'S' again! But, if one have *what* again? One wants to say: the *same sensation* again; but why *sensation*? For 'sensation' too is a word of our common language (cf. §261). And what counts as *the same*? What one had (and concentrated one's attention on) should, if it were really analogous to a sample in a public ostensive definition, give one a rule against which to measure subsequent uses of 'S'. ('The table is one metre long if it is *this* ↗ length' – and I point at a metre-rule.) But here one cannot compare what one now has with a sample (cf. Exg. §265). In this sense the normal criterion for remembering correctly the connection between 'S' and what it signifies (viz. correct application in accord with an appropriate explanation) is suspended.

Of course, it may seem to one that 'S' is connected with *this* (and one focuses one's inner eye on something). But is it? And what is *this*? And *what* connection does 'S' have with it? There is no answer. And in the absence of a distinction between seeming right and being right, there is no such thing as right. Hence there is no such thing as remembering correctly *or* remembering *incorrectly* the connection between 'S' and the postulated 'sample' sensation, not because memory is fallible (then one might remember incorrectly), but because there is no criterion of correctness, nothing that *counts* as right.

2   The manuscript material underlying this remark runs to many tens of pages. Some salient points from published and unpublished sources are:
(i) PG 194 (Z §248) gives a machine analogy for something that superficially appears like a proposition but is not one. Imagine a design for a steamroller consisting of a motor inside a hollow roller. The crankshaft runs through the middle of the roller and is connected at both ends by spokes with the wall of the roller. The cylinder of the engine is fixed onto the inside of the roller. This looks like a machine, but it is a rigid system. Unwittingly we have deprived the piston of all possibility of movement.

RPP I §397 comments on the unobvious depth of the analogy. One sees immediately that the machine cannot function, since one could roll the cylinder from outside even when the 'motor' is not running. But one may not see straight off that it is a rigid construction and not a machine at all. This is analogous to a private ostensive definition. For here too there is, as it were, a direct and an indirect way of gaining insight into the impossibility. (Presumably what W. meant was this: it is immediately obvious that another person cannot understand my private ostensive definition, and hence that a mutually intelligible language cannot incorporate such linguistic (explanatory, normative) devices. It is less obvious, but is the salient point of the arguments against the possibility of a private language, that such devices are, as it were, 'perfectly rigid', that I have unwittingly deprived ostensive definition of any possibility of functioning even in my own case.)

(ii) One can concentrate one's attention upon one's pains or on a colour, etc. And there is such a thing as impressing upon oneself the meaning of a word. In the case of private ostensive definition we delude ourselves into thinking that by concentrating one's attention on one's sensation, as it were pointing at it inwardly and repeating a sign 'S', one can impress upon oneself the meaning of 'S'.

Gazing at, concentrating one's visual attention on, an object is not pointing at something *for oneself* (Vol. XII, 189; LSD 38), although looking intently at something may well serve to indicate to someone *else* what one is speaking about. *A fortiori*, concentrating one's attention upon one's toothache is not a kind of pointing at it. Similarly, one can impress on one's mind what a word means, as one does when learning a foreign tongue. One can check whether one has done so successfully by running through the list of words in one's mind. But, of course, it is an open question whether one remembers *correctly* – which can be resolved by looking the words up in a dictionary. For here there is a distinction between being right and seeming to oneself to be right (MS. 179, 47). In the case of a private ostensive definition one is not actually impressing upon oneself the meaning of a word (but merely concentrating one's attention on one's pain and saying 'S'), and there is no distinction in one's later use of 'S' between being right and seeming right, hence no such thing as right.

(iii) The private, pseudo-ostensive definition is meant to establish the meaning of 'S', in order that the name be used for the sensation on later occasions. The definition should therefore provide a standard for correct use in the future. But on what occasions should 'S' be used? When one has 'a certain sensation'! But that does not describe an (unspecified) occasion for its use, for the 'certain sensation' is *unspecifiable*! 'What seemed to be a definition didn't play the role of a definition at all. It didn't justify one subsequent use of the word' (LPE 291). We fail here to see the disanalogy between genuine ostensive definition and this pseudo-ostensive definition. If one gives a name to an object, one can revert to the original in order to justify subsequent uses of the name. 'Aber wenn ich nun dem Erlebnis einen Namen gebe, wie greife ich dann vom Namen auf seinen Träger zurück, auf das *das*, was ich benannt habe? Die Definition sollte mich ja *zurückführen*, aber hier ist ja nur eine Hälfte der Definition, sozusagen, erhalten geblieben' (Vol. XV, 243). ('But when I give [an] experience a name, how do I then reach back from the name to its bearer, to the *this* which I named? For the definition was supposed to *guide me back*, but here there remains, so to speak, only half of the definition.') Of course, it seems otherwise. For we are inclined to think that our memory supplies the other half.

(iv) We are, in these reflections, prone to allocate to the faculty of memory tasks which it makes no sense for it to fulfil.

> Was mich zurückführt, ist also mein Gedächtnis; aber nun nicht in dem Sinne, in welchem es noch durch andere Tatsachen kontrolliert werden kann und man von richtiger oder falscher Erinnerung reden kann, sondern sein Ausspruch ist hier *allein* massgebend. Wir müssen also hier sagen: Die Definition, die ich jetzt gebe, *ist* die gleiche die ich damals gegeben habe, *wenn* mein Gedächtnis es mir sagt. (Vol. XV, 243f.)

> (So what leads me back is my memory; but not in the sense in which it can be checked against other facts and in which one can speak of correct or false memory, but rather its pronouncement alone sets the standard here. So here we must say: The definition that I now give *is* the same as I gave before, if my memory says so.)

W.'s point does not concern the *fallibility* of memory, and the argument is not a form of scepticism concerning memory. 'I cannot remind myself in my private language that this was the sensation I called red. There is no question of my memory's playing me a trick – because (in such a case) there can be no criterion for its playing me a trick. If we lay down rules for the use of colour-words in ordinary language, then we can admit that memory plays tricks regarding these rules' (LSD 8). Scepticism about memory requires that it *makes sense* to talk of remembering *incorrectly*. But here there is no correctness or incorrectness; only that we sometimes write 'S' and sometimes do not (cf. Exg. §265). In fact we mislead ourselves here in talking of *memory* at all, for what reason do we have in the private language story, for saying that *as he remembers*, this is what he called 'S'? Is it because of the peculiar character of the mnemonic *experience* (the *feeling* or flash of recognition)? That leads to an infinite regress, for how does the imagined user of the private language know that *this* feeling is what he previously called the experience of remembering (Vol. XV, 244f.)?

(v) One is inclined to object that surely if I had a certain sensation and named it 'S', I can *recognize* when it occurs again! But, first, how is one supposed to discern the experience of recognizing *as* recognizing. 'Recognize' is a word in our public language, and there are characteristic expressions (*Äusserungen*) of recognition and criteria for whether someone recognizes something, none of which apply in the envisaged case (MS. 180(a), 29; cf. MS. 124, 227). Secondly, 'recognize' is a success-verb. 'We use "recognize" where we can say "it *is* the same and he *recognized* it".' But we cannot say this in the case of a person's avowals of sensation, since the criterion of its being the same is his saying that it is the same. Here there is no distinction between appearance and reality, and we cannot say 'He has toothache but does not recognize it' or 'He has no toothache, but it seems to him that he has' (LSD 111f.). One can say 'I have the same toothache as before', but not 'This is the same toothache and therefore I recognize it'. 'This really means that it is impossible to recognize it wrongly – in fact that there is not any such thing as recognition here' (LSD 111). Elsewhere W. calls into question the very idea of 'recognizing' one's sensation even in a public language.

(vi) Vol. XV, 258ff. discusses the unintelligibility of a private memory sample of a sensation. Surely 'S' in the diary tells *me* something, precisely because I remember what is called 'S'. But why 'remember'? How do I know that what I am doing is called 'remembering'? The answer cannot be that I have the experience of remembering that I previously used the word thus. The justification can only be an *outer* one, for it is either an explanation by means of words or by means of a sample. One could also put it thus,

Mann kann die Vorstellung nicht als Muster nehmen, denn sie wäre dann wie ein Muster das zerstört würde, also keinen Nützen hat. Die Erinnerung aber, kann mir nur insofern helfen, als sie als 'Erinnerung' beglaubigt ist//wird//.

(One cannot take the image as a sample for it would be like a sample that would be destroyed and so is of no use. But a memory can only help me in so far as it is ratified as 'memory'.)

2.1   'concentrate my attention on the sensation': LPE 315 queries what it is like to concentrate on an experience – 'If *I* try to do this I, e.g., open my eyes particularly wide and stare.' Cf. Exg. §275, 2.

Section 259

1   A coda on §258: 'whatever is going to seem right to me is right'. The private ostensive definition purports to be a rule of the putative private language. But what the rule for the use of 'S' is turns out to be whatever *seems* to me to be the rule. But this makes no sense. The rules for the use of names of sense-impressions are the 'balance on which impressions are weighed'; but one cannot weigh impressions on the *impression* of a balance (cf. §267 and Exg.), any more than an image of the result of an imagined experiment is the result of an experiment (§265).

1.1   'on which impressions are weighed': the text here is opaque. Are these impressions the impressions *of rules* referred to in the previous sentence? Or is this a reference to impressing on oneself the connection between a sign and what it signifies, discussed in §258? The latter possibility can be dismissed, since *Eindrücke* does not etymologically echo *sich einprägen*. The former can be ruled out by reference to MS. 129. Page 51 of the MS. begins the following sequence of remarks: PI §§272, 274, 275, 277 (from page 1 of the MS., indicated by W.), 278 and 280 (from pages 23 – 4, indicated by W.), followed by a draft of the present section (also relocated from page 24). In this context it is obvious that the 'impression' in question is a *visual impression* ('visuellen Eindruck' (PI §277)), a private impression of a picture ('Sein privater Eindruck des Bildes' (PI §280)) or colour-impression ('Farbeindruck' (PI §§275, 277)), which is also re-ferred to as a *sensation* (PI §§272, 274). Hence this remark becomes clear if this sentence is read thus: 'The balance on which sense-impressions are weighed is not the *impression* of a balance.'

2.1   'is not the *impression* of a balance': MS. 129, 24 adds 'Wollte man nun fortsetzen: "sondern eine wirkliche Waage", so wäre dies zwar wahr; aber irreführend, weil der Ton nicht auf dem Unterschied zwischen wirklich und unwirklich ruht'. ('If one now wanted to continue: "but a real balance", this, to be sure, would be true; but misleading, for the matter does not rest on the difference between real and unreal.') This remark was crossed out. Perhaps W. here is alluding to the fact that in saying 'I have a pain' or 'I have a visual impression of red', I do not 'weigh' my sense-impression 'on a balance' at all. I just *say* these words – although 'This is not the *end* of the language-game: it is the beginning' (PI §290). It is *others* who assess my sense-impression on the balance that weighs the public criteria for being in pain or having a red visual impression.

SECTION 260

1   Reverting to the diary record of a 'private' sensation, how should we describe what the diarist is doing in §258? Should we conceive of him writing 'S' when he believes that he is having the same sensation as he previously named 'S'? This is how he conceives of the matter. W. replies ironically: is it not rather that he believes that he believes it? Why so? Because if, as argued, it is merely an illusion that 'S' is a meaningful sign, then there is no such thing as *believing* that one has S again (any more than there is such a thing as believing that la-di-da). By the same token, of course, there is no such thing as believing that one believes a nonsense. But one may say 'You just think (imagine, believe) that you believe something here, but you don't really have any belief at all'.

This is confirmed by the opening question of §260(b), for it does indeed follow from the argument that the diarist made a note of nothing whatever. But this should not be surprising; making a mark or marks on a calendar is not *per se* making a note of something. That requires that the marks have a function in the practice of speaking a language (PI §51), but 'S' in the private language has no such function.

(c) offers an analogy: there is such a thing as talking to oneself (as indeed there is such a thing as keeping a diary about one's headaches), but not every case of speaking when one is alone is a case of talking to oneself. The analogy suggests that babbling when alone is not talking to oneself. But the point may be more general: not all solitary coherent speech is talking to oneself (see Exg. §243, 2); complex criteria different- iate, for example, thinking one is talking to someone (although no one else is present) from reciting poetry in practice for tonight's perfor- mance, from prayer, exclamation, or talking in one's sleep or in delirium, and all of these from talking to oneself, as well as from babbling. Similarly, writing marks on a calendar (or in a diary) may be doing a multitude of different things, such as registering an appointment for next week or recording an appointment, making a note of a birthday or a wedding, keeping a record of one's pains, etc. Or it may be none of these, but just doodling. Whether it is one or another depends on the context, and the variegated criteria that fix the different concepts of making appointments, keeping records, etc., and the use of the marks in other speech-activities.

2   MS. 129, 44 contains PI §260 (a)–(b), but instead of (c) continues:

> Frage Dich, was der Sinn, der Zweck, einer Notiz ist. Denke *so*: Ist es nicht merkwürdig, dass wir manchmal Zeichen in einen Kalender einschreiben – wozu tun wir das eigentlich?

> (Ask yourself, what is the sense, the purpose, of a note. Consider: Is it not curious that we sometimes write signs in a calendar – why do we actually do this?)

W. does not answer (but goes straight on to PI §261). Vol. XII, 136 explores one possibility in the imagined case of the diarist. Perhaps, when he reads his diary later, it will enable him to recollect his experiences. Can we then say that the diary tells him something? But what does this consist in? Surely in the experiences of recollection which he has when he reads it! But, W. concludes, not everything that makes us recollect something can be said to communicate something to us. If looking at a row of trees makes him remember something, one would not say that the row of trees tells him something. The moral is that one should look closely at the language-game of communicating informa- tion, of telling someone something, and examine the analogue of this language-game when it is played by oneself. This is parallel to the examination of what counts as talking to oneself.

2.1   (i) 'Well, I *believe* that this is the sensation S again': Vol. XVII, 26ff.
explores the question differently. Does the following black spot △
rest on these struts and this foundation (cf. RFM 378)? And does my use
of the word 'black' rest on *recognizing* the colour, and my use of 'pain' on
my *remembering* that I previously called *this* 'pain'? A *picture* is involved
here, and it clashes, not with the facts, but with *other pictures*. If we claim
that 'When he later has a certain feeling, he says "I have a pain" ', this
makes it appear as if one could find out, by identifying the feeling (which
one, as it were, looks at), whether he uses the word correctly. Someone
who claims this lacks a clear picture of the use of this sentence. One form
of expression here clashes with another (one language-game is being
projected onto another). We are inclined to say 'If I later have this feeling,
then I say "I have a pain" ' (as we might say 'If I later see this colour, then
I say "That object is eau-de-Nil" '). But should one not say 'If I later
believe that I have the same feeling . . .', or even 'If I believe that I believe
this'? (For in the language-game with colours, one *can* intelligibly say 'If I
later believe that I see this colour, then I say . . .'). But it obviously
makes no sense to say: 'I believe that what I have now is a pain, because it
is the same as what I had before, and what I had before I called "pain".' It
looks as if the sentence 'If I later have *this* feeling . . .' articulates a
criterion of identity for pain which determines the correctness of my
saying 'I have a pain' (as 'If I later see *this* ↗ colour, then I'll say . . .'
articulates a criterion of identity for such-and-such a colour, in as much
as it presents a defining sample). But this is a complete misrepresentation
of the language-game with 'pain', as well as a misinterpretation of 'If I
have the same feeling then I say . . .'. For this phrase does
indeed say something about our language-game, but not what we
initially think it does. It says something about the grammatical relationship between 'same feeling' and 'pain', viz. that we use 'pain' always for
the same feeling, not for a different one on every day of the week (which
would be possible too).

    (ii) 'perhaps you believe that you believe it': a further strand could be
added to the argument, parallel to Exg. §258, 2(v). The diarist is not in
the position to insist that he *believes* that it is S again, for how does he
know that *this* is believing and not something else? For 'belief' too is a
word in our common language with public criteria for its (third-person)
application, not the name of a 'private experience' (cf. §261).

SECTION 261

1   In §260 the interlocutor retorted in astonishment 'Did the man who
made the entry in the calendar make a note of *nothing whatever*?' The

story was that when the diarist has a certain sensation, he writes 'S', which is a sign he has associated with the sensation (§258). So surely he is making a note of a *sensation*! Not so, for 'S' so far has no function (§260). But 'sensation' is a word of our common language for the (third-person) use of which there are public criteria. We often know whether someone else is feeling this or that sensation, and different people may have the same sensation. *In as much as 'S' is meant to name what can be known only to the person speaking* (PI §243) *and cannot be had by anyone else* (cf. PI §253), 'S' cannot be the name of a *sensation* (cf. PI §257); 'S' cannot be stationed by this signpost any more than a sign pointing north can be placed at the North Pole.

One may remonstrate that when the diarist has what he wishes to designate by 'S' he surely *has something*, not *nothing* (cf. Exg. §§294, 296, 304). But this is of no avail, for 'has' and 'something' too are words of common language, with rules for their correct use. A person may *have* pains, but also emotions, thoughts, and love affairs, not to mention adventures and debts. In each case there are criteria for saying of him 'He has . . .' which are familiar to us all. But what criteria justify saying of the envisaged user of a private language that he *has* . . .? 'Something' too is a word of our public language, with rules for its common use. I may have something in my pocket (a penny), but not a pain; something may cross my mind (a thought), but not a penny. If I say 'I have something in my pocket' and am asked what it is, I must be able to produce it or provide a description, even if only of the form 'I don't know what it is; it is round, flat, and metallic, but it is not a coin'. If I look through a microscope and say 'I see something but I don't know what it is', I must be able to describe what it looks like, e.g. 'It is irregular in shape, covered with small dots, etc.' In short, 'something' is a place-holder for a sample or (provisional) description – it is not itself, as it were, a *minimal description*. The use of 'something' is complex and variegated, depending upon what it is a place-holder for (see Exg. §294, 1). But it is a mistake to think, as the interlocutor here intimates, that its role is to signify what is, as it were, so minimal that it cannot be gainsaid. What justifies saying of the diarist that at any rate he has something? Something about which nothing can be said provides no such justification (cf. PI §304).

We, as philosophers, are reduced to trying to characterize what role 'S' has in the private language by an inarticulate noise. We now want a sound *unconnected with grammar* to name what the diarist has, for 'something' was wrongly supposed to be the next best thing to such a noise in so far as it seemed to have a location independent of any signpost at all. But while an inarticulate sound can be given the role of an expression signifying something, this is possible (intelligible) only in a language-game. And what seems to be a language-game of keeping a diary of 'private' experiences is not one at all. §270 picks up the theme.

2.1   'So the use of this word stands in need of a justification which everybody understands': i.e. the use of the word 'sensation' in our common language. But when I say that I still have a pain in my shoulder, the same burning sensation I had yesterday, do *I* have a justification? No, of course not. But this is just what misleads us here. For now it seems that if I say this and have no justification, then I am unjustified in saying it, i.e. that I should not say it. Is it not the *pain* that justifies my saying 'I have the same painful sensation as yesterday'? Here we misconstrue the grammar of 'justify' and edge ourselves, quite naturally, into the position under attack. MS. 124, 227f. clarifies this in the sequel to an early draft of PI §260.

> Mit welchem Recht reden wir hier von 'gleich', von 'Empfindung', 'wiedererkenn-en', und 'glauben'? Denn das sind ja alles Worter unsrer allgemeinen Sprache.
> Er hat ja eben kein Kriterium der Gleichheit! – Aber wenn er's nicht hat, dann haben wir's ja auch nicht, und doch reden wir von gleichen Empfindungen. – Ja, aber wir brauchen hier kein Kriterium; so wenig wie eines dafür, dass wir Schmerzen haben. Denn wir in unsrer Sprache benützen die *Äusserung* des Schmerzes. Und wir *benutzen* sie zu verschiedenen Zwecken. Während wir vorgaben, dass jener Mensch in seiner privaten Sprache die Empfindungen wie *Dinge* benennt, die er in einem Guckkasten sieht, in den nur er allein schauen kann.

> (With what right do we talk here of 'the same', of 'sensation', 'recognizing', and 'believing'? For these are all words of our common language.
> He has no criterion of sameness! – But if he hasn't one, then neither do we, and nevertheless we talk of same sensations. – Yes, but we need no criterion here; as little as we need one for our having pains. For we, in our language, use the *manifestation* of pains. And we *use* it for different purposes. Whereas we took it that that person names sensations in his private language like *things* which he sees in a peep-show which only he can look at.)

3   James nicely exemplifies these confusions:

> Any fact, be it thing, event, or quality, may be conceived sufficiently for purposes of identification, if only it be singled out and marked so as to separate it from other things. Simply calling it 'this' or 'that' will suffice . . . The essential point is that it should be re-identified by us as that which the talk is about . . . .
> In this sense, creatures extremely low in the intellectual scale may have conception. All that is required is that they should recognize the same experience again. A polyp would be a conceptual thinker if a feeling of 'Hollo! thing-umbob again!' ever flitted through its mind.[14]

---

[14] James, *Principles of Psychology*, Vol. I, pp. 462f.

Section 262

1   One can give an ostensive definition of, say, a new colour-word, but that presupposes the grammar of colour, which provides 'the post where the new word is stationed' (§257). A bare ostensive gesture, *a fortiori* a mere concentration of one's attention on a sensation, does not give a sign a *technique of application* (cf. PI §§30, 33 – 6). The proponent of the possibility of a private language thinks that he can dispense with this, for it seems that he can supply the technique for the use of 'S' by inwardly undertaking to use 'S' in such-and-such a way. But how does he undertake this? His answer is given in §§263 – 4. It is clear that he cannot have found the technique ready-made, since then it would involve the grammar of 'sensation', which is a word of common language with public criteria for its application (in third-person cases). So he must invent it! Of course, he will deny this, insisting instead that he reads the technique of using the word off *the nature* of the private object.

Note that PI §34 has pointed out that 'to intend the definition in such-and-such a way' does not stand for a process which accompanies giving a definition, and §205 (cf. §337) that such intentions are *not* independent of pre-existing techniques.

Section 263

1   This clarifies what the wayward interlocutor thinks his invented technique of application for 'S' is, viz. to call *this* 'pain' (= 'S') in the future, and also how he thinks he undertakes to use 'S' thus, viz. by concentrating his attention on his feeling. But, as argued, the 'this' provides no criterion of identity for pain (PI §253), and concentrating one's attention on a feeling is not a criterion for intending to use a word in accord with a certain technique of application.

Section 264

1   This makes it clear that the interlocutor is firmly caught in the web of the Augustinian picture. The entire grammar of an expression seems to unfold from knowledge of what it stands for, i.e. acquaintance with the object named. This conception yields a distorted picture of understanding and of the criteria of understanding.

SECTION 265

1   It seems to us that by a private ostensive definition one can correlate a sign with a sensation, and that by concentrating one's attention one can impress upon oneself this connection, so that in future one will re-member it right (PI §258). W. has already argued that in this case there is no criterion, i.e. no standard, of correctness. Here the same point is made by means of a contrastive analogy.

We consult a dictionary to justify translating 'Tisch' as 'table'. We can imagine someone with a vivid visual memory trying to remember what 'Tisch' means by calling to mind the image of the relevant page of the dictionary. Whether he remembers what it means can be checked against the actual dictionary. But could he not have a purely private dictionary, i.e. one that exists *only* in the imagination? Could he not consult his mental dictionary to see what a certain word means? Of course, it would be a purely subjective justification for the use of the word in question!

Note that the 'private dictionary' is analogous to a private table of samples correlated with words, as might be envisaged by the defender of the possibility of a private language. If there can be public tables of samples (e.g. colour-charts) surely there can be private ones which exist only in the imagination? Hence one might think that the process envisaged in §258 might yield something akin to a mental table of samples.

But the idea of justification by reference to a private dictionary is incoherent. For justification consists in appealing to something independent. Otherwise 'whatever is going to seem right to me is right. And that only means that here we can't talk about "right" ' (PI §258). The interlocutor objects, for we surely do appeal from one memory to another for confirmation; e.g. as I remember, the next train leaves at 12.35 but if unsure, I might call up an image of the timetable I was looking at yesterday, and if, as I thus imagine it, the time that follows 11.15 is 12.35, I shall rest satisfied. This is possible, for it parallels the above case of trying to remember what 'Tisch' means. In both cases calling up a mnemonic image can have a confirmatory role only because it is an image of something objective and hence can itself be tested for correctness. Here there is a manifest difference between remembering correctly and remembering incorrectly. But in the case of a dictionary that exists only in the imagination, *a fortiori* in the private diarist's case, there is no such distinction. He endeavours to remember what a word means *only* by reference to his memory of what it means. And *that* cannot be checked for correctness. There is here no *possibility* of an appeal to something independent, hence the manoeuvre he has in mind is like buying a second copy of *The Times* to check whether what is written in the first copy is correct. If the only thing *it makes sense* to appeal to in trying to remember what a word means is his memory of what it means, then 'whatever is going to seem right to me is right. And that only means that here we can't talk about "right"' (§258). §265(b) drives the point home.

1.1   (i) 'etwa ein Wörterbuch': 'a dictionary, for instance'.

    (ii) 'an eine unabhängige Stelle appelliert': 'consists in appealing to an independent authority'.

    (iii) 'Nein; denn dieser Vorgang . . .': 'No, for this process must actually call forth the *right* memory.' The right memory here is the memory of what a certain word *means*, and the intelligibility of remembering correctly presupposes that something *counts* as correct. In the timetable case, misremembering involves an error which it *makes sense* to check against the actual timetable. Here, however, there is no further check; whatever is called forth is 'right'. But that means that there is no right or wrong – for the balance on which impressions are weighed cannot be the impression of a balance (§259). The issue is *logical*, not epistemological.

2   LSD 8f. confirms that scepticism about the reliability of memory is not at issue (cf. Exg. §258, 2(iv)).

    Philosophers who conceive of ordinary language as discourse between speakers of private languages, i.e. who view public language as the congruence of private languages, imagine that each person possesses his own 'private dictionary'. W. discussed this aberration in Vol. XV, 87ff. (cf. 'Private ostensive definition', p. 111). It is a bogus explanation, which does no work at all (see Z §552).

    Vol. XII, 249 has this preceded by the following discussion. One wants to say 'Surely I say that I have pains because that is how it really is'. But is that supposed to explain the use of the expression 'I have pains'? How can it do so when it presupposes it? One might, however, say this in contrast to saying '. . . because that is part of the role I am learning by heart'. What one would really like to say is 'Surely I say I am in pain becuase *this here* is the case'. Of course, if one says this and accompanies it with a demonstration which, after all, 'this here' demands, no one will want to contradict this explanation. The interlocutor now queries: 'Whence then the illusion that the words are a description of a feeling?' That is not an illusion, W. replies; the illusion is that the sentence 'Pains are *this* feeling' is an explanation even when it is unaccompanied by a *demonstration*. One would have to speak here of an explanation which can *only* be laid down in one's memory.

2.1   (i) 'No; for this process has got . . .': Vol. XII, 249f. was even more
emphatic – 'Nein; denn es ist ~~(hier)~~ wesentlich, dass dieser Vorgang //
Prozess // erfahrungsgemäss // wirklich // hilft, die *richtige* Erinnerung
hervorzurufen' ('No; for it is essential ~~(here)~~ that this event // process //
in fact // actually // helps to call forth the *right* memory'). There
PI §265(b) is followed by a further analogy: it is as if, when playing dice,
one were to determine the value of a throw by a further throw.

    (ii) '(As if someone . . .)': Vol. XVI, 126 offers a different simile –
isn't this as if I let my mouth confirm that what my hand writes is
correct?

Section 266

1   The first of three remarks elaborating §265. The clock is the analogue
of one's memory. I can look at the clock to see what time it is, as I can
'consult my memory'. But I can also look at the clock face to guess what
time it is (e.g. if it loses time or perhaps has stopped) or move the hands
of a clock (that has stopped) till their position strikes me as right. In each
such case, however, there is an external, independent check on what time
it actually is – a way of determining whether the clock is *right*, whether
my guess is *correct*, whether its look's striking me as right is a true
intuition. But that is just what is *absent* in the case of looking up the table
(dictionary) in one's imagination.

1.1   '(Looking at the clock in the imagination)': cf. PI §607.

Section 267

1   A further variant on §265(b). Just as the image of the result of an
imagined experiment is not the result of an experiment, so too imagining
justifying the choice of dimensions for an imagined bridge is not
justifying an imagined choice of dimensions. Justification of dimensions
for an imagined construction takes the same form as for an actual
construction, viz. appeal to laws of mechanics, properties of materials,
etc. Hence one must cite genuine calculations and experiments to justify
an imagined construction being envisaged thus rather than otherwise.
Imagining calculations and experiments is to *imagine justifications*, not to
justify anything at all. Of course, an engineer might employ mental
images heuristically in elaborating his justification for his choice of
dimensions for a bridge (whether actual or only imagined in wishful
thinking). He might call to mind a page of an integral table in carrying
out a calculation or review an experiment in his mind's eye. But any such

justification is parasitic on ascertaining the reliability of his imagery in relation to the objective standard of actual table and concrete experiment. It is these that carry the real burden of justification.

The idea of a private language is incoherent precisely because it fails to distinguish imagining a justification for using a word and justifying the use of a word in one's imagination (e.g. by recollecting a page in an actual dictionary).

1.1   'Aber würden wir . . .': 'would we . . .'.

SECTION 268

1   Giving oneself a 'private definition' in the manner described no more has the consequences of a genuine definition (viz. determining a standard for the correct use of an expression) than my right hand's putting money into my left has the consequences of a gift. The latter does not comply with the grammar of 'giving a gift', and similarly the former does not accord with the grammar of 'giving a definition'.

SECTION 269

1   A provisional summary linked to the last sentence of §268.

1.1   'Sounds . . . which I "*appear to understand*" ': e.g. 'speaking with tongues'; this too might be called 'a private language'.

SECTION 270

1   In §258 we were asked to imagine wanting to keep a diary about the recurrence of a certain sensation (perhaps a pain or a feeling of nausea (Vol. XV, 256)). To do so on the private language model of associating the sensation with a sign 'S', giving oneself a private ostensive definition of 'S', inwardly undertaking to call THIS 'S', remembering what one previously inwardly called 'S', have all been shown to be incoherent. On those presuppositions no definition of the sign can be formulated; there can be no criterion of correctness for its use. A sensation, unlike a public sample, cannot (logically) provide one with, or be used as, a private standard for the correct use of a word.

Now we are to envisage a genuine use for the entry of the sign 'S' in my diary. Suppose I discover that whenever I have a particular sensation, my blood-pressure, as measured by a manometer, has risen. So now I might keep a diary for medical purposes and enter 'S' whenever I think my blood-pressure has risen, i.e. whenever I have the sensation experientially correlated with rising blood-pressure. I might report to my doctor that my blood-pressure must have risen last Tuesday and Thursday, for I entered 'S' in my diary on those days (cf. Vol. XV, 257). This is perfectly intelligible.

But might I not misidentify the sensation, think I recognize it, but be mistaken? The criticism of the private language theorist's conception, after all, turned on the unintelligibility of a private standard of correctness for the use of 'S' as the name of a sensation and on his inability, within the constraints which he has set, to determine what he 'has' as the same again. Does the same difficulty not arise here? No! To be sure, if I recognized the sensation, then I might misrecognize it. If I had to *identify* my sensation, then it would make sense for me to identify it wrongly; and I would need a criterion of correctness against which to check my identification. If I had none (and a private object cannot provide one), then the inference about the rise in my blood-pressure would be unfounded. But 'S' here (in §270) is not assigned a meaning by private ostensive definition. I write 'S' in my diary whenever I believe my blood-pressure to have risen on the ground that I have had the particular sensation which I have found to be correlated with rising blood-pressure. It makes no sense to speak of my making a mistake about whether I have a certain sensation, for 'I think I have a certain sensation, but I may be wrong' is nonsense. The supposition of misidentification here (unlike the case in §258) is vacuous – but not because I happen to have an unbroken record of correct identifications, rather because no question of *identification* arises.

I can show that my inference about my blood-pressure is not unfounded because, *ex hypothesi*, I *am* able to say that my blood-pressure is rising, and I am able to say this *precisely because* of my sensation. (I don't infer it from *nothing*!) The supposition that I might regularly misidentify the sensation is wholly vacuous, an ornamental knob which does not connect with the mechanism. How do I *know* that I have the sensation? That too is a senseless question. Does this not mean that what I really discovered was that whenever I *believe* I have it, my blood-pressure rises – but my belief might be mistaken? No, it makes no sense to talk of *believing* one has a sensation (see 2 below).

The private language theorist will doubtless feel that W.'s story deprives him of the very thing – the private object that functions as a defining paradigm – which makes 'S' a sensation-word rather than an empty mark. §270(b) is a response to the interlocutor's puzzlement that we can speak of a *sensation*-word here *without* the collateral of a paradigm. What is *our* reason[15] for calling 'S' the name of a sensation here? W.'s

---

[15] Not: what is *my* reason? The question is whether my use of 'S' satisfies the *public* criteria for sensation words.

reply is schematic: 'perhaps the kind of way this sign is employed in this language-game'. Evidently this stands in contrast to the pseudo-sensation-name in §§258, 260f. There the sign had no genuine use at all. Here it is used to register the occurrence of a particular sensation indicating (as I have discovered) that my blood-pressure has risen. And, presumably, I might explain this to the doctor. Further, I might say 'Look, I wrote "S" in my diary four times last week, so my blood-pressure must be brought under control', or 'The pills you gave me are working, for that particular sensation is occurring less frequently – see, I wrote "S" only once last week'. Perhaps, too, the doctor might talk of my S-sensation.

Similarly, the private language theorist conceived of the private paradigm as providing a criterion of identity for the sensation. How else could one determine that what one has is the same again? Has W.'s story not eliminated the very thing that makes it intelligible to speak of the recurrence of the *same* sensation? No; I do not recurrently write 'S' in my diary because I observe that what I recurrently have matches a paradigm, anymore than I clutch my jaw when I have toothache because what I have is this ↗, and one clutches one's jaw when one has *this*. Rather, I just write 'S' or 'S again'. And in this language-game with blood-pressure-indicative sensations, *that* I recurrently write 'S' is a criterion for others to say in these circumstances: 'He has the same peculiar sensation, so his blood-pressure must be rising.'

1.1   (i) 'Nehmen wir an . . .': 'Let's suppose that I regularly make a mistake in identifying it.'

(ii) 'die Annahme dieses Irrtums . . .': 'The supposition of this mistake was mere show.'

(iii) 'Perhaps the kind of way . . .': It is unclear what qualification, if any, is intended by the 'perhaps'. MS. 165, 229 has the rather more emphatic 'Nun vielleicht eben die Art und Weise . . .'.

2   The above interpretation is controversial. The source material is therefore given in some detail. The origin of the blood-pressure example is MS. 165, 145ff. Its introduction is in a context in which it is perspicuously genuine sensations that are at issue. We can, W. notes, on the basis of our sensations, make *immediate* inferences and predictions about processes in our brain, nerves, and organs. That is the point of the otherwise confused claim often made that one's states of consciousness are only another aspect of brain processes seen 'from the inside'. Then:

Wenn Du Schmerzen hast und daraus auf hohen Blutdruck schliesst, wirst Du doch nicht sagen wollen, Du habest aus *nichts* auf hohen Blutdruck geschlossen.

Und wie ist das Experiment zu beschreiben: Du beobachtest Deinen Blutdruck und siehst zu, wie er von Deinem Schmerzzustand abhängt. Dabei aber rufst Du nicht durch äussere Mittel die Schmerzen hervor, sondern vergleichst nur ihren Verlauf mit dem des Blutdrucks. Denk Dir nun, statt Kreuzchen in einen Kalender einzutragen wenn er Schmerzen hat, mache er dies Experiment! Ist das kein Experiment? Wird es nur dadurch zu einem, dass er einen Ausdruck der Schmerzen hat? Kann er nicht eben die Veränderung des Blutdrucks richtig, für jeden sichtbar, voraussagen.

Und hier spielt wieder das '*richtige*' Wiedererkennen seiner Empfindung gar keine Rolle, denn es genügt dass er sie wiederzuerkennen *glaubt*, da dass wichtige Resultat das *richtige* Voraussagen der körperlichen Erscheinung ist. Und daher muss es auch falsch sein, wenn ich sage, er *glaube* die Empfindung wiederzuerkennen.

(If you have pains and infer therefrom a high blood-pressure, you would not want to say that you inferred a high blood-pressure from *nothing*.

And how is this experiment to be described: You observe your blood-pressure and watch how it depends on the state of your pains. But you do not produce the pains by external means, rather you compare their course with that of the blood-pressure. Now imagine that instead of entering little crosses on a calendar when he has pains, he makes this experiment! Is it not an experiment? Does it only become one by his having an expression of the pains? For can't he just predict correctly every perceptible change in the blood-pressure?

And here again the '*correct*' recognition of his sensation plays no role at all, for it suffices that he *believes* that he recognizes it, since the important outcome is the *correct* prediction of the bodily phenomenon. And hence too it must be wrong when I say, he *believed* that he recognized the sensation again.)

The theme is resumed only on p. 227 of the notebook. There, preceded by a draft of PI §260(b), we find the first draft of PI §270(a). It is quite close to the final formulation. This is followed by:

Wie eher, wenn wir so sagen wolten: Er ist geneigt, immer wieder das selbe Zeichen ('E') zu gebrauchen // einzutragen //; darum sagen, wir, er habe die gleichen Empfindungen. (Ähnlich etwa: Er ist geneigt beim Beten nach oben zu schauen, darum sagen wir, Gott sei in der Höhe.) (MS. 165, 228f.).

(How if we wanted to put it like this: He is inclined always to use // enter // the same sign ('S') again; therefore we say he has the same sensation. (Perhaps like: He is inclined to look upwards when praying, therefore we say, God is on high.))

That is, the use of the same sign does not *rest on* an inner identification or recognition, but is a criterion for *others* to judge that the speaker (or diary-keeper) has the same sensation. (Cf. LPE 287: 'What is the criterion for his connecting the word always to the same experience [of having a red visual image]? Is it not often just that he calls it red?')

This remark is followed by a draft of PI §270(b), which opens, however, with a version of the first two sentences of PI §260:

'Empfindung' ist aber ein Wort der allgemeinen Sprache. Welchen Grund haben wir 'E' die Bezeichnung für eine Empfindung zu nennen? Nun, vielleicht eben die Art und Weise wie sie in diesem Sprachspiel (Steigen des Blutdrucks) verwendet wird. (MS. 165, 229f.)

(But 'sensation' is a word of common language. What reason have we for calling 'S' the name for a sensation? Well, perhaps just the kind of way in which it is used in this language-game (rising blood-pressure).)

This is evidently meant to contrast with the vacuous employment of 'S' in the private linguist's diary. For the next remark is a full draft of PI §261 (this begins on the last page of the notebook (p. 230) and continues on p. 42, where W. had evidently left an empty page). This in turn is succeeded by another draft of §270(b).

It is noteworthy that the three paragraphs from MS. 165, 145ff. were transcribed with only minor modification into MS. 124, 282f. They do not, however, occur in MS. 129. MS. 129, 46 has PI §270 after PI §§258, 260, 261; it is followed by PI §§209(b)–(c): we hanker for a *deeper* explanation or a deeper understanding.

2.1   '*richtig* wiedererkannt habe, oder nicht': MS. 165, 227 adds 'oder ob Du den Glauben richtig als Glauben erkennst' (or whether you recognize the belief correctly as belief).

SECTION 271

1   One might monitor the fluctuations in one's blood-pressure (given the scenario of §270) by writing 'S' in one's diary whenever one has the sensation found to be correlated with rises in blood-pressure. The supposition that one might be mistaken in identifying one's sensation is vacuous (one does not *identify* one's sensation). A similarly vacuous supposition (free-wheeling cog) is examined here: can we imagine a person who cannot remember what 'pain' means, and so calls different things 'pain', but nevertheless uses the word whenever he hits himself, burns or cuts himself and screams, etc., etc.? No! If he uses 'pain' as we all do, then he does remember what it means (which is not to say that he remembers what inner thing is named 'pain').

Note that it would be a mistake to assimilate §271 into the argument of §270, as if what makes the hypothesis of error a mere show in §270 is that I might misidentify the sensation *and* misremember which sensation indicates rising blood-pressure. §271 is a *parallel* vacuous hypothesis, *not* part of the argument of §270.

2   LSD 9 supposes someone to have learnt what 'toothache' means ('Now I know what "toothache" means' sounds as if he has been given a sample, but that, W. emphasizes, is wrong). The next day he says 'Now I have a toothache, I know what it is like, etc.'. Would it make sense here

to ask 'What if he has something entirely *different* today?' Only if one doubts whether he has learnt what 'toothache' means.

2.1   'whose memory could not retain . . .': the absurdity of the supposition can be invoked to dissolve the illusion of a 'private' object: 'Always get rid of the private object in this way: assume that it constantly changes, but that you do not notice the change because your memory constantly deceives you' (PI p. 207).

SECTION 272

1   Pain has occupied centre-stage hitherto; now W. switches to colours. Pain seemed to be defined by reference to a private sample; but that is an illusion, not because it is defined by reference to a public sample, but rather because it is not defined by reference to a sample at all. Colour-words are defined by reference to colour-samples, but because we typically apply colour-words such as 'red' without recourse to samples or colour-charts, we are inclined to misconstrue this and to project upon colour-concepts features of the grammar of 'pain' *as conceived on the private language model*. And we are further encouraged to do this by misconstruals of scientific investigations into light and visual perception. Bedazzled by such misunderstandings, it is easy to think that the real samples that define colour-concepts are private sense-impressions or 'sensations' (cf. 1.1 below), and that the last court of appeal for the application of colour-words is a private ostensive definition. §§272 – 8 dispel this illusion.

What is characteristic of a 'private language' is not that each person has his own exemplar by reference to which he explains and uses the words of his language. For that, after all, is perfectly intelligible; we might have our own tape-measures or colour-charts, which we could compare to ensure that we mean the same by '1 metre' or 'red'. Rather is it the supposition that each person's exemplar is essentially private, and hence that nobody knows whether others mean by 'red' *this* (and one concentrates one's attention upon one's own sense-impression) or something else. The immediate consequence of this would be that it is intelligible, though unverifiable, that what one section of mankind calls 'red' differs from what the rest call 'red'.

W. evidently holds this assumption to be unintelligible. But note that the objection to this assumption is not that it would be unverifiable and therefore meaningless. W. is not relying on the principle of verification as a premise in an argument. One should not argue: it is unverifiable, so it must lack meaning. Rather, one should ask: what is called 'having a red visual impression'? What are the criteria for saying of two people that 'they have the same colour-impression'? When is one licensed to say 'I have a different colour-impression of this than you?' We should examine the use of these phrases (for they do have a use) and the ways in which they are explained. The deep objection to the assumption of §272 is the one already spelt out, viz. that each person would not know what he *himself* means by 'red', for if the meaning of 'red' were 'determined' by a mental table of samples, then whatever seems right is right, and that means that there is no such thing as right (PI §§258, 265).

1.1   'eine Rotempfindung': the German 'Empfindung' is somewhat more flexible than the English 'sensation'. It is potentially misleading to speak of *sensations* of red (where? – in the eye or in the brain?), but W.'s point is clear enough. §§276 – 7 talk, with no sense of discontinuity, of *Farbeindruck*.

2   W. discussed the problem of 'spectrum inversion' *in extenso* in LPE, LSD, and Vol. XV, 87ff. (cf. 'Private ostensive definition', p. 111, for part of this discussion).

3   In MS. 124, 291 this occurs *after* §273 and is followed by §§274 – 5, then 'James ist eine Fundgrube für die Psychologie *des Philosophen*' ('James is a rich source for the psychology *of philosophers*'). On this topic, James, like von Helmholtz and numerous others before and since, argued:

> The real colour of the brick is the sensation it gives when the eye looks squarely at it from a near point, out of the sunshine and yet not in the gloom; under other circumstances it gives us other colour-sensations which are but signs of this – we then see it looks pinker or blacker than it really is . . . But all these essential characteristics, which together form for us the genuine objectivity of the thing and are contrasted with what we call the subjective sensations it may yield us at a given moment, are mere sensations like the latter.[16]

SECTION 273

1   We communicate to each other information about the colours of objects, obey orders to paint the wall blue or requests to bring something red. So does 'red', for example, signify something 'confronting us all'; but further, strictly speaking, each of us should have another word to name his own 'private' sense-impression of red? (If so, of course, the latter word could be understood only by the speaker himself.) Or is it rather that 'red' is actually ambiguous, signifying both something with

---

[16] James, *Principles of Psychology*, Vol. I, p. 286.

which everyone is acquainted and, in addition (for each person), something epistemically private? Or is it that it signifies (*bezeichnen*) something known to us all, but *refers* (*sich beziehen*) to a 'private' sense-impression? These questions stem from a misconstrual of the use of defining samples and misunderstandings of meaning, explanation, and understanding.

1.1   (i) 'bezeichne': name, signify, or designate; it is important to co-ordinate this translation with §293.

(ii) 'etwas "uns allen Gegenüberstehendes" ': this does not occur in early drafts (MS. 165, 178; MS. 124, 290f.) but only in MS. 129, 50. It seems to be a quotation from Frege's *The Basic Laws of Arithmetic*, Introduction, p. xviii, where there is an implied play on 'Gegenstand' and 'gegenüberstehen': 'Since the number one, being the same for everyone, confronts everyone in the same way, it can no more be investigated by making psychological observations than can the moon.' Frege thought that

> no one has another's idea, only his own, and no one even knows how far his idea – e.g. of red – coincides with another's; for I cannot express what is peculiar to the idea I associate with the word 'red'. To be able to compare one person's idea with another's, one would have to unite them in the same consciousness, and one would have to be certain that they had not changed in being transferred.[17]

Hence he nicely exemplifies the confusions of §273 in this remark:

> The word 'white' ordinarily makes us think of a certain sensation, which is, of course, entirely subjective; but even in ordinary speech, it often bears, I think, an objective sense. When we call snow white, we mean to refer to an objective quality (*so will man eine objektive Beschaffenheit ausdrücken*) which we recognize in ordinary daylight, by a certain sensation . . . Often . . . a colour-word does not signify (*bezeichnet nicht*) our subjective sensation, which we cannot know to agree with anyone else's (for obviously our calling things by the same name does not guarantee as much), but rather an objective quality. (FA §26)

Cf. BB 72f.

It is noteworthy that parallel to the temptation to conceive of 'red' as meaning both something known to oneself alone and something 'confronting us all' is the temptation to think that 'pain' means both something essentially private *and*, in a quite different sense, something confronting us all, viz. such-and-such behaviour. This strategy was essayed in *Philosophical Remarks*, Ch. VI.

[17] G. Frege, 'Review of Husserl's *Philosophy of Arithmetic*', repr. in Frege, *Collected Papers on Mathematics, Logic and Philosophy*, ed. B. McGuinness (Blackwell, Oxford and New York, 1984), p. 198.

3   The conception here alluded to is enshrined in the representational idealist tradition running from Descartes to Boyle, Locke and Newton, through Reid and von Helmholtz, to the present day.[18] On the one hand, what 'confronts us all', colour 'as it is in the object', is 'a certain disposition of the superficial parts of the object to trouble the light to reflect after such-and-such a determinate manner'.[19] On the other hand, 'the more proper, though not the usual acceptation of the word colour',[20] is the private sensation which reflected light causes 'in us'.

SECTION 274

1   The switch in §273 from 'signify' (*bezeichnen*) to 'refer' (*sich beziehen*) is of no avail, but it is what one is inclined here to say (cf. §254). It is a hallmark of the misguided thought that I know what I mean by 'red' *because* I can call up a private sample of red in the imagination. Of course, I do know what I mean by 'red' (and can tell you); and equally, I can call up a visual image of red at will. But in telling you what I mean by 'red', I would use a public sample (or refer you to one); and a visual image of red is not a sample of red.

1.1   (i) 'more psychologically apt': why so? 'beziehe sich auf' here implies something one draws out from within oneself.
       (ii) 'auf die eigene Empfindung': 'at my own sensation'.

SECTION 275

1   W. elaborates upon the 'particular experience in doing philosophy' mentioned in §274. The thought that colour-words signify or refer to something 'private' does not cross one's mind when using colour-names in the bustle of life, but only in philosophical reflection as in §273, i.e. when language is idling (PI §132). Also, he might have added, when misconstruing scientific theory concerning the nature of physical objects and their light-reflective propensities and misunderstanding the causal explanations given in physiological psychology.

.1   '(Consider what it means "to point to something with the attention")': cf. Exg. §258, 2(ii).

---

[18] See P. M. S. Hacker, *Appearance and Reality* (Blackwell, Oxford and New York, 1987), Ch. 1.
[19] R. Boyle, *The Experimental History of Colours, Works II* (London, 1744), p. 19.
[20] Ibid., p. 6.

2   BB 66 remarks: 'To get clear about philosophical problems, it is useful to become conscious of the apparently unimportant details of the particular situation in which we are inclined to make a certain metaphysical assertion.' For example, (a) One is more tempted to say 'Only this is really seen' when staring at unchanging surroundings than when one looks around while walking (BB 66). (b) One is inclined to think that 'red' means one's own visual impression when one looks at a bright colour in which one can 'immerse oneself' (PI §277). (c) One is inclined to locate 'the self' in the head when one says 'self' to oneself and concentrates one's attention while trying to analyse its meaning (PI §413). (d) 'The phenomenon of *staring* is closely bound up with the whole puzzle of solipsism' (LPE 309).

This preoccupation with the phenomenological context of the metaphysical urge evidently dates back to 1916, when W. succumbed to it:

> If I have been contemplating the stove, and then am told: but now all you know is the stove, my result does indeed seem trivial. For this represents the matter as if I had studied the stove as one among many things in the world. But if I was contemplating the stove *it* was my world, and everything else colourless by contrast with it. . . .
> For it is equally possible to take the bare present image as the worthless momentary picture in the whole temporal world, and as the true world among the shadows. (NB 83)

(See 'The world of consciousness', §1.)

Vol. XII, 224ff. reflects on different ways of seeing things: as we normally do; as 'the visual room' which is 'a world' which does not belong to a subject; as objects painted on a screen (cf. LPE 311), etc.

> Und worin besteht es denn: die Dinge so und so sehen? – Manchmal und teils darin, dass man den Blick ruhen oder wandern lässt und darin, wie er wandert; oder darin, dass man ganz *Auge* ist, und in dem was wir dabei sagen und *nicht* sagen; in Gesten, die wir machen; und vielem andern.
>
> Manchen dieser Eindrücke erhalten wir nur, wenn man auf einen Fleck starrt; manchen nur, wenn alle Gegenstände um uns in Ruhe sind, nicht wenn sich etwas bewegt; manchen wohl nur im Zimmer wenn alle Entfernungen klein sind; und wenn die Menschen immer im Freien philosophierten, würden sie auf manche Gedanken nicht kommen.
>
> Man kann sagen: wenn wir philosophieren, feiert nicht nur unsre Sprache, sondern auch unser Blick. Denn während ich den Ofen heize, sehe ich ihn anders, als wenn ich beim Philosophieren auf ihn starre – denke ich nicht an den 'visuellen Ofen', das Sinnesdatum, etc.

> (And what does seeing things thus-and-so consist in? – Sometimes, partly, in letting one's gaze rest or wander, and in how it wanders; or in that one is wholly *an eye*, and in what one then says and does *not* say; in gestures we make; and in much else.
>
> Some of these impressions we obtain only when we stare at a spot; some only when all objects around us are at rest, and not when something moves; some indeed only

indoors when all distances are small; and if people always philosophized in the open, there would be some thoughts that would never occur to them.

One may say: when we philosophize, it is not only our language that goes on holiday, but also our gaze. For when I am heating the stove, I see it differently from how I do when I philosophize and am staring at it – I do not think of 'the visual stove', the sense-datum, etc.)

3   Schlick nicely exemplifies this sort of 'experience when doing philosophy':

when I look at the blue sky and lose myself in the contemplation of it without thinking that I am enjoying the blue, I am in a state of pure intuition, the blue fills my mind completely, they have become one, it is the kind of union of which the mystic dreams.[21]

SECTION 276

1   Here the interlocutor reverts to the initial questions in §273. Note that the first sentence (in the German) is in quotation marks.

1.1   (i) 'meinen': in contrast to 'bezeichnen' and 'sich beziehen' in §273.

(ii) 'and name our colour-impression': the characterization of how something sensibly impresses one is not a description of what one perceives (RPP I §1081), though it may subserve such a description. (If the impression is blurred, it does not follow that what one sees is blurred – though it may be if it is a poor photograph.)

SECTION 277

1   This connects the phenomenology of illusion with the misconceptions of colour-words under scrutiny. §274 noted the 'particular experience when doing philosophy' of, as it were, casting a sidelong glance at one's own sensation, etc. The experience is one of a philosophical illusion, and it is facilitated by the fact that one's gaze is idling. In these circumstances the misconstrual of grammar is smoother and easier. When one looks at a red object and says 'That's red' (meaning that the object is the colour known to us all), and when one looks at it, thinking 'red' to mean one's current sense-impression, one does not attend to the object in the same way. But, of course, the difference in attention is not like the difference between looking at the shape and looking at the colour of an object.

---

[21] M. Schlick, 'Form and Content: an introduction to philosophical thinking', repr. in *Gesammelte Aufsätze* (Georg Olms Verlag, Hildesheim, 1969), p. 194.

There is a genuine difference in the mode of attention, but one is not attending to different things. Rather, when one 'immerses' oneself in the colour, it is easier to generate the illusion that there is one use of colour-words according to which they mean something wholly private, viz. one's own current visual impressions of colours.

1.1   'I immerse myself in the colour': cf. LSD 101.

Section 278

1   The interlocutor thinks that this proposition should be accompanied by an 'inward glance' at the visual impression; and that makes no sense. But this proposition does have a use, e.g. 'Ah! *I* know how the colour green looks to me – it looks cool and fresh and sleek, whereas red looks hot and angry', or, having put on colour-distorting spectacles, I might be at a loss to specify how green looks to me and then exclaim 'I know how green looks to me – it looks like the colour of the faded rug in the attic'.

Section 279

1   An analogy for the misconception discussed in §278. The sense-impression is no more a confirming measure of 'how green looks to me' than laying my hand on my head and saying 'I know how tall I am' is a measure of my height, confirming what I say. 'How does green look to you?' is answered by pointing at something 'outer' and saying 'Like *that*', not by 'pointing' inwards.

2   Vol. XII, 339 adds in parentheses 'Ich bin hier' ('I am here'). One might analogously claim 'But I know where I am, viz. *here*'. Hence the joke 'Mummy, mummy, where is Daddy? We're lost!' – 'No, dear. Daddy is lost – we're here!'

3   In Chapter 1 of *Alice in Wonderland*, Alice eats the cake but is not sure whether she will grow larger or smaller. 'She ate a little bit, and said anxiously to herself, "Which way? which way?" holding her hand on the top of her head to feel which way it was growing, and she was quite surprised to find that she remained the same size.'

Section 280

1   A final analogy to illuminate the illegitimacy of the supposition of perceptual predicates' (e.g. 'red') having a double meaning (cf. §273). A

theatrical or cinema director may sketch on paper roughly (*etwa*) how he imagines a scene. On the model of §273 it might seem that such a picture has two distinct representative functions. For others it represents the scene they are to create as the person envisages it. It tells them how he imagines the scene. But for him it represents his mental image of the scene which only he knows (since only he *has* it). Indeed, his visual impression of the picture he has painted *tells him* what he has imagined in a way in which, for others, it cannot. For in his case, his visual impression *of* what he has painted must surely *coincide* with the mental image he had when he imagined the scene!

This is a muddle. To paint what I imagine is not to *copy* a picture that is already 'painted' in my imagination (although I can, of course, imagine painting something, and then go on to paint what I imagined painting). The director's sketch does indeed represent how he imagines the scene; i.e. to the question 'How do you think it should look?' he might produce the sketch and say 'Like that'. This is what is *called* 'representing what I imagined it should look like'. But it is erroneous to think that the picture represents *to him* what he imagined in any different sense, for it does not represent it in virtue of *resembling* his mental image, any more than the verbal expression of what he thought *resembles* his thought. It informs others how he imagined things should look, but it does not inform him! What makes the picture a *good* representation of what he imagined? Not its likeness to his mental image, but rather his avowed acknowledgement that *that* was what he had in mind. But that acknowledgement does not rest on an 'inner glance' at his mental image. 'The image is not a picture, nor is the visual impression one. Neither "image" nor "impression" is the concept of a picture, although in both cases there is a tie-up with a picture, and a different one in either case' (Z §638). Hence it is a mistake to think that when I paint a picture to show you how I imagine a scene, the picture is a piece of information or a representation *for me*. It is an articulation or expression of how I imagine the scene, not an 'outer' picture of an 'inner' picture. Moreover, an impression of a picture is not a *representation* of a picture (cf. PI §366).

Similarly, although hearing the word 'red' may call forth a mental image of red (or of a field of poppies or a sunset), the answer to the question 'What do you mean by "red"?' is given by pointing to a sample. And if I ask myself 'What do I mean by "red"?', the answer is no different.

1.1   'Sein privater Eindruck des Bildes sagt ihm . . .': 'His private impression of the picture tells him . . .'

2   In MS. 129, 23 this remark follows PI §§291, 278 and is followed by PI §259. It is thus linked with the important theme of the logical

heterogeneity of *description*. Cf. Z §637: 'The descriptions of what is seen and what is imagined (*des Vorgestellten*) are indeed the same kind, and a description might be of the one just as much as of the other, but otherwise the concepts are thoroughly different.'

MEN, MINDS AND MACHINES

1. *Human beings and their parts*

'It comes to this: only of a living human being and what resembles (behaves like) a living human being can one say: it has sensations; it sees; is blind; hears; is deaf; is conscious or unconscious' (PI §281). This grammatical remark crystallizes a crucial array of connections in Wittgenstein's philosophy of psychology. Its consequences, both within philosophy and without – in psychology and neurophysiology, as well as in so-called cognitive science – are dramatic.

A wide range of expressions are predicable literally or primarily only of human beings and of creatures that behave like them. For the criteria for the application of such expressions consist in behaviour patterns in specific contexts against a background of widely ramifying complex capacities manifest in behaviour. Among these expressions are psychological terms such as sensation-names and perceptual verbs, the large vocabulary of thought and belief, consciousness and attention, desire and will, as well as emotion, mood and attitude, decision, motive and intention.

The first and paramount corollary is that it makes no sense save metonymically, metaphorically, or in a secondary use (cf. Exg. §282) to ascribe sensations, perceptual capacities and their exercise, thought and experience either to parts of the human body or to the body itself. This principle is a grammatical one, not an empirical generalization or a metaphysical necessity. It is not a matter of fact that it is the human being who is hungry, not his body – which needs food, or his stomach – which is empty. It is not a metaphysical principle, due to the essential nature of bodies and thought, that it is the person who thinks, ponders, and reflects – and not his brain. It is grammar that excludes attributing toothache to the brain or good eyesight to the 'visual' striate cortex. No sense has been given to these forms of words, no conditions of application have been laid down for the correct use of 'His brain has toothache' or 'His brain's eyesight is deteriorating'. One may be tempted to ask whether our grammar is right, whether it may not be unjustified? Could it not be overtaken by scientific progress?

A fuller answer will emerge below, but for the moment we should bear in mind some of Wittgenstein's arguments previously discussed (cf. Volume 2, pp, 329 – 38). Grammar is not justified by the facts; indeed there is no such thing as justifying grammar by reference to reality on the model of verifying an empirical proposition by reference to what makes it true. Grammar consists of rules for the use of words and has no such justification. It determines what we count as possible descriptions of how things are in reality, fixing a logical space which the facts, so to speak, may then occupy or fail to occupy. Grammar is autonomous, not answerable to, but presupposed by, factual propositions. In this sense, unlike means/ends rules, it is arbitrary. But it has a kinship to the non-arbitrary. It is moulded by human nature and the nature of the world around us. Facts about us and about the world condition the language-games we play and give point to our employing the concepts we have. Radical changes in us or in the world could rob our language-games of their point. But they could not show our concepts to be correct or incorrect, since there is no such thing. (The concept of a unicorn is not defective because there are no unicorns.) But concepts may be more or less useful for certain purposes, more or less appropriate relative to certain goals and concerns.[1]

It follows that although we are at liberty to introduce new words and new uses of words into our language, we cannot justify these grammatical innovations by reference to facts to which they correspond. For there is no such thing as such a correspondence between concepts and reality, nor can any empirical discovery contravene grammar and show it to be 'incorrect'. In the customary use of our psychological vocabulary, these expressions have no application to the body and its parts (or to inanimate things), save in metonymical, metaphorical, figurative, or secondary uses, which are severally explained by reference to the primary application of the terms to human beings and to what behaves like them. Hence the latter cannot be appealed to in order to license the literal application of these expressions beyond the bounds fixed in our grammar. If neurophysiologists, psychologists, artificial-intelligence scientists, or philosophers wish to change existing grammar, to introduce new ways of speaking, they may do so; but their new stipulations must be explained and conditions of application laid down. What may not be done is to argue that since we know what 'to think', 'to see', or 'to infer' mean and know what 'the brain' means, therefore we must know what 'the brain thinks, sees, and infers' means. For we know what these verbs mean only in so far as we have mastered their existing use, which does not license applying them to the body or its parts, save derivatively. Nor may one cross the new 'technical' use with the old one, as, for example, neuroscientists typically do in their theorizing. For this produces a

---

[1] The concept of phlogiston proved to be useless, but not incorrect, for the purposes of chemistry. It was the *theory* of combustion which employed the concept of phlogiston that proved to be incorrect. Of course, many theoretical concepts in science are embedded in a theory, in as much as they are wholly explained by reference to other theoretical terms. Nevertheless, the fact that the theory proves false or incorrect does not show that the concept is incorrect, for *concepts* neither correspond nor fail to correspond with reality.

conflict of rules and hence incoherence *in the neuroscientists' use* of these terms.

Typically, such extensions of the psychological vocabulary by scientists or cognitive scientists is not explained *de novo*, but is held to be justified, i.e. rendered true or correct, by scientific discovery or theory. This is the first error. Further, the new application is held to be wholly transparent by reference to existing use. This is the second error. Failure to apprehend these mistakes results in a blindness to the consequent incoherences in the novel applications of the terms. These incoherences do not lie simply in failure to conform to the ordinary use of the psychological terms, but rather in the conflict, *in the innovators' use*, generated by the extension of the application of the vocabulary beyond what existing grammar licenses, coupled with reliance upon existing grammar (i.e. existing rules for the use of the terms) to explain what these expressions mean (cf. RPP I §548). Scientists could, of course, introduce wholly new terminology; but it is no coincidence that they do not. Were they to do so, they would have to explain its use from scratch. Moreover, it would lack the explanatory force which appears to cling to their extended use of our existing vocabulary. For their aim is to explain what thinking, perceiving, etc. are by reference to the 'thinking' or 'interpreting', 'inferring' or 'hypothesizing', allegedly engaged in by the brain and its parts (or by a machine). We shall return to these matters in §4 below.

Parts of the body: One may hurt one's hand, but it is not the hand that *suffers*; it is the injured person. My hand may hurt, but it does not hurt itself; it hurts *me*, and it is I who have hurt myself. I may have a pain in my hand, but my hand does not have a pain in its thumb. I may be conscious of a throbbing pain in my hand, but my hand is neither conscious nor unconscious of it.

This is how we speak. And if we cannot logically justify it, if there is no such thing as that sort of justification here, we can nevertheless display the roots of our style of discourse. For in an important sense these articulations of grammar are not arbitrary, but reach deep into our instinctive behaviour. 'It is a primitive reaction to tend, to treat, the part that hurts when someone else is in pain' (Z §540), but 'if someone has a pain in his hand, then the hand does not say so . . .[2] and one does not comfort the hand, but the sufferer: one looks into his face' (PI §286). This sort of behaviour is *pre-linguistic* – 'a language-game is based *on it*, . . . it is the prototype of a way of thinking and not the result of thought' (Z §541). Just look at a mother tending her injured child, and equally at a child's reaction to his mother's having hurt herself. One is

---

[2] Wittgenstein added in parenthesis '(unless it writes it)' – which is, I take it, a (rather poor) joke.

filled with pity for the person, not for the person's hand (PI §287)! It is the *person* who expresses or manifests pain, *in his behaviour*. It is he who cries out, contorts his face with pain, weeps, and nurses his injured hand. His pain-avowals are an extension of his primitive pain-behaviour. We commiserate with him, ask him whether his pain is getting less, try to cheer him up, distract his attention from his suffering, and make allowances for him because he is in pain.

What goes for pain goes, *mutatis mutandis*, for other psychological expressions too. It is human beings, not their sense-organs, that see, look around, watch, and observe what is in view. A person sees *with* his eyes, and we can say whether he sees and what he sees by noting how he keeps a moving object in sight, avoids impediments in his path, or looks for things. His behaviour constitutes the criterion for saying 'He sees, looks, has noticed . . .'. Similarly, it is human beings and animals that can be said to be conscious or unconscious, awake or asleep. They, and not some parts of them, regain consciousness after having been stunned or anaesthetized. And so too it is the *person* who expresses his thoughts, opinions, and beliefs in his utterances and manifests them (defeasibly) in his deeds (cf. PI §360). His emotions are exhibited in his face, tone of voice, bodily responses, and in his behaviour.

Of course, there are some predicates that apply, in certain contexts, to a person and to parts of his body interchangeably. 'A gripped the hilt' and 'A's hand gripped the hilt' *generally* mean the same. We say of the blind that they are sightless, and we also speak of sightless eyes. But sightless eyes are not eyes that cannot see, they are eyes with which a person cannot see or eyes of the dead. We talk of warnings falling on deaf ears, but it is not the ears that cannot hear, but the person who refuses to listen. Numerous metonyms and secondary uses of expressions involve applying psychological verbs to parts of the body: 'My eyes have seen the glory of the coming of the Lord', we say; we speak of the heart aching with grief – but it is the person who sees or grieves (and this use of 'ache' is a secondary one). We say that someone has a good brain (i.e. is intelligent), urge someone to use his brain (i.e. to think), and wonder what is going on in his head (i.e. what he is thinking). In extra-theoretical contexts such turns of phrase are harmless. But unless taken figuratively, metonymically, or as secondary uses, as they often are not in psychology or cognitive science, they are typically nonsense. And if they are taken figuratively, metonymically, etc., then it is wholly futile to appeal to them to vindicate psychologists' or neuroscientists' extension of the application of psychological predicates to the brain as part of a theory which purports to explain vision or thought. For the criteria justifying the literal application of psychological verbs are characteristic forms of behaviour of a person. Eyes, ears, hearts, and brains do not *behave* as human beings. Hearts beat and pump blood, but they do not fall in love and express it in amorous glances, shy blushes, or in writing sonnets to their mistresses. Eyes respond to, i.e. are causally affected by, light, but do not look for their friends in a crowd; and although they may twinkle with glee, the glee is not the eye's. Ears respond to sound-waves, but they do not answer what their owner hears, do not tap feet to heard rhythms, do not listen attentively and smile in response to what is heard. And brains do not think; for there is no such thing as a brain expressing a thought or manifesting those distinctive patterns of behaviour and action in the circumstances of life that constitute criteria for thinking.

The body: There are predicates which can be applied indifferently both to people and to their bodies. 'A is bitten all over with mosquito bites' and 'A's body is bitten all over' in most contexts mean the same. 'She is beautiful' and 'Her body is beautiful' are sometimes interchangeable. This cuts no metaphysical ice, but only shows that in certain sentential contexts 'A' and 'A's body' are inter-substitutable. But not, typically, in psychological contexts. It is true that 'I ache all over' and 'My body aches all over' are interchangeable; but it is not my body that feels ill – I do, and I have aching sensations all over my body – but my body does not *have* aching sensations all over *its* body. It makes no sense to say 'A's body is thinking (is in pain, is conscious)', for behaviour, *pace* behaviourists, is not an attribute of a body (cf. 'Behaviour and behaviourism', §4). We are prone to forget how *peculiar* is the locution 'A's body' (and 'my body') and how it differs from genitives applied to other physical objects, e.g. 'A's bodkin'. Of course, here too we can envisage a different grammar. Instead of 'A is in pain', one might say 'A's body is in pain', and instead of 'I have a headache', it would be said 'My body has a headache'. But this shift in grammar would ramify (BB 73): rather than saying 'A must take an aspirin and lie down, should consult a doctor and work less hard', one would say 'A's body must take an aspirin, lie down, etc.'. One would not say 'I am going to London', 'I am thinking (expecting, hoping)', or 'I would like (want, prefer, etc.)', but rather 'My body is going to London (is thinking, etc.)'. And instead of 'A is in pain, but isn't showing it', one would say 'A's body is in pain, but his body is not showing it', and so on. And it will be A's body that speaks, that compliments my body for the work it has done or insults my body for the offence it has caused. Bizarre as this seems, it again makes little difference, *as long as one does not cross this new form of representation with the old one*. It will not be licit to say 'I can say what I feel (think, want) without observing my behaviour', for the correct form of expression will be 'My body can say what it feels without observing its behaviour'. In this form of representation, certain uses of 'my body' will have as privileged a position in grammar as 'I' does in our form of representation, and significant distinctions we draw will be obliterated or obscured.

2. *The mind*

It is in general wrong to ascribe psychological predicates to the body and its parts, save metonymically or metaphorically. It does not follow that it is correct to apply them to the mind. Notoriously, Descartes did just that, attributing all psychological properties to an immaterial substance, the mind or soul, which he thought to be only causally related to the body. It is, he held, the mind which has sensations, sees (or seems to see), hears (or seems to hear), is angry or pleased, thinks and doubts, has desires, intends and decides. This conception, which has dominated philosophical reflection for centuries, is incoherent in many respects. For present purposes we need to recall how the expression 'the mind' is actually used in our language, and so to bring the word back from its metaphysical use to its common-or-garden employment. We do not use the word 'I' as we use the phrase 'my mind', and although 'His mind is preoccupied (in a turmoil)' means the same as 'He is preoccupied (in a turmoil)', we cannot typically replace 'he' by 'his mind' in the generality of contexts of verbs of sensation, perception, emotion, thought, and will.

Puzzled about the nature of the mind, philosophers and psychologists raise the question 'What is the mind?' and endeavour to answer it by offering a definition. Or they paraphrase it immediately by 'What sort of entity is a mind?' and wonder whether it is an immaterial entity in causal interaction with the brain or is actually identical with the brain or stands to the brain as a programme to a computer. But 'What sort of entity is a mind?' is as pernicious a question as 'What sort of entity is a number?' Substantives are substance-hungry, but abstinence is to be recommended. 'How is the word "mind" used?' is the question we should address if we wish to clarify the nature of the mind (cf. PI §370). It is tempting to answer it by offering a definition. It has been suggested that the mind is the capacity to acquire intellectual abilities, i.e. abilities to engage in activities which involve operating with symbols.[3] This is illuminating, connecting the notion of a creature which has a mind with that of a creature with concept-exercising abilities and with the capacity to acquire them. But it is wrong; for it provides no standard of correctness for such (licit) uses of the word 'mind' as 'A thought crossed my mind', 'He has a quick (devious, dirty, small) mind', 'I have made up my mind', etc. And although these phrases are largely restricted to concept-employing creatures, it is not awry to say of a horse that it has a mind of its own when it stubbornly refuses to obey the will of its rider. To search for a *Merkmal*-definition of 'mind' is arguably as futile, and

[3] A. J. P. Kenny, 'The Origin of the Soul', in A. J. P. Kenny, H. C. Longuet-Higgins, J. R. Lucas, and C. H. Waddington, *The Development of Mind*, Gifford Lectures 1972/3 (Edinburgh University Press, Edinburgh, 1973), p. 46.

certainly as unhelpful for philosophical clarification, as searching for a definition of number. What is needed is a description of the use of the word 'mind' that will provide a surview of its grammatical articulations. Here only a pen-sketch will be essayed.

The English word 'mind' is connected primarily with the intellect and the will. At the most general level it is associated with intellectual faculties: a person is said to have a powerful, agile, subtle, or devious mind if he is skilful, quick, ingenious at problem-solving, or if his solutions, plans, and projects display subtlety or cunning. Hence too it is connected with corresponding intellectual virtues and vices: a person has a tenacious, idle, vigorous, judicious, or indecisive mind according to the manner in which he grapples with problems requiring reflection and according to the typical upshot of his reflections. (Curiously, however, we do not characterize a person's *mind* as wise, intelligent, or foolish.) A person is of sound mind if he retains his rational faculties, and is said to be out of his mind if he thinks, proposes, or does things that suggest unreason where reason is meet.

Numerous ordinary uses of 'mind' are bound up with (a) thought, (b) opinion, and (c) memory. (a) One turns one's mind to something when one starts to think about it, and one puts one's mind to it when it needs resolving. Ideas come to, flash through, or lurk, just out of reach, in the back of one's mind. And sometimes, when one cannot think or recollect, one's mind goes blank. (b) To know one's mind is to have formed one's opinion, and to tell one's mind is to express it. To give someone a piece of one's mind is to tell him harshly what one thinks of him, and to be of one mind with another person is to agree in opinion or judgement. (c) To keep or bear something in mind is not to forget it, and to call to mind (and *remind* oneself) is to recollect. Something out of mind is forgotten or not thought about ('Out of sight, out of mind'), and someone who is absent-minded is forgetful and inattentive.

Other connections are with the will. To make up one's mind is to decide, whereas to be of two minds is to waver between alternatives; to change one's mind is to withdraw one's previous opinion, judgement, intention, or decision and form one afresh. To have a mind to do something is to be inclined or tempted to do it, and to have half a mind to do something is to be sorely tempted, perhaps against one's better judgement.

Other uses fade off in other directions, e.g. broad- (or narrow-) minded, small- and petty-minded, having a dirty mind, having a mind like a razor, displaying presence of mind, having things on one's mind and hence no peace of mind, and so on. But this brief sketch suffices for drawing some morals.

Numerous pictures are bound up with this rich terminology, pictures of space (in, out of, through, or across the mind), of room (broad, narrow, small), and so of parts (half a mind, one's whole mind), of agency (quick, agile, powerful), and hence of virtues and vices (tenacity, indolence). But these pictures are not a theory of the mind, and our uses of these phrases no more commit us to a theory than does our talk of sunrise and sunset. Our terminology no more presupposes that 'the mind' is an 'entity' of any sort than our talk of numbers commits us to the view that numbers are 'entities'.

On the rebound from Cartesianism, it is tempting to argue that in talking of the mind we are indulging in a fiction, pretending that there is an entity of a strange sort, an immaterial homunculus or a non-physical space occupied by ethereal things (ideas, sense-data, or experiences). But this is as misguided as the supposition that in talking of numbers, we pretend that there exist Platonic objects in an abstract realm. 'What sort of entity is a mind?', like 'What sort of entity is a number?', can only be answered by insisting that a mind, like a number, is not an entity of any sort – not even a fictional or 'pretend' entity. This may seem drastic: for does that not mean that there are no minds, that minds do not exist? That too is confused, as is the thought that if one denies Platonism, then one is committed to the view that numbers do not exist. The moot question is rather: what does it mean to say that minds (or numbers) exist? To be sure, decisive people have a mind of their own, and quick-thinking people have agile minds. There can be no question but that when pondering, thoughts cross one's mind, and that when imagining things, one has things before one's mind's eye. These are not 'ontological commitments' or metaphysical revelations, but humble grammatical propositions. All they commit us to are uses of words.

It is philosophy and psychology (of scientific folk) that misconceive the *pictures* embedded in ordinary languages, misinterpret these pictures as theories, and construct alternative and equally absurd theories in response to their own misinterpretations of these pictures. The idiom of inspecting one's mind, seeing with the mind's eye, or searching one's mind for this or that, of introspecting, etc., if misconstrued, fosters the philosophical mythology of the transparent mind and its counterpart, the elusive mind, as well as the misconceived psychological methodology of Wundt's introspective psychology. In response to these confusions, psychological behaviourism denied the existence of the mind and held our ordinary discourse to be ridden with primitive fictions. Similarly, some contemporary philosophers look forward to a scientific millennium in which our current psychological vocabulary is replaced by something truer to the facts, e.g. a neuroscientific language embodying a true theory of human organisms. These muddles stem, *inter alia*, from adverting to pictures as if they were theories and disregarding their (wholly atheoretic) uses. The task of philosophy here is to describe the grammar of the mental. The task of psychology is to construct empirical theories (where theorizing is appropriate) within the framework of well-understood psychological concepts (including technical terminology where it is required). It is not errors in our language that are responsible for absurd theories of the mind (although that is not to say that new terms and distinctions are not needed in empirical psychology). It is our misconstruals of the uses of our expressions, our asking misconceived questions and trying to answer rather than to dissolve them.

Does this mean that the mind is just an aspect of the body? 'I'm not that hard up for categories,' Wittgenstein replied (RPP II §690). Height, weight, and build are aspects of the body – not having a thought in mind, making up one's mind, or having a mind of one's own. But equally, thinking, perceiving, having emotions, wanting, intending, and resolving are *not*, *pace* Cartesians, properties of, or activities performed by, the mind. It is living human beings (and what behaves like them) that reflect, ponder, and cogitate. It is people who love or hate, hope or despair. It is not my mind that makes up its mind, steels its will, and acts – it is I.

3. *Only in the stream of life . . .*

That people have such-and-such sensations is manifest in their behaviour: in their cries and groans of pain, the grimaces of their faces, their scratching, their rubbing and assuaging their limbs, and in their articulate avowals. That people see is evident in their looking, watching, scrutinizing, and reacting to what is visible; that they hear is manifest in their listening and responding to what is audible, etc. Their wants, intentions, and purposes are expressed in their tryings, strivings, and goal-directed behaviour and speech. These are grammatical propositions that characterize human life; and the use of the rich and variegated psychological vocabulary is part of our form of life, not part of an explanatory theory that might prove false and be rejected. Psychological and neurophysiological theories may come and go, but the propositions that people love and hate, make up their minds and pursue their aims, have things in mind and call things to mind, are no more theoretical than that white is lighter than black or that colours can be seen but not heard. It is not a matter of *opinion* that people have minds (cf. PI p. 178).[4] For what could show that *people* lack minds? Of course, we employ these psychological expressions in explanations of behaviour; we say that someone cried out because he hurt himself, moved aside because he saw the impediment in his path, jumped because he was frightened. Such explanations may, in

---

[4] 'Ich habe nicht die *Meinung*, dass er eine Seele hat'. There is no precise equivalent of 'mind' in German. 'Mind' is more restricted than 'Seele' or 'Geist', and so too is 'soul'.

their context, be right or wrong; but they are not part of a verifiable or falsifiable *theory* of human behaviour. And the use of 'I have a pain', 'I am frightened', 'I want (wish, expect, etc.)' are not reflexive applications of a theoretical vocabulary, any more than 'I cried out in pain', 'I ducked because I saw it coming', or 'I jumped with fright' are *theoretical* explanations.

Our psychological vocabulary has behavioural, species-specific roots and highly acculturated branches, foliage, and fruits. The expressions we employ in characterizing other people's thoughts, feelings, and experiences and in explaining what they do and say in terms of their experiences, beliefs, desires, and purposes have a use only in the stream of human life. Our use of psychological words in manifesting and avowing our own experiences or in giving expression to our thoughts and opinions is part of the weave of our life; it is constitutive of human life and not simply part of a theory about it.

These expressions make sense only in this complex weave, 'For concepts are not for use on a single occasion' (Z §568):

> How could human behaviour be described? Surely only by sketching the actions of a variety of humans as they are all mixed up together. What determines our judgement, our concepts and reactions, is not what *one* man is doing *now*, an individual action, but the whole hurly-burly of human actions, the background against which we see any action. (Z §567)

It is important to stress that 'One pattern in the weave is interwoven with many others' (Z §569). One cannot, as it were, isolate one pattern in this tapestry by removing a number of the threads.

> The concept of pain is characterized by its particular function in our life.
> Pain has *this* position in our life; has *these* connections. (That is to say: we only call 'pain' what has *this* position, these connections.) (Z §§532f.)

The concept of pain is bound up not just with characteristic pain-behaviour in circumstances of injury or illness, but also with pity and commiseration, fear and anxiety, cruelty and mercy. It is interwoven with special attitudes towards the sick (both care *and* disdain), with *concepts* of health and welfare and hence with that of the good of a being. And *this* example is a relatively simple one: 'Only surrounded by certain normal manifestations of life [*Lebensäusserung*] is there such a thing as an expression of pain. Only surrounded by an even more far-reaching particular manifestation of life, such a thing as the expression of sorrow or affection. And so on.' (Z §534). It only makes sense to say of a creature that it feels pain if it is a creature which can (logically) manifest it in behaviour. Hence the concept gets a firm grip with respect to humans and mammals, but starts to slip with lower creatures (RPP II §659) and has no application to the inanimate. And a far more complex setting of behaviour and behavioural manifestations of sophisticated capacities is necessary for the concepts of dissimulating or pretending to be in pain (cf. Exg. §249).

If that is so, how much more complex a behavioural setting is required for us to attribute fear, hope, expectation, and relief, let alone expecting, hoping, wanting, or wishing for something not here and now, but tomorrow, next week, or at the end of the year.

> We say a dog is afraid his master will beat him; but not, he is afraid his master will beat him tomorrow. Why not? (PI §650)

> Why can a dog feel fear but not remorse? Would it be right to say 'Because he can't talk'? (Z §518)

> Only someone who can reflect on the past can repent. But that does not mean that as a matter of empirical fact only such a one is capable of the feeling of remorse. (Z §520)

These emotions, and hosts of other experiences, are intelligibly predicable only of language-using creatures. 'There is nothing astonishing about certain concepts only being applicable to a being that e.g. possesses a language' (Z §520). Only of creatures with a far more complex repertoire of behaviour than dogs have, in particular only of those who have mastered the techniques of using a language, does it make sense to say that they have opinions, wonder whether, reflect or ponder on, guess or surmise that something is the case. Here the weave of life must be dense and rich – as it is with us. A creature that can hold opinions, reflect on problems, come to or sometimes jump to conclusions is a creature that can behave in endlessly variegated, subtly differentiated ways. It must be capable of expressing its opinions (or keeping them to itself), of articulating its reflections, and of acting on its conclusions. It must be a creature who can say to itself, and of whom it can be said, that it is justified or unjustified, has good grounds or lacks them, makes mistakes and occasionally corrects them, resolves to act on its conclusions. It must have goals, take pleasure in attaining them, and be disappointed at failure. The applicability of such concepts as opining, reflecting, wondering, guessing, surmising, etc. is not severable from the applicability of a wide range of other concepts – of desire and will, motive and intention, satisfaction and disappointment, etc. For the criteria for the application of the former involve the application of the latter.

4. Homunculi and brains

The asymmetry between first- and third-person psychological utterances and the assumption that first-person present-tense psychological utterances are uniformly descriptions of inner states uniquely accessible to their owner induces the thought that psychological predicates signify attributes of the mind rather than of the whole human being. Further pressures are generated by scientific reflections on the nature and mechanisms of perception. If vision is explained by the production of a retinal image of what is in view, and if that image is conceived as being transmitted to some part of the brain and, in some sense, reconstituted there, it is tempting to think that for a person to see an object, it is necessary that something other than the person, viz. his mind or soul, should see an internal picture of that object. Descartes argued that the retinal image, by stimulating the optic nerve, causes an image to be reproduced on the pineal gland. He rightly warned that although, in his view, the picture generated in the brain resembles the object perceived, the resultant sensory perception is not caused by that resemblance, for that would require 'yet other eyes within our brain with which we could perceive it'.[5] It is obviously futile to try to explain what it is for a human being to see (or to think, reason, or infer) by reference something else's seeing (thinking, reasoning, or inferring). For this both generates a regress and demands an explanation of what it is for this other thing (mind or brain) to see (think, reason, or infer). Descartes' warning, which is apt, might suggest that he carefully avoided the 'homunculus fallacy'. But this would be wrong. For he erred in two respects: First, he held that it is in the pineal gland that 'the two images coming from a single object through the two eyes . . . can come together in a single image or impression before reaching the soul, *so that they do not present to it two objects instead of one.*'[6] But since the soul does *not see* what is on the pineal gland, it is not necessary that there be there one image as opposed to two or none. Whatever is there is not the *object* of perception. Secondly, no matter what is registered on the pineal gland or for that matter in the 'visual' striate cortex – no matter whether it is an image, a 'map', or any other so-called internal representation – it is not something that can intelligibly be said to be 'presented'. For to whom is it 'presented'? In short, it is a conceptual confusion to attribute sight to the soul or mind.

Where Descartes misguidedly ascribed perceptual and intellectual predicates to the soul, contemporary psychologists and neurophysiologists ascribe them to the brain. Three examples make this vivid:

---

[5] Descartes, *Optics* in *The Philosophical Writings of Descartes*, tr. J. Cottingham, R. Stoothoff, D. Murdoch (Cambridge University Press, Cambridge, 1984), Vol. 1, p. 167 (*Oeuvres de Descartes*, eds Ch. Adam and P. Tannery, rev. edn (Paris, Vrin (C.N.R.S.), 1964 – 76). Vol. VI. p. 130. Hereafter AT followed by volume and page numbers.)

[6] Descartes, *The Passions of the Soul*, in *Philosophical Writings*, Vol. I, p. 340 (AT XI, 353).

we can thus regard all seeing as a continual search for the answers to questions posed by the brain. The signals from the retina constitute 'messages' conveying these answers. The brain then uses this information to construct a suitable hypothesis about what there is . . .

. . . it is the cortex that asks meaningful questions, and so dictates the whole scanning process through its connections with the mid-brain . . . the real problem is to find out how the cortex uses the message it gets from the retina to answer the questions and to ask others. This is the serial process that we call visual perception.[7]

Impressed by Helmholtz's incoherent idea that 'perceptions' are 'unconscious inferences', scientists find themselves

driven to say that such neurons [as respond in a highly specific manner to, say, line orientation] have knowledge. They have intelligence, for they are able to estimate the probability of outside events – events that are important to the animal in question. And the brain gains its knowledge by a process analogous to the inductive reasoning of the classical scientific method. Neurons present arguments to the brain based on the specific features they detect, arguments on which the brain constructs its hypothesis of perception.[8]

Suspicious of the Cartesian conception of the mind, scientists are prone to substitute the brain. Hence, seeing is held to be

probably the most sophisticated of all the brain's activities: calling upon its stores of memory data; requiring subtle classifications, comparisons and logical decisions for sensory data to become perception.[9]

If it is nonsense to say that a person's mind has toothache, smells the scent of roses, or intends to go to London, it is 'nonsense on stilts' to suppose that a brain classifies and compares, asks questions and answers them, constructs hypotheses and makes decisions. These are predicates of human beings, applied on the basis of sophisticated behaviour and presupposing complex capacities. It is no more the brain that sees than it is the mind.

Nothing which a brain can intelligibly be said to do constitutes a behavioural manifestation of pain. It is not brains that feel pain, but people (and animals) who have brains and manifest pain in their behaviour. If one replies that surely, when a person is in pain, the C-fibres in his brain are firing and this is a criterion for being in pain, one merely manifests further confusion over the concept of behaviour in general and the criteria for pain in particular. Brains do not groan or cry

[7] J. Z. Young, *Programs of the Brain* (Oxford University Press, Oxford, 1978), pp. 119, 124.

[8] C. Blakemore, *Mechanics of the Mind* (Cambridge University Press, Cambridge, 1977), p. 91.

[9] R. L. Gregory, 'The Confounded Eye', in R. L. Gregory and E. H. Gombrich (eds), *Illusion in Nature and Art* (Duckworth, London, 1973), p. 50.

out; they do not limp on their sprained ankle or rub their bruised shoulder. My brain does not ask for an analgaesic, excuse its inattention by reference to a headache, ask to be left alone, or call for a doctor. The firings of C-fibres are not a behavioural manifestation of the brain's being in pain, but at best an inductively discovered condition for the possibility of a person's having a pain.

A fortiori it makes no sense to say that a brain calculates, constructs hypotheses, asks or answers questions. These are intelligibly predicable only of language-users, not of a *part* of a creature who has mastered the techniques of using a language. A brain cannot speak or write – not because it is dumb or illiterate, but because it makes no sense to say 'His brain spoke (or wrote)'. The brain can neither use nor misuse a language. There is no such thing as a brain expressing an opinion ('I think it is going to rain') or acting on a belief (e.g. taking an umbrella), let alone arguing, disputing, hypothesizing, or conjecturing; nor does it make sense to attribute to a brain misunderstanding or reactions to other people's opinions and beliefs such as indignation, resentment, or delight.

But scientists do speak thus of the brain. Can it not be argued that these are derivative or secondary uses? Not so. 'He has a good brain' means the same as 'He is intelligent'. 'My brain isn't working today' means the same as 'I can't think clearly today'. These and many other phrases are quite harmless. But the claims that the brain asks and answers questions, makes subtle classifications, comparisons, and 'logical decisions' are not metonymical. These are not the questions and answers, comparisons and decisions, of a person; indeed, they are not held to be anything of which the person is aware. Rather they are putative explanatory hypotheses which are meant to explain perception, much as the theories of certain theoretical linguists, who attempt to explain how we can understand what we hear, are prone to suppose that the brain engages in complex logico-linguistic analysis of acoustic inputs. Far from being harmless *façons de parler*, these are pernicious; for they are low-grade nonsense in the guise of high-powered theory.

5. *Can machines think?*

It might seem that the above arguments are refuted by the simple observation that we talk of *machines* as calculating, computing, and even thinking, say that they have more or less powerful memories, and speak, in relation to such machines, of artificial intelligence. Artificial-intelligence scientists insist that they are already building machines that can think and see, recognize and identify, make choices and decisions. Chess-playing machines can 'beat' chess-masters, and computers can 'calculate' far more efficiently and quickly than mathematicians. If all this is to be taken at face value, it seems to show, first, that the grammatical remark that these predicates, in their literal use, are restricted to human beings and what behaves like human beings is either wrong *simpliciter* or displays 'semantic inertia' that has been overtaken by the march of science, for machines actually do behave like human beings. Secondly, if it makes literal sense to attribute epistemic and even perceptual predicates to machines which are built to simulate certain human operations and to execute certain human tasks, it seems plausible to suppose that the human brain must have a similar abstract functional structure to that of the machine design. In which case, surely, it must make sense to attribute the variety of psychological predicates to the human brain after all. And if that is so, then are not the answers to the centuries-old philosophical questions about the relation of mind to body and about the nature of thinking or consciousness to be found in physiological psychology and artificial-intelligence theory?

Philosophical problems stem from conceptual confusion. They are not resolved by empirical discoveries, and they cannot be answered, but only swept under the carpet, by conceptual change. Fifth-generation computers will doubtless be able to execute astonishing tasks. But their existence will do nothing to clarify the question of whether it makes literal sense to attribute psychological predicates to machines that are not, and do not really behave, like human beings. The fact that we now apply a limited range of epistemic verbs to our gadgets no more shows an enlightened 'semantic momentum' stemming from insight into the true nature of the mental than does the fact that we have always applied these expressions to dolls or spirits and ghosts (PI §282).

Wittgenstein addressed the question briefly in the 1930s and obliquely in the *Remarks on the Foundations of Mathematics*. In the *Blue Book* he wrote:

'Is it possible for a machine to think?' (whether the action of this machine can be described and predicted by the laws of physics or, possibly, only by laws of a different kind applying to the behaviour of organisms). And the trouble which is expressed in this question is not really that we don't yet know a machine which could do the job. The question is not analogous to that which someone might have asked a hundred years ago: 'Can a machine liquefy a gas?' The trouble is rather that the sentence, 'A machine thinks (perceives, wishes)' seems somehow nonsensical. It is as though we had asked 'Has the number 3 a colour?'. (BB 47)

Wittgenstein's point is not that thinking, being in some sense ethereal, gaseous, non-physical, cannot be a property of a machine because it must, of its nature, be a property of something that has a 'spiritual nature', viz. the mind. On the contrary, he had already repudiated that in *Philosophical Grammar* (PG 106):

In the consideration of our problems one of the most dangerous ideas is the idea that we think *with*, or *in*, our *heads*.

The idea of a process in the head, in a completely enclosed space, makes thinking something occult. . . .

It is a travesty of the truth to say 'Thinking is an activity of our mind, as writing is of the hand'. (Love in the heart. The head and heart as loci of the soul.)

As argued above, it is not a person's mind that thinks for him, nor does he think with it. But replacing that Cartesian idea by the supposition that it is the brain that thinks is equally awry. It makes no more sense literally to attribute thinking to the brain than to assert (or deny) that the number 3 is green. One may say 'Hush! I'm thinking. Don't disturb me!', but not 'Hush! My brain is thinking. Don't disturb it!' One may add, 'Wait a moment and I'll tell you', but not 'Wait a moment, and my brain will tell me, and then I'll tell you'.

Nor is Wittgenstein's point that thinking is an emergent property of sufficiently complex material structures, whether biological or electro-physical. For it is not as if, once the 'machinery' of the brain becomes exceedingly complicated, a super-physical 'world' of experience springs into being. He noted that

It seems to us sometimes as though the phenomena of personal experience were in a way phenomena in the upper strata of the atmosphere as opposed to the material phenomena which happen on the ground. There are views according to which these phenomena in the upper strata arise when the material phenomena reach a certain degree of complexity. E.g., that the mental phenomena, sense experience, volition, etc., emerge when a type of animal body of a certain complexity has been evolved. (BB 47)

He added that there is obviously something right about this. Clearly, psychological faculties are empirically related to cerebral development, 'for the amoeba certainly doesn't speak or write or discuss, whereas we do' (ibid.). Nevertheless, the picture of the mental as an emergent 'world', as it were, is wholly misconceived (see 'The world of consciousness', §2). And although neurological complexity (crudely speaking) is empirically requisite for possession of perceptual, volitional, and cognitive faculties, the kinds of features and the nature of their 'complexity' (if any) that underlie, and constitute criteria for attributing such faculties and their exercise to a being are quite different from this. Psychological concepts are not concepts of ethereal properties or processes, and the presuppositions and conditions of their application concern issues logically independent of neurological complexity, or indeed of the 'computational' complexity or power of a machine.

Has Wittgenstein not been overtaken by scientific progress? Are computers not precisely prosthetic organs of thought (cf. Z §607)? Or, if not *organs*, at least machines that can think for us, faster and more efficiently than we can? Can't we say, when we press the appropriate keys on our computer and wait for an answer to flash upon the screen,

'Now it's thinking'? Yes, we can joke thus; as we can pat our dear old car and say 'She's temperamental today'. But the *behavioural* criteria *in the circumstances of life* for saying of something that it is thinking can no more be exemplified by a computer than a number can turn green. It is not, and does not behave like, a human being, and what it does is not a criterion for saying that it is thinking.

It might seem that the 'Turing test' circumvents this objection. If a computer could be so programmed that the typed answers displayed on its machine screen were indistinguishable from those a human being might type out in response to questions, is the machine not behaving precisely as a human being? Not so! It takes more – but not *additively* more – to perform a speech-act than to make a noise or generate an inscription. Human beings are no more uncomprehending programmed typing-machines than computers have a form of life. The appearance of typed messages on a screen may be the *product* of human behaviour or of a machine programme put to certain human purposes. But it is not a form of human behaviour.[10]

It is now known that Wittgenstein read Turing's famous paper 'On Computable Numbers'. His only *direct* comment on it is brief and bewildering: 'Turing's "machines". These machines are *humans* who calculate' (RPP I §1096). It is possible to make sense of this enigmatic remark, however, by reference to the presuppositions of Turing's discussion and other remarks of Wittgenstein on the concepts of calculation, following rules, and mathematics.[11] Accepting a version of Church's thesis, viz. that all effective number-theoretic functions (viz. algorithms) can be encoded in binary terms and that these binary-encoded functions are machine-computable, Turing sketched an abstract notion of a computing machine by analogy with human beings calculating:

We may compare a man in the process of computing a real number to a machine which is only capable of a finite number of conditions $q_1, q_2, \ldots, q_R$ which will be called 'm-configurations'. The machine is supplied with a 'tape' . . . running through it, and divided into sections . . . each capable of bearing a 'symbol'. At any moment there is just one square, say the r th bearing the symbol $G(r)$ which is 'in the machine'. We may call this square the 'scanned symbol'. The 'scanned symbol' is the only one of which the machine is, so to speak, 'directly aware'.[12]

---

[10] Similarly, the pattern in a carpet may be the product of a human being making the carpet or of a Jacquard loom, but it is not a form of behaviour.

[11] The following discussion is indebted to S. G. Shanker's 'Wittgenstein versus Turing on The Nature of Church's Thesis', in *Notre Dame Journal of Formal Logic*, 28, No. 4 (Oct. 1987), pp. 615 – 49.

[12] A. Turing, 'On Computable Numbers, with an application to the *Entscheidungs-problem*', §§1 – 2, *Proceedings of the London Mathematical Society*, 42 (1937), pp. 230 – 65.

Using the expression 'computer' to mean a person computing, Turing continues:

The behaviour of the computer at any moment is determined by the symbols which he is observing, and his 'state of mind' at that moment . . . Let us imagine the operations performed by the computer to be split up into 'simple operations' which are so elementary that it is not easy to imagine them further divided. Every such operation consists of some change of the physical system consisting of the computer and his tape. We know the state of the system if we know the sequence of symbols on the tape, which of these are observed by the computer . . . and the state of mind of the computer . . . The simple operations must therefore include:

   (a) Changes of the symbols on one of the observed squares.
   (b) Changes of one of the squares observed to another square within L squares of one of the previously observed squares . . .

The operation actually performed is determined . . . by the state of mind of the computer and the observed symbols in particular, they determine the state of mind of the computer after the operation is carried out.

    We may now construct a machine to do the work of this computer. To each state of mind of the computer corresponds an 'm-configuration' of the machine . . .[13]

Notwithstanding the crudity of Turing's conception of a *state of mind* and of his notion of determination, he successfully demonstrated that given binary encodability, recursive functions are ideally suited to mechanical implementation by means of electrical circuitry. But given that we can now construct, partly due to Turing, ingenious machines to relieve us of computing tasks, does it follow that computers (in the contemporary sense of the term) can calculate, let alone think? Or is it rather that by using our machines, we can now arrive at the results of complex calculations without anyone (or anything) literally calculating, as we can now find out what is happening on the other side of the moon without anyone (or anything) going there to look (viz. by means of spacecraft television cameras)?

    Calculating devices were invented long before computers, ranging from the humble abacus to the slide-rule and the mechanical calculating machines invented in the nineteenth century. No one was tempted to say that these gadgets could literally calculate or think. Are electronic computers in principle any different? It is tempting to insist that they are, not merely because the tasks that they can be used to undertake are so much more complex, but also because they surely follow rules. For do we not programme them with ever more sophisticated algorithms, and do they not follow these instructions meticulously? No; one can no more literally instruct a computer to do anything than one can instruct a tree, though one can make a tree grow in a certain way, and one can make a computer produce the result of vastly complex calculations. One can

[13] Ibid., §9.

replace a complex rule with a sequence of simpler rules compliance with which will ensure the same outcome, and human beings can typically follow such simple rules quite mechanically, i.e. without reflecting (RFM 422). But a machine cannot follow a rule mechanically, no matter whether the rule is simple or complex, since it makes no sense to talk of a machine *following* a rule.

This grammatical remark should be obvious from previous discussions of following rules (cf. Volume 2, 'Rules and grammar', 'Accord with a rule', 'Following rules, mastery of techniques and practices'). A machine can execute operations that accord with a rule, provided all the causal links built into it function as designed and assuming that the design ensures the generation of a regularity in accord with a chosen rule or rules. But for something to constitute following a rule, the mere production of a regularity in accord with a rule is not sufficient.

A being can only be said to be *following* a rule in the context of a complex practice involving actual and potential normative activities (cf. Volume 2, pp. 44 – 8, 254 – 69) of justifying, noticing mistakes and correcting them by reference to the relevant rule, criticizing deviations from the rule, and, if called upon, explaining an action as being in accord with the rule or teaching others what counts as following the rule. The determination of an act as being done *correctly* in accord with a rule is *logical*, not causal. For transformations of signs to constitute calculating or inferring, the nexus must be normative. Must it not be deterministic? Must not the consequences flow with the inevitability of a machine? To this one might reply ironically with Wittgenstein, 'What sort of machine? One constructed of the usual materials – or a super-machine? Are you not confusing the hardness of a rule with the hardness of a material?' (RFM 220). A causal nexus determines an outcome causally, not normatively; but the determination that underlies the steps in a calculation or in a logical inference is not causal.

'We are calculating only when there is a *must* behind the result.' But suppose we don't know this *must*, is it contained in the calculations all the same? Or are we not calculating, if we do it quite naïvely?

How about the following: You aren't calculating if, when you get now this, now that result, and cannot find a mistake, you accept this and say: this simply shows that certain circumstances which are still unknown have an influence on the result.

This might be expressed: if calculation reveals a causal connection to you, then you are not calculating.

Our children are not only given practice in calculation but are also trained to adopt a particular attitude towards a mistake in calculating, towards a departure from the norm.

What I am saying comes to this, that mathematics is normative. (RFM 424f.)

The transformation of signs constitutes calculating or inferring only in so far as it is normative. And such transformations are normative only if they have a function apart from the transformation – viz. as determining a sense and as constituting a measure ('This is how things *must* be!'). What makes a sign-game into mathematics is the use of the signs *outside* mathematics: 'Just as it is not logical inference either, for me to make a change from one formation to another (say from one arrangement of chairs to another) if these arrangements have not a linguistic function apart from this transformation' (RFM 257). The point is vividly made by imagining calculating machines occurring in nature, in impenetrable caskets. 'And now suppose that . . . people use these appliances, say as we use calculation, though of that they know nothing. Thus e.g. they make predictions with the aid of calculating machines, but for them manipulating these queer objects is experimenting' (RFM 258). No matter how reliable the resultant predictions, the people are not making calculations with the machines, any more than one makes calculations with a crystal ball. And could one say that the machines are making calculations independently of human beings? No, no more than one can say that the revolving globe tells the time independently of human beings' conventions of time-measurement.

The internal relation between a rule and what correctly accords with it is manifest in the employment of the rule in the practices of life, in using the rule as a canon of correctness. There can be no accord with a rule if there is no following of that rule, and following a rule requires regularities of behaviour in the context of normative activities. One can programme a machine to execute an algorithm. If its parts do not malfunction, its causal connections will ensure the correct output. But what makes the output *correct* is not the causal inevitability with which it is produced. In what seems almost to be a direct reply to Turing, Wittgenstein wrote:

> Does a calculating machine *calculate*?
>
> Imagine that a calculating machine had come into existence by accident; now someone accidentally presses its knobs (or an animal walks over it) and it calculates the product of 25 × 20.
>
> I want to say: it is essential to mathematics that its signs are also employed in *mufti*. (RFM 257)

But, one could add, our calculating machines are always in uniform, never in *mufti*. We use these machines (computers) to save us the tedious labour of calculating; but it does not follow, and is indeed nonsense to assert, that the machine infers or draws conclusions. One could readily build a computer from a very large toy railway-set with a huge number of switch-points and storage depots for different types of carriages to be shunted into until called upon for further operations (i.e. a 'computer memory'). This computer would be cumbersomely large and slow, but in essence its operations would not differ from the latest gadgetry on the computer-market. Would any one say, as hundreds of trains rush through complex networks of on/off points according to a pre-arranged timetable (a programme), depositing trucks in sidings or depots and collecting others, 'Now the railway-set is calculating', 'Now it is inferring', or 'Now it is thinking'? Does it make any difference if the 'railway-set' is miniscule and the 'trains' move at the speed of electric current?

Turing conceived of a human being computing a real number as having his behaviour *determined* 'by the symbols which he is observing, and his "state of mind" at that moment . . .'. In particular, it is these that 'determine the state of mind of the computer after the operation is carried out'. It is clear that Turing was thinking here of causal, psychological determination, and that he failed to see that the determination of the correctness of a computation cannot be causal. Again, Wittgenstein identified the crux of the matter:

> *There are no* causal connections in a calculation, only the connections of the pattern. And it makes no difference to this that we work over the proof in order to accept it. That we are therefore tempted to say that it arose as the result of a psychological experiment. For the psychical course of events is not psychologically investigated when we calculate. (RFM 382)

One might say that Turing's philosophical speculations (as opposed to his mathematical insights into computability) conflated a human who is, as it were, a calculating machine with a human calculating mechanically.

> A human calculating machine might be trained so that when the rules of inference were shown it and perhaps exemplified, it read through the proofs of a mathematical system (say that of Russell), and nodded its head after every correctly drawn conclusion, but shook its head at a mistake and stopped calculating. One could imagine this creature as otherwise perfectly imbecile. (RFM 258)

Of this creature one could not say that it knows any mathematics, understands mathematical notation, calculates, or draws inferences. But we might use it to save us the labour of calculating and checking proofs. And in a society which used logical and mathematical formulae and derivations (only valid ones!) solely as decorations for wallpaper, this human calculating machine might be used to check whether the wall-paper was 'correctly' decorated (cf. LFM 34ff.)! Of course, *we* can do calculations mechanically, without reflecting (RFM 422), but – and here we come full circle to Wittgenstein's sole direct remark on Turing's machines – 'if calculating looks to us like the action of a machine, *it is the human being* doing the calculation that is the machine' (RFM 234).

A creature that can calculate mechanically can also calculate thoughtfully or reflectively. If it can think, it must also make sense to say of it that it ponders, mulls over, and reconsiders (but it makes no sense to consider or reconsider *mechanically* (RPP I §560)); hence that it is, from time to time, pensive, reflective, or in a contemplative mood. It is a creature which can be said to be collecting its thoughts before it speaks, to be wrapt or engrossed in thought. It must be capable of having beliefs and opinions, hence it must make sense to say that it is incredulous or opinionated, open-minded or bigoted. It may be of a sceptical cast of mind or tentative and hesitant. It may be shrewd, prudent, and wise or short-sighted and poor in judgement.

This array of attributes and dispositions is in turn embedded in a wider network. For this battery of psychological predicates can only be applied intelligibly to a being who can manifest such features and dispositions in behaviour, express its thoughts, beliefs, and opinions in speech and action. ('What a lot of things a man must do in order for us to say he *thinks*' (RPP I §563).) And that in turn makes sense only in the context of richly differentiated behaviour within a form of life.

Intellectual and cognitive capacities cannot be severed from conative and affective ones, and these in turn are bound up with perception, pleasure, and pain. We, who can think, reason, and conjecture, hold opinions and beliefs, also place trust in certain judgements on which we act, rely on what we are told for our plans and projects, have hopes and expectations. We are pleased at certain outcomes, disappointed at others, surprised or amazed at the turn of events. We not only act in pursuance of our goals, but also set ourselves goals. The achievement of our ends affects our welfare and prosperity, and we respond to our successes or failures with joy, pleasure, and delight or with grief and distress.

What prevents the literal applicability of concepts of thought, reason, and inference to our calculating devices are not deficiencies in computational power, which may be overcome by fifth-generation computers. Rather, it is the fact that machines are not alive. They have no biography, let alone autobiography. The concepts of growth, maturation, and death have no application to them, nor do those of nutrition, health, and reproduction. It makes no sense to attribute to a machine *will* or *passion*, *desire* or *suffering*. The concepts of thinking and reasoning, however, are woven into this rich web of psychological faculties. It is only of a living creature that we can say that it manifests those complex patterns of behaviour and reaction within the ramifying context of a form of life that constitute the grounds, in appropriate circumstances, for the ascription of even part of the network of psychological concepts.

Thought, inference, and reason are capacities of the animate. And these capacities are bound up with a vast network of further faculties, of perception, pleasure and pain, emotion and volition, which are exercised and exhibited in endlessly varied behaviour within the stream of life. Could we not imagine an inorganic being with behavioural capacities akin to ours, a being which manifests perception, volition, pleasure and pain, and also thought and reasoning, yet neither grows nor matures, needs no nutrition and does not reproduce? Should we judge it to be alive for all that, to have a life, a biography, of its own? Or should we hold it to be an inanimate creature? There is surely no 'correct' answer to this question. It calls for a decision, not a discovery. As things are, we are not forced to make one, for only what is organic displays this complex behaviour in the circumstances of life. But if we had to make such a (creative) choice or decision, if Martians were made of inorganic matter, yet displayed behaviour appropriately similar to ours, it would surely be reasonable to disregard the distinctive biological features (absent in the Martians) and give preference to the behavioural ones. If in the distant future it were feasible to create in an electronic laboratory a being that acted and behaved much as we do, exhibiting perception, desire, emotion, pleasure, and suffering, as well as thought, it would arguably be reasonable to conceive of it as an animate, though not biological, creature. But, to that extent, it would not be a machine, even though it was manufactured.

Machines, unlike living creatures, do not *have* a body, although they are bodies (cf. 'Behaviour and Behaviourism', §4). Only what can (logically) die can have a body.[14] Machines and their parts have purposes and functions: viz. those which they were designed to fulfil. The organs of a living creature have functions the non-fulfilment of which adversely affects the normal (species-specific) capacities of the creature. But its body has no intrinsic function or purpose. A living being may be used by another for a purpose or to fulfil a function, as we use animals and other human beings for purposes that are not their own. But it does not itself have an intrinsic purpose, even though it may, unlike a machine, be capable of adopting purposes and goals. Human beings, in particular, can set themselves ends; and in so doing, they manifest preferences, likings, and dislikings. In pursuit of their ends they exhibit motives and intentions the fulfilment of which is marked by satisfaction and pleasure. In the achievement of their ends, their welfare is typically affected and their happiness sometimes augmented. It is only of living creatures, not of machines, that we say that they have a good, and only of such creatures can it be said that they flourish or prosper. Circumstances can beneficially or deleteriously affect the condition of a machine, be good or bad *for* it. But they cannot affect the welfare or the good of a machine, since it makes no sense to say of something that has no life that it is well or that it is doing well. What is lifeless has no welfare.

---

[14] Of course, a car has a body attached to its chassis; but that is not the sense in which an animal (but not a plant) has a body. Plants, unlike machines, can die, but they do not have bodies. A dead plant is not a corpse, for a living plant is not sentient.

   Thinking is a capacity of the animate, manifest in the behaviour and action characteristic of its form of life. We need neither hope nor fear that computers may think; the good and evil they bring us is not of their making. If, for some strange and perverse reason we wished to create artificially a thinking thing, as opposed to a device that will save us the trouble of thinking, we would have to start, as it were, with animality, not rationality. Desire and suffering are the roots of thought, not mechanical computation. Artificial intelligence is no more a form of intelligence than fool's gold is a kind of gold or counterfeit money a form of legitimate currency.

EXEGESIS §§281 – 9

SECTION 281

1   Sensation-words (or words for inner experiences) are tied up with
natural behavioural expression (PI §§244, 256). The categorial implications of this are now examined (§§281 – 6). Does it follow that there is
no pain without pain-behaviour and, *pari passu*, no perception without
perceptual response in behaviour, no thought without the expression of
thought (cf. PI §360)? This is a misunderstanding. Of course one can
have pains and not manifest them, see or hear things and not respond to
every passing sight or sound, think various thoughts and not voice them.
(Yet what is intelligible as happening some of the time may be senseless if
envisaged as happening all the time!) W.'s point is not reductionist.

Only to a living human being (not a corpse) and what behaves like a
human being does it make sense to attribute psychological predicates *or
their negations*. Of a human being we may say that he sees or is blind, also
of a dog or a horse. But a tree or a table neither sees *nor is blind*; a robot
that responds to verbal instructions does not hear, and if it is malfunctioning, it is not *deaf*, a computer, no matter how complex, is not
conscious, nor is it *unconscious* (or should we say 'One day it will
awake'?). One might add that the same applies to predicates of behavioural manifestations of the inner and their negations (e.g. 'smiles',
'laughs with amusement' (or 'ironically', 'cruelly', etc.)) and a wide
range of predicates of action.

The theme of §281 is resumed in a different vein in PI §§357 – 61.

1   (i) 'It comes to this . . .': note that a seemingly metaphysical question
is transformed into a grammatical one about what one can intelligibly
say.

(ii) 'only of a living human being and what resembles it . . .': but also
pots in fairy-tales or dolls in play (cf. PI §282) and spirits (PI §360). But
these are essentially secondary uses *parasitic* on the primary application to
human beings (cf. Exg. §282, 1), and *different* from it (the gods hear our
prayers even if our words are drowned by noise, indeed even if
unspoken, and our deeds are not concealed from their sight even by
opaque solid doors).

(iii) 'and what resembles (behaves like)': how far must the resemblance
reach? There is no clear answer, but not because of *ignorance*. Our
concepts of possessing a perceptual faculty, of consciousness, of susceptibility to pain are essentially indeterminate at *this* boundary. It makes no

sense to attribute pain to a table (save in fairy-tales) or a plant, but what of a wriggling fly (PI §284)? Here the concept gets a foothold – but no more; can a fly have aching joints?

(iv) 'it has sensations': why the asymmetry with 'sees; is blind; hears; is deaf'? 'Insensible' implies lack of consciousness, and numbness is itself a sensation. But one might say: has pain; is free of pain.

(v) 'it sees; is blind': whether it sees or fails to see this or that is not in question, but only whether it has or lacks a visual faculty.

2   MS. 165, 95f. introduces these reflections (and those of §282) in the context of the question of whether W. had not made things too easy for himself in the builder's language-game (PI §2) in as much as he had supposed circumstances (the construction of a building, building components, etc.) which are so similar to ours:

Nein, die Sprache ist ein Teil des menschlichen Lebens und was diesem ähnlich ist. Und wenn im Märchen Töpfe und Pfannen mit einander reden, so gibt das Märchen ihnen auch noch andre menschliche Attribute. Ebenso wie ein Topf auch nicht lächeln kann, wenn er kein *Gesicht* hat.

(No, language is a part of human life and of what resembles it. And if pots and pans talk to each other in a fairy-tale, still the tale gives them other human attributes too. Just as a pot can't smile, if it has no *face*.)

Later (MS. 165, 126f.) W. queries whether one who lacks a language can imagine things. But that amounts to the question of whether it makes sense to say of one who can give no expression to the imagination that he imagines something. Well, can a fountain-pen imagine things? And if not, why not? But in a fairy-tale one can talk of a fountain-pen's imagining things!

MS. 179, 56 picks up the theme of PI §281: the interlocutor concedes that W. is *not* arguing that there can be no sensation which is not expressed, but now further queries whether W. is not claiming that a creature that has no *capacity* to express sensations could have none.[22] W. replies: we couldn't // wouldn't // talk of sensations if there were no natural expression of sensations. 'Doesn't see' and 'is blind' mean the same (as do 'doesn't hear' and 'is deaf'); one does not say 'This man is blind, but perhaps he still sees'. (By implication, one cannot say 'The table does not see', for that is not like 'The table does not grow'; one does not know what it would be for a table to see! (cf. Z §129).) Does this mean that if there were no expression of sensation, there would be no

[22] That one may have sensations when paralysed is no objection. For neither the criteria for being in pain nor the criteria for *not* being in pain are satisfied. But after recovery from total paralysis, the criteria for *having been* in pain or not having been in pain are obvious enough.

sensations in the world? Can't one imagine them? – One then thinks of sensations floating around the world (as Hume did[23])!

Vol. XII, 338 observes that there can be a psychology only for beings whose behaviour resembles that of human beings.

SECTION 282

1   The interlocutor invokes ascription of psychological predicates to inanimate objects in fairy-tales as an objection to §281. W. concedes the point, but not as an objection. In fairy-tales pots are not inanimate; if they see and hear, they also talk, and to that extent resemble (behave like) human beings. If they see and hear, what do they see and hear *with*? And if they talk and smile (MS. 165, 96), do they not have mouths?

The interlocutor rightly objects that we surely *understand* fairy-tales. They relate what is not the case, but they are not *nonsense*! But, W. replies, this oversimplifies. Is it not a kind of nonsense to talk of pots seeing and hearing? Certainly we do not think that as a matter of empirical fact pots do not perceive or talk. We do not even have a clear picture of what it would be for a pot to talk. There are many different kinds of nonsense, and neither such a fairy-tale nor 'Jabberwocky' is nonsense as mere babbling is. (Just as Escher's 'impossible' etchings are not scribbles.)

Such uses of psychological predicates, like children's ascription of pain to dolls, are essentially secondary uses. A secondary use of an expression is parasitic on the primary one in as much as the secondary use would not have the significance it does if its prototype did not exist (it, as it were, echoes the primary use). Can one imagine ascribing pain to and pitying *only* dolls? The parenthetical analogy clarifies the parasitism: children who play trains but do not know what trains are or what they are for would not understand their game as our children do. It could not make the same *sense* to them as it does to us. (Similarly, imagine playing monopoly in a society lacking the institution of money and private property.)

1   'is a secondary one': PI p. 216 elaborates – talking of days of the week as fat or lean or of vowels as coloured are secondary uses of terms. 'It is only if the word has the primary sense for you that you use it in the secondary one.' (Imagine colour-words being used *only* of vowels!) The

---

[23] Hume thought that as *a matter of fact* there were no 'perceptions' that did not exist in 'bundles', i.e. in relations of causation and resemblance to others. James was agnostic, maintaining that we have no means of ascertaining whether in the room there is a mere thought that is no one's thought.

meaning of the relevant word is *explained* by reference to paradigms involved in the primary, not the secondary, use.

2   MS. 124, 239 adds, after PI §282(a) – (b) and a remark about children playing, the observation that in magical and religious rites, inanimate things are treated as if they were animate. MS. 179, 67 notes that the child who says that his doll is ill does not believe that the doll is alive. *One* language-game can be played thus, *another* not. (If the parent rushed the doll to the hospital, the child would not understand what was going on, for *that* was not the language-game it was playing.)

2.1   (i) 'the fairy-tale only invents what is not the case: it doesn't talk *nonsense*': RFM 264 observes that in a fairy-tale the dwarves might pile up as many gold pieces as there are cardinal numbers. 'What can occur in this fairy-tale must surely make sense.' (As much, and as little, as the pot calling the kettle black!)

(ii) It might appear that the example of playing trains is a poor illustration of the relation of a secondary to a primary use of an expression, precisely because the children of the alien culture *can* play trains i.e. stand in a line holding on to each other and then shuffle along shouting 'chuff-chuff' and 'toot-toot', etc. But a secondary use of an expression is essentially parasitic on the primary use and without it has no sense. W. might defend his analogy by querying in what sense it is *trains* that they play. LW §800 observes, 'Only children who know about real trains are said to be playing trains. And the word "trains" in the expression "playing trains" is not used figuratively, nor in a metaphorical sense.'

SECTION 283

1   §283(a) reverts to §281, viz. that only to living human beings and what behaves like them can one attribute sensations, etc. What gives us the idea that beings (*Wesen*), which are objects (*Gegenstände*), can feel? W. explores this question in order to undermine the false dilemma upon one horn or the other of which Cartesians and anti-Cartesian materialists impale themselves. For it seems that sensations, perceptions, indeed consciousness itself, must be attributable either to physical things, viz. bodies (and if bodies, why not stones?), or to quite different things, indeed different substances, viz. minds or souls, which some bodies have. But can a *body* have a pain? And if not, is it the soul which the body has that has the pain? But how can a body *have a soul*? And how does one get oneself into this pickle? *Inter alia*, by the natural thought that experience is 'private'.

It is tempting to think that we teach children sensation-words by getting them to associate such words with the sensations which they have (cf. Z §545). Then a child knows what 'pain' *means*; now he must learn to apply the word to objects outside himself, in conformity with the way we all use the word. So he must not ascribe pain to stones, plants, etc. But, apart from the requirement of conforming to our use of 'pain', why should he not ascribe the idea of what he has to stones? (If he can imagine some other *person's* having what he has (cf. IP §302), why can't he imagine a stone's having it too? If he is to imagine a pain he does not feel on the model of a pain he does feel, why should he not imagine a stone's having one?)

§283(c) starts by strengthening the supposition. Can't I imagine that I turn into a stone while my pain continues, and would that not be a case of a stone's having a pain? If I can imagine it, surely it makes sense. In which case the grammatical remark of §281 is wrong. Consequently, W. places pressure on the supposition: in what sense will the stone have pains? Since stones cannot manifest pain (i.e. there *is no such thing* as a stone manifesting pain), how could the pain, which we suppose to continue after I turn to stone, be the stone's? Indeed, why, in this case, should it be *anyone's* pain?

One might reply that *ex hypothesi I (a bearer of pain) continue* to feel pain, and I can surely have a pain without manifesting it. This is correct, but (a) I do not *identify* myself as the bearer of pain when I have a pain or say to myself that I am in pain. (Nor, indeed, does *what* I say when I say to another 'I am in pain' identify the bearer. Rather it is my saying it, which is typically an *expression* of pain, that identifies who is in pain.) (b) That there is *sometimes* pain which is not manifest (a point conceded by implication in §281) does *not* imply that it is intelligible that there be bearers of pain who logically cannot manifest it (e.g. statues and stones). (c) If it is further argued that there is no such thing as *unowned* pains (suffering without sufferers), hence that in the imagined petrification *I* am the bearer of the pain, then it is partly conceded that the stone is not, or not directly, the bearer of the pain.

§283(d) takes up this point: one thinks here that *I* continue to have pain after *my body* has turned to stone. So the bearer of pain is the soul (self, mind, *res cogitans*, 'that which in us perceives and thinks'[24] (cf. BB 69, 73f.))and the stone has pains 'indirectly' in as much as its soul has a pain. But this is nonsense. For stones do not *have* souls (or pain): it is people, living beings, who laugh and weep, act and react, i.e. *behave* in an infinite variety of ways in the circumstances of life, who *have* souls. The representational form of ownership misleads us here, for we think that

---

[24] I. Newton, *Optics: or a Treatise of the Reflections, Refractions, Inflections and Colours of Light*, 4th edn (William Innys, London, 1730), p. 345.

'having' signifies a relationship between two substances (as indeed it does in 'A has (owns) a house'). But '*my body*' does not signify a relation of ownership between me and my body,[25] although it may be said that he who sells himself into slavery, sells his body but not his soul. (Yet note that he who sells his soul to the Devil does not cease to *have* a soul when he dies!) 'I have a body' is at best a grammatical proposition or a rhetorical exclamation, as is 'I have a soul (or mind)'. But 'My body has a soul' is nonsense. So too, it is absurd to suppose that a stone, e.g. my petrified body, might *have* a soul.

§283(e) reiterates the grammatical observation of §281: only of what can manifest pain in behaviour can one say (truly or falsely) that it *has* pain. And what thus manifests pain in behaviour is *a living human being* (and animals that behave like one). Mere bodies do not exhibit pain, indeed do not *behave* – for it is not the body that weeps and cries out, clenches its teeth and resolves not to complain, etc. Living human beings *have* bodies, but they are not identical with their bodies (cf. 'Behaviour and behaviourism', §4).

§283(f) is ironic (a supposition confirmed by §286 and BB 73f.), indeed a *reductio ad absurdum*. One must surely attribute pain *either* to a body *or* to a soul which some body has! (Either I or my materialist adversary must be in the right!) What *else*, the Cartesian will ask, is there to attribute pain to? Well, nothing *else*, no *third thing* over and above body and soul, but *not these either*.

1.1   (i) 'drawing my attention to feelings in myself': the supposition is that adults get the child to name his sensations by private ostensive definition. Cf. PI §258: 'I concentrate my attention on the sensation, and so, as it were, point inwardly.'

(ii) 'Seele': in this context, 'soul' or 'mind' indifferently.

(iii) 'Only of what behaves': frequentative, not occurrent.

2   MS. 165, 150ff. discusses this theme in the context of the general observation that the absurdity against which W. battles is that semi-solipsism which says that I am intimately acquainted with sensations in as much as *I* have them, and that I then generalize my own case. But the *concept* of pain is acquired in learning a language, and from this concept how can one arrive at the idea that there can be sensations without a bearer? That must rest upon a misconstrual of the concept. But 'to smell a rat is ever so much easier than to trap it'.

Then follows the supposition that one might turn to stone (or that one's body might disappear – the one supposition is just as good as the other) yet one's experience continue. But *which* experience? It is no good

---

[25] Much of the early debate about natural rights turned on this misconception.

saying 'The one I am having now', for in order that that should make sense, I must have a criterion for the persistence of the same sensation. (For 'sensation' and 'same sensation' must have the same meaning for me as for others.) Why must I have such a criterion (after all, as things are, I don't employ a criterion in my own case)? Because on this supposition the sensation is severed from its expression and left hanging in the air[26] (cf. PI §288(c)). Then follows (after a detour through PI §421) a draft of PI §290: in the actual language-game with 'sensation' I do *not* identify my sensations but simply use the same word; but with us this is the beginning of the language-game, not its terminus (see Exg. §290).

MS. 124, 240f. explores the same issue in the context of a variant of PI §282. Couldn't my pains persist though I changed to stone? Would they cease to be *pains* just because I had lost the ability to express them? To be sure, the *stone* does not *have* pains! One would have to say that it is just a matter of fact that hitherto my pains were had by a human being, or indeed by *something*. But what this 'having' really means is that their actual expression is a cry (for he who cries out, flinches, etc. is he who is said to *have* the pain). And (by implication) is that supposed to be just a matter of fact?

W. adds that someone might take what he has said as a proof that it does make sense to say that a stone has pains or that one can never know whether a stone has pains or not, or even that disembodied or indeed unowned pains can exist. If one is stupid enough, he concludes, one can draw all manner of inferences here. In the sequel he explores how one slides down this slippery slope. It *is* curious that one is inclined to say that one's pains could persist though one had changed to stone. One supposes this because one can imagine opening one's eyes and finding that one's body is insensible, that one might see one's leg being cut off but feel nothing at all, that it might feel as if one were moving one's limbs, but they were motionless, etc. Indeed, one could imagine seeing one's body carted away, although one's visual field did not change save for no longer containing part of one's body. But now, *does* it make sense to suppose that there is before me in space a disembodied being who sees without eyes, indeed sees from a particular vantage-point in space, hears without ears, etc.?

MS. 129, 19 has PI §283 *after* PI §302.

SECTION 284

1   Living beings are said to feel; stones and other inanimate things are not. One cannot even get the idea of ascribing pains to stones (except in

---

[26] MS. 124, 285 adds here 'and needs a new underpinning'.

fairy-tales), save by the philosophical *cul-de-sac* of §283, for the concept of pain can get no grip in the absence of (the possibility of) behaviour that expresses pain. We *react* differently to what is alive, *respond* differently in countless ways. These natural reactions are not the product of a theory or hypothesis, nor are they the foundations for one, but rather the bedrock of our language-games. Furthermore, we do not merely see living people *move* in certain ways, we see them smile amicably, scowl in anger, grimace in pain as well as *acting* intentionally, deliberately, etc.

1.1   (i) 'pain seems able': The 'seems' is noteworthy. The category boundaries are *not* clear, and this indeterminacy is an important feature of such concepts (see Exg. §281, 1.1(iii)).

(ii) 'das Lebendige'/'das Tote': 'the living'/'the dead': There is no suggestion in §284(b) that the living are 'things'.

(iii) ' "from quantity to quality" ': a Hegelian, and later a Marxist, term of art signifying an abrupt qualitative change resulting from a marginal quantitative change. Here W. responds to the interlocutor's query as to whether the 'mere movement' of a creature can make a difference between the unintelligibility and the intelligibility of predicating pain by pointing out that here there is a *categorial* difference. CV 74 invokes the same phrase apropos the change in the *character* of a musical theme when played at different tempi. (Cf. also MS 165, 120 and RPP II §145.)

SECTION 285

1   This illustrates the 'transition from quantity to quality' of §284. The difference between a friendly smile, a wry, sarcastic, ironic, or cruel smile may be no more than a *minute* difference (a thousandth of an inch) in the orientation of the lips, but we recognize it – and not by *measuring* the difference. And we describe facial expressions thus, and would not explain our different descriptions by reference to measurement. For we *react* differently to such different facial expressions (cf. LA 30f.). And we can *reproduce* such expressions without looking in the mirror, i.e. without checking on the precise disposition of our features. It is an important fact of human nature that we are immensely sensitive to the play of features on a human face. We *see* friendliness in a face; we do not *infer* it from such-and-such a facial configuration which we know (by looking in the mirror?) accompanies our own friendly feelings.

2.1   'Think, too, how one can imitate . . .': cf. Z §220.

SECTION 286

1   This is a direct continuation of §283(f):[27] *does* one have to say of a body that it has pains? Isn't it, rather, absurd – the Cartesian may urge – to say that? And in acknowledging that it is absurd, are we not recognizing the truth of a metaphysical thesis? '. . . it is as though we looked into the nature of pain and saw that it lies in its nature that a material object can't have it. And it is as though we saw that what has pain must be of a different nature from that of a material object; that, in fact, it must be of a mental nature' (BB 73). This is doubly confused. For, in the first place, it is not the soul that feels pain, but the human being. And, secondly, the absurdity of attributing pain to the body is not because of gross factual (or even 'metaphysical') error. That it is not my hand that feels pain, but I in my hand is a *grammatical* truth.

'Is it the body that feels pain?' looks like an empirical question, but as soon as one reflects upon how it might be decided, what experiments might determine it, it becomes evident that it is not. We do not say 'This body feels pain' any more than we say 'This body must take an aspirin' or 'This body must keep a stiff upper lip'. Of course, we *could*; but that would involve a shift in grammar and an alteration of concepts (cf. BB 73f.). How does our existing grammar (our attribution of pain to a *person* and our ruling out such attributions to a body as senseless) show itself? With what features of our life does it smoothly mesh? If someone has hurt his hand, his hand does not avow pain; *he* does. He may nurse his hand, but we comfort *him*.

1.1   'Wie macht es sich geltend': 'plausible' smacks of *belief*, which can be true or false; so better, 'validate itself', 'show itself', or 'claim recognition'.

2   Vol. XVI, 243ff. has the interlocutor query whether one can say 'My *body* loves, meditates, intends, etc.' Why not?, W. replies. This way of speaking is, after all, not yet 'occupied', i.e. this logical space has not yet been made (it is neither true nor false that my body loves). The interlocutor misunderstands: would it be *true* to say such a thing? It would be true, W. responds, if the corresponding proposition in our current notation were true.

---

[27] In MS. 129, 20 and MS. 179, 69f. it follows directly after PI §283.

SECTION 287

1   A coda to §286: one comforts the *sufferer*, not his hand. *What* one pities
(the object of one's pity) is not the hand, but the person whose hand it is.
That comes out in the fact that one looks into his face, talks to him, puts
one's arm around his shoulder. And this constitutes the natural
background of the *grammatical* fact that it makes no sense to pity a hand.

SECTION 288

1   Having clarified the concept of the subject of sensations (§§281 – 7),
W. now reverts to first-person sensation-sentences, building on the
example in §283. The supposition of turning to stone yet one's pain
continuing is one which severs the concept of pain from the criteria of its
application to others, in as much as pain, in this case, could not
intelligibly have any behavioural expression. Given this supposition,
how do I (who have turned to stone) know that what persists is *pain*? The
interlocutor balks: I *can't* be in error here; 'I have a pain' is a Cartesian
thought, and *cogitationes* are transparent. If I have a *cogitatio*, I *know* that I
have it; it means nothing to doubt whether I am in pain!
      It is true that it means nothing, but not because I *know* that I am in
pain. Doubt is excluded not by certainty, but by grammar! An expression of doubt about whether one has a pain or something else (barring
borderline cases, e.g. 'It's unpleasant but it doesn't really *hurt*') can only
signify that the speaker does not know what the word 'pain' *means*. For
since there is no such thing as doubting whether one is in pain, an
expression of doubt here is a criterion for not knowing what the word
means.
      One can explain what 'pain' means to a person who does not know
this English word, perhaps by enacting injury and showing how
someone behaves when he hurts himself, viz. by crying out 'Ow! That
hurts!' Or one might prick the learner with a pin, and when he starts and
cries 'Ow!', one would say 'See, that's what pain is'. This explanation
(see 1.1 below) might be understood, misunderstood, or not understood,
like any other. How the person goes on to use the word after having been
given the explanation will show (is the criterion of) whether he now
understands what 'pain' means. What if he insists that he *does* know what
'pain' means (and perhaps, indeed, does generally use it correctly), but
nevertheless does *not* know whether what he now has is pain? We should
not know what to do with him, any more than we should know what to
do with someone who claims to remember believing things before he
was born. Here is an abnormality for which our concept of understand-

ing is ill-tailored (and that is no coincidence, for were it tailored for these cases, it would not fit normal ones – and, moreover, it would not *be* our concept of understanding). Criteria for understanding are here satisfied cheek by jowl with a criterion for not understanding.

The expression of doubt (and the claim to knowledge) have no room in the language-game *we* play with avowals of sensation. So how can W. query whether, on the supposition that one has turned to stone, one might not be mistaken in thinking one's pain continues? Precisely because that supposition abrogates the normal language-game: it severs pain from the possibility of its behavioural expression, and hence the concept of pain from the criteria for its application (to others). In our language-game there are criteria in behaviour for whether a person is in pain, and for whether what he has is the same pain as he had previously. The sufferer who avows his pain and its continuity does not employ these (or any other) criteria in his avowals, but others do; and it is these criteria that *give sense* to 'pain' and 'same pain' both in my utterance 'I still have the same headache' *and* in the judgement that another person's pain is still as severe as before. But in the envisaged case there is no longer *any such thing* as the behavioural expression of pain (stones do not *behave*, and though the Laocoön wonderfully expresses suffering, it does not do so *behaviourally*, but by the *depiction* of behaviour). So a criterion of identity for the sensation *is* required here, i.e. something must be determined as *counting* as having pain, and having the same or different pain. But if the (petrified) bearer of the (imagined) sensation needs a criterion of identity for it (unlike the bearer of pain in our language-game), then the possibility of error exists (as it does in third-person ascriptions of pain based on criteria in the normal language-game). Hence it *looks* as if I might legitimately doubt whether what goes on, when I turn to stone, is pain or something else. But, to be sure, it only *looks* thus, for the argument is a *reductio ad absurdum*. The envisaged 'sensation' is no sensation at all; there is no such thing as a *non-behavioural* criterion of pain, for the *concept* of pain is determined by its behavioural criteria.

.1   'by pricking him with a pin and saying "See, that's what pain is" ': this is a perfectly licit explanation of what 'pain' means, but one which is liable to be misconstrued by philosophers. For one is immediately tempted to think that this explanation will be understood if the learner *has* what we *have* when we are pricked, and associates the word 'pain' with what he has. Thinking along these lines, it will seem that the explanatory device of pricking the learner is a means of producing in him a private sample of pain which will be 'qualitatively' identical with the private samples we use to give the word 'pain' its meaning. These are precisely the misconceptions which the private language arguments strive to eradicate.

Since the pain produced by pricking the learner is not a sample of pain (for reasons elaborated in PI §§243ff.), how can the envisaged explanation *be* an explanation? Clearly we are demonstrating (explaining) to the pupil when to use the expression 'I have a pain' or 'It hurts'. If, as normal, he flinches and cries 'Ow!', we can teach him to replace his cry with an avowal of pain and also to say of others who display pain-behaviour in similar circumstances that they are in pain. But if his limb is anaesthetized and he does not react to the pinprick, or if he is abnormal and merely giggles, our explanation will misfire.

Such an explanation of a sensation-word is not an explanation by means of a sample, even though it may look like one, save that the sample is 'private'. But there is no such thing as a 'private' sample.

2.1   (i) LSD 110f. examines the explanation of 'pain' by pinching someone. Here W. declared that in so doing one gives a sample of pain. But, he queried, is the *sensation* the sample or the *pinching*? In so far as one is inclined to say that only the person pinched knows what the sensation was and that the sensation was that which was *present*, then the sensation could not have been the sample. The reason W. gave was that samples are akin to words in that (a) they must endure: 'a sample is, just as a word is, something which lasts', (b) they must be publicly accessible: 'I show you the sample, you see it, I see it, we look at it for five minutes.' A fleeting sense-impression therefore cannot be a sample. On the other hand, one can say that the sensation is the sample if (a) one means that it's that sensation which is called 'pain', not just the pinch, so that if the learner were anaesthetized, he would not understand, or (b) if, when one pinches him, one says 'It's this sensation' (presumably parallel to 'Red is this *colour*').

This reasoning is unhappy (and is not repeated elsewhere). First, while relative permanence of the written word resembles that of, e.g., colour-samples, this is not mirrored by the spoken word. Yet if one says 'Repeat after me "Abracadabra"!' the quoted word is a sample to be reproduced by the hearer. Many samples are no more permanent than this, e.g. explanations of verbs that employ samples ('*This* [and I thump the table] is what is called thumping') or explanations of names of sounds or notes ('This [striking the keyboard] is middle-C'). Secondly, the reason why a sensation cannot be a sample used in defining a sensation-word is not because it is fleeting, for a persistent pain would be no better than a momentary one. Rather it is because sensations, though they can be exhibited (i.e. manifested) in behaviour (PI §313), cannot be exhibited *as samples*, as objects for comparison. There is (and can logically be) no *technique* of employing them (laying them alongside reality like measures) as standards for the correct use of a word in a *practice* (see 'Private ostensive definition', §3).

It is this point that makes it unintelligible that sensations should function as samples in a genuine (public) language. And although it *seems* as if they might function as private samples in a 'private' language, this, as has been argued, is an illusion. MS. 130, 209f. (≃ Z§§546 – 8) demonstrates this nicely in a pertinent context. Suppose someone always pricks himself with a pin when he says 'I'm not certain whether he is in pain', supposing thereby to have the meaning of 'pain' vividly before his mind to ensure that he knows *what* he is to doubt about the other man. But would his pain tell him what he is to doubt about the other? How would the pain *he* feels engage with his doubt about someone *else*'s pain? Is he in a better position to doubt whether another person has a pain because *he* has one? In order to doubt whether someone else has a cow, must I have a cow? Can he doubt whether someone else has *this* (and he pricks himself)? It is as if one were told 'Here is a chair. Can you see it clearly? – Good – now translate it into French!' In order to doubt whether someone else is in pain, one needs, not pain, but the concept of pain.

In short, it is the *use* that makes something a sample for this or that, and there is no such thing as using a sensation as a paradigm for the correct application of a word.

(ii) 'I might *legitimately* begin to doubt afresh': MS. 124, 246f. (derived from MS. 165, 143f.) interpolates here

Der Satz 'Wenn ich mich nun irrte und es gar nicht Schmerzen wären' ist Unsinn, weil ein Kriterium der Identität der Empfindung vorgespielt wird das es gar nicht gibt. (Ähnlich wie im Satz: 'Ein Anderer kann nicht *diese identischen* Schmerzen haben, die ich jetzt habe.'

(The sentence 'Suppose I were in error and it wasn't pain at all' is nonsense, for it gives the illusion of a criterion of identity for the sensation which does not obtain. (Just as in the sentence: 'Another cannot have *these identical* pains which I now have.'))

Then follows the rest of (c). The back-reference to PI §253(c) is noteworthy: in both cases an 'inner' criterion of identity is misguidedly intimated.

SECTION 289

1   The expression of doubt has no place in the language-game with avowals of pain. It is, however, tempting to think that the reason for this is Cartesian certainty, indubitability, about 'inner experience'. Am I not 'immediately acquainted' with the sensation which *makes it true* that I am in pain, and is it not the occurrence of this sensation that is *described* in saying 'I have a pain'? Of course I cannot justify this certainty to

others, but surely I am justified *before myself* – by the immediate private experience!

This is precisely the misconception against which W. wars. That which seems here to be founded on the bedrock of experience (the foundation of all empiricist architecture) is actually free-floating. This seems absurd. If it were so, what would stop it slipping from beneath our feet? That which is most certain would become unreliable, subject to the eroding waters of sceptical doubt! But these fears stem from misunderstandings. The earth too is free-floating, but does it slip from beneath our feet? Does the fact that it is unsupported in space make our buildings less well-founded? It is true that I cannot doubt whether I am in pain, but not because that is the most certain kind of empirical knowledge I have.

What does it mean to claim that in avowing pain I am justified before myself? It seems that I fit the word 'pain' to what I experience. If another could experience what I have, he would agree that my description 'I have a pain' fits this experience, i.e. that I am using the word correctly on this occasion to describe my experience. But, of course, this experience is 'private', and another cannot know what I am calling 'pain'! This incorporates all the confusions hitherto raked over. First, in what sense am I *calling* something 'pain' when I say 'I have pain'? Certainly not in the sense in which I call something 'a magnolia' when I point at a tree and say 'That's a magnolia'. Secondly, in the thin sense in which I can be said to be calling something 'pain' when I say 'I am in pain', another *can* know what I am calling 'pain'. Does the dentist *not* know what I am talking about when I say 'I have toothache'? Thirdly, would someone else (the dentist, for example) *not* admit that I am using the word 'pain' correctly when my cheek is swollen, I flinch if my tooth is touched, I chew on the other side only, etc. It is mistaken to think that *I* have a justification for using the word 'pain', and equally fallacious to suppose that another can have no justification for judging me to be using it correctly.

It is a mistake to think that to use a word without evidential grounds or without a defining paradigm is to use it wrongfully. It is easy to see why one is tempted to think thus, for one is inclined to suppose that W. is suggesting that when one sincerely says 'I am in pain', there are just the words and nothing else, viz. no *pain* (Vol. XVII, 10f.). And surely, when one says 'I am in pain', one has a *reason*, viz. that one *is in pain* (cf. MS. 162(b), 92)! This is confused. Of course when one sincerely avows pain, one *is* in pain. But *that one is in pain* is not a reason (a grammatical justification) for saying that one is in pain! To think otherwise is like thinking that the reason it is right to say that $\frac{\delta x^2}{\delta x} = 2x$ is *because it is so* (MS. 158, 83). But, of course, there is all the difference in the world between being in pain and saying 'I am in pain', and saying 'I am in pain' without being in pain – the difference, in fact, between sincerity and a lie (cf. PI §304). Nevertheless, there *is* such a thing as a reason for saying 'I am in pain', e.g. to elicit sympathy, or, differently, because these words belong to the role I am acting in a play. But that a sincere avowal of pain does not rest on a grammatical justification does not derogate from its role in the language-game: 'You have to regard the utterance (without a reason) with the same respect as a statement that rests on a reason, not as something that *lacks support*' (MS. 158, 83f. (in English)). For this utterance is the beginning of the language-game (cf. Exg. PI §290).

1.1   'es zu Unrecht gebrauchen': 'to use it wrongfully' (as in RFM 406).

2   Vol. XVII, 10f. queries how one knows that in saying 'I have pains' one is using the word 'pain' correctly? One does not *know*, W. retorts, i.e. there is here no criterion, rather the word forces itself upon one. And that is why it seems that one *must* have a justification for using it, an inner justification. But even if one had what one imagines, i.e. an inner image of pain, it would not be a justification, for the existence of an inner object cannot justify the use of a word. But this gives the false impression, W. adds, that he is arguing that there are just the words of the utterance and nothing else.

Later (Vol. XVII, 42f.) W. contrasts 'He has the same pain as I' with 'I now have the same pain as I had earlier'. In the first case there is a criterion of identity, but what of the second? Should one say 'I *know immediately* that it is the same'? Do I then know immediately that the word 'same' fits here, or that such and such a picture (an inner image) fits? And in what way does it 'fit' (i.e. is there here a technique of comparison determining what *counts* as 'fitting')? The interlocutor queries: does this mean that one just *says* the word 'same' without its being somehow justified? 'The word "just" is wrongly applied here', W. responds. The suggestion that 'same' is here used without justification discomforts one much as the claim that the earth floats free in space without support disturbs some people.

MS. 162(b), 71ff. examines the temptation to say that we can never really know whether someone else is justified in saying that he has a certain experience, since it depends precisely on *his* experience. This is wrong: we can know it perfectly well. For the 'experience' is not the justification of the use – not, that is, in the grammatical sense.

How do I know that I can imagine purple, but not the (unsurveyable) figure |||||||||||||||? How do I know that what I imagine is purple, or that what I sometimes imagine is not the figure |||||||||||||||||? The image is no justification, but the material picture (at which one may point, saying 'That's what I imagined') is.

But there is indeed a justification for the use of the words 'I can imagine that.' Suppose someone said 'I can imagine what Pavlova experienced during that dance'. One might query 'How can you imagine that; what have you experienced that is similar to that?' And he might reply, 'The most similar experience that I have had was to imagine what Mozart felt while composing.'

2.1   'To use a word without a justification . . .': RFM 406 (= MS. 124, 132) has PI §289(b) in the context of a discussion of sameness (see Exg. §292, 1).

AVOWALS AND DESCRIPTIONS

1. *Descriptions of subjective experience*

The classical picture of the relation between the mental and the physical represents a complex web of grammatical structures as delineating two co-ordinate worlds, the world of 'subjective experience' and the world of physical objects (see 'Privacy', §1). The former is conceived to be private, directly accessible only to its owner, the latter to be public, accessible to all. The objects, events, and processes in each domain can be described, for do we not distinguish between descriptions of objects of experience that are in the physical world and descriptions of our experiences of objects? Indeed, there is much more in the subjective domain than perceptual experiences of objects; for we experience sensations, emotions, and moods; we have desires and intentions; and we think, believe, and form judgements; and these too, and much more, we represent in words.

Perception is our source of knowledge of the world around us. We find out how things are by looking, smelling, listening etc. We, so to say, perceive the facts, read off their description from what we thus perceive, and portray what we apprehend in words, in accord with rules (cf. PI §292). It is altogether natural to think that the inner, subjective world is likewise perceived; and here too, it seems, we read off a description, e.g. 'I have a toothache', 'I think it is raining', 'I want a drink', from the facts accessible to us alone. Of course, perception of the inner does not involve a sense-organ, but we do talk of *being aware* of our pains, of rising anger or feelings of joy, just as we talk of being aware of the ticking of the clock or of a curious smell in the room. So it seems as if, despite the absence of sense-*organs*, we have a faculty of inner sense whereby we can apprehend how things are with us subjectively. We dub this faculty 'introspection' and conceive of ourselves as reporting events and processes in our subjective world by introspective scrutiny of the facts, which we then represent for the benefit of others (or for our own future use) in descriptions.

Many further factors induce the picture of first-person psychological utterances as descriptions of states of affairs in an inner world. After all, one is inclined to say, propositions such as 'A has a toothache' ('is angry', 'wants a drink', 'intends to go', etc.) are surely descriptions of a person, characterizing his mental state. If A says sincerely 'I have a toothache', that provides adequate grounds for describing him as having a toothache, i.e. for saying 'A has a toothache'. And if the latter sentence is a description, so too is the former first-person utterance. For surely 'I have a toothache' said by A says *of* A just what 'A has a toothache' says of him. The former symmetry between first- and third-person psychological sentences seems to make this an inescapable conclusion. Indeed, a natural inclination to cleave to the pre-theoretical *Urbild*, the Augustinian picture of language, that words are names and sentences *au fond* descriptions of states of affairs makes it natural to imagine that 'I have a pain' describes exactly what 'He has a pain' said of me describes.

Not only is there a first/third-person symmetry to induce this thought, but there is also an equally obvious tense symmetry. For does not 'I had a pain yesterday' express exactly the same proposition as 'I have a pain' said yesterday? And does not 'I had a pain yesterday' describe how things were with me? It is, after all, just what I might say in response to the doctor's query 'How were things yesterday?'.

Further weight is given by the equally natural thought that truth consists in correspondence with the facts, for a true proposition, after all, is a proposition which describes things as they, in fact, are. The proposition that A has a pain is true if and only if A has a pain, i.e. if that is how things are, i.e. if it is a fact that A has a pain. But equally, A's utterance 'I have a pain' may be true or false, for A may be lying. It is true if and only if he has a pain, so one and the same fact makes the two assertions true. Indeed, some philosophers have argued that the two utterances express the same proposition or make the same statement. Surely then, they describe the very same fact and are true in virtue of what they thus describe.

These considerations emphasize a logical symmetry between first- and third-person psychological sentences. But the price that has to be paid for conceiving of both alike as descriptions is high. For if one thinks of, e.g., 'I have a pain' as a description after the manner of 'He has a pain', then it seems that it is one which is *justified* by the facts. So I am in a position to assert such a proposition only in so far as I know or believe it to be true. I must compare it with reality, i.e. verify it. This, it seems, I can do, for it is I who have the pain; indeed, am I not in a uniquely privileged position to do so? The justification here appears to be private, in as much as only the subject really knows whether his description is true. For only he can compare the proposition directly with the reality that makes it true (or false).

This conception of the descriptive status of first-person psychological utterances generates a fundamental epistemological asymmetry side by side with the apparent logical symmetry. For while 'He is in pain', for example, allegedly describes the same state of affairs as 'I am in pain' said by him, one who asserts the former is not in a position to compare it directly with the facts. The grounds upon which he asserts third-person psychological propositions consists in what people do and say. From their 'external' behaviour he must infer the existence of their mental state, which, if it obtains, makes his assertion true. Hence judgements about the mental states of other people are essentially conclusions of inferences from the observed to the unobserved. The character of such inferences has been variously construed by philosophers. One common strategy is to claim that the argument is *analogical*, that we attribute mental states to others by analogy with our own case. An alternative is to represent the arguments as *theoretical*, as a matter of an inference to the best explanation. Postulating inner states, unobservable to outsiders, as it were, provides the best available explanation of the manifest behaviour. A more radical option (methodological solipsism) is to argue that other people's states of mind are second-order logical constructions.

In this essay we are concerned with only one strand in this web of confusion, viz. the mischaracterization of avowals of experience (*Äusserungen*) as descriptions of experience and the misconception of avowals and reports of experience as a matter of reading a description off the facts presented to one in introspection.

2. *Descriptions*

One paradigm of description which Wittgenstein often employed as an object of comparison is giving a word-picture of perceptible states of affairs, events, or objects. Here one characteristically observes what lies within one's perceptual field and depicts it in words, as it were reading the description off the facts. What one says may be true or false, accurate or inaccurate, detailed or rough-and-ready. To be sure, there are many different language-games that constitute describing, and they are less alike than one might think. Many different things in different contexts count as describing what one sees; contrast describing a scene with describing a painting of a scene, or describing a scene, whether actual or painted, with describing the impression it makes. Even when the words used are the same, e.g. in describing a scene and in describing a corresponding dream, the difference of context shows that the use to which the words are being put is wholly different, as is evident from the different kinds of criteria of success or failure, correctness or mistake, etc. which apply to the descriptions in these distinct contexts. Describing what one hears is importantly different from describing visibilia, and describing what happened *at* a play is altogether unlike describing what happened *in* the play. Furthermore, describing what one perceives is unlike describing how something ought to be or ought to be done, as different as a picture is from a blueprint. Again, the description of a blueprint is quite different from the description of a fictitious episode in a novel. And numerous further specific language-games with descriptions have distinctive features of their own, e.g. describing one's dreams, describing something from memory, or describing how one imagines something. In each case, what is called 'describing' or 'a description' interlocks with quite different grammatical joints. What counts as improving or refining one's description, checking it, correcting it, varies from case to case.

This diversity is important (PI §291), but for present purposes it will suffice to contrast the simple paradigm of describing what is visible before one, e.g. the room in which one is sitting, with a range of first-person present-tense psychological propositions, such as an utterance of pain, an exclamation of anger, or an expression of intention. This will serve to highlight the differences between the language-games and to cast doubt upon the traditional supposition that such utterances as 'I am in pain' are standardly and uniformly employed as descriptions of a state of affairs. Subsequently, reminders of what we actually call 'describing one's state of mind' and 'describing one's pain', as well as 'reporting how one feels', will be adduced.

The activities (and the concepts) that belong to the language-game of describing one's surroundings are, in the first place, observing, scrutinizing, examining, and investigating (LW §51). Here too there must be room for the ideas of perceptual competence and observational conditions: if one has poor eyesight, one may put on spectacles to see more clearly, and if it is dusk, one may turn on the light to improve visibility. The upshot, in certain cases, is identifying (or misidentifying) and recognizing. In giving a description of a room, one strives for accuracy (Is the table mahogany or teak?), and one may refine one's description on closer scrutiny. One may make mistakes and correct them after further investigation (Actually, it is padouk!). It makes sense here in many cases to consult authorities (Is the Piranesi print one of the *Vedute* series or not?) and to elaborate one's description accordingly. Hence too, one may ask others for their considered judgement. It makes sense here to answer the challenge 'How do you know?' and also 'Why do you think that?', for in certain cases one has grounds or evidence for one's identifications and characterizations. And one may be certain (and yet wrong) or tentative and unsure of one's attribution or identification. In respect of certain features there is such a thing as expertise, and some people are better than others in carrying out the task of giving a detailed and accurate description.

The contrast between this simple paradigm and many typical first-person present-tense psychological utterances is marked. 'I have a toothache', 'I intend to go', 'I think he is in London', 'I am furious with you', 'I expect him to come' are very different kinds of sentences. But they have in common the following feature: used spontaneously in an appropriate context, they diverge dramatically from the paradigm of description just spelled out. First, such utterances are not grounded in perception. If asked how one knows that there is an octagonal table in a certain room, one may reply 'I saw it'. But one does not perceive one's toothache, intention, thought, anger, or expectation. Of course, it is tempting, especially in the case of sensations, emotions, and moods, to say 'I know that he has a pain (is angry, is cheerful) because I see how he behaves, but I know that I have a pain (etc.) because I feel it'. But to feel pain, angry or cheerful is just to have a pain, be angry or cheerful. So 'I know I have a pain because I feel it' amounts to 'I know I have a pain because I have it', i.e. because it is true, i.e. because I am not lying (LSD 13). But that I am not lying is neither a source of knowledge nor a ground for my assertion. Secondly, in as much as such utterances are not based on observation, it makes no sense to speak here of conditions of observation; one cannot, as it were, improve the conditions of visibility so that one may better apprehend one's toothache. There are no organs for perceiving one's pains, emotions, or thoughts, and one cannot be more or less skilful is feeling toothache or in feeling cheerful. Thirdly, one does not identify or recognize one's sensations, thoughts, or intentions, although one may realize that the pain in one's chest is angina pectoris or that one's intentions are disreputable. Consequently, there is no room for misidentification of the sensation, but only for mischaracterization of the cause of the pain (e.g. it is indigestion, not angina). For 'I thought I had a pain in my chest, but I was mistaken' makes no sense. Fourthly, there is no such thing as checking what one has said by looking more closely, comparing one's sensation, emotion, or thought with paradigms. It makes no sense to consult others or to look up authorities to find out whether one has a sensation, what one intends to do, or what one thinks. Fifthly, one's utterance does not rest on evidence, and it is senseless to ask 'How do you know that you have a toothache?' or 'Why do you believe that you intend to go?'. For finally, knowledge and ignorance, certainty and doubt, have no place here – but only indecision (see 'Privacy', §3).

These grammatical differences cast doubt on the suppositions that such first-person utterances are parallel to the corresponding third-person propositions, that they describe one's 'inner world' as observation statements describe the 'public world'. These doubts are strengthened by the fact that the supposition that they are such descriptions must in the final analysis rest on the intelligibility of private ostensive definition, on the independence (in these cases) of truth and truthfulness, and on the thought that the relevant psychological concepts are names of private objects, events, and processes. These misconceptions are assailed by Wittgenstein in the private language arguments.

3. Natural expression

The traditional philosophical conception of first-person psychological utterances is so natural, so firmly rooted in superficial analogies of form, in similes and metaphors that are in constant (and harmless) use, that it can only be combatted by showing that it is eminently avoidable. We are not *forced* to conceive things thus by the very facts of the matter, any more than we are forced to conceive of mathematical propositions as descriptions of relations between abstract objects that are real but non-actual. We are constrained only by our natural disposition to advert of similarities of form and to overlook differences in use, to theorize rather than to describe, to explain instead of clarifying the rules for the use of our expressions.

The classical picture conceives of the language-game with 'I have a pain' as beginning with the sensation, which the sufferer observes *in foro interno*, identifies, and then represents in a description which communicates to others what is directly accessible only to him. But on the contrary, Wittgenstein argued, this language-game begins with natural expressive behaviour in certain circumstances (PI §§244, 290). We cry out when we injure ourselves, groan and scream; we grimace and clutch the part that hurts, assuage the injured limb. It is in these primitive, instinctual forms of pre-linguistic behaviour that the language-game with 'pain' is rooted, not in observations of private objects in an ethereal realm. We do not ask a child who has hurt himself how he knows that it hurts or whether he is quite sure that it does; we comfort him.

Note that something similar holds for a wide range of rudimentary psychological states, reactions, and conditions – although not for all, and not for more developed forms. A child who wants a toy reaches for it and tries to get it. The child's anger is manifest in striking out, contorted features, and screams of rage. If the child expects to be given a piggyback, he jumps up and down in eager anticipation, if he is frightened, he blanches, cries, and runs to Mummy. We do not wonder whether the child who tries to reach his toy and screams in frustration has correctly identified his desire. And we do not query, of the frightened child, whether he has recognized his feelings. These are primitive forms of behaviour characteristic of our species. They are antecedent to our language-games and provide the behavioural bedrock for them.

The exclamation 'It hurts', the groan 'I have a toothache', the cry 'I've hurt myself' are manifestations (*Äusserungen*) of pain, not descriptions; they are comparable to moans or screams of pain rather than to descriptions such as 'He has a toothache' or 'He has hurt himself'. Avowals of pain are learnt extensions of natural expressive behaviour, and are themselves forms of behaviour: 'words are connected with the primitive, the natural, expressions of the sensation and used in their place. A child has hurt himself and he cries; and then adults talk to him and teach him exclamations and, later, sentences. They teach the child new pain-behaviour' (PI §244). The importance of this observation is not as a contribution to (armchair) learning theory, but rather as a way of pinpointing and illuminating crucial features of the grammar of such utterances. An avowal (*Äusserung*) of pain, such as 'It hurts' or 'I have a pain', no more rests on 'introspective evidence' than does a scream or a groan of pain, and it is no more a description of an observed inner state than is a moan. For in the most rudimentary case, 'It hurts' is simply a partial replacement of a cry, groan, or scream of pain. The spontaneous avowal, like a moan, is an expression of pain, as crying out in alarm is an expression of fear or laughter of amusement. Like natural, non-linguistic forms of pain-behaviour, an avowal of pain is a criterion for others to assert 'He is in pain'. It is not an empirical discovery, established by inductive correlation, that when people hurt themselves, they typically cry out, clutch their injured limb, and assuage the pain. There is no such thing as non-inductive identification of pain other than by reference to pain-behaviour; for in one's own case one does not identify one's pain at all, one has a pain which one (typically) manifests in behaviour. The behavioural manifestation of pain, whether natural or linguistic, is not a *symptom* of pain. We learn the use of 'pain' by learning to say 'He is in pain' when someone behaves in these characteristic ways in circumstances of injury or illness and by learning to extend our own natural pain-behaviour by using such sentences as 'It hurts' or 'I have a pain'.

To view avowals of pain as forms of pain-behaviour akin to moans or cries of pain is not to identify pain with pain-behaviour. To moan is not to say 'I moan', and to cry out 'I have a pain' is not to say 'I am manifesting pain-behaviour'. We do not use the word 'pain' as we use the phrases 'manifestation of pain' or 'expression of pain'. Indeed, it is an essential aspect of this language-game that someone can be in pain and not groan or moan, and so too that one can hurt oneself and not cry out 'It hurts'. Conversely, one can pretend and dissimulate, groan or exclaim 'I have a pain', and yet not be suffering at all. This makes it appear as if pain and its manifestations are logically independent. But that is not so: unless injury and illness were associated with these forms of behaviour, we should have no use for the concept of pain (cf. LPE 286). For pain-behaviour *is* logically connected with pain, not, of course, by way of entailment, but rather by pain-behaviour's constituting a criterion for a person's being in pain. It makes no sense to say 'Here is pain, and here is behaviour – it just happens that they are associated' (cf. LSD 10). While pretence is sometimes possible, it is absurd to suppose that all pain-behaviour might be pretence. For the very concept of *pretending to be in pain* is parasitic upon the concept of *being in pain*. There are criteria for pretending to be in pain no less than for being in pain. Pretending to be in pain must be *learnt*, and the prototype for pretending to be in pain is manifesting *pain*. Numerous concept-involving capacities and skills must be acquired by a human being before it can intelligibly be said of him that he is pretending to be in pain. The idea that a new-born child might be pretending thus is absurd, for his behaviour lacks the necessary articulations, his capacities are too limited, and the weave of his life is as yet too simple (cf. Exg. §249).

As with a moan, so too with an utterance of pain, it makes no sense to ask 'How do you know?' or 'Why do you believe that?'. One does not learn or find out that one has a pain; there can be no question of error or mistake, and so too no room for knowledge or ignorance, certainty or doubt. Hence the concept of justifying an utterance of pain has no application in the manner in which a description of a feature of a room can be justified. It makes no sense to justify one's avowal by reference to perception; nor does it make sense to cite evidence. One cannot justify what one says by producing a sample as one can justify saying that the curtains are eau-de-Nil by displaying a sample of that colour. One can, of course, insist that one said one was in pain because one *was* in pain, as opposed to acting the role of someone injured or to reading out a text. Here one draws a contrast between language-games, but that is not a ground for assertion.

It is important to emphasize that Wittgenstein was not *assimilating* avowals to the natural expression of 'inner states'. An avowal of pain is not *just like* a groan, and it would be as misleading to say that it has the same logical status as a groan as it is to assimilate it to a description (LSD 11). For there are differences as well as similarities. An utterance (*Äusserung*) of pain, unlike a moan, is articulate; it is a linguistic expression consisting of words in grammatical combination. A sentence that can be used in a spontaneous avowal has other uses too. It can be embedded in the antecedent of a conditional, it has an intelligible negation, and there are tense transforms of such a sentence. These cases are not expressions or manifestations of inner states and must be treated differently. Similarly, while the spontaneous use of such sentences in appropriate circumstances is a form of expressive behaviour, they can also be used coolly in reports or explanations (see below).

These features, however, must not blind us to the distinctive grammatical differences between avowals and descriptions, differences that remain significant even in reports and genuine descriptions of how one feels, of one's pain, or one's own mental states. It is evident that the connection between the word 'pain' and the sensation of pain is altogether unlike the connection between the word 'red' and the colour or the word 'dumb waiter' and the piece of furniture. One can say that the word 'pain' is the name of a sensation, as one can say that the word 'red' is the name of a colour or 'dumb waiter' the name of an article of furniture. But the expression 'is the name of a sensation' is as unlike 'is the name of a colour' or 'is the name of a piece of furniture' as 'is the name of a number' is unlike 'is the name of a numeral'. One can explain what 'red' or 'dumb waiter' means by ostension. One can label a colour-sample 'red' and hang a name-plate from a dumb waiter. But there is no such thing as a mental sample of pain, and the notion of a private ostensive definition of 'pain' is a philosophical misconception. One cannot stick a label on a sensation of pain, and this name/object model has no application to sensations. Rather ' "pain" is the name of a sensation' amounts to no more than ' "I have a pain" is an expression of pain (*Schmerzäusserung*)' (RPP I §313). For the word 'pain' is connected to the sensation of pain by way of its connections with behavioural expressions of pain, and one such connection consists in the fact that 'I have a pain' *is* an expression of pain (PI §244).

Just as the name/object model is inappropriate for sensation-names, so too the central paradigm for ' "w" refers to . . .' has no genuine use here. Of course, one can say 'The word "pain" refers to the sensation of pain', as one can say that the word 'red' refers to the colour red. But in the latter case one can point to the colour and add 'Namely *that*'. The move from talking of referring to physical objects or their perceptible properties to talking of referring to sensations is a shift in language-games, which calls out for a fresh explanation of what is meant here by 'referring' (cf. Z §434). The tempting idea that the speaker knows expactly what he refers to when he says 'I have a pain', since he can, as it were, cast a sidelong glance at the private sensation is a piece of philosophical mythology (PI §274). But, of course, one can say: 'The word "pain" refers to the sensation of pain, not to pain-behaviour' – this is a grammatical remark, and it draws an important distinction.

This schematic account of the rudiments of the grammar of 'pain' can and should be generalized, but not mechanically. It does not provide, as it were, a blueprint for the grammar of sensation-words in general, let alone for all psychological expressions. Although it is illuminating to compare the spontaneous utterance 'I have a pain' with a groan and to view it as a partial substitute for and learnt extension of this natural pattern of pain-behaviour, one cannot say the same of the report 'I have a dull nagging pain in the lumbar region' or 'I have a throbbing pain in my knee'. There is no natural expressive pain-behaviour that differentiates dull, nagging pains from throbbing ones. Numerous bodily sensations, e.g. of pressure, of swelling, sensations of tingling, of a hot flush, of heartburn, etc. have little if any distinctive, differentiating natural expression. Their primary behavioural manifestation *is* linguistic. (Does it make sense to say of a mouse that it has tingling sensations, feels nauseous, has a nagging ache in its shoulder?) Nevertheless, these more refined forms of verbal expressive behaviour are rooted in the more primitive ones. Once the primitive linguistic extension is grafted onto the natural expressive behaviour, further linguistic extensions grow. For the mastery of a language opens up the possibility of ever more subtle, refined, and linguistically differentiated pain-*behaviour*.

It may seem *prima facie* curious to suggest that the possibility of experience should be conditioned by the possibility of its expression. For we are inclined to think of experience as *given*; and whether it can be expressed and how it is expressed seem to be further matters. But this is obviously misconceived, as is evident as soon as one recollects that the criteria for having a certain experience lie in what a creature does (and *says*), and hence that the possibility of enjoying a given experience (and the intelligibility of ascribing or denying such-and-such an experience to a creature) turns upon the possibility (intelligibility) of its expression. It makes sense to say that a dog wants a bone now, but not that it now wants a bone next Sunday, for nothing in the behavioural repertoire of a dog would count as the expression of a desire to have a bone next Sunday. But the child who learns to use the exclamation 'Want!' in conjunction with a pointing gesture, instead of reaching for an object and crying, and who subsequently learns a tensed language becomes able to want things which it *could not* previously want, e.g. a new teddy bear for Christmas. The vast majority of our desires have no natural, pre-linguistic behavioural expression; but their expression is nevertheless rooted in the primitive behaviour of striving to get or crying for something or other.

4. *A spectrum of cases*

The affinity between spontaneous avowals and natural expressive behaviour must not mask the fact that the uses of first-person psychological sentences are heterogeneous. Some approximate to primitive cries and gestures, and others are far removed from those paradigms. Wittgenstein was not suggesting that there is no such thing as reporting, informing, telling others how things are subjectively with one. But what is called 'telling someone what one feels', 'describing one's state of mind', or even 'observing one's emotional state' are much more unlike reports, descriptions, and observations of the physical world than one thinks.

The uses of first-person psychological sentences constitute a whole spectrum of different cases. At one end of this spectrum there is a disparate cluster of exclamations, such as 'It hurts!', 'How nice to see you!', 'What a surprise!', that merge with spontaneous avowals such as 'I have a toothache', 'I'm furious with you!', 'I'm delighted', 'I do hope he'll come'. Here too are expressions of desire and intention, such as 'I'm hungry', 'I want a drink', 'I'll go', and avowals of thought and belief. Despite negative affinities (viz. *not* constituting descriptions, reports, observations, etc.), there are great differences. A groan of pain may be wrenched from me, but 'I'm furious with you!' is a flash of anger, and 'I am delighted' may be a gesture of pleasure. 'I want a drink' is often a request, and 'I prefer red wine', said when offered a mixed tray, is the expression of a choice. 'I don't believe it!' is often a cry of incredulity'; 'I think it is getting late' may be a suggestion that it is time to go, and 'I believe . . .' may be used as a polite denial, a tentative judgement, a confession of faith, or a passionate commitment. 'I feel great joy' and 'I'm so happy to see you!' are expressions of joy and delight, not statements of inner observations. But does 'joy' not designate (*bezeichnen*) something inner? 'No, "joy" designates nothing at all. Neither any inward nor any outward thing' (Z §487). The model of 'object and designation' is altogether inappropriate here (cf. PI §293).

The diversity is indefinitely large, and how we draw distinctions will be partly determined by our purposes in so doing. Relative to a given purpose, our differentiation of cases will depend upon the circumstances of utterance, the sentential context, and the accompanying behaviour – the tone of voice, facial expression, and gesture. But in all these cases the concept of *description* gets no grip. These fragments of expressive behaviour are no more assertions about one's state of mind than are such corresponding exclamations as 'You swine!', 'Water!', 'Red wine, please', 'No!', or 'Let's go!'. Of course, one can make inferences from them about the speaker's feelings, desires, attitudes, and beliefs, but that does not show that they are true or false descriptions. For one can make similar inferences from the corresponding exclamations, and no one would call those 'descriptions' (cf. RPP I §463). Indeed, the concepts of truth and falsehood are typically out of place here, although dissimulation and deception are possible in such contexts, as indeed they are with groans, smiles, or laughs. Similarly, the more such utterances approximate to exclamations, the less room there is for evaluating them as sincere or insincere; for this dimension of evaluation gets a firmer grip in relation to the articulate expression of one's inner life, confessions, and telling others how one feels or what one thinks. The innocent and the sincere are they who interpose nothing between their inner life and its outward articulation which would censor or distort.

Of course, these sentences can be used differently; but whether they are employed as articulate expressions of feelings, emotions, or attitudes or as reports is not determined by investigating what 'want', 'believe', or 'think' signify:

> We ask 'What does "I am frightened" really mean, what am I referring to when I say it?' And of course we find no answer, or one that is inadequate.
> The question is: 'In what sort of context does it occur?'

I can find no answer if I try to settle the question 'What am I referring to?', 'What am I thinking when I say it?' by repeating the expression of fear and at the same time attending to myself, as it were observing my soul through the corner of my eye. (PI p.188)

The roles of these expressions in our language-games cannot be clarified by 'semantic investigations' or by thinking about what stands *behind* them, what they report or describe. For in numerous contexts they do not report or describe anything. We need to look around, not behind – at the context and circumstances of use in the stream of life.

Between exclamations, avowals, and expressions on the one hand and genuine descriptions of mental states on the other lie hosts of inter-mediate cases of reports, articulations of thought, feeling, and attitude. I may vent my feelings so that you should appreciate my response to your behaviour, as when I say 'I'm very angry with you for breaking your promise'. This is not a spontaneous reaction of anger, but it is not a description of my state of mind either. 'I'm looking for my book', 'I intend going to London next Sunday', or 'I should like to spend next summer in Rome' are not spontaneous avowals but are uttered with the intention of conveying information. But they are not descriptions; nor do they rest on observation or evidence (RPP II §§176f.).

'I'm frightened' may be an exclamation of fear; but in a different context it may be uttered as a piece of information or as an explanation of why my hands are shaking. It can even be said with a smile as one wryly confesses one's trepidation (LW §§17, 20f.; PI p. 174). One can report what one thinks or intends, and such a cool confession of what one has in mind is not a spontaneous expression. Nevertheless, it is not a descrip-tion of anything either. To tell you what I think is not to describe an inner object or process with which I am uniquely acquainted (RPP I §572); for what I think is no object, and I am not 'acquainted' with my thoughts. If one insists that it is perfectly licit to talk about describing one's thoughts, Wittgenstein will issue no prohibitions, but only draw one's attention to grammatical differences:

If someone wants to call the words the 'description' of the thought instead of the 'expression' (*Ausdruck*) of the thought, let him ask himself how anyone learns to describe a table and how he learns to describe his own thoughts. And that only means: let him look and see how one judges the description of a table as right or wrong, and how the description of thoughts; so let him keep in view these language-games in all their situations (RPP I §572)

My expression of my thoughts may be faulty, but not because I am insufficiently observant – rather because I am insufficiently articulate. What I say may be wrong, but not because I have misidentified my thought. My confession of my thoughts may be inadequate, but not because I have made a mistake – rather because I have been untruthful or have held something crucial back, have exaggerated or understated.

Informing, telling, confessing, and reporting states of mind, sensations, and attitudes may be truthful or untruthful. One may lie about one's pains, feelings, and thoughts. But a lie about what one feels or thinks is unlike a lie about what another person feels or thinks. I tell a lie about A if I know him to be upset and assert that he is not, with intent to deceive. But I lie about my feelings or thoughts if I feel or think such-and-such and deny that I do, with intent to deceive. Moreover, when I say what I think or feel, my sincere confession is a criterion for my thoughts and feelings. But when I say, in all honesty, that A is upset, that does not guarantee (*ceteris paribus*) the truth of what I say.

In cases of confessing, reporting, or telling what one thinks, intends, or feels, one can typically answer the questions 'Why did you say that?' or 'What did you mean by that?'. But unlike similar questions asked of descriptions of objects, the answers here do not rest on observation and do not allude to features of an object being described. Rather, they characterize the point of the utterance, not its grounds, for it has none. Or they paraphrase the utterance to render it more perspicuous (PI p. 188).

Describing one's state of mind is indeed something one can do: but it is a much more specialized language-game than one might initially think (LW §50). Such descriptions are likely to be more accurate, refined, and observant in proportion to one's degree of self-consciousness or self-awareness. But self-consciousness is not consciousness of a 'self'. Whether a use of a form of words counts as a description of a state of mind is dependent upon the context and manner of utterance, e.g. upon antecedent discourse and upon the tone of voice of the speaker, his intentions and purposes (LW §43). The concept of a *state* of mind is far more restricted than philosophers typically assume. Intending, believing, thinking, for example, are not states of mind; and to say what one intends, believes, or thinks is never to describe one's mental state. States of mind have genuine duration (RPP II §722); hence they are typically described in the imperfect or continuous tense, interwoven with descriptions of what one did, how one reacted, what one was thinking about. 'I can't keep my mind on my work today; I keep on thinking of his coming' (PI §585); 'I have been afraid of his arrival all day long . . . immediately upon awakening I thought . . . then I considered . . . time and again I looked out of the window . . .' (RPP II §156); or 'I have been hoping for the whole day . . .' (RPP II §722) can legitimately be called 'descriptions of a mental state'.

A highly self-conscious person is one who attends to his emotional and conative life, who registers the ebb and flow of his passions, reactions, and attitudes. Such a person reflects upon his responses, analyses them, and searches for patterns that inform them. His descriptions of his mental states will typically be sensitive, detailed, and articulate. But even here, at this end of the spectrum of first-person psychological propositions, the relevant descriptions are very unlike descriptions of the 'outer'. They may be observant, but do not generally rest on observation. They may, in various ways, be inadequate or defective, but not because of misperception. Their typical flaws are likely to be forms of *self-deception*, rooted in a defect of the will rather than of the intellect, let alone of the senses. One who deceives himself about his state of mind, his motives, or intentions may or may not also deceive others. But if he does, it will not be because he is truthfully reporting a mistaken observation, but because he is being untruthful – with himself, and so too with others. There is no such thing as self-deception with respect to sensations, but our emotional life and avowals of motivation are run through with the distorting influence of the will and fantasy. So here, unlike the case of sensations and spontaneous avowals that are expressions of the 'inner', there is room for knowledge and error, i.e. self-knowledge properly speaking, and self-deception or failure to realize the pattern of one's reasons and desires. But this kind of knowledge, ignorance, and error is altogether unlike knowledge, ignorance, and error regarding what is 'outer'.

The spectrum of uses of first-person psychological sentences to which Wittgenstein drew attention involves subtle gradations. A corollary of that fact is that one often cannot say of a particular utterance that it lies at this or that point on a scale – for avowals, reports, and descriptions may occur in blends. If someone were to say 'I have spent the whole day in fear [and here he might elaborate in detail] . . . and now too I am full of anxiety', it would be misguided to try to classify his utterance as either avowal or report or description. 'Well, what should we say', Wittgenstein remarked, 'other than that here we have the use of the word "fear" in front of us?' (RPP II §156).

SECTION 290

1   §290(a) smoothly continues the argument. One says 'I am in pain' without justification. Whereas I identify the pain of another by reference to behavioural criteria (including his verbal behaviour), I do not identify my sensation by criteria, nor does a 'private' sample justify my utterance. Indeed I do not *identify* my sensation (for there is here no possibility of any misidentification). Rather, I repeat an expression the use of which is a manifestation or expression of pain, a learnt extension of natural behavioural manifestations of pain (cf. PI §244). My utterance no more rests on justifying grounds than do my groans of pain. But this is not the end of the language-game; it is the beginning. In this respect the language-games with avowals are altogether different from the language-games with descriptions of physical objects. *There* the language-game terminates with a description[28] (e.g. of my room) which may be true or false, ill-informed or well-informed, more or less accurate, perceptive and skilful, or crude. And *that* language-game begins with observation, perhaps with careful scrutiny. Its terminus is subject to correction, improvement, and refinement.

§290(b) indicates one source of confusion. We are inclined, when philosophizing, to project the features of one language-game onto another. We think that the concept of *description* is uniform across language-games. (And at root, we think, all words are names, all sentences descriptions!) We take 'I have a pain' to be a description of the speaker's state of mind, and so conceive this language-game to begin with the sensation, which is observed, identified, ascribed to a subject (I) to whom one refers in the description which is the terminus of the language-game. For when I describe my room, e.g. 'The sofa-table has a K'ang-Hsi vase on it', I observe the items in the room, identify them, satisfy myself that I know how things are, and refer to them in the description I give. But these language-games are altogether different. I do not observe my sensations, nor do I identify them. There is no question of my knowing or not knowing how things are with me here. The first-person pronoun thus used is not a referring expression (see 'I and my self', §4), and in an avowal such as 'I have a pain' I do not ascribe

---

[28] Of course, the language-game may continue, e.g. with an argument about the correctness of the description, in which case the description is the terminus of the first phase of the game.

an experience to a person to whom I refer (cf. Exg. §§404 – 10). An avowal of pain is not a description of one's state of mind, nor is it a description of one's pain (see 'Avowals and descriptions', §2).

2   This theme preoccupied W. throughout the late thirties and early forties, and becomes even more prominent in the *Remarks on the Philosophy of Psychology* and *Last Writings*. The following is a selection of only a few remarks leading up to the *Investigations*.
    LPE 302 observes:

There seems to be a *description* of my behaviour, and also, in the same sense, a description of my pain! The one, so to speak, the description of an external, the other of an internal fact. This corresponds to the idea that in the sense in which I can give a part of my body a name, I can give a name to a private experience (only indirectly).
    And I am drawing your attention to this: that the language-games are very much more different than you think.
    You couldn't call moaning a description! But this shows you how far the proposition 'I have toothache' is from a description . . .
    In 'I have toothache' the expression of pain is brought to the same form as a description 'I have 5 shillings'.

    And in the lectures (LSD 11) W. nicely crystallized this thought: 'What we call the description of feeling is as different from the description of an object as "the name of a feeling" is different from "the name of an object" ' (cf. LSD 44).
    Vol. XVI, 114 gives a striking analogy: I explain draughts to a fool. I show him the initial positions and the black and white pieces. He says, 'I understand: and whoever gets the white has won'. I reply, 'No, this has as yet nothing to do with winning and losing'. This is similar to: with someone's utterance 'I have pains', the language-game only begins.
    Subsequently (Vol. XVI, 133) W. elaborates: Another person can no more *check* that what he has is really what we call 'pain' than I can,[29] for there is no such thing in this language-game. The language-game begins with his *saying* that he has pains, not with his *knowing*. The great difficulty here is not to present matters as if there were something one cannot do, i.e. as if there were an inner object from which one derives a description, but which one cannot show anyone else; as if the language-game really began not with the expression (*Äusserung*) of pain but with the 'private object'. On p. 137 W. queries whether his remark that the language-game begins with the expression of pain is a grammatical truism (as it should be). He compares it with 'The game begins with *telling one's dream*, for this of course does not mean that one does not believe someone who says, 'Last night I dreamt . . . ! One can appar-

[29] Of course, I can check – but not in the way envisaged. And in *that* way, he cannot check either.

ently say both: the game begins with the dream, and the game begins with telling it.

This hesitation disappears in the longer discussion in Vol. XII, 242ff. in which the material is reworked. One is tempted to say that I can never really *know* whether another has said the ABC to himself in his imagination. But can he know that? What if one said 'He too cannot know this, he can only say it'? So does he *not* know? No, that would be wrong too! (He *cannot* know, not: he does not know – and the *cannot* here is logical, not epistemological; it signifies senselessness, not ineradicable ignorance.) To say that he does not know would mean that he doubts, is uncertain. Rather, there is here no question of either knowing or doubting. The language-game begins with someone saying that he imagines . . . The language-game begins as it were with a description which does not correspond to something described (cf. Vol. XVI, 133); but this grammatical remark could also be wholly misleading. The conception of remembering as an inner process makes it possible for us to make an assumption about this process, apparently without concerning ourselves about how and whether this inner process is expressed. But now this assumption is *empty* as long as it is not coupled with an assumption about the outer process. Then follows a re-draft of Vol. XVI, 137 (see above), with the comparison of expressions of pain with telling a dream, but without the qualifying clause. For presumably W. came to think that although it may appear that one *can* say that the game begins with a dream, this is *far more* misleading than to block that route. 'The language-game only begins with the expression (*Äusserung*)', W. concludes, *is* the difference between a description of an inner experience or process and a description of a physical fact or fact of the 'outer world'.

Earlier in the volume W. remarked:

Eine Äusserung der Empfindung kann man vergleichen dem Blatt das ein Kartspieler erhält. Es ist ein Ausgangstellung des Spieles, aber noch kein Ergebnis desselben. (Vol. XIII, 170)

(A manifestation of a sensation is comparable to the hand which a card-player holds. It is a starting-point of the game, but not the outcome of one.)

MS. 165, 160f. contains the first final draft of PI §290, followed by a remark contrasting a description of a room, which, as a matter of fact, only I have seen, with a description of something which only I *can* (logically) 'see'.

SECTION 291

This highlights the conclusion of §290. The form of the sentence 'I have a pain' does not show that it is a description (although in certain circumstances, such a sentence might be used as a *report*, e.g. the doctor asks 'How are you this morning?', and I reply 'I have a pain in my back'). But that is not to say that there is no such thing as a description of one's own state of mind (see 'Avowals and descriptions', §4). In the grip of the Augustinian picture of language, philosophers are prone to conceive of the essential role of propositions as describing. The *Tractatus* did so in claiming that the essential function of propositions is to describe states of affairs and that the general propositional form is 'This is how things are'. More recently, it has been extensively argued that the sense of a sentence, no matter whether it is declarative, interrogative, or imperative, is given by its *truth-condition*, which specifies how things must be for it (or, with more refinement, for its sentence-radical) to be true. Hence we think of propositions as word-pictures (descriptions) of the facts (and may, as in the *Tractatus*, make this idea into the pivot of a general account of the essential nature of any possible language).

This is misleading. First, it disregards the *diversity* of pictures: still-lives, portraits, landscapes, mythological or fictional representations, historical paintings, ornamental designs, maps, diagrams (Vol. XII, 233), not to mention *trompe l'oeil* pictures, abstract paintings, collages, etc. Secondly, the idea abstracts from the diverse *functions* of pictures: we think primarily of pictures that hang on the wall, that are there to be looked at. (Although *even here* one should distinguish the different function of a picture of the Pantocrator in a Byzantine church from that of a picture of the crucified Christ or of the Madonna of Mercy, and these from a picture of Charles I by van Dyck glorifying the monarch, and that too from Bosch's moralistic fantasies, and these from genre-paintings, from *mementi mori*, etc.) So we tend to forget such pictures as machine drawings, cross-sections of mouldings, architectural blueprints with elevations and measurements, which are *used* in making or building things or in checking whether they are properly constructed.

By analogy, we should examine the different *uses* of propositions, for although they may all appear as if they are descriptions of how things are, they are not. '25 > 24' sounds like 'John is taller than Mary', but it is not a description of how things are in the realm of numbers, since there is no such thing as a realm of numbers, and propositions of arithmetic are not descriptions of anything. 'Nothing can run faster than a cheetah' and 'Nothing can be red and green all over' look alike; yet the latter is not a description of an impossibility, but the expression of a grammatical rule. So too 'I have a pin' and 'I have a pain' look alike, but while the former describes a state of affairs, the latter is typically an *Äusserung*.

Furthermore, within the domain of what *can* legitimately be called 'descriptions' there is much greater logical diversity than comes to the blinkered philosophical eye. A description of my room, a fictional description of a house, a description of my state of mind, and a description of a project are very different. They are subject to different kinds of fault, are correctable or improvable in altogether different ways, and involve different skills. A Proust may excel at describing his state of mind, but not because his inner vision is so superior to normal mental eyesight. A Tolstoy may wonderfully describe the lives, thoughts, and feelings of his characters, but not because he can see possible worlds in the realm of fiction. A Marlborough may describe his campaign plans in meticulous detail, and things may happen just as he planned; but the excellence of his description is not a matter of the foresight of the gypsy crone reading off the future from a crystal ball – although it is, in another sense, a matter of meticulous foresight.

2   Vol. XII, 219f., in the course of a long discussion of descriptions, observes that we do not note, e.g., the fact that the description of a landscape, coupled with an ostension that it is in such-and-such a place, lends itself to a further possibility of application; viz. it enables one to find one's way. Contrast this with a description of one's visual impression (i.e. of how things visually strike one). We forget that what we call 'description' can occupy different positions in the language-game.

SECTION 292

1   The conception of a proposition as essentially a description, *a fortiori* the conception of a proposition as a word-picture of the facts, is often associated with the thought that we 'read it off from the facts'. For it seems that we observe that things are thus-and-so, and that we then make use of names correlated with the observed things to frame a proposition describing the fact observed. In this way it appears as if a fact is portrayed mechanically according to the rules of correlation that give words their meanings and that the description can be straightforwardly compared with reality to check on its truth.

This, however, is doubly misleading. First, in the case of first person psychological utterances, 'there is no comparing of proposition and reality. (Collating.)' (LPE 294). In one's expressions of sensation or perception, of memory or intention, there is no such thing as observing *in foro interno* an array of psychological facts accessible only to the eye of the mind, which one then *describes* for the benefit of others. Secondly, given that the first point is accepted, the comparison of 'I have pains' with 'The rose is red' becomes misleading in a different way. It encourages the misconception that whereas the latter is well-founded, resting firmly upon a rule (viz. an ostensive definition of 'red' by reference to a sample) which can be invoked to justify the proposition and employed in comparing the proposition with reality, the psychological utterance is free-floating and hence vulnerable, for it is unjustified. Though this conception is in one sense quite correct, it misrepresents matters. For the avowal, though unjustified in the sense elaborated (cf. Exg §289), is as firm as the earth beneath our feet, as reliable (barring insincerity, etc.) as the natural cry of pain, exclamation of joy, or snarl of anger. And on the other hand, we forget that even in cases where we can characterize propositions as having a grammatical justification, e.g. by reference to a sample which is a constituent of a rule, the rule does not contain its own application. The sample does not guide us in its use. Rather, *we* have to apply the rule (and employ the sample) in a general practice. W. insists that when one says 'I am in pain', one says so without justification, and this seems to deprive one of any right to say it. But that thought rests on a misconceived comparison. For one has here a confused picture of normative compulsion. One has as much right (though no justification) to say 'I have a pain' in appropriate circumstances as one has to say 'That thing is red' (even though in this latter case one can adduce a grammatical justification or rule).

Note that W.'s point is not to show that expressions (*Äusserungen*) of the 'inner' and judgements of the 'outer' are equally shaky and vulnerable, that a kind of naturalistic scepticism is something we must live with, a part of the human condition. On the contrary, it is to remind us that though the earth is unsupported in space, it is as firm as firm can be, and we need not fear falling!

SECTION 293

1   W. reverts to the issue of privacy. One is inclined to think that one knows what 'pain' means only from one's own case, for it seems that it is the sensation one *has* that gives the word its meaning (cf. §283). One is 'intimately acquainted' with one's own sensations (for, one argues, '*I* have them', and no one else can have *my* sensations). And what one *has* is conceived as a private sample that defines 'pain'. This is the *semi-solipsism* against which W. wars (MS. 165, 150) – 'semi-solipsism' since the proponent of this philosophical mythology does *not* argue that he is the only person who has pain (indeed, the only person who *can* intelligibly be said to have pain). Rather does he claim that others likewise know what 'pain' means from their sensation; i.e. he generalizes his own case. But can one generalize this one case so irresponsibly, particularly when one has not the slightest guidance as to *how* one should generalize it (MS. 124, 255)?

Note that the problem of 'generalizing one's own case' here does not address the question of how I know that others are in pain, but rather how I know how others assign meaning to 'pain'. For 'the essential thing about private experience is really not that each person possesses his own exemplar, but that no one knows whether other people also have *this* or something else' (PI §272). The solipsist, of course, argues that it is unintelligible that anyone but he should have *this*. But the 'semi–solipsist' pretends that each person, in his private language, names his sensations, as if they were objects in a peep-show into which only he can peer (MS. 124, 228).

§293(b) explores an analogy: 'beetle' is the name given to whatever is in each person's box, into which no one else can look; and everyone says he knows what a beetle is (what 'beetle' means) by looking into his own box. But here (a) every person might have something different in his box, and (b) what is in each person's box might change constantly. If (a) were the case, no one could know it (PI §272). If (b) were the case, it would make no difference to the meaning of 'beetle', which simply signifies whatever is in the box. Now suppose that 'beetle' had a use in the *common* language of these people. One point is clear: it would not be used as the name of a thing; it would not be used as we use names of ordinary objects. (One might say here that the phrase 'Whatever is in my box' is not the name of an object. But, of course, 'beetle' in each person's envisaged 'private' language is not used as the phrase 'Whatever is in my box' is used in ordinary language.) If 'beetle' were to have a use in their common language, then it would have no connection with what is in each person's private box – which might, as far as mutual communication by means of a common language is concerned, be empty. It would not even mean merely *something* (cf. PI §261). If what is in the box is relevant to the meaning of 'beetle', then no one else can understand what I mean by 'beetle'; and if 'beetle' is understood by others, it cannot signify what is in each person's private box.

§293(c) draws the conclusion: *if* we construe the grammar of the expression of sensation on the model of object and name, then the object drops out of consideration as irrelevant. If we think of 'pain' as the name of a sensation we have on the model of names of objects (in a generalized sense of 'object'), then solipsism is unavoidable. A public language cannot be construed as the confluence of private languages that happen to coincide. (A good angel is always necessary (RFM 378), but even a good angel could not engineer *this*!) And the incoherence of solipsism is a consequence of the logical impossibility of a private language.

1   (i) 'Nun, ein Jeder . . . ': 'Well, everyone . . . '.

(ii) 'One might even imagine such a thing constantly changing': cf. §271 and the method of demonstrating that the hypothesis of a private object is an idle wheel in the mechanism.

(iii) 'Gegenstand und Bezeichnung': 'Bezeichnung eines Dinges' was translated in the previous paragraph as 'name of a thing', so better 'object and name'.

2   LSD 124 clarifies how the 'private object' drops out of consideration as
      irrelevant. Suppose that each person has a private object which no one
      else can see. Everyone has mastered the colour-vocabulary, and now a
      game of describing the colour of one's private object is introduced.
      Suppose someone, quite sincerely, looks into his private box, sees a blue
      object, and says 'red'. Is he wrong? No, he is neither right nor wrong,
      for there is no technique of applying colour-words to private objects *on
      the model* of *applying them to public ones*. There is no *method* of comparing a
      sample with a private object. (Of course, we can say what colours our
      after-images are; but does it make sense to say 'He had a red after-image,
      knew what colour-words mean, but believed his after-image was blue'?)
      It makes no sense to say 'Play the same game with the private object', for
      nothing has been determined to *count* as *the same*. (Contrast 'Play the
      same game as tennis, only without the ball' with 'Play the same game as
      chess, only the winner is he who gets checkmated'). Of course, the
      premise of the argument is *absurd* (for this argument is a *reductio*), for does
      it really make sense to say 'It was blue but he said it was red'? One might
      respond by saying 'All right, let's lay down a rule for application of
      colour-words to what is "internal" – viz. that it shall make no difference
      (i.e. they shall be applied just as they are applied to what is "external")'.
      W. replies ironically, 'Yes, that's just it, it *doesn't* make any difference.'

2.1   'not even as a something'; cf. MS. 158, 80; the 'something' is an idle
      wheel in the mechanism.

                            SECTION 294

1   This draws together the argument of §261 and §293, but here, unlike
      §293(a), W. is not concerned with the private object as a pseudo-sample
      which is purportedly used to give a meaning to a sensation-word, but
      with the private object as an object of description. To conceive of a
      sensation, sense-impression, or mental image conjured up when recol-
      lecting or imagining something as a *private picture* is to conceive of it as an
      object that can (logically) be *described* in the sense in which a public
      picture can be described. So to say of another that he has a private picture
      before him is already to make an *assumption* about what he has (e.g. we
      assume, in the analogy of §293, that he has a beetle in his box). In
      particular, this assumption implies that we too can or do describe more
      closely what he has. For the idea of a describable object which is *logically*
      describable by only one person is incoherent. It is the correlate of the
      equally incoherent idea of a rule that can *logically* be understood and
      followed by only one person. For the private object, which we envisage
      as being described by the person who has it, is also conceived as being

used as a private sample in the mental ostensive definition of a word which only he can understand.

But we must admit that we have not the faintest idea of what kind of thing it might be that he has before him (cf. §§261, 272). That is to say, even the *category* of the thing is undetermined; for we cannot say that he has a *sensation* (or *mental image of a colour*) before him, since these expressions too are words of common language which need (and have) rules for their use. So with what right do we say that, despite our total ignorance, at any rate we know that he has *something*. For the word 'something' is not, as it were, a minimal description that cannot be faulted. In its significant use it is akin to a variable the value-range of which is determined in advance. 'Something happened in the street just now' determines an *event*; 'Something is at the back of the drawer' determines a physical *object*. 'Something crossed my mind' determines a thought or idea; 'He did something astonishing' determines an act; 'I felt something in my leg' determines a sensation (a twinge or pain) or bodily state (a swelling or a lump); 'He told me something interesting' determines a piece of information; 'I thought I heard something' determines a noise – in short, the use of 'something' commits one to something, not to nothing. And what it commits one to is a more or less determinate range of possibilities, *not* a minimal piece of knowledge that is indefeasible. But the misguided philosopher's use of 'something' here is cut free of these constraints, hence is comparable to 'He has something; but I don't know whether it is money or debts or an empty till', i.e. if that is all I know, then I know *nothing* about what he has, not even whether he has anything of whatever kind. For if nothing can count as something, then having a mere something before one counts for nothing!

2   This derives from Vol. XII, 205ff. We imagine that there is such a thing as a subjective regularity, which exists only for the subject and only he can know, etc. But this is incoherent, for we have no reason for calling whatever he purports to have 'a regularity', or for thinking that what he purports to be doing is rightly called 'a (language) game', or indeed that what we are dealing with is 'a language'. That is, we employ here a picture of a 'private object' which only he can see. But is this really a picture? It is of the nature of such a picture that we can make further suppositions about this object and about what he does with it; it is not enough to say that he has a private something and does something with it! Then follows a comparison of a description of a dream or of a sense-impression. Here too one cannot say that what the person describes is something (an inner picture) which only he can see. After a lengthy detour, a draft of PI §294 occurs on p. 209, followed by the remark 'Isn't it like this – you first imagine for yourself what it is that he has before him (viz. a private picture), which you then explain as being

quite groundless (since we admit that, *ex hypothesi*, we cannot know what he has before him), and yet you still insist that he has something before him!'

Vol. XVI, 58 has the last sentence of PI §294 followed by the query 'How do you know he has a private picture before him?', to which the interlocuter replies 'Because I have one before me'. This W. denies; one *says* that, but there are neither more nor less grounds for using this figure of speech in one's own case than in the case of others. One wants to reply that one imagines something vividly, one sees it before one, but one's neighbours cannot see it, for it belongs to oneself alone. But, W. retorts, it is here just a metaphor to talk of seeing something 'before one' or 'in one's mind's eye'. If someone else imagines the same, does he not see the very same thing before him? One might reply, 'He surely can't have the same pains as I'. But why not? What is the criterion of identity? Then follows PI §398.

Section 295

1   A deflationary remark on §293(a). If the proposition that one knows what 'pain' means only from one's own case were empirical, then it might be otherwise – i.e. one might know what 'pain' means without reference to one's aches and pains. But that the private language theorist will not wish to concede, for, he will insist, one *cannot* know what 'pain' means unless one has had pains (cf. §315). Yet if it is not an empirical proposition, is it a *grammatical* one? If it were, then it would be a rule of grammar that someone who had never suffered pain but who used the word 'pain' correctly did *not* know what the word 'pain' meant, even though he said of others that they were in pain only when they had hurt themselves and of himself that he had no pain. But we employ no such rule; on the contrary, such a rule would conflict with what we mean by 'understands or knows the meaning of "pain" '.

Suppose everyone *did* say (as so many philosophers have) that they know . . . only from their own case. This remark gives no information, either empirical or grammatical; but it might be viewed as a picture, an iconographic representation in words of a segment of our grammar. What fragment of our language might it illustrate? W. gives no clue here (nor do the MS. sources 124, 258f. and 129, 60). But whatever W. had in mind here, the moral is clear enough. When doing philosophy, we adduce such pictorial representations as if they were descriptions. But we misinterpret such a picture as a description of the facts, rather than as an emblem – as if we were to take the sand-glass of Father Time to be the master-clock of time-measurement. Other such illustrated turns of speech are manifest in our talking of the flow of time (the river of time), in our pictures of the mental as inner, and in our representation of the laws of logic as adamantine.

SECTION 296

1   The interlocutor reverts to §294, for it constantly strikes him as if W. is denying that when one emits a cry of pain, there is *any pain*! But no one would deny that when one stubs one's toe and cries out, one cries out *in pain*. Or that when one cries out thus, one cries out *because* one has hurt oneself. Or that the pain is sometimes frightful. Or that it is important. But this is news from nowhere. The almost irresistible temptation to object that 'there is *something* accompanying my cry of pain' is rooted in the ideas that an inner 'something' defines the concept of pain, that 'pain' means this inner accompaniment of a cry of pain, and that the verbal expression of pain is *justified* by reference to it. But these moves have been shown to be futile. They reflect multiple misconceptions of the grammar of 'pain' and, more generally, of the grammar of the expression of sensation (§293). Like 'I know . . . only from my own case' the interlocutor's remark here conveys no information. It is merely another pictorial representation of our grammar.

2 Vol. XVII, 7ff. has a twenty-page discussion of this.

SECTION 297

1 In §296 the interlocutor insists, quite rightly, that when he cries out in pain, he is *not just behaving*. But this truism is accompanied by a complete misconstrual of the grammar of sensation, manifest in his insistence that there is *something* accompanying his cry of pain (§296). Moreover, he conceives of the pain which he expresses in his utterance 'I have a pain' as akin to a private picture which he describes (§294), so that 'I have a pain' is read off these inner facts and portrayed in words according to rules (§292). He thinks that he knows what the word 'pain' means by reference to the private picture that is before him, viz. his pain or what he conjures up in his imagination when he imagines a pain (§293(a), §300). That is, he thinks not merely that *pain* enters into the language-game with sensation-words, but that a private *picture of pain* does too. It gets described; and it also functions as a private sample or paradigm that defines what 'pain' means.

The analogy of §297 is meant to undermine this conception. In a picture of water boiling in a pot ('a kettle' would be more vivid here) picture-steam comes out of the pictured pot. But it would be absurd to claim that there must also be *something* boiling in the picture of the pot. Rather, the picture is a picture *of* water boiling in the pot; we do not need to add anything to the picture of a kettle with steam coming out of its spout to make it a picture of water boiling in the kettle. Indeed, we could not; that is already what it is a picture of.

Here the pot (or kettle) in the picture is the body, the steam is the behaviour (the cry of pain), and the water is the pain. 'There must be something boiling in the picture of the pot' resembles 'Somebody who expresses pain must have *something* that accompanies his cry of pain (something important and frightful).' It is as misguided to treat pain as *something* which accompanies an avowal of pain as it is to say that *something* must be boiling in the picture of the pot if picture-steam comes out of a picture-pot. (How can picture-steam come from nothing, given that steam cannot come from nothing?!)

Elaborating further: in the language-game with pain (as in the picture of the boiling pot) no *picture* or *paradigm* of pain plays any role, just as no picture of bubbling water plays any role in the picture of water boiling in a (closed) pot. But it is a picture of water boiling in a pot for all that!

This analogy points both backwards and forwards in the text. Looking backwards to §294, it clarifies the absurdity of making an assumption about what he has before him (viz. a private picture). This is as absurd a *assuming* that there is something boiling in the picture of the pot. It also makes clear why the interlocutor's remark in §296 stems from misunderstanding. For the 'something' that 'accompanies' one's cry of pain is not important *because* it gives meaning to the word 'pain' as a picture or paradigm which one knows only from one's own case (§295). The metaphor points forward to §300, for in the language-game with pain, there is no such thing as a *picture* (paradigmatic sample) which plays a role in the grammar of 'pain'.

2   This derives from Vol. XII, 207 (Vol. XVI, 56f.) introduced above (Exg. §294, 2). In our conception of a subjective regularity we employ a picture (a simile) of a 'private object' which only its owner can see; but we must make it clear to ourselves that this is *only a simile*. W. examines the case of someone describing his dream. Here too, one is inclined to say that he saw a picture (or image) before him which he describes for us. But a picture that is described is something visible to all. That is evidently not in question here; so one might say that the 'picture' described when describing a dream is not a 'material' picture, but rather akin to one's *sense-impression* of a material picture. But then one cannot characterize it as 'a picture which only I can see' (for I don't *see* my sense-impression, and others do not *overlook* it). Rather, the *Vorstellungs-bild* is the picture which is described when one describes *what* one imagines (cf. PI §367), i.e. to describe what one imagines is not to

describe an *image* but a state of affairs, which one has imagined. To characterize one's sense-impressions, imaginings, or dreams as *pictures* (i.e. something from which one can read off a description) is to employ the *simile* of a 'material' picture. Then follows PI §297.

SECTION 298

1   'This *something* is the important thing' (PI §296) is the interlocutor's refrain; and he thinks that he can pick out the 'something' (without committing himself to what sort of thing it is) by pointing inwardly. Yet nothing but misunderstanding engenders this thought. Dozens of false pictures succeed each other here, false pictures of the 'inner' and 'outer', of meaning and understanding, of language and explanation, of experience and knowledge, of doubt and certainty, of naming and describing, of the use of 'having' and of 'something', all reinforcing one another. Hence the strength of the inclination to make such empty remarks as 'This is the important thing', 'I have *something*' (§294), or 'I know . . . only from my own case' (§295).

2   In MS. 124, 259f. this is followed by the remark that 'Yes, but there is something there all the same . . . ' (cf. PI §296) already incorporates the wrong picture. For one says 'something' in order to leave open the possibility that it need not always be the *same*, but only something upon which the cry of pain can rest.

SECTION 299

1   That we are inclined, even irresistibly inclined, to make such philosophical observations as 'I surely have something (at least that's certain)' or 'I know . . . only from my case' does not mean that one is being forced (by the facts!) into making an *assumption* (for these are not meant as empirical observations which could be otherwise (§295(a)). Nor does it mean that one has here immediate or intuitive knowledge which inclines one irresistibly. On the contrary, what we, when doing philosophy, 'are tempted to say' in all these cases is the raw material of philosophy, something for philosophical treatment (PI §254).

2   BB 59f. emphasizes that the solipsist's 'Only I feel real pain' is not stating an opinion (parallel to 'an assumption' in §299). 'That's why he is so sure of what he says. He is irresistibly tempted to use a certain form of expression; but we must yet find *why* he is.'

SECTION 300

1   This examines one of the things which we are 'irresistibly inclined to say' (PI §299) when we surrender ourselves to philosophical reflection on the 'inner' and the 'outer'. Grasping W.'s remarks here is made difficult by the fact that while 'image' corresponds to 'Vorstellungsbild', it does not uniformly correspond to 'Vorstellung'. The English 'image' is much more closely associated with what can be pictured or sculpted (as in 'graven images') than is the German 'Vorstellung'. It is with some strain that we speak of 'auditory images', and 'image of a taste' or 'image of a smell' is surely going too far. But 'Die Vorstellung des Geschmacks von Zucker' is perfectly licit, as is 'Die Vorstellung des Schmerzes'. However, the latter is unhappily translated as 'image of pain'. Moreover, although we speak of the memory of an event still being fresh or of the memories that come flooding back to one, there is in English, unlike German, no corresponding expression for 'imagination' and its cognates. The divergences make the accurate translation of W.'s remark here and in related texts almost impossible. Consequently the verbal form 'imagining pain' has, with misgivings, been adopted as a rough rendering of 'Die Vorstellung des Schmerzes', and, at the cost of clumsiness, the German 'Vorstellung' has often been retained in what follows.

    We are tempted to say that it is not just the picture of behaviour, or *paradigm* of behaviour, that plays a role in the language-game with 'He is in pain', but also the picture or paradigm of pain. Many reasons incline us to think thus: (a) It seems that I know what 'pain' means only from my own case, which furnishes me with a picture or paradigm of pain. (b) It appears that when I say 'I have a pain' I describe the inner facts (as I describe a picture) in words, just as when I say 'I have a penny' I describe 'outer' facts. (c) To say of another that he is in pain is not to describe his behaviour, but, it seems, it is to attribute to him what I have when I am in pain; and here one must be able to recollect what it is that one has when one has a pain (and is that not an 'inner picture'?). (d) We readily think that to understand a sentence, one must be able to imagine something for every word; in particular, to understand what 'I am in pain' means, one must know what it would be like to be in pain, i.e. to imagine it (PI §449(a)). So surely to understand the sentence 'He is in pain', one must be able to imagine pain. Does this not show that the picture or paradigm of pain plays a role in the language-game?

    The point upon which W. focuses here is a confusion concerning the relationship between the concept of a mental image and that of a picture. Clearly, pictures are objects of comparison, and equally clearly, mental images can correspond to pictures. So we are inclined to think that mental images are likewise objects of comparison. Indeed, we are prone to conceive of mental images *as* pictures. They seem to be just like pictures, save for being mental! This is multiply confused. Imagining pain (*Die Vorstellung des Schmerzes*) is not having a picture of pain (*ist kein Bild*). One can imagine a toothache or remember a headache, but this does not furnish one with a picture; there is nothing here employable *as* a picture or a paradigm, not even as a picture which only oneself (as it happens) can see. The description of the imagined is not a description of an inner picture, but a description of what one imagines (e.g. the face that launched a thousand ships (cf. PI §367)). Similarly, the description of the recollected is a description of what I remember, perhaps only hazily, not a description of a hazy picture. There is no such thing as using a *Vorstellung* of pain (as one *can* use a picture of something) as a sample or paradigm. Even in those cases where one can intelligibly talk of (vivid) images (*Vorstellungsbilder*), one's mental image is not a sample or paradigm, for there is no such thing as a method of projection for a mental image. One cannot lay a mental image alongside reality for comparison. But it is important that if, e.g. I imagine a shade of red (and perhaps have a vivid image of it), I can paint what I imagine, and *that can* be used as a paradigm. 'That ↗ is how I imagined the backcloth to be', I might say to the scene-painter, while pointing at a patch of paint. Here the image of red is replaceable by a paradigm (picture) of red. But nothing corresponds to imagining a pain (*die Vorstellung des Schmerzes*) as a red sample corresponds to imagining, having an image of, red. Hence the *Vorstellung* of pain is not replaceable by anything that can function as an object of comparison.

It is obvious that when I imagine a toothache, I cannot compare the *Vorstellung* directly *with another's behaviour* to determine whether he has such a toothache. Nor can one lay it alongside another person's toothache for comparison, as one can lay a sample of red alongside an object to determine whether the object is to be said to be red (cf. BB 53). And one cannot paint a picture of the imagined toothache, as one can paint imagined toothache-behaviour or the colour one imagined. Indeed, the *Vorstellung des Schmerzes* is not replaceable by *anything* that could be called a picture or paradigm of pain, for there is no such thing. There is such a thing as a picture of someone's being in pain. Also such a thing as imagining a pain, and such a thing as imagining someone to be in pain without showing it (cf. PI §393 and Exg. §302) – and here one does *not* imagine pain-behaviour.

How does the *Vorstellung* of pain enter the language-game? *Not* where we would expect it (cf. Z §636), but in all sorts of ways: for we tell each other to imagine how awful this or that pain must be, we empathize with each other, saying 'I can well imagine it, it must have been dreadful', and so on (see 2.1 below).

1.1   *this* image': viz. of pain; other images (*Vorstellungsbilder*), of course, are replaceable by pictures.

2   Much material underlies this remark. Some of the salient points are as follows: (a) An image is not a kind of picture and cannot be used as one (WWK 97; cf. Exg. §301). (b) One can imagine another person's pain no less than his pain-behaviour. If one imagines another person's pain-behaviour or his black eye, one can replace the imagining by a painted image. This picture can be compared with what it is a picture of to see whether it is correct. 'The sense in which an image is an image is determined by the way in which it is compared with reality. This we might call the method of projection' (BB 53). But now, if we vividly imagine that someone suffers pain (and perhaps imagine that, by a great effort of will, he does not show it), is there any such thing as comparing the imagined pain with his actual pain? 'If you say, you compare them "indirectly" via his bodily behaviour, I answer that this means you *don't* compare them as you compare the picture of his behaviour with his behaviour' (ibid.). (c) An 'image of pain' contrasts with an 'image of pain-behaviour'. In the latter case, one can show another person what one's image is like. In the former, one might ask 'How did you learn the expression "imagining pain"?', but one cannot *point* at an image (LSD 39). (d) The idea that a picture of pain plays a role in the language-game stems from thinking of imagining pain as having a private picture of pain. W. draws an analogy with his example of a private table of colours which is apparently consulted (privately) by each player, but which actually plays no role in the game. The impression that there is a (genuine) private table in the game (and a *picture* of pain in the language-game) stems from the *absence* of a table (and a picture) coupled with the similarity of the game to one played with a table (picture) (Z §552). Here, one might say, the language-game with 'pain' is deceptively similar to the language-game with *colours*. (e) Imagining or remembering pain cannot serve to *define* 'pain' (Vol. XVII, 10). (f) One is misled by the fact that descriptions of what is seen and what is imagined are of the same kind (indeed, the same description may, in different contexts, serve both roles). But the concepts are otherwise utterly dissimilar. Imagining is more a doing than a receiving, a creative act (RPP II §111 = Z §637). Yet the similarity inclines one to compare a description of one's imaginings to a description of a picture, which, one adds, is an 'inner' one!

2.1   'Wohl tritt die Vorstellung des Schmerzes in einem Sinn ins Sprach-spiel ein': Vol. XII, 84, after a draft of PI §449, has:

   Damit meine ich natürlich nicht, dass es in manchen Sprachspielen nicht wesentlich ist, dass man an gewissen Punkten den Übergang von den Worten zur Vorstellung mache – Wenn wir dem Arzt mitteilen, wir hätten Schmerzen – in welchen Fällen ist es nützlich, dass er sich einen Schmerz vorstellt? – Und wie ist es übrigens: sich einen Schmerz vorstellen? Geschieht dies nicht auf sehr mannigfache Weise. (So mannigfach, wie: sich an einen Schmerz erinnern.)

(Naturally I do not mean that it is not essential in some language-games that the transition at certain points from the words to imagining be made – when we tell a doctor that we have been having pains – in what cases is it useful for him to imagine a pain? – And doesn't this happen in a variety of ways? (As great a variety as: remembering a pain.)

SECTION 301

1   An image, which one may have when one imagines or remembers something, is not an 'inner picture'. But a picture may correspond to such an image, for one can often paint a picture of what one imagines and say 'This is how I imagined it' (cf. §280). Is this always possible, i.e. does it always *make sense*? No; for it is clear from §300 that though I can imagine a severe toothache, no picture corresponds here as a picture of someone clutching his swollen jaw corresponds to imagining someone manifesting a bad toothache.

2   This remark derives from MS. 130, 33, where it occurs in a list of chapters or section-headings for a book. W. never did collect together the huge mass of remarks on mental images and their relation to pictures. In the *Investigations* the subject is taken up in §§363ff.
     It is noteworthy that already in 1930 W. categorially differentiated mental images from pictures, thus taking a stand against the pervasive tradition in philosophy and psychology:

> An image of 'yellow' is not a picture of yellow that I have seen in the sense in which I carry a picture of my friend, for instance, in my wallet. An image is a picture in an entirely different, formal sense . . . *An image of colour has the same multiplicity as the colour.* That is what its connection with reality consists in. (WWK 97)

This is partly right and partly wrong. That an image must have in one sense the same multiplicity as that of which it is an image is clear enough – that I cannot even imagine something that is both red and green all over is not due to the poverty of my imagination. But, in a different sense, the multiplicity of the image differs from that of which it is an image. One might say that the yellow imagined must have the same multiplicity as the yellow seen, but the image of yellow does not have the multiplicity of the patch of yellow. For I can *look* at the latter, but not at the former, examine it more closely, be deceived in respect of its shade, show it to someone else, fail to notice features of it (e.g. that it has an orange tinge at the corner), etc.

In *Philosophical Remarks* W. noted that:

speaking of images as 'pictures of objects in our minds' (or some such phrase) is a metaphor. We know what a picture is, but images are surely no kind of picture at all. For, in the first case I can see the picture and the object of which it is a picture. But in the other, things are obviously quite different. We have just used a metaphor and now the metaphor tyrannizes us. (PR 82)

In Vol. VI, 241 he wrote:

Sagt aber der Realismus die Vorstellungen seien doch 'nur die subjektiven Bilder der Dinge', so ist zu sagen dass dem ein falscher Vergleich zwischen der Vorstellung von einem Ding und dem Bild des Dinges zu Grunde liegt. Und zwar einfach weil es wohl möglich ist ein Ding zu sehen *und* sein Bild (etwa nebeneinander) aber nicht ein Ding und die Vorstellung davon.

Es handelt sich um die Grammatik des Wortes 'Vorstellung' im Gegensatz zur Grammatik der 'Dinge'.

(If realism says that images are 'just subjective copies of things', it must be pointed out that this rests on a false comparison between the image and the picture of a thing. And simply because it is quite possible to see a thing *and* its picture (perhaps side by side) but not a thing and the [mental] image of it.

This has to do with the grammar of the word 'image' in contrast to the grammar of 'things'.)

Despite this warning, in PG 102, 147 he made just this comparison, but later (LPE 285) noted that 'In part of their uses the expression "visual image" and "picture" run parallel; but where they don't, the analogy which does exist tends to delude us.' In MS. 164, 164f. things finally crystallize:

Ein Spiel kann Einer wohl mit sich selbst spielen. Und kann er es nicht doch in der *Vorstellung* mit sich selbst (oder mit andern spielen)?

Wann aber würden wir sagen er habe z.B. Schach mit einem Andern in der Phantasie gespielt? Wie weiss er dass es Schach war? Hatte er Schach-in-der-Vorstellung gelernt? Nun, wir könnten ihm ja ein wirkliches Schachspiel zeigen und ihm fragen 'War *das* was Du Dir vorgestellt hast?' Wenn er ja sagt so hatte er also ein Vorstellungsbild einer Schachpartie. Aber welcher Art war das Bild? Was für eine Projektion des Schachspiels war es? Darauf gibt es keine Antwort und es ist keine Frage denn die Vorstellung ist eben kein Bild. Vergleiche ich sie einem Bild so wäre es eines von dem niemand, auch ich nicht, wüsste wie es ausschaut. Denn auf die Frage, *was* ich mir vorstelle kann auch ich nur *für* mich auf die für Andere sichtbaren Gegenstände zeigen. Die Antwort für mich besteht z.B. nicht darin, dass ich mir auch noch eine zeigende Finger vorstelle. Denn der wäre ja nur einer unnötigen Farce. Aber das Konzentrieren meiner Aufmerksamkeit ist für mich kein zeigen.

(Someone can, of course, play a game by himself. And can he not do so by himself (or with others) in his imagination?

But when would we say, e.g., that he had played chess with someone else in his imagination? How does he know that it was chess? Did he learn chess-in-the-imagination? Well, we could show him a real chess game and ask him 'Was *this* what you imagined?' If he says 'Yes', then he did indeed have a mental image of a chess game. But what sort of picture was it? What sort of projection of a chess game was it? There is no answer to this, and it is no question, for the image is not a picture. If I compare it with a picture, it would be a picture which no one, not even I, knows what it looks like. For in response to the question *what* I imagine, even I, for myself, can only point at objects perceptible to others. The answer, for me, does not consist, e.g., in my further imagining a pointing finger. For that would just be a redundant farce. But concentrating my attention is, for me, not a kind of pointing.)

In *Investigations* §370 the guiding principle is specified: 'One ought to ask, not what images are or what happens when one imagines anything, but how the word "imagination" is used.' The subsequent extensive writings on this theme (RPP I, II and LW) explore the connections between the concepts of image, picture, and visual impression. The general conclusion is epitomized in RPP II §112 (Z §638): 'The image is not a picture, nor is the visual impression one. Neither "image" nor "impression" is the concept of a picture, although in both cases there is a tie-up with a picture, and a different one in either case.' (See 'Images and the imagination', §§4 – 5.)

SECTION 302

1   W. further explores the incoherence of the supposition that the picture of pain (i.e. imagining pain, wrongly conceived as involving a private picture or paradigm) enters the language-game with 'He has a pain'.

Of course, I can imagine someone else being in pain, even someone being in severe pain and not showing it. Here I would imagine what effort he must make not to wince, how he must be saying to himself 'This is ghastly, but keep smiling', etc. (cf. PI §391). But it is incoherent to suppose that I imagine another person's pain *on the model of* my pain. For in imagining *his* pain, I do not imagine that my pain is in his head – that would be to imagine that *I* feel a headache in his head (which, W. argues, is possible (see 1.1 below)). Rather, I must imagine that *he* has a headache. But now, how am I to imagine a headache I do *not* feel on the model of one which I *do* feel? For, after all, this is *not* like imagining a house I do not see on the model of a house which I do see; rather it is like imagining a negative integer on the model of a natural number. (And it would not make sense to give myself a headache and say 'Now, imagine that he has *this*' (Z §§546f.).)

The nexus between §302(a) and (b) is not immediately obvious, but can be clarified. To imagine someone else's pain on the model of one's own *seems* simply to involve making a transition in the imagination from pain in my body to pain in his. But §302(a) has shown that that confuses imagining *my* having a pain in his head with *his* having a pain in his head; i.e. the *location* of a pain does not determine a subject. (Phantom pains, which are not 'in' anyone's body, are not therefore 'unowned', and pain at the juncture point of Siamese twins may be suffered by one of the twins or the other or both.) I have to imagine not *my* having a pain in his body, but *his* having a pain in his body. The location of a pain can be determined by pain-behaviour (pointing at the painful spot and/or assuaging the injured limb), the pain-behaviour *of the subject*. And the subject of the pain is *he who manifests it*. To imagine someone else's being in pain is not to imagine that someone else 'has' *this*, or that *this* is located in his foot; that would suit imagining someone else having my pin in his foot. Rather is it to imagine *someone's* suffering (though not necessarily to imagine him *expressing* his suffering). But I cannot imagine *someone's suffering* 'on the model of my pain', since my pain – for me, as it were – has no owner (see 2 below).

1.1   (i) 'which would also be possible': W. seems to have found intelligible, at least in certain circumstances, the idea of my feeling a pain in another person's body (cf. WWK 49; PR 92; BB 49f.). It is the act of pointing that determines the place of a pain one suffers (BB 50). If I am groaning with pain and am asked where it hurts, I might (perhaps with my eyes closed) point to the locus of my pain and find that I have pointed to my neighbour's limb. This, W. suggests, would be a case of feeling pain in another's body. The supposition, however, seems more problematic than this (see Exg. §253, 1.1(i)).

    (ii) 'die leidende Person ist die, welche Schmerz äussert': 'the suffering person is he who manifests pain'.

2   LSD 7 remarks on the inclination to say 'I can imagine him to have a toothache, for I can imagine that he has what I have'. But, W. observes, 'When I have a shilling, I can imagine him to have what I have. So also if I have a black eye. But is it the same sort of transition when we take "*seeing*" or "*toothache*"? "Having" is used in an entirely different sense when we speak of "having a toothache" and "having a blackeye".' Vol. XVI, 24ff. reflects on the asymmetry between 'I have . . .' and 'He has . . .'. To say 'If I can have an image of such-and-such, so surely can someone else' makes it appear as if my having an image shows me what it is for someone to have an image, just as a clock in a drawer shows me how I must imagine a clock's being in a drawer. But 'I have . . .' *for me* signifies nothing (one might say that my having . . . does not have the multiplicity of 'X has . . .'). Do I experience *my having* a pain or just a pain? I *say* 'I have a pain' to another; for myself, I just groan. And the

groan corresponds perhaps to the word 'pain', but not to 'I'! Of course, my groan may show someone *else* that I am in pain, viz. in virtue of the fact that *I* groan. But if, when I am in pain, a groan escapes from me rather than from someone else, that is not because I chose to groan with *my* mouth. That is, I do not *thereby* express the fact that *I* and *not someone else* groans.

Vol. XII, 161 elaborates the distinction between imagining another to be in pain and imagining my having a pain in another's body. If I am told 'You know what it is like when *you* feel pain; now just make the transition to someone else!' then there are different transitions I can make; and that shows that one cannot say '*This* is what "pain" signifies, and you know what "I have", "You have" mean, etc. so you know what "He has pains" means.' These are *two* misleading pictures, W. claims. Presumably one misleading picture is the compositionalist conception of sentence-meaning (viz. that the meaning of a sentence is composed of the meaning of its constituents), the other the conception of the meaning of 'having pain' (viz. as given by private ostensive definition). One must learn to see the expression '*I have* pains' as just as derivative (*übertragenen*) as 'The straight line cuts the circle at two imaginary points' (p. 162). The latter does not indicate an intersection of line and arc, and the former does not signify a kind of ownership, nor does it specify a possessor. Then follows PI §426: the misconception we have of attributing pain to others is comparable to our misconceptions in set-theory of infinite series as unsurveyable totalities which only a god can survey.

Does not the whole matter turn on the fact that the words 'I have pains' correspond to a groan and that it is the groaning of the sufferer that leads us to him, whereas *I* could moan with pain and in a certain sense not know *who* is in pain (cf. PI §§404ff.). The person who moans is he of whom one says '*He has* the pains'; and that is why one cannot say that the moan (indeed, the wail 'I have the pain') *states* who has the pains (pp. 163f.).

We are misled by the superficial similarity of 'I have' and 'he has'. But it is not as if 'I' and 'he' are, as it were, pointers in '. . . has pains', the former pointing at my body, the latter at another person. One is tempted to say that I know that another person has a pain because I observe his behaviour, but I know that I have a pain because I feel it. But this is senseless, since 'I feel pain' means the same as 'I have pain'. It looks as if one employs two different senses (seeing and feeling) to determine the subject of pain (as one *looks* for an object or *listens* for it). One can say that in the one case my visual impressions lead me to the location of (his) pain, and in the other my feeling of pain. But my feeling of pain does not lead me to the *owner* of the pain (pp. 164f.).

MS. 179, 66 has the first sentence of §302. In parentheses W. adds that it is misleading to say that the emphasis here (viz. 'pain which I *do not feel*' and 'pain which I *do feel*) is wrong, that I just have to imagine pains which *I do not* feel on the model of pains *I* do feel. The primitive pain–behaviour can point to the location of the pain, but not to a person. The person who suffers is he who moans.

See also BB 68f.

SECTION 303

1   In the grip of a misguided picture which seems to fix the sense of 'pain' unambiguously (PI §426), we are driven to say 'I can only *believe* that someone else is in pain, but I *know* it if I am' (cf. §246). For it seems as if in order really to *know* whether another is in pain, one would have to 'see clearly into the breast of another, and observe that succession of perceptions, which constitutes his mind',[30] but, we think, only a god can see thus into human consciousness (just as only a god can survey an infinite totality). So it appears as if the form of expression we use were designed for a god, who knows what we cannot know (§426).

This is a muddle. In truth, the insistence upon substituting 'I believe he is in pain' for the confident assertion 'He is in pain' (or, indeed, for 'I know he is in pain') is not an expression of justifiable epistemic caution based on experience. Rather it is the replacement of one way of talking (*Redeweise*), one form of expression, by another. For evidently *there is no such thing*, on this conception, as *knowing* that someone else is in pain (cf. BB 54).

Of course, it *looks* otherwise. For one is inclined to say 'He knows whether he is in pain, I can only believe it', and this looks like an explanation of an epistemic limitation. But it is not, for (a) he neither knows nor is ignorant (PI §246), and therefore (b) the appearance that there *is* such a thing (on this conception) as *knowing* that he is in pain (but *I* fall short of achieving it) is doubly mistaken. In so far as he can be said to know that he is in pain, he does not know that *he*, as opposed to *someone else*, is in pain (and that means that he need not know *who* is, i.e. having a pain identifies no bearer). So what he is alleged to know merely by feeling pain is not what I allegedly can only believe but not know. For what I believe (and may indeed know) is that A (someone else) is in pain, but what A (allegedly) knows is not that A is in pain, but rather that *he* is in pain.

The proposed exclusion of 'I know that' as a prefix to 'He is in pain' does not rest on *doubt* about the suffering of others, for then one would not say that I *can* only believe . . . , i.e. it would make sense for me to know, and one could specify the circumstances under which one knows that another is in pain, e.g. when doubt is put at rest. But the global

---

[30] Hume, *A Treatise of Human Nature*, Bk. I, Pt. iv, Sect. 6.

exclusion of knowledge (which is a mere grammatical move) does not differentiate circumstances wherein one *merely* believes *because* there is some doubt from cases where there is no doubt at all. Hence §303(b): just try, in a case when someone is writhing in pain or a baby is screaming with colic, to say 'There is some doubt here; I only *believe* he is in pain'. Here it is perspicuous that the interlocutor's demand is no more than a demand to employ a different *form* of words, not (as it is presented as being) an expression of strict epistemic standards.

2   LPE 302 remarks:

One could from the beginning teach the child the expression 'I think he has toothache' instead of 'he has toothache', with the corresponding uncertain tone of voice. This mode of expression could be described by saying that we can only believe that the other has toothache.

But why not in the child's own case? Because there the tone of voice is simply *determined* by nature.

In this way of speaking, one might say, the difference between an *expression* of toothache and a *statement* of toothache is marked by the different forms of words 'I have . . .' and 'I think he has . . .'. So here the proposition 'We can only believe that the other has toothache' would be a grammatical proposition to the effect that *others* cannot *express* A's toothache, but can only *state* that he has one. But, of course, provision of a distinction between certainty and doubt regarding another's toothaches has yet to be made.

Vol. XVI, 119f. pursues matters further:

Und warum soll man nicht sagen: 'Man kann nie *wissen*, dass einer blind ist, nicht sieht, die Tatsachen können es nur höchst wahrscheinlich machen'? Warum soll man nicht auch diese Ausdrucksform// *diese* Ausdrucksweise// gebrauchen, so kompliziert// sehr verwickelt // und irreführend wie sie ist?

Wenn ich annehme, dass er die und die Erscheinung vor sich sieht – auch gegen alle äussere Evidenz, so nehme ich eigentlich ein Bild an.

Wie geht die Annahme eines Sachverhaltes in die Annahme einer Ausdrucksform über? Wie geht das arbeitende Rad in ein leerlaufendes über? Die Annahme leistet keine Arbeit.

(And why shouldn't one say 'One can never *know* that someone is blind, cannot see, the facts can only make it highly probably'? Why shouldn't this form of expression // this mode of expression // be used too, complicated // thoroughly entangled // and misleading as it is?

If I suppose that even contrary to all external evidence he sees such and such an appearance before him, then I am really accepting a picture.

How does the supposition of a state of affairs go over into the acceptance of a form of expression? How does a working cog go over into a free-wheeling one? The supposition ceases to do any work.

BEHAVIOUR AND BEHAVIOURISM

1 Behaviourism in psychology and philosophy

Behaviourism in empirical psychology originates with the work of J. B. Watson in the USA during the 1910s. Reacting against W. Wundt's introspective psychology on the Continent and against E. B. Titchener and William James in the USA, Watson repudiated the prevailing orthodoxy that psychology is the study of consciousness. On the contrary, he insisted, 'the subject matter of human psychology is the behaviour of the human being'.[1] Psychology is a purely objective branch of natural science, and its ultimate goal is the control and prediction of behaviour.

Not only is consciousness not the subject-matter of psychological science, but the very concept of consciousness is unusable. The committed behaviourist, Watson declared, will drop 'from his scientific vocabulary all subjective terms such as sensation, perception, image, desire, purpose, and even thinking and emotion as they were subjectively defined.'[2] This is not merely because these concepts are insufficiently sharply defined for 'scientific purposes'. Rather, there is no such thing as consciousness as traditionally conceived. 'The belief in the existence of consciousness', he wrote contemptuously, 'goes back to the ancient days of superstition and magic.'[3] The scientific psychologist 'can do without the terms "mind" and "consciousness", indeed he can find no objective evidence for their existence'.[4] Hence 'the behaviourist recognizes no such things as mental traits, dispositions, or tendencies'.[5]

For psychology to mature into a natural science, it must confine itself to what can be observed, viz. behaviour. Like physics, its explanations and predictions must rest on functional dependencies between observable data. Customary explanations of human action in terms of 'subjective' psychological concepts are dismissed as pre-scientific mythology.[6] The

---

[1] J. B. Watson, *Behaviourism* (Kegan Paul, Trench, Trubner, and Co., London), p. 2.
[2] Ibid., pp. 5f.
[3] Ibid., p. 2.
[4] Ibid., p. 18.
[5] Ibid., p. 98. It is noteworthy that Watson equivocated between the radical claim that consciousness, the mind, mental traits, etc. are fictions, the claim that there is no evidence for their existence, and the claim that 'scientific', 'objective' psychology need pay no heed to them. His repudiation of the dualist (Cartesian) confusions of introspectionist psychology led him to embrace a distorted conception of behaviour, of what is or is not observable, and of what is 'objective'.
[6] B. F. Skinner was subsequently to refer to ordinary explanations of actions in terms of desires, reasons, and motives as 'explanatory fictions'.

data of psychological science are environmental stimuli on the one hand and movements of the organism on the other – not only movements of the whole body, but also changes in respiration, blood pressure, and retinal reactions. Although Watson indignantly rejected the criticism that the behaviourist is merely 'a muscle physiologist',[7] he saw no incongruity in claiming that the glands are organs with which we *behave*, since the action of the glands is no less a response to stimuli than the movement of the limbs or the utterance of a sentence.[8] Behaviour amounts to any movement of or in an organism. The crudity of this conception of behaviour unsurprisingly gave rise to conceptual difficulties in demarcating the domain of psychological investigation and in characterizing what is to count as a legitimate description of its data.

Behaviourist psychology, according to Watson, aims to discover scientific laws correlating external stimulus and behavioural response. Subsequently, psychologists were to distinguish *molar behaviourism*, which restricts its investigation to functional relations between stimulus and 'gross observable reactions' of organisms, and *molecular behaviourism*, which would, it was hoped, explain the laws discovered by molar behaviourist science in terms of underlying physiological laws. Intentions, purposes, and desires were bypassed as explanatory fictions, and explanations of behaviour were ventured in terms of stimulus conditioning, 'drives', etc. Speech was explained not by reference to thought, but in terms of causal conditioning:

The fact that every object and situation in the external environment is *named* is of vast importance. Words not only can and do call out other words, phrases and sentences, but when the human being is properly organised they can call out all of his manual activity. The words function in the matter of calling out responses exactly as did the objects for which the words serve as substitutes.[9]

Knowledge was held to be no more than causally generated 'verbal habits'; and self-knowledge, far from involving 'introspecting' one's mind, was argued to be no different in kind from knowledge of other people.

The capacity for thought and the traditional association of thinking and consciousness constituted a locus of forceful objections to the behaviourist programme. Watson tried to forestall them by denying that

---

[7] Watson, *Behaviourism*, p. 15.

[8] Ibid., p. 77.

[9] Ibid., p. 233. Here Watson cleaves to an almost pure and primitive version of the Augustinian picture of language. He continued thus: 'Wasn't it Dean Swift who had one of his characters who couldn't or wouldn't speak carry around in his bag all the objects of common use so that instead of having to say words to influence the behaviour of others he pulled out the actual object from his bag and showed it? The world would be in this situation today if we did not have this *equivalence for reaction* between objects and words.' The reference is to *Gulliver's Travels*, Pt. III, §2, 'A Voyage to Balnibarbi'.

thinking is an incorporeal mental activity. It is, he argued, nothing more than talking to oneself – i.e. sub-vocal word-behaviour.[10] The muscular habits learned in overt speech are responsible for implicit or internal speech – which is what thinking is. This claim was held to be an empirical thesis supported by evidence derived from the observation of children's behaviour:

The child talks incessantly when alone . . . Soon society in the form of nurse and parents steps in. 'Don't talk aloud – daddy and mother are not always talking to themselves.' Soon the overt speech dies down to whispered speech, and a good lip reader can still read what the child thinks of the world and of himself . . . The great majority of people pass on to the third stage under the influence of social pressure constantly exerted. 'Quit whispering to yourself', and 'Can't you even read without moving your lips?' and the like are constant mandates. Soon the process is forced to take place behind the lips. Behind these walls you can call the biggest bully the worst name you can think of without even smiling.[11]

Rather surprisingly, Watson considered this sub-vocal talking to be a form of 'word-behaviour',[12] presumably because he thought it to be a matter of laryngal movements. Even more curiously, he held that the deaf and dumb, who speak by means of manual sign-language, 'use the same manual responses they employ in talking in their own thinking', and even that in their dreams they talk to themselves using finger-language with great rapidity![13]

Such confusions are rife in Watson's writings. Nevertheless, the official ideology was to view the mental as primitive mystification, rather as contemporary cognitive scientists view what they call 'folk psychology'. Similarly, all teleology was to be swept away in favour of the mechanics of bodily behaviour. The advance of science was identified with the elimination of final causation and its replacement by efficient causes in proper explanations of phenomena. In parallel with the physicist or engineer, 'It is part of the behaviourist's scientific job to be able to state what the human machine is good for and to render serviceable predictions about its future capacities whenever society needs such information.'[14] Refinement and sophistication were added to this theory of human conduct by Hull and Skinner, but the spirit of behaviourism remained essentially the same.

The immediate impact of Watson's behaviourism upon philosophy is evident in Russell's *Analysis of Mind* (1921), which Russell had given to Watson for comments while in manuscript (AM 6). In the Preface he

[10] Ibid., pp. 238ff.
[11] Ibid., pp. 240f.
[12] Ibid., p. 243.
[13] Ibid., p. 241. The muddle is exemplary. To think is not to talk to oneself, and to make finger-signs while asleep is neither to think nor to talk to oneself.
[14] Ibid., p. 271.

wrote 'I think that what has permanent value in the outlook of the behaviourists is the feeling that physics is the most fundamental science at present in existence.' This idea was to bear fruit in Carnap's physicalism in the 1930s and in the Vienna Circle's dream of 'unified science'; but because of Russell's neutral monism, it is in fact far less prominent in the book than one would expect from his declaration. His stance was a curious admixture of classical empiricism with Watsonian behaviourism, tenuously held together by neutral monism. Unlike Watson (in his more radical pronouncements), he did not deny the existence of consciousness, although he agreed that consciousness is not definitive of the mental. Rather, it is to be analysed in terms of mental imagery, its meaning relation to what it is an image of, and belief or expectation.[15] Both mind and matter, he argued, are logical constructions. Laws of physics and laws of psychology alike are causal, but the latter are distinguished from the former by their concern with *mnemic* causation, which may have neural foundations. The raw data out of which both mind and matter are constructed are appearances, which, viewed subjectively, are sensations.

The unhappy synthesis of empiricism and behaviourism is evident in Russell's account of desire: ' . . . desire, like force in mechanics, is of the nature of a convenient fiction for describing shortly certain laws of behaviour' (AM 32). All that can actually be observed in animals or in other human beings consists in bodily movements, physiological processes, and emitted sounds (AM 43f.). Mechanical movements depend only upon properties which animal bodies share with matter in general, but 'vital' movements depend for their causation upon the special properties of the nervous system (AM 47). The explanation of animal action in terms of desire is behaviourist; e.g. a hungry animal is restless until it finds food, when it becomes quiescent. That which brings a restless condition to an end is said to be what is desired (AM 32). The concept of desire in the case of animals is explicable in terms of behaviour cycles, viz. 'a series of voluntary or reflex movements of an animal, tending to cause a certain result, and continuing until that result is caused, unless they are interrupted by death, accident, or some new behaviour cycle' (AM 65). The 'purpose' of a behaviour cycle is the result that terminates it in a condition of quiescence, and the animal is said to 'desire' the purpose while the behaviour cycle is in progress.

In his account of *human* desire, however, Russell immediately introduces familiar empiricist apparatus. What sets a human behaviour cycle in motion is a sensation of discomfort (for which no behaviourist account is offered), which causes bodily movements likely to lead to the cessation of the discomfort and its replacement by sensations of pleasure (AM 68). Unconscious desire is merely a tendency to a certain behaviour

---

[15] AM, Ch. XV; Russell's account here is reminiscent of Hume's.

caused by sensations of discomfort. Conscious desire, however, is desire accompanied by a true belief as to its 'purpose' (AM 72), i.e. as to what state of affairs will cause quiescence. The traditional view that we have immediate knowledge of our own desires which does not depend upon observation of our actions is false. 'I believe that the discovery of our own motives can only be made by the same process by which we discover other people's, namely the process of observing our actions and inferring the desire which could prompt them. A desire is "conscious" when we have told ourselves that we have it' (AM 31). But a belief as to the purpose of our own desire 'may very well be erroneous, since only experience can show what causes a discomfort to cease' (AM 72). (It is unclear whether 'false consciousness' is or is not meant to instantiate what he called 'conscious desire', for he was evidently pulled both ways.)

An equally curious admixture of crude behaviourism and classical empiricism is visible in Russell's account of language and meaning. The essence of language, he held, lies in the use of fixed associations in order that a sensible sign may call up the idea of something else. That of which it is intended to call up the idea is said to be the meaning of the sign; and the salient puzzle which Russell addresses is 'what is the relation of the word to the individual which makes the one mean the other?' (AM 191). His answer is that this relation 'is of the nature of a causal law governing our use of the word and our actions when we hear it used' (AM 198). In four respects, understanding words can, he argued, be given a behaviourist analysis. Active understanding is merely a matter of suitable circumstances making a person use the relevant word properly (AM 197, 199). Passive understanding consists in the hearing of the word causing a person to behave appropriately. One is further said to understand a word if one associates it with another word (say, in a different language) which has the same stimulus effects on behaviour, and if one associates the word with the object it 'means', so that the word acquires some of the same causal efficacy as the object.

Does understanding not require that a person know, i.e. be able to say, what the word means? Not so, Russell insisted (in company with Watson). Understanding language is more like understanding cricket than it is like knowing dictionary definitions (AM 197): 'it is a matter of habits, acquired in oneself and rightly presumed in others. To say that a word has a meaning is not to say that those who use the word correctly have ever thought out what the meaning is: the use of the word comes first, and the meaning is to be distilled out of it by observation and analysis.' Indeed, 'There is no more reason why a person who uses a word correctly should be able to tell what it means than there is why a planet which is moving correctly should know Kepler's laws.' This behaviourist understanding 'may be reduced to mere physiological causal laws' (AM 199).

With respect to two important domains of language-use, Russell
parted company with Watson and cleaved to his empiricist forbears.
Memory-statements and imaginative narrative, he held, must be
accounted for in terms of mental imagery. Moreover, these two functions are of the essence of *thinking*, since it is only thus that words,
through their connection with images, 'bring us into touch with what is
remote in time or space' (AM 203). In understanding a word, 'there is a
reciprocal association between it and the images of what it "means".
Images may cause us to use words which mean them, and these words,
heard or read, may in turn cause the appropriate images. Thus speech is a
means of producing in our hearers the images which are in us' (AM 206).
The meaning of a word 'is wholly constituted by mnemic causal laws'
(AM 210). As Wittgenstein was later to picture this classical empiricist
conception, 'Uttering a word is like striking a note on the keyboard of
the imagination' (PI §6).

Analysis of Mind constituted an unhappy half-way house between
classical empiricism and logical behaviourism. The latter emerged, under
the title of 'physicalism', in the Vienna Circle. In *Der Logische Aufbau der
Welt* (1928), Carnap attempted a wholesale reconstruction of empirical
concepts and knowledge on a methodological solipsist foundation. He
held that from the purely logical point of view of 'construction theory' a
materialist foundation which reduces the psychological to the physical
(behavioural) was perfectly possible. Indeed:

> A materialistic constructional system has the advantage that it uses as its basic
> domain the only domain (namely, the physical) which is characterized by a clear
> regularity of its processes . . . Since the task of empirical science . . . consists, on the
> one hand, in the discovery of general laws, and, on the other hand, in the explanation
> of individual events through their subsumption under general laws, it follows that
> from the standpoint of empirical science the constructional system with physical basis
> constitutes a more appropriate arrangement of concepts than any other. [16]

He noted (not quite accurately) that the behavioural psychology of
Watson, Dewey, and others (referring to the bibliography in Russell's
Analysis of Mind for more details) reduced all psychological phenomena
to the physical, i.e. observable behaviour. 'Thus a constructional system
which is based upon this position would choose a physical basis . . . such
a system would be quite possible and practicable.' However, Carnap
himself opted for a constructional system with a phenomenalist or, as he
called it, 'an autopsychological basis', on the grounds that it should
conform to the epistemic order of propositions. Consequently he gave a
logical behaviourist analysis of the heteropsychological, arguing that

---

[16] R. Carnap, *The Logical Structure of the World*, tr. R. A. George, (Routledge and Kegan
Paul, London, 1967), §59.

propositions about other people's experiences, etc. are second-order logical constructions, reducible in the first instance to propositions about their behaviour. The autopsychological, however, was not reduced to the behaviour of the subject, but constructed out of the 'given' – i.e. bare 'unowned' sense-data.

In 1932, however, under pressure from Neurath, Carnap shifted ground. The principle of the unity of science (methodological monism) and the demand for 'intersubjective verification' triumphed over the epistemological rationale for choosing a phenomenalist base for construction. In two articles in *Erkenntnis*, 'Die physikalische Sprache als Universalsprache der Wissenschaft'[17] and 'Psychologie in physikalische Sprache',[18] he defended the thesis that 'all sentences of psychology describe physical occurrences, namely, the physical behaviour of humans and other animals'.[19] This, he argued, 'coincides in its broad outlines with the psychological movement known as "behaviourism"'.[20] The general physicalist thesis that 'physical language is a universal language', i.e. that all empirical sentences are translatable into physicalist ones, when applied to psychology, yields a form of *logical behaviourism*.

Unlike radical versions of psychological behaviourism, Carnap's logical behaviourism did not imply that mental states, etc. are fictions – i.e. that there really are no such things. Rather, the claim was that all psychological sentences are translatable into an array of 'physicalist' ones. Accordingly, Carnapian physicalism stands to psychological behaviourism somewhat as linguistic phenomenalism[21] stands to idealism. A corollary of physicalism was that the laws of psychology are actually physical laws, and it seemed reasonable to suppose that they might ultimately be deducible from general physical laws that apply to inorganic matter.[22]

The supposition of the reducibility of third-person psychological propositions to behavioural ones was already defended in *Logische Aufbau* and 'Pseudoproblems in Philosophy' (1928). In 'Psychology in Physical Language', Carnap argued that such propositions are equivalent to assertions that there exists a physical microstructure of the person's body which is responsible for certain kinds of behaviour and behavioural disposition. This significantly modified the behaviourist analysis, since it admitted into the analysans not only propositions about behaviour, but

[17] Carnap, *Erkenntnis*, II (1931), pp. 432 – 65, published in English as a monograph *The Unity of Science*, tr. M. Black (Kegan Paul, London, 1934).
[18] Carnap, *Erkenntnis*, III (1932/3), repr. as 'Psychology in Physical Language', tr. G. Schick, in A. J. Ayer (ed.), *Logical Positivism* (Allen and Unwin, London, 1959), pp. 165 – 97.
[19] Carnap, 'Psychology in Physical Language', p. 165.
[20] Ibid., p. 181.
[21] 'Linguistic phenomenalism', as opposed to Mill's modal phenomenalism.
[22] Carnap, 'Psychology in Physical Language', p. 167.

also propositions about physiological changes within the body (as, indeed, Watson had) and essential reference to (as yet unknown) states of the central nervous system. This did not, however, prevent members of the Vienna Circle from referring to the doctrine as 'logical behaviourism',[23] with the proviso that the term 'behaviour' must include 'internal behaviour'[24] and dispositions to behave in certain ways.

The most significant change relative to *Logische Aufbau* lay in the account Carnap now gave of first-person present-tense psychological sentences. These, he claimed, are reducible to sentences about one's bodily state, behaviour, and behavioural dispositions. The argument was thin, to say the least, and the range of examples amounted to a starvation diet. The sentence 'I now am excited' in the so-called *system-language* was alleged to be rationally supported by the protocol sentences 'I feel my hands trembling', 'I see my hands trembling', 'I hear my voice quavering', etc. It has, Carnap insisted, precisely the same content as 'My body is now in that condition which, both under my own observation and that of others, exhibits such and such characteristics of excitement'.[25]

From the point of view of Wittgenstein's response to behaviourism, it is not necessary to trace the story any further. But it is clear enough what different routes remained to be explored. A stricter psychological behaviourism (molar behaviourism) would disregard physiology and concentrate upon searching for laws correlating stimulus and behavioural response. A stricter logical behaviourism would search for analyses which restrict the analysans of psychological statements to specifications of behaviour and behavioural dispositions. Materialists would go in the other direction, identifying the mental with states of the central nervous system. Carnap himself later opted for yet another line of attack, suggesting that scientific psychological concepts are not dispositional, but are 'hypothetical constructs' within a theoretical structure.[26] This in turn, cross-fertilized with the mechanist thesis derived from Turing and Craik, led to contemporary computational functionalist theories (see 'Men, minds, and machines', §5).

2 *Wittgenstein: first reactions*

When Wittgenstein resumed philosophy in 1929, behaviourism was definitely in the air. There is no evidence to suggest that he read Watson's

[23] See C. G. Hempel, 'The Logical Analysis of Psychology' (1935), repr. in translation in *Readings in Philosophical Analysis*, ed. H. Feigl and W. Sellars (Appleton, Century, Crofts, Inc., New York, 1949), p. 381.

[24] See Carnap, 'Logical Foundations of the Unity of Science' (1938), repr. in *Readings in Philosophical Analysis*, ed. Feigl and Sellars, p. 412.

[25] Carnap, 'Psychology in Physical Language', p. 191.

[26] Ibid., p. 197, and *idem*, 'The Methodological Character of Theoretical Concepts', in H. Feigl and M. Scriven (eds.), *Minnesota Studies in the Philosophy of Science*, Vol. 1.

book, but he certainly read Russell's *Analysis of Mind*, in which Watson's ideas are discussed. It seems likely that at some stage he at least looked at Carnap's *Logische Aufbau*[27], and he definitely read the first of the *Erkenntnis* articles in 1932, which occasioned a quarrel. Wittgenstein accused Carnap of plagiarism, and held that Carnap's ideas concerning physicalism were derived from the *Tractatus*, conversations Wittgenstein had held with Waismann and Schlick in which Carnap had participated, and reports of Wittgenstein's new ideas circulated to members of the Vienna Circle by Waismann. He abruptly severed relations with Carnap.

The quarrel is *prima facie* puzzling, as Wittgenstein never went so far as to give a 'physicalist' or 'logical behaviourist' account of first-person present-tense psychological utterances. It is true, of course, that in 1929/30 he gave a kind of logical behaviourist analysis of third-person psychological propositions. But Carnap had done something very similar in *Logische Aufbau*, long before he met Wittgenstein. Until the full correspondence with Schlick and Carnap is published, it will be impossible to be certain about the details of this quarrel. The following is, therefore, a conjectural reconstruction.

The *leitmotif* of Carnap's first *Erkenntnis* article is the 'unity of science', i.e. the claim that 'all empirical statements can be expressed in a single language, all states of affairs are of one kind and are known by the same method'.[28] This thesis involved three corollaries: (a) That there are no philosophical propositions, and no special domain of philosophical knowledge, since the whole task of philosophy consists 'in clarifying the notions and statements of science'.[29] (b) Statements in logic and mathematics 'are tautologies, analytic propositions, certified on account of their form alone. They have no content, that is to say, assert nothing as to the occurrence or non-occurrence of some state of affairs.'[30] (c) 'Contentful' (empirical) statements do not divide into mutually irreducible kinds (e.g. physics, biology, and the *Geisteswissenschaften* – psychology, history, and the social sciences); rather, 'all statements in Science' (i.e. all cognitive statements) can be translated into, and are reducible to, the intersubjective language of 'physics'. It is noteworthy that the details of Carnap's thesis of the reducibility of psychological propositions to behaviouristic ones are *not* discussed in *The Unity of Science*, but are

---

[27] It is referred to explicitly in PLP 197, 270, 407, and perhaps in a conversation with Waismann in 1931 (WWK 182). It is possible, however, that the latter allusion is *not* to *Logische Aufbau* but to conversations with Carnap. Had Wittgenstein read it before 1932, the quarrel with Carnap would perhaps have been precipitated before publication of Carnap's first *Erkenntnis* article.

[28] Carnap, *The Unity of Science*, p. 32.

[29] Ibid., p. 33.

[30] Loc.cit. To be sure, this is an oversimplification of Wittgenstein's view of the propositions of mathematics, since he did not claim that they were either tautologies or analytic, but rather that they were pseudo-propositions (TLP 6.2).

explicitly[31] postponed for discussion in the subsequent paper, 'Psychology in Physical Language', which was published a year later.

In a letter to Schlick[32] dated 8 August 1932, Wittgenstein remonstrated that Carnap's central ideas were taken without acknowledgement from him. Certainly the only acknowledgement was to Neurath, who had coined the term 'physicalism' and who had, Carnap wrote, persuaded him to abandon the methodological solipsist base of *Logische Aufbau*. It seems that Carnap had said, or written, to Schlick that Wittgenstein had not touched on the matter of physicalism. Wittgenstein objected: 'Dass ich mich nicht mit der Frage des "Physicalismus" befasst hätte, ist unwahr (nur nicht unter diesem – scheusslichen – Namen) und in der Kürze, in der die ganze "Abhandlung" geschrieben ist.' ('That I had not dealt with the question of "physicalism" is untrue (only not under that – horrible – name), and with the brevity with which the whole of the *Tractatus* is written.') Moreover, he continued, Carnap's account of ostensive definition was derived from conversations at which Waismann was present. His conception of a hypothesis likewise came from Wittgenstein and not, as Carnap had insisted (presumably in a letter to Schlick), from Poincaré and Reichenbach, whose notions of grammar and proposition were quite different. The distinction between formal and contentful forms of speech (*inhaltliche Redeweise*), Wittgenstein remonstrated, went not one jot beyond his own work, and he expressed incredulity that Carnap could pretend that he had not understood the concluding propositions of the *Tractatus* on the proper method of future philosophy, but had arrived at that conclusion independently.

It seems that Wittgenstein thought (with some justice) that the general principles of 'the unity of science' or 'physicalism' were explicit in the *Tractatus*.[33] That he paid no attention to Carnap's reduction of first-person psychological propositions to behavioural ones is not surprising, since this programme was not carried through in the first *Erkenntnis*

---

[31] Carnap, *The Unity of Science*, p. 72.

[32] See M. Nedo, *Wittgenstein: sein Leben in Bildern und Texten* (Suhrkamp, Frankfurt, 1983), pp. 254f.

[33] He was surely right that the conception of philosophy as logical analysis of propositions of 'natural science', i.e. empirical propositions, and as exposure of the nonsensicality of metaphysical propositions originates in the *Tractatus* (e.g. TLP 6.53). The claim that *all* empirical propositions are analysable into truth-functional combinations of elementary propositions can be taken to be equivalent to the thesis of the unity of science, but is non-committal with respect to a physicalist basis as opposed to a methodological solipsist (or phenomenalist) one. It is evident that a version of the latter emerges explicitly in the *Philosophical Remarks*. What remain very unclear are Wittgenstein's references in 1929 to a distinction between 'primary' and 'secondary' languages, which he had previously advocated and now repudiated. For if the secondary is not reducible to the primary, then the thesis of unity must have been abandoned. It is noteworthy that his remarks on primary and secondary language are not only obscure but are also equivocal, sometimes repudiating the distinction and sometimes using it (PR 51, 58, 84, 88, 100, 103, 158, 168, 267).

article. The analysis of third-person psychological propositions in terms
of observable behaviour, however, was arguably implicit in the *Tractatus*
and had been explicitly advocated by Wittgenstein since 1929 (WWK
49f.; PR 88 – 95). The general thrust of this quasi-behaviourist account is
evident in Waismann's *Thesen* (1930/31), which, it is plausible to assume,
Carnap had read:

> A proposition cannot say more than is established by means of the method of its
> verification. If I say 'My friend is angry' and establish this in virtue of his displaying a
> certain perceptible behaviour, I only *mean* that he displays that behaviour. And if I
> mean more by it, I cannot specify what that extra consists in. A proposition says only
> what it does say and nothing that goes beyond that. (WWK 244)

The behaviourist pressure was premised upon the suppositions that
first-person psychological sentences express genuine propositions, that
these are verified by reference to immediate experience, and that
psychological concepts such as pain are systematically ambiguous.
Wittgenstein clarified the predicament with a nice example:

> Suppose I had stabbing pains in my right knee and my right knee jerked with every
> pang. At the same time I see someone else whose leg is jerking like mine and he
> complains of stabbing pains; and while this is going on my left leg begins jerking like
> the right though I can't feel any pain in my left knee. Now I say: the other fellow
> obviously has the same pain in his knee as I've got in my right knee. But what about
> my left knee, isn't it precisely the same case here as that of the other's knee? (PR 93)

Consequently, he concluded:

> The two hypotheses, that others have pain, and that they don't and merely behave
> as I do when I have, must have identical senses if every *possible* experience confirming
> the one confirms the other as well. In other words, if a decision between them on the
> basis of experience is inconceivable. (PR 94f.)

Of course, what this means is not that we can never know whether
others are really in pain, but rather that to ascribe pain to others is not
really to talk of anything over and above their behaviour. This would be
made explicit in a different form of representation in which one never,
for example, attributed toothache to other people, but only characterized
their behaviour as being akin to one's own when one has toothache
oneself. Of course, one would then talk in pitying tones of people who
display toothache-behaviour (but are not said to have toothache), and
one would differentiate genuine toothache from simulated toothache by
reference to behaviour (cf. PR 93). The central point is that one cannot
traverse the bounds of sense, e.g. attributing what I have – my toothache
– to others, in thought. 'Philosophers who believe you can, in a manner
of speaking, extend experience by thinking, ought to remember that you
can transmit speech over the telephone, but not measles' (PR 95).

The misunderstanding of the radical asymmetry between first- and third-person psychological propositions is a source of both solipsism and behaviourism. These doctrines are the opposite of each other (LWL 112), each apprehending correctly that one member of any pair of such propositions is logically unlike the other, and each doctrine misconstruing that insight.

The logic of our language is so difficult to grasp at this point: our language employs the phrases 'my pain' and 'his pain', and also the expressions 'I have (or feel) a pain' and 'He has (or feels) a pain'. An expression 'I feel my pain' or 'I feel his pain' is nonsense. And it seems to me that, at bottom, the entire controversy over behaviourism turns on this. (PR 94)

Later in the 1930s, when his own views had changed dramatically, Wittgenstein was to compare behaviourism and finitism in mathematics:

we want to see the absurdities both of what the finitists and of what their opponents say – just as we want in philosophy to see the absurdities both of what the behaviourists say and of what their opponents say.

Finitism and behaviourism are as alike as two eggs. The same absurdities and the same kind of answers. Both sides of such disputes are based on a particular kind of misunderstanding – which arises from gazing at a form of words and forgetting to ask yourself what's done with it . . . (LFM 111)

Here Wittgenstein was thinking primarily, if not exclusively, of psychological behaviourism, rather than of logical behaviourism. This is evident from the later remark 'Finitism and behaviourism are quite similar trends. Both say, but surely, all we have here is . . . Both deny the existence of something, both with a view to escaping from a confusion' (RFM 142). Psychological behaviourism misguidedly denied the existence of experiences (pains, desires, emotions, etc.) in order to escape from the confusions of introspective psychology which conceived of the mental in Cartesian, dualist, terms. But both alternatives are absurd. In *Philosophical Remarks* Wittgenstein had sought to escape from the horns of this dilemma by construing third-person propositions as 'hypotheses' the symptoms of which are behaviour (see 'Criteria', §1). Subsequently he was to find a quite different resolution.

Two features of Russell's quasi-behaviourist drift in *Analysis of Mind* caught Wittgenstein's attention when he returned to philosophy, viz. Russell's account of desire (and related intentional concepts) and his rudimentary causal theory of meaning (which was also mooted in Carnap's *Erkenntnis* article). Wittgenstein's objections were rooted in ideas concerning the pictoriality of the proposition which originated in the *Tractatus* and persisted in modified form despite abandonment of the picture *theory* of the proposition. In both cases the criticisms apply with equal force to psychological behaviourism as conceived by Watson.

The key defect in Russell's theory of desire is that an internal relation, viz. between desire and its fulfilment, is taken to be an external relation. There is an internal relation between a proposition and the fact that makes it true, and so too there is an internal relation between a desire and what fulfils it:

> for me, there are only two things involved in the fact that a thought is true, i.e. the thought and the fact; whereas for Russell, there are three, i.e. thought, fact and a third event which, if it occurs, is just recognition. This third event, a sort of satisfaction of hunger (the other two being hunger and eating a particular kind of food) could, for example, be a feeling of pleasure . . . (PR 63)

The consequences of Russell's account are the following absurdities: (a) that we often do not find out what we wanted until our desire is satisfied, i.e. until the behaviour cycle has terminated in a state of quiescence; (b) that we are often mistaken about what we wanted (e.g. it would make sense to say 'I thought I wanted to go to London, but I actually wanted a piece of cake'); (c) that if we do know what we want, our knowledge must rest on induction from past experience (e.g. 'This feeling of dissatisfaction has, in the past, been alleviated by an apple, so I must want an apple'); (d) that if one wants something one has never had before, one cannot know what one wants.

The postulated causal, external, connection between desire and its fulfilment is what produces these incoherences. 'I believe Russell's theory amounts to the following,' Wittgenstein wrote (PR 64); 'if I give someone an order and I am happy with what he does, then he has carried out my order. (If I wanted to eat an apple, and someone punched me in the stomach, taking away my appetite, then it was this punch that I originally wanted.)' On Russell's theory it makes no sense to say 'I wished for an apple, but a pear has satisfied me', for if the pear has satisfied me, then what I wished for was really a pear (BB 22). But this is absurd, since we distinguish between fulfilling a wish or desire and producing gratification that may ameliorate an unfulfilled wish or desire. Furthermore, on Russell's account, it is not a tautology, but an empirical truth, that if someone sincerely says that he wants an apple, then his desire will be satisfied by an apple (PLP 117). But saying 'I should like an apple' does not mean 'I believe that an apple will quell my feeling of discomfort'; and this latter proposition is not the expression of a wish or desire at all (PI §440).

By contrast, Wittgenstein insisted that the connection between a proposition and what makes it true, a desire and its satisfaction, an expectation and its fulfilment, and an order and its execution is in every case *internal*:

> The fulfilment of an expectation doesn't consist in a third thing happening which you could also describe in another way than just as 'the fulfilment of the expectation', thus for example as a feeling of satisfaction or pleasure or whatever.

For expecting that *p* will be the case must be the same as expecting that this expectation will be fulfilled; whereas, if I am wrong, expecting *p* would be different from expecting that this expectation will be fulfilled.

Isn't it like this: My theory is completely expressed in the fact that the state of affairs satisfying the expectation of *p* is represented by the proposition *p*? And so, not by the description of a *totally* different event. (PR 65f.)

Describing an expectation by reference to what is expected is to give an internal description (PR 68); and if there were only an external connection, then no connection at all could be described, since we only describe the external one by means of the internal one (PR 66). With Pavlovian behaviourism obviously in mind, Wittgenstein added 'Salivation – no matter how precisely measured – is *not* what I call expecting' (PR 70).

He connected this insight explicitly with his earlier ideas in the *Tractatus*:

Expecting is connected with looking for: looking for something presupposes that I know what I am looking for, without what I am looking for having to exist.

Earlier I would have put this by saying that searching presupposes the elements of the complex, but not *the* combination that I was looking for.

And that isn't a bad image: for, in the case of language, that would be expressed by saying that the sense of a proposition only presupposes the grammatically correct use of certain words. (PR 67)

With the abandonment of the metaphysics of logical atomism, however, the apparent metaphysical harmony between language and reality is disclosed to be a harmony *within language* (see Volume 2, 'Accord with a rule', pp. 86 – 91). Desire and the characterization of its satisfaction, expectation and the description of its fulfilment, make contact in language. For 'the desire that *p*' = 'the desire that is satisfied by *p*'s being the case'. The articulate expression of a desire (wish, expectation, or command) contains a 'picture' of what will fulfil it. It makes no sense to suppose that one only finds out later what one really wanted or to think that one's expression of desire is a hypothesis confirmed or disconfirmed by a later experience of gratification. The failure to discern this internal relation, to apprehend the unintelligibility of the primary characterization of a desire or expectation other than in terms of its fulfilment, vitiates the Russellian and causal, behaviourist theory of desire.

A similar flaw lies at the heart of the behaviourist theory of meaning. Wittgenstein was willing to concede that language learning is rooted in training that antecedes explaining what expressions mean (PLP 111 – 14). Such training is not unlike setting up a causal mechanism by way of stimulus conditioning, which approximates to the behaviourist conception. It does not follow, however, that in general 'the pronouncing of a word is now a stimulus, now a reaction' (PLP 113f.) as Watson and, with qualification, Russell suggested, let alone that its meaning consists in 'a causal law governing our use of the word and our actions when we hear it used' (AM 198). Suppose we trained a dog to behave in such-and-such a way or built a machine (a calculating machine) to perform such-and-such a task, given the stimulus of a sign 'p'. Now contrast (a) The sign 'p' means the same as the command to do so-and-so and (b) The animal (or machine) is so conditioned (or constructed) that the occurrence of the sign 'p' brings about so-and-so. The causal account of language in effect reduces the explanation of meaning given in (a) to the description of a causal nexus given in (b). But (a) specifies a convention, a rule for the use of the sign 'p' – an explanation within the 'calculus' (network of rules) of language; whereas (b) describes a causal mechanism. The truth of (b) is wholly independent of the truth of (a), and the convention is independent of the reactions of the dog or machine. A dog, however well trained, may misbehave, and a machine, however well constructed, may malfunction. But that what it does *is* misbehaviour or malfunctioning is determined by reference to the stipulated convention of meaning. Otherwise, what meaning a sign has would always be a matter of a hypothesis about what reaction it will call forth, and its meaning would not be determinable in advance of the behavioural consequences of its use from occasion to occasion. Hence too, one could not determine that the machine was malfunctioning, since what 'p' means would just be whatever response it produces (PLP 114 – 16).[34]

The meaning of an expression, Wittgenstein argued, is not its effect. It is what is given by an *explanation* of meaning. And explanation consists in a move *within* language; it is a rule for the use of a sign, an articulation within the grammatical network of the language. Although training in the rudiments of word-use may be behaviouristically conceived, it rapidly progresses to explanations of meaning, to asking and being given answers to the question 'What does "x" mean?', and hence to progressive mastery of a *normative*, not a causal, structure. (At this stage, Wittgenstein favoured comparing it with a *calculus* of rules, a simile which he later progressively relinquished.) Moves within this structure are justified by reasons, not causes, and it is these normative connections that constitute the meanings of expressions. The meaning of an expression is the correlate of understanding, for one is said to understand an utterance when one knows what it means. The criteria of understanding include both *correct use*, which is not a causal concept, and *giving correct explanations*, e.g. by paraphrase, examples, ostension, or exemplification, which are rules for the use of expressions. The correctness of use is

---

[34] This contrast between a causal and a normative connection lies at the heart of Wittgenstein's response to the idea of a 'Turing machine' (see 'Men, minds, and machines', §5). It is also a pivotal point in the contrast between experiment and calculation in mathematics (RFM 194 – 9, 364 – 6, 379 – 82, 389 – 92).

determined by the practice of measuring applications against the yard-stick of explanations.

Although Russell's comparison of understanding a language with understanding cricket (AM 197) is apt, since in both cases a technique is mastered and a practical skill is acquired, his claim that understanding is independent of knowing what the expressions one understands mean is incoherent – as absurd as the idea that one might know how to play cricket without knowing the rules. Russell remarked that there is no more reason why a person who uses a word correctly should be able to tell what it means than there is why a planet which is moving correctly should know Kepler's laws (AM 199). This reveals his conflation of the nomic with the normative. Planets do not move *correctly*, whereas people do use expressions correctly or incorrectly. But it only makes sense to say of a person that he uses a word 'correctly' if there is a standard of correctness which he satisfies; and that is what is given by accepted explanations of meaning. The first steps in the rudiments of language learning may be mere training (which antecedes understanding). But the introduction of explanations of meaning, questions about what expressions mean, criticisms of use as incorrect, etc. transform behavioural regularities (which can (perhaps) be represented in terms of stimulus and response according to causal connections) into normative behaviour justified by reasons (which cannot intelligibly be so conceived). Contrary to what Russell asserted (AM 197), the supposition that the meaning of a word is 'to be distilled out of [its use] by observation and analysis' is incoherent. For whatever causal connections between utterance and behaviour are established by training (or stimulus/response conditioning), they cannot determine the logical (grammatical) consequences of the use of a symbol, as opposed to its putative causal consequences. Hence they cannot determine the differentiation of correct from incorrect use; and so they bypass the question of the meaning of an expression altogether.[35]

3 *Crypto-behaviourism?*

A crucial development in Wittgenstein's thinking occurred in 1932/3 when he abandoned the view that first-person psychological utterances are the 'genuine propositions', denied that they get compared with reality (viz. immediate experience) for verification, and repudiated his earlier view that they are objects of knowledge or ignorance. Instead he came to view them as expressions (*Äusserungen*) or manifestations of the

---

[35] Wittgenstein was equally critical of Russell's associationist explanation of meaning in terms of imagery and 'mnemic causal laws', but this theory and its flaws do not belong to a discussion of behaviourism.

'inner' and to see their occurrence not as a *symptom* for a hypothesis, but as a *criterion* of the mental. The ramifications of this change are explored in other essays ('Privacy', 'The inner and the outer', 'Men, minds, and machines' and 'Criteria').

That Wittgenstein repudiated psychological behaviourism is obvious enough. He did not argue that pain, for example, is a mere fiction, but rather that pain, conceived as a 'private object' that lies behind pain-behaviour, is a *grammatical* fiction (PI §307). He acknowledged the difference between pain-behaviour with pain and pain-behaviour without pain and denied that pain is a mere nothing (PI §304). But, more enigmatically, he also denied that pain was a something and justified this *prima-facie* obscure remark as a rejection of 'the grammar which tries to force itself on us here'. He also repudiated the picture of an inner process associated with, for example, the notion of remembering (PI §305). Contrary to the empiricist tradition, he denied that feeling or 'experiencing' pain is a pre-condition for understanding the word 'pain' (PI §315), and that clarification of the meaning of the verb 'to think' requires any introspective scrutiny of thinking (PI §316). One might harbour the suspicion that his repudiation of psychological behaviourism goes hand in hand with acceptance of a form of *logical* behaviourism.

The case for such an interpretation seems to be strengthened by closer examination of the transformation in Wittgenstein's philosophy in 1932/3 when he abandoned his earlier conception of first-person psychological sentences. For did he not insist that what appear to be reports of an inner realm of mental objects are in fact merely verbal *behaviour*? The verbal expression of pain, he argued, is new pain-behaviour which replaces crying (PI §244). The utterance 'Now I understand' or 'Now I know how to go on' is not a description of a mental state, but a signal (PI §180) or an exclamation that corresponds to an instinctive sound or a glad start (PI §323). The words with which one expresses one's memory are a *memory-reaction* (PI §343), and the expression of expectation is a *verbal reaction* (Z §53). Is this not a logical-behaviourist account of first-person psychological propositions?

In *Philosophical Remarks* Wittgenstein surely gave an analysis of third-person psychological propositions in terms of behaviour. Although he subsequently claimed that behaviour is a criterion of the inner, did he not continue to insist that third-person psychological propositions are verified, and can at least on occasion be conclusively verified, by reference to behaviour? It is characteristic of those who oppose logical behaviourism to claim that the subject of experience knows directly and with certainty what experiences he is having, whereas others know or perhaps only believe on the basis of indirect evidence. But that is precisely what Wittgenstein denied. It is nonsense to say 'I know I have a pain', and others often do know, with certainty, that I am in pain (cf. PI

§246); furthermore their evidence – viz. my behaviour – is *not* indirect
(LPE 278). Did Wittgenstein not claim that the *body* is the best picture of
the soul (PI p. 178), and that if one sees the *behaviour* of a living thing one
sees its soul (PI §357)? But remove the poetry from these remarks, and do
we not have before us a form, indeed an extreme form, of logical
behaviourism? Small wonder that the *Philosophical Investigations* and
Concept of Mind have seemed to many bemused philosphers to be sisters
under the skin.[36]

There is no denying that Wittgenstein's philosophical psychology
shares significant features with behaviourism. Negatively, like (logical)
behaviourists, Wittgenstein repudiated the traditional philosophical conception of the inner. Experience is not hidden behind behaviour; nor
does it accompany behaviour as music which only I hear can accompany
my singing. The mental is not a private world accessible only to its
owner, and experiences are not private ethereal objects inhabiting such a
realm. The subject does not have a privileged access to his mental states
and does not know better than others how things are with him (indeed,
in typical cases it makes no sense to talk either of knowledge or of
ignorance). Like the (psychological) behaviourists, Wittgenstein was
willing to accept the idea that language-learning with us is founded on
brute training, which presupposes for its success a variety of natural
forms of behaviour and reactions.[37] Far from first-person present-tense
psychological utterances being reports of parades upon an inner stage, he
conceived of them as extensions of, and often partial substitutes for,
natural, primitive, expressive behaviour. Contrary to the empiricist
tradition, he did not conceive of language-use as a translation, for the
benefit of others, into 'word-language' from language-independent
thoughts. On the contrary, 'our language-game is behaviour' (Z §545),
and the capacity to think is in general parasitic upon the capacity to
express one's thoughts in utterance and behaviour. Parallel to logical
behaviourism, Wittgenstein argued that the ascription of psychological
predicates to other people is *logically* connected with behaviour; we
would have no use for these expressions if they were not bound up with
behavioural criteria (LPE 286). The inner is indeed verified by reference

[36] This is in fact doubly erroneous. First, Ryle's *Concept of Mind* is mischaracterized as
'logical behaviourist'. Secondly, Wittgenstein's account differs extensively from Ryle's,
both on numerous points of detail (e.g. doing mental arithmetic, tunes going through one's
head, imagining) and on general issues of principle (the explanation of first-person
psychological utterances and the characterization of self-knowledge).
[37] This seems to be an empirical claim, and to that extent lies outside the bounds of
logical grammar. Arguably Wittgenstein would have held it to be a platitude, a remark on
the natural history of human beings, not a novel curiosity but an evident truism (cf. PI
§415). Though he would have repudiated Skinnerian theories of language, Chomsky's
argument in favour of an innate knowledge of universal grammar as a *sine qua non* of
language-learning would, I suggest, have struck him as yet another house of cards.

to the outer, and doubts about the inner, e.g. over dissimulation, are settled by reference to more evidence consisting of the outer. For even a person's sincere avowal is a form of behaviour. Behaviourists were surely right to note the importance of the fact that avowals license predictions; if people's avowals of understanding were not in general followed by successful exercises of appropriate skills, these forms of words would have no use. And if people's expressions of pain were not integrated into more general patterns of pain-behaviour, their words would be meaningless. Finally, Wittgenstein, like the behaviourists, denied that the empirical study of human psychology is to be pursued by 'introspection', i.e. by noticing what goes on in one's own case when one thinks, is angry, or desires this or that, and describing what one observes for the benefit of the psychologist. Nor is it a study of the inner at one remove – an examination of unobservables by means of registering their effects, like particle physics. Everything suggests that he would have repudiated as incoherent the classical conception of psychology as the investigation of a special 'realm of consciousness'.

Despite these important converging lines, it is fundamentally misguided to classify Wittgenstein's descriptions of the grammar of psychological expressions as a form of logical behaviourism. The convergence is explained by the common repudiation of (roughly speaking) Cartesianism and the classical empiricist Cartesian inheritance. To escape from these confusions, the radical psychological behaviourist denies the existence of the mental, and the logical behaviourist reduces the mental to behaviour. Wittgenstein did neither. To a first approximation, what he did was to explore the grammar of the expression or manifestation (*Äusserung*) of the inner. In his detailed examination of the relation of behaviour to what it is a manifestation of, of the logical status of avowals of experience, of thinking and imagining, of intention and desire, and of the very *concepts* of body and behaviour (i.e. of what *counts* as behaviour), his account diverged dramatically from logical-behaviourist strategies.

In *Investigations* §571 Wittgenstein pointed out that it was misleading to suggest that psychology treats of processes in the psychical sphere just as physics does in the physical. The physicist observes the phenomena (e.g. movements of bodies) that he theorizes about, but the psychologist observes the *Äusserungen*, i.e. the expressive behaviour, of human beings. This is an apt warning against introspectionist psychology. But does it then follow that the psychologist deals only with behaviour and not with the mind (PI p.179)? Not so; for although the utterances (*Äusserungen*) of human beings are *also* forms of behaviour, they are uses of language too – and they are not *about* behaviour. Wittgenstein developed this theme at greater length in the *Remarks on Philosophical Psychology*:

So does psychology deal with behaviour (*say*), not with human states of mind? If someone does a psychological experiment – what will he report? – What the subject says, what he does, what has happened to him in the past and how he has reacted to it. – And not: what the subject thinks, what he sees, feels, believes, experiences? – If you describe a painting, do you describe the arrangement of paint strokes on the canvas – and *not* what someone looking at it *sees*?

But now how about this: The observer in the experiment will sometimes say: 'The subject said "I feel . . .", and I had the impression that this was true,' – Or he says: 'The subject seemed tired.' Is that a statement about his behaviour? One would perhaps like to say: 'Of course, what else should it be?' – It may also be reported: 'The subject said "I am tired" ' – but the cash value of these words will depend on whether they are plausible, whether they were repeating what someone else said, whether they were a translation from French, etc.

Now think of this: I recount: 'He made a dejected impression.' I am asked: 'What was it that made this impression on you?' I say: 'I don't know.' – Can it now be said that I described his behaviour? Well, can one not say I have described his face if I say 'His face became sad'? Even though I cannot say what spatial alterations in the face made this impression?

It will perhaps be replied: 'If you had looked closer, you would have been able to describe the characteristic changes of colour and position.' But who says that I or anyone could do this? (RPP I §287)

The report 'He was dejected' is about both behaviour and state of mind, but not side by side, as if one were an accompaniment of the other. Rather, about one in one sense and the other in another (RPP I §288).[38] The dejected look is not a *sign* of sadness, as a flushed face is a sign (an empirically correlated symptom) of fever (RPP I §292). It manifests, makes visible, the person's mood.

The relations of behavioural expression to what it is an expression of are not external. The inner is not related to its outward manifestations as an unobservable entity to its causal effects (e.g. as an electron is to its traces in a cloud chamber). The relation is internal or grammatical. But the mental is not, *pace* logical behaviourists, reducible to behaviour. 'He is in pain' does not *mean* 'He is behaving (or is disposed to behave) thus-and-so'. Nor is pain-behaviour related to pain as symptom to hypothesis. Rather, it is a *criterion* of pain. It is possible for pain to occur without being manifest, and it is possible for pain-behaviour to be displayed without there being any pain. This grammatical relation, though distinct from entailment, nevertheless allows for certainty, although it is defeasible (see 'Criteria').

A verbal utterance which constitutes the expression of an inner state, etc. is *also* a kind of behaviour; but it is not *only* a kind of behaviour. It is

---

[38] PI p. 179, rephrases this: 'aber nicht im Nebeneinander; sondern vom einen durch das andere'!

an articulate use of language. The utterance 'I have a toothache' is not *about* my clutching my cheek or about my groanings and wincings. It is akin to a cry of complaint; but the complaint is not about my behaviour, it is about my toothache, which is a sensation. And sensations are not patterns of behaviour. Nevertheless, the grammar of 'about' in the context of an *Äusserung* is unlike the grammar of 'about' in the context of a description – it signifies what the *Äusserung* is an expression of. Such an avowal is not uttered on the grounds of my observations of my own behaviour (*pace* Carnap's logical behaviourism), and I do not *know it to be true* on the same grounds as others, since I cannot be said to know or to be ignorant of its truth. It is *groundlessly* uttered, and it is not *verified* by reference to behaviour or *anything else*! The verbal manifestations of pain, joy, or desire are not *correlated* with what they manifest. For one cannot say '*This* is pain, and *this* is pain-behaviour – they normally go together, therefore . . .'. The logic of expression (*Äusserung*) is not the logic of correlation of distinct domains, and the grammar of psychological words used in verbal manifestations of the mental is not the grammar of names of objects (PI §293). One might say that behaviourism, no less than dualism, failed to appreciate the grammatical (logical) significance of the fact that 'I have a pain' is an *expression* of pain.

4 *Body and behaviour*

The Cartesian sundering of mind from body constituted *inter alia* a methodological demarcation of the domain of the physical sciences. Bodies as such belong within that domain. What differentiates a corpse from a living human being (as opposed to a living animal, which is merely a 'biological machine') was held to be the fact that the living human being is animated by a mind. Here lies the gap in the otherwise seamless web of efficient causation in nature. For the mind can control, via the pineal gland, the movements of the body. Although the total quantity of motion in the physical universe, like the quantity of matter, is conserved, the direction of movement, in the case of human beings, is subject to 'outside intervention'.

The distortions in the resultant conception of the mind tend to overshadow the no less important Cartesian misrepresentation of the concepts of the human body and of human behaviour.[39] Though Descartes conceded that 'I am not merely present in my body as a sailor is present in a ship', but am rather 'very closely joined and, as it were, intermingled with it, so that I and the body form a unit',[40] the

---

[39] I am indebted here to J. W. Cooke's 'Human Beings', in P. Winch (ed.), *Studies in the Philosophy of Wittgenstein* (Routledge and Kegan Paul, London, 1969), pp. 117–51.
[40] Descartes, *Meditations on First Philosophy*, 'Sixth Meditation', in *Philosophical Writings*, Vol. II, p. 56 (AT VII, 81).

intermingling is causal, and the unity contingent. I *have* a body; but according to Cartesians it is conceivable that I might not have had one, and it makes sense to suppose (for the sake of argument against hyperbolic doubt) that I do not have one. The body is explicitly conceived to be a *machine*. The mind or soul is the entity that has, owns, the body – and ownership consists in the two-way causal interaction between this pair of substances. The mind *controls* the body which it 'owns'. 'When a *rational soul* is present in this machine it will have its principal seat in the brain, and reside there like the fountain-keeper who must be stationed at the tanks to which the fountain's pipes return if he wants to produce, or prevent, or change their movements in some way.'[41] My body, therefore, is that body impact upon which causes me to have sensory experiences and which moves in compliance with my will. My behaviour consists in those movements of my body which are caused by me.

This conception could hardly help sowing the seeds of scepticism about other minds. In the *Meditations* Descartes wrote:

if I look out of the window and see men crossing the square, as I just happen to have done, I normally say that I see the men themselves . . . Yet do I see any more than hats and coats which could conceal automatons? I *judge* that they are men. And so something which I thought I was seeing with my eyes is in fact grasped solely by the faculty of judgement which is in my mind.[42]

The seeds duly germinated. Although Berkeley repudiated the Cartesian duality of mind and matter and rejected the attendant conception of material substance, he accepted without demur this picture of what is visible in the behaviour of human beings. 'A human spirit or person is not perceived by sense', he insisted;[43] 'We do not see a man, if by *man* is meant that which lives, moves, perceives, and thinks as we do: but only . . . a certain collection of ideas.' All we see of 'other spirits' are 'several motions, changes, and combinations of ideas'. For

is it not the soul which makes the principal distinction between a real person and a shadow, a living man and a carcass? . . .

By the person Alciphron is meant an individual thinking thing, and not the hair, skin, or visible surface, or any part of the outward form, colour, or shape, of Alciphron . . . And in granting this, you grant that, in a strict sense, I do not see Alciphron, i.e. that individual thinking thing, but only such visible signs and tokens as suggest and infer the being of that invisible thinking principle or soul.[44]

---

[41] Descartes, *Treatise on Man,* in *Philosophical Writings,* Vol. I, p. 141 (AT XI, 131).
[42] Descartes, *Meditations,* 'Second Meditation', in *Philosophical Writings,* Vol. II, p. 21 (AT VII, 32).
[43] G. Berkeley, *The Principles of Human Knowledge,* CXLV, CXLVII.
[44] Berkeley, *Alciphron,* 'Fourth Dialogue', §§4f.

Mill shared this conception:

> In the case of other human beings . . . I must either believe them to be alive, or to be automatons: and by believing them to be alive, that is by supposing the link to be of the same nature as in the case of which I have experience, and which is in all respects similar, I bring other human beings, as phaenomena, under the same generalization which I know by experience to be the true theory of my own existence.[45]

What grammar has put together, philosophers can only sunder at the cost of nonsense. Do we *believe* that other human beings are not automatons? Do we observe only physical movements and grimaces? And do we infer, on the basis of analogy with our own case, that our spouses and children are sad or joyful, amused or annoyed? Does the rich tapestry of human social life, of empathy and mutual understanding, of shared experience and emotion, hang upon an analogical thread?

   Behaviourism is first cousin to 'the problem of other minds'. Cartesians pictured the soul's relation to the body rather like that of an immaterial hand within a visible glove. In one's own case, one can feel one's hand and see the movements of the glove; in the case of others one can see only a glove and its movements, and one infers the existence of an invisible hand by analogy. Behaviourism (by and large) rightly repudiated the Cartesian conception of the mind, but accepted the correlative conception of the body – as it were, an empty glove that moves in accord with the laws of stimulus and response (molar behaviourism), which are probably ultimately reducible to laws of physics (molecular behaviourism). But philosophical enlightenment, a surview of our concepts of both inner and outer, of psychological expressions and of behavioural ones, can be achieved only by repudiating *both* halves of the classical diptych.

   Wittgenstein explicitly addressed the question of whether one believes other people not to be automatons. Characteristically, he faulted the question itself. In certain circumstances, one can say 'I believe he is suffering'. But can one also say 'I believe he is not an automaton' (PI p. 178)? No! – but not because I am *certain* that he isn't one. For what would it be like if he were an automaton? One might object that one can surely imagine this. Perhaps so, Wittgenstein replied, but then one would imagine him going about his business as if in a trance, with a glazed look in his eyes (cf. PI §420). But can one look at children playing and say to oneself 'Perhaps they are automatons'? Is one to suppose here that other human beings, behaving as they normally do, are unconscious (PI §418)? That is obviously absurd. Is it, then, that they are supposed to

---

[45] J. S. Mill, *An Examination of Sir William Hamilton's Philosophy*, ed. J. M. Robson, in *Collected Works of John Stuart Mill*, Vol. IX (University of Toronto Press, Toronto, 1979), p. 191.

lack consciousness? What does that mean? That they lack something which *I* have? 'I am conscious' has a use in special circumstances, but not as a report of an experience (PI §416; see 'The world of consciousness', §3). 'Consciousness' does not signify a private experience which I apprehend directly in my own case and problematically infer in the case of others; and to say that human beings are conscious or 'possess consciousness' is not to make an empirical statement at all (PI §418). When people behave *thus*, we say that they are 'fully conscious'; and when conscious they may further be conscious of a noise in the next room or of being overdressed for the party. People can, when drugged for example, behave like automatons, i.e. mechanically, moving jerkily, etc. But it makes no sense to ask of human beings behaving normally whether they may not be automatons for all that.

But surely, one may still object, human beings have bodies, and one *sees* their bodies (and not their souls). Does it not make sense to ask whether *those bodies* are not automatons? The question again is awry. One can ask whether those bodies (decaying corpses, for example) are human bodies as opposed to bodies of some other kind of primate. One can point at a person, indeed at the body *of* a person, and say 'That body is a human body' – which would be a grammatical explanation of the expression 'human body'. But the question 'Are those bodies automatons or human beings?' presupposes that it is legitimate, just like that, to say that human beings are bodies. This subtly distorts the grammar of 'a body', as well as that of 'human being' (or, indeed, 'animal') and 'mind' or 'soul'. (Do we *not* see a soul in anguish or a first-rate mind at work?) This distortion, in a philosophical context, is highly misleading. Human beings and animals *have* bodies; this is a grammatical proposition. And the grammar of 'having a body' has distinctive features which are obscured by replacing this phrase with 'being a body'. The grammatical distinction earmarks the qualitative difference between the living and the dead, the animate and the inanimate, the sensible and the insensate (PI §284).

I may be proud of my body without being proud of myself, and ashamed of myself without being ashamed of my body. It makes sense to say 'I am N.N.' on introducing myself to a stranger, but 'I am a body' is no introduction. Nor does it characterize me, as does 'I am a diabetic' or even the grammatical proposition 'I am a human being'. (Human *beings*, although they are space-occupants, are not human *bodies*.) Unless it is an emphatic insistence that I have physical needs, it is quite useless outside philosophy. And within philosophy its only use is as a misleading denial of the confused metaphysical claim that I am a mind.

One might venture another throw. If my body is healthy or, alternatively, out of condition, then I am healthy or out of condition, respectively. If my body is *n* stone in weight, then I weigh *n* stone; and when I die, my body will be a dead body, a corpse. So is it not correct to say that I *am* my body? But what is this supposed to mean? It surely cannot mean that I am *identical* with my body. For, first, it is no more an identity-statement than 'I am N.N.' (see 'I and my self', §4). Secondly, I will cease to exist before my body ceases to exist, for when I die I leave my remains behind. My body will then be a corpse, but I will not. Thirdly, although it is true that in some contexts 'I' can be replaced by 'my body', nevertheless, (a) the very phrase '*my* body' presupposes the distinctness of the grammars of 'body' and 'person' (or 'human being'); and (b) in most contexts the expressions are *not* intersubstitutable.

'I am *this*↗ body' avoids the complications of 'my body' but otherwise fares no better. One cannot say, pointing at oneself, 'This body intends to go to London, has made up its mind, is trying to resolve a philosophical problem.' We must again call to mind Wittgenstein's remark that 'only of a living human being and what resembles (behaves like) a living human being can one say . . .' (PI §281). He did not write 'only of a living human *body*'.

The terrain here is strewn with mines, and one must tread with care. To repudiate the sentence 'I am my body', and to deny that a person is identical with his body or that a human being is a (human) body is not to affirm that I, or any other person, is identical with something else distinct from the body – a mind, soul, or self. 'Who am I?' is answered by 'I am N.N.'. 'What am I?' can be answered in various ways (soldier, sailor, tinker, tailor – or a miserable sinner, a misanthrope, etc.) But to deny the identity of myself or of another person with a body does not force one to adopt Cartesianism. It is noteworthy that even 'I am a human being', unless employed, for example, to remonstrate against maltreatment, has no function save as a grammatical explanation of the expression 'human being'. For as with 'He isn't an automaton', here too one might say: 'What information is conveyed by this and to whom would it be information? To a *human being* who meets [me] in ordinary circumstances? What information *could* it give him?' (cf. PI p. 178). 'He is a human being' would need a very special context to make any sense; but it is true that one might have occasion to explain that General Motors, unlike General Montgomery, is *not* a human being. Obviously something similar applies to 'I have a body'; it is more like 'this rod has a length' than like 'I have two hands'. But this rod may well have a length of two metres, and I may have a body of such-and-such characteristics.

Some human beings have beautiful bodies, others have ugly ones; but they are not their bodies. The grammatical form of ownership is doubtless misleading. To say that a person *has* such-and-such a sort of body is not to imply that the person is a Cartesian mind which owns that body. If it seems so, we should remind ourselves that a person is also said to *have* a decisive mind. To have a beautiful body, unlike having a beautiful car, is not to own or be in possession of something. Nor does 'having' here function in the same way as in 'I have two hands'. It makes sense to lose one's hand, but not to lose one's body. My hand is part of my body, but my body is not a part of anything. 'Having a body' does not signify a two-way causal interaction between a person and the body he has. A person's body is not like the car he drives, but not because he 'is more intimately intermingled' with it. The body of a living creature is not a machine, and a person does not control his body as a driver controls a car. Machines do not *have* bodies, and the bodies of living creatures, unlike machines, do not have intrinsic purposes. Only what is alive can be said to have a body, and not *everything* that is alive – for plants and trees, though they have branches and foliage, do not have bodies. Only animals, in particular self-moving, *sentient* creatures, have bodies (which become corpses on death). And it is not the body that is sentient, conscious, or unconscious, that sees or hears – but rather the creature whose body it is. Having a body, one might say, is a (formal) mark of *sentient life*. 'Our attitude to what is alive and to what is dead, is not the same. All our reactions are different' (PI §284). The same holds of what lacks life – of sticks and stones, and of what is not self-moving and is insensate – like trees and plants.

What then gives me the idea that living beings can feel (PI §283)? *Not* (as Mill thought) that I transfer the idea of feelings from my own case to objects outside myself. The idea that it must be either the body or the soul (or mind) that is conscious or unconscious, that sees or is blind, is excited or indifferent presents a misguided Cartesian dilemma – and it is this which must be repudiated. It is misconceived to think that categorially different properties, such as thinking on the one hand and walking on the other, must belong to categorially distinct substances, and equally erroneous to think that 'mind' and 'body' signify such substances. Sensation, perception, emotion, etc. are attributed to *human beings* and to creatures that *behave like them*; and neither minds nor bodies *behave*. Animals bark or purr, eat and drink, chase each other, search for food, etc; but these are not actions or activities attributable to their bodies. Human beings, unlike other animals, talk, ask questions and answer them, issue orders and obey them; but it is neither their *bodies* nor their *minds* that engage in these transactions. The category of human being, is, as one would expect, fundamental to our language-games. We react spontaneously in distinctive ways to other human beings, to our mothers and fathers, siblings and other children, long before we learn to speak. We are not of the *opinion* that our parents and companions are human beings. Our attitude towards them is an attitude towards *human beings*; and such attitudes come before opinions (alternative draft of PI p. 178 in MS. 169). Our language-games are rooted in these forms of pre-linguistic behaviour (cf. Z §545), and the question of whether 'these bodies' (of Mother and Father, and all the others) might not be automatons does not arise, nor can it intelligibly be raised.

Nevertheless, it might be replied, does the concept of a human being not stand in need of justification. Is not the attribution of pain, joy, and the rest based on *behaviour*? Do we not see the mere behaviour (which is, as Wittgenstein stresses, a *criterion* for the inner) and infer from it that such-and-such experience is being enjoyed? Does Wittgenstein himself not say that 'if one sees the behaviour of a living being, one sees its soul'?

Further confusions still need to be unpacked. First, as Wittgenstein remarks in a different context:

> Here we are in danger of wanting to make fine distinctions. – It is the same when one tries to define the concept of a material object in terms of 'what is really seen'. – What we have rather to do is to *accept* the everyday language-game, and to note *false* accounts of the matter *as* false. The primitive language-game which children are taught needs no justification; attempts at justification need to be rejected. (PI p. 200)

The child does not *learn* to respond to his mother's behaviour as to a human being. He responds – and later learns a language. Those responses might have been different, as they are in cases of autism. But had they generally been different, the human forms of life as we know them would not have arisen. The child does not see his mother's behaviour *as* the behaviour of a human being. For seeing human behaviour for what it is antecedes aspect-perception, which presupposes mastery of a technique. On the contrary, it is seeing human behaviour as the behaviour of automatons which could be said to be a limiting case of aspect-perception (PI §420).

Secondly, the relationship between behavioural concepts and psychological concepts is complex. Wittgenstein's analogy with the misconceived attempt to define 'material object' in terms of 'what is really seen' is apt. He noted elsewhere, apropos this very issue: 'It is like the relation: physical object – sense impression. Here we have two different language-games and a complicated relation between them. – If you try to reduce their relations to a *simple* formula you go wrong' (PI p. 180). One way in which this complicated relation gets oversimplified was built into Cartesianism *ab initio* and was inherited unquestioningly by behaviourism, logical and psychological alike. If one views the body as the vehicle of the soul, if one thinks that one does not really 'see the men themselves' but only 'hats and coats which could conceal automatons' (Descartes), then one is bound to think of human behaviour as 'several motions, changes' of 'the outward form, colour, or shape' of a 'mere body' (Berkeley). (This aberration is parallel to the thought that we do not even see 'the things themselves' but only their mere appearances, sense-data or impressions.) The consequent distortion of the concept of behaviour is the seed-bed of the philosophical problem of 'other minds'.

Disillusionment with Cartesianism bred behaviourism, which rightly rejected the Cartesian (and empiricist) conception of the mind, but accepted the associated conception of the body and behaviour. Hence the declared goal of C. L. Hull, for example, was to show how, from 'colourless movements' (as opposed to intentional, goal-directed behaviour) and 'mere receptor impulses as such', one can deduce or construct psychological concepts such as purpose, intention, desire, etc.[46] Logical behaviourists pursued, more or less self-consciously, a similar objective. And it has been thought that Wittgenstein differed from the Vienna Circle primarily in introducing a novel, and perhaps dubious, logical relation to mediate between (mere) observable behaviour and psychological state, viz. that of a criterion.

This is to overlook completely the fact that Wittgenstein repudiated the Cartesian and behaviourist conceptions of body and behaviour, as well as the Cartesian picture of the mind. Behaviour is indeed the criterion of the mental, but behaviour is not mere 'colourless movement'.[47] Wittgenstein parted company with the prevailing tradition in four crucial respects. First, when he wrote of the distinct criteria of thinking, pain, anger, joy, wish, fear, intention, etc., the term 'behaviour' includes not merely the play of facial expression and gestures, but also the surroundings, the occasion of these expressions and gestures (RPP I §129; cf. §314). Hence for example, 'Pain-behaviour and the behaviour of sorrow. – These can only be described along with their external occasions. (If a child's mother leaves it alone it may cry because it is sad; if it falls down, from pain.) Behaviour and kind of occasion belong together' (Z §492). The behaviourist might go along with this. After all, he too describes behaviour in the context of a specific stimulus. But the characterization of the occasion in purely causal (stimulus) terms will obliterate or distort the crucial distinction between reason and cause, and hence too the difference between the causes and objects of emotions and the propriety of the behaviour (e.g. *obeying* an order) with respect to its occasion (viz. the issuing of a command).

Secondly, and connected with the latter point, behaviour which is, *inter alia*, a criterion for the mental includes not only what people do antecedently to learning, but also what they do, and in particular what they *say*, after having learnt. If someone has learnt to use the words 'I am glad' where others say 'I am frightened', then 'we shall draw unlike conclusions from like behaviour' (RPP I §131). So behaviour includes the use of the techniques of a language, and hence too what the speaker *means*

---

[46] C. L. Hull, *Principles of Behaviour* (New York, 1945), p. 25.

[47] It is noteworthy that in PR (ch. VI) and even in BB (pp. 51f.) Wittgenstein drifted close to this position. (And this gave rise to Waismann's 'language strata' conception (F. Waismann, 'Language Strata', repr. in A. G. N. Flew (ed.), *Logic and Language*, 2nd series (Blackwell, Oxford, 1953).) Only gradually did he liberate himself from this misconception.

by what he says, and also whether he speaks *sincerely* or *plausibly* (cf. RPP I §287).

Thirdly, Wittgenstein denied that we see only 'colourless movements':

> 'I see that the child wants to touch the dog, but doesn't dare.' How can I see that? – Is this description of what is seen on the same level as a description of moving shapes and colours? Is an interpretation in question? Well, remember that you may also *mimic* a human being who would like to touch something, but doesn't dare. And what you mimic is after all a piece of behaviour. But you will perhaps be able to give a *characteristic* imitation of this behaviour only in a wider context. . . .
>
> But now am I to say that I really 'see' fearfulness in this behaviour – or that I really 'see' the facial expression? Why not? But that is not to deny the difference between the two concepts of what is perceived. . . . 'Similar expression' takes faces together in a quite different way from 'similar anatomy'. (RPP I §§1066 – 8)

The supposition that we do not 'really' see the anger, sorrow, or amusement in a person's face is as absurd as the idea that we do not 'really' see the furniture in the room around us, but only sense-data or appearances. Behaviour, as Wittgenstein construes it, is indeed a criterion for the mental, but it does not follow that anger, sorrow, or amusement are, as it were, hidden behind the face that manifests them: 'In addition to the so-called sadness of his facial features, do I also notice his sad state of mind? Or do I *deduce* it from his face? Do I say: "His features and his behaviour were sad, so he too was probably sad"?' (LW §767).

The mind, human emotions and moods, desires and purposes, thought and belief are no more hidden behind their behavioural *expression* than the meaning of a word is hidden behind the utterance of a word. It is true that we may suppress our emotions, conceal our intentions and keep our thoughts to ourselves, but when we do not, when we express our feelings, manifest our purposes, and articulate our thoughts, they do not lie behind our expressive behaviour.

Fourthly, although what is 'outer' (behaviour) is a criterion of what is 'inner', far from the inner being describable only in terms of the outer, it is – a little paradoxically at first blush – the outer, or at least much of what is most important to us about it, that is essentially and unavoidably describable in terms of concepts of what is inner. The apparent paradox vanishes as soon as one recollects that, for example, we *recognize* facial expressions as joyous or sad, glum or preoccupied, amused or contemptuous, etc. And we describe facial expressions thus, in the rich vocabulary of the inner, of mood, emotions, attitudes, etc., and could not describe them in terms of *facial measurements* from which the character of the expression and hence too of what it manifests might be inferred (cf. PI §285). Indeed, not only the description of facial expression, but also of gesture and action, is run through with the vocabulary of the 'inner', something strikingly obvious when one remembers the character of adverbial modification of descriptions of action. We could not even describe (let alone distinguish) gesturing angrily or in despair, shuddering fearfully or in disgust, chortling joyously or with amusement, prancing expectantly, happily, or with surprise save in our psychological vocabulary. Our attributions of anger, despair, fear, disgust, joy, amusement, etc. do not rest on observations of 'colourless physical movements'. On the contrary, what we *see* is expressive behaviour – and we would be hard put even to describe the bare physical movements.

'The human body is the best picture of the human soul' (PI p. 178) not because the soul is something bodily (MS. 124, 7), but precisely because the soul is manifest in behaviour.[48] Only a creature with eyes can cast a loving look or a contemptuous gaze, weep with joy or grief. Only a creature with a mouth can smile, with sympathy or cruelty, in amusement or cold anger. But for these forms of expression to be possible a highly complex behavioural repertoire in widely varying circumstances is presupposed. The soul of a fish, if it had one, would be a poor thing. The articulations of the human face and body in the circumstances of human life are not externally related to what it makes sense to say of the human soul. Commenting on Fraser's report that the Malays conceive the human soul as a homunculus corresponding exactly in shape, proportion, and colour to the body in which it resides, Wittgenstein wrote: 'How much more truth there is in this view which ascribes the same multiplicity to the soul as to the body, than in a modern watered down theory' (GB 74).

---

[48] One must again bear in mind that 'Seele' does service for both 'mind' and 'soul'.

SECTION 304

1   So strong is the inner/outer picture under which we labour, the model of object and name, the idea that the 'image' of pain (*die Vorstellung des Schmerzes*) enters the language-game as a paradigm, the supposition that having a pain is knowing something which others cannot know, that when W. repudiates these misconceptions, it will appear as if he is a behaviourist (cf. §307), denying that there is any difference between pain-behaviour accompanied by pain and pain-behaviour without pain. We do not see that these pictures are merely *emblematic* representations of our grammar, not pictures of the facts. Hence W.'s description of the grammar of sensation-words looks to our astigmatic vision as if it were a denial of something we all wish to affirm.

Why, in particular, does he appear to be denying the difference between pain-behaviour with and without pain? Because he denies that pain is an inner object, a *something*, which its owner may scrutinize and describe for the benefit of those who cannot perceive it. And is that not tantamount to saying that pain is a *nothing*? (If it isn't a something, it must be a nothing!) No; this is to misunderstand him altogether. What he is doing is rejecting the grammar of name and object (§293) which tries to force itself upon us here. To deny that a pain is a mental object (a kind of substance, only in an ethereal realm), to deny that having a pain is akin to having a penny, to deny that one can have a pain now which is just like one's pain yesterday, only not the same, is not to say that pain is a nothing. It is rather to insist that the grammar of pain is not the grammar of objects – indeed, not even the grammar of items that can be said to be *something*, let alone of what can be said to be *nothing*. For 'I have something in my mouth' – 'What is it?' – 'A toothache' is surely appropriate only in the Looking Glass world. And *nothing* is, as it were, the *absence* of something (e.g. there is nothing, no money, in the purse; nothing, no noteworthy event, happened in the street; nothing, no sound, could be heard). But it is, of course, no part of W.'s argument that *pain* is the absence of something.

The argument that repudiated the name/object model for 'pain' reached the conclusion that a nothing would fulfil the *apparently* requisite roles of private sample, of justification for saying 'I am in pain', or of a private picture before the mind's eye *no less well* than a something about which nothing can be said. Why 'a something about which nothing can

be said'? This ground has been raked over. (a) The something, unconnected with behavioural manifestation, has no criteria of identity; one
cannot even say that one *believes* that it is the same as before (§260). (b) It
does not belong to any superior category such as 'sensation' or even
'something' (§261). (c) If the word for it has any use, it does not matter at
all if one recognizes the 'something' correctly or not (§270). (d) It would
not matter for the imagined language-game with a name for such a
something whether each person had something different answering to
the name, or even nothing at all (§293). (e) The something, thus
conceived, is like the water in the picture of the boiling kettle; it is not
boiling in the picture – indeed, it is not picturable. In short, *nothing at all*
will fulfil the role of such a something, about which nothing can be said.

This seems paradoxical, but is not. It is merely to repudiate the idea
that the grammar of pain can be coherently represented on the model of
correlating a word with an object. But the appearance of paradox will
disappear only when one frees oneself from the trammels of the
Augustinian picture of language, according to which language always
functions in the same way (the function of words is to name, sentences
are combinations of names that describe a state of affairs). According to
that pervasive *Urbild*, the purpose of communication by means of
language is equally uniform, viz. to convey thoughts (PI §363). Ridding
oneself of this picture will enable one to see the role of verbal manifestations of pain, and so too of expressions of intention, emotion, or mood,
the grammatical character of telling one's dream or recounting one's
recollections. It will also bring home to one how *specialized* is the activity
of conveying one's thoughts to another (see 'Thinking: the soul of
language', §4). The bulk of our discourse, contrary to philosophical
tradition, is not to communicate our thoughts, reflections, or ruminations. Everything will appear different when seen from the correct
logical point of view! One will distinguish between *expressions* (*Ässerungen*) of the inner and *reports* of the inner (which are not descriptions);
and one will be led to examine in detail just what *are* descriptions of
mental states.

2   MS. 124, 19ff. elaborates: not only do 'He has pains' and 'He behaves
thus-and-so' mean something quite different, but their uses are far *more*
different than philosophers who attack behaviourism imagine! For when
they emphasize and try to show us this difference, they represent the uses
of the two kinds of sentences on the model of the same schema. W.'s
observation here is penetrating: both behaviourism *and* dualism labour
under related confusions. (See 'Behaviour and behaviourism', §§3 – 4.)

The theme of a something or a nothing is given a forty-page
investigation in Vol. XVII, 7ff. Cf. also MS. 166, 24ff.

3   'to convey thoughts': this venerable misconception was a pivotal point
in Frege's conception of communication by means of language.

Section 305

1   This involves a parallel movement of thought to §304. The question
'Surely remembering involves an inner process?', like 'Surely pain is not
a nothing?', is what is misleading. If one affirms the interlocutor's
proposition, one subscribes to a mythology of mind; if one denies it, one
seems to be denying what is most obvious.
      What needs to be denied here is not a fact, but a picture that informs a
description. It is the picture that is misguided; it leads to the morass of
'inner perception' that dogs empiricism (and much empirical psychology). For then we think that the 'inner process of remembering' is *seen*
by the recollecting person, and that he who remembers must *know* that it
is *memory* that he is invoking. And how should he know that save by
reference to (privately) observable features of the inner process, such as
vivacity (Hume) or familiarity (Russell)? The phrase 'inner process' is
immensely misleading; we think that there are two broad genera of
processes, outer ones and inner ones. So an inner process is a *process*, just
like fermentation in a vat, only it happens to be 'inner'! (See 'Thinking:
methodological muddles and categorial confusions', §§3 – 4.) To insist
that the form of words 'inner process of remembering' incorporates a
misguided picture is not to deny that people remember things, nor is it to
insist that remembering is behaving.

2   PG 85 connects the objections to the picture of psychological processes
with parallel objections to the picture of numbers as objects. What does
remembering *consist of*? (*That* surely is a misguided question!) W. notes
that remembering is not at all the mental process one imagines at first
sight. The most varied things may happen when I say 'I remember that
p'; and also nothing at all, save just rightly saying it! 'The psychological
process of . . . is in the same case as the arithmetical object three. The
word "process" in the one case, and the word "object" in the other
produce a false grammatical *attitude* to the word.'
      Vol. XII, 252, contains PI §305 followed by the remark that when
someone says 'You surely know that when you remember a certain thing
you experience something inner', one is inclined to answer 'Yes'; i.e. one
is inclined to use this picture. But what next? What happens with it now?
(It is noteworthy that in Vol. XVII, 7ff., having discussed the some-
thing/nothing schema at length and observed that he is searching for the
magic words that will break the spell here (p. 22), W. notes that

'Yes – and now what?' or 'What are these words good for?' are the *entzaubernde Wort* (p. 39), the spell-breaking word. For in the grip of philosophical illusion, one constantly describes a picture here, not the application of a picture; one describes an imaginary, free-wheeling (*leerlaufende*) language-game behind the real one. Asking what the consequences are, what the function in the language-game of the inner 'something' is, will therefore break the spell; for reflection will show that it has *none*.) Vol. XII, 253 continues: if we are, in certain circumstances, inclined to repeat to ourselves idle sentences (*leerlaufende Sätze*), why should there not also be idle dialogues, such as the above exchange. The interlocutor queries 'You surely don't want to say that nothing went on within you!' – Well, W. replies, I said: I remembered . . . Should there have been something *else* going on? After all, you didn't mean a process in the sense of 'eating' or 'knitting'. Nothing is being denied here, W. concludes, save the wrong picture that is imposed by the expression 'inner process', just as calling the number three 'an object' imposes the wrong picture.

Vol. XVI, 134f. explores a different route: 'Remembering is surely an inner process' is a grammatical remark which actually says that the language-game begins with the *expression* of the memory. The grammatical remark gives the *appearance* of justifying us in making assumptions about a person's inner processes of remembering; but one could say that just because remembering is an inner process, an assumption about the inner processes of remembering is quite senseless if it is not an assumption about the expression of these processes.

SECTION 306

2   Vol. XII, 246 contains this, preceded by a remark on the vacuity of assumptions about an inner process that are not coupled with assumptions about its outer expression (parallel to remarks just quoted from Vol. XVI, 134f.). W. then gives an analogy for the *picture* of remembering as an inner process. It is as if we had inherited a form of language that represented all things as the product of casting a material (a 'stuff') in a form, so that in this language one could not talk plainly of a table, but always of the matter of the table having been introduced into the form of the table. Then one would be led to believe that simply to talk about the table is a kind of linguistic crudity, in that one should distinguish first the matter and then the form into which it enters. The result of philosophy here would be that one *did* talk plainly of the table and viewed this as a perfectly good form of expression. PI §306 follows; clearly 'mental process of remembering' is analogous to 'matter and form of a table' in

the imagined form of representation. For here too it seems that if we talk about remembering without mentioning a mental process, it appears as if we are being crude and imprecise.

SECTION 307

1   W.'s riposte here epitomizes the argument of §§304 – 6. (See 'Behaviour and behaviourism', §3.)

2   In MS. 124, 5f. a draft of this occurs, preceded by a variant of PI §217(c), quoted in Exg. §217, 2.1(iii). Then:

> Aber bist Du nicht doch nur ein verkappter Behaviourist? Denn Du sagst, dass *nichts* hinter der Äusserung der Empfindung steht?
>
> Sagst Du nicht doch im Grunde, dass alles Fiktion ist, ausser dem Benehmen? – Fiktion? So glaube ich also, dass wir nicht wirklich etwas empfinden, sondern nur Gesichter machen/schneiden/?!// So glaube ich also, dass wir nicht eigentlich empfinden; sondern bloss so tun?// Aber Fiktion *ist* der Gegenstand hinter der Äusserung.// Fiktion aber ist *wirklich* die Erklärung der Äusserung mit dem/mittels des/privaten Gegenstand/Gegenstands./ vor unserm innern Sinne.// Fiktion ist es, dass unsre Worte, um Bedeutung zu haben// etwas zu bedeuten// auf ein Etwas anspielen müssen, das ich, wenn nicht einem Andern, doch mir selbst zeigen kann. (*Grammatische* Fiktion.)

> (But aren't you just a behaviourist in disguise? For you say that *nothing* stands behind the expression of the sensation?
>
> Aren't you at bottom saying that everything except behaviour is a fiction? – Fiction? So I believe that we don't really have sensations of anything, but only make/pull/faces?!// So I believe that we don't really have sensations but only pretend to?// But the object behind the expression *is* a fiction?// What is really a fiction is the explanation of the expression by the / by means of the/ private object before our inner sense. It is a fiction that in order for our words to have a meaning // to mean something // they must allude to something, which I, if not another, can show myself. (A *grammatical* fiction.))

The proposition that nothing stands behind the expression of a sensation, W. continues, is a *grammatical* one; it does not say that we do not have sensations. The interlocutor protests: 'Aren't you saying that "The soul is just something bodily"?, that when you have described people's behaviour, you have described everything?' But, W. retorts, he who *gives expression* to his pain does not describe his own behaviour! Yet, the interlocutor queries, if nothing stands behind the expression (*Äusserung*), does that not mean that it is not the expression of something (*nicht der Ausdruck von etwas ist*)? No, W. replies, for what it expresses, is not what we have agreed to call *thus*.

3   J. B. Watson argued in *Behaviourism* that belief in the existence of mental states, of consciousness, is mere superstition; that there is no objective evidence for the existence of minds (see 'Behaviour and behaviourism', §1).

Section 308

1   This describes, and prescribes the antidote to, the natural dialectic of reflection in the philosophy of psychology. Dualism insists that there are mental states and processes; after all, we experience them, are intimately acquainted with them, know them by introspection. Behaviourism insists that this is a pre-scientific mythology, that there are no mental states and processes, that these are fictions; and logical behaviourism argues that mental states are just logical constructions out of behaviour and dispositions to behave. Torn between these poles, materialism attempts a synthesis: there are indeed mental states and processes, only they are identical with brain-states, which cause behaviour. But this too is unsatisfactory for a multitude of reasons, and we replace it by something more up to date, viz. functionalism: mental states and processes are functional states of an organism that cause behaviour and are 'realized' in the nervous system. And so on. Far from this 'Hegelian' development being Reason successively approximating to the Real, it is a picture of Reason caught in the Hall of Mirrors: one illusion after another captures our attention for a while before we move on to the next.

The initial error escaped our attention, for it seemed altogether innocent. We talk of states and processes and very carefully avoid committing ourselves to characterizing their nature. *That*, we think, will become clear in the course of subsequent investigations. What could be more careful than such a procedure? But it is precisely here that the error lies: for the expressions 'state' and 'process', although vague, have specific grammars. Their unreflective adoption in psychology commits us to a definite (and misleading) way of looking at things. In one use of the expression, a state is an array of objects, with various properties, standing in certain relations to each other; that is how we talk of the state of the room (as tidy, the books being in the bookcase, the furniture in place) or of the garden (as untidy, with untrimmed bushes, weeds, and an unmown lawn), the state of the economy or the nation. Rather differently, we talk of being solid, liquid, or gaseous as three states of matter. A physical process is a more or less regular sequence of causally related events, themselves constituted by the transformation of substances; it goes on in time, has successive phases, can be slowed down or speeded up, interrupted, reversed, etc. We have a definite concept of what it is to know such a process better, but that concept does not apply in the same way in the domain of the mental! If we apply our 'definite concept of what it means to learn to know a process better' to the psychical sphere, we shall, *inter alia*, think that the subject of psychical states and processes can 'see' them, observe their obtaining, going on, and changing, and then report back to the psychologist what he has found out about these inner processes accessible directly only to him.[31] (James exemplifies this (see Volume 1, p. 602; MU p. 328). So if we say that 'reading is a quite particular process' (PI §165), we might try to find out more about this peculiar mental process by reading and attending to what happens. Is it too quick? Try reading Cyrillic! (MS. 152, 5; cf. Exg. §165).

Is it still obvious that talking of mental states and processes, *and leaving their nature undecided*, is innocuous? We do indeed talk of mental states (e.g. of intense concentration, nervous agitation, deep depression) and of processes (e.g. of adjusting to new situations, coming to terms with the loss of a loved one, of the growth of self-knowledge). But instead of examining the rather special uses of 'mental state' and 'mental process', which vary from case to case, philosophers (and psychologists) transpose the expressions 'state' and 'process' from the physical to the mental domain, leaving their nature undecided, as if *the facts*, if we are lucky, will reveal it to us. But *their nature is their grammar* (PI §373), and if we do not determine it, i.e. determine the *grammatical* differences between *mental* process and *physical* process, we shall unavoidably project the grammar of the latter onto the former. This will force upon us whole ranges of questions which, in the domain of the mental, make scant sense; or, at least, not the sense one expects, for one will be using the wrong paradigm. (See 'Thinking: methodological muddles and categorial confusions', §§3 – 4.)

1.1   'And now the analogy . . .': presumably the analogy between physical states and processes and, e.g., remembering, understanding, thinking. For there is indeed an analogy. But if we project upon these concepts our quite definite idea of what it is to come to know a *physical* process better, we fall into nonsense, and the analogy crumbles.

2   In many places W. issued warnings about the promiscuous and misleading application of the concepts of state and process to the mental. Thus:

We say that understanding is a 'psychological process', and this label is misleading, in this as in countless other cases. It compares understanding to a particular *process* like

---

[31] It is noteworthy that in Vol. XII, 333 a version of PI §571 occurs between two different drafts of PI §308.

translation from one language to another, and it suggests the same conception of thinking, knowing, wishing, intending, etc. That is to say, in all these cases, we see that what we would perhaps naively suggest as the hallmark of such a process is not present in every case or even in the majority of cases. And our next step is to conclude that the essence of the process is something difficult to grasp that still awaits discovery. (PG 74f.)

In this context in the *Grammar* W. suggested that understanding signifies a whole family of interrelated processes in specific contexts. But in *Zettel* he insisted 'But don't think of understanding as a "mental process" at all. – For *that* is the way of speaking that is confusing you' (Z §446 ;cf. PI §196; see also Volume 1, 'Understanding and ability', §§6 – 8). Similarly, we are puzzled as to how our thought is connected with what or whom we are thinking about, and so 'we think of meaning or thinking as a peculiar *mental activity*; the word "mental" indicating that we mustn't expect to understand how these things work' (BB 39). We wonder what the nature of imagination is and expect the answer to be given by a *description of process*; but 'One ought to ask, not what images are or what happens when one imagines anything, but how the word "imagination" is used' (PI §370). The present tense of expressions of ability, e.g. 'He is capable of . . .', 'He is able to multiply', 'He can play chess', etc., wrongly suggest that 'the phrases are descriptions of states which exist at the moment when we speak' (BB 117), and this gets in the way of seeing that potentialities are not shadowy actualities, and that earlier and later performances are *criteria* for having abilities at a particular time.

Despite these remarks, W. himself was sometimes willing to indulge an inclination to the promiscuous use of 'mental state', albeit with qualifications. Thus in *Investigations* §§572f. he observed that expecting, opining, hoping, knowing, being able to do something are states. The qualifications are (a) that these are *grammatically* states, arguably implying that grammar (the mere forms of expression that can be taken in at a glance) here misleads us (for 'sleeping' is *grammatically* an activity, 'refraining' is *grammatically* an act, etc.); (b) that only examination of the criteria for, e.g., reaching an opinion, having an opinion, changing an opinion, will show *what* gets treated *grammatically* (formally) as a *state* here. Similarly, in *Remarks of the Philosophy of Psychology* he characterized seeing (RPP I §1; RPP II §43), believing (RPP I §704), hearing, and having a sensation (RPP II §45) as *mental states*. On the other hand, in the same work he explicitly denied that believing, knowing, intending, etc. are states of consciousness, stressing their lack of 'genuine duration' (RPP II §45). There seems to be an unclarity in his thoughts in this text, which he surely would have remedied had he lived to prepare these notes for publication. His most important remarks on this subject are two late, methodological observations. The first warns against taking these very general concepts as ultimate logical categories, sharply defined and providing pre-prepared pigeon-holes for everything:

> The concept of experience: Like that of happening, of process, of state, of something, of fact, of description and of report. Here we think we are standing on the hard bedrock, deeper than any special methods and language-games. But these extremely general terms have an extremely blurred meaning. They relate in practice to innumerable special cases, but that does not make them any the more *solid*; no, rather it makes them more fluid. (RPP I §648)

The second manifests a sharpened awareness of the misleading character of such questions as 'Is X (where 'X' holds a place for a psychological expression) a mental state (process, activity, act, disposition, etc.)?' Apropos expecting someone, knowing since this morning that he is coming, W. wrote:

> Wenn man fragt: ist dies ein Zustand der Seele – so sieht man, das weder die Antwort 'Ja' noch die Antwort 'Nein' etwas nützt. Es gibt zu viele (psychologische) Kategorien, die man alle 'Zustände der Seele' nennen könnte. Die Einteilung // Klassifizierung // hilft hier nichts mehr. Man muss die Begriffe einzeln von einander unterscheiden (MS. 167, 6).

> (If one asks: is this a state of mind – one sees that neither the answer 'Yes' nor the answer 'No' helps. There are too many (psychological) categories all of which could be called 'states of mind'. The division // classification // no longer helps here. One must distinguish the concepts from one another individually.

2.1   'the first step': Vol. XII, 322 elaborates:

> Der erste Schritt ist die unschuldige pneumatische Auffassung wobei man (aber) die 'Art' der Vorgänge oder Zustände offen lässt. Der nächste aber ist, dass man sieht: welcher *Art* immer dieses etwas ist, wovon man reden will – es erkläre nichts und sei eine unnütze Fiktion. Gibt man nun aber dieser Fiktion auf, so scheint man alles Geistige zu leugnen und dadurch zu sagen, es gäbe nur Körperliches.

> (The first step is the innocent ethereal conception in which one (nevertheless) leaves open the 'kind' of processes or states. But the next is that one sees that no matter what *kind* of thing this something is of which one wants to talk, it explains nothing and is a useless fiction. But now if one gives up this fiction, it seems as if one is denying everything mental and thereby saying that there is only the bodily.)

3   The disease of thought here diagnosed was, and still is, pervasive. W. himself succumbed to it, as is strikingly evident in his 1919 letter to Russell (R 37). Frege was similarly infected (PW 145). So was James, who (apparently innocuously) assumed 'a direct awareness of the process of our thinking as such, simply insisting on the fact that it is an even more inward and subtle phenomenon than most of us suppose'.[32] Similar

---

[32] James, *Principles of Psychology*, Vol. I, p. 305.

cautious confessions of ignorance about the *nature* of mental states, activities, processes, or acts are to be found in Moore, Russell, Ramsey, etc., coupled of course with complete confidence that *there are such*; and so a *picture* is prepared into which subsequent reflections will be made to fit!

SECTION 309

1   Ryle asked 'But what has the fly missed, that has never got into the bottle and therefore never looked for or found the way out of it?' This is misleading, and the tempting answer that 'It has missed philosophical insight' is equally so. The correct answer would be: nothing at all save the experience of being trapped – but has there ever been such a fly? Only a clod or a god could resist being drawn into the fly-bottle of philosophical bafflement, a clod because he barely flies (thinks), a god because he already sees both the way in and the way out, so is not tempted in.

He who always knows his way about the grammar of his language and never loses his bearings, who is not even inclined to conceive the grammar of number-words on the model of the grammar of names of objects or the grammar of mental states on the model of physical states or the grammar of moral discourse on the model of empirical discourse or the grammar of infinite sets on the model of finite sets, etc., has no need for philosophy. For he would see immediately that the verb 'to be' is not used like the verb 'to eat', that the predicate 'is true' has a quite different kind of use from 'is blue', that 'time flows' and 'time passes' signify in a different way from 'the river flows' or 'the storm passes', and so forth. Such a person already possesses philosophical insight and does not need to work his way through the quagmires of philosophical confusion in order to attain it.

But we are not like that. The grammars of our language are immensely difficult for us to survey; philosophical questions masquerading as factual questions about the nature of things come naturally to us, and we are enmeshed in philosophical confusions that spring from the language we use, from the endlessly misleading forms of language which mask categorial differences from our eyes.

Die Menschen sind tief in den philosophischen d.i. grammatischen Konfusionen eingebettet. Und, sie daraus zu befreien, setzt voraus, dass man sie aus den ungeheuer mannigfachen Verbindungen herausreisst, in denen sie gefangen sind. Man muss sozusagen ihre ganze Sprache umgruppieren. – Aber diese Sprache ist ja so entstanden // geworden //, weil Menschen die Neigung hatten – und haben – *so* zu denken. (BT 423)

(Human beings are deeply embedded in philosophical, i.e. grammatical, confusion. And they cannot be freed w<u>ithout f</u>irst being extricated from the extraordinary variety of associations which hold them captive. You have, as it were, to reconstitute their entire language. But this language grew up // became // as it did because human beings had – and have – the tendency to think in this way.')

Moreover, we *love* our chains:

Das was den Gegenstand schwer verständlich macht ist – wenn er bedeutend, wichtig, ist – nicht, dass irgendeine besondere Instruktion über abstruse Dinge zu seinem Verständnis erforderlich wäre, sondern der Gegensatz zwischen dem Verstehen des Gegenstandes und dem, was die meisten Menschen sehen *wollen*. (BT 406f.)

(What makes it difficult to understand the matter – if it is significant, important – is not the lack of some special instruction in obstruse things necessary for its understanding, but the conflict between the right understanding of the matter and what most men *want* to see.)

For who among us would not prefer the glitter of gold encrusted with jewels brought into view by metaphysics to the heap of rusting iron and old stones revealed when the spell is lifted.

It is not just philosophers who are drawn into the fly-bottle, but scientists, psychologists, mathematicians – in fact all who reflect on the nature of the soul, the relation of mind to body, the character of thought, the scope of possible knowledge, the strangeness of mathematics, etc. 'Philosophy is a tool which is useful only against philosophies and against *the philosopher in us*' (TS. 219, 11; my emphasis).

To ask what the fly which has never got into the bottle has missed is rather like asking what the man who has never been ill has missed. Doctors are not likely to become redundant (or iatrogenic diseases to cease to multiply!).

2   LPE 300 has the first occurrence of the fly-bottle metaphor: 'The solipsist flutters and flutters in the flyglass, strikes against the walls, flutters further. How can he be brought to rest?' PI §309 occurs in Vol. XIV, 142f. and Vol. XIII, 92, with the addendum 'Dieser Weg zu finden ist, unter gewissen Verhältnissen u<u>nmögli</u>ch; unter andern ganz leicht; und unter wieder anderen ungemein schwer' ('To find this way is in certain circumstances i<u>mpossib</u>le; in others altogether easy; and in yet others extraordinarily d<u>ifficul</u>t.') When is it impossible? Perhaps when the will to illusion cannot be broken!

SECTION 310

1   W. now reverts to §304: viz. the difference between pain-behaviour accompanied by pain and pain-behaviour without any pain. §310(a) sets

the scene: I avow pain; the hearer may believe, disbelieve, be slightly suspicous, etc. §310(b) follows up the interlocutor's question in §304(a): does not the hearer's response 'It's not so bad' *prove* that he believes that there is *something* behind my pain-behaviour, something to which he *refers* in saying that *it* is not so bad? No; his attitude is what it is, commiseration or gentle reproach. It is an attitude towards a soul, towards a human being, a person (PI p. 178). That the hearer may take up this or that attitude manifests his belief that I am in pain or his suspicion that I am not suffering as much as I make out, but *that* is not proof of a philosophical thesis (mythology) that pain is *a something* behind pain-behaviour. His attitude, expressed by his utterance 'It's not so bad', could also be expressed by instinctive noises and gestures. Would they prove that he believes that pain is an inner object known only to its owner? – No more than an instinctive cry of pain proves that the sufferer believes that he has something no one else could have!

2   In MS. 165, 171 this is followed by a contrast with the role of the truth or falsity of a statement in other language-games. If I look out of the window and say 'The wind has blown the tree over', you may rush to the window and see whether I was pulling your leg or speaking the truth. Clearly this is disanalogous to the way in which we establish whether in saying 'I am in pain', you were only pulling my leg.

.1   'His attitude to me . . . .': cf. Z §545.

SECTION 311

1   §304 agreed with the interlocutor that of course there is all the difference in the world between pain-behaviour without pain and pain-behaviour with pain. But this is readily misunderstood as a concession to his *picture*; for the interlocutor eagerly explains the difference on his preferred model. It seems that the difference is such as can only be exhibited or displayed to oneself, privately. I can exhibit publicly the difference between a broken and an unbroken tooth, but pain-behaviour with pain differs from pain-behaviour without pain only by the presence of *pain*; and *that*, the interlocutor insists, I can exhibit only to myself.

But, W. retorts, for the 'private exhibition' one does not have to prick oneself with a pin (and, even if one did prick oneself, that would be *having* a pain, not *exhibiting* a pain to oneself). It should suffice that one imagines a pain. Then one can say to oneself that when pain-behaviour is accompanied by *this*, it is pain-behaviour *with* pain, otherwise not! But what does one *do* when one imagines pain? Perhaps one screws up one's face a little! Does *that* tell one what it is that one is imagining? Although one can imagine pain-behaviour with pain and pain-behaviour without pain, to imagine anything presupposes a grasp of what is to be imagined. Hence here it presupposes that the difference is crystal-clear to one *prior* to one's imagining these two cases. Moreover, to imagine a pain is not to *exhibit* pain to oneself. There is no such thing as a *private* exhibition of the private.

1.1   (i) 'Den Unterschied aber . . .': 'I can, however, exhibit . . .'.
        (ii) 'You screw up your face a bit': to imagine pain is not to have a picture of pain before one's mind, for there is no such thing. You can imagine pain all right, but not by way of a mental image (*bildliche Vorstellung*) of pain (cf. Exg. §§300f.). Of course, when you imagine pain, a mental image may cross your mind too – perhaps an image of something brown or violet-brown (MS. 161, 52)!

2   The illusion of a 'private exhibition' of experience, of displaying the 'content' of experience before one's mind, is discussed in various passages in RPP I. One is sorely tempted to say that one knows what toothaches are like, that one is acquainted with them, and so too with the experiences of seeing different colours, feeling emotions, remembering, intending, etc. In all these cases one is inclined to say that one has a 'privileged access' to the phenomena, and surely one can 'parade these experiences before one's mind', exhibit them to oneself! W. responds acidly, 'So I know, do I, what it means to parade these experiences before one's mind? And what *does* it mean? How can I explain it to anyone else, or to myself? (RPP I §91). The very concept of the content of experience thus invoked in philosophy 'is the private object, the sense-datum, the "object" that I grasp immediately with the mental eye, ear, etc. The inner picture' (RPP I §109; cf. RPP I §896).

SECTION 312

1   §311 argued that there is such a thing as a public exhibition or display of the public (e.g. the difference between a broken and an unbroken tooth), but no such thing as the *private* exhibition of the private. Yet it may seem that the cases of the tooth and of the pain are similar, for do I not note the difference between a broken and an unbroken tooth by *seeing* it; and does not the visual sensation (or sense-impression) in this case correspond to the sensation of pain in the other?
      W.'s answer comes in two stages. First, I can exhibit (display) the visual impression *privately* as little as I can exhibit (display) pain to myself privately; i.e. there is no such thing as a *private exhibition*. For neither

having (or imagining) a pain, nor having (or imagining) a visual sense-impression, count as exhibiting a pain or as exhibiting a visual sense-impression even to oneself. Does it follow that one *cannot* exhibit pain or exhibit having a visual sense-impression? No, one *can* exhibit pain and one *can* exhibit having a visual sense-impression – only not *privately* (cf. §313). To exhibit these to myself does not differ from exhibiting them to someone else. Of course, a sensation of pain does not correspond to a visual sensation or sense-impression; for having a pain is not involved in perceiving an object. But that does not affect the argument.

§312(b) gives the (opaque) second stage of W.'s reply. The absence of an object perceived does not hinder a public exhibition of pain. One can indeed imagine a closer association between pain and perception. If surfaces of plants had areas on them which produced pain on touch, and if it were useful to notice these patches and their shapes (e.g. if they correlated well with the nature, medicinal or nutritious character, of the plants), then the sensation of pain had on touching these plants would be akin to perceiving. What one perceived by touching and having a sharp pain would be conceived as a pain-patch, and these pain-patches thus apprehended would be important in identifying or characterizing the plant. Sensitivity to pain on touching plants would then be a faculty for apprehending features of the world around us (some people might be better than others at discerning whether a plant was such-and-such).

How does this bear on §312(a)? Perhaps as follows: one would display the difference between a broken and an unbroken tooth by pointing at them; one would display having a visual sense-impression of a broken tooth by looking at one and maybe saying 'Aha! This looks like a broken tooth!' or otherwise giving expression to how it strikes one visually. How then does one, in a parallel manner, exhibit feeling pain? We do not, as it happens, talk (much[33]) of pain-patches. But that does not matter. In the envisaged story one could exhibit pain-patches to touch as one exhibits red patches to sight. One would, further, exhibit feeling pain, e.g. by touching a pain-patch on a plant and drawing one's hand back and exclaiming 'Ow!' One can, in this sense, exhibit the sensation of pain for oneself no less well than one can exhibit the visual sense-impression of a broken tooth. The fact that we do not speak of pain-patches as we speak of colour-patches is irrelevant to the nature of exhibiting seeing or pain. But there is nothing private about such exhibiting. Pain is not an object of perception, and sensitivity to pain is

---

[33] We do a little, as in '*stinging* nettles', '*burning* sand', '*painful* shoes'; but it is easy to see why we do not extend this. Almost anything can cause pain, hence its capacity to do so is a poor guide to its nature. Most things that can cause pain do not always do so when touched. And pain so caused typically persists *after* contact is broken.

not a sense-faculty; but that is no impediment to the *ppublic* exhibition of (feeling) pain.

The argument here is puzzling. A visual sense-impression or sensation (*Gesichtsempfindung*) corresponds to the sensation of pain only in the sense that neither can be exhibited 'privately' (see 2(ii) below). That one can exhibit the sensation of pain publicly, i.e. *manifest* pain, is a point which gets no significant support from the story of pain-patches; nor does it need it. Whether or not there are pain-patches on objects which are perceptible by touch, the concept of a sensation of pain is fundamentally different from the concept of a 'visual sensation' or a visual sense-impression. The concept of a visual impression of X is parasitic on the concept of X. So, for example, the concept of a visual impression of red is parasitic on the concept of red, and the latter can be defined ostensively by reference to a red patch, used as a sample. But the concept of pain is not parasitic on the concept of its cause. It is determined by the criteria for pain. Even if we talked of pain-patches, the concept of a pain-patch would be parasitic on the concept of pain, not vice versa. A pain-patch would *cause* pain on touch, but it would be mistaken to suppose that a red patch *causes* a visual impression of red (though this cannot be argued here). §312(b) does not really seem to advance the argument at all.

1.1　　(i) 'visual sensation': arguably a stretched use of 'sensation'. Are there such things as *visual* sensations as opposed to visual impressions? The best candidate for the title would be the sensation of being dazzled; but that is not what W. has in mind.

(ii) 'that we can infer important properties from them': as things are, of course, we cannot infer important properties of objects from the fact that they can cause us pain, but only 'accidents' of objects (e.g. that they are, at the moment, hot). Indeed, that is one reason why we do not talk of pain-patches.

2　　(i) MS. 165, 176f. imagines getting an electric shock from certain areas on the surface of things. Sensitivity to pain could be employed (in these circumstances) in discerning features of the external world in a similar way to tactile sensation (cf. RPP I §697).

(ii) Z §§665ff. argues that I can exhibit something to myself only in the way I exhibit it to others. I can exhibit my good memory by interrogating myself and answering (the dates of the English monarchs, for example); and this serves both for others and for myself.

SECTION 313

1　　This draws the conclusion from §312. One *can* exhibit pain, but not as the interlocutor envisaged. We need to bring to mind what is *called* exhibiting (or displaying) pain. W. does not here note the manifold *differences* between exhibiting pain and exhibiting red, but concentrates on the reminder that the former is no less public than the latter. That much is true. But it is surely misleading to suggest that one can exhibit pain *as* (in *the same way* as) one can exhibit red.

2   In MS. 165, 178 and MS. 124, 290 this is followed by PI §§273ff., which clarifies that exhibiting red is not a private exhibition either.

SECTION 314

1   A concluding remark: the philosophical problem(s) about sensation are not to be resolved by studying (concentrating on) one's sensations. For it is nonsense to suppose that the 'nature' of pain, for example, can be read off the sensation. And it is misguided to construe the grammar of 'pain' on the model of name and object. Rather, one should proceed by analysing the concept of sensation (cf. PI §§383f.), which is done by studying the *use of the word* 'sensation' (cf. Z §§546 – 8).

This remark is the hook upon which §§316ff. hang.

SECTION 315

1   The ideas that understanding the word 'pain' turns on the possibility of my giving myself a *private* exhibition of pain (or, more generally, of the 'inner') and that it is only from my own case that I know what 'pain' means (PI §§311, 293(a)) go hand in hand with the thought that a necessary condition for understanding the word 'pain' is to have felt pain. But is this meant to be an empirical truth? Have we discovered that people who have never suffered pains do *not* understand the word? Clearly not. (Have we ever come across such a person? Is our immediate inclination to assent to this claim based on our experience with such people?)

Confronted by the fact that the apparent obviousness of the claim is not based on social surveys, we are inclined to insist that one could not *imagine* pain without having previously felt pain. (For are 'ideas of the imagination' not faint copies of antecedent impressions?) And surely, it seems that 'using a sentence involves imagining something for every word' (PI §449). Is it not obvious that 'I must know what it would be like if I were in pain' (ibid.)?

This common line of thought is confused. First, it is, for many reasons, misguided to think that in using a sentence with understanding one must imagine something corresponding to it. For example, in the case of the order 'Imagine a red circle here', must I already obey it in order merely to understand it (PI §451)? Secondly, the phrase 'knowing what it would be like' equivocates precisely over the matter at issue. Does it mean 'knowing what ". . . " means'? Or does it mean 'having experienced . . .'? And in the case of pain, if I *have* felt pain, *do* I therefore know *what it is like*? The experience of pain is surely not a sufficient condition for knowing what it is like! (Does an injured cat know what it is like to have a pain?) Indeed, what is it like? That is, what *kind* of answer does this question invite? It obviously steers us in the direction of answering 'Like *this*' – and thumping ourselves on the chest; but then, what is *this* like? The answer is modelled on 'I know what magenta looks like, viz. like *this*' – and pointing at a sample. But this model, as has been shown, has no application here. Thirdly, if one knows what 'pain' means, does one *not* know what it is like to have a pain?

To this question, one might be inclined to reply 'Yes, one does, but one cannot know what "pain" means unless one has had pain!' This is where we started. How can one get off the merry-go-round? Only by asking a different question: viz. 'What are the criteria for knowing what "pain" means?' If a person uses the word 'pain' correctly, says of others that they are in pain when they exhibit pain, says that they are no longer in pain when they exhibit relief from pain, etc., would we deny that he understands what 'pain' means? Would we investigate his medical history before pronouncing on his linguistic competence? Since it is evidently not an empirical claim that one must have felt pain if one knows what 'pain' means, is it a grammatical truth? No; we do not have a rule that prohibits saying of a person that he knows what 'pain' means if, although he uses it correctly, he has never suffered pain. (No more need a person have debts in order to know what a negative number is!)

2   LSD 35f. pinpoints *one* source of the confusion here in the misguided projection of the grammar of colour-words on to the grammar of sensation-words:

> Suppose someone who has never had a toothache, but has heard the word. Then one day he has a toothache, and says 'Now I know what "toothache" means'.
>
> But then suppose I ask him, 'Well, what *does* it mean?' Or: 'Does it mean what I had?'
>
> When I have a sample of red, then if you ask me 'Well, what *does* "red" mean?', I can answer 'It means *this*'. In the case of toothache, the temptation is to say 'Well, I know, although I can't express it'. There is a suggestion that you have a private ostensive definition. And I say you have not got one.
>
> Just as there is an inclination to say that the ostensive definition of 'red' might be secret – recorded in my diary (which no one else sees); but further, that it is *essentially* secret.

2   'Is experience to teach me . . .': Z §267 elaborates: 'Is it supposed to be an empirical fact that someone who has had an experience can imagine it, and that someone else can *not*? (How do I know that a blind man cannot[34] imagine colours?) But: he cannot play a certain language-game (cannot learn it). But is this empirical, or is it the case *eo ipso*? The latter.' That the blind cannot play (or can only partially master) the language-game with colour-words *is* a grammatical proposition. So too is the remark that, synaesthesia apart, the blind cannot imagine colours. For they do not know what colour-words mean: they can neither use them nor explain them as we do (as they are to be used and explained). So they do not know *what* they are to imagine when told to imagine a red expanse, for example.

---

[34] The German transcription and translation alike have omitted the negation (see MS. 162(b), 33).

THE INNER AND THE OUTER

1. *Semi-solipsism*

The traditional picture of the mental represented avowals of experience and expressions of thought as descriptions of inner states based on introspective scrutiny of private objects. A complement of that conception is an equally distorted picture of the nature of third-person psychological propositions. For a corollary of the idea of first-person 'privileged access' is the idea of 'indirect access' to other people's states of mind, thoughts, beliefs, or experiences. This aberration, which Wittgenstein referred to as 'semi-solipsism' (MS. 165, 150), is one of the targets of his critical investigations.

It is striking that few of the originators of the *philosophical* conception of the mind which we have inherited from the Cartesians and British empiricists dwelt at any length upon the nature of our knowledge of the 'inner world' of other subjects of experience. Berkeley was an exception, and his account of what he called 'our knowledge of spirits' is one of the more curious elements in that strange metaphysics which he constructed to replace the incoherences of representational idealism:

It is plain that *we* cannot *know the existence of other spirits* otherwise than by *their operations* or *the ideas by them excited in us*. I perceive several motions, changes, and combinations of ideas, that inform me that there are certain particular agents *like myself*, which accompany them, and concur in their production. Hence the knowledge I have of other spirits is *not immediate*; as is the knowledge of my ideas; but depending on the intervention of ideas, by me referred to *agents or spirits* distinct from myself, as effects or concomitant signs.[1]

The 'intervening ideas', of course, are my ideas of the 'motion of limbs' of the body of another person, which ideas are conveyed to my mind by God. Indeed, Berkeley held, our knowledge of each other is less certain, more indirect, than our knowledge of God. If we cannot *see* God, we cannot see each other either, and our knowledge of others is mediated by God's activity in producing in us ideas.

A human spirit or person is not perceived by sense, as not being an idea; when therefore we see the colour, size, figure, and motions of a man, we perceive only certain sensations or ideas excited in our minds; and these being exhibited to our view in sundry distinct collections, serve to mark out unto us the existence of finite and created spirits like ourselves.[2]

[1] Berkeley, *The Principles of Human Knowledge*, CXLV.
[2] Ibid., CXLVIII.

It is difficult to see how this form of 'semi-solipsism' can be prevented from collapsing. For if other people's bodies are merely collections of ideas in *my* mind, conveyed there by God's causal (volitional) activity, then *those ideas* cannot, contrary to Berkeley's insistence, be conceived as being 'accompanied' by 'certain particular agents like myself'. The only mental substances involved in this story are myself, whose ideas these are, and God, who causes them. In Berkeley's tale, there is only room for tea for two. An idealist cannot build anything upon an analogical argument.

Mill propounded a more explicit version of the analogical argument without the encumbrance of the Deity.

> I observe that there is a great multitude of other bodies, closely resembling in their sensible properties . . . this particular one [viz. my own], but whose modifications do not call up, as those of my own body do, a world of sensations in my consciousness. Since they do not do so in my consciousness, I infer that they do it out of my consciousness, and that to each of them belongs a world of consciousness of its own, to which it stands in the same relation in which what I call my body stands to mine, . . . Each of these bodies exhibits to my sense a set of phaenomena (composed of acts and other manifestations) such as I know, in my own case, to be effects of consciousness, and such as might be looked for if each of the bodies has really in connexion with it a world of consciousness.[3]

This has a superficial cogency. But again, as with Berkeley, it is propounded in the context of an idealist metaphysics. For Mill argued that material objects, including human bodies, are no more than permanent possibilities of sense-experiences. Neither philosopher noticed the tension between his idealism and his account of knowledge of other people's experience.

The analogical argument sits more comfortably in a philosophical context which is not idealist. Like Berkeley and Mill, a proponent of such an argument conceives of the 'world of consciousness' as externally related to the 'world' of visible human bodies. We cannot *perceive* the minds or experiences of other people, but only their bodies and behaviour – and bodily behaviour *seems* to be just a matter of the movement of a physical object in space (see 'Behaviour and behaviourism', §4). The 'inner' therefore appears to be *hidden* behind the 'outer' and to be inferred from perceptible behaviour by analogy. Another person's pains, one is inclined to think, are hidden from me but accessible to him – I cannot feel them, but he can. Similarly, his thoughts are hidden from me, unless he reveals what he thinks. Hence, it seems, I can know only *indirectly* that he has a pain or thinks this or that, whereas he knows *directly*. For I have to *infer* that he has a pain, but he does not.

---

[3] J. S. Mill, *An Examination of Sir William Hamilton's Philosophy*, in *Collected Works*, Vol. IX, p. 192.

It seems obvious that what lies within is the *cause* of behaviour. For do people not cry out *because* they are in pain? And is pain not something 'inner'? They reach for a glass of water because they want a drink, and they make assertions because they believe what they say. So an inference from behaviour to a thought or experience that lies behind it must surely be an inference from an effect to a hidden cause. Hence we are prone to think of human behaviour as akin to the movements of a puppet manipulated by hidden strings, Cartesians conceiving of these strings as being controlled by the mind (via the pineal gland) and materialists conceiving of them as being pulled by the brain.

2. *Inside and outside*

Our knowledge of the experiences of others, in comparison with what philosophers think of as self-knowledge, seems distinctly shaky. Do I not know what I feel, want, or think directly, by introspection? But I know how things are with another person only on the basis of what he does and says, how he reacts and responds to circumstances. One is tempted to claim that one can never really know, but only *believe*, how things are with another person (PI §303). We are inclined to think that the belief or supposition that another person has a pain is just the belief or supposition that he has what I have when I have a pain (PI §350). I know what pain is, one wants to say, from my own case. To say that someone else is in pain just is to say that he has the same as I have so often had. This seemingly innocuous claim is one of the struts supporting the argument from analogy and also its updated version, the 'inference to the best explanation'. The *sense* of the third-person pain-attributions seems perspicuous and unproblematic. The philosophical problems appear to arise only with respect to knowing their truth. This is precisely where we go wrong.

'If one has to imagine someone else's pain on the model of one's own', Wittgenstein urged, 'this is none too easy a thing to do: for I have to imagine pain which I *do not feel* on the model of the pain which I *do feel*' (PI §302). For it is not as if I have to imagine that the pain I have in my knee is in my ankle, or even that I feel pain in someone else's ankle. Rather, I have to imagine someone else having *this*, which I now have. But what does it *mean* for another person to have *this*? This question antecedes any epistemological qualms. But surely, all one needs to suppose is that someone else has the *same* pain, and we have clarified that this is perfectly possible! Indeed so, but for an explanation in terms of *sameness* to get any grip, it must be determined what is to count as another person's being in pain. Wittgenstein elucidated the point by an analogy: one cannot explain what it is for it to be five o'clock on the sun by saying that it is five o'clock on the sun if it is five o'clock here and it is the same time there (PI §350). On the contrary, we can say that it is the same time on the sun as it is here if it is five o'clock here and also five o'clock there. But that presupposes an explanation of what it is for it to be five o'clock there. Similarly, if I have a pain and someone else has a pain, one can say that we have the same experience. But we have yet to explain what is to count as someone else having a pain. One's own pain does not furnish one with a criterion for being in pain, since one does not identify one's pain by criteria (PI §290); one just says 'I have a pain' (or groans), without any grounds or justification. A fortiori, one's own pain gives one no criterion for the identification of the pains of others.

But, of course, for one's *avowal* of pain to count as an avowal of *pain*, it must fit in with, be an extension and partial replacement of, one's natural pain-behaviour. For, just like natural expressions of pain, an avowal of pain is a criterion for others to judge that one is in pain. Hence ascription of pain (as well as sense-impressions, emotions, moods, desires, etc.) to others is rendered intelligible not by analogy with or by extrapolition from one's own case, but by reference to the behavioural manifestations of pain, etc. The behavioural *expressions* of the 'inner' are not mere symptoms (inductive evidence) of how things are, but critera. Hence it is a mistake to think that they are *mere* behaviour, nothing but externalities (just noises and movements). But as long as one is in the grip of the picture of the 'inner' and the 'outer', it is wellnigh impossible to think of the behavioural expression of the mental as anything other than an outward sign (symptom) of an inner, hidden state or experience.

It is noteworthy that one does not say, save when doing philosophy, that toothache is something 'inner' (LSD 18), any more than one says that pain is something mental. And that is right, for what would it be for toothache to be 'outer'? Indeed, what is toothache *in*? The mind? There is no such thing as mental toothache, and toothache is, by definition, in one's tooth. We talk of *physical* pain and contrast it with mental suffering, viz. anguish and grief. But we *compare* toothache and its behavioural expression with 'internal' and 'external' (LSD 18). The comparison is not silly, for it is true that I do not say that I have toothache on the grounds of observation, whereas I judge another to have toothache only in so far as I see him clutch his swollen jaw and hear him groan (cf. LPE 278). But, Wittgenstein observed, 'We must get clear about how the metaphor of revealing (outside and inside) is actually applied by us; otherwise we shall be tempted to look for an inside behind that which in our metaphor is the inside' (LPE 280).

Someone may have a pain and not manifest it; he can see something and not say what he sees; and he can think such-and-such and not voice his thoughts. But if he groans with pain, says what he sees, and expresses his opinions, then he has 'revealed' what is, *in our metaphor*, the inner. If he screams with pain as the doctor prods him, one cannot say 'Well, that is only behaviour – his pain is still concealed'. If he tells us, in no uncertain terms, what he thinks about so-and-so, we cannot say 'These are only words – he has kept his thoughts to himself'. And if he *shows* us what he sees, then we too can see what he sees, even though we do not look inside anything (LPE 279). This, in each case, is what we *call* 'exhibiting pain', 'expressing one's thoughts', 'showing what one sees'. For it is not as if, in such cases, he always leaves something behind which he keeps to himself.

There is indeed such a thing as concealing one's pain, hiding one's feelings, keeping one's thoughts secret. But to have a pain, feel annoyed, or think such-and-such is not *per se* to conceal anything. I hide my pain when I stifle my groans, but by the same token I reveal that I am in pain when a scream finally bursts from my lips. I conceal my feelings when I exercise self-control, but I reveal them when, e.g., I give vent to my anger. I do not conceal my thoughts merely by thinking them and not saying what I think, although it is true that that will often leave others bemused and may even mislead them (and hence it is *comparable* to hiding (RPP II, §§586ff.)). Rather, one hides one's thoughts by writing them down in code, by keeping one's diary under lock and key (LW §974), or by communicating them to one's wife in a language which the children do not understand (RPP II, §§563f.). But if the code is broken, the diary read, the foreign language understood, one's previously hidden thoughts are perfectly public.

Parallel to the confusions of 'inner' and 'outer', of 'concealed' and 'revealed', is a misuse of 'direct' and 'indirect'. It is wrong to say that I know only *indirectly* that he has pain, sees such-and-such, thinks this or that, whereas he knows directly. For, in the first place, it is wrong to say that he *knows*. Secondly, it only makes sense to talk of indirect knowledge if it also makes sense to talk of direct knowledge. For this distinction is meant to draw a contrast (and in *other* domains does). But there *is* no more direct way of knowing that another person is in pain , than by seeing him moan and writhe. Similarly, there is no more direct way of seeing what he sees than by his showing what he sees, and no more direct way of knowing what he thinks than from his sincere confession. If a friend opens his heart to me, I cannot say 'I know only indirectly what he thinks and feels'. That would be appropriate if my information were *hearsay*, but a confession from the horse's mouth, so to speak, is not second-hand. Knowing indirectly that someone is in pain might be a matter of noticing the empty bottle of analgesics by his bedside or seeing that he has gone to lie down (as he always does when he feels unwell). But there is nothing *indirect* about witnessing the agony of childbirth. Not to have had such pains does not imply that witnessing them gives one only *indirect* knowledge of their severity, and to have suffered the pangs of childbirth is not to *know* anything directly, but to have *experienced* such pains, i.e. to have had them.

It is tempting to try to cash the metaphor of direct/indirect in the currency of inference. For one is inclined to say that he knows that he is in pain without inference, i.e. directly, whereas I know that he is pain by inference from his behaviour, i.e. indirectly. But this is in part nonsense and in part wrong. As argued, it is nonsense to say that he knows that he is in pain. What is true is that he does not say that he has a pain on the grounds of observation, whereas I do. But it is misleading to say that because I assert that he is in pain on the grounds of observing his winces, groans, or writhing, therefore I know that he is in pain by inference, i.e. indirectly (cf. LW §767). When someone writhes on the ground with a broken leg, one does not *infer* (draw the conclusion) that he is in pain from evidence; one *sees* that he is suffering. The doctor infers that his patient has an appendicitis from the character and location of the patient's *pain*, but it would be highly misleading to say that he infers that his patient is in pain from his screams of agony. If asked 'How do you know he is in pain?', one might answer 'I saw him writhing in agony', but it would be absurd to say 'I saw only his behaviour, but I inferred that he was in pain'. To see him writhing in agony *is* to see that he is in pain. But if I hear that someone has severe arthritis, then I might infer that he has pain.

One might object: to be sure, we can see *that* another person is in pain, but one cannot see his pain; surely that is inferred! The objection is incorrect. First, do we not say 'I could see his agony' or 'I was witness to his suffering'? Is it elliptical to say 'I saw the pain in his face'? (Although, to be sure, the pain I could see in his face may well be the pain of a broken leg)? Secondly, in so far as it is true that I cannot *see* or otherwise perceive his pain, neither can he. I see the manifestations of pain which he exhibits; but when he exhibits pain, it is *manifest*. It can be said that I cannot see his pain only in the sense in which I cannot see sounds or hear colours (LW §885). From the fact that I know he is in pain by observation or know his thoughts because I heard his confession, it does not follow that my knowledge is inferential, any more than the fact that I know that there is a picture on the wall because I can see it implies that I infer that there is a picture there.

Nevertheless, one may object, I may be wrong. I may see him writhing on the ground and say, 'He is in pain'; yet it might all be simulation and pretence. Similarly, he may confess that he thinks such-and-such and yet be totally insincere. And does this not show that his pain and his opinions are something 'inner', hidden behind his behaviour, and that my judgements about them are inferences from the 'outer', and hence that my knowledge is indirect and fallible? It is true that there is such a thing as pretending, that one can hide one's thoughts and feelings, even lie and dissimulate. Indeed, this is one thing that might legitimately be meant by saying that thoughts and feelings are private (RPP I §570). But under the spell of the misleading model of 'inner' and 'outer' we misconstrue the implications of these possibilities. For they no more show that our judgements about other people's mental states, etc. are inferential and our knowledge indirect than the possibility of illusion and hallucination show that our judgements about objects in our field of perception are inferential and our knowledge indirect.

The possibility of lying, deceit, and pretence shows that our judgements about other people are fallible; it does not show that their feelings, desires, and thoughts are hidden behind their behaviour as the movement of a clock is hidden behind its face. We judge another to be in pain, sorrowful, or overjoyed in as much as we take his behaviour to be an expression of pain, a manifestation of grief or joy. And we may, indeed, be deceived; for he may be pretending. But to be deceived here is not to think that there is something inner behind the behaviour when in fact there is not. It is to think that his groans are a manifestation of pain whereas they are mere pretence, that his sighs express grief whereas they are deceitful. That he is not in pain or not sorrowful is shown by *other things he does*, by what he said earlier or how he acts later, by subtle and barely noticeable deviations from the characteristic pattern of expression of pain or sorrow. These do not show the absence of something behind the behaviour, but the presence of something *in* the behaviour which is other than what one initially thought. It is misguided to think of moaning with pain as behaviour *plus* an inner experience, just as it is misconceived to think of saying something and meaning it as behaviour plus an inner act of meaning. One might rather say that moaning without pain or saying something and not meaning what one said is behaviour *plus* something, for here there is something which is absent in the case of sincere behaviour, viz. a dishonest purpose! We are systematically misled in this domain by our picture of 'outside plus inside' (LSD 10).

Expressions of pain, manifestations of sorrow, etc. are criteria for saying of a person that he is in pain, grieving, and so forth. The possibility of lying, deceit, and pretence shows that these criteria are, *in certain circumstances*, defeasible. It does not show that the observable criteria for being in pain, grieving, etc. are criteria for something hidden behind what is on view. But while agreeing that such criteria are defeasible, one must emphasize that their defeasibility is circumstance-dependent. Lying, deceit, and pretence are essentially parasitic activities, language-games that must be learnt and are learnt only after the 'host' activity has been mastered (cf. Exg. §§249f.). It would be unintelligible to suppose that the smile of an unweaned infant is pretence (PI §249);

indeed, 'it is senseless to say: the expression may always lie', for the language-games with expressions of feeling are based on games with expressions of which we do not say that they may lie (LPE 293). And that is not an *assumption* that might prove to be wrong. It makes sense to attribute deceit and pretence to a creature only within a highly complex weave of life, in which a wide range of other capacities is manifest. Hence one cannot attribute dishonesty and dissimulation to a dog (PI §250 and Exg.). Moreover, even if a creature does possess those capacities and has mastered those techniques, the intelligibility of attributing pretence to it is still circumstance-relative. If someone falls into a fire and screams with pain, it would be absurd to say 'He may be pretending' (cf. LPE 318). There are certain kinds of behaviour of which one may say 'One *can't* pretend like that' (Z §570), e.g. throwing oneself off the roof while pretending to be distraught. There are even circumstances in which one may say of a person 'He *thinks* he is pretending' (PI p. 229). The possibility of pretence gives no grounds whatever for the sceptical anxiety that maybe all behaviour is mere pretence (Z §§570f.). For here, as elsewhere, it is false that what happens sometimes might happen always (PI §§344f.).

One may still object: if Wittgenstein does acknowledge that 'pain' does not mean the same as 'pain-behaviour', that experience and thought are distinct from their public expression, must he not also acknowledge that what is 'inner' is the cause of the behaviour that we call 'its expression'? Is it not pain that causes me to cry out, desire that causes me to act, or fear that makes me blanch and tremble? And given that this is so, might it not be that the causal mechanism, with which I am intimately acquainted in my own case, is different in other people?

The causal conception of the mind and its relation to behaviour is too large to tackle comprehensively here; all that can be done is to sow seeds of doubt that may be cultivated elsewhere. We do say 'I asserted that because that was what I was thinking' or 'I insisted on that point because I remembered it happening'. But it does not follow that my thinking was an inner event or my recollecting an inner process which caused me to speak. Rather, such explanations are given in order to distinguish sincerely expressing one's opinions, from, e.g., pulling someone's leg, being deliberately provocative, or acting as devil's advocate, or, in the case of citing one's recollections, in order to make explicit the source of one's knowledge, viz. that one witnessed such-and-such and so was not merely repeating hearsay. 'Because' here does not identify a *cause*. One may concede that we often shrink from something because we are afraid or reach for something because we desire to have it. But it is not obvious that these explanations are causal. We contrast shrinking from something out of fear from shrinking from it out of disgust or disdain. These explanations *characterize* the action, but it is not evident that they do so by identifying a cause. It is as misleading to conceive of dancing with joy, chortling with amusement, or weeping with grief as behaviour plus inner process as it is to conceive of plaintive, joyous, or triumphant music as sounds plus plaint, joy, or triumph (cf. LSD 10f.). Similarly, saying something and meaning it is not saying plus an inner activity of meaning. In all these cases the inner/outer picture makes the causal model of explanation seem compelling, even inevitable. But if the grip of that mesmerizing picture has been weakened, we should examine afresh the plausibility and apparent inevitability of that model.

The dominant philosophical account of causation conceives of the causal relation as non-logical (external), inductive (hence requiring the possibility of independent identification of the relata), and nomic (instantiating a general law). The mental and its behavioural expression, however, do not unquestionably fit this account. Although one can have toothache and not show it or feign toothache without having it the behavioural manifestation of toothache is not logically independent of toothache (LSD 10). For the behavioural manifestations of toothache are the identifying criteria for toothache, not inductive evidence for it (LSD 134f.). It is not as if we can envisage the possibility of people having excruciating toothache but happily chewing their food, laughing, and joking. Nevertheless, when I have a toothache and inadvertently bite on the infected tooth, is it not the pain that makes me cry out? Of course; I *could not help* crying out, could not stifle the cry, so severe was the pain. But to admit that is not to admit that the pain caused me to cry out in the sense in which the sun causes wax to melt. If anything caused me to cry out in that sense, it was biting on the infected tooth. The pain is not a third object or event that *mediates* between the biting and the crying, even though it is true that one can feign toothache, i.e. bite and cry out without having a pain. But it is misleading to conceive of crying out with pain as crying out *plus* an inner experience that is its cause (LSD 10).

The sceptical supposition that the 'causal mechanism' might be different in other people, that they might cry out and moan when they injure themselves even though they have no pain but, perhaps, a pleasant sensation of warmth is as absurd as the supposition that they might all be automatons. If someone suggests that for all we know the blind really see, but only behave as if they do not, and that the sighted are really blind, but only behave as if they saw, it is obvious that his suppositions sever the concepts of seeing and blindness from their behavioural manifestation. In so doing, he deprives these words of any content; for such behaviour is what we *call* 'stumbling blindly', 'showing that one sees', etc. (LPE 286). These suppositions have no more content than the corresponding idea that maybe things cease to exist when no one perceives them. It is not, as some philosophers would have it, that everything speaks against such suppositions, but rather that nothing could *conceivably* speak for them.

3. *The indeterminacy of the mental*

We can know of the inner states, desires, and thoughts of another person, and often do. We can be as certain that someone else is suffering or joyful as that $2 + 2 = 4$. But to insist upon these platitudes is not to hold that the language-games that concern the 'inner' are logically of the same kind as those concerning the 'outer'. On the contrary, it was precisely because of a disposition to project the grammar of the 'outer' upon that of the 'inner' that philosophers were led to the sceptical absurdities that Wittgenstein exposed. But lurking behind those sceptical qualms is an important truth that characterizes the category of the mental.

We say of some people that they are transparent to us, that we know without a doubt what they are thinking or feeling, what mood they are in, or what they want. On the other hand, one human being may be a complete enigma to another – a phenomenon that is strikingly evident when one encounters an alien culture. Even if one speaks the language, one may fail to understand the people; their motives and reasons may be opaque to one, and their reactions puzzling. We cannot find our way around with them (PI p. 223). This is not because we do not know what they are saying to themselves. The phenomenon of opacity, though made vivid in alien contexts, is familiar at home too. For we often fail to understand someone, not only when he is successfully concealing his feelings, but also when he is doing his utmost to make himself intelligible (MS. 169, 86). The nexus between reason and action is elastic, and the transparency of reasons is both culture-relative and, to a degree, agent-relative.

We may agree with Hume that 'were there no uniformity in human actions, and were every experiment which we could form ·of this kind irregular and anomalous, it were impossible to collect any general observations concerning mankind; and no experience, however accurately digested by reflection, would ever serve to any purpose'.[4] Indeed, the behaviour would not be human, and our psychological concepts would get no grip, for their use depends upon a uniformity in the weave of life. Nevertheless, there is an *essential* unpredictability about the mental (MS. 173, 78). Not only are the important fine shades of behaviour unpredictable, but it is often impossible to foresee what another person will do *even though* one knows his beliefs and motives. It does not *follow* from the fact that he intends such-and-such, has

---

[4] Hume, *An Enquiry Concerning Human Understanding*, §65.

such-and-such beliefs, etc., that he will act. Two people may have the same beliefs and desires (even the same strength of desire by any available criterion of how much one wants such-and-such), and yet the one may act and the other refrain; and there may be no non-trivial explanation of why they behaved differently. One cannot say what the essential observable consequences of an inner state are, e.g. of someone's being pleased. There are, of course, characteristic consequences; but one cannot say exactly what is to be expected of him and what not (he may weep with relief, jump with joy, or just smile). His responses cannot be described in the same way as reactions characterizing the state of a physical object (MS. 174, 27). The limited predictability of human behaviour is not that of an only partly understood mechanism, and its unpredictability is not always a function of our ignorance, as if, were we better informed, we would always be able to predict with certainty.

Corresponding to this essential unpredictability of behaviour is a logical indeterminacy in explanation of behaviour, a feature upon which Kant dwelt in the *Groundwork of the Metaphysic of Morals*.[5] Wittgenstein did not elaborate this, but focused upon a related form of radical indeterminacy. We typically do not know what another person is thinking unless he tells us. Sometimes we guess, and the person may affirm (or deny) that that was what he was thinking. Yet in some cases he may be wrong; his memory may be deceiving him, or he may have let himself be talked into the conviction that he previously thought thus-and-so. And whether he really thought this or is merely imagining himself to have done so is essentially undecidable (RPP I §§568ff.; PI p. 222). The criteria for someone's guessing correctly what I thought consist in my confessing that he has guessed right; but one does not always have to believe such a confession, even if deception is ruled out (RPP II §692). Here, Wittgenstein suggested, there may be criteria, but none that are certain (MS. 174, 21), or criteria which some take as certain and others do not (MS. 174, 20). Our ignorance or uncertainty about what goes on in someone else is not uniform. We cannot read off what he is saying to himself from his behaviour, but must ask him. Sometimes we cannot understand what he says. Often we do not know what mood he is in, and his intentions may be obscure. In each case the ignorance is of a different kind, and is removed, if at all, in different ways (LW §957). Occasionally it cannot be definitively removed, for nothing counts in those circumstances as settling the matter beyond doubt. In certain circumstances, we cannot say whether one person feels more pain than another or merely gives stronger expression to his suffering (RPP II §647).

---

[5] Kant, *Groundwork of the Metaphysic of Morals*, ch. II.

It is tempting to explain these various uncertainties by invoking the picture of the inner and the outer. Viewed from this perspective, one might naturally insist that 'While you can have complete certainty about someone else's state of mind, still it is always merely subjective, not objective certainty' (PI p. 225). But this is misleading. We can contrast subjective with objective certainty in the language-games with indirect, as opposed to direct, observation. I may be 'subjectively certain' that you have money in your purse, even though I cannot see it, while you are 'objectively certain', for you can. But there is no such contrast here, for it is not as if 'objective certainty' does not exist *because* we cannot see into another person's soul. He cannot see into his soul either, and his lack of doubt is not determined by his certainty; *both* are grammatically excluded. The claim that there is no objective certainty signifies the same as the claim that one cannot see into another's soul (MS. 169, 4f.). So 'Here I can't achieve objective certainty' is not like 'You can't know what is in a locked box', but is akin to 'You can't kick a goal in tennis' (RPP I §567). Of a clock one can say 'I don't know what is going on inside'; but with a human being, one might say, this indeterminacy or uncertainty is *postulated* (RPP II §§665f.) – it is impossible to look inside, i.e. there is no such thing. What looks like a defect in knowledge or a shortcoming in the available evidence, which we are inclined to express in the claim that there is no objective certainty, betokens a difference in language-games (PI p. 225). This uncertainty, if it is to be called such, might be said to be *constitutional* (RPP I §141). The *only* way to recognize pain is from the 'outer'; but that is no defect, for it lies in the nature of the language-game (RPP II §657).

One is inclined to say that one can be more certain about propositions concerning physical objects or about mathematical propositions than one can about the experiences of others. But that is wrong; I can be as certain that someone is in pain as of any mathematical proposition (PI p. 224). Nevertheless, one might respond, there is a difference in kind, even if not in degree. This is correct; but it would be wrong to represent the difference as a psychological one, e.g. a difference between objective and subjective certainty. In so far as there is an 'objective uncertainty' about the mental, it consists in an indefiniteness in the nature of the game, in the rules of admissible evidence (LW §888).

In conceding that there is a 'constitutional uncertainty' about the mental, Wittgenstein was not claiming that we can never know that another person is in pain (PI §246). On the contrary, there are indeed cases where only a madman would take an expression of pain to be insincere. There is an *unmistakable* expression of joy or sadness, and there are circumstances in which we *know* that someone is in pain or that he is not (MS. 169, 101). The 'uncertainty' in question, the philosophical uncertainty, does not relate to each and every particular case, but to the method of establishing the inner (Z §555; RPP I §682; LW §239). What are the peculiarities of the 'rules of evidence'?

One distinctive feature is that although the connection between the inner and the outer is not just empirical but logical (MS. 173, 73), our concepts of the mental do not bring behaviour, occasion, and inner process (or experience) into necessary connection (*zwangsläufige Verbindung*), for behaviour and occasion do not *entail* the inner process (MS. 169, 68f.). In certain circumstances I may be *certain* that someone is in pain, but another person in the same circumstances may not be convinced. I cannot offer him a *proof*, and neither he nor I will be judged to be irresponsible or incapable of judgement (RPP II §685; cf. MS. 169, 62f.). Of course, this discrepancy has its limits; but what is significant is that it lies in the logic of our concepts, not in ignorance of fact. Within this penumbra of indeterminacy there is such a thing as better and worse judgement, just as in art there are connoisseurs (LW §§917, 925, 927). In general, better attributions issue from the judgements of those who have looked at and compared numerous paintings, even though they might be unable to explain their reasons to a jury, as opposed to giving intimations to other connoisseurs. Similarly, those with a wide knowledge of mankind are more likely to give better *prognoses* regarding the genuineness of people's feelings than others. These judgements require experience. 'Learning' and 'teaching' here are peculiar, for though there are rules, they do not form a system. One does not acquire a technique, but learns correct judgements. A good teacher here does not impart a method, but teaches one to look, gives one *tips*, makes one sensitive to *imponderable* evidence, to subtleties of glance, gesture, and tone of voice (PI pp. 227f.). In judgements about the inner there is a dimension of particularity: one can judge the nuances of a person's behaviour better if one knows him well, and one can better judge the significance of a person's manifestations of feeling if he is an old acquaintance. And typically one cannot describe what it is in the conduct that is decisive (MS. 174, 27).

We operate in this domain with elastic, flexible concepts (LW §§244, 246; MS. 169, 74), and these concepts inform our behaviour and shape the contours of our lives. This does not, of course, mean that 'anything goes', that these concepts could be distorted as one pleases. But it does mean that there are phenomena of an essentially undecidable character (RPP I §568), that evidence for the inner is defeasible (cf. RPP II §692), that there is a logical indeterminacy in the concepts. How is this to be explained? Could we not replace these concepts with sharper ones? No; not without a fundamental change in our nature. For 'Concepts with fixed limits would demand a uniformity of behaviour. But where I am *certain* someone else is uncertain. And that is a fact of nature' (Z §374;

RPP II §683). Being sure that someone is in pain, doubting whether he is, 'are so many natural, instinctive, kinds of behaviour towards other human beings, and our language is merely an auxiliary to, and further extension of, this relation. Our language-game is an extension of primitive behaviour. (For our *language-game* is behaviour)' (Z 545; RPP I §151). We are all too prone to look upon our linguistic activities from the perspective of *thought* and the communication of thought. But our language-games are rooted in instinctive behaviour, and where there is lack of uniformity in that behaviour, it is reflected in our concepts: 'Instinct comes first, reasoning second' (RPP II §689), and 'There is uncertainty of behaviour which doesn't stem from uncertainty in thought' (RPP II §660). Our flexible, elastic concepts of the inner are not employed merely for *description* of the mental but for its constitutive *expression*; we manifest and give shape to our inner lives in these patterns of linguistic behaviour. The use of these concepts is part of our form of life. They are not concepts devised for the description and theoretical explanation of an independently existing reality (as are the concepts of physics); rather they *inform* the reality which they are *also* used to describe and (sometimes) to explain.

Wittgenstein conceived of the 'constitutional uncertainty' of the inner not as a consequence of defective evidence, but as a reflection in the rules of evidence of disagreement in human attitudes and responses that antecede our language-games. He recommends us to look at this uncertainty in the light of the (different) question of whether an insect feels pain (RPP II §661). For here too people react differently, and their disagreement is not resolvable by factual investigation. The non-uniformity in our instinctive reactions of trust and mistrust towards each other is one source of the constitutional uncertainty of psychological concepts. There is no such uncertainty in numerous other language-games, and that too is determined by the character of our reactions. Disputes over the correct result of a calculation are rare and can be settled conclusively (PI p. 225). Mathematicians do not in general disagree over the result of a calculation, and this fact determines our concept of mathematical certainty – not because 'mathematically certain' means the same as 'generally agreed by mathematicians', but because if mathematicians did not generally agree then we would not have our concept of mathematical certainty. Similarly, although there is such a thing as colour-blindness, there are ways of establishing it, and those who are *not* colour-blind generally agree in their judgements about colours (PI p. 227). There is no such agreement, however, in many applications of concepts of the inner.

It is still tempting to attribute the penumbra of uncertainty that characterizes these concepts to the fact that they signify what is 'inner', hidden 'behind' overt behaviour. Indeed, it is tempting to misconstrue the constitutional uncertainty of the mental as confirmation of the idea that the 'inner' is hidden. But this is a mistake. We do not disagree about other people's mental lives *because* their inner world is hidden from us; on the contrary, it is partly because of our (sometimes irresolvable) disagreement about people's motives, beliefs, and feelings that we cleave to the misleading picture of the 'inner' hidden behind the 'outer'. We need to be reminded that we recognize a sign of something inward to be trustworthy by reference to something outward, viz. antecedent or subsequent behaviour. So the distinction between what is certain and what is uncertain does not depend on the contrast between inner and outer (MS. 169, 101f.). Rather, the uncertainty depends upon the irregularity of the outer. Our inability to understand another person does not, in these cases, turn on our ignorance of what is going on within him, but on the consequences of his inner state. One aspect of our uncertainty consists in our inability to foresee his actions (MS. 173, 77); another turns on our inability to render his actions intelligible to ourselves (MS. 173, 87f.). For, given that a sincere avowal is a verbal reaction, rather than a description of an inner state which only the agent can observe, it is not determined what the consequences of this signal are (MS. 173, 94). An avowal is a behavioural manifestation of the inner, but it is a piece of behaviour that lies within a complex weave of circumstances, response, and consequence. This pattern is not wholly regular, and the irregularity of the pattern determines the penumbral uncertainty of our concepts of the inner (LW §211). The tapestry of human life is not machine-made. Irregularities are part of its texture. Some threads break off, others are knotted. These anomalies in the pattern are a feature of our nature, and their reflections in our concepts are not shortcomings.

CHAPTER 2

Thought

(§§316 – 62)

INTRODUCTION

§§316 – 62 examine the nature of thinking. The grand-strategic role of this 'chapter' is to undermine the idea that it is *thinking* that breathes life into otherwise dead signs. Having demolished the conception of private ostensive definition as fixing the foundations of language, W. now turns to the equally tempting picture of an inner process of thought as constituting the soul of language. This too is a mythology. The strategy perspicuously builds on previous clarifications. Part A (§§316 – 26) is a preliminary investigation of the 'dual-process' conception of thought. §316 applies the principle of §314 (viz. one cannot clarify philosophical problems about sensations by studying one's headache) to thinking. §317 emphasizes the difference between the relation of pain to a cry (its expression) and of a thought to a proposition (which expresses that thought). The appearance of a parallelism encourages the false notion that the use of a proposition is to communicate an inner process going on in one's thinking apparatus to which one has privileged access. But 'expression' means something quite different in each case. §318 provides a further reason for our conceiving of thinking as an introspective inner process, viz. our idioms of a thought crossing one's mind in a flash and of the lightning speed of thought. §§319 – 20 clarify these idioms, and §321 – 3 harken back to the discussion of sudden understanding in §§179 – 84 and bring those earlier clarifications to bear on the current issue. What 'a thought's going through one's mind like lightning' or 'seeing the solution in a flash' mean is no more to be answered by describing an inner process than sudden understanding is to be clarified by answering the question of what *happens* when one suddenly understands. §§324 – 6 repudiate the suggestion that one's conviction that one understands (has grasped a thought, seen the solution to a problem) when one has a flash of insight or understanding rests on induction from similar experiences in the past. This conviction requires no reasons and is typically justified.

The structure of Part A:

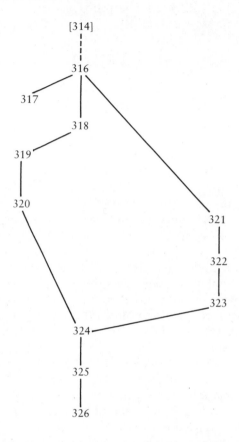

Part B (§§327 – 41) investigates the relation between thought and speech, misunderstandings of which lie at the heart of the dual-process conception introduced in the preceding remarks. §327 raises the question of whether one can think without speaking, a question which sounds as if it is about the interdependence of two processes. To answer it, the concept of thinking must be clarified, but, of course, not by observing what goes on in oneself when one thinks (cf. §316). First steps are taken in §328, which reminds us of the senselessness of error in saying that one is thinking (but that is not because the inner process is so well lit that one cannot but see it), and of the dissimilarity between the flow of thought and the flow of speech. §329 elaborates the opening sentence of §318: speech with thought (i.e. which is not parrot-like) is not a *pair* of activities. §330(a) poses the central problem perspicuously: is thinking a kind of speaking? It seems to be a concurrent process the occurrence of which distinguishes speech with thought from parrot-like speech. §330(b) and §§331 – 7 attempt a variety of antidotes to this insidious poison. In an appropriate context, the only thing that may *happen* outwardly *or* inwardly when one thinks such-and-such is that one makes a gesture, pulls a face, etc. (§330(b)). §331 invites us to imagine people who can think only aloud. §332 concedes, as a behaviourist would not, that speech with thought often involves mental processes concurrent with speech. Nevertheless that accompaniment is not what is meant by 'a thought'. §333 offers an analogical case in which the pressure is lower. We say 'only someone convinced would say that', but we do not think of the conviction as an inner accompaniment of the speaking, and no more so is the thought when someone speaks with thought. §334 brings to light another phrase which incorporates the misleading dual-process picture, viz. 'You really wanted to say . . .' – as if what one wanted to say coexisted in thought with whatever one ill-advisedly said. But when we look at the actual use of this phrase, it is obvious that that is not how things are. §335 deals with a parallel case: we often, as we say, try to find the right phrase to express our thought; and that looks like trying to find the right phrase to *translate* such-and-such an expression from another language. So this picture makes it appear as if the thought 'is already there' in our mind, and we are just looking for its correct outward expression. But here too, scrutiny of the application of this picture dissolves the illusion. §336 adduces a similar, very natural idea (to a non-German speaker), viz. that one *could not* think a sentence with the word order of German. So one has the picture of thinking the thought and then translating it into word-language. §§337 – 8 embroider the equally tempting converse thought: viz. that surely one must have *intended* the whole construction of the sentence in advance of uttering it, i.e. one must have constructed it in *thought*? But this idea misconstrues the concept of intention. To intend to do something does not mean that one does it in thought in advance of doing it. §§339 – 41 bring this part of the discussion to a head. Thinking is not an 'incorporeal process'. One must examine the use of the word, not guess it. Speech with and without thought is comparable to playing a piece of music with and without thought, and playing a sonata with thought does not mean accompanying it with an inaudible process!

The structure of Part B:

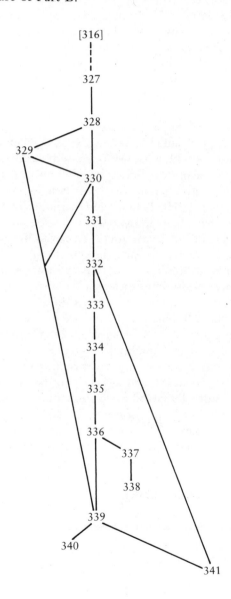

Part C (§§342 – 52) reverts to the question of §327: can one think without speech? James presented the Ballard case as an empirical proof that one can think sophisticated thoughts even though one cannot speak at all. W. queries not the truth of Ballard's claim, but its intelligibility. 'I remember that I thought . . .' is not a report of an inner event (§343) that one apprehended in the past, and it is unclear what, in Ballard's case, could possibly *count* as his having had thoughts which he could not have expressed or articulated in any way at all. §344 raises much the same question again, not on the grounds of apparent empirical confirmation, but on logical grounds. For we all often think without voicing our thoughts; so the supposition that people who cannot speak an audible language might nevertheless speak to themselves in the imagination (i.e. think) is just a form of the supposition that what sometimes happens can (logically) always happen. §§344 – 5 challenge the cogency of the latter inference. The criteria for someone's saying something to himself in the imagination lie in his *behaviour*, and we say it only of someone who is able to speak (hence not of a parrot, which can mimic what it hears but cannot speak, has not mastered these techniques). §346 challenges this, for can we not imagine that God gives understanding to a parrot, who now speaks to itself? But to invoke God is precisely to lift the constraints of the language-game! §347 attempts another route to establishing the independence of thought from the possibility of speech, viz. that I know what talking to oneself in the imagination means *from my own case*, and if I lost the power of speech I could still talk to myself. W. challenges the premise. §348 is reduced to defending only the letter of the proposal of §344, while abandoning its spirit. It queries whether deaf mutes who have learned only gesture-language might not nevertheless talk to themselves in their imagination in vocal language. The idea is fishy, W. retorts, for we are applying a picture in a context where it has no grip (§349). §§350 – 1 investigate analogous illegitimate cases of attempted extrapolation. §352 examines a misuse of the law of excluded middle which we commonly indulge in when we insist that there must be an objective fact of the matter, viz. either they talk to themselves or they do not, etc.! But the law of excluded middle *presupposes* the sense of its constituent propositions and cannot be used to establish it!

The structure of Part C:

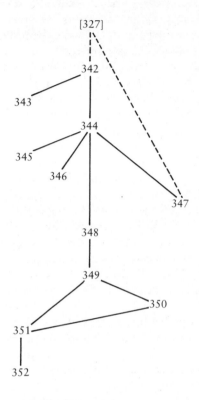

Part D (§§353 – 6) interpolates a brief set of remarks on verification. The link with the foregoing is twofold. First, §352, like §350, showed that appeals to identity or the law of excluded middle, far from clarifying the meaning of propositions about thinking, actually presuppose the meaning to be given. But what is it given by? Second, §340, concluding the prior discussion, stressed the need to examine the use of problematic expressions. The examination of whether and how a proposition is verified *is* an examination of an aspect of its use, and hence can clarify its meaning and contribute to a description of its grammar (§353). And this is what needs to be done with words such as 'thinking', 'saying something to oneself in the imagination', etc. §354 emphasizes the fluctuation betwen criteria (fixed by grammar) and symptoms (inductive correlations) and identifies this fluctuation as a source of the misguided thought that nothing exists but symptoms. §§355 – 6 embroider on an example given in §354. The structure of these four remarks is linear.

Part E (§§357 – 62) reverts to the theme of talking to oneself in the imagination, which was broken off at §349. We do not say that maybe a dog talks to himself. Why not? Because the verifying grounds for such a proposition, the criteria for saying of a creature that it talks to itself in its imagination, lie in its behaviour, in what it does and *says*. But, of course, I don't say that *I* am thinking on any such grounds. §358 is a digression: my avowal that I am saying something to myself does *not* make sense because of an underlying 'act of meaning' I might perform. §359 switches from the dog to a machine and the question of whether a machine can think? Or be in pain? A single thrust resolves the question: a human body comes as close as can be to such a machine, but we do *not* say 'My body thinks' or 'My body has toothache!' §360 echoes §281: a machine cannot think; but that is no empirical statement, for we say only of a living human being and what is like one that it thinks! §§361 – 2 clarify the point of §360 by examining the idea of attributing thought to something that is both inanimate (unlike the dog) and does not execute intelligent tasks (unlike a computer), viz. a chair. §362 concludes this 'chapter' by emphasizing that the expression 'to speak to oneself' is not taught indirectly by inducing the learner to give himself a private ostensive definition.

The structure of Part E:

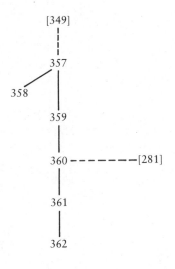

Correlations

PI§	PPI(I)§	MS. 129	MS. 124	MS. 165	Vol. XII	Others
316	255	68–9	274–5			MS. 179, 48
317						Vol. XIII, 134; BT 222[1]
318	256	70–1	215–16			MS. 180(a), 15–17
319	257	71	218			
320	258	71–2				MS. 180(a), 17–18
321		185f.[2]				
322		186				
323	259	72–3	217–19			MS. 180(a), 18–19
324	260	73–4	220–1	137		MS. 180(a), 19–20
325	261					MS. 130, 8–9
326		11				
327	262	10		206–7		
328	263	10		207–8		
329						Vol. X, 151
330	264	90–1		59–61; 2		
331						MS. 130, 23
332					103–4	
333						Vol. X, 225
334						Vol. XI, 53
335						Vol. XI, 48
336		102–3				
337		103				
338					302	
339	265	91–3		61–2; 3–4		
340		106		20–1		
341	266	115	282	135		
342	267	4–5		195–6		
343		152			181	
344	268	3, 69		133–4[3],	192[4], 209[5]	
345	269	5–6, 69–70	279[6]	197–8[7]		
346	270	3–4		209–10		
347	271	4		194		
348	272	6–7		198–200		
349					140	
350					141	
351					142–3	
352					148–50	
353						Vol. VIII, 99; Vol. XI, 72
354						Vol. XI, 73
355						Vol. XI, 74
356						Vol. XI, 74
357	273	7		200–1		
358	273.1[8]	93		5		
359						Vol. XIII, 129
360		177–8		61		
361	275–6	9–11		204–6, 208, 211–12		
362	277	11		212–13		

[1] PI §317(a) only.
[2] PI §321(a) only.
[3] PI §344(a) only.
[4] PI §344(b), but without the last sentence.

[5] PI §344(b), last sentence only.
[6] PI §345(c) only.
[7] PI §345(a) and (b) only.
[8] On p. 183 of the typescript.

THINKING: METHODOLOGICAL MUDDLES AND CATEGORIAL CONFUSIONS

1. *Thinking: a muddle elevated to a mystery*

It is natural to raise questions about thinking. Indeed, one who does not is lucky, or immune to puzzlement (LPP 236). It is noteworthy that anyone who does ask such questions is himself a thinking person; thinking is no novelty to him. And yet it will sometimes strike him as peculiarly baffling. When scrutinized from the wrong angle or when in the grip of a paradigm that does not fit the concept, thought appears to do very mysterious things.

If the dull substance of my flesh were thought,
Injurious distance should not stop my way;
For then, despite the space, I would be brought,
From limits far remote, where thou dost stay.
No matter then although my foot did stand
Upon the furthest earth remov'd from thee;
For nimble thought can jump both sea and land,
As soon as think the place where he would be.[1]

And when my thought of A traverses 'injurious distance', I think of *just him*, and my thought as it were nails him (Z §§13 – 17). So it is like a super-ballistic missile, only faster and more unerring than any physical missile could be! Even more mysteriously, I can think of someone even though he no longer exists – indeed, even if he never existed (PG 103). But I could not hit Santa Claus with a ballistic missile! Furthermore, just as I can think of someone even though he does not exist, so too I can think that such-and-such is the case even though it is *not* the case. But if what I think does not exist, if there is no such thing, how can I think it?

Not only can we readily generate the illusion that thinking can *do* mysterious things, but we also succumb to the idea that it operates in mysterious ways. It *connects* ideas in the mind, we say; and then we wonder how this strange connection is effected: by associative mechanisms, predicational glue, or whatever. Thinking sometimes seems to operate on images; but sometimes it seems to use words as its material. And when we mystify ourselve thus, it does indeed seem that thought is mysterious, that we need to find out what the materials of thought are and how the mind goes to work on them.

---

[1] Shakespeare, Sonnet XLIV.

It is equally easy to make thinking appear occult. In thought, we say things to ourselves – which no one else can hear, as in our imagination we picture things to ourselves – which no one else can see. One's thoughts can seem like super-private property: no one else can know what I am silently thinking; at best they can guess. One's thoughts seem hidden from the sight of all save oneself, hidden in the most secure hiding-place, one's own mind.[2] We all remark on the uncanny speed of thought; it

> . . . can wing its way
> Swifter than lightning flashes or the beam
> That hastens on the pinions of the morn.[3]

Mozart was rumoured to be able to think through, 'hear', in a flash a whole concerto that he was composing. People often see the solution to a complex practical or theoretical problem in a moment. 'Now I have it!' they may exclaim, and it takes them half an hour to explain what they have thus grasped instantaneously.

Thought seems like an elusive, intangible material that is difficult to control. Thoughts often flit across our minds uncalled-for; occasionally they press in on us willy-nilly and we cannot banish them; sometimes they are apparently buried in the recesses of the mind and cannot voluntarily be brought to the light of consciousness. Hence thinking seems like a complex process undergone by an immaterial stuff in the receptacle of the mind. It then strikes us as being as mysterious as a flame, impalpable, in perpetual motion, endlessly fascinating and mesmerizing (Z §125).[4] So we are prone to conclude that 'thinking is an enigmatic process, and we are a long way off from complete understanding of it' (RPP I §1093).

It is characteristic of philosophers that having tied a knot in their reflections on thinking, they respond to the knot by constructing a theory. The apparent mysteries of thinking will be resolved, they fancy, by producing a good theory about the nature of thought. Frege notoriously conceived of thinking as a mysterious process ('perhaps the most mysterious of all' (PW 145)), a process of grasping immaterial objects that are like physical objects, only non-spatial and timeless (PW 148). It is the task of psychology, he proclaimed, to explain this mental process. Wittgenstein in the *Tractatus* entertained equally bizarre ideas (see 'Thinking: the soul of language', §1). His conception of

---

[2] The privacy of thought is further examined in 'Privacy', §2.
[3] J. G. Percival.
[4] But, Wittgenstein adds, why should something impalpable seem more mysterious than something palpable? Is it because we want to grasp it (Z §126)? And if so, is that not because of analogies between names of objects and expressions that superficially resemble names of objects but are not such names?

thinking as a kind of language (NB 82), stripped of its logical atomist elements, has an analogue today in the writings of cognitive scientists and speculative neurophysiologists. Thinking is conceived to be a mental process that is neurologically 'realized'. What this 'language of thought' is remains to be seen; it is a mystery that will be duly resolved by a good theory.

These programmatic theories, however, are but echoes of misunderstandings of conceptual articulations. The aura of mystery which thus surrounds thought is nothing more than a product of a distorted vision. The 'uniqueness' of thought, the mystery of understanding language through the medium of thought, is a *superstition* (not a mistake) produced by grammatical illusions (PI §110). The task of philosophy is not to construct theories about cognitive processes which scientists can then elaborate and test; it is rather to destroy those illusions.

It is noteworthy that thinking does not strike us as in the least mysterious when we think (PG 154; PI §428), but only when we think about our thinking, wonder what to say about our 'cognitive activities', let ourselves be guided by language along the smooth rails of a compelling analogy which leads us astray. Thinking (or understanding or meaning) is not a queer experience like the experience of weightlessness, but as commonplace and humdrum as walking or eating. Nor is it strange because it has curious and unanticipated *effects* (BB 5); on the contrary, the effects of thinking are typically transparent. X took an umbrella because he thought (believed) it was raining, and that is intelligible precisely because *that it is raining* is a *reason* for taking an umbrella. If anyone, even a child, is asked what he is thinking, he will answer with as much ease as if asked what he is doing. The question will not strike anyone as a question about a mystery. But one might wonder how he knows that what he is doing is thinking or that what he is thinking is that p rather than that q – and one is straight away caught in a net of grammar.

One might respond by observing that there is nothing mysterious about things falling to the ground and other things floating or flying. This too is commonplace, but it needed the theory of gravity to explain the phenomenon. Water plays a familiar role in our lives, but the fact that it expands below 4° Centigrade is extra-ordinary, and its inner structure, which needed to be discovered, is what explains its properties, including this one. Is thinking (understanding, meaning, etc.) not similar? No; for what *mystifies* us about thinking is not anything that could be explained by a *theory* or by theoretical *discoveries*, any more than the beauty of a Mozart symphony could be explained by acoustics or psychology. There *are* discoveries to be made about our ability to think: e.g. how and why such-and-such capacities are impaired by alcohol, fail with age, or vary with gender. But these domains of relative *ignorance* are not what give us the (false) impression that thinking is mysterious. The 'speed of thought', the possibility of thinking about the non-existent or what is not the case, the transparency of thought and its privacy, are not features that could be demystified by the discovery of hidden inner structures (cf. LPP 236f.). They are, rather, muddles felt as problems (BB 6).

The sense of mystery here stems from *philosophical* bafflement. We know how to use the verb 'to think' (or 'to mean' or 'to understand') and how to teach its use to our children, to explain to them what it means. But we lack a surview of that use and of those explanations. When faced with questions about the nature of thought, we are as lost as when faced with parallel questions about the nature of the number 1 (PG 108). We sense a mystery because we lack a clear view of the grammar of such expressions, and hence naturally gravitate towards misleading grammatical analogies. Number-words resemble names of substances, so we think of numbers as objects, though we add that they are not concrete and are not located in space and time. Similarly, 'to think' *in some of its uses* resembles such activity-verbs as 'to speak' or 'to write', and we naturally conceive of thinking as an activity, though we add that it is an activity of the mind (as speaking and writing, crudely speaking, are activities of the body). We then project features of physical activity onto thinking, and then straight away (rightly) find thinking thus conceived to be a mystery. 'We interpret the enigma created by our misunderstanding as the enigma of an incomprehensible process' (PG 155).

Consequently, Wittgenstein argues, we do not need a theory or hypothesis to resolve our difficulties. We want to clarify the nature of thinking, but not as a physicist investigates the nature, the hitherto unknown structure, of water. It is not new empirical facts about thinking that will dispel the mystery that seems to surround thought, but a rearrangement of familiar *grammatical* facts. Recourse to laboratories *at this point* merely compounds confusion:

'Thinking is an enigmatic process, and we are a long way off from complete understanding of it.' And now one starts experimenting. Evidently without realizing *what* it is that makes thinking enigmatic to us.

The experimental method does *something*; its failure to solve the problem is blamed on its still being in its beginnings. It is as if one were to try to determine what matter and spirit are by chemical experiments. (RPP I §1093)

Will the philosophical clarification of thinking not rob us of an *appropriate* sense of mystery in the face of such things as thinking, dreaming, sensation? Not at all! What will disappear is the *bogus* mystery. And once that has gone, why should thinking or dreaming be any more mysterious than a table? Why should they not be *equally mysterious* (RPP I §378)? But *this* mystery is no longer ignorance or a conceptual muddle, but rather wonder before the contingency of all that exists.

2. *Methodological clarifications*

The suggestion that our sense of mystery about thinking is a pseudo-mystery, a mere mystification consequent on having a mistaken idea of the use of *words*, is repulsive (RPP I §§548f.). It seems to trivialize our inquiry; we want to investigate the essence of thinking, and Wittgenstein tells us to examine the use of words. Surely words are arbitrary; and that this word is used *thus*, that one *thus* is arbitrary too. Yet the nature of thinking is anything but arbitrary!

The objection rests on incomprehension. It is grammar that determines the essence of something (cf. Exg. §§371f.). The rules for the use of the word 'think' constitute what is to be called 'thinking', and that *is* the essence or nature of thinking. Of course, words are arbitrary; what is called 'thinking' could have been called something else. The use of the sign 'thinking' could have been different; but if it had been different, it would not have the meaning it has, and so it would not have signified *thinking*. Investigating the grammar of the word 'thinking' and seeking to lay bare the essential nature of thought are one and the same endeavour (cf. PI §370).

One should indeed concede that there is something wrong in saying that our philosophical bafflement stems from having the wrong idea of the use of the word 'thinking' (LPP 243f.). If someone has the idea that 'to think' means to be quiet, then he has a wrong idea of the use of this expression. He misunderstands the word, does not know what it means, and cannot use it correctly. But no philosophical troubles stem from such misunderstanding. Philosophical confusions typically arise when one does know how to use a word correctly, i.e. in accord with established use, but lacks a synoptic view of its use. Hence when called upon to resolve questions which seem factual but are not, e.g. 'Can machines think (perceive, wish)?' (BB 16, 47f. and Exg. §359), one flounders in a morass of confusion and in effect *misdescribes* one's own (correct) practice of using the word 'to think' in the bustle of daily life. This produces a philosophical conflict.

We might say that we form a wrong *picture* of thinking. This, Wittgenstein noted, sounds less repulsive than attributing our difficulties to misdescriptions of the use of mere *words* (RPP I §§548f.). But properly understood, this is no concession at all. It is *of* thinking that we thus form a wrong picture, and what makes it a wrong picture of *thinking* as opposed to something else is the association of the picture with the use of a word. We have a picture of thinking as an inner process or activity, a picture which is embedded in certain misleading aspects of the grammar of the verb 'to think'. We may even give it a concrete representation, e.g. in a drawing of a man with 'bubbles' coming from his head in which his thoughts are written. But is this sketch also a picture of the thoughtful tennis-player? Is the drawing of the thinking man also to be used with regard to one who speaks with thought or understanding? And while speaking can be called 'an activity', is the thought that informs it a *further* activity?

Why, then, do we form a wrong picture? Many factors contribute. We are misled by superficial features of grammar, and are impressed by the fact that 'thinking', like 'speaking', has the grammatical appearance of an activity-verb (forgetting altogether that 'sleeping' has too). We take figurative speech, e.g. 'Use your brains!' or 'I wonder what is going on in his head', literally, and imagine that it is an obvious fact that we think *with* our brains, *in* our heads. Metaphors such as 'A thought flashed through his mind' lead us astray. Partial convergence of different expressions, e.g. 'thinking' and 'saying . . . to oneself', induce the wrong *expectations*, and when we note that thinking does not satisfy them overtly, we conclude that it must be very mysterious! 'Here one tells oneself: "It must be like this! – even if I cannot immediately get rid of all the objections." ' (RPP I §555). Wittgenstein gave an analogy for the way a wrong picture can play havoc with our philosophical reflections: imagine that the word 'giant' did service for 'big'. The picture we would form for ourselves of what it is to be big would be of a giant; and now imagine that one had to describe the queer employment of the word 'big' with this picture in mind[5] (RPP I §554)!

These grammatical sources of confusion feed, and in turn are fed by, more general culture preconceptions. Both the Greek and the Judaeo-Christian sources of European civilization foster the picture of thinking as an activity of the spirit or soul, part of the essential nature of humanity, separable from the body and its activities, hence more pure and incorruptible, enabling us to contemplate eternal truths that transcend the changing, destructible world of matter. This cultural mythology has partly philosophical origins, and it plays a role in strengthening philosophical prejudices and preconceptions. These are as evident among materialists as in the works of the dualist and idealist traditions. Since Wittgenstein's day, the computer revolution has set up fresh pressures, new sources of confusion. We use machines to carry out complex calculating tasks. Bedevilled by misconceptions about thinking, conceiving of calculating as 'pure thought' (cf. Frege's subtitle for *Begriffsschrift*), and divorcing thinking from its behavioural manifestations, many philosophers and artificial-intelligence scientists conceive of these machines as capable of thought. (Typically, those who demure object to this absurdity for the *wrong* reasons: e.g. because computers are

[5] E.g. big mouse/big elephant; big gap in the path/big gap in the argument; big smile, big fuss, big deal, big party.

not *conscious*). The more sophisticated these machines become, the greater the temptation to think of ourselves on the model of our creations (see 'Man, minds, and machines, §5). We understand (because we designed) the inner processes that occur in a computer; surely our own thinking must involve an analogous inner process! Like the Cartesian, the modern materialist has no qualms about the claim that thinking *is* an inner process. But, in his view, it takes place in the brain rather than in the mind.

We form a picture of thinking as an inner accompaniment of speech, which can go on alone and much faster. We suppose the concept of thinking to have a simple unified use with smooth contours (RPP I §554). But that is an illusion. The use of this expression is far more erratic than we expect, and also much more *specialized* (RPP II §234); hence the danger of using 'think' in a global, highly generalized way is great. The concept is a widely ramified one, like a traffic network connecting many out-of-the-way places (Z §110; RPP II §216). Compare, e.g., speaking 'with thought' (i.e. non-mechanically), speaking thoughtfully, thinking before speaking, speaking before thinking, thinking while speaking, speaking while thinking, speaking to oneself in the imagination, thinking of something or someone, thinking up a solution to a conundrum, a thought crossing one's mind in a flash, engaging in an activity attentively and with intelligence, etc. Of course, we are tempted to say that one feature unifies all these: viz. an activity of or process in the mind. In all these cases, the mind is not idle; something is going on inside it which does not occur when a person is in a stupor, and it is this that constitutes thinking (RPP II §§217 – 21). But it is precisely this idea which should be investigated. To be sure, the *picture* we all have of thinking is of an invisible auxiliary activity; but this may be just where we go wrong (RPP II §§226ff.). For this picture forces on us a wide range of *bad questions*, and in our attempts to answer them, we generate further confusion and mystification.

3. *Activities of the mind*

The verb 'to think' is multi-faceted, being connected with opining ('I think we ought to . . .'), believing ('I think she is in the garden'), conceiving, imagining, fancying, and envisaging ('That is just how I thought it would be). It is also bound up with doing things attentively, carefully, with due consideration. And, what is prominent in philosophical investigation, it is related to reflecting, musing, meditating (whether aloud or *in foro interno*), as well as to deliberating, speculating, reasoning, and inferring. Grammarians see in this latter use of 'to think' an 'activity-verb'. Like 'to run' or 'to talk', but unlike 'to know' or 'to understand', it has a progressive aspect, readily admits an imperative, can form a pseudo-cleft sentence with a Do pro-form ('What I did was to think hard'), can be qualified by manner-adverbs (e.g. 'quickly', 'laboriously', 'reluctantly'), and takes 'for . . . sake' constructions ('I thought hard for N's sake').[6]

Philosophers and psychologists alike find it natural to conceive of 'thinking' thus used as the name of an activity. (Moreover, they will be prone to generalize this categorial classification to all thinking.) 'What are you doing?' may get the answer 'Drawing a picture' or 'Thinking about tomorrow's party'. Thinking is something we engage in. It can absorb us; we concentrate on it; give ourselves over to it whole-heartedly. It often takes time, for though I may think of the answer to your problem in a flash, it may take an hour to think up the right solution, or I may spend a sleepless night thinking about it. One can think voluntarily or involuntarily, willingly or reluctantly. 'Thinking is a mental activity' seems a truism which no sane man would deny.

The concept of an activity, like the concepts of an act or an action, as well as those of happening, process, state, object, fact, etc., looks like a hard, clearly defined categorial concept, part of the bedrock of any conceptual scheme. But, Wittgenstein warned, 'these extremely general terms have an extremely blurred meaning. They relate in practice to innumerable special cases, but that does not make them any the more *solid*; no, rather it makes them more fluid' (RPP I §648; see Exg. §308(2); cf. LPP 265). Fluid though it is, the idea of an activity does involve the notion of a constituent series of successive (and occasionally simultaneous) acts systematically related to each other. Moreover, a detailed description of an activity will specify such acts and their manner of performance. Walking and running are activities, as are playing football or cricket. These are simple paradigms. However, as we move away from them, the concept blurs. Is talking an activity? One might well say so; but note that it would be something of a joke to answer the question 'What is your favourite activity?' by 'Talking', although one might reply thus to 'What is your favourite pastime?'. If talking is an activity, what of listening? At a piano recital, the pianist is hard at work at the keyboard; is the audience hard at work in their seats? And what of sleeping through a lecture or a concert? No one would call that 'an activity', even though the sleeper breathes, moves, and snores occasionally. 'Listen' and 'sleep' qualify as 'activity-verbs', and 'What is he doing?' can be answered by 'Listening' or 'Sleeping'. But the latter is certainly, and the former arguably, not what we call 'an activity'.

What of thinking? Someone who works with care and attention, concentrating on what he is doing and considering various options as he

---

[6] Cf. R. Quirk, S. Greenbaum, G. Leech, J. Svartvik, *A Grammar of Contemporary English* (Longman, London, 1972), pp. 92ff.

goes along will typically intersperse his work with auxiliary activities (otherwise, at least in certain kinds of cases, he would be doing whatever he is doing mechanically). He will pause with X in his hand and examine it, stop periodically and consider things, frown, shrug his shoulders, and resume his labour, etc. However, these activities are *not* the thinking, any more than when one speaks with thought, the speaking *is* the thinking. But it is striking that the concept of thinking is formed on the model of an imaginary auxiliary activity (as the concept of the differential quotient is formed on the model of a kind of imaginary quotient). One imagines the thinking as that which must be flowing under the surface of these expedients if they are not, after all, to be mere mechanical procedures (RPP II §§226 – 8). Thinking seems to be the invisible stream which carries and connects these actions. And so we assimilate the grammar of 'thinking' to that of 'speaking', and this comparison plays havoc with our attempt to get a clear picture of thinking.

The conception of thinking as an activity of the mind that *may* (but need not) accompany certain physical activities is strengthened when we examine the notions of reflecting, musing, and pondering. Here, it seems, we have the activity of thinking pure and simple, unaccompanied by any physical activity. If we carefully scrutinize these phenomena, we will discover what this inner activity really is. So it seems that 'in order to get clear about the meaning of the word "think" we watch ourselves while we think; what we observe will be what the word means' (PI §316). As long as we do not think too fast, we should be able to discover what the real activity of thinking is by observing what happens in our minds when we cogitate. 'But', Wittgenstein retorts, 'this concept is not used like that' (ibid). We must compare the uses of 'thinking' with what are called 'activities'.

One engages in typical physical activities by doing things, acting in certain ways, with one's body, limbs, or other organs. One writes by moving one's hand, as one swims by moving one's limbs or sings by using one's mouth and vocal cords. If thinking is an activity, it is an activity we engage in *without using any organ at all*. I do not think up another verse to my poem by doing something with my brain, and when I am thinking my way through a difficult problem, I am not performing any constituent acts with my brain (cf. BB 6f.). Of course, thinking may be protracted, as when I struggle to think my way through a conundrum. Am I then engaged in an activity? One might reply that that is indeed so: I wrack my brains! But what exactly do I do then? I frown, very likely close my eyes, perhaps beat my brow with my fist. But *that* is not thinking, nor is it something I do with my brains (but rather with my face and fist). We must not be misled by the instruction 'Use your brain!'. Like 'Let your heart tell you want to do!', it is a metaphor. 'He's got a good brain' is like 'He's got a warm heart', not like 'He's got good teeth'. This is obvious enough when one recollects that the brain is not an organ one can move at all. One does *nothing* with one's brain, for it is not an organ over which one has any *control*. Might thinking then not be an activity of the brain, not after the pattern of writing's being an activity of the hand, but rather on the model of digestion's being an activity of the stomach? But this is too is wrong. For while we say that I digest my food, for me to digest my food *is* for my stomach to do so, and I need know nothing about its chemical activities. But it is I, not my brain, that thinks. And when I think, I can say what it is that I think. It would be absurd to say 'My brain is thinking it over, but I don't yet know what conclusion it has reached!'

In response to this, one is inclined to shift ground. Granted that thinking is not an activity of the brain, surely, being a *mental* activity, it is an activity of the *mind*? Here we cast the mind in the role of an immaterial object. But the mind is not an ethereal appendage with which one can do things. 'It is a travesty of the truth to say "thinking is an activity of our mind, as writing is an activity of the hand" ' (PG 106). 'I think with my mind' is more akin to 'I love . . . with all my heart' than it is to 'I chew with my teeth'.

One might concede that the mind is not an organ with which one thinks, yet insist that mental activities, unlike physical ones, are engaged in without the use of any organ. For surely things *go on* in one's mind when one is thinking; one's thinking, like an activity, takes time, can be interrupted and resumed. The mind is not idle, but active, while one is engaged in thought.

These parallels between the grammar of thinking and the grammar of activities are misleading, for they induce us to overlook important differences. Nothing *need* go on when one thinks. First, when one speaks or writes with thought and concentration, nothing typically 'goes on' in one's mind, apart from the fact that one is thinking about what one says or writes. All one's attention is on what one is saying or writing, and any actual images or 'inward speaking' that may occur typically mark a lapse of concentration. Secondly, an interruption or break in thinking is altogether unlike a hiatus in an activity. A long pause in a speech is a period during which one is not speaking. But if one is thinking about rearranging a room, e.g. thinking whether this piece of furniture would look better there, and one gets a tape-measure and measures the size of this or that, and while doing so says nothing to oneself, one has not therefore ceased thinking about rearranging the room, that the chest will look better there, or how to hang the pictures (cf. PI §328). Thirdly, when one is reflecting on what to do or musing on a passage one has just read, interior monologue or mental imagery is neither necessary nor sufficient for the truth of 'He is thinking (musing, reflecting)', although they may and often do accompany the thinking. It is not sufficient, since reciting the multiplication-table or the alphabet in one's mind is not thinking (cf. RPP II §193). It is not necessary, since someone's report of what he has thought after musing or reflecting would not be undermined by his denying that he talked to himself in his imagination when he thought up the solution to such-and-such a problem. That is to say, the criteria which justify saying that someone is thinking about, over, or up something or other are not the criteria for someone's saying something to himself or for having an array of mental images; and the absence of criteria for the latter are not defeating conditions of the criteria for the former. We may indeed ask someone in a brown study what he is thinking, and he may tell us. But to tell us his reflections is not to report what images or words crossed his mind. The 'stream of thought' which so fascinated James (to whom we owe the memorable phrase) is largely a meaningless babble, and it is philosophical confusion to think that a description of the 'stream of thought' such as Joyce presented in *Ulysses* is a description of the real activity of (Bloom's) thinking. This is so far from the truth that a comprehensive description of any mental goings-on when one is thinking might well hardly *ever* even mention *what* one is thinking.

Of course, the answer 'He is thinking about . . .' can be given to the question 'What is he doing?' But note how it differs from answers that describe typical activities. Specifying an activity engaged in (e.g. playing cricket, negotiating a contract, building a wall) intimates what is going on, what kinds of things are being done (e.g. bowling, batting, or fielding; telephoning, drafting, or arguing; brick-laying, mortar-mixing, or pointing bricks). But when one is told that a person is thinking about, over, or up something or other, one does not and need not have the faintest idea of what is going on in his brain or what images or jumbled words flit across his mind (cf. Z §88). Rather, what one knows is what is *aimed* at, viz. a solution, answer, plan, or project. And if one is told what, after due reflection, he thought, one knows his conclusion, opinion, or considered judgement.

One might still object. Surely, at least in cases in which one thinks through an argument, one goes through a definite activity of thinking first that x follows from a and b, that given x and c, it follows that y, and y implies z. This is misleading. If one has thought through an argument, then the *expression* of what one thought will be an ordered sequence of thoughts or propositions. In so far as there is anything that can be called 'the structure of thought (or of thinking)' it is the structure of the expression of the argument which is thought through. But one must not conflate the *logical* stages of an argument with a psychological process or activity. Specification of the argument one has thought up or thought through is not a description of a psychological process. To report what one thought when one thought through an argument is not to describe what one *said* to oneself; nor is it to describe a series of *mental* images that crossed one's mind. A picture of what went on in one's mind, as it were, would not be a picture of the argument one thought of.

Nevertheless, one might respond in a reductive spirit, thinking is, at least in certain cases, an activity. It is not a *further* activity over and above talking (writing, engaging attentively in any non-mechanical task); rather, one might say that *in these circumstances* saying such-and-such or doing so-and-so *is* to think. But this too would be misleading, as if thinking is sometimes talking, at other times walking, sometimes singing, and occasionally diving! (Here we can see how the idea that thinking is an activity forces bad questions on us, for is it the *same* activity as talking, etc. or is it a *different* activity?) It is indeed correct that to do something thoughtfully, with attention or concentration, reflectively or with due care, is not to accompany the activity with an inner activity of thinking, concentrating, reflecting, or attending. But to say that in these circumstances the thinking *is* the doing is as misleading as to say that when one eats one's breakfast hastily, the hurrying *is* the eating; or that when one loiters with intent, the intending *is* the loitering. At best, the claim is an unclear gesture in the direction of what Ryle called the 'adverbial' character of thinking.[7]

Activities that are voluntary are typically taught, and thinking is indeed often voluntary. But there are not, and could not be, special lessons at school in thinking, over and above the run-of-the-mill lessons in arithmetic, physics, history, and so on. One learns to think, to use one's wits more effectively, in the course of learning these subjects. For, of course, thinking is not a specific technique with teachable procedures which one can learn. If one is faced with a difficult problem in arithmetic, physics, or history and asks a friend how to solve it, the reply 'Try thinking, it sometimes does the trick' is at best a poor joke.[8] There are indeed teachable procedures of a rigorous kind for certain types of problem-solving, e.g. code-cracking, but they typically eliminate or greatly reduce the need for thinking. Activities can be practised, but one cannot practise thinking *per se*; rather, one improves one's ability to think

[7] G. Ryle, 'Adverbial verbs and verbs of thinking', in *On Thinking* (Blackwell, Oxford, 1979). It is noteworthy that although Ryle's reflections in many respects run on parallel tracks to Wittgenstein's, they also diverge significantly. Where Wittgenstein stressed the misleading character of apparent categorial expressions and emphasized their indeterminacy, Ryle was prone to view them as sharp. Hence, where Ryle was inclined to categorize different uses of expression in apparently ready-made pigeon-holes, Wittgenstein described the irregularity and diversity of use. The temptation to 'systematize', to impose more order upon the untidy skein of our use of words than is actually there must be resisted on pain of distortion and falsification (RPP I §257).

[8] See J. F. M. Hunter, *Understanding Wittgenstein* (Edinburgh University Press, Edinburgh, 1985), pp. 173 – 85.

clearly by practising essay-writing or problem-solving in arithmetic or physics, and so forth.

Should we conclude that thinking is *not* an activity? Wittgenstein sometimes did (MS. 124, 215): 'Vom Worte "denken" konnte man sagen, es sei nicht ein Tätigkeitswort' ('One could say of the word "thinking" that it is not an activity word'). But one could – and Wittgenstein often did – take a gentler line. One might say that it is only *misleading*, not wrong, to say that thinking is an activity (cf. BB 6). It is misleading in as much as it commonly induces the wrong pictures of thinking, which then, *in certain contexts* – in psychology and philosophy – lead one astray, just as talk about 'imaginary numbers' once led many mathematicians astray (LPP 124 – 6, 244, 286). In some humdrum contexts there is nothing misleading about it at all: when the doctor explains my insomnia by saying 'Your mind is too active', he just means 'You lie awake thinking' (LPP 244). If one wishes to contrast stupor or mechanical action with the innumerable different kinds of cases of thinking and of thoughtful or intelligent action, one might well say that in all the latter cases the mind isn't idle, that something is going on in it. This is picturesque and draws a distinction (RPP II §217).

But when doing philosophy, one is prone to say 'Thinking is a mental activity', in order to distinguish it from *physical* activities. This *is* misleading, as misleading as saying that while numerals are physical objects, numbers are immaterial objects, real but non-actual, as Frege claimed. This makes the difference between numbers and numerals appear *too slight* (PI §339) and wholly obscures the role of arithmetical propositions, leading philosophers of mathematics up the garden path. Similarly, saying that thinking is a mental activity typically leads philosophers and psychologists into futile investigations about the 'materials' of thought (words, images, internal representations) and about mental operations allegedly constitutive of thinking (e.g. the psychologist's supposition that thinking about whether two drawings are of one and the same object at different orientations involves rotating images in mental space at constant velocity). It may generate wild mythologies of symbolism, such as pseudo-theories about the innate 'language of thought'. It induces the wrong pictures of thinking and generates misleading questions. It is, therefore, a move best avoided. Rather than locating the erratic and widely ramified concept of thinking in the deceptive, apparently determinate category of *activity*, we should, from case to case, investigate what are the criteria for someone's thinking. This will reveal *what* gets treated grammatically as an *activity* here (cf. PI §573), i.e. what in the superficial grammatical *form* looks like the name of an activity but has in numerous respects a quite different use from verbs signifying paradigmatic activities.

4. *Processes in the Mind*

In philosophy and psychology we talk of thought-processes as little known and perhaps mysterious, certainly complicated, processes in the mind. The picture we have here (unlike the picture of thinking as an activity of the mind) is of a space in which these processes take place, as the fermentation of grape-juice occurs in a vat (cf. PG 100). We are then prone, rather inchoately, to conceive of thinking as a process of an ethereal 'mind-stuff' (as James called it). The picture is reinforced by the use of common phrases such as 'When I was talking to him, I didn't know what was going on in his head.' The sense of mystery associated with the idea of thought-processes is exacerbated by such phenomena as calculating prodigies, of whom neither we nor they can say *how* their feats are performed. Hence we suppose that hidden mental mechanisms are at work, mechanisms which must be investigated by psychology.[9]

It is almost universally agreed that thinking goes on in the head. The idea is far more compelling than the similar notion that one loves with one's heart. The latter is transparently metaphorical, but the former, we suppose, is a literal truth. However, if thinking really did take place in the head, then the question 'Where did you think that up?' would have answers such as 'Two inches behind my left eye', '39 mm below where I thought that we should go to London tomorrow', or 'Diffused right throughout the cranial cavity'. But these replies make no sense. The only licit kind of answer is 'In the train as I was going to London' or 'In the library'. Of course, it could be *given* a new sense: the cranial location of thinking might be stipulated to mean that part of the brain which, when probed with a micro-electrode, would cause one to cease to think of *A* (cf. BB 9). But that is not the sense of 'Where did you think of *A*? or 'Where did you think that up?' And note that by parity of reasoning, one might also stipulate a cranial location for digestion. If someone insists that thinking takes place in the head, one should press him to explain what it would be for human beings to think in their stomachs. For presumably it is an empirical truth that is in question, and hence contingent. The correlation between thinking and parts of the cerebral cortex had to be *discovered*. So what would creatures, otherwise akin to us in appearance and behaviour, be like if they thought in their stomachs? Is it that their *brains* would be in their midriff? Or is it that whereas we clutch our heads and groan 'Let me think!', they would clutch their stomachs?

---

[9] Under pressure from the alleged analogy between the workings of the brain and of the computer, many scientists hold that the hidden mechanisms are neural, forgetting that *whatever* neural mechanisms there are, they are not *thinking mechanisms*, and their operation is not a thought-process.

We are tempted to conceive of thinking as a process or activity which occurs in the head for a variety of reasons. (a) We draw an analogy between speaking, writing, and thinking. One does the first with the mouth and the larynx, the second with the hand, so surely one must do one's thinking with something, e.g. one's brain. But, as argued, this is wrong, for there is *no* organ of thought (BB 7). One does not think *with* anything – save with a pen in one's hand or with the wireless on! (b) We have a rather primitive picture of ourselves as located at the invisible apex of the cone of vision the base of which is our visual field, so we think of ourselves as looking *out* from our heads, and hence of our thinking as occurring in our heads (LWL 25). (c) We conceive of thoughts as the product of thinking and imagine them to be *stored* in our heads, for, after all, we remember what we thought, and how could we remember our thoughts unless we retained them? Memory, as Locke put it, is the storehouse of ideas, and the brain, the moderns add, is the storage depot. But, of course, this is confused. Whatever neural structures and events may be necessary for a person to think or remember that *p*, what he thinks no less than what he typically thinks about cannot be in the head (cf. PG 143). What one thinks, namely *that p*, is not an object and no more has a location, in the head or anywhere else, than does the fact that *p* which makes that thought true. It makes no sense to talk of *that p* as having a place; 'Where is the thought that *p*?' is like 'Where is your visual space?' (AWL 54).

Of course, the head is more closely connected with thinking than it is with digesting or walking, but not because one thinks with or in one's head as one digests food in one's stomach or walks with one's legs. Rather, it is because one clutches or beats one's head when one wracks one's brain, closes one's eyes to think better, and so forth. One reads a person's thoughts *on his face*, not on his feet; it is his *eyes* that light up when he has 'cottoned on', that twinkle when he is fondly pulling one's leg, and so on. This explains why we favour the *picture* of thinking as going on in the head. But when we proceed to claim that thinking literally goes on in the head, that the brain is the organ of thinking, or that thinking is a process or activity of the brain, we are misconstruing the use of the picture no less than when we conceive of thinking as an activity of or process in the mind (RPP I §§278f.; cf. PG 106, 143).

We would often like to know 'what is going on in someone's head', i.e. what he is thinking (PI §427). But that is no reason for being interested in what processes are going on inside him. What he is thinking is given by specification of a proposition, viz. he is thinking that such-and-such, not by a description of an inner process (RPP I §§579f.). And we find out what he is thinking by what he says and does. What goes on in his mind or brain while he is thinking almost never interests us when we are concerned with *what he thought* (Z §88). For to say what one is thinking, like saying what one intends, is not to describe an experience. And one does not read off what one thinks, any more than one reads off what one intends, from observation of any inner processes. It is a fundamental misconception to suppose that thinking is a mental, incorporeal process that accompanies talking with thought, and sometimes, as when one is musing or reflecting, goes on without it.[10] Though one may talk with thought or just babble, the thought is not detachable from the talking any more than when one eats with haste, the haste is detachable from the eating. They are not like Peter Pan's shadow (cf. PI §339). And likewise, a description of one's musing or reflecting is not a description of an 'incorporeal process'.

A superficial reaction to these claims would be to accuse Wittgenstein of propounding theses (which he is supposed to eschew) or of denying what we all assert (which he is committed to not doing). Furthermore, it may seem that he is a behaviourist in disguise. For is he not denying that anything goes on in the mind and insisting that thinking *is*, or is *reducible* to, just saying or doing? This is wrong. He is denying nothing but the misleading picture of an 'inner (incorporeal) process' that goes with the concept of thinking (cf. PI §305). 'Thinking' is not the name of an introspectible inner process; but to insist on that is not to deny that people think, nor is it to *equate* thinking with saying or doing. Wittgenstein does not deny that when one is thinking, a variety of things may cross one's mind – words, phrases, mental images, and the rest. But a description of *this* 'stream of consciousness' would *not* be a report of what one was thinking or of the *reasoning* underlying the conclusion reached. Nevertheless, is he not insisting (contrary to what we all know!) that nothing *has* to go on in my mind when I think, hence that thinking might be *nothing*? This misconstrues his argument: the images and jumble of words are indeed incidental to what I thought, but he is not denying that I was thinking about such-and-such, and that I concluded that . . . Should anything else have been going on (Vol. XII, 253)? What is repudiated is merely a misleading picture that is fostered by the similarities between the verb 'to think' and process-verbs such as 'to grow', 'to change', 'to deteriorate'.

As with 'Thinking is a mental activity', so too with 'Thinking is an inner process': one *can* say such things if thereby one wishes simply to differentiate thinking from corporeal processes like digestion (cf. PI §339) or (rather more profoundly) to point out that in as much as thinking is 'inner' (in as much as the concept is a psychological concept displaying first-/third-person asymmetry) the language-game with 'thinking' *begins* with the expression of thoughts and manifestations of thinking (cf. Vol. XVI, 134f.). But it is misleading, for thinking is not, as

[10] See James, *Principles of Psychology*, Vol. 1, Ch. VII, for an example of such confusion.

it were, just like a physical process, only mental! The physical analogues of engaging in thought are not physical processes like digestion or breathing, but the *soundness* of digestion, the *quickness* of breath, the *irregularity* of heartbeat (RPP I §661). Having 'a mental life', i.e. thinking, wishing, believing, doubting, having mental images, being sad or merry, and so on, is not analogous to: eats, drinks, walks, runs, but to: moves now fast, now slow, now towards a goal, now without a goal, now continuously, now in jerks (RPP I §284). Here Wittgenstein anticipated (but did not elaborate) Ryle's comparison of verbs of thinking to so-called adverbial verbs.

The concept of a process has a familiar application in the physical sphere, where we talk of physical, chemical, or biological processes, in the description of certain regulated human activities and sequences of actions, as when we talk of legal and constitutional processes, and in the characterization of industrial and other artefactual processes. But this model of a process, when applied to the mental in philosophical or theoretical contexts, distorts the phenomena, creating misleading pictures and giving rise to false expectations. In this respect 'Thinking is an inner, incorporeal, or mental process' is akin to 'Sensations are inner, mental objects'. The 'mental process of thinking' need involve no changes in or transformations of a substance (as the process of fermentation does) or any essential sequential array of acts by agents (as legal processes do) or the processing and transformation of particulars (as manufacturing processes do). What 'goes on' in thinking, unlike what is manifest in its articulate expression, is not a sequential array of stages or phases in a 'process of thinking'. In short, we have here, one might say, the *form*, but not the substance, of a process. This is not to say that we do not have some use for the notion of a psychological (but not 'incorporeal'!) process; but it is highly specialized, as in 'the painful process of coming to terms with the loss of a loved one'. When in philosophy we extend it beyond these rather narrow confines, confusion and obfuscation ensue.

Finally, to round off this discussion of thinking and its subsumption under putative categorial concepts, is thinking an *experience*? No, it is categorially quite distinct. We do not compare thoughts as we compare experiences (Z §96); the relation of thinking to duration is unlike that of experiences to duration (RPP I §105), and so is its relation to hedonic values. Two people think the same, their thoughts converge, if they both agree that such-and-such is the case or that if so-and-so, then probably such-and-such. They think the same thought, have the same idea, if the expressions of their thoughts say the same thing. But this is not like having the same experience. In one sense of that expression, two people have the same experience if they do or undergo the same things (which one may like, and the other may hate). In another sense, in which having a pain is said (perhaps misleadingly) to be an experience, two people can be said to have the same experience if, e.g., they both have a pain of similar intensity, duration, phenomenal character, and location. Experiences in this sense have a 'content': a pain, which may be sharp and throbbing or dull and nagging, or a perceptual experience, which may be enjoyable (smelling jasmine) or unpleasant (smelling hydrogen sulphide). But in this sense of 'content', the putative experience of thinking has *no* content. To say *what* I thought is not to specify the *content of an experience*; it is not to say 'what it was like'. Moreover, if one expresses a thought in speech, no one would say that the first word one speaks is the beginning of the experience of thinking that thought or that the experience of thinking occurred just then. And if one says that the beginning and end of the experience of thinking is the beginning and end of the utterance, one would not know how to answer the question of whether the experience is uniform throughout or constantly changing, like the words of the utterance (RPP II §257).

The moral of the tale is that there is no substitute in philosophy for the description of the particular case. The grammar of each concept needs to be examined in its own right. There are no short-cuts by way of invoking apparent categorial concepts to give us our bearings. On the contrary, if our first step is to take it for granted that, e.g., thinking is a mental activity (or remembering a mental process, sensation an inner object) the exact nature of which must now be investigated, then we go wrong at the very start. 'The decisive movement in the conjuring trick has been made, and it was the very one that we thought quite innocent' (PI §308). The concepts of activity, act, process, object, when invoked in philosophical psychology, lead us astray, imposing upon us misleading pictures, creating a false aura of mystery, and ensuring that we remain in a state of confusion (PI §339). 'One cannot guess how a word functions. One has to *look at* its use and learn from that ' (PI §340).

THINKING: THE SOUL OF LANGUAGE

1. *The strategic role of the argument*

The psychological hinterland of the austere logical doctrines of the *Tractatus* is notoriously obscure. The declared aim of the book is to set a limit to thought, or rather to the expression of thoughts (TLP, Preface p.3). Only in language can that limit be set, and the *Tractatus* accordingly concentrates on delineating the essential nature of any possible represent-ation. The bare minimum about the psychological nature of thinking is given, for Wittgenstein believed that his task as a critical philosopher was purely logical. His study of language *corresponded* to traditional philo-sophical investigations, of a similarly critical nature, into thought-processes. But such enterprises typically got entangled in inessential psychological questions. With his method too, he was aware, there was a similar risk (TLP 4.1121), and he carefully screened out psychological concerns. The result is that the psychological presuppositions of the book are barely visible and must often be read between the lines or gleaned from the occasional remarks in the *Notebooks 1914 – 16* and correspondence.

This much seems clear: a propositional sign contains the possibility of expressing its sense (TLP 3.13).[1] It has that possibility in virtue of its logical multiplicity: the combinatorial possibilities in syntax of its constituent names, which must be logically isomorphic with what they represent. It only constitutes a proposition, however, if it is given a content. Tacit in the *Tractatus*, but explicit in the *Notebooks 1914 – 16*, is the idea that content is, as it were, injected into names by mental acts of meaning: '*By* my correlating the components of the picture with objects, it comes to represent a situation and to be right or wrong' (NB 33f.; cf. NB 53, 68, 70). Although there can be superficial vagueness in sentences, what one *means* by a constituent expression must always be 'sharp' (NB 68), for one can always explain that 'I *know* what I mean; I mean just THIS' and point with one's finger (NB 70). A proposition is not a Platonic object, but a propositional sign in its projective relation to the world (TLP 3.12). The method of projection is to think the sense of the proposition (TLP 3.11). When we use a propositional sign as a projection of a possible situation, i.e. use it 'thinkingly', with understanding, then it

---

[1] Here I follow A. J. P. Kenny's interpretation of TLP 3.13; see 'Wittgenstein's early philosophy of mind', repr. in his *The Legacy of Wittgenstein* (Blackwell, Oxford and New York, 1984), pp. 1 – 10.

is a proposition (*sinnvolle Satz*). It is, therefore, thought-processes (acts of meaning, thinking, understanding) that connect language with reality, link names with their meanings, and infuse sentences with life.

Further complications and irresolvable tension were added by the account of a thought as a psychological fact. A thought, like a proposition, is a picture or representation of a situation, although, unlike a proposition, it is not a perceptible one (TLP 3 – 3.1; NB 82). 'A thinks that *p*' is of the form ' "*p*" says that *p*' (TLP 5.542), which involves the correlation of *facts* by means of the correlation of their objects. The thought that *p* therefore is a psychical fact which, like a sentence, represents a situation. So a thought just is a kind of proposition, and thinking is a kind of language (NB 82). In response to Russell's queries, Wittgenstein wrote:

> I don't know *what* the constituents of a thought are, but I know *that* it must have such constituents which correspond to the words of language. Again the kind of relation of the constituents of thought and of the pictured fact is irrelevant. It would be a matter of psychology to find it out . . . [The] psychical constituents . . . have the same sort of relation to reality as words. What those constituents are I don't know. (R. 37)

The tension in this account is between the idea that a thought is a representation and thinking a kind of language, on the one hand, and the idea (as Wittgenstein later put it) that thought 'is the last interpretation' (cf. BB 34). Whereas a language of perceptible signs may stand in need of an interpretation (in order to disambiguate, clarify vagueness, etc.), thought does not. For *me*, there can be no gap between what I think and what I mean. The underlying idea is both natural and mystifying.[2] It makes sense to ask what a sign 'N' (a name) means or to wonder what the sense of a sentence '*p*' is. But if I *think* of N or *think* that *p*, it makes no sense for me to wonder who I mean or what I am thinking. However, if a thought is a proposition in the language of thought, this remarkable power of transparent, unerring correlation between the thought-constituents and what they represent must itself be explained. Two moves might seem to be available, and it is unclear which Wittgenstein opted for. One might argue that thought-constituents *intrinsically* represent the objects they represent. To this there are two objections: first, that if so, then they do *not* have the same sort of relation to reality as words; second, that far from explaining how this mystifying relation is possible, the reply that it is intrinsic merely disguises the original

---

[2] It is mystifying if one lacks a surview of the grammar of 'thinking' and of the relation of thought and its expression. For how is it possible for me to think of just N? Even though he is not here, but in America, and looks just like his twin N.N., I can still 'nail him' with my thought! And how can I even think that *p*, if it is not the case that *p*? (See 'Thinking: methodological muddles and categorial confusions', §1).

question in the form of an answer. Alternatively, one might argue that thought-constituents *are* related to reality as words are, i.e. extrinsically. The mechanism of correlation would be by means of the Will, but not the Will as a phenomenon, rather the Will as an aspect of the metaphysical self. This, however, is mere mystery-mongering. As Wittgenstein was later to realize (see §3 below), this feature of our thoughts can be clarified only by relinquishing the ideas that thoughts are kinds of propositions and that there is any such thing as a language of thought. But if these ideas are abandoned, one must also relinquish the related idea that it is thought that breathes life into otherwise dead signs.

It is important to note that the conception of thoughts and of thinking in the *Tractatus* is exceedingly general. When Wittgenstein said that 'a logical picture of facts is a thought', his idea applied not merely, for example, to opining, but to judging, believing, wondering, guessing, and also to doubting, supposing, and assuming. In all these cases, and very likely also in the case of wishing, hoping, expecting, and so on, it seems that we *represent*, or *picture to ourselves*, a certain situation. The differences between these psychological verbs was of no concern to Wittgenstein; what was of logical (and metaphysical) importance was the nature of representation, and of thought *qua* psychic representation, in general.

It is natural for a philosopher to conceive of thought and of thinking in this generalized manner. It seems that a logical investigation into representation just is an investigation into the nature and limits of thought. Niceties about the differences between thinking, knowing, meaning, understanding, and judging seem irrelevant at this level of generality. Moreover, ordinary language (for what it is worth to such a philosopher) seems to support the natural philosophical intuition. In many contexts 'I think' *is* interchangeable with 'I imagine', 'I believe', 'I mean', and the possibility of expressing intentions, desires, and beliefs in the form 'I think I'll go now', 'I think I'd like a drink', or 'I think it's raining' suggest that all these are, or involve, thoughts and thinking processes. Finally, a venerable tradition in philosophy supports this generalizing penchant. The Cartesian use of *cogitare* subsumed almost the whole range of the mental; Kant's use of *denken* covered anything 'representable in thought'; and although Frege's *Gedanke* was a Platonic object rather than a psychological one, *thinking*, engaging with this timeless entity, incorporates or is a constitutent of, conceiving, understanding, supposing, believing, and judging, as well as questioning.

Wittgenstein's anti-psychologism had induced him not to investigate the concepts that informed the psychological presuppositions of the *Tractatus*; only the essence of any possible symbolism seemed relevant to his concerns. Hence what it is to understand symbols and their use, what it is to mean something by a symbol, what kind of process (if any) thinking might be: these and related questions were allocated to psychology. When the edifice of the *Tractatus* collapsed, Wittgenstein started digging down to the foundations of the ruin. In the 'Big Typescript' (1932/3), his first effort at compiling a book incorporating his new ideas, Chapter 6 is entitled 'Thought and Thinking'. It is preceded by the following sequence of chapter themes: understanding, meaning, the proposition and its sense, instantaneous understanding, and the nature of language. It is evident that although in one sense his anti-psychologism is unabated, he now began to think that *philosophical* investigations into these psychological *concepts* is of paramount importance for the clarification of philosophical problems about meaning and representation.

The discussion of thinking in the 'Big Typescript' corresponds very roughly to that of Chapter V, §§63ff. of Rush Rhees's compilation *Philosophical Grammar*.[3] The aim of the chapter is to undermine the supposition that it is thought which lends life to mere signs, that makes sounds or marks mean something; and hence too to explode the idea that behind the intelligent use of any sentence lies a mental process of thinking the thought which that sentence expresses. For this destructive purpose, Wittgenstein continued to use the words 'thought' and 'to think' in the very wide sense sanctioned by the tradition of which the *Tractatus* had been the culmination. This is clear also from an opening passage of the *Blue Book*, where the same target is in view:

It seems that there are *certain definite* mental processes bound up with the working of language, processes through which alone language can function. I mean the processes of understanding and meaning. The signs of our language seem dead without these mental processes. . . . We are tempted to think that the action of language consists of two parts; an inorganic part, the handling of signs, and an organic part, which we may call understanding these signs, meaning them, interpreting them, thinking. (BB 3)

Despite this highly general and largely critical interest in thoughts and thinking, Wittgenstein's criss-cross journeys through this landscape led him into adjacent areas. Hence he also considered issues that bear only tangentially on his central theme: e.g. the location of thought, the purpose of thinking, and the possibility of a machine's thinking.

Few of the remarks from Chapter 6 of the 'Big Typescript' were incorporated into §§316 – 62 of the *Investigations* (though the discussion of the purpose of thinking in §§466 – 75 derives from those early reflections). Nevertheless, many of the themes recur: e.g. that thought is something ordinary and unmysterious, that thinking is not an inner

---

[3] For details of the relationship between the 'Big Typescript' and *Philosophical Grammar*, see A. J. P. Kenny, 'From the Big Typescript to the *Philosophical Grammar*', repr. in his *Legacy of Wittgenstein*, pp. 24 – 37 and S. Hilmy, *The Later Wittgenstein* (Blackwell, Oxford and New York, 1987), Ch. 1.

process, the absurdity of the idea that in French the order of words mirrors the order of thinking, and the question of whether machines can think. Moreover, the position of §§316 – 62 in the grand strategy of the *Investigations* has a similar rationale. Implicit in Augustine's conception of language is a beguiling picture of the nature of thinking and of the relation between thought and speech:

> Augustine describes the learning of human language as if the child came into a strange country and did not understand the language of the country; that is, as if it already had a language, only not this one. Or again: as if the child could already *think*, only not yet speak. And 'think' would mean something like 'talk to itself'. (PI §32)

The misconceptions about thinking, meaning something by one's words, saying something with thought or understanding, that are implicit in this picture and which surface in sophisticated philosophical theories constitute Wittgenstein's target (and the presuppositions of the *Tractatus* are not far from the bull's-eye). Confusions about thinking in this very general sense contribute as much to our philosophical perplexities about the nature of language and linguistic representation as vice versa.

The strategic role of §§316 – 62 is likewise clear. The private language arguments have shown the incoherence of the idea that the foundations of language lie in private objects that constitute, or explain, the meanings of primitive indefinables of language. It is a natural extension of this classical philosophical picture that an inner process of thinking gives our discourse its life, differentiates it from mere noises, and is what we communicate to each other by means of a verbal vehicle when we talk. (It is no coincidence that the discussion of thinking here is followed by an examination of imagining, for part of the private language 'syndrome' is the idea that the imagination plays an essential role in language, for it seems that one must have an image of a sensation or experience if one is to understand the words that name them. And surely to understand what another person says is a matter of having the right array of images called up in response to his words!)

However, as in the 'Big Typescript', so too here, Wittgenstein's reflections carried him beyond the narrow confines of the immediate strategic purpose – e.g. in the brief discussion of machines' thinking – and of the restriction to human beings of predications of 'thinking' (a theme that links up with §§281 – 3). It is obvious that while writing the notebooks that are the immediate source of the bulk of this section, Wittgenstein's interests were moving markedly in the direction of themes in philosophical psychology. In his lectures on that subject in 1946 – 7, he dwelt more extensively on questions concerning the nature of thinking, and in the notes he wrote during the immediate post-war period on the philosophy of psychology (MSS. 130 – 8), his treatment of thinking is more fine-grained, concerned with the very specialized use of 'to think' and with its differences from other related psychological verbs.

In this essay, the later writings on thinking are treated as of a piece with those in *Investigations*, Part 1. They grew out of that seed-bed, and the only shift in the analysis of thinking is the sharpening of focus, the diminution of the global use of 'think', and the concentration on philosophical psychology. But there is no significant, discernible conflict between the 1944 – 5 remarks on thinking and those of 1946 – 8.

2. *The dual-process conception*

The idea that thinking is an inner process which accompanies speaking but may go on independently of it is indeed intuitively persuasive. The conception of thought as that which gives 'life' to otherwise 'dead' signs is compelling for quite mundane reasons. A machine can emit words, but they are, 'as far as it is concerned', just noises. A parrot can utter words, but it cannot *say* things or *tell* one things. It can croak 'Tea is ready' or 'Polly is pretty', but it cannot *say that* tea is ready or *that* Polly is pretty. It can utter words, but it does not *mean* them or *understand* them; it does not *think* what it utters. What a robot or parrot emits are just noises; the words are lifeless, without a soul. An alien script, prior to decipherment, is just a sequence of dead marks. Only when we can understand what thought they express do they come to life.

These observations, which are roughly right, make it seem plausible to suppose that what *animates* dead signs is something that lies behind them. And philosophers construct theories about the nature of this 'something'. On a Fregean view, it is a sense, an abstract entity distinct from the sign, which we attach to it. 'It rains' and 'Es regnet' are different signs to which the same sense is attached in the same context. If I, here and now, utter the English sentence and you utter the German one, we both grasp the same thought, which is neither English nor German. According to this conception, sense is logically independent of language, but it gives language life.[4] For language is 'alive' for one only in so far as one thinks or understands the senses attached to sentences. Thinking is a psychological process of coming into intellectual contact with, grasping, these lexical souls. Speech is the communication to others by means of a linguistic vehicle of the sense one has 'grasped'.

An alternative picture that has a similar rationale cuts out the Platonism. On this conception – e.g. in the *Tractatus* – a continual process of

---

[4] An economist of Fregean bent would think of paper money as paper with a value attached to it (cf. PG 106f.; BB 4). He might, absurdly, suppose that what gives a £5 note its value is its being attached to the value of £5, which is the *same* value (today) as is attached to $7.72. If he were a philosophical materialist rather than a Platonist, he might find incoherent the abandonment of the gold standard!

meaning or *thinking* accompanies one's cogent, non–mechanical speech and breathes life into otherwise meaningless signs. Yet another picture informs the tradition of the British empiricists, who conceived of thinking as a transaction with ideas or images which accompany intelligent speech. Speaking is accordingly a *translation* from the imagist 'language of thought' into word-language, which will generate in the mind of the comprehending hearer a similar play of representations.

It is indeed true that a sign can be lifeless for one, as when one hears an alien tongue or sees an unknown script. But it is an illusion to suppose that what animates a sign is some *immaterial thing*, abstract object, mental image, or hypothesized psychic entity that can be attached to it by a process of thinking (BB 4). One can try to rid oneself of these nonsensical conceptions by simple manoeuvres. In the case of the idealist conception, imagine that we replace the mental accompaniment of a word, which allegedly gives the expression its 'life', by a physical correlate. For example, instead of accompanying the word 'red' with a mental image of red, one might carry around in one's pocket a small red card. So, on the idealist's model, whenever one hears or uses the word 'red', one can *look* at the card instead of conjuring up a visual image in thought. But will looking at a red slip of paper endow the word 'red' with life? The word plus sample is no more 'alive' than the word without the sample. For an object (a sample of red) does not have *the use* of the word laid up within it, and neither does a mental image. Neither the word and the sample nor the word and the mental pseudo-sample dictate the use of a word or guarantee understanding.

In the Fregean (Platonist) case, one should ask of a given sentence, e.g. 'It is raining' (which allegedly has 'life' conferred on it by being associated with its sense), what sense it has. The reply 'Its sense is: that it is raining' does not animate the dead sign. The question 'What is the sense of the sentence "*p*"?' *if it is not a request for a paraphrase of 'p' into other symbols*, has no more sense than 'What sentence is formed by this sequence of words?' (cf. BB 161; PI §502). Explaining the sense or meaning of an expression is not to refer one to something extra-linguistic, i.e. to something other than an expression (Vol. (IV, 237) or sample (which belongs to the means of representation). Understanding, according to Frege, 'would be something like seeing a picture from which all the rules followed, or a picture that makes them all clear' (PG 40). It seemed to Frege, Wittgenstein claimed, that no adding of inorganic signs, as it were, can make the proposition live, from which he concluded that 'What must be added is something immaterial, with properties different from all mere signs' (BB 4). He did not see that such an object, a sense mysteriously grasped in thinking, as it were a picture in which all the rules are laid up, 'would itself be another sign, or a calculus to explain the written one to us' (PG 40). If anything can be said to give a sign life, it is its *use* (as what gives a £5 note its value is what one can *do* with it). This is not something that *accompanies* a sign; hence to say what sense or meaning an expression has does not involve pointing at or ineffably showing some accompanying entity that is that sense, but rather to give *another expression* with the *same use*. To understand a sign, i.e. for it to 'live' for one, is not to grasp something other than the sign; nor is it to accompany the sign with an inner parade of objects in thought. It is to grasp the use of the sign itself (AWL 54; BB 4f.).

Recognizing such philosophical theories as confusions will not help unless one can free oneself from the urge to construct theories to dispel the apparent mysteries of thinking and meaning. One must locate the sources of the confusions and come to see that they can be dispelled only by grammatical clarifications, not by theories of thinking or of meaning. Many compelling considerations contribute to the idea that thinking is an inner process that accompanies speaking (which is not thoughtless) or listening with understanding.

(i) One can speak mechanically, without thought, or speak with thought. Surely thinking, the inner activity, is the accompaniment that makes the difference! One can think without speaking, and is that not to engage in the inner activity without communicating it to others in speech, for is not speech a matter of telling others what one has been thinking? Indeed, thinking often seems to be a kind of talking to oneself *in foro interno*, the soul conversing with itself (Plato). Moreover, one can say one thing and think another, so thinking is obviously quite different from saying. The one is an outer activity, the other looks like an inner activity that typically, but not uniformly, accompanies the outer.

(ii) A second array of factors contributing to the dual-process picture of thought and speech turns on the natural idea of a medium of thought. One can speak in English, French, or German; but is it not an open question what one *thinks in*? It is very tempting to suppose that some languages, especially one's own, have a word-order that corresponds to the order of thought, whereas others, such as German or Latin, say, do not (PI §336). Here it seems as if one thinks *in* a certain medium, perhaps in ideas or images, which one then translates into word-language. This picture is strengthened by our natural talk of having an idea before our mind, which we then express in words, as if we first think the idea and then translate it into English (BB 41). We sometimes look for the right word to express our thought, and superficial reflection on this suggests that we think the thought in 'Mentalese', as it were, and then look around for the right translation. For do we not sometimes exclaim 'What I said does not express my thoughts at all well! Let me try again!'? These considerations suggest a non-linguistic medium of thought, but others push in the opposite direction. Does the Englishman speaking German haltingly not think *in* English and then translate what he wants to say into German? And when he has thoroughly mastered the alien tongue, is one not tempted to say that he knows German so well that he even thinks in it?

(iii) We often understand something in a flash or think of a complex solution to a problem at a stroke. We naturally enough speak of the lightning process of thought. Hence it can seem as if thinking without speaking is a very rapid process (like the ticking of a clock with a broken escapement), whereas speech slows the thinking down (PI §318). We say 'Think before you speak!' like 'Wash before you eat!', and both orders appear to prescribe one activity before another (BB 148). As James noted, we ordinarily know what we are going to say before we say it, and this induces the idea that the thought must have been completed by the time the first word is uttered (PI §337). We use such phrases as 'What you really wanted to say was . . . ', which intimate the picture of the thought articulated in 'Mentalese' and of thinking as an inner activity of generating thoughts (PI §334).

The premises of the first array of considerations are correct, but they do not confirm the dual-process conception. Wittgenstein clarified this with a wide range of arguments, illustrations, and reminders. When one thinks without speaking, one is not doing what one does when one articulates what one thinks, only minus the speaking. For to speak with thought, i.e. non-mechanically, is not to speak *and* do something else as well (PI §332), as becomes obvious when one is asked to say something with thought and then just to do what one did when one said it with thought, only without saying it. What characterizes speaking without thought (viz. mechanically, unthinkingly, without understanding) is not the absence of an accompaniment. Indeed, it is sometimes the *presence* of an accompaniment which explains one's lack of thought, e.g. a violent headache or the distraction of one's attention ('I'm so sorry, I wasn't thinking when I said that, my mind was on the music'). One should compare speaking with thought not to singing and playing the tune on the piano as accompaniment, but to singing *with expression*, i.e. with modulation of the voice, accentuation, intensity, etc. These are obviously not *accompaniments* of singing (BB 148; cf. PI §341), and no more so is thinking when one speaks with thought. One can indeed imagine people who only think aloud (PI §331); but no one would imagine that when such people speak with thought, they say things twice!

The lack of thought in speech, in one sense, is manifest in the mechanical, monotonic mode of speech and in the lack of expression in voice and face. In another sense, it is marked by the inappropriateness or ineptness of what one says. In neither case, however, is the lack of thought a matter of the absence of an inner process accessible only to oneself. Lack of thought is characterized by one's inability or unwillingness to explain or justify what one said and by one's reluctance to stick by it. The function of 'When I said that, I wasn't thinking' or 'I didn't mean anything in particular when I said that' is not to make a report on introspected goings-on or their absence. If it were, it would make sense for the speaker to be mistaken as to whether he was thinking when he said what he said. But does it?[5] Even if certain ideas crossed his mind, indeed even if he *was thinking* (of something *else*), his words (viz. 'I wasn't thinking') are not nullified; for this utterance is a *disclaimer*, a denial of *intent* (cf. RPP II §§250ff.), not a report of mental happenings. 'I didn't mean anything by it, I was just saying it' is indeed, in a sense, indubitable or incorrigible, but not because it describes an experience (RPP II §253). 'I wasn't thinking' often means 'I didn't take *that* into account' (as I should have).

Any analytic investigation of the fine grain of the concept of thinking must distinguish the various ways in which an utterance may be thoughtless and in which something may be said unthinkingly. One may say something wholly mechanically (as when one repeats a line of poetry 500 times to commit it to memory), or one's words may be a spontaneous exclamation which one did not utter intentionally and, perhaps, should not have uttered at all. Here too one might say 'I wasn't thinking'. A remark is said to be thoughtless if it is indiscreet, insensitive, or inconsiderate; or, rather differently, if it is unreflective where reflection was meet, foolish where a little thought would have prevented the folly.

To be sure, saying that p and thinking that p are not the same, and one can say that p while thinking that not-p. But saying something and 'not thinking it' is not cutting out one activity or process. Saying something 'with thought', as opposed to saying it unthinkingly (in one or other of the *different* senses in which a remark may be thoughtless, mechanical, unthinking, unthoughtful), typically involves a *commitment*. One might compare it to playing a card in a game of cards. One must be prepared to defend what one says, to explain it, act on it in appropriate circumstances, take credit or incur debit for it, stand by it, and so on. One might say that to express one's thoughts, to say what one thinks, cannot be a description, report, or communication of an inner process or activity, because no such description of an inner process or activity could have the consequences in the language-game of the expression of thought.

Turning now to the second set of considerations, one should challenge the supposition that one thinks *in* anything, for it is highly misleading (cf. LPP 247f.). One speaks in a language, but does one think in a

---

[5] Some philosophers would argue that introspection, though a kind of 'inner' perception, is nevertheless infallible. But this purchases immunity to the above objection at the price of a mystery; for how can it be that a faculty of knowledge is guaranteed against error? See 'Privacy', §3, and 'The inner and the outer', §2.

language? Is the parallelism between speech and thought that simple? If I speak thoughtfully in English, am I at the same time thinking in English *in addition* to speaking? Enough has been said to make it obvious that this is erroneous. Of course, I may talk to myself *in foro interno* in English or in German. But, in the first place, not all 'talking inwardly' is thinking: reciting the multiplication-tables, going over one's speech in one's imagination to make sure that one knows it by heart, and 'counting sheep' in order to stop one from thinking and so to induce sleep are not. In the second place, one should note how peculiar and particular is the very notion of talking to oneself in the imagination. Talking audibly and talking in the imagination are no more two different ways of doing the same thing than experimenting in the laboratory and experimenting in one's imagination are two different ways of doing the same thing (cf. RPP I §574; PI §265). Reflect on the fact that we do not say 'After I said that to myself, I didn't talk to myself again for the rest of the day' or 'I am tired of listening to myself talking to myself', etc. We are inclined to think that talking in whispers stands to talking to oneself *in foro interno* as talking loudly stands to talking quietly, but this comparison is wrong. The last member of the series 'shouting, talking loudly, talking quietly, whispering' is 'moving one's lips silently', not 'talking to oneself in the imagination', let alone 'thinking'.[6] To be sure there *is* a close relationship between 'saying inwardly' and 'saying' (as there is between 'calculating in one's head' and 'calculating'). But it is not to be explained by saying that the 'inner' is just the same as the 'outer', only hidden from view (PI p. 220). It is manifest, rather, in the possibility of telling someone what one was saying to oneself (and that is *not* akin to relating a soliloquy one overheard!) and also in the outward actions that often accompany inward speech (e.g. I may sing inwardly and beat time with my hand).

Of course, one does say 'I can speak in German, but I can't think in German', signifying thereby that before I can say something in German, I must, by and large, first decide what I want to say and be *able* to say it in English, and then struggle to find the German words. But it does not follow that it makes sense to say of a native English speaker that he thinks *in* English, unless that just means that when he talks in his imagination what he thus says is in English (i.e. the answer to 'What were you saying to yourself?' is, e.g., 'I came, I saw, I conquered', not 'Veni, vidi, vici'). One may indeed say of an Englishman that he speaks German so well that he even *thinks* in German, but that just means that he *does not* first think of what he wants to say and then pause to try to think of the German word for such-and-such. Although it is in general true that the capacity for thought is bound up with the capacity to manipulate symbols, this is not

---

[6] Interestingly, Watson fell into this trap (see Behaviour and behaviourism', §1, and Exg. §330).

because unexpressed thoughts must be *in* a language, but rather because the *expression* of thoughts in speech must be. It is highly misleading to suggest that one thinks *in* anything, although it is both true and important that whatever one thinks must be *expressible* in words, images, or whatever.[7] We are doubtless deceived by the analogy between an English speaker hunting for the right German word in order to say such-and-such and an English speaker hunting for the right word in his own language to express his thought. But the analogy is deceptive; for in the first case he can *say*, in English, what he thinks, but in the second he cannot. And this is *not* because he has thought *in* images or 'non-linguistic symbols' and has not found the right translation, so that he, so to speak, knows what he thinks and is now looking for the words to express his subjectively perspicuous thought (cf. RPP II §565; PI §§335f.). 'The word is on the tip of my tongue' just means that the right word escapes me for the moment, but that I hope to find it soon (PI p. 219) and am on the verge of producing it. Similarly, 'I know exactly what I want to say, but I can't think of the words' is either nonsense or just means 'Give me another moment for the thought to crystallize and then I'll tell you what I think'.[8]

The third group of considerations ((iii) above) is equally confused. We do indeed speak of the lightning speed of thought, but this is a metaphor. One cannot literally *measure* the speed of thinking a thought, but only how long it takes someone to reach a conclusion (or a determinate phase of an argument) on a given occasion. Thoughts, like propositions, but unlike loaves of bread, do not come in slices; hence one cannot say 'Now he has thought half the thought, now two-thirds of it; now he has almost finished' (cf. PI §§318f.; PG 39). To say that thinking in a flash is the same as speaking with thought only very much faster is confused. The flashing of a thought, the sudden insight, is manifest in the exclamation 'Now I have it', followed by an expression of the thought or delineation of a scheme (PI p. 176). But 'Now I have it' is a jolt or glad start of sudden understanding. Though we say 'It flashed through my mind', we hardly ever ask 'How did it flash through your mind, what was it like?' (RPP I §239). What went on, if anything, is irrelevant to the thought's having flashed through your mind; what we are interested in is what you can now do, what conclusion you have reached in a flash. One should compare seeing or understanding a complex thought or plan in a flash not to running through it verbally at high speed, but rather to jotting down the whole theme of a lecture in a few key words: they are an epitome of those ideas in as much as I *can* run through the whole lecture on the basis of those jottings (PI §319).

[7] This point was further developed by Ryle in his essays on thinking.
[8] Searching for the right expression is *not* comparable to the efforts of someone who is trying to make an exact copy of a line which only he can see (RPP I §580).

It is perfectly correct to say that one typically knows what one is going to say before one says it. But one must not be misled by this turn of phrase. It does not imply that one has already said what one wants to say to oneself *in foro interno*. Nor does it imply that it *always* makes sense to ask 'How *long* before you said such-and-such did you know what you were going to say?' Rather, what it means is that when someone is interrupted, he can normally continue; and if he cannot, he says 'I've forgotten', not 'How should I know what words were going to follow?' Knowing what one was going to say is of a piece with knowing, being able to say, what one intended. One is no more surprised at what one ordinarily says than at what one normally does. And the intention to say such-and-such, like the intention to do such-and-such, does not 'contain' a model of what it is an intention of, from which one might read off what one meant (RPP I §§173ff.; Z §§1f.).

Equally, we do remark 'What you really wanted to say was . . . '; but that is not a guess at what he said to himself inwardly and failed to articulate overtly. Rather, this form of words is used to lead him (with his consent) to something *else*, which coheres in certain ways with the context and antecedent utterances, and so forth (cf. Exg. §334). It resembles certain uses of 'What you *really* want is . . . ', where it had never crossed one's mind that that was what one wanted, but which, once mentioned, crystallizes the will. Similarly, 'Think before you speak!' is not like 'Wash before you eat!' but more akin to 'Pause before you jump!' or 'Don't speak precipitously!' It is not an invitation to engage in an activity, but, e.g., *to take such-and-such factors into account* in one's reply.

The dual-procession conception of thinking is a mythology of the mind based on multiple misunderstandings. It exemplifies how, when doing philosophy, we misinterpret the very expressions we use comfortably in our daily transactions, 'like savages, primitive people, who hear the expressions of civilized men, put a false interpretation on them, and then draw the queerest conclusions from it' (PI §196). We are taken in by pictures embedded in language because we do not scrutinize their *use*.

The use of the word 'thinking' serves much more specialized purposes than its form suggests (RPP II §234). One must reflect on what role 'to think' has in characterizing people ('Yon Cassius has a lean and hungry look; he thinks too much: such men are dangerous'); what follows from the fact that when such-and-such occurred, I was thinking or musing; what are the implications of saying something with thought, as opposed to saying it mechanically (e.g. that I take responsibility for it, explain why I said it, justify my thinking thus as well as my saying what I think). If someone reads something with thought, i.e. attentively, then he may be impressed by it, he can say what he has read (Z §91), evaluate or criticize it, develop it further, and so forth. Someone who engages in a certain activity with thought (as opposed to doing it automatically) *considers* alternatives, makes choices, expects certain consequences, and so on (RPP I §§560ff.). The expression 'to think' is used as a very special sort of signal or indicator of antecedents and consequences, as well as of aspects or modes of speech and action, rather than to report on parallel covert activities or processes. And that, of course, is why *whether someone thought* on a given occasion is often determined by what comes before or after. Hence too it is only in very special circumstances that one can say that something was done without thinking (Z §95).[9] If thinking were an inner accompaniment of animated speaking, for example, then it would be intelligible that a highly animated, sophisticated conversation take place, only without any thinking. But this is not intelligible (Z §93; RPP II §238), not because it contradicts all our experience of human beings and their conversational capacities, but rather because what did or did not go on *in foro interno* is of no interest and has no bearing on whether the participants were thinking.

3. *Thought, language, and the mastery of linguistic skills*

It is tempting to wonder whether one can think without language. Indeed this question is a natural foil to the dual-process conception of speaking with thought or understanding, for one wants to get *behind* language in order to find what 'gives language life'. In connection with this confusing question, we harbour various conflicting pictures. On the one hand, we entertain the idea of wordless thoughts flashing across the mind in an instant; we suppose the play of images to constitute thinking; and we wonder whether, or fondly assume that, animals, especially our own pets, think even though they cannot speak. So we are inclined to advocate the intelligibility of thought without language. On the other hand, we are captivated by the venerable picture of thinking as the discourse of the soul with itself. For thought must be articulate; one must be able to distinguish the thought that p from the thought that q, even if one does not *say* what one thinks. And hence it seems that thinking that p must involve saying it *to oneself*. Therefore we are disposed to contend that only one who can talk, at least *in foro interno*, can think. Both pictures are given apparent support by scientific theorizing. On the one hand, psychologists try to collect evidence of 'wordless thought' by asking people to describe what happens when they think, and take their answers as evidence about the medium and process of thinking. On the other hand, theoretical linguists and 'cognitive scientists' argue that there must be an *innate* language of thought if human beings are to be able to learn a natural language.

[9] There is a parallel here with pretending.

Both pictures induce a conception of speech as a translation or encoding of thoughts. Hence we suppose, in conformity with tradition,[10] that given that we cannot directly transfer our thoughts to the mind of another, we translate our 'inner thoughts' into a natural language as an *indirect* means of communicating them. This confusion dovetails neatly with another, which turns on a muddle over the identity of thoughts (see 'Privacy', §2). According to one picture, successful communication consists in conveying to the hearer the thought that is in the mind of the speaker. Here the thought is conceived as an ethereal object and the sentence uttered as its vehicle, which will transport it from speaker to hearer. According to a different picture, the sentence is akin to a potion which will generate in the mind of another not the identical, but an exactly similar, thought to the thought in the mind of the speaker. These knots will be disentangled later.

The original question 'Can one think without language?' is doubtless as confused as the dogmatic answers 'All thinking is in language' and 'There is non-verbal thought'. As a first step towards clarifying matters we must side-step the original question, approaching it only indirectly by way of a different one: viz. whether the capacity to think is logically bound up with having mastered a language. This indirect approach will prove more fruitful than a direct strategy. William James cited the Ballard case as empirical proof that one can think even though one has not mastered a natural language and cannot speak one. Wittgenstein challenged the intelligibility of the story (PI §342 and Exg.). Given that the young Ballard could not speak any language, what would have *counted* as an expression of his alleged pre-linguistic thoughts about God and creation? If nothing in his behavioural repertoire would so count, then what would be the *criterion* for his having thought that *p* rather than that *q*, or indeed his not having thought anything at all? In the normal case the criteria for whether someone thinks such-and-such include his avowing this, i.e. his *expressing* what he thinks. And it makes sense to attribute unexpressed thoughts to a person only in as much as the possibility of his expressing them is intelligible. The question of how he *knows* that he thinks such-and-such cannot arise, for it is nonsensical, as is the question of whether he is certain or has doubts as to whether he thinks that *p* or that *q*.[11] But if, as in the Ballard case, we cut out the possibility of any behavioural expression of thoughts (viz. in avowals that *this* is what one is thinking), then doubts break out in respect of his memory-claim in later years. How could Ballard be sure that he had

---

[10] Cf., e.g. Hobbes, *Leviathan*, Ch. IV; Arnauld, *The Art of Thinking*, Introduction; Locke, *Essay Concerning Human Understanding*, Bk. III, Ch. i, Sect. 2; I. Watts, *Logick or the Right Use of Reason*, Pt. I, Ch. iv, Sect. 1. These confusions are equally evident in Frege (see FA §60; PW 105, 142, 269f.), Russell, (AM, Ch. XI), and their current heirs.

[11] We are concerned here with ignorance, not indecision.

correctly translated those 'wordless thoughts' of his childhood into words? The question is absurd; but it points to something vital, viz. that with the abrogation of the normal language-game with the avowal of thoughts, we need a criterion of identity for what a Ballard might have thought, *and so does he*.[12] Since there is none, the question of how Ballard knows that that was what he thought, of whether he is sure that he has correctly translated his wordless thoughts, *does* arise – and can have no answer! And that shows not that he may be mistaken, but that the story is incoherent.

One might object to the drift of Wittgenstein's reflections. Do we not say of animals that they think? And yet they do not speak! But we must distinguish. For, first, we simply do not say of amoebas, crabs, or fish that they think, any more than we say it of chairs or tables. One would not know what it would be for a chair or a table to think, or even a fish (Z §129; PI §361); and this is not due to ignorance of fact or to epistemic qualms. Secondly, we must distinguish between thinking (opining, believing) that *p* and thinking (reflecting or pondering), e.g. thinking something over, thinking up a solution, thinking whether things are thus or not, or whether one ought to act in a certain way. In the former use, we do sometimes say of the higher animals that they think such-and-such (e.g. that a dog, hearing its leash being take off the peg, thinks it is going to be taken for a walk) – but only where their behavioural repertoire is sufficiently rich for something to *count* as an expression of such-and-such a thought or belief (e.g. the dog's joyful prancing at the door). This might be called 'primitive thought', describable via primitive *behaviour*, not via a 'thinking accompaniment of behaviour' (cf. Z §99); but the possibilities are very limited, as limited as the behavioural repertoire. Similar considerations apply to the second use: we do say, e.g. of Köhler's apes, that they found the solution to the problem of reaching the bananas – but only because their having solved the problem is expressed in their behaviour. (Note, however, that in Ballard's case *nothing* would count as behaviour expressing the fact that he thought that God created the universe, and furthermore that nothing would count as his thinking *about* or pondering on God and the origins of life.) Nevertheless, we hardly ever predicate 'is thinking' of any animal other than ourselves (Z §129). We do not say that, for all we know, dogs talk to themselves *in foro interno*, precisely because dogs do not talk; we only say of a creature that it talks to itself in the imagination if it is a creature that *can* talk (MS. 165, 200f.). For the criteria for someone's talking to himself thus consist in what he *says* when asked or when relating a certain

---

[12] A remark on thoughts in the spirit of *Investigations* §288. Note that this point is *not epistemological*, but logical. The question at stake is not 'How do we know?' but rather 'What counts as having such a thought?'

episode (cf. PI §376). Similarly, with rare exceptions, we do not say of an animal that it is thinking something over, thinking up a plan or project, or even just thinking about something. Köhler's apes could be seen as a limiting case (RPP II §224; RPP I §561), where we can discern a pale anticipation of *considering*, a glimmer of reflecting on options, even though the creatures have not mastered a language.

These arguments may impel us into the converse fallacy, viz. that if, with the exception of the above kinds of limiting cases, only a language-user can be said to think, then thinking must be inward speaking. But we have already shown that idea to be incoherent. One must not confuse the necessary capacity for the (outer) expression of thought with the actuality of inner vocalization. Mechanical 'inner' speaking is no more thoughtful than mechanical 'outer' speaking; moreover, one can think up, think about, reach the conclusion that something or other is the case without talking to oneself in the imagination at all. One may be inclined at this point to suggest that such 'wordless thoughts' are thought in images, for they must surely be *in* something! But that is just as confused. One does not think *in* images at all, although when one is thinking of something or about something, images may cross one's mind, and in certain cases conjuring up a mental image of X may serve a heuristic purpose (e.g. when solving problems in geometry). But having an image of X before one's mind is not thinking *in images* in the sense in which one speaks *in English*; 'thinking in images', like 'thinking in English', is not on the same level as *speaking in* a language. The words one utters when one speaks are the *expression* of one's thought; the images one may conjure up while thinking are *not* an expression of one's thought but an aid to thought or an accompaniment of thought.

There is, however, a deeper objection to the idea that thinking, taken in a wide sense, is inward speaking (as opposed to being occasionally accompanied by inner speaking): viz. that if it were so, then a report of thinking could not mention what or whom was *meant* (RPP I §180). For it is an essential feature of the linguistic expression of thought that the user of the linguistic sign can say whom he meant (e.g. by the sign 'N' in the sentence 'ϕN' or what he meant (by 'ϕN'). Of any sign one uses, it is always possible when the sign has been specified to raise the question of what one meant thereby (if anything). However, if thinking *were* just inner speaking, then a report of what one thought *would leave out what one meant*. All it could do would be to adduce further *signs*. But that is absurd, for there is no difference here between thinking that p and meaning that p. One can say of an expression one has used that 'By "N" I mean *this*', but one cannot say of a 'thought-constitutent' 'By "N" I mean *this*'. For then it would not be a language of *thought* at all, but would have to be 'thought out' like any other symbolism. Signs have a use (and misuse). But thinking of something, thinking that things are

thus-and-so, meaning or intending such-and-such *in foro interno*, is not a
use of signs, even though it typically presupposes the mastery of the use
of signs that would express what one thinks, means, or intends.

> The point is that one has to read off from a thought that it is the thought that
> such-and-such is the case. If one can't read it off (as one can't read off the cause of a
> stomach-ache) then it is of no logical interest. . . .
>   If a thought is observed there can be no further question of an understanding: for if
> the thought is seen it must be recognized as a thought with a certain content; it does
> not need to be interpreted! – That really is how it is; when we are thinking, there isn't
> any interpretation going on. (PG 144f).

Hence if one supposes the meaning, the thinking, to be a process
accompanying the saying, and conceives of it as couched 'in the language
of thought', i.e. as a further *sign*, one generates a dilemma. Either the
meaning, the sentence-in-thought, can be interpreted, and the question
of what one *meant* ('in thought') can, absurdly, arise; or, the meaning
cannot be interpreted, and the question of what one meant (thought)
cannot, absurdly, be answered (BB 34f.; PG 144ff.)!
   To put the same point differently: the idea that *I interpret* my thought
that ϕN as being a thought about N, is absurd. The thought is 'the last
interpretation', it 'reaches right up to reality' (does not fall short of it).
But the price one must pay for this is that thinking is *not* 'having
representations' *in* a symbolism of any kind. And if thinking *is*, as some
philosophers suppose, a matter of having 'internal representations', the
the question of what one means by such-and-such an internal representation must, absurdly, arise *in one's own case*.[13] Hence the contention that
'All thinking is *in* language', no less than 'There is wordless thought', is
deeply confused.
   These confusions can be made to disappear only when one abandons
the conception of thinking (or meaning something) as an inner process or
activity of any kind.

> If I try to describe the process of intention, I feel first and foremost that it can do
> what it is supposed to do only by containing an extremely faithful picture of what it
> intends. But further, that that too does not go far enough, because a picture, whatever
> it may be, can be variously interpreted; hence this picture too in its turn stands
> isolated. When one has the picture in view by itself it is suddenly dead, and it is as if
> something had been taken away from it, which had given it life before. It is not a
> thought, not an intention; whatever accompaniments we imagine for it, articulate or
> inarticulate processes, or any feeling whatsoever, it remains isolated, it does not point
> outside itself to a reality beyond.
>   . . . We want to say 'Meaning is surely essentially a mental process, a process of
> consciousness and life, not of dead matter,' But what will give such a thing the

---

[13] This argument pin-points a fatal incoherence in contemporary speculation in cognitive
psychology. Further investigation, however, would be out of place in this context.

specific character of what goes on? – so long as we speak of it as a process. . . . It could be said: we should call any process 'dead' in this sense. (PG 148)

Although *mastery* of a language is by and large a prerequisite of thinking, since what one can think is co-extensive with what one can express (although not necessarily only verbally), it does not follow that thinking is speaking to oneself in the imagination. And it does not follow from the latter point that 'wordless thought' is 'in' pictures or images.

Once these absurdities are dispelled, one can see how the classical pictures of communication by means of language are based on multiple misunderstandings. Both the 'vehicle' model, viz. that I convey the thought I have in mind to others by means of an uttered sentence that is its linguistic *vehicle*, and the causative or 'potion' model, that the sentence uttered *induces* in the hearer the same (exactly similar) thought that is in the mind of the speaker, conceive of speech as the *indirect* communication of thoughts in default of a direct means of apprehending or grasping the thought in question. It only makes sense to talk of communicating something indirectly if it also makes sense to talk of communicating it directly. The classical pictures labour under the misconception that I apprehend the thought I am thinking 'immediately', and that I could only communicate it directly to someone else by letting him 'see' what is in my mind. Since this is impossible, one must make do with indirect communication of thoughts. But this is a muddle. For, first, even if the hearer could look into my head or, *per impossibile*, into my mind, he would not discern there what I was thinking, i.e. what I *meant* (cf. PI p. 217). Secondly, the pictures confusedly suppose that the thoughts are *in* my head, and that communicating consists in transporting them to or generating them in your head. (The causative model is vividly, pictorially, manifest in de Saussure's famous 'speech circuit' diagram.[14]) But what I think, the thought I entertain, is no more *in* my head than the fact that makes what I think true is *in* the world. Is the thought in my *mind*? One may say that – although, for more reasons than one, it is highly misleading. But 'This is what I have in mind' or 'I have a thought in mind' are just ways of saying 'This is what I think' or 'I have thought of something'. Hence to conceive of communication as the transference of thoughts from my brain or mind to yours is a muddle. If I send you a letter, the letter which was in my possession will then be in yours, but I do not thereby lose the thoughts I expressed in the letter (unless I forget what I said). Communicating or expressing thoughts is not transferring or transporting objects of any kind. Thirdly, the alternative picture is no less confused. The causative model implicitly assumes that the thought allegedly generated in your mind by my utterance is not identical with

---

[14] F. de Saussure, *Course in General Linguistics*, tr. R. Harris (Duckworth, London, 1983), p. 11.

the thought in my mind, but only exactly the same, just as we are inclined to think that your headache cannot be identical with mine but only exactly the same (cf. PI §§253f.).[15] But this misguidedly projects onto thoughts a distinction between being identical and being exactly similar, which has appliction paradigmatically to material objects (see 'Privacy', §2). If I think that p, and you think that p, then we do indeed think the same (and not a 'just exactly similar' *or* a 'numerically identical') thought. Fourthly, for someone to understand what I say when I tell him what I think, it is not necessary that he should think what I think, 'have the same thought' as I, but only that he should *know* what I think (and said). It must be possible for him to *express* that thought, i.e. to say what *I* think; but it is not necessary that he should have or think it. The *pictures* underlying the concept of communication, viz. the pictures of *conveying* or *producing* thoughts, are deeply misleading. Finally, we can indeed distinguish various ways of communicating thoughts indirectly. We might call writing a letter 'indirect' by contrast with talking to the recipient; or we might contrast overtly telling someone something with communicating that message to him by a wink or a gesture; or we might contrast telling him something by word or letter with getting someone else to pass the message on to him. But in none of these cases is speaking to him conceived as *indirect* communication; there is no *more* direct way of letting someone know what one thinks than telling him!

4. *Making a radical break*

The pictures of thinking, of speaking with thought, of communicating our thoughts, mislead us in numerous ways when we are doing philosophy. One deep root of our troubles lies in a supposition which Wittgenstein criticized in the context of his discussion of the name/object model as misapplied to the concept of pain and its relation to pain-behaviour (PI §304). For of thinking too we might say that our paradoxes and bewilderment will only disappear 'if we make a radical break with the idea that language always functions in one way, always

---

[15] James writes:

. . . no one of them [thoughts] is separate, but each belongs with certain others and with none beside. My thought belongs with my other thoughts, and your thought with your other thoughts . . . each of these minds keeps its own thoughts to itself. There is no giving or bartering between them. No thought even comes into direct *sight* of a thought in another personal consciousness than its own. Absolute insulation, incredible pluralism, is the law. *Principles of Psychology*, Vol. I, pp. 225f.)

It was in response to such a muddle that Frege fell into the converse confusion of reifying thoughts (propositions, what we think) in order to ensure that different people can think the *numerically* identical thought.

serves the same purpose: to convey thoughts – which may be about houses, pains, good and evil, or anything else you please' (PI §304). This idea not only plays havoc with our endeavour to see utterances (*Äusserungen*) aright (not to mention ethical judgements); it also distorts our view of the very phenomenon from which it is derived, viz. the expression of thought. 'As if the purpose of the proposition were to convey to one person how it is with another: only, so to speak, in his thinking part and not in his stomach' (PI §317(b)). Numerous sentences we utter express a thought. But it does not follow that uttering such sentences is the outward manifestation of the inner state, process, or activity of thinking as a cry of pain is the outer manifestation of physical suffering (PI §317(a)). In saying '*p*', I may, *in certain contexts*, be expressing a thought; but it does not follow that I am communicating a thought that is 'in me', a thought that I am thinking or have in mind. We must remind ourselves how specialized is the language-game of saying what we think, of communicating our thoughts, of telling them to others.

You regard it much too much as a matter of course that one can tell (*mitteilen*) anything to anyone. That is to say: we are so much accustomed to communication (*Mitteilung*) through language, in conversation, that it looks to us as if the whole point of communication lay in this: someone else grasps the sense of my words – which is something mental: he as it were takes it into his own mind. If he then does something further with it as well, that is no part of the immediate purpose of language. (PI §363(b))

We are misled by the use of 'a thought' and 'to express a thought' into a too facile, smooth, and simple conception of the grammar of these expressions (RPP I §554). We say that a sentence 'S' expresses the thought that *p*, as we say that the sentence expresses the proposition that *p*. But it does not follow from the fact that a person uttered the sentence 'S' that he thought that *p* and expressed his thought in words in order to communicate his thought to his hearer. The phrase 'to express a thought', when applied to a person, has a quite particular grammar, which is abused when we take it for granted that every utterance of a sentence that can be said to express a thought (or proposition) involves the speaker's expressing his thought. (And something similar applies to the phrases 'to express a proposition' and 'to formulate a proposition'[16].) So, for example, it would in most contexts be wholly misleading to suggest that one is expressing one's thoughts, saying what one thinks, or telling someone what one thinks, when one utters such sentences as 'Yes,

---

[16] For example, though one might say that the antecedent phrase of a conditional sentence 'If *p*, then *q*,' expresses the proposition that *p*, it would be quite wrong to say of someone who asserted the conditional (or asserted that not-*p*) that he expressed the proposition that *p*.

I'll go, 'I saw him yesterday', 'Then she burst into tears', 'No, I didn't', 'Really, how interesting!', 'It's the second on the left', 'I can see John over there', 'It's two o'clock', and so on. Even if we do wish to say that declarative sentences typically express thoughts or propositions (though not necessarily what the speaker is thinking), we are prone to be duped by failure to note the diversity of propositions and their functions. *A fortiori* the utterance of sentences expressing propositions does not have as its core, uniform function the conveying of the speaker's thoughts. It would be misleading to suggest that my saying 'But 25^2 is not 624' is an *expression* of my thinking (or of my thought) that 25^2 is not 624 (although I do think that 25^2 is not 624); rather, it is an expression of my thinking that you have made a mistake. The focal range of the phrase 'to express one's thoughts' is in the area of expressing one's opinions, reflections, and ruminations, in answering the question 'What do you think about this?' or 'What were you thinking just then?' It is in such contexts that we tell others what we think, express or confess our thoughts on this or that. These are very special moves in a language-game, and they call forth very particular kinds of response, e.g. agreement or disagreement, interest or amusement, admiration or disappointment. But reports, announcements, expressions of intent, declarations, repudiations, etc. are not, in that sense, expressions of thoughts. Romeo's passionate declarations of love communicate to Juliet not his *thoughts* but his passion; a war correspondent's reports from the front communicate to his readers what he has witnessed, what has happened, and only incidentally what he thinks about it.

Making a radical break with the idea that language always functions to convey thoughts enables us to recognize a familiar landscape distorted in our minds by misleading pictures. By reminding ourselves of the way such expressions as 'a thought', 'to have a thought', 'a thought's occurring to one', or 'a thought's crossing one's mind' are used, we can shake ourselves free of the philosophical illusions that pervade traditional reflections on this subject. By attending carefully to the use of 'thinking', 'confessing one's thoughts', 'telling someone what one thinks', and 'expressing (or communicating) one's thoughts', one will be liberated from the beguiling fallacies that beset one in this domain of philosophy.

Section 316

1   This opens the investigation into the concept of thinking. The point of departure is parallel to one of the exploded fallacies with respect to the concept of sensation. Just as we are prone to study our aches and pains in order to get clear about philosophical problems regarding sensations (PI §314), so too we are inclined to suppose that by watching ourselves while we think, we will observe what the word 'thinking' means, i.e. the stream of thought, the inner phenomenon of thinking.[1]

W.'s riposte is terse and supported only by an analogy. The concept of thinking is not used like that. But like what? The point arguably cannot be that the *meaning* of the word 'think' is not an object, event, or process which one might observe; for it has been established that the meaning of an expression is never an object, event, or process of any kind, but is rather what is given by an explanation of meaning, a rule for the *use* of the expression in question. But of course there are many expressions which *are* explained by pointing at an object which one may observe and saying '*That↗* is X' or '*That↗* is what is called "X" ' or even ' "X" means *that↗* F' (e.g. 'That is red', 'That is what is called "red" ', or ' "Red" means that colour'). To be sure, what is pointed at is not a meaning; rather, by pointing at a sample, one gives an explanation of meaning.

It is surely correct that just as 'pain' is not explained by private ostensive definition, so too 'thinking' is not thus explained. But it is not W.'s purpose here merely to distinguish the 'inner' from what is ostensively defined by reference to samples. More is intended, as is made clear by the parenthetical analogy. The categorial differences between thinking and having sensations, neither of which are ostensively defined, are no less than those between sensations and material objects or colours.

Whereas I can observe (attend to) the course of my pains (their waxing and waning, etc.) and report what I note to the doctor, to observe what goes on 'in me' while I am thinking (pondering, reflecting) is *not* to observe the course of my thoughts. Although there are phenomena of thinking, thinking is not itself a phenomenon (Z §471; RPP II §§31ff.). And 'it is very noteworthy that *what goes on* in thinking practically never

---

[1] James, *Principles of Psychology*, Vol. I, Ch. IX, provides a vivid illustration of this perennial temptation.

interests us' (Z §88), for, of course, these inner goings-on are not my thoughts, and only rarely would one be able to derive what I was thinking from my report of what went on when I thought whatever I thought (cf. BB 147). Telling someone what I think is not giving them a report on inner goings-on. Thinking is not an *experience*; and to tell you my thoughts is not to describe the character of an experience I have suffered or enjoyed. Reporting my pains is categorially altogether unlike reporting my thoughts, and were I to describe what went on in my mind when I thought up such-and-such, what I had to say (if anything) would typically be irrelevant to the question of *what* I thought. It is *this* feature to which the parenthetical analogy draws attention. Observing the last move of a game of chess will not clarify for one what 'mate' means; similarly, observing what goes on in one when one thinks will not clarify for one what 'thinking' means. *That* is not how one learns to use the verb 'to think'. How far does the analogy stretch? In the case of chess one can say that *in these circumstances* of the game, moving this piece thus *is* to mate one's opponent. But in typical cases of thinking one *cannot* say 'In *these* circumstances, such-and-such's going on in me (such-and-such pictures crossing my mind, such-and-such fragmentary sentences occurring to me, etc.) constitutes thinking that so-and-so'. (It is noteworthy that BB 147f. drifts towards this erroneous view.) What then did thinking such-and-such *consist in*? Why should it *consist in* anything? (Cf. Exg. §335, 2.1.)

2.1   'It would be as if . . . ': MS. 179, 48 uses a different simile. It would be like observing a piece of cheese in order to see how the cheese increases in price (cf. PI §693).

SECTION 317

1   If we suppose that thinking is an inner process the observation of which will clarify what 'thinking' means (§316), we may be tempted into further error. We may take pain (something 'inner') and its outer expression as a paradigm on which to construe thinking and its verbal expression. Just as a cry is an expression of pain, so too, we will then argue, a proposition (the utterance of a sentence expressing a proposition) is an expression of thought. ('In a proposition a thought finds an expression that can be perceived by the senses' (TLP 3.1).) It will then seem that the utterance of a proposition is an outward expression of something inner. This misconception is firmly associated with the Augustinian picture of language. Hobbes, for example, imagined that 'the general use of speech is to transfer our mental discourse into verbal,

or the train of thoughts into a train of words. . . '.[2] The proposition uttered is then conceived as an outward mirror of the inner processes going on 'in the thinking mechanism'.

(b) clarifies why the parallel is misleading. When the doctor probes our abdomen, we cry out when it hurts, and the purpose of the cry (in such a case) is to let him known how it is with us in our abdomen. But if we construe the relation between thought and the expression of thought on that model, it will seem that the purpose of the proposition is to let the hearer know how things are 'in the thinking mechanism'. But to utter a sentence which expresses what one thinks does not have as its purpose to let another know what images crossed one's mind or what words one said to oneself. The answer to the question 'What do you think about . . . ?' is not a description of an inner process.

1.1   (i) 'Der Schrei, ein Ausdruck . . . ': 'a cry, an expression of pain; a proposition, an expression of thought'.

(ii) 'Denkapparat': thinking device or mechanism.

2   BT 222 has §317(a) (*without the words* 'Misleading parallel') as a hand-written addition to the section entitled 'Gedanke und Ausdruck des Gedankens' ('Thought and expression of thinking'). Underneath is a further addition indicating the target aimed at: 'Das Denken ein Vorgang in einem ätherischen Mechanismus' ('Thinking a process in an ethereal mechanism'). These two inscriptions could even be alternative titles for the section. The drift of the argument is evident from the following excerpts:

> Der Gedanke ist wesentlich das, was durch den Satz ausgedrückt ist, wobei 'ausgedrückt' nicht heisst 'hervorgerufen'. Ein Schnupfen wird durch ein kaltes Bad hervorgerufen, aber nicht ausgedrückt.
> Man hat nicht den Gedanken, und *daneben* die Sprache. – Es ist also nicht so, dass man für den Andern die Zeichen, für sich selbst aber einen stummen Gedanken hat. Gleichsam einen gasförmigen oder ätherischen Gedanken, im Gegensatz zu sichtbaren, hörbaren Symbolen.
> Man hat nicht den Zeichenausdruck und daneben, für sich selbst, den (gleichsam dunkeln) Gedanken. Dann wäre es doch auch zu merkwürdig, dass man den Gedanken durch die Worte sollte wiedergeben können.
> D.h.: wenn der Gedanke nicht schon artikuliert wäre, wie könnte der Ausdruck durch die Sprache ihn artikulieren? Der artikulierte Gedanke aber ist in allem Wesentlichen ein Satz. . . .
> Der Gedanke ist kein geheimer – und verschwommener – Prozess von dem wir nur Andeutungen in der Sprache sehen . . . . (BT 222ff.)

---

[2] Hobbes, *Leviathan*, Ch. IV.

(Thought is essentially what is expressed by a proposition, where 'expressed' does not mean 'produced'. A cold is produced by a cold bath, but not expressed by it.

One has not got thought and *side by side* with it language. – For it is not as if one has signs for others, but for oneself only dumb thoughts. As it were, a gaseous or ethereal thought as opposed to perceptible or audible symbols. . . .

One does not have the symbolic expression and side by side with it, for oneself, the (as it were, shadowy) thought. For then it really would be too remarkable that one should be able to reproduce thoughts in words.

I.e.: were the thought not already articulate, how could its expression by means of language articulate it? Rather the articulate thought is in all essentials a proposition. . . .

Thought is no secret – and indeterminate – process of which we see mere indications in language . . ..

W. here linked the concept of thought with the concept of its expression, and was inclined at this stage to advocate, as an *Übersicht* of the concept of thinking, an identification of thinking with operating with symbols (as he linked understanding with mastery of a system of symbolism (cf. BT 93, 143; PG 106, 131)). The *contrast* between the expression of thought (viz. essentially articulate) and the expression of pain (viz. an inarticulate cry) was not emphasized in this text.

Some unpublished dictations to Waismann, roughly contemporaneous with the 'Big Typescript', made W.'s reflections at this stage even clearer. He characterized his position as 'die Gleichung von Gedanken und Ausdruck des Gedankens' (the equating of thinking with the expression of thinking' ('Denken', p. 2)), a remark comparable to 'Der Ausdruck der Erwartung ist die Erwartung' ('The expression of expectation is the expectation' (BT 355)). This, he noted, runs contrary to the traditional conception ('die traditionelle Auffassung'), which construed the expression of thought as a *translation*. Equating thinking with its expression, he argued, gives a valuable *surview* of the grammar of the words 'denken' and 'Gedanke'. (Similarly, the notion that believing is an inner experience is an obstacle to clarifying the use of the word 'believe'. By contrast, 'Die Ersetzung des Glaubens durch seinen Ausdruck liefert uns mindestens einen konzisen Auszug aus der Grammatik des Worte(s) "Glaube"/"glauben" '('Glaube', p. 3). ('Replacing believing by its expression gives us at least a concise epitome of the grammar of the word "belief"/"believe".')

It is noteworthy that this elaboration of the intentionality of thought (including expectation, understanding, belief, and desire) turns on contrasting thoughts with pains.

Der Glaube [das artikulierte Glauben, dass wir einem neuen Weltkrieg entgegen gehen] ist kein gleichbleibender Zustand, der den Satz begleitet, also nicht von der Art eines Gefühles. ('Glaube', p. 1)

(The belief [the articulate believing that we are approaching a new world war] is not a constant state which accompanies the sentence, hence not akin to a feeling.)

Acknowledging that a belief is articulate is incompatible with taking belief to be a mental state like a feeling or a sensation. For toothache, for example, is amorphous or inarticulate ('Intention', p. 1). Hence too, W. summed up his treatment of understanding in this way:

> Die Ansicht, gegen die ich mich in diesem Zusammenhang kehren möchte, ist die, dass es sich bei dem Verstehen um einen *Zustand* handelt, der in mir vorhanden ist, wie z.B. die Zahnschmerzen. ('Intention', p. 1)

> (The view against which I should like to turn in this connection is that according to which understanding is a state, which is present in me, like toothache, for example.)

PG 107 emphasizes that though we speak of thought and its expression, the expression of thought by a sentence uttered is not a causal mechanism, like a drug, designed to induce in the hearer the same thought which I have and express in my utterance. This misconception informed classical empiricism; thus Locke argued that each man will 'use these sounds as signs of internal conceptions; and . . . make them stand as marks for the ideas within his own mind, whereby they might be made known to others, and the thoughts of men's minds be conveyed from one to another'.[3] This picture was duly enshrined as the foundation-stone of modern theoretical linguistics in the writings of de Saussure. This conception of communication by means of language views discourse as a form of *thought-transference*. But, W. queries, what sort of process might actually be called 'thought-transference' or 'thought-reading'?[4] Clearly, if I learn what you think from hearing you express your views on a certain matter, I should not be said to read your thoughts off your words. But I might read your thoughts *on your face*. Reading your letter is not a case of thought-reading, but reading *between the lines* of your restrained prose might be so called. Similarly, telling me what you think is not a case of thought-transference; but if you put your

---

[3] Locke, *An Essay Concerning Human Understanding*, Bk. III, Ch i, Sect. 2.
[4] LWL 25f. (1930) emphasizes that thought is a symbolic process:

Language is not an indirect method of communication, to be contrasted with 'direct' thought-reading. Thought-reading could only take place through the interpretation of symbols and so would be on the same level as language. It would not get rid of the symbolic process. The idea of reading a thought more directly is derived from the idea that thought is a hidden process which it is the aim of the philosopher to penetrate. But there is no more direct way of reading thought than through language.

This is partly right and partly wrong. W. would subsequently certainly not have claimed that thought is 'a symbolic process' or, indeed, a non-symbolic process (see PG 106 for the beginning of the shift in his position); and one would expect greater subtlety in handling the notions of thought-reading or thought-transference. The following account is not W.'s, though it is intended to be in the spirit of his later reflections.

hand on my brow, and we both concentrate, and I say such-and-such, and that *was* what you were thinking, then this might, in certain circumstances, be called 'thought-transference'.

Vol. XIII, 134 has a draft of PI §317 followed by:

Frag nicht: "Was ist der Gedanke?" – denn diese Frage stellt // zeigt // ihn Dir schon als ätherisches Wesen hin // dar //.

(Do not ask: "What is the thought?" – for this very question already presents // shows // it to you as an ethereal entity.)

2.1   'Ausdruck': In a dictation to Waismann ('Ausdruck und Beschreibung'), W. distinguished two different senses of 'expression'. The sense in which a groan is an expression of a pain differs from that in which an utterance is an expression of a wish (expectation, thought).

Section 318

1   This introduces *one* factor which induces the idea that thinking is an inner process which accompanies overt activities. When we speak or write thoughtfully, that idea would *not* strike us as apt. Here thought does not seem separate from its verbal expression; it does not seem to accompany its expression, only half a pace ahead as it were. We are not inclined for the most part, in such cases, to suppose that we think faster than we speak. But we do talk of the speed of thought, of a thought flashing through our head, of solutions to problems becoming clear in a flash. These pictures suggest that thinking is an inner, high-speed process. For it seems as if in lightning-like thought we think, just as we ordinarily do in speech that is not thoughtless, only very much quicker. Then it *will* seem as if in ordinary speech, the thought *accompanies* the words, keeping in step with them, hence proceeding relatively slowly. It is as if speech were the escapement that prevented the clockwork from running down all at once, and hence as if lightning-like thought was the same, only without the escapement!

1.1   (i) 'Wenn wir denkend sprechen': 'think while we talk' carries precisely the connotations W. is trying to *avoid*: viz. the suggestion of a dual process. So better, though still not quite right, 'when we speak thoughtfully', or 'when we speak with thought'.

(ii) 'wie beim nicht gedankenlosen Sprechen': 'as is the case with speech that is not thoughtless'.

2   MS. 124, 216f. (=MS. 180(a), 15ff.) has this in a quite different, but revealing, context. Pp. 212f. have PI §241 (viz. agreement in form of life

is not a kind of subjectivism about truth) followed by the objection that one can imagine each person having a unique language of his own which is used *only* for reflexive speech-acts (see Exg. §243). Then follows a draft of §243(a): an explorer might learn how to translate the monologuists' languages. A fresh issue is then raised (pp. 214f.): if a monologuist orders himself to climb this tree, and if, on the other hand, *I* order myself to climb this tree, then in the latter case (but not the former) the utterance could be used to order another person! So is the *thought* of the order the same in both cases? This, W. responds, can be answered as one pleases, as long as one does not imagine the thought to be an *accompaniment* of speech. Thinking does not accompany speaking like the text which the tune of a song accompanies, but is more akin to the expressiveness with which the song is sung (cf. BB 148; PI §341). The verb 'to think', one might say, is not an activity word. Then follows a draft of PI §318. Instead of the last sentence, W. replies to the question: 'Ich glaube, das wird man nicht sagen wollen' ('I think that one would not want to say that'). Then follows an allusion to Mozart's letter (see Exg. §148) about hearing a whole composition in a flash: with what right does Mozart claim to have heard a piece of music in his head? How did he know that a piece of music corresponded to what he heard? We say 'I saw the solution in a flash', but if we see it in abbreviated form, how do we know that *this* is what the abbreviation is an abbreviation of? Then follows the first sentence of PI §323 and PI §319.

MS. 130, 236 queries whether the 'lightning speed' of thought is a psychological property of many people's thinking? Is it comparable to the speed of talking or writing? Can one *measure* the speed of thought (as one can measure a secretary's shorthand rate)? And why can't one? We are left to answer that ourselves (cf. Exg. §§319f.): it is evident that the speed of thought is not the speed of an *activity* (and is hence unlike the speed of writing), but the time taken to achieve something (hence more akin to how long it takes to hit the bull's-eye). Of course, we can measure how long it took a person to think of the answer to a problem.

BB 148 cites other phrases which induce the picture of thinking as an inner process that accompanies outer activities, e.g. 'Think before you speak', 'He speaks without thinking', 'What I said didn't quite express my thought', 'He says one thing and thinks just the opposite', 'I didn't mean a word of what I said'.

SECTION 319

1   This, and the next remark, divert us from the misleading picture of high-speed inner processes towards the more fruitful analogies that will reduce the pressure that forces us into myth-making. One can indeed

sometimes 'see a whole thought before one in a flash' or understand a thought in a flash, but this is not comparable to being able to enunciate a long sentence incredibly fast. Rather, it is comparable to making a note of a complex thought in a few words or a fragmentary diagram.

What makes such an opaque note, typically unintelligible to others, an epitome of a given thought? MS. 124, 218 answers: the use which I make of it. My terse lecture notes suffice for me to give the lecture, are adequate reminders of what I had in mind, and provide the basis for writing up these ideas in an article, etc. Note that although an epitome of a thought may be a reminder, not every reminder is an epitome of a thought (e.g. a knot in a handkerchief is not). For a note or diagram to be an epitome of a thought, there must be an internal relation between the sign *thus used* and the articulate expression of the thought.

1.1   'Ich kann . . . einen Gedanken ganz vor mir sehen': 'I can see a thought completely in my mind's eye in a flash'. A curious turn of phrase, seemingly equivalent here to completely understanding or grasping a thought in a flash. Grasping a thought, seeing the solution to a problem, does not involve articulating the thought in one's imagination, but the dawning of a capacity (hence 'in a flash') to say what the solution is or otherwise to act on it.

2   MS. 124, 218 has this preceded by the example of the Mozart letter and that of seeing the solution to a problem in a flash. Then follows the first sentence of PI §323. The lightning-like thought is more akin to suddenly being able to do something than to doing something suddenly, and the thought or solution one sees in a flash is more of a pointer than a product.

MS. 130, 236f. imagines people who only think aloud and who draw pictures where we imagine things. This provides a clue, for what would lightning-like thought look like here? Presumably a few muttered words, a scrawl on the drawing pad!

SECTION 320

1   A further, related analogy to clarify understanding a whole thought in a flash. What crosses my mind when I suddenly grasp it, see the solution, etc. can be related to what I say in elaborating what I think as the formula of a series is to the sequence of numbers I write down. The analogy is not, of course, that what crosses my mind in a flash is a rule in accord with which the spoken thought is expressed. It is twofold. First, what actually happens, the picture that comes to mind or the key word that occurs to me, etc. (the analogues of a note or a few pencilled dashes (§319)) do not *contain* or *constitute* an inner, private expression of the

thought any more than the algebraic formula *contains* the sequence that is developed in accord with it. Secondly, my conviction that I have understood such-and-such an idea in a flash, seen the solution to a certain problem at an instant, etc. is akin to my conviction, on seeing an algebraic function, that I can work out its values for a sequence of arguments. In the case of certain formulae, my conviction will be said to be well grounded, in as much as I have learnt how to compute such functions. In other instances my certainty is justified by success.

1.1   (i) 'blitzartige Gedanke': an explicit reference to the first sentence of §319: 'blitzartig einen Gedanken ganz vor mir sehen'.
        (ii) 'kann sich . . . verhalten': 'can stand to the spoken thought as the algebraic formula to the sequence of numbers'.
        (iii) ' "wohlbegründet" '/'nicht begründet': ' "well grounded" '/ 'without any grounds' would make clearer the connection that is explicit in the German.

SECTION 321

1   We misguidedly suppose that we can clarify what 'thinking' means by watching ourselves while we think (§316), and we similarly suppose that the concept of sudden understanding can be clarified by observing what happens when one suddenly understands. W. here sheds light on the former confusion by elucidating the latter. As argued in §§151 – 5, 179 – 84, whatever happens when one suddenly understands something (and all sorts of things may happen (§151)) it is not the process or experience of understanding; for understanding is neither a process nor an experience. It is in this sense that the question 'What happens . . . ?' is misleading; for in as much as the answer is meant to clarify the meaning of 'sudden understanding', the question, as it were, faces the wrong direction.

Taken at face value, the question might be understood as a query about the psychical accompaniments, the (inner) tokens, of sudden understanding. These may be very variegated; but they are merely inessential inner accompaniments of understanding. For (a) one may understand, and be justified in saying so, even though *no* inner event occurred (§151(d); Z §136); (b) any inner event is compatible with one's not understanding (including saying the answer to oneself, for one may simply have learnt it by heart without understanding it!); (c) one's avowal of understanding is not justified by such a token's occurring (cf. §§151, 179(c)).

Of course, there is a different sense in which there are tokens of understanding: e.g. a sudden intake of breath, a gleam in one's eye, a change of expression. But these are tokens of understanding *for another*.

There is no reason to suppose that the person who suddenly sees the solution to a problem or understands a complex thought feels these physical changes at all, even if he does once his attention is drawn to them. He does not say 'Now I know!' on the grounds that he felt his facial muscles relax and his breathing-rate change!

1.1   '((Posture))': an allusion to a parallel point concerning our capacity to say how our limbs are disposed. Here too one is tempted to say that one knows that one's arm is bent because one has such-and-such sensations. After all, if one's arm were anaesthetized and lacking any sensation, one would *not* be able to say whether it was bent or not! Nevertheless, it does *not* follow that when it is not anaesthetized and I say rightly that it is bent, I do so on the grounds of any sensation, *even if*, when my attention is drawn to the matter, I do have such-and-such sensations! (See RPP I §786 and N. Malcolm, *Ludwig Wittgenstein, A Memoir* (Oxford University Press, Oxford, 1984), p. 42).

2   PI p. 218 briefly explores the case where *nothing went on*, and yet I exclaimed 'Now I know!' Why am I so sure that I knew? Does it follow that I did *not* really know? Of course not. One is looking at this language-game wrongly, for one is viewing it from the perspective of games with evidential grounds, games in which it makes sense to ask 'What grounds do you have?', 'How do you know?' But this is not like that. We need to remind ourselves what the *signal* (cf. PI §180) 'Now I know!' is for. It is, one might say, an announcement; but whether it was correctly used is to be seen by its *sequel*, not by its antecedents or grounds. The 'knowing' is not an accompaniment of the exclamation, *a fortiori* not its grounds.

SECTION 322

1   The question of what 'sudden understanding' means is not answered by describing what happens 'within one' when one suddenly understands. But this in turn may mislead one; for if one finds that when one 'peers into one's mind' one cannot find any describable event or process which *constitutes* understanding, one may jump to the conclusion that understanding is a 'specific indefinable experience' that lies behind such events as one *can* describe. But this says nothing unless we have laid down criteria which determine what counts as the occurrence of this alleged 'specific indefinable experience' (cf. LPE 287, 291; LSD 42; RPP I §200).

1.1   'was *legen wir fest* . . . ': 'what *do we fix* as a criterion of identity for its occurrence?'

Section 323

1   This complements §§180 – 2. 'Now I know how to go on!' is not a description of a state of understanding, justified by reference to evidence accessible only to the speaker. It is rather an exclamation (comparable to 'Of course!'), and corresponds to an instinctive (natural) sound or gesture. But my feeling that I can go on or my feeling of certainty does not *guarantee* that I can go on. Sometimes I will *not* be able to do so. In some cases I may then say 'I thought I understood, but I didn't' (cf. PI p. 53n.); in others I should say, 'When I said I knew how to go on, I *did* know' (just as I might insist that when I said 'I can pick up that weight' I *could* pick it up, even though when I tried to do so, I slipped a disk and was unable to (cf. §182)). This would be legitimate if my chain of thought were disrupted, my attention distracted, or my concentration interrupted by some intervening event.

   (b) adds that a persistent illusion of understanding might afflict someone, in the sense that he is always exclaiming that he has understood, but can *never* actually go on. This would be a strange form of aberration. It is noteworthy that it is *not* intelligible that we all suffer such persistent illusions of comprehension. For 'Now I understand' and 'Now I have it' would not retain their meanings in such circumstances.

2   MS. 124, 218f. has, after the first sentence, the sentence 'Wie das Lachen einem Witz, so folgt dieser Ausdruck und etwa Worte wie "jetzt hab ich's!" ' ('This expression, and perhaps such words as "Now I have it!", follow, as laughter does a joke!') This is apt, for the laughter is a *reaction of understanding*, not a consequence of an inner event that assures one that one has understood. On p. 219, after §323(b), W. compares the feeling of certainty that we can elaborate a thought with the feeling of certainty that we can continue a tune if given a few bars. It is of great interest that this feeling is usually not deceptive.

Section 324

1   The feeling of certainty is, on the whole, reliable. Would it be correct to say that my certainty that I can continue the series rests on induction, viz. that whenever in the past I have had the feeling that I can go on, I have always been able to go on successfully, and since I now feel that I

can go on, I am certain that I shall be able to? §179 has already repudiated this suggestion. I should indeed be surprised if I could not continue the series 2, 4, 6, 8, . . . , as I should be surprised if I dropped a book and it remained hanging in the air. But my certainty that the book will fall is not 'based on' induction (cf. §326), and likewise my certainty that I can continue the series of even integers beyond 8 does not rest on any *grounds*. That I *am* justified in being certain is evident in my unhesitatingly continuing 10, 12, 14, 16, . . .

SECTION 325

1   This explores the first sentence of §324. What exactly is meant by saying that my certainty that I can continue the series (when I have seen how to go on, had the experience of sudden understanding) is based on induction? W.'s reply is analogical: a philosopher might say that my certainty that fire will burn me is based on induction. But if that is supposed to mean that I *reason* myself into this certainty by arguing that in the past fire has always burned me, so it will burn me now, that is obviously wrong. First, I do not do so. On the contrary, 'The belief that fire will burn me is of the same kind as the fear that it will burn me' (PI §473); and no one would say that my fear is based on induction, any more than one would say that the dog's fear of fire is so based. Secondly, if it were based on induction, would it justify this rock-solid certainty? After all, 'it is *only in the past* that I have burnt myself' (PI §472). But *nothing* could induce me to put my hand into a flame; it is here that we see the meaning of certainty, what it amounts to (PI §474). I neither have nor need reasons for a belief as deeply rooted, as animal, one might say, as that (PI §477).

Should one then say that the previous experience of burning myself (and bear in mind that *one* experience suffices!) is the *cause* of my certainty? That is an empirical matter, to be determined within the framework of the system of hypotheses or natural laws of the empirical theory which we invoke. Hence it is not a matter upon which philosophy need pronounce.

Note that W. is not 'repudiating inductive reasoning'. One *can* produce reasons for opinions, beliefs, and assumptions about the future, and such-and-such statements about the past are 'simply what we call a ground for assuming that this will happen in the future' (PI §480). And if someone challenged this language-game, insisting that information about the past could not convince him that something would happen in the future, we would not understand him (PI §481). All this may be admitted while denying that our certainty that fire will burn us *rests* on any reasons at all. Far from our patterns of inductive reasoning justifying such reactive beliefs and expectations, it is the fact that we respond to experience in this way that constitutes the framework within which the activity of inductive reasoning and justification takes place (cf. PG 109f.).

So too, one's certainty that one can continue an algebraic series after having seen the formula and exclaiming 'Ah, I have it!' does not rest on reasoning, even though it may be true that typically, when one has this experience (sudden illumination), one can go on. But is this confidence *justified*? Granted that I am not confident on the ground that . . . , is my confidence justified, as it were, in the eyes of others? The answer was given in §320. In some cases it will be said to be well grounded, in as much as I have learned to compute such functions, etc. In other cases no grounds will be given, but my *success* will justify my certainty *ex post actu*. This is what we *accept* as justification.

2.1 'the *cause* of my certainty, not its ground': cf. C §429; I believe I have five toes on each foot (although being shod, I cannot see them) but:

> Is it right to say that my reason is that previous experience has always taught me so? Am I more certain of previous experience than that I have ten toes?
>
> That previous experience may very well be the *cause* of my present certitude; but is it its ground? (C§429)

SECTION 326

1   A coda to this series of remarks. That chains of reasons terminate is a recurrently emphasized point in W.'s reflections (cf. Exg. §217), particularly in clarifying the notion of the *boundary* of a language-game. The point is made, as here, in association with inductive reasoning (PG 111), following a rule (BB 14f., 143; PG 97; Z §301), and in emphasizing the danger in philosophy of looking for explanations and justifications beyond the point at which it ceases to be intelligible to give further reasons (RFM 199; Z §§314f.). We expect fire to burn us; this is how we *respond* to being burnt. We are surprised if we find that we get stuck in running through the series of even integers; this is something we *can* do. These *regularities* set the framework within which our reasonings take place.

SECTION 327

1   This opens the investigation into the relation between thought and speech. 'Can one think without speaking?' has the appearance of a question about the interdependence of a pair of processes or activities (like 'Can one talk without breathing?'), the one 'inner', the other

'outer'. To answer, one must clarify the concept of thinking. W. replies ironically, taking us back to §316. 'Thinking' is not the name of an introspectively observable inner process that typically accompanies speaking, but may also go on (perhaps very much faster) without it.

Section 328

1   This begins the answer to the question raised in §327. What does one *call* 'thinking'? To answer this we must examine the use of the word, not observe what goes on in us when it is correct to say 'I am thinking'. What is the word used *for*? W. does not answer here (but see 'Thinking: the soul of language', §§2, 4); rather, he examines one feature of the use of 'to think' which is pertinent to the picture of thought as an inward, introspectively observable process. Is there room for *error* or *misidentification*? Someone may sincerely exclaim 'Now I understand!'or 'I've got it!' yet *not* have understood. Does it make sense for a person to make a parallel mistake in the case of thinking?

The first question, 'Are there circumstances . . . ?', seems rhetorical and invites the answer 'No'. The second question, 'Has he interrupted the thought . . . ?', seems likewise to invite a negative answer (as is made clear in §330) and also in some way to confirm the response to the first question. This requires clarification.

Suppose someone is thinking about how to rearrange his room. The portrait would look excellent in *that* niche, he thinks, and it might be a good idea to put the chest below it, *if* it fits. And he takes out a tape–measure and measures the chest and the niche. Does he *stop* thinking if he says nothing to himself while measuring? If someone enters and asks 'What are you up to?', could he not correctly reply 'I was thinking about moving the chest into the niche'? And before he started measuring, *must* he have *said* anything to himself? And if he did, need it be more than 'Hm, that will look good'? But saying 'Hm, that will look good' is not, *per se*, thinking that the portrait will look excellent in the niche, and even better if we can fit the chest in beneath it! In short, a train of thought is *not* like a train of words. A train of words is interrupted by a hiatus of silence. But a train of thought need not (though it may) be broken off by an activity during which nothing is said to oneself. For whether or not I say something to myself while measuring is *irrelevant* to whether I am (still) thinking about how to rearrange the room and what it would look like. What *is* relevant is whether, having measured, I pause bemused and ask myself 'Now, what was I doing?' or 'What *was* I thinking about?'

How does this bear on the previous question, viz. whether there is room for error in saying 'I am thinking?' The picture we have of error here is of a process of thinking going on, but my not noticing or recognizing it, or, conversely, of my misidentifying a certain mental going-on as thinking when it is really something else. We may, like Descartes, think it impossible to err; but then we would be hard put to explain *why* it is impossible. But, of course, this is the *wrong* picture; nothing at all need be going through my mind as I measure the chest of drawers, but I am nevertheless thinking about the rearrangement of the room. And conversely, I may be frantically saying things to myself (e.g. reciting the alphabet) in order to *avoid* thinking about something (perhaps while being subjected to a lie-detector test).

PI pp. 222f. resumes the discussion and confirms the above interpretations. Three important points are made. (a) Assume that someone can always successfully guess my thoughts. What is the criterion for his guessing right? Obviously, my truthful confession. But might *I* not be mistaken. Can my memory not deceive me? Might it not *always* do so when I truthfully say what I thought? This is now perspicuously a wheel that does not engage with the mechanism. For 'now it does appear that "what went on in me" is not the point at all (Here I am drawing a construction line.)' Why so? Because (b) 'The criteria for the truth of a *confession* that I thought such-and-such are not the criteria for a true *description* of a process. And the importance of the true confession does not reside in its being a correct and certain report of a process. It resides rather in the special consequences which can be drawn from a confession whose truth is guaranteed by the special criteria of truthfulness.' Here, as in the case of a dream-report, we have *laid down* no criterion to distinguish truth from truthfulness. A truthful report *is* a true report. (c) Imagine a game of *guessing* thoughts. Suppose I am putting a jigsaw together; the other person cannot see me, but guesses my thoughts. He says 'Now, where is this bit?', '*Now* I know how it fits!', 'I have no idea what goes in here', etc. He may well be guessing right, but *I need not be talking to myself either out loud or silently at the time.*

1   (i) 'Nun, was nennt man . . . ?': 'Well, what does one call "thinking"?'

     (ii) 'hat er das Denken unterbrochen . . . ': 'has he interrupted the thinking . . . '.

     (iii) 'says . . . to himself': saying things to oneself in one's imagination, talking to oneself inwardly, is more problematic than springs to the eye. It is scrutinized later (cf. Exg. §§344, 347 – 9, 357, 361).

.1   (i) 'Are the circumstances in which . . . ?': MS. 165, 207f. has here 'Hat man das Wort "denken" so zu benutzen gelernt, das man sich fragt: "War, was ich getan habe, wirklich ein Denken?"?' ('Did one learn to use the word "thinking" in such a way that one asks oneself "Was what I was doing really thinking?"?') This even more obviously invites a negative answer.

(ii) 'says . . . to himself': MS. 165, 203f., prior to its draft of PI §327 (on p. 206), makes explicit the problematic character of this concept. If saying something, or talking, means producing appropriate *sounds*, then saying something to oneself *without producing sounds* is none too perspicuous a notion. If I tell someone to use the word 'sugar' for something which is just like sugar, only neither sweet nor edible, it is by no means obvious what he should call 'sugar'. This is followed by 'The chair talks to itself . . . ' (cf. PI §361) and then PI §§327 – 8.

SECTION 329

1   A further argument against the misconception of thinking as an inner process. When I speak with thought, or indeed when I 'think aloud' (ruminate), there are not two simultaneous processes going on: speech and a parade of meanings, or senses, before my mind (cf. §318). The language itself is the vehicle of the thinking. What I have said *is* what I think, not a description of something else, which is my true thought (seen from afar, as it were); nor is the sentence I utter a *translation* of my thought, as if the thought *an sich* were in 'Mentalese' and my overt utterance translates it into English. The thinking is not a process *behind* the utterance.

1.1   (i) 'When I think in language': this is an unhappy expression, for while I can speak in English, German, or French and say things to myself in English, German, or French, when I speak, and do not speak thoughtlessly but reflectively, I am not 'thinking in language'. It is possible, however, that 'in der Sprache denken' is intended to be equivalent to 'denkend Sprechen' (§318) and accordingly could be translated 'When I think in speaking', i.e. when I speak with thought.

(ii) 'the vehicle of thinking': surely an unhappy metaphor since vehicles carry passengers, and thinking does not need transportation. But when I speak with thought, the thinking is not distinct from the use of language. Moreover, whereas I may communicate my thoughts in speech, the words are not vehicles and communicating is not transporting thoughts.

2   Z §100 describes someone engaged in a practical activity requiring thought. Nothing needs to be said *sotto voce* or *in foro interno*. Z §101 concludes: 'Of course we cannot separate this "thinking" from his activity. For the thinking is not an accompaniment of the work, any more than of thoughtful speech.'

SECTION 330

1   *One* conception of thought is as an inner process running parallel to overt speech (when it is not thoughtless). Many considerations induce this false picture. One is cited here: we do distinguish speech with thought from talking without thinking, and these very phrases intimate that thinking is a process that may accompany speech or may go on by itself.

(b) endeavours to break the hold of this picture of parallel tracks by reminding us what it is to utter a sentence without thinking the thought that it expresses and what it is to think that very thought without expressing it.

(i) To say 'Yes, this pen is blunt. Oh well, it'll do' and to *think it* is not to say it and simultaneously do something else in the confines of one's mind, e.g. observe 'meanings' going through one's mind (§329) or go through the *mental process of grasping (Erfassen) a thought,* conceived as an abstract entity (cf. Frege, PW 145). It is rather to say it and mean it, i.e. to say it seriously, not as a joke, a white lie, or an example of an English sentence, etc. If this is correct, then, of course, I cannot while reading W.'s text say 'Yes, this pen is blunt . . . ' and think it; at the very least I need a blunt pen. Alternatively, W. might simply mean: say the sentence *with understanding* (this interpretation is supported by BB 43(b)).

(ii) To say 'Yes, this pen is blunt. Oh well, it'll do' *without* thinking it can likewise be given various interpretations. I can *read* the sentence; then, of course, I do not mean or think that my pen is blunt, etc. Or I might hold a pen in my hand and utter the sentence, but *not* think that the pen is blunt or not think that it will do. Or I might utter the sentence parrot-wise, concentrating 'my attention on something else while I was speaking the sentence, e.g., by pinching my skin hard while I was speaking' (BB 43).

(iii) To think that the pen is blunt, but that it will do nevertheless, without saying anything even to oneself might, in appropriate contexts, amount to no more than testing the point of the pen, making a face, and then shrugging one's shoulders and continuing one's writing. The moral of (iii) is that what here constitutes thinking that the pen is blunt but that it will do is *not* something that needs to accompany the utterance 'The pen is blunt. Oh well, it'll do' in order that the utterance not be thoughtless.

A parallel argument is applied to meaning what one says in PI §§507 – 11 (cf. MS. 165, 9ff.).

1   (i) 'While taking various measurements': an answer to the final question of §328.

(ii) 'Aber was hier das Denken ausmacht': 'But what constitutes thinking here'.

2   MS. 165, 3 has this, followed by a draft of PI §339(b), which adds a further reason for the misconception of thinking as an inner process that accompanies speech. One might, as a grammatical remark, say that thinking *is* a process, only an incorporeal one. This has a point, for it draws attention to the grammatical differences between 'thinking' and 'eating'. It is nevertheless ill–advised, for it makes the differences look *too slight* (see Exg. §339). And it is misleading in generating the picture of parallel activities, vocal and mental.

BB 41ff. has an earlier discussion of this theme. The following points bear on the matter: (a) The aim of the investigation is to rid us of the supposition that there *must* be a mental process of thinking independent of the process of expressing a thought. (b) A parallel experiment to PI §330 is suggested, viz. to say and mean 'It will probably rain tomorrow' and then to think it, but without saying anything either aloud or to oneself.

If thinking that it will rain tomorrow accompanied saying that it will rain tomorrow, then just do the first activity and leave out the second. – If thinking and speaking stood in the relation of the words and the melody of a song, we could leave out the speaking and do the thinking just as we can sing the tune without the words. (BB 42; cf. PG 155)

This, though correct, is a less refined position than that in PI §330. (c) Speaking and meaning what one says is distinguished from speaking without thought, but not necessarily by what happens *at the time one speaks*. The distinction may lie in what happens before or after one's utterance.

Z §§93 – 6 supplements this. The distinction between 'thinking' and 'not thinking' applies to an utterance only in rather special circumstances. One would not know how to apply it to a normal conversation for example; i.e. if asked what that very conversation would look like if one of the participants was speaking without thought, one would not know how to reply. Certainly any such distinction would have nothing to do with concurrent inner processes. If we *must* speak of thinking as an experience, then it is exemplified in the experience of speaking as well as anywhere. But thinking is not an experience, for we do not compare thoughts as we compare experiences. We compare thoughts by comparing what is thought, viz. *that* such–and–such. We compare experiences by comparing what was done or undergone and what it was like, e.g. how one responded to it hedonically, etc.

SECTION 331

1   A further blow at the conception of thought under attack. We can (up to a point)[5] imagine people who can think only aloud. Are we then to imagine that with them speech with thought consists in saying everything twice?! This move exemplifies W.'s strategy: 'If you are puzzled about the nature of thought, belief, knowledge, and the like, substitute for the thought the expression of the thought, etc.' (BB 42).

2   BB 42 objects to the strategy on the grounds that the expression of thoughts may always lie, for we may say one thing and mean another. W. responds that we could imagine beings who do their private thinking by means of 'asides', and so lie by saying one thing aloud, followed by an aside asserting the opposite.

SECTION 332

1   A thought is not the accompaniment of an utterance, even if the utterance has an accompanying mental process. Saying *in foro interno* 'Oh, it would be so nice!' and conjuring up images of snow falling, snow-covered fields, roaring log fires in the hearth, etc. might well constitute all that happens when thinking that a white Christmas would be welcome. And if asked 'What are you doing?' one might well reply 'Thinking of a white Christmas'. But the sequence of images that cross one's mind is not the thought that a white Christmas would be welcome.

Similarly, saying something with understanding is not to accompany the saying with anything, any more than listening to *Tosca* with enjoyment is accompanying the listening with a sensation (for then one might obtain the very same enjoyment from a gin and tonic!). An analogy illuminates the point further: to sing a tune with expression is not to *accompany* the song with its expression, even though there are various repeatable, autonomous things one does while singing expressively. The 'with' of 'with thought or understanding' is the 'with' of 'with expression, humour, seriousness', not of accompaniment. Similarly, to do something with thought is akin to (and, indeed instantiated by) doing it with care, attention, or concentration; hence that notion is, to use Rylean terminology, *adverbial*.

---

[5] But only for certain uses of 'think'. For it is not clear what the thoughtful tennis-player is meant to be saying to himself as he lobs, smashes, drives, etc., or whether someone who only thinks aloud would have time to articulate an ordinary tennis-player's thoughtful tactics in the thick of the game.

Note that the criticism of the dual-process conception of thinking is *not behaviourist*. W. does not deny the occurrence of mental events and processes. The criticism is *grammatical* (not theoretical or 'ontological'): these goings-on are not what we *call* 'thinking' or 'a thought'.

1.1   (i) 'While we sometimes call it "thinking" to accompany a sentence by a mental process': it is unclear that W. has in mind here, unless it is a phenomenon such as that described above. In general, 'In philosophy, the comparison of thinking to a process that goes on in secret is a misleading one' (RPP I §580).

(ii) 'Say a sentence and think it; say it with understanding': this suggests that what W. has in mind by 'denkendes Sprechen' just is saying it with understanding and perhaps, in certain cases, also meaning what one says.

(iii) 'aber "Gedanke" nennen wir nicht jene Begleitung': 'is not what we call . . .'

SECTION 333

1   Yet another move against the conception of thinking as an accompaniment of speech (§330). 'There's been no happiness in your life, but wait, Uncle Vanya, wait. We shall find peace. We shall find peace,' Sonya exclaims in the closing lines of *Uncle Vanya*. Reflecting on this, we might indeed say that in such circumstances only someone convinced can say these words, that conviction (in this particular case, faith) burns bright in them. And similarly we say of many a remark that one *cannot* say such a thing without thought (if *that* is talking mechanically, then my name is Jack Robinson!), i.e. that particular remark, said in these circumstances, uttered in that way, cannot be called 'mechanical' or 'without thought'! But we would not wish to say that the conviction with which a passionate declaration is made is something that exists side by side with the utterance, as breathing with walking. True enough, one can be convinced that such-and-such without saying anything, and one can say that things are thus-and-so without being convinced (which is not the same as saying it without conviction). But it does not follow that when one says something with conviction, one's conviction accompanies one's utterance; rather, it informs or infuses it, so that one's words are charged with faith. And speech with thought is not an overt activity masking an accompanying covert one, any more than meaning what one says consists of a pair of activities.

1.1   'What if someone were to say . . . ?': a second analogical argument. To sing a tune *from* memory is not to reproduce publicly what one is hearing 'privately', but to reproduce publicly what one previously heard publicly. To sing from memory, one does not have to 'hear it in one's mind', but to have heard it in the past. Similarly, to speak with thought, one does not first have to recite what one is about to say in one's mind and then say it out loud.

SECTION 334

1   A further phrase that misleadingly intimates the dual-process picture is 'So you really wanted to say . . . '. For it suggests that the thought which we articulate for him was actually present in his mind. (Normally, when *he* says what he thinks, he, as it were, pulls a string of beads out of a box through a hole in the lid, revealing what was present in the box; in this case, *we* pull the beads out of his box, bringing them to light. But they are present in the box all the same; otherwise they wouldn't be 'what he really wanted to say'! (cf. BB 40).)

But this is to misconstrue the use of this phrase. We see the picture, as it were, but do not advert to its application. The function of 'You really wanted to say . . . ' is to lead someone from one form of expression to another, which does not have such-and-such unwarranted or misleading implications or which highlights more perspicuously such-and-such a point.

To clarify this, W. gives a mathematical example. For more than 2,000 years mathematicians tried to find a general method for trisecting an angle with a compass and rule, until it was shown that such a construction is impossible, that there is no such thing. But this is problematic; for what is it that mathematicians were trying to do? (If there is no such think as checkmate in draughts, then there is no such thing as trying to checkmate in draughts.) What has the impossibility proof effected? No one would want to say that it has shown that mathematicians were not trying to do anything! But one could say that the proof gives them a clearer idea of what they were trying to do (LFM 87). How so?

Suppose we have a method of constructing polygons with a rule and a fixed pair of compasses, so that we can construct an octagon, a 16-sided polygon, etc. Now we are asked to construct a 100-sided polygon in this way. We repeatedly fail; then someone proves that it cannot be done. The proof shows that if we want to construct an n-sided polygon in this way, then n must be a power of 2. The last power of 2 before 100 is 64; after that is 128, so 100 does not occur in this series. The proof changes our idea of constructing an n-sided polygon by bisections. Before the proof one would explain what one was trying to do in one way, viz. by drawing circles and lines; after the proof one would give a different explanation of what one was trying to do, viz. to see whether 100 is a power of 2. To be sure, one may say that our idea of what we were trying to do is changed by the proof; but one could also say that this is a different way of expressing the *same* problem, that *this is what we had in mind* (LFM 87f.)! So too, in the case of trisecting an angle with compass and rule, the proof transforms the question into the question of whether one can solve a general cubic equation with square roots: 'the proof gives us a new idea of trisection, one which we didn't have before the proof constructed it. The proof led us a road *which we were inclined to go*; but it led us away from where we were, and didn't just show us clearly the place where we had been all the time' (BB 41). Of course, we say: that is what I meant (had in mind), since the proof led me along a road I was *inclined* to go. 'The process was one that led from one symbolism to another, and led with my consent' (PLP 400).

These examples cast light on what kinds of things may persuade us to give up one expression and replace it by another, and also what is *meant* by 'So you really wanted to say . . . ', 'So what you really had in mind was . . . ', or 'What, in effect, you were trying to do (aiming at) was . . . '. In particular, it shows that although what you really wanted to say was . . . , that does not mean that that thought was already present somewhere in your mind.

2   Vol. XI, 47f., preceding the draft of §334 (on p. 53), reflects on those cases where someone says something equivocal. On being asked what he meant, he may be none too clear, and may ask us for a clarification of a word or for a formulation that will capture his point perspicuously. And here we will often reply: 'What you really wanted to say was . . .'. But this can easily be misunderstood, for it *need* not be a description of a process in which one says one thing while wanting to say another (viz. a slip of the tongue); nor is it as if what one really wanted to say had already been said inwardly.

2.1   'The concept "trisection of the angle with ruler and compass" ': this is discussed at length in PG 387 – 92, the primary purpose of which is clarification of the nature of an impossibility proof, and hence of a 'search' for the construction. LFM 86 – 90 examines a parallel case and brings it to bear on the description or re-description of what one meant or what one was trying to do. See also PLP 398 – 400.

SECTION 335

1   This introduces yet another phrase, and experience, which induce the idea that thought is an inner process which underlies thoughtful speech. 'To make an effort to find the right expression for our thoughts' is

misleadingly akin to the phrase 'to make an effort to find the right English expression for Goethe's sublime thoughts'; i.e. it suggests that in expressing our thoughts we *translate* from the thoughts, which are already *there* ('in' images or 'Mentalese'), into English! Equally, it is deceptively similar to the phrase 'to make an effort to find the right expression to describe such-and-such (a view, a picture, an artefact)'; i.e. it suggests searching for the right words to describe something in view.

The picture is not wholly inappropriate, though it is misleading. There are all sorts of *different* cases in which this turn of phrase is legitimately used. In many cases there is a co-ordination of words (the expression of thought) and something else. But the something else is not itself the thought that then gets expressed in words. Sometimes it may be a mood, a frame of mind, which crystallizes into a word, and I write to my friend 'I am feeling despondent'. Or a picture may cross my mind, and I try to describe it (but to describe a picture before my mind is as different from describing a picture before my eyes as describing how I intend to act is from describing my intentional action). Or as I write in German and get stuck, searching for the right expression of my thoughts, an English word occurs to me and I try to hit on the German one, for this will express what I wanted to say. And so on.

§335(b), in two brief questions, highlights the gulf that can open between the picture and its application, in particular in cases where one is not merely looking for a translation or paraphrase. Does one have the thought before finding the expression? – Does the farmer have the fruit before the seed has grown? If one fails to find the 'right expression', can one deliver the thought in some other way? Not always; and does one not then say, after a pause, 'No, it's gone' or 'I thought I had the answer, but it's gone'? (And, of course, this figure of speech perpetuates the picture!) And in such cases what did the thought *consist in*, before one found the right words to express it? It did not *consist in* anything. For although all sorts of things may have occurred, none of them constitute thinking such-and-such a thought.

1   'consists in': the question 'What does X consist in?' makes sense only for very particular kinds of things. Applied to thinking or thoughts, it makes none. PI §678 emphasizes a parallel point explicitly: 'What does the act of meaning (the pain or the piano tuning[6]) consist in? No answer comes – for the answers which at first sight suggest themselves are of no use. – "And yet at the time I *meant* the one thing and not the other." Yes – now you have only repeated with emphasis something which no

---

[6] I have a toothache and can hear a piano being tuned. I say 'It'll soon stop'. Which did I mean, the pain or the tuning? (PI §666).

one has contradicted anyway.' And Z §16 embroiders further: 'The mistake is to say that there is anything that meaning something consists in.' Cf. BB 86 on 'comparing from memory'.

SECTION 336

1   A further context in which the dual-process conception of the relation of thought to the expression of thought seems irresistible is when one imagines that one could not straightforwardly think a thought in the expression of which the main verb comes only at the end of the sentence (as the main verb comes at the end of a Latin sentence). For how would one know what one was thinking if one had to wait until the completion of the thought? So one supposes that one first has to think the thought and then to express it in a sequence of words in the curious order of Latin or German. Only altogether superior languages strictly mirror the sequential ordering of thought-constituents!

1.1   'einen Satz . . . denken': better perhaps 'think a proposition', although that too is strained. Nevertheless, W.'s point is clear.

2.1   'A French politician': Vol. V, 177 suggests that it was Briand. The observation, W. points out, is most significant even though sheer nonsense, for it earmarks a particular conception of thought and its expression.

SECTION 337

1   This introduces the diametrically opposite thought, which neverthe- less still induces the dual-process conception. I surely know what I am going to say before I say it. The sentence I am about to utter is surely already complete in thought before I begin to speak; otherwise how would I know how to complete the sentence? And if it was in my mind in the form of the intention to say such-and-such, then, contrary to the thought of §336, must it not have been there in the ordinary word-order?
    This is a confusion exacerbated by a misleading conception of inten- tion as *containing* a picture of its own satisfaction. But that conception was undermined by §§197 and 205. It is the *expression* of an intention that can be said to depict what will satisfy it. I can, of course, intend to play chess now; but that does not mean that my intention *contains* all the rules of chess (§197). It is *not* true of an intention to play chess or, for that matter, of uttering a certain sentence, that 'the existence of a custom, of a technique, is not necessary to it' (§205). Chess is defined by its rules, but

these are not 'contained in' the intention to play chess. They are present in the mind of the intending player only in the sense that he has mastered them and can say what they are. Far from an intention being independent of any custom or technique, 'an intention is embedded in its situation, in human customs and institutions'. If the technique of chess did not exist, I could not even intend to play a game of chess. Hence it is *not* imaginable that two people should intend to play chess in a world in which no games exist (cf. §205 and Exg.). Hence too, in so far as I intend the construction of a certain sentence in advance, that is possible just because I speak the language, have mastered its techniques. To intend to say such-and-such does not mean that what one intends must already 'exist in one's mind' in advance of saying it.

The argument is left incomplete here, and W. does not return to it until §§633 – 7. There, the following points round the matter off: (a) If I was interrupted, but still know what I was going to say, that does *not* mean that I had already thought it before, only not said it, unless one takes the certainty with which I continue as a *criterion* of the thought's having been completed before. (In that case the confident continuation will be an aspect of the *grammar* of 'He had completed the thought, but not the sentence, when he was interrupted', not a symptom of antecedent psychological processes.) (b) Nevertheless, the situation and the things which did cross my mind will typically contain all sorts of things to help me continue the sentence (like reminders or cryptic notes). (c) However, these 'hints' are not *interpreted*, for I do not choose between alternatives; I remember what I was going to say!

1   (i) 'of the sentence (for example) . . . ': similarly, I intend to sing the whole sequence of notes when I begin to sing a tune (cf. §333), but that does not mean that I must first sing it or hear it in my mind (see Z §2).

      (ii) 'embedded in its situation': (cf. PI §581, where the argument is applied to the parallel case of expectation). One cannot intend to play chess unless there is a practice of playing games; one cannot intend a deed of knight-errantry in the twentieth century or a violation of copyright in the twelfth.

2   MS. 130, 239f. returned to this theme, comparing James's idea that the thought is already complete at the beginning of the sentence with the idea of the lightning speed of thought and with the concept of the intention to say such-and-such. To say that the thought is already finished by the beginning of the sentence[7] means the same as: if someone is interrupted after the first word and is then asked 'What did you want to say?' he can often answer the question. But here too James's remark *sounds* like a

---

[7] And why not, W. adds in parenthesis, by the beginning of the *previous* sentence?

psychological one, but isn't. For if it were, then whether thoughts are complete at the beginning of the sentence would be something to be discovered by asking individual people. But although we sometimes cannot answer the question of what we were about to say, in this case we say that we have *forgotten*. After all, is it conceivable that in such cases people would say 'I only said that word; how should I know what was going to follow it'?

3   The passage in James to which W. was alluding in the above remark (and Z §1) is in *The Principles of Psychology*, Vol. I, Chap. IX, e.g. 'Whatever things are thought in relation are thought from the outset in a unity, in a single pulse of subjectivity . . . ' (p. 278), and again, 'even before we have opened our mouths to speak, the entire thought is present to our mind in the form of an intention to utter that sentence.' A dim inkling that there is no more any such thing as thinking half a thought than there is such a thing as half a proposition is here confused with a piece of putative psychological phenomenology! W. seems to have James in mind in PG 107f., and his diagnosis fits perfectly James's curious diagrams of the stream of thought: ' . . . we are comparing the thought with a thing that we manufacture and possess as a whole; but in fact as soon as one part comes into being another disappears. This leaves us in some way dissatisfied, since we are misled by a plausible simile into expecting something different' (PG 108). LW §§843f. compares James's claim with the idea of a 'germinal experience', e.g. having a mental image which one 'knew' to be of N. N. without interpretation or recognition. One knew it from the beginning; but, of course, knowing is not an experience! Similarly James's claim that the thought is complete when the sentence begins wrongly treats *intention* like an experience. Of course, 'It has *not* been there from the beginning' would be wrong, for 'The thought is *not* complete from the very beginning' means: I didn't find out or decide until later what I wanted to say. And one obviously does not want to say that.

SECTION 338

1   §337 concluded that I can intend the construction of a sentence in advance only in so far as I can speak the language in question. In this sense, the intention is 'embedded in its situation, in human customs and institutions'. §338 expands the point, but this time gives the diagnosis before identifying the error into which we are typically tempted.
     One can say something only if one has learned to talk, so to *want* (and to intend) to say something, one must have mastered a language. But one

can obviously want to speak (or dance or exercise any other skill) without doing so. And when we reflect on this, our mind reaches for the *image* of speaking, dancing, etc., and we misguidedly think that intending to ϕ must contain a 'representation' of ϕ ing; for otherwise what would make it an intention to ϕ (rather than to ψ)? And how would we know that *that* was what we intended?

2   Vol. XII, 300ff. incorporates this in a long discussion of 'I wanted to say'. It opens by dwelling on the oddity of remembering that I wanted to say something on some previous occasion. It appears odd in as much as there seems no event *to* remember! (hence akin to 'I meant . . .'). So could one substitute 'It seems to me that yesterday I wanted to say . . .' for 'Yesterday I wanted to say . . .'? But one can also say 'I *know* that yesterday I wanted to say', and one says this with conviction. It is the expression of one kind of remembering; has it then no use? And sometimes one believes someone who avows this ('Yes, I could see on your face that you were about to say that'), and sometimes one does not.

The grammar of 'wanting to say something' is related to 'being able to say something', and the grammar of 'I then wanted to say . . .' to 'I could then have continued . . .'. The one is a case of remembering an intention, the other of a recollection of understanding. One does not learn what is called 'wanting to say something' by having a state or process pointed out to one!

Then follows PI §338, followed by 'Als wäre nämlich das Tanzenwollen einen *Plan* für den Tanz machen. Aber man kann doch auch einen Plan machen *wollen*.' ('As if wanting to dance were making a *plan* for the dance. But one can also *want* to make a plan.') Clearly that route generates a senseless regress.

In MS. 124, 228f. the interlocutor objects to W.'s suggestion that hoping, believing, fearing, expecting, etc. that such-and-such is the case essentially involve a technique of thinking (hence customs and practices) without which there can be no thinking. For, he argues, it is obvious that one knows immediately that one can hope, whether or not one has hoped or thought before. It is evident that a single act of hoping can exist irrespective of what is earlier or later! If you had said, W. replies, that you are *inclined to say* this, rather than that it is obvious to you, then there would be no disagreement, for I too am often inclined to say this!

1   'grasp at the *image* of . . .': LA 30 remarks that we conceive of imagery as the international mental language. BB 5 explores the suggestion that what gives life to a sign is a mental image we correlate with it.

1   This is the leading member of a triad of concluding remarks to this
phase of the argument. The picture of thinking that is embodied in the
many expressions examined in the preceding remarks is of a process that
runs parallel to, and is essentially detachable from, i.e. logically
independent of, speaking. Closer scrutiny of each such phrase and of
each experience picked out by one phrase or another has shown the
picture to be wholly misleading. When we examine how these expressions are used, it becomes clear that we have been taken in by a picture.

Thinking is not an incorporeal process which gives life and sense to
speech. What makes dead signs live is not something immaterial. (And
what makes a body a corpse is not the loss of an immaterial substance.)
We do indeed use signs with understanding and thought; we mean
something by them. But what gives them life is not the accompanying
processes of understanding, thinking, and meaning, but the *use* we make
of them in the stream of human life. And understanding, thinking, and
meaning are not processes. Though we speak with thought, thought is
not detachable from speaking as Schlemiehl's shadow is detachable from
Schlemiehl. Rather, as was intimated in §332, thought infuses speech as
expression informs the singing of a tune (but whether the singing was
expressive can be heard immediately, whereas whether the utterance was
made with thought can often be discerned only by reference to antecedent and subsequent events).

Even this negative point is misleading, however, not because a
categorial point is being made (which looks like a *truth*, but is in fact the
expression of a *rule*), but rather because the expression 'an incorporeal
process' has not had any clear sense assigned to it. We know about
biological processes and are acquainted with industrial processes of
manufacturing materials or artefacts; we speak of *psychological* processes,
e.g. of maturation or adaptation to the loss of a loved one or of preparing
oneself mentally for an ordeal. But the notion of an *immaterial* process is
unclear: is inflation an immaterial process? What of the rise and fall in the
morale of the nation? And that of an *incorporeal* process is even more
obscure. We introduce the suspect expression 'incorporeal process' when
floundering around for an explanation of what 'thinking' means. Thinking, we say, is not a physical or corporeal process, as digestion is. Rather,
thinking is a process that takes place in the mind. And one then thinks of
the mind as a gaseous medium that is little understood and in which
extraordinary things mysteriously occur (cf. PG 100; BB 3ff.; and
'Thinking: methodological muddles and categorial confusions', §4).

§339(b) explains how one might, less crudely, introduce the term
'incorporeal process' in this context. One might do so in the course of

distinguishing between different grammatical categories.[8] 'To eat' falls in one category, we would then explain, whereas 'to think' falls in another. But this is still too crude. There is some point to the distinction, but it is still misleading (just as it is misleading to call 'to sleep' an activity-verb!). It makes the differences between *concepts* look too slight, as if 'to eat' signified an activity performed with the mouth and 'to think' signified an activity in just the same way, only not performed with a corporeal organ! This is visibly similar to Frege's distinction between actual and non-actual (but real) objects (GA, p. xviii; cf. PG 108f.), numerals being actual and numbers non-actual. (And he too was prone to explain what a non-actual object is by claiming that it is just like an actual object only not in space or time (PW 148)!) The expression 'incorporeal process' is unsuitable, for it adverts only to the similarity of surface grammar (e.g. to those rather obvious features, alluded to above, which 'to think' shares with 'to eat') and seems to save us the trouble of a careful examination of differences in *use* by offering us an apparently acceptable category, viz. 'incorporeal process', to capture the difference. (As does 'abstract object', when invoked to explain what numerals name!) In this sense, the jargon actually bars the way out of confusion.

1   (i) 'the Devil takes the shadow of Schlemiehl': see Adelbert von Chamisso's tales entitled *Peter Schlemiehl*.
     (ii) 'da ich die Bedeutung . . .': 'because I was trying to explain . . .'.

1   'look *too slight*': perhaps like the difference between -1 and +1, whereas what we are dealing with is comparable to the difference between -1 and $\sqrt{-1}$ (cf. RPP I §108).

Section 340

1   The grammar of an expression, particularly of an expression which is so deeply woven into our lives as 'to think', cannot be *guessed* on the basis of mere unreflective familiarity with the word. Yet that is precisely what is being done when one too easily pigeon-holes *thinking* as an 'incorporeal process' or erects philosophical theories on the assumption that thinking is an activity of the mind. The correct method is to *look* at the use of 'to think' and its cognates in widely varying sentential contexts

---

[8] See R. Quirk, S. Greenbaum. G. Leech, J. Svartvik, *A Grammar of Contemporary English* (Longman, London, 1972), pp. 94ff. Grammarians distinguish between *dynamic* verbs and *stative* verbs, and within the category of dynamic verbs they distinguish *activity-* and *process*-verbs from other subcategories. We might think to follow them, only refine matters further. Just as they distinguish *concrete* from *abstract* nouns, we might distinguish physical or concrete activity- and process-verbs from incorporeal activity- and process-verbs.

and diverse circumstances. Then it becomes evident that thinking is not an inner process that accompanies speaking, that it is not an activity of the mind in the way that writing is an activity of the hand, that it is not logically independent of speech, etc.

A powerful prejudice, however, stands in the way of investigating philosophical problems thus. It is not obvious to what W. is alluding — or indeed why he suggests only *one* prejudice. Perhaps what he had in mind is the impression of trivialization which this method produces. We are asking deep questions about the essence of things; and not just any old things, but the most fundamental things in our experience – time, matter, mind, thought, experience, etc. – and we are told to examine how mere *words* are used! But words are merely arbitrary names, and what we are interested in are the immutable natures of things (cf. §§370 – 3)! And to investigate those, surely we must examine the entities named, not their alterable, arbitrary, dispensable *labels*! This interpretation is rendered plausible by RPP I §§548 – 50. Alternatively, the prejudice to which W. is alluding may be 'our craving for generality'. We are, after all, seeking the *essence* of things, what is common to *all* cases of, e.g., thinking, meaning, and understanding. This craving for generality fosters contempt for the particular case; for if someone suggests, on the basis of a particular example and context, that *here* and in these circumstances *this* is what is called ' . . .', we will dismiss this as irrelevant, because it is *insufficiently general*. And this prejudice prevents us from examining the multitudinous interwoven, overlapping, particular cases that together make up the use of the expression in question and constitute the 'essence' that we are seeking. This interpretation rests upon BB 16 – 20.

Either way, the prejudice is not *stupid*. (a) Our interest in words is very different from that of the grammarian's. We are not especially concerned with the *English* verb 'to think', as opposed to the German 'denken' or the French 'penser'. We may concede immediately that we do *not* want to talk only about words. But, as W. clarifies with respect to philosophical investigations into the faculty of imagination (PI §370), the question as to the nature of thinking is as much about the word 'thinking' as is the question how the word 'thinking' is used. And this question is not to be decided – either for the person who does the thinking or for anyone else – by pointing; nor yet by a description of any process. The first question also asks for a word to be explained; but it makes us expect a wrong kind of answer. (b) Similarly our craving for generality is not stupid. We are indeed concerned with clarifying the essences of things (PI §92), but we have a wrong conception of what constitutes the essence of something. In the kinds of cases that are of philosophical concern, essence is expressed by *grammar* (PI §371), for what define number, proposition, proof, thought, sensation, etc. are grammatical structures

(BB 19). Moreover, the essence of a thing need not be determined by common properties at all, but by a multitude of overlapping family-resemblances.

2   In both MS. 165, 20 and MS. 129, 106 this follows a draft of PI §§440 – 1, hence was stimulated by the peculiarities of the concepts of desire and wish and their internal relation to their fulfilment.

Z §§110 – 14 emphasizes the diversity, unruliness, and indeterminate boundaries of the use of 'to think'. Its use does not conform with what we unreflectively expect, and its description is difficult; one cannot guess how it functions from a couple of examples.

SECTION 341

1   A coda to §§327ff. Far from thought being an inner accompaniment of speech with thought, speaking with thought ('nicht gedankenloses Sprechen') is comparable to playing a piece of music with thought. And no one would think that the difference between playing a sonata with thought and without thought consists in an inner (and hence inaudible) accompaniment of the music. On the contrary, it consists in the expressiveness with which the piece is played (cf. Z §§163f.), in the pattern of variation of loudness and tempo that manifest the player's understanding of the piece (PI §527).

2   W. frequently compared language with music, understanding a language with understanding music, experiencing the meaning of a phrase in language and in music (see esp. Z §§156 – 77). He emphasized the 'strongly musical element in verbal language. (A sign, the intonation of voice in a question, in an announcement, in longing; all the innumerable *gestures* made with the voice.)' It is these, *inter alia*, that distinguish speech with and without thought.

SECTION 342

1   After the careful examination and repudiation of the dual-process conception of thinking, W. returns to the question posed in §327: Can one think without speech? James argued that one must think *in a material*; with most of us, mental images are the 'mind-stuff' of thought (as was ascertained, James observes, by Galton's experiments [9]). However, can a deaf and dumb man weave his tactile and visual images into a system of

---

[9] James, *Principles of Psychology*, Vol. II, pp. 50ff.

thought? '*The question whether thought is possible without language* has been a favourite topic of discussion among philosophers. Some interesting reminiscences of his childhood by Mr Ballard . . . show it to be perfectly possible.'[10] The idea that this question can be settled empirically, by asking the deaf and dumb, is what W. challenges.

The challenge is powerful. The first move opens the question of whether Ballard has correctly *translated* his wordless thoughts about God and the world into words. But, forewarned by what W. has already clarified, it should be obvious that this question is odd. For no amount of play of images constitutes thinking that such-and-such is the case. (It is, at most, the 'logical germ' of a thought (cf. LW §843).) There is no such thing as *translating* a play of images into the verbal expression of thought; rather, one *expresses* the thought that occurs to one *when* such-and-such images, as it happens, cross one's mind. To express this thought is not to *translate* it. But Ballard, before he had mastered sign-language, had no means of expressing thoughts about God and the world; i.e. nothing in his behavioural repertoire could *count* as the expression of the thought that God had created the world. But if so, what constituted thinking this thought? (Could he also play mental chess before he learnt how to play chess?)

The second move is subtle: the question of whether one is sure that one has correctly translated one's wordless thought into words is not a question which normally exists, so why does it raise its head *here*? The normal non-existence of the question is not because the answer is usually too obvious, viz. that ordinarily all human beings do translate their thoughts correctly into language. Rather, the question is *senseless*. It is senseless not only because we do not *translate* our thoughts into words, but also because it makes no sense for a person to be mistaken about what he thinks. This is not because he knows what he thinks in the sense in which he might know what someone else thinks; rather, both knowledge and ignorance are grammatically excluded (cf. PI p. 222). Equally, error about one's own thoughts is ruled out; it makes no sense (save in special cases) to suppose that a person might think that *p*, but mistakenly think that he thinks that *q*! In these respects one's sensations and one's thoughts are on the same level. So why does this otherwise meaningless question arise here? The answer was given in PI §288(c):

That expression of doubt has no place in the language-game; but if we cut out human behaviour, which is the expression of sensation, it looks as if I might *legitimately* begin to doubt afresh. My temptation to say that one might take a sensation for something other than what it is arises from this: if I assume the abrogation of the normal language-game with the expression of a sensation, I need a criterion of identity for the sensation; and then the possibility of error also exists.

[10] Ibid., Vol. I, p. 266.

Mutatis mutandis, the same applies here. What happens to a person when he thinks something, i.e. what images cross his mind, and so forth, does not constitute a thought; nor does it furnish a criterion of identity for the thought. And, of course, it makes no sense for *him* to doubt whether he thinks what he says he thinks. (It is absurd to suppose that he might *mistake* the thought that it is cold today for the thought that Shakespeare wrote *Hamlet!*) But if, as in the Ballard case, we cut out the verbal or symbolic behaviour which articulates the expression of thought, then it *looks* as if one might legitimately doubt. For if one assumes the abrogation of the normal language-game with the expression of thoughts, then one needs a criterion of identity for the thought – and then the possibility of error exists!

The third move follows from the second. We should not say that Ballard *mis*remembers, any more than we should say 'He misremembers' if we heard someone say 'I distinctly remember that some time before I was born I believed . . .' (cf. PI §288). For what would it be for him to remember *correctly* what he thought before he could talk (or what he believed before he was born)? Rather, we should just treat these 'recollections' as a queer memory-phenomenon, an aberration, a 'queer reaction which we have no idea what to do with' (PI §288).

2   Vol. XII, 202f. observes that if someone were to say of something that today he sees it as red, but that yesterday he saw it as green, then in certain circumstances we should accept this, e.g. if we had an appropriate physiological explanation. But if someone recurrently made such claims, for which nothing else spoke, we would say not that he remembers yesterday seeing it thus, but that he *says* that he remembers, and we might add 'But what that actually means, I don't know'. And if someone now said that this person has what we call 'the experience of remembering', we would be inclined to brush this aside as irrelevant to whether he remembers or not, i.e. to view any 'inner experience' in these circumstances as idle. In parenthesis W. adds 'James' quotation from Ballard'; i.e. something counts as a mnemonic experience only within a context in which something counts as remembering, not vice versa.

Section 343

1   This confirms the interpretation of §342, for 'memory-reaction' here stands in contrast to the supposition entertained *faute de mieux* in §342 that Ballard's words are a *translation* of his memory.

2   PG 181f. elaborates the point that to avow or report a memory is not to translate an experience into words. Rather, one is, for example, asked

a question about what one did, and one answers with certainty. And isn't *that* the 'experience' of remembering. One is inclined to ask what *makes* one certain, and that very question invites the answer; a mental picture, off which one reads what happened (a stored photograph in the medium of the mind!). But the correct answer is: nothing *made* me certain; I *was* certain. It is a mistake to suppose that memories expressed in language are, as it were, mere threadbare representatives of the real memory-experiences (cf. PI §649). Vol. XII, 181 remarks that one does not normally read off what one remembers from any inner picture. Rather, one says, 'I remember doing . . .', and one's words are the manifestation (*Äusserung*) of memory; expressing them is itself the memory-phenomenon (experience), not the description of an inner picture.

SECTION 344

1   Another probe at the supposition that thought is independent of the capacity to speak. Is it not imaginable that people should never speak any language aloud, yet still speak a language to themselves *in foro interno*, in the imagination? The interlocutor observes innocently that this supposition merely suggests that it is imaginable that people should always do what they sometimes do. And it is true that we often say something to ourselves in the imagination, without expressing our thought aloud in any way. But this generalization is not licit. The fact that 'some things have property F' makes sense does *not* ensure that 'All things have property F' makes sense; it is a fallacy that 'some' and 'all' are topic-neutral. In particular, the transition from 'It is possible that people should sometimes speak to themselves in the imagination' to 'It is possible that people should always speak to themselves in the imagination' is not licit. For our criterion for someone's saying something to himself in the imagination is what he tells us (and related behaviour). And a pre-condition for that is that he *can speak* in the ordinary sense of the term, i.e. *not* in the sense in which a parrot or gramophone can. (We do not say that maybe the parrot speaks to itself in its imagination!)

1.1   'nur in ihrem Innern zu sich selbst sprächen': 'if people only spoke inwardly to themselves'. It is important to bear in mind that it is speaking to oneself *in the imagination*, or *inwardly*, that is at issue, not talking only to oneself (which has been countenanced in PI §243). Evidently in this context (and in the succeeding remarks up to §362) W. is treating speaking to oneself in the imagination as a kind of thinking, as is made quite explicit in §361. It is noteworthy that PI p. 211 cuts finer here: ' "Denken" und "in der Vorstellung sprechen" – ich sage nicht "zu sich selbst sprechen" – sind verschiedene Begriffe.' (' "Thinking" and "speaking in the imagination" – I do not say "speaking to oneself" – are different concepts.') One can think without speaking in the imagination, as when one talks with thought or works intelligently or hits on a solution to a problem, etc. And one can speak in the imagination without thinking, as in a daydream or in reciting a poem in the imagination or in doing a mechanical calculation 'in one's head'. And speaking to oneself need not be in the imagination, but can be aloud; while, conversely, not all one's internal speakings are addressed to oneself.

2.1   (i) 'Like: "An infinitely long row of trees . . . " ': the absurdities that result from attempted extrapolation from the finite to the infinite are examined in PR 165 ff. and 306ff. It is no explanation of what is *meant* by 'infinitely long row of trees' to say 'You know what "a row of trees" means, you know what "the row comes to an end after the nth tree" means, well – an infinite row of trees is one that *never* comes to an end!' For no criterion for the row's being infinite has been given, since 'never' here does not refer to a time *interval* (as it does in 'He never coughed during the whole hour'). So it incorporates the very problem it appears to resolve!

(ii) '. . . if, in the ordinary sense of the words, he *can speak*': MS. 165, 192 embroiders. We do not say that maybe a dog speaks to itself in a European language. And if someone agrees that this is *highly improbable*, this is a misuse of the word 'improbable'. Of someone who has not learnt to speak, we do not say that he speaks to himself.

SECTION 345

1   This amplifies the general critical point of §344. The supposition that if F(a) makes sense, then so too does (x)F(x) is indefensible. Although the topic–neutrality of the quantifiers is a postulate of the formation-rules of the predicate-calculus, that alone suffices to show that it does not capture the 'logical form' of generality and of inferences involving generality in natural languages. W. here gives a pair of examples where an inference of this kind is patently invalid.

2   PG 265ff. dwells on the inadequacy of the Frege–Russell notation for generality, and criticizes the conception of generality in TLP. There are many different *kinds* of generality, as many different 'logical forms' of generality as there are different logical forms concealed by the subject–predicate grammatical form.

In many other writings W. pointed out, in particular cases, the illegitimacy of parallel transitions from the intelligibility of a singular proposition to the intelligibility of its generalization. Thus, for example, it makes sense to order someone to write down any cardinal number, but not to write down all cardinal numbers (PG 266). 'There is a circle in the square [(∃x) . fx]' makes sense, but not 'all circles are in the square [∼ ∃x . ∼ fx]' (ibid.). LPE makes parallel points about deception (293), lying (295), and someone's always seeing as red what we see as green (316). Z §571 argues for the unintelligibility of the supposition that all behaviour might be pretence. More generally, a condition for the existence of our mathematical practices is that mistakes be the exception, not the rule; and even more generally, a condition for the existence of shared language-games and for the possibility of communication is that there be agreement in judgements. Note that the *reasons* for faulting the transition are not uniform.

SECTION 346

1   A further objection to the claim that thought (speaking to oneself in the imagination) is possible only for those who *can* speak. Why is it an important fact that I imagined a deity in order to imagine a parrot's saying things to itself? Because this abrogates the rules of our ordinary language-games (God sees, even *in the dark*; He hears my *inaudible* prayers). By the same token, the expressions must be given a new role in this different language-game, or else they are senseless. So 'Couldn't we imagine God giving a parrot understanding . . . ' amounts to 'Let's forget about sense, and let our imagination roam beyond the bounds of sense' – which is excellent advice for a would-be Lewis Carroll.

SECTION 347

1   The interlocutor plays the private-language card: surely I know *from my own case* what it means 'to speak to oneself in the imagination'. And if so, then the concept of thus speaking to oneself (which one often does when thinking) *is* detached from any public, behavioural criteria. For would anyone deny that if I were deprived of the organs of speech I could still talk to myself thus?

      W. does not deny the latter claim. What is awry is the former one: viz. that I know what speaking to oneself in the imagination is from my own case. A putative 'private' paradigm can have no role in explaining the common (shared) concept of speaking to oneself. So *if* I know only from my own case, then I do *not* know what is called 'speaking to oneself in the imagination', but only what *I* call this – which I cannot explain to anyone! (And hence, not to myself either!)

..

SECTION 348

1   The interlocutor's objections weaken, but also grow more subtle. Granted that the intelligibility of the occurrence of inner speech depends on being able to speak publicly, hence on something's *counting* as an expression of thought, is it not intelligible that a Ballard, having learnt a gesture-language, should then talk to himself in his imagination in a *vocal* language? If so, then in this *thin* sense, the question of §344 would get an affirmative answer (but not that of §327, save trivially).

W.'s riposte is delicate: it is not obvious that one *does* understand the supposition. Certainly one cannot argue: 'You know what "being able to communicate only by means of a gesture-language" means; and you know what "talking to yourself in vocal language" means; so you must know what it means to say that someone who communicates only by means of a gesture-language talks to himself in a vocal language!' (The bankruptcy-order on compositionalism should not be lifted here!) What can one *do* with this claim? Have we been told *when* to say that a deaf mute is talking to himself *vocally* in his imagination? And when he allegedly does so, does he *pronounce* the words he says to himself correctly? in an English or Welsh accent? Or is it not rather that these questions get no grip here? (The supposition is analogous to the idea that the blind have vivid visual images of shapes they feel.)

SECTION 349

1.1   'this supposition': not the supposition that these deaf mutes who have mastered a gesture-language nevertheless talk to themselves in a vocal language, but rather the supposition that someone (a normal speaker) engages in internal monologues. Hence 'these words', which have a familiar application in ordinary circumstances, are 'speaking to oneself inwardly in a vocal language'.

2   This originates in Vol. XII, 139f. in a different context. After an early draft of PI §243(a) (see Exg. §243, 2) W. examines the sentence 'I assume that a picture crosses his mind' (Z §531). One cannot assume that such a picture occurs to a stove. But why not? Is it because a stove lacks human form? W. leaves the question hanging, and turns to examine the supposition. After all, it amounts to no more than words and a picture, and a pretty crude picture at that, viz. of a human head with an image nebulously in it.

Then follows PI §349, in which, in this context, the 'supposition' is that 'a picture crosses his mind'. The 'falling away of its application' is exemplified by the attempted application of the phrase to the stove. In such cases, bereft of the normal human context, the phrase and crude picture stand naked. The (genuine) application, W. concludes, is a timely wrapping for the sign.

What gives expressions such as 'talking to oneself vocally in the imagination' or 'a picture crossing one's mind' their sense is a very specific context of application. When this does not obtain, the expressions lack any genuine use, and all that remain are words, a primitive picture, and philosophical bewilderment.

SECTION 350

1   The target of this remark was identified in §349, viz. that if a supposition makes sense in one circumstance, then it makes sense in any circumstance; hence too, if one understands what an expression means in one context, then one must understand it in any context.

The interlocutor's opening remark insists that the intelligibility of the supposition that another has pain is guaranteed by extrapolation from one's own case, viz. what is supposed is that *he* has the same as I have when I am in pain. This runs parallel to the claim that the supposition that a deaf mute talks to himself vocally in the imagination just is the supposition that he does what I do when I talk to myself vocally in the imagination.

W.'s objection is that the explanation by means of *sameness* does not work here, and he explains why not by an analogical case. One cannot explain what 'It is 5 o'clock on the sun' means by saying that it is the same time as here when it is 5 o'clock here. For obviously enough, if it is 5 o'clock on the sun and 5 o'clock here, *then* it is the same time there as here. But that presupposes, and does not explain, the intelligibility of 'It is 5 o'clock on the sun'. Given our methods of measuring terrestrial time (by reference to the sun's zenith) and our conventions of time-zones relative to Greenwich, we can readily explain what it is for it to be 5 o'clock (GMT) here (in Oxford). But nothing has been stipulated as to how to measure time on the sun; nothing has been laid down as the appropriate ground for saying 'It is *n* o'clock on the sun'. The method of determining time by reference to the sun's zenith has no application to the sun itself; hence the expression 'It is 5 o'clock on the sun' has no sense. This is not to say that we could not *give* it a sense by stipulation; we could. But it is to say that we cannot explain what sense it *has* by saying that it is the *same* time as here.

Pari passu, one cannot explain what it is for another to have a pain by saying that it is for him to have the same as I have when I am in pain. To be sure, if he has a throbbing pain in his leg and I have a throbbing pain in my leg, then we both have the same pain. But equally, if the stove has a throbbing pain in its leg, it too has the same pain! The question is, when should one say 'He has a pain'? The explanation by sameness does not work, because in my own case I neither have nor need a criterion for determining whether I am in pain. Hence my own case furnishes me with no criterion for judging another to be in pain, just as our method of measuring terrestrial time provides us with no method for measuring time on the sun.

1.1   'the stove has the same experience': the reference to the stove is somewhat surprising here; for what has the stove got to do with this discussion? In Vol. XII, 141 this perspicuously picks up the reference in the draft of PI §349 (see Exg.) to the questionable intelligibility of the supposition that a picture might occur to the stove.

2   Vol. XII, 141 has the first draft of this. After the second sentence, it has 'Die Frage is ja eben: wie *appliziere* ich diese meine Erfahrung auf den Fall des Andern?' ('The question is just: how do I *apply* this experience of mine to the other's case?') This, though deleted in PI, is answered by 'If one has to imagine someone else's pain on the model of one's own, this is none too easy a thing to do: for I have to imagine pain which I *do not feel* on the model of the pain which I *do feel* (Vol. XII, 160; PI §302; see Exg. §302, 2).
    Vol. XV, 224 invokes the analogy with time-measurement in a related context. If one concedes, as one must, that one can have a certain experience without expressing it, then surely another can have the same experience? I'll concede everything, W. responds, as long as I know what I am conceding! The question is, what counts here as *the same experience*? How do we 'measure' the two experiences to determine that they are the same? For, *ex hypothesi*, the ordinary scales on which we weigh experiences, viz. behavioural expression, have been excluded here. Might the person (e.g. a deaf mute) not subsequently say: 'I once had such-and-such an experience'? To be sure, under normal circumstances that is a criterion for what he experienced. But not always: e.g. 'I remember that before I was born I dreamt . . .'. These moves are akin to insisting that since you concede that it may be 5 o'clock here, even though you haven't looked at your watch, you must concede that it may be 5 o'clock on Mars. But one must not forget what Einstein taught the world: that the method of measuring time belongs to the grammar of the time-expression.
    RPP II §§93f. invokes the analogy again: could we not imagine a creature that lacked sense-impressions but had mental images? Surely a 'higher being' could know what mental images such a creature had? But this is by no means obvious; one can talk about this, but that doesn't

show that one has thought it through. In parenthesis W. added ('5 o'clock on the sun').

SECTION 351

1   Despite the clarifications there is still a temptation to reply 'Pain is pain – whether *he* has it or *I* have it; and however I come to know whether he has pain or not'. Why so? And what does this objection seem to achieve?

At a very general level one is tempted to cut the cackle and insist that there is an objective 'fact of the matter' as to whether someone is in pain, irrespective of how and whether we find out that he is. For has not W.'s preoccupation with how we *know* that another is in pain or talking to himself in the imagination, etc. allowed epistemological concerns to distort our grasp of 'ontological realities'? More locally, if the objection is correct in insisting on the objectivity of pain and on the independence of the *truth* of propositions about another's pain from how we know whether he is in pain, then we should equally insist that whether deaf mutes talk to themselves vocally, whether people who cannot speak can nevertheless say things to themselves in the imagination, is equally an objective matter independent of whether we know that they do or not. (And something similar applies to the question of whether the blind can have 'ideas of colour' without any preceding 'impressions'.) Tactically, the objection seems to rebut the time-measurement analogy of §350. For while a case has been made out for denying that 'It is 5 o'clock on the sun' has any use (is meaningful), no such case has or could be made out for 'He is in pain'. One could not, therefore, say '5 o'clock is 5 o'clock, whether it is in Oxford or on the sun!', as one surely can say 'Pain is pain, whether *he* has it or *I* have it!'

W., however, immediately concedes that pain is pain, whether *I* have it or *he* has it. Who would wish to deny *that*? This parallels the move in §350: viz. if he has a throbbing headache in the temples and I have a throbbing headache in the temples, then we have the *same* pain. But just as the latter concession still precludes an explanation by sameness of what it means for him to have a pain (viz. he has the same as I have when I have a pain), so too this apparent concession gives nothing away; for the question still remains: what is it for him to have a pain?

Similarly, W. concedes that if another has a pain, then he has a pain however I might happen to find that out. For, to be sure, the *truth* of propositions about others' inner states is independent of how, and indeed whether, we establish it in a particular case. It is the *meaning* of such propositions that is at issue, in particular that their meaning cannot intelligibly be explained by extrapolation from one's own case. And the clarification of meaning is a matter of reminding ourselves how certain expressions are *to be used*; hence it is a grammatical investigation, not an epistemological one. (Although that is not to say that the question of how such propositions are verified is irrelevant (PI §353); it is rather to insist that whether we know is a matter of the truth of our judgements; how we can know, i.e. what method is to be followed, may well be part of the grammar of an expression.)

The concession, it is evident, grants the interlocutor little. He would like it to license such sentences as 'The stove is in pain' – pain is pain, whether *I* have it, *he* has it, or the *stove* has it! He would then argue that, as a *matter of fact*, the stove is never in pain! The proposition is meaningful, but false. But this he cannot do (for what would it be for the proposition to be true? – It would be for the stove to have what I have when I am in pain! But *this* roundabout was brought to a halt in §350). W.'s move recapitulates the argument of §349; we have the words and certain images or pictures; but they have no application here.

The second half of the remark adds a further example to clarify the illegitimacy of the compositionalist extrapolation that W. is criticizing. The interlocutor might argue that 'Above is above, whether it is above the wardrobe or above the earth'. But that is precisely wrong. For 'above' and 'below' applied to objects and structures on the earth do not have the same meaning when applied to the earth (globe) itself.

.1   (i) 'Damit könnte ich mich einverstanden erklären': 'I might go along with that.'

(ii) 'cannot be used in the ordinary way': the subsequent parenthetical example explains one deviation. If A lives on the fifth floor and B on the fourth floor, A may rightly say that he lives above B, but B cannot say that he lives above A; whereas if we say that the Antipodeans are 'below' us, they *can* say that we are 'below' them.

.1   'We are indeed all taught at school . . .': PG 381f. contrasts W.'s concern with mathematics with a mathematician's. The latter has been trained to *repress* these kinds of question, and finds them repulsive. 'That is to say, I trot out all the problems that a child learning arithmetic, etc. finds difficult, the problems that education represses without solving. I say to those repressed doubts: you are quite correct, go on asking, demand clarification!'

Section 352

1   Just as we are inclined to insist that 'pain is pain, whether *he* has it or I have it' (§351), so too we are tempted to invoke the law of excluded

middle in this context and to insist that either X is in pain (talks to himself vocally in his imagination, has an image in his mind) or X is not in pain (etc.), no matter whether X is a normal person, a deaf mute, or a stove!'

But this is deceptive. The law of excluded middle, if presented in the form 'p v $\sim p$' is a *tautology which says nothing at all*. Or, more accurately, on the assumption that 'p' and '$\sim p$' are indeed expressions of propositions, then 'p v $\sim p$' is an empty tautology. Why then does it seem to say something, indeed something quite definitive? If we take 'p' to be a proposition the sense of which is perspicuous, it would not even occur to us that 'p v $\sim p$' says anything. It conveys no information whatever, not even the grammatical truth that if 'p' is a proposition then either it is true that p or it is false that p. But if the sentence 'p' is, in one way or another, problematic, if its sense flickers, as it were, then we can derive from the tautology 'p v $\sim p$' the illusion of a picture of how things are, viz. either like *this: p* or like *this*: $\sim p$! And now, it seems, all we have to do is to find out which of these is true. This gives us the illusion that there is no problem about sense or meaning at all, but only a problem about how to establish truth (and, in that sense, an epistemological problem which takes meaning to be given!).

It is indeed remarkable that we can be taken in by the form of a tautology. For the question with which we are concerned is not whether it is true that p or it is true that $\sim p$, but rather, what it is for p to be true. Or, more accurately, what does 'p' mean: 'When someone sets up the law of excluded middle, he is as it were putting two pictures before us to choose from, and saying that one must correspond to the fact. But what if it is questionable whether the pictures can be applied here?' (RFM 268). But these are precisely the cases we are concerned with: viz. whether it makes any sense to talk of a stove having a pain or of a picture's occurring to it, or whether 'these deaf mutes talk to themselves inwardly in a vocal language' expresses a proposition at all. And if, in our contortions, we have rendered the proposition 'He is in pain' problematic (e.g. by arguing that it is to be understood by analogy with 'I am in pain'), then insisting that 'Either he is in pain or he is not in pain, there is no third possibility' achieves nothing. For we owe an explanation of what it is for him to be in pain. This law of excluded middle gives us a picture, a picture of a pair of pictures one of which corresponds with reality and the other of which does not. And this seems to fix the sense of 'He has this experience' and 'He does not have this experience' absolutely unequivocally. But that is exactly what it does *not* do.

The argument is parallel to that of §350, but with a further irony. In §350 the interlocutor attempts to invoke sameness in order to explain attributing pain to another; whereas only if one has laid down what it is for another to be in pain and has found out that someone is in pain is one in a position to say that he has the same as one has oneself if one is in pain. Here we try to invoke a tautology in order likewise to by pass the difficulty of clarifying the sense of 'He is in pain', whereas 'Either he is in pain or he is not in pain' only *has* a sense if 'He is in pain' has a sense – which we still need to explain. And the irony is that if 'He is in pain' has a sense, then, of course, the sense of 'Either he is in pain or he is not in pain' is, like that of all tautologies, zero sense!

1   (i) 'unendlichen Entwicklung von π': 'infinite (decimal) expansion of π'.

(ii) 'either the group "7777" occurs or it does not': a famous and much discussed matter. Though invoked here merely as an example, W. examined it at length elsewhere (WWK 71 – 3; PR 146ff., 206ff.; AWL 140, 189 – 201; PG 451ff.; RFM 266ff.). A number of points are noteworthy to avoid misinterpretation here:

(a) W. is not arguing that, contrary to classical logic, there are propositions, such as 'There are four consecutive 7s in the infinite expansion of π', to which the law of excluded middle does not apply – i.e. of which one cannot say: either this or its negation is true. This was what Brouwer thought, and it was for this that W. criticized him:

> Brouwer talks of a range of propositions for which the law of excluded middle does not hold; in this branch of mathematics this law does not *apply* . . . Brouwer has actually discovered something which it is misleading to call a proposition. He has not discovered a proposition, but something having the appearance of a proposition . . . To say the law of excluded middle does not hold for propositions about infinite classes is like saying 'In this stratum of atmosphere Boyle's law does not hold'. (AWL 140)

But it is absurd to conceive of laws of logic on the model of laws of science! If the law of excluded middle does not 'apply', then (*ceteris paribus*) we are not dealing with a proposition.

(b) W. was not therefore impugning the validity of the law of excluded middle or the principle of bivalence. On the contrary, the principle that every proposition is either true or false (which might be expressed, not by a particular tautology '*p* v ~*p*', but rather by the statement *that* '*p* v ~*p*' *is a tautology*) partially *defines* what a proposition is (AWL 140). Hence one might say in the spirit of PI §136 that, contrary to Brouwer's view, the law of excluded middle does not 'fit' propositions (so that one could intelligibly ask whether it *applies* to *this* proposition), it 'belongs' to propositions! (But for later qualms about the excluded middle in relation to certain conditionals, see RPP I §§269 – 74.)

(c) W.'s agreement with Brouwer that the law of excluded middle does not apply to 'There are four consecutive 7s in the infinite expansion of π' does not rest on an awareness of limitations on human recognitional capacities. If it did, it would make sense to suggest that God sees the whole of the infinite expansion of π, but that we, with our 'medical limitations' (as Russell put it) cannot see so far. But that is precisely what W. repudiated: ' "Can God know all the places of the expansion of π?" would have been a good question for the schoolmen to ask. In all such cases the answer runs, "The question is senseless" ' (PR 149). It is senseless in so far as it treats infinity as a quantity and an infinite decimal as a series. But the concept of an infinite decimal is a concept of the unlimited technique of expansion of a series (RFM 278f.)

(d) It would be a complete misunderstanding to suggest that W. was trying to restrict mathematics to finitistic statements, let alone that he was doing so *on the grounds* that the law of excluded middle does not apply to infinitary statements. What he was doing in his discussion of this issue was drawing attention to grammatical differences between statements dealing with finite totalities and those dealing with infinite processes. It makes sense to talk of an infinite series containing a certain pattern only in certain circumstances, e.g. if the law of the series determines a recurring decimal. For then the criterion for the occurrence or non-occurrence of the pattern is its occurrence or non-occurrence *in the period* (AWL 190). But no such criterion obtains in the case of a lawless (irregular) infinite decimal. Here the question 'Do four consecutive 7s occur in the expansion?' *makes no sense*. One can only intelligibly ask 'Do four consecutive 7s occur in the first *n* places of the expansion?', for this question is a finite (extensional) one, and in the absence of periodicity we cannot take the former question about the infinite decimal extensionally.

It is important not to fall into a further fallacy here. In recent years the value of π has been calculated (by a computer) to 100,265 places.[11] There are four consecutive 7s beginning at the 1589th place. It is tempting to see this as a proof that there are four consecutive 7s in the expansion of π, and hence as a refutation of W.'s claim that the question makes no sense. It is, one might argue, a proposition which is not *falsifiable*, hence it is unlike finitistic mathematical propositions; but it is verifiable, and has now been verified! But this is a confusion. What has been determined is that there are four consecutive 7s after the 1589th place, i.e. in *an* expansion of π, not that there are four consecutive 7s in *the* expansion of π. For 'there isn't any series that is called *the* expansion of π. There are expansions of π, namely those that have been worked out . . .' (PG 480). The confusion becomes perspicuous when we reflect on whether we should say that before the calculation had been carried through until the

[11] D. Shanks and J. W. Wrench, Jr, 'Calculations of π to 100,000 decimals', *Mathematics of Computation*, 16 (1962), pp. 79 – 99. (see S. G. Shanker, *Wittgenstein and the Turning-Point in the Philosophy of Mathematics* (Croom Helm, London, 1987), p. 102).

1589th place, we did not know whether the proposition made sense? Were we then trying to answer a question which we did not know made sense? But is there any such thing as trying to answer such a question? Here we are perspicuously in the grip of a *picture* of an infinite series; it is there, we think, and all we have to do is to walk down this road and we will find what we will find (either that there are four consecutive sevens or that there are not)! But 'there are . . .' in mathematics is not a prediction about what we will find. The further expansion of π is a further expansion of mathematics.

.1   'Entweder es schwebt ihm ein solches Bild vor': 'either such a picture crosses his mind'. In Vol. XII, 148 this occurs after a discussion of what it is to understand the sentence 'He imagines a red circle'.

Section 353

1   Having examined a variety of false pictures and temptations that should be resisted, we are left at an impasse. Neither extrapolating from one's own case nor appealing to the law of excluded middle is of any avail in trying to make clear whether the suppositions that concern us (e.g. that deaf mutes speak to themselves vocally in their imagination) make sense. For both moves presuppose the meaning of third-person ascriptions of thought to be given. But *how* is it given? §340 noted that one must *look at* the use of a word ('thinking') and learn from that. Now a concrete suggestion, implicit in the foregoing, is made: whether and how a proposition is verified is part of its grammar, and a description of it is a clarification of the meaning of an expression. And that is indeed *one* task that needs to be done in elucidating the nature of thought, of talking to oneself in the imagination, etc.

2   Though derived immediately from Vol. XI, 72, this remark can be traced back to 1930/31, i.e. when W. had only just returned to philosophical work (Vol. VI, 238; Vol. VIII, 99; ETB 270, 449, 590). It was at this stage that he introduced the principle that inspired the Vienna Circle,[12] viz. that the meaning of a proposition is determined by its method of verification. The atomism of the *Tractatus* was repudiated in

[12] This is confirmed by Carnap, 'Intellectual Authobiography', in R. A. Schilpp (ed.), *The Philosophy of Rudolf Carnap* (Open Court, Illinois, 1963), p. 45; B. Juhos, 'The Methodological Symmetry of Verification and Falsification', in his *Selected Papers on Epistemology and Physics*, ed. G. Frey (Reidel, Dordrecht, 1976), pp. 134ff.; V. Kraft, *The Vienna Circle, the origins of neo-positivism* (Greenwood Press, New York, 1969), pp. 31, 197; and F. Waismann, 'A Logical Analysis of the Concept of Probability', first published in *Erkenntnis*, 1 (1930 – 1), repr. in translation in his *Philosophical Papers*, ed. B. McGuinness (Reidel, Dordrecht, 1977); see esp. p .5. Cf. also Waismann's 'Theses', in WWK 243ff.

1929 and replaced (briefly) by the conception of a language as an interconnected system of propositional systems (*Satszysteme*) and a tripartite distinction between types of proposition or 'propositions' in different senses of the term. 'Genuine' propositions concerning immediate experience were distinguished from 'hypotheses', and both were sharply differentiated from mathematical propositions. It is important to note that W.'s verification dictum was employed for a very specific purpose, viz. as a determinant of what kind of *propositional system* a given proposition belongs to and of what kind of proposition it is. Thus 'This is red' is compared with reality in a similar way to 'This is blue'; hence they both belong to the same propositional system, which differs from the propositional system of 'This is hot' and 'This is B-flat'.

> You can only search in *a space*.[13] For only in a space do you stand in relation to where you are not.
>
> To understand the sense of a proposition means to know how the issue of its truth or falsity is to be decided.
>
> . . . You cannot search wrongly: you *cannot* look for a visual impression with your sense of touch.
>
> You cannot compare a picture with reality unless you can set it against it as a yardstick. (PR 77)

Furthermore, if a proposition can be conclusively verified, then it is a different kind of logical structure from one which cannot be verified, viz. a hypothesis (WWK 210; PR 285). Vol. IV, 108 (a precursor of PI §353) argues that if one wants to know what a proposition means, one can always ask how one knows it. Does one know that there are so-and-so many permutations of three elements in the same way as one knows that there are six people in the room? No, and that is why they are propositions of different *kinds*! (Cf. PR 200; PG 458f.) In these senses, clarification of how a proposition is verified is obviously a contribution to its grammar. W., of course, abandoned his distinction between genuine propositions and hypotheses, and replaced his conception of propositional systems by the much more flexible and richer conception of language-games. But this did *not* mean that he had to abandon the simple point that how a proposition is verified is an aspect of its grammar, as long as this point is not taken as a dogmatic *thesis*[14]: 'How

---

[13] E.g. in visual space for colours, in auditory space for sounds.

[14] Hence his reported remark many years later:

> I used at one time to say that, in order to get clear how a certain sentence is used, it was a good idea to ask oneself the question: How would one try to verify such an assertion? But that's just one way of getting clear about the use of a word or sentence . . . Some people have turned this suggestion about asking for verification into a dogma – as if I'd been advancing a *theory* about meaning.

See D. A. T. Gasking and A. C. Jackson, 'Wittgenstein as Teacher', repr. in K. T. Fann (ed.), *Ludwig Wittgenstein: the Man and his Philosophy* (Dell Publishing Co., New York, 1967), p. 54.

far is giving the verification of a proposition a grammatical statement about it? So far as it is, it can explain the meaning of its terms. In so far as it is a matter of experience, as when one names a symptom, the meaning is not explained' (AWL 31). Of course, there are many sorts of propositions for which it makes no sense to ask how they are verified; but that very fact is an important feature of their grammar and is a mark that distinguishes them from other kinds of propositions.

Section 354

1   The preceding remark has suggested that clarifying how and whether a proposition can be verified is a contribution to characterizing its grammar. But if it is a proposition of the kind for which it makes sense to ask how it is verified, not any sort of verification belongs to its grammar (AWL 31, quoted in Exg. §353). One can verify whether Cambridge won the boat race by reading *The Times*, but that *The Times* reports that it did is not part of the grammar of the proposition; it is merely a 'symptom' (cf. M 266).

But though there is in one sense a sharp distinction between criteria (fixed by convention) and symptoms (discovered inductively), in another sense there is not. For there is often a widespread fluctuation, especially in science, between symptoms and criteria. As long as certain phenomena are virtually always concomitant, there is no need to decide whether $e_1 \ldots e_3$ define h as its criteria, whereas $e_4 \ldots e_7$ are merely inductive evidence, or vice versa. And for certain purposes in one context, one may take $e_1 \ldots e_3$ as criteria, and for other purposes in another context one may treat $e_4 \ldots e_7$ as criteria. Hence it is very often the case that one cannot ask globally whether a certain theory (e.g. Newtonian mechanics) treats such-and-such as a criterion for so-and-so. Rather, one must ask whether *this* specific argument does so, or whether this person, in this argument, is doing so (see 'Criteria', §2).

This fluctuation between criteria and symptoms can make it appear as if there were nothing at all but symptoms. And, by implication, the troubles besetting us in this investigation into thinking stem from failure to distinguish criteria from symptoms and from overlooking their fluctuation (but this has not been shown). Hence we are inclined to think that all we *ever* have to go on when it comes to judgements about another's thoughts, mental images, or interior monologues are symptoms. But avowals (*Aüsserungen*) of the 'inner' are *not* symptoms; they are *criteria*.

W. applies pressure to the supposition that there are nothing but symptoms by invoking an example from a different area. We say, quite correctly, that experience teaches us that when the barometer falls, it rains. This is an inductive correlation, the fall of the barometer being a symptom of rain. But we are wrongly inclined to say likewise that experience teaches us that when we have certain sense-impressions, it rains. We even defend the claim that this is a matter of experience by citing the indisputable fact that sense-impressions may deceive us, i.e. having a visual impression of rain does not *entail* that it is raining, so the relation must be inductive or experiential!

The conclusion does *not* follow. It may indeed look to me as if it is raining, yet *not* be raining. But that possibility does not imply that the proposition that normally when it looks to one as if it is raining, then it is raining is an empirical proposition, discovered to be true by inductive correlation. For the *concept* of 'looking to a person as if it is raining' is not independent of the concept of its raining. That this (false) visual impression is one of *rain* is founded on a *grammatical* nexus; we explain what 'It looks to me as if it is raining' means by pointing to the *rain* and saying 'When it looks like *that* ↗, then it looks as if it is raining!'

So far, so (tolerably) good! But in order to illustrate the point at stake, W. would have to claim that its looking to me as if it is raining (my having a visual impression of rain) is a *criterion* (not a symptom) of its raining. Yet that, surely, he would not want to do! We do not say that it is raining *on the grounds* that it looks to us as if it is raining, as we say that A is in pain on the grounds that he fell and is groaning. 'It looks to me as if it is raining' is not my *evidence* for the fact that it is raining; indeed, I *need* no evidence, I can *see the rain*! It is true that if asked 'How do you know that it is raining' I would have an answer: viz. 'I can see it.' But that answer does not supply the questioner with my *evidence* for the rain. We learn to say 'It's raining' in circumstances in which we have certain visual and tactile impressions, but *not on the grounds* of having those impressions. On the contrary, we learn to characterize the impressions only after having mastered the concept of what the impressions are impressions of – viz. *rain*!

2   Like §353, this derives from Vol. XI, 72ff., written in 1933/4. It is noteworthy that prior to this draft there occurs the following:

> Wie weiss man, wenn es regnet? Wir sehen, fühlen, den Regen. Die Bedeutung des Wortes "Regen" wurde uns mit diesen Erfahrungen erklärt. / Ich sage, sie sind 'Kriterien' dafür, das es regnet / 'Was ist Regen?' und 'Wie sieht Regen aus?' sind logisch verwandte Fragen. – Die Erfahrung habe nun gelehrt, dass ein plötzliches Fallen des Barometers und ein Regenguss immer zusammengehen, dann werde ich ein solches Fallen des Barometers als ein *Symptom* für das Niedergehen eines Regengusses ansehen. Ob ein Phänomen ein Symptom des Regens ist, lehrt die Erfahrung, was als Kriterium des Regens gilt, ist Sache der Abmachung (Definition)/unsere Bestimmung. (Vol. XI, 72)

(How does one know whether it is raining? We see, feel, the rain. The meaning of the word 'rain' is explained to us with those experiences. / I say, they are 'criteria' for its raining. / 'What is rain?' and 'What does rain look like?' are logically related questions. If experience has taught that a sudden fall of the barometer always goes together with rainfall, then I shall consider such a barometric fall as a *symptom* of rainfall. Whether a phenomenon is a symptom of rain is taught by experience, what counts as a criterion of rain is a matter of stipulation (definition)/our determination.)

This is followed by a version of Z §438: nothing is commoner, especially in science, than for the meaning of an expression to oscillate, due to a fluctuation between criteria and symptoms. This long remark is followed by a draft of PI §§354 – 6.

It is noteworthy that this sequence of remarks was *not* tailored for the purpose of clarifying an aspect of the grammar of psychological expressions in general, let alone 'thinking' or 'speaking to oneself in the imagination' in particular. Furthermore, it is a relatively early remark which antedates W.'s exploitation of the concept of a criterion in philosophy of mind. Arguably it fulfils its current role poorly. First, though we can distinguish symptoms from criteria in the case of psychological features, it is less than obvious that the difficulties encountered thus far are due to any *fluctuation* between the two. Rather, the appearance of there being nothing but symptoms in the case of ascribing psychological predicates to other people arises through the inner/outer picture of the mind and through failure to grasp the grammatical nature of the first-/third-person asymmetry in the case of psychological terms. Secondly, though its seeming to me as if it is raining is not a symptom of rain, it is not a criterion either – at least, not if W. conceives of a criterion as a *justifying ground* that is fixed by convention. For the concept of its looking to X just as if it is raining *presupposes*, and does not determine, the meaning of 'It is raining' (cf. Z §§422ff.), and that it looks to me as if it is raining is not my reason or ground for judging it to be raining, although I might, in certain circumstances, use this form of words to *draw back* from the judgement that it is raining.

The general point at issue in connection with psychological predicates is perhaps better made by RPP I §292. One is inclined to think that psychologists, who study the workings of the mind, are handicapped relative to other scientists. For unless they engage in introspective psychology, are they not condemned to study the phenomenon of the human mind from afar, indirectly as it were? For what they observe are the words spoken by their subjects and their behaviour, but these are surely only *signs* of the mental processes the psychologist is interested in! This is confused. It is true that words and behaviour that are *learnt by heart* are of no interest here to the psychologist. But the expression 'signs of mental processes' is misleading, for we speak of the colour of the face

as a sign of fever, i.e. as inductive evidence. But the utterances
(*Aüsserungen*) and behaviour of a subject are not uniformly symptoms,
but *criteria* of the mental.

SECTION 355

1   This repeats the conclusion of §354. Because sense-impressions can be
deceptive (it may look to me as if it is raining, yet not be) one is inclined
to think of sense-impressions as mere symptoms of what they are sense-
impressions of. But that they are not symptoms (inductive evidence, i.e.
externally related to what they are impressions of) is shown by the fact
that we understand what our sense-impressions are impressions of. We
'understand their language', for we are not at a loss as to whether the
sense-impression we are having is one of rain or of a pink elephant.

1.1   'is founded on convention': characterizing how things strike one
visually by 'It looks to me as if it is raining' requires mastery of the rules
for the use of these expressions. And it is correct to use these words only
if it looks to me like *that* ↗ – and here one points to rain! (cf. Z §§418ff.)

SECTION 356

1   The opening move provides a link with §352 which is perhaps the
primary rationale for the occurrence of §§354 – 6 in the argument. For
here too one vacuously invokes the law of excluded middle while
brushing aside the question of verification, of the circumstances justifying the use of the proposition, as irrelevant to its meaning.
     How the information that it is raining has reached one, one is inclined
to insist, is irrelevant to the truth or falsity of the proposition in question.
And so, indeed, it is, if that simply means that truth is independent of
whether or how it happens to be known. But *meaning* is not so
independent. One learns to use the expression 'It is raining' when one has
certain visual, auditory, or tactile sense-impressions, i.e. when it looks
like *that* ↗, sounds *thus*, or feels like *this*. One knows (verifies) that it is
raining by perceiving the rain (or someone tells one that it is, or one
infers that it is from one's visitor's wet umbrella). But it is misleading to
characterize perceiving the rain as a matter of information being *transmitted* to one; in perception one often acquires information, but not by
information *reaching* one, rather by perceiving how things are. What
gives this 'information' the character of information about something is
that one is now in a position to give someone else that information, e.g.
to *say* 'It is raining'. It is not that one was *given* information oneself (e.g.

in the form of ambient light), for light hitting the retina does not give the retina or anyone else information, and though one's optic nerve transmits electrical impulses to one's 'visual' striate cortex, this too is not a case of one's eyes giving one information or even giving one's 'visual' striate cortex information. Hence the opening claim here is muddled. How I know is *not* 'another matter', but the heart of the matter in this case, for I did not acquire the information that it is raining by acquiring some other information (viz. that it looks to me as if it is raining) from which it follows.

SECTION 357

1   After the two pertinent digressions, §§349 – 52 (on the apparent sense of a supposition involving illegitimate extrapolation and the failure of the law of excluded middle to support its sense) and §§353 – 6 (on the relevance of verification to meaning), W. now returns explicitly to the theme of the antecedent remarks and picks up the thread of §348, viz. the investigation of the concept of talking to oneself in one's imagination. §348 expressed doubt over the intelligibility of supposing deaf mutes to speak to themselves vocally in the imagination. The issue turns upon the limits of intelligible applications of this expression and, as has now been argued, on what verifies the judgement that someone says something to himself in the imagination.

We do not say that perhaps a dog talks to itself. Is that because we are so well acquainted with its soul (or mind)? If one is caught in the net of the inner/outer picture one will, of course, deny that one is 'acquainted with its soul' at all. And one will also be prone to agnosticism in respect of the question of whether possibly the dog talks to itself. But one should jettison the philosophical ideas that accompany that picture anyway. (I am not *better* acquainted with my soul than those who know me well; indeed, I am not *acquainted* with my soul at all.) One sees the soul of a living being in its behaviour, and in this sense one might (perhaps ironically) *agree* that we do not say that possibly a dog talks to itself because we *are* well acquainted with its soul. For nothing in the behavioural repertoire of a dog could count as a criterion for its talking to itself in its imagination.

The interlocutor questions this; for after all, I do not say that *I* am saying something to myself in the imagination on the grounds of *my* behaviour. W. agrees immediately. I do not say that I am thinking, in pain, or that I intend such-and-such on the grounds of observing my behaviour either. But the first-person avowal or report *makes sense* only in as much as I generally do, in my behaviour, give others grounds for saying of me 'He is talking to himself in his imagination' ('He is thinking, in pain, intends to . . .'). The concluding sentence provides the transition to §358.

1.1   (i) 'Well, one might say this': it is not clear what it is that one might say – that we are so well acquainted with the soul of the dog and hence do not say that perhaps it speaks to itself, or that if one sees the behaviour of a living thing, one sees its soul. In MS. 165, 200f. the 'this' is perspicuously anaphoric (see below).

(ii) 'One sees its soul': after all, one might say, a dog is wholly transparent to us, one sees its delight, its fear, its anger – there is neither simulation nor repression.

2   MS. 165, 200f. and the later MS. 129, 7 have the draft of this remark following directly after PI §348.

MS. 165, 200f. has, in place of the third sentence

Nun, man *könnte* so sagen. Nur vom Menschen sagen wir, er spreche zu sich selbst – und nur vom sprechenden Menschen. Nur von dem, was/der/sich so und so benimmt.

(Well, one *could* say this. Only of a human being do we say, he speaks to himself – and only of a human being who can speak. Only of/that which/one who/behaves thus-and-so.)

This links the remark far more clearly with §348, to which it offers an answer, and also with §281 and §283 ('only of a living human being and what resembles (behaves like) a living human being can one say . . .'), which is appropriate given that it is succeeded in draft by §361 ('The chair is thinking to itself . . .') and §327, rather than §§359 – 60. But prior to §361, MS. 165 interpolates two further remarks.
    The first picks up an earlier remark (MS. 165, 7) 'Denk Dir, statt in einen Stein würdest Du in ein Grammophon verwandelt' ('Imagine that instead of being turned into a stone [see PI §283] you were turned into a gramophone') and observes that a gramophone 'speaks', so could one not suppose that it has a soul and *means* with it what it says? This might be difficult to imagine, W. says ironically, but is it impossible? The second stresses the problematic character of the concept of speaking to oneself. If speaking means to emit sounds, then the transition from the concept of speaking to the concept of speaking to oneself in the imagination (i.e. when no sounds are emitted) is none too perspicuous. It is comparable to telling someone to use the word 'sugar' for something that is just like sugar, only neither sweet nor edible.

2.1   'If one sees the behaviour of a living thing [being] one sees its soul': cf. PI p. 178: 'The human body is the best picture of the human soul,' and

RPP I §280: 'What better picture of believing could there be, than the human being who, with the expression of belief, says "I believe . . ."?'

Section 358

1   §357 argued, in conformity with the thrust of the private language arguments, that though my avowal that I am saying something to myself in the imagination rests on no grounds, in particular not on my own behaviour, nevertheless it only makes sense because I do (sometimes) manifest such-and-such behaviour. Hence, of course, 'I am in pain' or 'I was saying to myself that . . .' do not make sense simply because I mean something by them. Indeed, quite generally, it is not mythical 'inner acts of meaning' which give sentences their sense, endow them with life.

1   (i) 'And here, of course, belongs the fact that one cannot mean a senseless series of words': a thought that had played an important role in W.'s reflections when working on TLP. One is tempted to argue that word-language allows senseless combinations of words (cf. PI §512), but that the language of thought (cf. R 37) does not allow senseless combinations of thought-elements. Hence one cannot *think* a nonsense (PI §511). So one cannot *mean* a nonsensical combination of words; hence 'Green ideas sleep furiously' is nonsense *because* one cannot mean it! An alternative route to the same thought, and one equally prominent in W.'s first philosophy, is that *meaning* the words one utters is what connects the words with reality (cf. 'Thinking: the soul of language', §1). But, one might then think, one cannot connect a senseless combination of words with reality precisely because they will not mirror the logical multiplicity of the facts (of representable states of affairs).
     (ii) 'a dream of our language': a nightmare of reason.

2   MS. 165, 5ff. has this at the beginning of a long discussion of meaning something. Immediately following the first draft is a remark, which surely echoes TLP 5.6ff., that one could imagine someone saying that actually each person talks only for himself, since only he *knows* what he means. But then he ought really to say that actually everyone really talks for *me*, since only I know how I understand the words!

Section 359

We do not say of a dog that maybe it speaks to itself, but what of a machine? Can it think? Many philosophers and artificial-intelligence scientists would claim that machines can think, or, alternatively, that we are on the brink of creating such machines. W.'s response here is oblique. Shelving the question of thinking until §360, he queries whether a machine could be in pain. Rather than replying, as most of us would, with a simple negative response, he shifts the question subtly. Is the human *body* a machine which thinks or is in pain? Surely nothing can come any closer to being such a machine? But we do *not* say of the body that it thinks or is in pain: my tooth hurts – but *I* am in pain, not my tooth (cf. §281 and 'Men, minds, and machines', §5.).

2   Vol. XIII, 129 contains the draft of §359 in the context of a long discussion of thinking and believing. Our philosophical unclarity about thought and belief, and more generally about what is problematic in psychology, is manifest in the picture we have of a hidden mechanism, whether in the brain or, ethereally, in the mind. We think that our difficulties would be resolved if only we knew more about the processes in these mechanisms. But it is not undiscovered processes which concern us here; rather it is the use of familiar 'processes' of belief, such as saying 'I believe . . .'. The mechanism which we do not understand is not in our minds or in our brains, but in our lives, where this expression is at home.

This is followed by PI §359, which is succeeded by the remark that the word 'I' in 'I have a pain' does not refer to a body, hence it does not stand for a machine either. This observation, one might say, is the mature wine from the reflections of PG 105, which pursued a different line of attack, closer to the strategy of PR, Ch. VI.

2.1   'It surely comes as close as possible to being such a machine': but not all that close; see Z §614: 'But you would never talk like that if you were examining the behaviour of a machine. – Well, who says that in this sense a living creature, an animal body, is a machine?' (My translation; cf. 'Behaviour and behaviourism', §4.)

Section 360

1   This applies §281 to the question raised in §359. It makes no more sense to anticipate the construction of machines that can think than to attempt to make machines to investigate the colours of numbers. Of course, that is not to say that we may not one day make thinking beings in laboratories, with or without organic material! (Cf. 'Men, minds, and machines', §5.)

1.1   (i) 'of dolls and no doubt of spirits too': these are 'secondary' uses, whose intelligibility is parasitic on the primary use.
(ii) 'Look at the word "to think" as a tool': cf. §421.

SECTION 361

1   This probes deeper the observation of §360 that we say only of a
human being and what is like one that it thinks. *If* someone were to say
that the chair is thinking to itself, we would wonder *where* it is thinking.
And that is highly significant, for when we are told that a human being is
talking to himself, we do *not* wonder where he is doing this (save,
trivially, where he is when he is doing it). Why does the question of
where the chair is talking to itself seem to demand an answer? Precisely
because if the contention that the chair is talking to itself is to make even
remote sense, we need to bring the chair within the ambit of the human
form, as it were. We must see it as a potential agent that could manifest
thought in action and expression. So, in a Disney film in which chairs are
animated, they have faces and mouths. Here, if we are told that the
armchair said something to itself, the question of where it did so would
not arise.

§361(c) belongs together with §362. One wonders, when doing
philosophy, what it is like to say something to oneself. It seems as if the
answer lies in careful introspection, careful observation in one's own case
of what happens when one says something to oneself in the imagination.
But, of course, that is not so at all. For typically, nothing *goes on*, save
that I said to myself that . . .; or if anything *else* goes on, it is irrelevant.
So to explain what it is *like* to say something to oneself is not to describe
an 'inner' event or process, but rather to explain the circumstances in
which one uses the expression – as, indeed, when one explains the
meaning of the expression. (The only thing that 'goes on', one might
say, is that one does *not* say anything aloud for a moment, as one reflects
and says to oneself that . . .)

1   (i) 'im Innern': 'inwardly', i.e. in his imagination.
(ii) 'What is it like to say something to oneself?': W. does not explore
here the contours of the concept of saying things to oneself (cf.
'Thinking: the soul of language, §2); he is concerned primarily with the
point that it is not a concept of *an experience*. One does not teach someone
what 'saying something to oneself' means by directing his attention to an
experience.
(iii) 'was da vorgeht': since this alludes to 'was geht da vor' in the first
sentence of (c), it should be similarly translated.

2   This derives from MS. 165, 204 and 211f., but its remote ancestor is
Vol. XII, 227ff. Apropos the private linguist who keeps a diary of his
experiences, it is noteworthy that it is not wholly clear what is meant if
one says that when he reads his diary, certain images come before his
mind. So is it a mistake to talk, without more ado, of the private linguist

as having, or as *perhaps* having, mental images? W. takes a round-about route. One cannot assume, without more ado, that a table has mental images. If that is because one does not assume that it has a mind, then why not assume that it does? It is surely because there must be both body *and behaviour*, for it is action that is the criterion for whether a being has a mind. After all, if asked to entertain the thought that the table sees an image before it, one wouldn't rightly know what one was meant to suppose, how to apply the expression 'to have an image' to a table in this context. Why can one do so in the case of a human being? It is important that when we conceive of a human as having an image before his mind, we look at his face and demeanour, not at his feet or his stomach. Is that because we think the image is *in* his head? That is the metaphor we use; but look at its application!

So one cannot imagine a table's seeing or having an image ('with what part?' one might ask), but only a human being doing so. But then the *objection* to the private linguist's imagining things in association with his diary-entry collapses, for we *can* suppose that this man sees an image before him! Not so: for 'we *can* suppose that . . .' really amounts to the fact that this is a well-entrenched English sentence with a use, that we can *ordinarily* get around with it. But then ordinarily we never stop to wonder how states of mind, like having an image before one, *adhere* to people (and not to tables); rather, we make use of our expression. (Just as we pay our bills with banknotes and don't stare at them trying to see how their value adheres to them.) This is not because we aren't thinking, but because we *are* thinking, and our thought is not in a cramp!

One's qualms over talking of the private linguist's having mental images stem from not knowing how to apply the expression correctly in these (non-ordinary) circumstances; hence the feeling that one does not know how the images *adhere to* this person! But what mental imagery 'adheres to' is what a person *says* and *does*, i.e. to his actions.

2.1   'where': for a discussion of the location of thought, see BB 7f. and 'Thinking: methodological muddles and categorial confusions', §4.

Section 362

1   As with so many psychological terms, we are prone to think that we teach the meaning *indirectly*, as it were guiding the pupil by remote control until he homes in on the private experience which *is* speaking to oneself in the imagination. Then he can give himself a private ostensive definition! This illusion was exposed by the private language arguments. In this context the supposition would be doubly erroneous, since, in addition, speaking to oneself is not an experience.

.1   'without telling him directly': cf. BB 185; LPE 285f.; PI p. 194; Z §545, all of which discuss aspects of the direct/indirect contrast in relation to learning, teaching, and understanding psychological expressions. But 'indirect' makes *sense* only if it is *intelligible* that what is done indirectly be done directly.

CHAPTER 3

Imagination

(§§363 – 97)

INTRODUCTION

The tenth 'chapter' runs from §363 to §397, but there is no sharp break separating it from the previous discussion. §361(c) argued that the concept of saying something to oneself is not linked with 'what takes place' when one says something to oneself, and §362 emphasized that this concept is not acquired by engendering an inner happening which then functions as a sample for a private ostensive definition. §363 switches to the example of imagining, but the example is incidental to the point of the remark, and the subject of the imagination only gradually comes to the forefront of the discussion.

§363 is linked to previous remarks via the idea that imagining (or having a sensation) is something that *happens*, an inner event, which one then communicates to others by means of speech. W. focuses upon a misconception of communication that characterizes the philosophical tradition, a theme he has touched on earlier in the book (§§6, 304, 317). That picture distorts the diversity of the language-game of telling someone something and mischaracterizes it as the transference of something mental (the sense of one's words) from the mind of the speaker to the mind of the hearer.

§364 reverts to the opening move of §363, for it seems as if W. is denying that there are any mental processes. The interlocutor takes up an example which seems to refute W. decisively, viz. calculating in the imagination. Surely this is an inner process, exactly like the outer process of calculating on paper, only without paper! This W. disputes, and it seems as if he is denying that calculating in the head is real calculating. But, of course, it is real calculating-in-the-head (as opposed to pretending to calculate in the head), just as characters in a drama may play a real game of chess (as opposed to pretending, in the play, to be playing a game of chess (§365)). Calculating in the head is neither more nor less real than calculating aloud, but it is not a mental process corresponding to a physical process, as one physical process may correspond to another (§366). Such a correspondence can obtain only when it makes sense to talk of a method of projection from one process to another, but the mental image of a sign is not a *representation* of the sign imagined.

§§367 – 8 digress: we think of a mental image as an inner picture, but to describe one's mental image is not to describe something visible to oneself alone. It is rather to describe what one imagines, and that is altogether different from describing what one sees. The criterion for what a person imagines is what he says and does.

§369 reverts to the matter raised in §363 (viz. what happens when one imagines something) and focuses on the special case of calculating in the head. Clarifying what is called 'calculating in the head' cannot be done by explaining that one adds one number to another, etc., *in one's head*. The correct method of conceptual clarification of concepts of the imagination is to describe how the word 'imagination' (or 'doing such-and-such in the head') is used (§370). This looks as if it bypasses the philosophical concern with the nature or essence of the imagination in favour of mere lexicography, but it does not. §§371 – 3 briefly pursue this issue: essence is expressed by grammar, and an investigation into the essential nature of this or that *is* a grammatical one. §374 picks up the methodological remark in §370: the claim that one cannot explain what images are by pointing (even in one's own case) or by describing what happens when one imagines something makes it sound as if there is something one cannot do, viz. display one's mental images (whereas in fact one is pushing against the bounds of sense). The best therapy here is to yield to the temptation to use the picture of a private object off which one reads a description and to investigate its application. Then it will become clear that it is incoherent.

A tree-diagram of the structure of Part A (§§363–74) is given on the next page:

The structure of Part A:

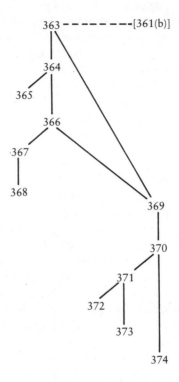

Part B (§§375 – 82) examines features of the conception of a 'private object' from which one derives a description. §375 opens the discussion with the old example of reading to oneself (cf. §156). One can teach someone to read to himself only if he can read; and one says that he can read to himself only if he can say what is written on the page he purports to have read. But he does not derive a description of what he has read to himself from scrutiny of the 'inner process' of reading to himself. §376 switches to the example of saying something to oneself (cf. §§361 – 2): what is the criterion of identity for two people to say the same thing to themselves or to have the same image? No inductive correlation with laryngal or brain-processes is possible in the absence of a non-inductive criterion. §§377 – 8 explore the question of the criterion of identity for mental images. In the first-person case no criterion at all is employed, either for characterizing one's mental image or for its identity with another's image (or a previous image one had oneself). One's avowal and behaviour, however, are public criteria for third-person statements about mental images and their identity. It is tempting to suppose that an avowal is justified by reference to one's recognition of the image one has. This futile manoeuvre is examined in §§379 – 82. Recognition presupposes the intelligibility of misrecognition. It only makes sense to speak of recognizing something *as* such-and-such if what is recognized can be picked out in some other way. It is unintelligible to interpose a 'process of recognition' between an experience and its expression, for then the question of how one identifies the process of recognition would, absurdly, arise. One is tempted to invoke a private ostensive definition as a rule to guide one in characterizing one's experience, but that is unintelligible. The ability to say what colour one has in view involves mastery of the technique of using colour-words, but rests on no grounds (§§380 – 1). Equally, the ability to say what colour one is imagining rests on no grounds, although, of course, it is parasitic upon mastery of the public vocabulary of colours (§382).

The structure of Part B:

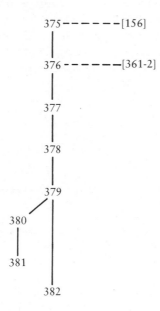

Part C (§§383 – 9) reverts to the theme of mental concepts and their analysis. §383 picks up the methodological remark of §370 and wards off a further misunderstanding. It may appear as if W. is propounding a form of nominalism and so denying that there are essences; but nominalism interprets all words as names and fails to describe their use – which is what is necessary for the clarification of a concept and hence for elucidation of an essential nature. §384 reminds us that describing the use

of a word does not fall short of clarifying the concept it expresses. §385
resumes the discussion of §369 concerning calculating in the head. The
concept of calculating in the head is parasitic upon the concept of
calculating, and the criteria for calculating in the head are internally
related to the criteria for calculating. §386 raises a worry parallel to that
of §364: there it was queried whether, on W.'s account, calculating in the
head is really calculating; now the interlocutor misinterprets W'.s qualms
about the relation between the concepts of calculating and calculating in
the head as qualms about whether he might not be mistaken in thinking
that he calculates in the head. But this mislocates his qualms, which arise
precisely because such doubts are excluded by *grammar*, not by the
unmistakable similarity between images and what they are images of.
§387 is an aside; §388 explores the correct observation that someone who
has mastered the colour-vocabulary knows that he can pick out a given
colour on sight. That capacity does not rest on having a mental image
which one compares with the colour one sees. §389 concludes the
discussion by locating a source of confusion in the thought that an image
of X is a super-likeness of X (it looks so like X that one *cannot* mistake it
for anything else!). But this confuses the absence of recognition or
identification in the case of one's avowal of what image one has with the
presence of an unmistakable criterion of similarity.

The structure of Part C:

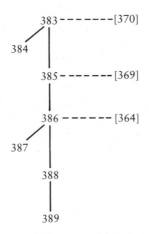

Part D (§§390 – 7) is concerned with the relation between imaginability and the bounds of sense. For someone to imagine something and for
what he imagines to make sense (as Lewis Carroll's imaginings deliberately do not), it must be possible to give an account of what it would be
for things to be as he imagines. Hence someone who insists that he can

imagine stones being conscious can be dismissed, in the light of §§281 and 284, as indulging in nonsensical image-mongery (§390). §391 gives a contrasting example: one can imagine people in the street being in frightful pain, but concealing it. However, merely saying so does not suffice. And attributing pain to the mind, i.e. something which is conceived as having no essential connection with the body, merely compounds the confusion. Rather, one must fill in a story, imagine artful concealment, etc. Then one can be said to be imagining this. §392 cautions against an error: that I imagine this or that is not a matter of *what goes on in me* but of the story I tell. §393 emphasizes that one can imagine (it makes sense to imagine) pain without pain-behaviour; but even here it would be wrong to suppose that a *picture* or *paradigm* of pain is involved (cf. §300). This becomes clear when one reminds oneself of natural contexts in which one might tell someone to imagine something. What goes on in his mind is irrelevant to whether he does imagine what we tell him to. That would be relevant only to empirical investigations into the heuristics of the imagination and the accompaniments of imagining (§394). §§395 – 7 conclude the investigation by emphasizing the shaky relation between imaginability and sense. That one cannot imagine anything in connection with a certain proposition does not mean that one does not understand it (§396), and that one can imagine something in such a case does not necessarily indicate the use of the sentence in question, for in some cases what one imagines is simply the expression of a misleading picture.

The structure of Part D:

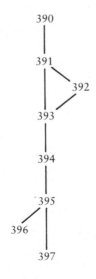

Correlations

PI§	PPI(I)§	MS. 129	MS. 124	MS. 165	Vol. XII	Others
363	278	49–50	262–3[1]; 280[2]	127–8[2]		
364	279–80	74–5	247–9			
365	281	75				
366	282	75–6	250–1			
367					207	MS. 164, 166
368						MS. 162(b), 97–8
369	283	76–7				
370					319	
371					340	
372						Vol. VI, 144; Vol. X, 157
373					340	
374					243–4	Vol. XVI, 134
375		125	281	131		
376					242	
377		115–16	281[3]	131[4]		MS. 180(a), 66[5]
378		118–19				MS. 180(a), 65–6
379		119				MS. 180(a), 71
380		116–18; 182				MS. 180(a), 65[6]; 71[7]; 74[8]
381		179–80				MS. 180(a), 68
382					120	Vol. V, 199[9]
383	284	190–1				
384		114–15	284	150		
385	285	77	252			
386(a)	286	77–9	272–4			MS. 179, 41
387	286[10]	79	273			
388					27	
389					28	
390		90		59		
391	288	13–14		53		
392	289	14				
393	290	14–15; 80–1; 131–2		54		MS. 179, 61–2
394	291	80–1; 132		54–5		
395	292	16				MS. 179, 63
396		194				
397	no known source					

[1] PI §363(b) only.
[2] PI §363(a) only.
[3] PI §377(a) and first sentence of (b) only.
[4] Only last sentence of PI §376 and first sentence of PI §377(b).
[5] PI §377(b) only.
[6] PI §380(b) only.
[7] PI §380(a) only.
[8] PI §380(c) only.
[9] PI §382(b) only.
[10] Two remarks have the same number in TS.

IMAGES AND THE IMAGINATION

1. *Landmarks*

The family of concepts constituted by 'imagine' and such cognates as 'imaginary', 'image', 'imaginative', 'imaginable' is difficult to survey. Their contours merge imperceptibly here and there with those of the adjacent psychological concepts of thought and conception, perception and illusion, creativity and invention. The application of the concepts of the imagination is, like that of many other psychological concepts (e.g. understanding, thinking, feeling), heterogeneous. The natural philosophical impulse towards generalization and imposition of unity upon diversity, however, drives us to raise such questions as 'What is the hallmark of the imagination?', 'What does imagining consist in?', 'What is the process of imagining?' These questions invite oversimplification and mystification, and lead us astray from the very start.

Striving to find a simple characterization of the essence of the imagination, philosophers have argued that it consists in the power to call up before the mind mental images, either in recollection and recognition (the reproductive imagination) or in fancy (the productive imagination). These images, sometimes thought to be or to be constructed from faint copies of perceptual impressions, are (mysteriously) deposited in cold storage in the mind, the 'storehouse of ideas' as Locke put it. In more modern vein, it has been argued that imagining consists in the production and combination of 'mental representations', or that the raw material of all imaginings consists of 'reproductions' of visual, auditory, tactual, etc. experiences that one has previously had. It is then tempting to think that such 'mental representations' or images constitute private objects of comparison that guide us in our use of words.

Approaching the philosophical – i.e. conceptual (grammatical) – questions about the imagination from this vantage-point obscures one's view of the manifold facets of the imagination and leads to multiple distortions and oversimplifications. First, one will be prone to overlook grammatical facts. Many licit uses of 'imagine' fail to conform to the conception of the imagination as a kaleidoscopic faculty for combining images or 'representations'. That Columbus imagined he had reached the Indies does not imply that he had any mental images or representations of the Indies. That I can well imagine flying to New York does not mean that I must have flown there or elsewhere before or that I see myself in my mind's eye in a 747. That I can imagine N's delight (disappointment, surprise, embarrassment) at such-and-such news does not mean the same

as being able vividly to imagine N's look of delight (etc.). It makes
perfectly good sense to imagine much which it makes scant sense to
picture to oneself, e.g. Queen Victoria's last thoughts, traditional virtues
ceasing to be valued, new philosophical questions or confusions. Awareness of this typically leads philosophers to claim that there are multiple
different senses of 'to imagine'. For to believe falsely (as Columbus did)
is not an exercise of the faculty of the imagination, and the creative
exercise of the imagination does not necessarily involve any mental
imagery. The tie-up between *image*, *imagine*, and *imagination* is doubtless
complex, although it is not obvious that one must conclude that there are
many different concepts of imagining.

   Secondly, philosophers are also prone to delineate the limits of the
imagination in ways that are highly questionable. One cannot, it is
sometimes argued, imagine something which one has not experienced or
which is not decomposable into what one has experienced.[1] After all, it is
rightly said, the congenitally blind cannot imagine the appearance of a
bowl of flowers and the congenitally deaf cannot imagine the sound of a
symphony. But must one explain this by reference to the supposition
that their storehouse of ideas or neural repository of mental representations is inadequately equipped? Similarly, it has been argued that since
the building-blocks of the imagination are experiences or their 'copies',
nobody can imagine anything which does not essentially involve his
experiencing something (e.g. being dead or asleep). Such suggestions
arguably draw the limits of the imagination too narrowly. (It is
improbable that Richard III could not have imagined being murdered in
his sleep; but if it is true, it would have been due to lack of imagination,
not to *logic*!) On the other hand, to claim that one can imagine being
Napoleon or a bat arguably draws the boundaries too generously. I may
be able to imagine what Napoleon thought or felt, and if I can do so, I
may be able to *act* the role of Napoleon (like Charles Boyer) all the better.
We also say, quite unproblematically, 'The disposition of forces at 11.30
a.m. at Waterloo was thus. Now, imagine you are Napoleon! What
would you do?' Here one is invited to reflect on what one would do
when faced by the options and predicaments that confronted Napoleon.
But, this usage apart, is there anything else that can be understood by the
order 'Imagine you were Napoleon (or a bat)!' What would it be for me
to be Napoleon? If it does not make *sense* for *me* to be Napoleon (or a
bat), does it make sense to imagine it? Is this any less absurd that
imagining my clock's being a symphony, as opposed to its being a
Tompion? For if it does not make sense, then there is nothing to imagine!
Yet some people actually think, or believe, that they are Napoleon. Of
course – but they are *mad*. Some lunatics think that they are pens (as in

---

[1] For Wittgenstein's ironic response to this conception, see Exg. §289, 2.

Peer Gynt). Is it so obvious that we understand what it is that they think? One might object that one can surely imagine what does not make sense – witness Lewis Carroll or much of science fiction! These are indeed nonsense. But there is nonsense and nonsense, some of it very entertaining. So one might say that to the extent that nonsense can be understood, to that extent it can be imagined.

Thirdly, and consequently, the boundary-lines between empirical and conceptual investigations are characteristically blurred. Investigations into the limits of the imaginable begin to look misleadingly like a curious kind of physics of the mind. One *cannot* imagine such-and-such, it is held, *because* one has not experienced anything like it, or *because* the building-blocks of the imagination are images, ideas, or representations. But one should query what this 'cannot' signifies. Are such claims meant to be empirical? Surely not, for then it would be at any rate logically possible, conceivable (imaginable?), that things be otherwise. Are they then non-empirical claims? If so, whence their necessitarian status? To attribute these alleged constraints to the 'essential nature of the mind' is to reproduce the very question in the guise of an answer. Whatever conceptual constraints there are upon the imagination are *conceptual* constraints, i.e. constraints laid down in our norms of representation, in what it makes *sense* to say and what it does *not* make sense to say. The conceptual limits of the imagination are the contour-lines, whether sharp or blurred, of the *grammar* of 'image', of the combinatorial possibilities of 'imagine' and its cognates which have a use in our language and for which we acknowledge certain explanations as correct explanations of meaning the giving of which constitute criteria of understanding.

Finally, we are prone to introduce questions about meaning in the form of questions about existence. There are heated debates among philosophers and psychologists alike over whether there really are such things as mental images, some insisting that there are, since they actually have them, others denying this, since 'introspection' in their own case reveals none. It is often held to be a simple fact of experience that certain people have mental images and others do not. But what is it the existence of which is being affirmed or denied? Does it make sense for psychologists to seek experimental confirmation for the existence of mental imagery in psychological laboratory tests? Should mental images be treated as theoretical constructs which must be 'postulated' as information-bearing structures, or 'data-structures', in the brain the existence of which would explain human behaviour? The dispute is not unlike classical debates over the existence of universals or continuing disputes over whether colours 'exist objectively'. The first question is not whether mental images exist, but rather what it means to say that someone has a vivid mental image of such-and-such and what the criteria are for having a mental image of something. Only when we have clarified what it would be for someone to have a mental image of something can we turn to the question of whether anyone does. And it might be hoped that the clarification of the first question will render the second as trivial as the question of whether any objects have shapes (or, for that matter, colours!).

The correct path through this morass was indicated by Wittgenstein:

> One ought to ask, not what images are or what happens when one imagines anything, but how the word 'imagination' is used. But that does not mean that I want to talk only about words. For the question as to the nature of the imagination is as much about the word 'imagination' as my question is. And I am only saying that this question is not to be decided, neither for the person who does the imagining, nor for anyone else – by pointing; nor yet by a description of any process. The first question also asks for a word to be explained; but it makes us expect a wrong kind of answer. (PI §370)

This is the route that will be followed in this essay. Before turning to the salient themes that preoccupied Wittgenstein, however, it is worth plotting some of the landmarks in the (English) terrain as a background against which to examine his observations. For not only is it difficult to 'look and see' how 'imagine' is used, especially if one thinks that one already has a clear picture of such a 'trivial' matter, but the temptation to tamper with the linguistic facts, the rules of grammar, is great:

> Mere description is so difficult because one believes that one needs to fill out the facts in order to understand them. It is as if one saw a screen with scattered colour-patches, and said: the way they are here, they are unintelligible; they only make sense when one completes them into a shape. – Whereas I want to say: Here *is* the whole. (If you complete it, you falsify it.) (RPP I §257)

The half-a-dozen foci of attention in this discussion are not the ground floor of a theory of the imagination, but rather poles of a description of grammar (cf. RPP I §633). One feature or aspect of the use of 'imagine', 'imagination', etc. is not offered as an explanation or justification of another; but there are multiple connections between them, some of which will be described. It should be noted that the grammatical web of 'imagine' and its cognates differs from that of the German 'vorstellen'. Hence, when we turn, in the next section, to examine Wittgenstein's remarks on the imagination, some strands in the network, e.g. the connection between 'imagine' and 'imaginative', will not be in view.

First, the concept of imagination is associated with the concept of a mental image. We are all familiar with the phenomenon of a tune 'running through one's head', and we commonly use such phrases as 'I can still hear his tone of surprise', 'I can readily call her face to mind', or 'I can visualize exactly what it should look like'. Hence we talk of visual, and sometimes of auditory, images, which may be vivid and clear or faint and obscure. The expression 'mental image' is, however, philosophically misleading, for it is constructed on the model of 'physical image' (cf. LW §442), i.e. a perceptible likeness (whether manufactured or natural), representation, or imitation of an actual or imagined form. A 'graven image' is a statue or bas-relief; a painted image is a figure in a painting. We also speak of a reflected image of an object in a mirror, and metonymically scientists speak of a pattern of light irradiation as 'an image'. Similarly, we refer to a counterpart, facsimile, or copy as 'an image', as when we say that a son is the very image of his father or that man is made in the image of God. It is all too easy to think of a mental image as a species of the genus *image*, i.e. 'just like a physical image, only mental'. This is no more illuminating than referring to the square roots of negative integers as being just like real numbers, only imaginary. The use of 'mental image' is no more closely related to that of 'physical image' than is the use of 'number' to that of 'numeral' (cf. LW §442). It is similarly misguided to think, as Hume and many after him did, that a mental image is a faint *copy* of a sense-impression.

Secondly, imagination is connected in *various* ways with perception. Although the august role given to the imagination by Hume and Kant in their very different accounts of perception and perceptual recognition of objects is arguably a case of miscasting, it is indisputable that it takes imagination to see or hear certain kinds of resemblances, forms of connectedness, or patterns of relationships. It takes imagination, for example, to hear a piece of music as a variation on a particular theme (PI p. 213); or to see certain kinds of 'quotations' in paintings, e.g. Michelangelo's *Isaiah* in Reynolds's *Mrs Siddons as the Tragic Muse*; or to see Marcel Marceau's Bip skating and skipping on ice where there is no ice in view and no skates to see. Although we can vividly imagine things disconnected from the physical space around us, e.g. call to mind the face of a childhood love or conjure up a vivid image of a long-vanished scene, we can also imagine things essentially connected with what we currently perceive. Here Leonardo's famous advice to painters is an apt reminder:

I cannot forbear to mention among these precepts a new device for study which, although it may seem but trivial and almost ludicrous, is nevertheless extremely useful in arousing the mind to various inventions. And this is, when you look at a wall spotted with various stains, or with a mixture of stones, if you have to devise some scene, you may discover a resemblance to various landscapes beautified with mountains, rivers, rocks, trees, plains, wide valleys and hills in varied arrangement; or, again you may see battles and figures in action; or strange faces and costumes, and an endless variety of objects, which you could reduce to complete and well-drawn forms. And these appear on such walls confusedly, like the sound of bells in whose jangle you may find any name or word you choose to imagine.[2]

---

[2] Leonardo de Vinci, *Trattato della Pittura*, §508.

When we engage in such exercises of fantasy, we *see* the stain marks on the wall as hills and valleys, the cracks perhaps as winding paths or rivers, the crumbling plaster maybe as figures in a landscape. Hence too, it should not be surprising to find Wittgenstein connecting the concept of imagination with the capacity to *see aspects*, to see the duck-rabbit now as a duck, now as a rabbit, or to see a triangular figure as an object that has fallen over (PI p. 207).

Thirdly, the faculty of imagination is associated with artistic creativity and no less so with intellectual creativity, with originality, insight, and deviation from stock solutions to problems. The great painter, architect, or landscape-gardener is credited with outstanding visual imagination. Though this may be connected with his power to visualise things vividly, note that it does not *follow* that before he produces his highly imaginative frescoes, buildings, or gardens, he *must* first have vivid visual images of what they should look like, let alone that he *copies* these. His powerful imagination is visible in the spontaneity, originality, etc., of his product, not invisible in his mind, and it is exercised in its production and not in what precedes it in his mind's eye. Still less does our correctly crediting a Shakespeare or a Tolstoy with extraordinary imaginative powers, an ability to visualize a scene vividly, involve necessarily attributing to them vivid mental imagery. The creation of great fiction or great poetry needs imagination, but the only imagery it *requires* is verbal. Telling a good story needs imagination, but one may make it up as one goes along, rather than rehearsing it in advance in the imagination. Even less essentially connected with images is the employment of imagination in the solution of purely intellectual problems, e.g. in mathematics or philosophy itself. The power of intellectual insight, the capacity to see or create fresh analogies and intermediate cases, to find illuminating connections between *prima facie* unconnected phenomena, all these are no less exercises of the imagination than the creations of fiction or the visual arts.

Fourthly, 'to imagine' is connected not only with intellectual creativity, but also more generally with thought, conception, or supposition. For short stretches the concepts of imagination run cheek by jowl with these adjacent concepts, even though they diverge elsewhere. A bridge of well-imagined construction is well-thought-out, just as Gilbert Scott's frequently ill-imagined additions to medieval buildings are ill-conceived. A mind so noble as to be unable to imagine things contemptible cannot conceive of acting dishonourably. The nexus of 'imagine' with supposition is evident in such sentences as 'He never imagined that he could surpass them all', 'The town was further away than he had imagined', 'One would imagine it impossible that any creature could survive an Arctic winter'. Of course, that such sentences, in an appropriate context, might be paraphrased in terms of 'suppose' ('guess' or 'suspect') does not show that the expressions are *everywhere* interchangeable. The imagination is a faculty, but there is no faculty for supposition, any more than there are powers or skills of supposition. From the fact that one cannot imagine something, it does not follow that one cannot suppose it. One can vividly imagine but not vividly suppose, and one can imagine but not suppose the consequences of a supposition.

Fifthly, 'to imagine' is associated with false belief, mistaken memory, and misperception. We may imagine ourselves half-way to our destination when we have barely covered a quarter of the distance. Suddenly, we may think we see a friend in the crowd, only to realize on closer scrutiny that we merely imagined this. And so too, we may claim to remember having done this or that or having seen or heard such and such, only to be told that we are imagining things. Note that someone given to false beliefs, to making erroneous memory-claims, or to misperception is *not* said to be exercising his powers of imagination or to have a rich imagination (save ironically!). Such propensity to false beliefs is not conceived to be a feature of the imagination *qua* faculty, since as a faculty the imagination is not primarily concerned with literal truth and falsehood, but with invention, originality, and creativity. Whence then this connection between 'to imagine' and the false? Perhaps via the notion of the imaginary or fictitious as that which has no 'real existence', or (misleadingly) that which exists 'only in the imagination'. Also by reference to the relation between the concept of imagining and the concepts of finding and making up. What we imagine we make up. We find truths, but we make up lies. Furthermore, what we imagine we often think to be as we imagine it. And if we are wrong, then we are said to be *merely* imagining things, i.e. misconceiving or falsely believing. But note that while the imaginary is unreal, the imagined need not be. For things may be just as I imagine them to be.

Finally, the imagination is connected with make-believe, pretence, play-acting, or idle fancy. The actor imagines the character he is playing feeling this or meaning that, and how he imagines the character informs his acting. The child who can play happily alone with only a few blocks of wood to do service for bricks and yet builds castles in the air, who can ride his rocking-horse in the company of King Arthur and his knights, who can make an armchair into the cockpit of a Spitfire, is rightly said to be imaginative. But note that this imaginativeness *need* not be connected with originality, creativity, or insight. However, although imagination can contribute to successful pretence, one may be good at imagining, yet poor at pretending, because lacking the knack for acting or deceit. And conversely, many a charlatan has a poor imagination. It is mistaken to conceive of imagining as a kind of pretending (as Ryle did); for pretending, unlike imagining, is necessarily a performance. One must engage in some activity or perform certain actions as a means of pretending. Someone who is good at pretending is a good actor, for he must typically so behave that things seem to be as he pretends they are. Skill at imagining is not a skill in acting but in conceiving or envisaging. One can pretend without for one moment imagining that things are as one pretends them to be; and when one imagines something, one does not normally engage in any pretence. Confidence tricksters pretend, artists, writers, and neurotics imagine. Pretending is often deceitful, sometimes convincing and difficult to see through. Imagining may be clear, correct, or accurate. One can make mistakes when one imagines how things are, since one can imagine that things are so-and-so and also think (rightly or wrongly) that they are. But one cannot pretend that things are so if one actually thinks they are.

Wittgenstein's interest in the imagination focused upon six interrelated themes: (a) the relationships between seeing, imagining, and having visual (mental) images (*Vorstellungsbilder*[3]); (b) the analogies and disanalogies between mental images and pictures; (c) the similarities and differences between mental images and sense-impressions, including hallucinations; (d) the 'voluntariness' of the imagination and the relationship between a mental image and what it is an image of; (e) the irrelevance of mental imagery to meaning and understanding utterances (see Exg. §§390–7); (f) the connection between the imagination, perception, and the seeing of aspects. The latter theme, dealt with in *Investigations*, Part II, is too extensive to be discussed here.[4]

2. Seeing, imagining, and mental images

'The tie-up between imagining (*Vorstellen*) and seeing is close; but there is no similarity' (RPP II §70). The concepts of sense-perception in general and of vision in particular are used in the *expression* of our imaginings; we say that we *hear* speech or melodies in our imagination and that we *see* the faces of distant friends when we call them up before the mind's eye (cf. RPP I §885[5]). But though perceptual concepts are used here, they are used *differently*. What is or can be perceived can also intelligibly be imagined, and can also be imagined as being perceived (though these are

---

[3] It should be noted that the German 'die Vorstellung', 'eine Vorstellung', or 'Vorstellungen' are not always readily translated into English (see Exg. §300, 1). A very large number of the remarks on the imagination in RPP I and II and LW (sometimes perhaps unavoidably) are mistranslated (e.g. RPP II §§64f., 69f., 72, 75, 77f., 80, 82f., 88, 93, 110f., 116, 119 – 21, 125, 130f., 138f., 141f., 145). I am indebted here and elsewhere to A. R. White's writings on the imagination.

[4] A further issue that briefly concerned him is the connection between the imaginable and the logically possible, cf. Exg. §251.

[5] Here Wittgenstein remarks that it is *essential* to imagining that concepts of sense-perception are employed in its expression. It would be wrong to suggest, however, that whenever we imagine X, we imagine perceiving X.

different in important ways), but, nevertheless, much can be imagined that cannot intelligibly be perceived (e.g. A's having a right to appoint his successor or a number which is the sum of its prime factors). The same *description* can represent both what one sees and, in a different context, what one imagines (RPP II §69), but these identical descriptions are differently used, are embedded in very different language-games. What it makes sense to say in response to someone's giving such a description in one language-game (e.g. 'Are you sure?' 'Did you look again, more closely?' 'Did anyone else see?' 'Might you not have made a mistake?') makes no sense in the other. Bits of one language-game resemble bits of the other, but the bits which resemble each other are not homologous (RPP II §139). We must distinguish the phenomena of perceiving (and seeing in particular) from the phenomena of imagining (and visualizing or having visual images), as well as distinguishing the *concepts* of seeing from the concepts of (visually) imagining (RPP II §130).

The differences between the observable phenomena of seeing and of imagining are manifest in the difference in the criteria that justify saying of someone that he sees a house and the criteria that justify saying that he imagines a house. The faculty of vision is exercised by the use of the eyes in appropriate conditions of visibility. One who sees can find his way around his environment by using his eyes, can follow moving objects with his eyes. Hence seeing is conceptually bound up with looking, watching, observing, or scrutinizing what is publicly visible to others. One can observe a sighted person *trying* to see something, or trying to see it better, by looking over there↗, moving closer to get a better view, straining his eyes by screwing them up. By contrast, one who imagines something may imagine it in darkness no less than in light, with his eyes closed (save in 'Leonardesque' types of cases) or simply staring blankly into space (RPP II §134). Indeed, one may try to imagine more *clearly* by *closing* one's eyes (RPP II §§72, 77). One does not *observe* one's mental images when one visually imagines things (RPP II §885) or look at them more closely, although one may imagine seeing those things from closer to. What a person sees is, *ceteris paribus*, visible to others, and that he sees what is thus visible is evident in his reactions to it (including what he says). What a person imagines and how he imagines it is visible neither to himself nor to others, unless he displays or manifests it in drawing or mime. The criteria for what he imagines are what he sincerely says he imagines, what he draws or enacts in explaining what or how he imagines.

Hence the concept of the visual imagination is bound up with other psychological concepts quite differently from that of vision. One can *overlook* features of what one sees, look more closely and *notice* things one had not seen before. One cannot overlook features of what one imagines, any more than one can overlook (as opposed to forget) an aspect of (as opposed to a consequence of) what one intends. It makes no sense to notice or fail to notice an aspect of one's vivid visual image of a scene, for one does not observe it.[6] Looking informs us about objects in our environment; but imagining gives us no information, either right or wrong, about how things are (RPP II §63), even though things may turn out as we imagined they would. Imagining, unlike looking, is not a way of finding out how things are. Verbs of perception have a use as success-verbs: if A sees a tree in the quad, then there is a tree in the quad; but if he imagines a tree in the quad, it does not follow that there is one there. One cannot order someone to stop *seeing* what is before his eyes, only to stop looking at it; but one can order someone to stop imagining (or day-dreaming about) this or that and to get on with his work. One can cease to look at an object, but one cannot 'banish' one's visual impressions of an object while one is looking at it. By contrast, it *makes sense* to talk of 'banishing' or trying to 'banish' one's mental images (one shakes one's head, ceases to stare into space, and concentrates on the task at hand), even though they sometimes recur obsessively (RPP II §§89ff.). One may be surprised at what one sees, and a look of delight may spread over one's face, but one is no more *surprised* at the visual images that cross one's mind (RPP II §88) than at one's own intentions, although one may be pleased at the ideas that thus occur to one, and *others* may be surprised at what one imagines. When looking at a luminous object, one may be dazzled or blinded by the light it emits, and look away or shield one's eyes. While one can imagine dazzling objects or imagine being blinded by them, one's vivid mental images of a dazzling object do not bedazzle one and there is no such thing as being blinded by an imagined object. While it makes no sense for me to see something differently from how it appears to me (although I can *try* to see a double-aspect figure differently from how it *now* appears to me), I can certainly imagine something's being different from how it appears to me. Wittgenstein invites us to compare and contrast teaching someone to obey the order

---

[6] A. R. Luria in *The Mind of the Mnemonist* (Penguin, Harmondsworth, 1968) relates how the mnemonist explained an error in his mnemonic performance. The performance consisted in manifesting his ability to recollect a large number of random objects called out by his audience. His mnemonic device was to imagine himself walking down a street in St Petersburg, and as each object was called out, he would imagine himself placing it at a particular position in the imagined stret. (The device is a variation upon an ancient one; cf. Frances Yates, *The Art of Memory* (Routledge and Kegan Paul, London, 1966).) When the audience had finished, he would recall the objects named by imagining himself walking down the street again, and would, as it were, read off the list of objects from his imagined scene. On one occasion he forgot an item, viz. a milk bottle. He explained this by claiming that he had imagined putting the bottle of milk in front of a white door, so that when he imagined walking down the street again, itemizing the objects in question, he did not *notice* the milk bottle against the white door! This makes *no sense*. (What would be the criteria for its *being there*, even though he did not 'notice' it?)

'Look!' with teaching them to obey the order 'Imagine!' These language-games must be taught quite differently (RPP II §139); they are played in altogether different contexts, for reflect when in real life we tell someone to imagine something! An actor may be having difficulty in interpreting the role he is playing, so the director may say 'Imagine Lear at this point being both hurt and furious, but determined not to reveal his feelings; and now speak the lines'; or, in narrating a series of events, we may say 'Can you imagine what would have happened if he hadn't done that?'; or, while choosing upholstery mateial, we may say 'Try to visualize the room! Will this colour go with the colours of the carpet?' Reactions and responses which belong to the language-games with 'Look!' do not belong to the language-games with 'Imagine!' or 'Visualize!' and the criteria for having complied in the one case are very different from those in the other. Imagining, unlike perceiving, is more akin to a creative, not a receptive, act (RPP I §111); and visualizing something is more closely akin to depicting than it is to seeing (cf. RPP II §115). It is comparable to an *activity* (RPP II §88), although this too can be misleading (RPP II §80).

The visual idiom dominates our discourse about the imagination. We talk of seeing things *in* (not 'with') our mind's eye, of visualizing or picturing things to ourselves.[7] We speak of visual images, perhaps of auditory ones, but not (in English) of gustatory or olfactory ones, although one can, of course, imagine tastes and smells. Those with the requisite facility draw things 'from the imagination' and not just what they currently see, and those who cannot draw can nevertheless describe how they visualize things. It is an interesting question, which Wittgenstein raised (RPP II §§66, 144), whether there could be people who could draw 'from the imagination' or from memory, describe vividly how something looked or how they envisage something, and accompany these performances, as we do, by first staring into space or closing their eyes, exclaiming 'Ah, now I know what it is like', etc., but *not* use the visual idiom, finding such expressions as 'I see him vividly before me' wholly inappropriate. Indeed, he added, the really important question is whether this question itself *makes sense* (RPP II §144). For are these forms of behaviour not precisely the criteria for saying of *us* that we form visual images of things, visualize things clearly or vaguely, see things in our mind's eye?

3. *Images and pictures*

The multitude of grammatical similarities between the visual imagination and visual perception is immensely deceptive. It inclines us to think

---

[7] Curiously, we do not speak of hearing things *in* (or *with*) the *mind's ear*, although we speak of hearing things 'in our head'. And, to be sure, there is no smelling things in the mind's nose!

of the 'inner picture' as differing from the 'outer picture' primarily in being private, as if the visual image were like a picture locked away in a room to which only the owner has the key. While it is true that in part of their uses 'visual image' and 'picture' run parallel, the concepts are very different. But the analogy which does exist tends to delude us (LPE 285). One must bear in mind that speaking of mental images as 'pictures in the mind' is only a metaphor (PR 82). It makes *sense* to see a picture and the object of which it is a picture (if it portrays an actual object or scene) juxtaposed; but there is no such thing as seeing a mental image of something actual juxtaposed with that of which it is an image. Hence too, the method of *comparison* of a picture (portrait) and what it is a picture of is altogether different from the relation between a visual image and what it is an image of. 'The room is quite different from how I imagined (visualized) it,' I may say, and I can tell you how – but not by comparing the room I see with my visual image of it (as I might compare the room with a picture of the room). Indeed, one cannot visualize – there is no such thing as visualizing – the room as it is,[8] any more than one can have a hallucination of it, *while* one is looking at it (cf. RPP II §63),[9] although I can say how I visualized it and how it differs from the way I imagined it as being.

One can imagine things which actually exist or things 'purely imaginary'. One can imagine existing things which one has previously perceived (as when one conjures up an image of an absent friend or childhood scene) or which one has only heard about. One can imagine fictitious things (the Olympian gods) and things which are as yet non-existent, but are to be made – as an architect imagines a building he is planning. In all cases of imagining what is depictable, there are obviously connections between the concept of a visual image that one conjures up when visualizing things and the concept of a picture. If asked 'What are you imagining?' one can sometimes (given the appropriate facility) give one's questioner a rough idea of what one is imagining by drawing a picture (PI §280; RPP II §63). But one does not *copy* one's visual image as one can copy a painting. A copy *reproduces* its original, but to reproduce one's visual image, if it means anything, would be to imagine or visualize *again* what one imagined previously.

Can one *draw* one's visual image? Certainly not as a *plein air* artist draws (but does not *copy*) the visible scene before his eyes. But artists also draw 'from the imagination', paint historical scenes as they imagine them (which is not necessarily as they imagine they appeared), produce

---

[8] But, of course, I can look at it and visualize what it will look like when redecorated.
[9] Although I might, while talking to an elderly man, suddenly imagine that I am talking to N. N., and he may actually *be* N. N. – but then I must not *know* his identity.

mythological and allegorical paintings, genre paintings of imagined scenes, paintings of imaginary objects, and so forth. Can one say in these cases that the artist depicts *his mental images*? That would be gravely misleading. To be sure, the artist depicts *what he imagines*; but he does not imagine his mental images, he imagines what his mental images are images of. Drawing what one imagines can be said to be drawing one's mental images only in so far as drawing what one perceives can be said to be drawing one's perceptions or sketching what one glimpsed can be said to be sketching one's glimpses. The *plein air* artist draws what his perceptions are perceptions of, and what the artist who draws from the imagination draws is what he imagines. It is confusing to call this 'drawing one's mental image'. Of course, one can draw 'from the imagination' – indeed, draw imaginary objects (think of Bosch doodling) – without having any mental images at all; but one nevertheless draws what one imagines. Even if one does vividly visualize the imaginary scene one means to depict, what one paints is what one's vivid mental images are images *of*.

A form of words can be used to describe what one sees or to describe what one imagines. A (naturalistic) picture of what one sees can be judged a good or poor likeness by visual comparison with its subject. *That* ↗ (and one points to the scene or person portrayed) is what is depicted, and the picture is compared with *that* for verisimilitude. If I draw a picture of what I imagine, perhaps to explain to my stage-designer what I have in mind, I may say 'That ↗ is what I imagined' – but then I point at my sketch, not at my mental image. A sketch of how I imagine something does not *resemble* the visual image I might have in imagining it, for it makes no sense to say that the sketch *looks like* the mental image. It *represents* what I imagine, as do *my words*.

Of course, how I imagine X may be similar to or identical with how X is. One may match's one's imagination against reality in two ways, depending upon the direction of fit. One may imagine the Sistine Chapel vividly, and when one sees it, one may find that it is just as one imagined it to be, or, perhaps, far more splendid than one had envisaged. Here one imagined it rightly or wrongly. On the other hand, reality may be matched against what one imagined and be judged a more or less adequate *realization* of one's imagination. 'That is exactly how I imagined it', the director may say to his stage-designer who has made a set in accord with his instructions; or he may say 'I imagined the backcloth there a much deeper shade of green'. Here the relationship between the imagination and the artefact is akin to the relationship between an intention and its execution. Our judgement of match or mismatch (irrespective of direction of fit) is not like that of picture and pictured (which may fit either way too), for we compare the actuality with the person's *expression* of his imagination – with what he *says* or does in manifesting what he had in mind, not with his image (and this comparison is not a 'second best' either).

One may object that this account of the visual imagination and the actuality imagined, or the pictorial representation of what is imagined, is true for *others*, but not for the person who is imagining. Surely he *sees* the mental or visual image before his mind's eye! Hence *he* can judge whether something correctly *realizes* what he imagined (or only resembles it more or less adequately) and whether his sketch correctly *represents* what he imagined, not by comparing them with what he *says*, but by comparing them 'directly' with his mental image (cf. PI §280). This is confused; for when the director 'sees the set vividly before his mind's eye', he does not *see* a visual image, but rather vividly imagines the set as he intends it to be. He does not *know* how he imagines it by examining the visual image, which he can be said to *have*, and then reading off its features. For were that so, it would make sense to suppose that he might *err* and think that he imagines it thus, while really imagining it otherwise. But that makes no sense. His mental image does not *inform* him of what he has imagined, as the sketch he draws *or words he utters* may inform his stage-designer of what he has imagined. For were that so, it might misinform him, misrepresent what he imagines, and he might misunderstand what it tells him. But that too makes no sense. The 'inner picture', unlike the 'outer picture' which he might sketch, is not a representation of what he imagines (PI §280). And if he sketches a picture to represent what he imagines, he does not judge its adequacy *as* a representation by comparing it with a 'private image' (as an architect compares the finished edifice with his blueprint and elevations to assure himself of its adequacy), but rather as he judges what he says or writes to be an adequate expression of what he *thinks*. He imagines whatever he imagines, and says that *this* is indeed how he imagined things or that it is not quite right but approximates to what he had in mind. How does he know? He does not *know*; he *says* so, and what he says is decisive (cf. LW §811).

Because perceptual concepts and concepts of the perceptible play such a dominant role in the expression of our imaginings, we are prone to exaggerate the affinity of the imagination to perception and to overlook the extent to which and the manner in which thought suffuses the imagination. When a composer tells the musicians at a rehearsal that he had imagined *that* chord being played louder, that is not because it *sounded louder* in his imagination, any more than if I expected an explosion to be louder or thought that it would be louder, there was something louder in my expectation or thought (BB 40). Similarly, when a choreographer tells his dancers that he had imagined a particular *pas de deux* much faster than they danced it, that does not mean that they danced more quickly in his imagination. If someone insists that 'They danced more quickly in his imagination' just means the same as 'He imagined them dancing more quickly', then we should point out that what is important here is to note that it does not follow from 'They danced more quickly in his imagination' that they danced more quickly. And when people imagine a rotating figure, it does not make sense to try, as some experimental psychologists do, to measure the velocity of rotation.

Imagining is comparable to depicting in the following respect. One does not imagine whoever 'resembles' one's mental image, but rather one imagines whoever it is one *means* to imagine (RPP II §115), even though one may imagine him wrongly. Something parallel holds for paintings: the resemblance between Caravaggio's features and the features of the severed head of Goliath in his famous painting does *not* mean that the painting is not a painting of David holding the head of the Philistine, but is rather of David holding the head of Caravaggio! But there is this difference: that if I intend to paint a picture of M from memory and inadvertently paint a good likeness of N, it is doubtful whether the *portrait* could be said to be a poor portrait of M. Rather, one might say that I had meant to portray M, but, perhaps guided by unconscious forces, had produced a portrait of N (cf. RPP I §262). On the other hand, if I imagine how M looks and visualize him as having features that actually characterize N, not M, nevertheless the visual image I have is *of* M, not N – it is M whom I imagined, even though I can be said to have imagined him wrongly. Similarly, I can imagine a closed box, and I can draw a picture of a closed box, but a picture of a closed box could also represent several other things. For this configuration of lines on paper could represent a wire structure or three adjacent quadrilaterals, etc., hence it might need an interpretation. But a mental image does not, in that sense, consist of a configuration of lines; it is an internal property of my visual image of a closed box that it is *of* a closed box (LW §450).[10] A mental image is, as it were, all message and no medium – like a thought.

The idiom of 'picturing something to oneself' inclines one to think that visually imagining something is like giving oneself a picture of that thing. But this is misconceived (LSD 137), for we distinguish an object from a visual image of an object, and both of these from a picture of an object. Why should we say that when we visually imagine a robin, for example, we give ourselves a *picture* of a robin, rather than that we give ourselves a robin? For one can imagine (have a visual image of) a picture

---

[10] Wittgenstein compares this with knowledge in a dream (ibid.). I may dream that there is a desk in such-and-such a room, and, in the dream, I *know* that there is a book in the desk. Here it makes no sense to wonder whether I might not have been mistaken.

of a robin no less than one can imagine a robin, and these are by no means the same. If one objects that when one imagines a robin, one does not *really* 'give oneself' a robin, one may reply that that is obvious, but that, equally, one does not *really* 'give oneself' a picture of a robin either! To picture something to oneself is not to give oneself a kind of picture (viz. a 'mental' one).

'The "mental (visual) image" [*Vorstellungsbild*] does not enter the language-game in the place where one would like to surmise its presence' (RPP II §110). In particular, it does not enter the language-game of imagining in the place in which a picture enters the language-game of describing, evaluating, and judging the verisimilitude or interest of pictures. The beginning of the language-game of imagining is not the visual image, which one then describes, any more than the beginning of the language-game with 'pain' is the sensation, which one then describes (cf. PI §290). The language-games with the visual imagination begin with the *expression* of what one imagines and how one imagines it, and the description of what one imagines is *fundamentally* unlike the description of a picture which one sees, examines in good light, compares visually with what it depicts, and so forth.

4. *Visual images and visual impressions*

If the analogy between mental (visual) images and pictures is potentially misleading, that between visual images and visual impressions is even more confusing. 'Images seem to be dull reflections of sense-impressions,' Wittgenstein remarked (RPP II §142); but 'when does this seem to be the case, and to whom?' Paradigmatically to philosophers caught in the web of grammar. In a famous argument, Hume wrote:

> We find by experience, that when any impression has been present with the mind, it again makes its appearance there as an idea; and this it may do after two different ways: either when in its new appearance it retains a considerable degree of its first vivacity, and is somewhat intermediate betwixt an impression and an idea; or when it entirely loses that vivacity, and is a perfect idea. The faculty, by which we repeat our impressions in the first manner, is called the MEMORY, and the other the IMAGINATION. 'Tis evident at first sight, that the ideas of the memory are much more lively and strong than those of the imagination, and that the former faculty paints its objects in more distinct colours, than any which are employ'd by the latter. . . . in the imagination the perception is faint and languid, and cannot without difficulty be preserv'd by the mind steddy and uniform for any considerable time. Here then is a sensible difference betwixt one species of ideas and another.[11]

Later empiricists followed Hume in his confusions. But it is not *just*

[11] Hume, *Treatise of Human Nature*, Bk. I, Pt. i, Sect. 3.

philosophers who are thus confused. Francis Galton, pioneer of the psychological questionnaire, concocted the following:

> Before addressing yourself to any of the Questions on the opposite page, think of some definite object – suppose it is your breakfast-table as you sat down to it this morning – and consider carefully the picture that rises before your mind's eye.
> 1. *Illumination.* – Is the image dim or fairly clear? Is its brightness comparable to that of the actual scene?
> 2. *Definition.* – Are all the objects pretty well defined at the same time, or is the place of sharpest definition at any one moment more contracted than it is in a real scene?
> 3. *Coloring.* – Are the colors of . . . whatever may have been on the table, quite distinct and natural?[12]

Faced with these questions, 'men of science', as Galton called them, commonly protested that mental imagery was unknown to them. But much to Galton's relief, among lesser mortals a different disposition prevailed. As he reported:

> *Many men and a yet larger number of women, and many boys and girls, declared that they habitually saw mental imagery and that it was perfectly distinct to them and full of color . . .* They described their imagery in minute detail, and they spoke in a tone of surprise at my apparent hesitation in accepting what they said. I felt that I myself should have spoken exactly as they did if I had been describing a scene that lay before my eyes, in broad daylight, to a blind man who persisted in doubting the reality of vision.[13]

Galton concluded that 'scientific men', as a class, have feeble powers of visual imagination.[14]

Confronted by confused questions, it is hardly surprising that one gives confusing answers. To untangle the knots in one's understanding of these matters, one must first clarify what it is for a mental image to be clear and vivid or dim and faint, what it is for imagined objects to be well-defined, and what it is for the colours of an imagined scene to be distinct and natural. Superficial similarities between the grammar of 'mental image' and the grammar of visibilia derail us before we even start. Certainly there is such a thing as clarity and unclarity in visual images. If someone says 'My visual image of N is much less clear (or exact) than the visual impression I have when I see him', then this is true in so far as he cannot describe N nearly as accurately by relying on his

---

[12] F. Galton, *Inquiries into Human Faculty*; quoted by James, *Principles of Psychology*, Vol II, Ch. XVIII, pp. 51ff.

[13] Galton; quoted in James, ibid.

[14] He also thought that the French 'possess the visualizing faculty in a high degree', since they excel in ceremonials and *fêtes*, tactics and strategy. 'Their phrase "figurez-vous" or "picture to yourself" ', he concluded, 'seems to express their dominant mode of perception' (ibid.).

imagination as he can when he sees N before him. But in certain circumstances (e.g. if one is very short-sighted and one has lost one's spectacles) one may see a person much less clearly than one can imagine him (RPP II §142).

Similarly, there is such a thing as imagining the colours of a scene clearly, vividly, and distinctly. One who imagines a stage-set in clear, vivid colours can tell his stage-designer to paint the sky in the backcloth just a little bit more blue ('I imagined it bluer than this,' he might say) or to lessen the contrast between the red and the orange ('I did not imagine them as clashing,' he may add). By contrast, one who does not imagine the colours of a scene vividly will hesitate in judging whether the effect is right. 'Is that what you meant?', his stage-designer may ask, and he may reply, 'I'm not sure; let's try a little less blue and see what it looks like.' And if he says 'I did not imagine that these colours would clash thus,' that indicates a fault in his imagination.

Hume and his followers thought that the lesser vivacity of mental images as opposed to visual impressions was a datum. This invites the question: what would it be like if one's images were very vivid indeed? Would one then *mistake* one's mental images for sense-impressions, after-images, or hallucinations? If one imagined *very vividly* a red expanse with green dots on it, would it prevent one from seeing what is before one's eyes, as a vivid after-image disrupts one's vision (LPP 313f.)? Of course not, for then it would not be a case of imagining at all. The mental image and the visual impression (or after-image) are not in the same logical space, and it makes no sense to conceive of them as competing in the vivacity stakes. Conversely, if someone reports that his mental images are *less* vivid than perceptions, one might ask whether they are so much less vivid that he hardly *notices* them? On Hume's conception this question ought to make sense; but it does not, for one does not notice or fail to notice one's mental images, any more than one *notices* what one means to do. That they are 'less vivid' than perceptions does not mean that they are less noticeable, like faint stains on one's shirt after laundering, as opposed to vivid ones before a wash. What is at issue *is not that sense of 'vivid'* (LPP 313). Indeed, one might say that one's *perceptions* cannot be said to be vivid at all! What one sees may be vivid: e.g. a red rose against dark green foliage. I may see you vividly silhouetted against the sunset, but I cannot be said to see you vividly. Granted one may gain a vivid, i.e. memorable or striking, impression of what one looks at, nevertheless one does not *see* it vividly, only more or less clearly and distinctly.

No matter *how* vividly one imagines something, one's mental images are 'less vivid' than one's perceptions, for the so-called lesser vivacity is an ill-denominated and poorly understood array of *grammatical* features, not phenomenological ones. (An analogue here would be the claim that one's family obligations are weightier than any burden one might have to carry, in that one may not lay them down or transfer them to someone else.) The vividness or faintness of a mental image does not lie *on the same scale* as the clarity or unclarity of a visual impression. My mental image of A may be more vivid than my mental image of B, and I may be able to visualize such-and-such much more vividly than you can. But my mental image can no more be more vivid than my visual impressions than a negative attitude can be more negative than a negative integer.

What does the 'lesser vivacity' of mental images as opposed to perceptions amount to? Primarily to the different relations of imagining and perceiving to the will (see below), to the fact that what we perceive, in an important sense, is not voluntary, and to the unintelligibility of mistaking imagining for perceiving – hence also to the exclusion of certain kinds of epistemic expressions in connection with talk of mental images and sense-impressions. If someone were to say 'I don't know whether I am now seeing a tree or just imagining one', one would take him to mean 'or just fancying that there is a tree over there'. If this is *not* what he means, then one would not know what he is talking about, no matter how vivid his mental images are (RPP II §96). For it makes no sense to suppose that one might confuse discerning with inventing. Hence 'I fancy I can still see him in the distance' does not mean 'Maybe I am imagining him [conjuring up an image of him] in the distance' (RPP II §74).[15] One can think one is inventing when one is, unawares, plagiarizing; but one cannot think one is imagining the words one is *reading*. One cannot *mistake* a mental image for an after-image (or hallucination) or a sense-impression (any more than one can mistake a weighty obligation for a heavy load). It is not that mental images are less vivid than sense-impressions *and that is why we do not mistake our imaginings for perceivings*, but rather: there is no such thing as mistaking a mental image for a sense-impression and that is *one* reason why philosophers are inclined to say that mental images differ in vivacity from sense-impressions.

The criteria for whether someone is imagining something are altogether different from the criteria for whether he is perceiving something or having a certain sense-impression. One who is imagining *behaves differently* from one who perceives something or other. And in one's own case, one could no more mistake an image for a visual impression than one could mistake drawing for seeing, even though what is drawn and what is seen may be the same thing (RPP II §113). Similar considerations apply to the contrast between imagining and having hallucinations. One

---

[15] But someone else might respond, 'Oh, you're just imagining it; he is no longer visible.' Here 'imagining' coincides with 'misperceiving', 'fancying', or 'thinking wrongly that you perceive'.

who has a hallucination typically takes himself to be perceiving what his hallucination is a hallucination of, as Macbeth took himself to be perceiving Banquo. But one cannot mistake – there is no such thing as mistaking – a mental image for a reality. I can vividly imagine roses in the vase on the table, but I cannot try to smell them (only try to imagine their smell or to imagine smelling them). Hence Macbeth's dagger, which he tried to clutch, was not an imagined dagger (RPP II §85), although it was an imaginary one. He no more saw it in his mind's eye than he imagined clutching it. Hallucinations are not subject to the will in the sense in which images are (see below). It makes no sense to conjure them up or 'banish' them (RPP I §653). Hallucinations, like after-images, disrupt one's vision; imagining at most disrupts one's attention.

Finally, what should be made of the question 'Do mental images exist?' Wittgenstein did not tackle this question, but his strategy suggests the following tactics. We can clarify what it is for someone to visualize things, to have a vague or clear mental image of something, to see things vividly in his mind's eye. We can spell out what it is that someone who has a good visual imagination can do, which someone who is a poor visualizer cannot. We can describe the forms of words which a person who vividly imagines a scene or object will be prone to use. In so doing, we are also elaborating the *criteria* for saying of someone that he has a clear mental image of such-and-such, that he visualizes things vividly. Does it then follow that mental images exist? The question is misleading, for it looks like 'Do unicorns exist?' If we deny the latter, at any rate it is clear to us what it would be for a unicorn to exist. But those who deny the existence of mental images or those who purport to be exercising proper scientific agnosticism have no *coherent* conception of what it is that they are denying or suspending judgement about – though they typically have in incoherent one. The question is also *wrong*, for being modelled on inquiries into the existence of objects, it invites spurious questions about coming into existence and ceasing to exist, duration and location. One can ask whether someone has a clear mental image of such-and-such, whether he visualizes it vividly, and to this there are typically answers. A vivid mental image may be before my mind's eye for half a minute or so, but it would be misleading to say that the image existed for half a minute; rather, my vividly imagining such-and-such went on for half a minute. Does it follow that mental images do *not* exist? No; it only follows that we should eschew this question. But whether some people visualize things clearly, have vivid mental images of how things were, are, or ought to be, of imaginary and fictitious objects, has an obvious and straightforward answer.

5. *Imagination, intention, and the will*

One reason why we are so readily misled in our reflections on mental images and the imagination turns on misconceptions about what makes one's mental image of N a mental image *of* N. For if one has a vivid mental image of N, there is no doubt in one's mind that it is N whom one is imagining. So one is inclined to think that one knows that one is imagining N because one knows that one's mental image is a (mental) image of N. It then appears that one knows that it is of N because one *recognizes* it as such (how else could one know it?) But if that is so, then it must have certain (recognizable) features in virtue of which it is a mental image of N.

This is a misunderstanding of the use of the expression 'a mental image of . . .'. For what makes my image of him into an image of him is not its looking like him (PI p. 177). A mental image does not *look like* anything, and I can imagine him otherwise than how he looks. I then imagine him wrongly (with blue eyes rather than grey ones), but it is still him that I imagine! When I say that I am imagining him now as he was when I last saw him, I am not designating something as a *portrait*, i.e. something which one could *investigate* as to who it is of (LW §§308, 314).

It is true that a face can come before my mind (or a tune can run through my head) without my knowing whose face (or what tune) it is. This is akin to having a description in mind, but not knowing whom or what it fits (e.g. 'There was a tall fellow at the party with grey hair and a lisp; now remind me who that was'). It does not follow that when a face comes before my mind as I imagine N, I recognize it as N's face. What *makes* it N's face then? The question is misleading; for it is more like 'What makes this remark a remark about *him*?' (LW §317) or 'What makes the intention to write to him an intention to write to *him*?' than it is like 'What makes this photograph a photograph of him?' If I avow 'I see him now vividly before me', what makes my avowal into an utterance about N is not its being backed by a mental image which looks like him. If someone wants to know whom I meant, he can ask me (LW §317). And if someone wants to know of whom my mental image is an image, my sincere avowal provides the criterion. But what criterion do *I* use? None (cf. PI §377).

Might I not be wrong? If I imagine King's College on fire, how can I be sure that it is King's that I imagine? Could it not be a different building, but one which looks like King's? After all, one's imagination is not so exact that half-a-dozen buildings might not fit the bill! This misconceives matters: of course, I do not doubt that it is King's I imagine on fire, but not because I *recognize* it as an image of King's, have grounds for believing that it is King's I imagine. Rather, I *say* 'It is King's I imagined', and *this* makes the connection (BB 39), as I say whom I *meant* or to whom I am writing or what I intend. How do I *know*? Knowledge is not in question here, nor is ignorance. 'I imagine . . .' is not a description which may or may not fit an object. Rather, it determines the content of my imagination, somewhat as my avowals of intention determine (and constitute criteria for) what I intend. What is at issue is my ability to say whom or what I imagine, have in mind, or mean. One should bear in mind that we could replace 'I see him vividly before me' or 'I have a vivid mental image of him' by 'Now I know what he looks like' or 'Now I'll tell you what he looks like'; i.e. these forms of words could, for certain purposes, fulfil the same role. But the latter pair do not have the misleading character of the former (RPP I §360) and do not suggest that any 'act of recognition' is involved here. Mental images are not objects seen, as it were, through a private telescope.

There is a venerable tradition of associating perception with the category of passive receptivity and imagination with the voluntary. This is partly right and partly wrong. The various modes of perception are essentially connected with looking, listening, sniffing, sampling (foodstuffs), and fingering (as well as groping, prodding, touching, etc.). These are exploratory activities subject to the will. One can decide to look at *this* or smell *that*, and if ordered to listen to *that* or feel *this* material, one can obey the order or flout it (cf. RPP II §139). On the other hand, seeing (as opposed to looking), hearing (as opposed to listening), etc. are not, in that sense, voluntary. One cannot order someone to stop seeing what is before his eyes (only to stop looking at it) or to stop hearing what is audible (only to stop listening to it), let alone to stop tasting what is in his mouth. One's perceptual *impressions*, unlike one's perceptual *activities*, are not (save in the case of perceiving aspects) subject to the will.

To say that the imagination is dependent on the will is correct but potentially misleading. One can decide to imagine something, as one can decide to look at or listen to something, but not to see or hear what one looks at or listens to. One can stop imagining and 'banish' the mental images before one's mind in a way in which one cannot 'banish' one's visual impressions. But it is also true that images sometimes beset one against one's will, recur obsessively, and preoccupy one. Of course, one can struggle against them; yet to call such obsessive images voluntary would be like calling a movement of one's arm 'voluntary' when someone forces one's arm *against* one's will (RPP II §86). So the kernel of truth in the claim that the imagination is voluntary needs careful separation from the husks of falsehood. Our concern is with grammar, with what it makes sense to say, not with empirical descriptions of phenomena.

First, to say that mental images depend upon the will gives a wrong picture both of the will and of mental images. We do not first become acquainted with mental images and then learn that we can bend them to our will (RPP I §900). We do not 'direct' them with our will, for the will is not a kind of motor that puts them into motion (RPP II §78). It is not as if we had here a genuine case of psychokinesis, as it were!

Secondly, one cannot compare the voluntariness of the imagination with the voluntariness of one's bodily movements. For others can typically say whether I moved, but whether I imagine something moving or not is determined wholly by what I say (subject, of course, to the proviso that what I say makes sense). So really moving objects drop out of consideration, for no such thing is in question here (RPP II §123).

Thirdly, to say that mental images are dependent on the will whereas visual impressions are not makes it appear as if mental images are just like sense-impressions, only subject to one's control. But that makes *no sense* (RPP II §124). For it represents the difference between mental images and sense-impressions ·as an empirical one, viz. that one can voluntarily affect the former but not the latter (RPP II §§89f.). But that is altogether misguided. Even if one's visual impressions (e.g. one's impressions of what one sees in a peep-show) coincided exactly with what one wanted, one would not think that one was vividly imagining things, for one cannot even begin to take an impression for an image (RPP II §§96f.). Conversely, suppose that at will one could produce pictures on a screen visible to others as well. In this case, would 'I see such-and-such on the screen now' be equivalent to 'I imagine such-and-such'? Obviously not; for others have no less authority than I in saying what is on the screen, and, indeed, I might err in saying what I see there. But 'I see such-and-such on the wall' and 'I imagine such-and-such' are equivalent in the case of Leonardesque exercises of the imagination, and, 'For me, what is on the screen now represents . . .' does correspond to imagining (RPP II §§119 – 20).

So what does the 'voluntariness' of mental images and of the imagina- tion amount to? It boils down to an array of grammatical (conceptual) features characterizing the use of 'mental image' and 'imagine'. In this respect it is like the 'vividness' and 'faintness' of mental images. For in both instances distinctive aspects of the grammar of 'imagination' are confusedly captured by a characterization which appears to be phenomenological. What specific grammatical features are concealed by the slogan 'Images are voluntary'? Such things as that (a) imagining is not a way of finding out how things are and so is unlike perceiving; (b) imagining is not a matter of observing the 'inner'; (c) imagining is more akin to drawing than to seeing; (d) one imagines whoever one means to imagine; (e) it makes *sense* for one to 'banish' one's mental images at will, unlike one's sense-impressions; and so on.

Wittgenstein's treatment of the imagination is, to be sure, incomplete. Many questions remain unanswered, but then his aim was not completeness (Z §465). It was rather to teach us how to fend for ourselves when we get lost in the jungles of philosophy (cf. PI p. 206). For the right way of handling any of these puzzles concerning our psychological concepts casts light on the correct treatment of others (Z §465). So it is here; seemingly intractable problems about the nature of the mind are shown not to be empirical problems at all. Hence they are not amenable to experimental methods, but exemplify how 'in psychology there is what is problematic and there are experiments which are regarded as methods of solving the problems, even though they quite bypass the thing that is worrying us' (RPP I §1039). The questions with which we have been dealing are not solved, but dissolved. They yield to a patient examination of the grammar of expressions. Confused questions and muddled answers about the imagination are shown to be rooted in the misguided projection of one language-game onto another and in failure to note how an expression (e.g. 'vivid', 'voluntary', 'picture') used in one language-game may occur in another language-game with a very *different* use. Here, as elsewhere in the philosophy of psychology,

The difficulty is to know one's way about among the concepts of 'psychological phenomena'.

That is to say: one has got to *master* the kinships and differences of the concepts. As someone is master of the transition from any key to any other one, modulates from one to the other. (RPP I §1054)

1   This opens the long series of remarks on imagining, but multiple strands connect it with antecedent discussions. One does not learn the use of the expression 'to say something to oneself' by learning to identify an inner process which is called 'saying something to oneself' (PI §361) and which constitutes a defining sample for a private ostensive definition (PI §362). Perhaps so, the interlocutor reasons, perhaps saying things to oneself is peculiar, but surely when one imagines this or that, something *happens*! And it is surely *that something* which one communicates to another when one tells him what one imagines! W. defers for a moment the consideration of the irrelevance of what happens when one imagines something to what it is that one imagines (cf. PI §§369 – 70). Instead he probes one very general feature which informs the interlocutor's picture. Given that something happens and that one then emits a noise (utters words), what for? On the interlocutor's conception of language and its use, it is to tell someone what has happened, viz. what image has come before one's mind. For does not language always function in one way, always serve the same purpose: viz. to convey thoughts – in this case thoughts about what happened when one imagined whatever one imagined (PI §304)? Is not the purpose of a proposition to convey to another how it is with one (PI §317), what is before one's mind? This uniform conception of communication (*Mitteilung*) by means of language, of telling someone something (*etwas mitteilen*), is now brought under fresh attack. For how is telling done? What is called 'telling someone something'? Is there only one such thing, only *one* technique of communicating, telling, something to someone?

(b) sharpens the critical focus of the remark: we take discourse for granted and operate with a primitive picture of interpersonal communication by means of speech. That primitive picture has roots in the Augustinian conception of language, according to which sentences are essentially descriptions of states of affairs. It can, as we have seen, be variously elaborated. A Fregean conception would argue that language typically functions 'to convey thoughts – which may be about houses, pains, good and evil, or anything else you please' (PI §304). A more psychologistic elaboration, characteristic of the British empiricists, German psychologism (including Husserl), and linguists following in de Saussure's footsteps, conceives of communication as a matter of encod-

ing ideas in the speaker's mind into words that will stimulate corresponding ideas in the mind of the hearer. ('Uttering a word is like
striking a note on the keyboard of the imagination' (PI §6).) Either way,
we conceive of the words uttered as a mechanism for producing in the
hearer a certain mental state, viz. that he should grasp the sense of those
words, entertain the thought that was in my mind, have the same
(exactly similar!) ideas I had. If this upshot has been achieved, then the
hearer has understood what the speaker has told him. What he then does
with the thought he has thus grasped is a further matter!

This compelling preconception distorts the heterogeneity of the roles
of sentences, misconceives both the range and the diversity of what can
be called 'a description', and misrepresents the concepts of thought and
idea, and *a fortiori* of thinking and having or entertaining an idea.
Equally, it twists out of all recognition the concept of *understanding* what
the speaker told one and (in all its elaborations) misconstrues what it is
for the speaker to mean what he says. Accompanying and reinforcing
these logico-linguistic misconceptions is a rich variety of misapprehen-
sions of psychological concepts and of their linguistic expression: of what
it is to tell someone that one is in pain, to communicate to another one's
fears or anxieties, to divulge one's intentions or motives, to recount one's
memories, or to elaborate what one imagines.

(c) shifts the example from imagining to pain, and elaborates with
respect to this example one absurd consequence of the picture delineated
in (b). If we think that the purpose of the proposition is to let another
know how it is with us (PI §317), then we will conceive of telling
someone that one has a toothache as aimed at inducing in him the
knowledge that one is in pain. And with all due philosophical humility,
we may leave the nature of the 'mental state or process' of knowledge
undecided (PI §308) – sometime we shall know more about this queer
phenomenon of knowledge. But this is not admirable caution; rather it is
already to have erred. For, on hearing someone groan 'I have a
toothache', knowing that he is in pain is not a mental state or process that
mediates between his utterance and one's response (e.g. 'Can I get you an
aspirin?'). The purpose of telling someone that I have a toothache is
misrepresented if conceived as a matter of inducing a 'mental state or
process of knowing' in the hearer, and the criteria for whether the hearer
has understood what I communicated to him lie in his *responses* to what I
said, not in a queer and as yet indeterminate mental process.

1.1   (i) 'to tell what happened', 'communication through language': note
that the translation masks the fact that 'mitzuteilen' and 'Mitteilung' are
cognates. The peculiarities of the English verb 'to tell' are not at issue
here.

(ii) 'Mitteilung durch Sprechen': 'communication through speech', in contrast with communication by means of gesture and non-linguistic behaviour (cf. MS. 124, 261f.). For does the child who has hurt his hand and cries and shows his bruised fingers to his mother for commiseration *not* communicate the fact that he is in pain to his mother? But would anyone conceive of this as the conveying of a thought from the child's mind to the parent's? Yet the linguistic avowal of pain grows out of, and in appropriate contexts may have the same function as, the primitive pain-behaviour the point of which is to solicit sympathy or aid (as in the above example).

(iii) 'etwas Seelisches': this characterization of the sense of one's words would seem to restrict the target to psychologistic conceptions of sense or meaning. Such a restriction is unnecessary, since the same picture informs Frege's model of communication through speech, save that sense is conceived Platonistically. MS. 124, 262 and MS. 129, 50 have here 'ein ätherisches Ding' ('something ethereal'). The explanation perhaps lies in MS. 165, 9ff. which examines the idea that a sentence has a sense because the speaker is conscious and *means* it. This meaning, it seems, is something mental ('dieses Meinen ist natürlich etwas Seelisches') and private. So one is inclined to wonder what *happens* when one means a sentence – for an act or process of meaning is conceived of as what connects the mere words (sounds) and the facts. Subsequently W. anatomizes the confusions implicit in this conception. It may be that he had this, rather than the equally confused Fregean picture, in mind in §363(b).

(iv) 'that he *knows* that I am in pain': the switch from the example of imagining to having pain disrupts the flow of the argument, and is not obviously significant. It is perhaps explained by the disparate MS. sources, §363(a) being derived from a discussion of imagining in MS. 165, 127f., and (b) – (c) from MS. 124, 262f., which focuses on the communication of the fact that one is in pain. MS. 129, 49f. brings the two together in the final MS. draft, and opens equivocally 'Wenn ich mir etwas vorstelle // etwas empfinde // . . .' ('When I imagine something // have a sensation // . . .').

(v) 'Die Uhr zeigt uns': *zeigt*, not *teilt mit*, hence better 'shows us the time', since the concept of telling the time is not a special case of the concept of telling someone something.

2   PG 39 and 107 observe that though we distinguish between a thought and its expression, we must not conceive of signs as a potion that will produce in the hearer the same kind of condition as in the speaker.

MS. 165, 9ff. is a remote ancestor: one is inclined to think that a sentence has a sense because I *mean* it, that my meaning it effects the connection between the mere words and the facts (cf. PI §358). This is, to be sure, confused. We talk of meaning a sentence we utter in contra-distinction, for example, to uttering a sentence as an exercise in a language class. In the former case we intend to tell someone something. What *happens* when we mean it? Is it always the same? And how does it *accompany* the utterance: word by word or by enveloping the whole sentence? Certainly there is a difference in the surroundings and accompanying circumstances of the two cases. But meaning the sentence is not an accompanying mental process comparable to a pain – that is not how 'to mean' is used.

MS. 165, 126ff. has the first draft of PI §363(a). It occurs in the context of a discussion of whether it makes sense to talk of someone imagining things who has not learnt a language, i.e. who cannot give expression to his imaginings. §363(a) here encapsulates the picture of one who contends that imagining is an inner process which is independent of its expression. If one *can* speak, one can then tell another about this inner event! W.'s queries in this passage therefore challenge this picture of telling someone what one is imagining. He adds: is the language-game of telling the same whether one tells someone about a physical process or a mental one? Of course, one wants to say that one means by one's words just that which happens, that one's words refer to a very specific inner event, a process analogous to an outer process which one's words describe. (This remark was then transcribed into MS. 124, 280).

MS. 124, 261ff. has the first draft of §363(b) – (c) in the context of a discussion of someone who has not learnt a language trying to elicit help or sympathy for his pain from another by means of gestures and facial expressions. Is this not a case of communicating to another the fact that he is in pain? It may sound as if such an account bypasses the very pain itself – for where in the gestures and grimaces is there a *reference* to the pain? But if it sounds so, W. responds, that is only because one has a wrong conception of what it is to communicate or tell someone something. That wrong conception is then spelled out in a draft of §363(b) – (c).

SECTION 364

1   It seems to the interlocutor as if W. is denying that anything at all goes on when one imagines something, as if he were suggesting that the mind is a complete blank. (Cf. MS. 165, 132: 'A complete blank?', W. retorts there, 'God forbid! what I am saying is the complete opposite of that.') The interlocutor switches to what seems an irrefutable example of something going on: calculating in one's head. Here, surely something *happens* – a calculation goes on, for the result does not just spontaneously

come to one, one works it out! Indeed, how would we *explain* how the calculator got the right result if not by reference to an inner process of calculating, an inner process that must be just like the outer process of calculating on paper except for the fact that it takes place in the mind.

The objection misfires, for it misconstrues the thrust of W.'s argument and rests on a distorted view of the concept of calculating in the head. In the first place, W. is not denying that various things may occur in one when one does a mental calculation; rather, what he is denying is that they constitute the calculating, that they are necessary or sufficient conditions for performing a mental calculation. If we were to hear what went on in the mind of a calculating prodigy, 'it would perhaps seem like a queer caricature of calculation' (Z §89).) Secondly, the interlocutor's citing this example as an instance of something's happening (§363) or taking place (§361) in the mind *as he understands these expressions* rests on a categorial confusion. Just as saying something to oneself *in foro interno* is no more an instance of saying something than an imagined experiment is a kind of experiment, so too, calculating in the head is not an instance of calculating *in the sense in which* calculating out loud or in a pocket notebook are. And when W. tries to disabuse him of his misconception, he interprets W.'s objections as a form of behaviourism. But W.'s point is to clarify the fact that the move from talking of calculating out loud or on a blackboard to talking of calculating in the head involves a grammatical transformation as radical as that involved in moving from talk of marrying women to talk of marrying money.

The interlocutor conceives of calculating in the head as a process precisely analogous to calculating on paper (PI §366), only without the paper. But this is absurd; it is akin to: 'Saying something to oneself is precisely analogous to saying something aloud, only without making a sound'. We do not have here an analogy resting on a correspondence of processes, as we do with calculating aloud, calculating on paper, calculating on one's fingers, and calculating on an abacus. Rather, we have a new *grammatical articulation* which introduces a *secondary*, parasitical use of 'to calculate'. For one can only learn what 'calculating in the head' is by learning what 'calculating' is (PI p. 220); and only if one has learnt to calculate, on paper or out loud, can one come to grasp what calculating in the head is (PI p. 216). This observation is a grammatical one, not a hypothesis belonging to learning theory, for the impossibility is a *logical*, not a psychological, impossibility. By contrast, one can learn to calculate with an abacus, even if one has not learnt to calculate on paper. This new grammatical articulation (viz. calculating *in the head*) was not forced upon us by the phenomena (no move in grammar is *forced* upon us). Instead of saying to someone 'Calculate the result in your head!', we might have adopted the form of words: 'Now get the result *without* calculating!' (RPP I §655). And if someone found himself naturally inclined to say 'I did the sum inwardly', we might correct him, saying 'You don't calculate *inside* anything! You calculate *unreally*', and he would thenceforth use this form of representation (cf. RPP I §657).

The interlocutor hypostatizes an 'inner process of calculation' analogous to an outer one in order to *explain* how it can be that the correct result was arrived at. But he fails to see that his explanation is no more comprehensible than the explanandum; in fact it is incoherent! It is, to be sure, extraordinary that human beings, having learned to calculate aloud or on paper, should then be able to produce the correct result of a calculation without writing or saying a word. That is a fact of our natural history. But to hypostatize an inner process of calculation, just like an outer one only inner, provides no more than a mirage of an explanation.

'Neurophilosophers' may postulate neural circuitry as a surrogate calculator, for, they may insist, it must be possible to explain calculating in the head. But all that neurophysiology could ever hope to explain is not the 'mental process' of calculating in the head, only the neural prerequisites for it. For neural activity, even if causally necessary for the exercise of one's capacity for mental arithmetic, is not *calculating*, any more than electrical current's moving through circuitry of silicon chips in a pocket calculator is calculating! Is this to argue that the phenomenon of calculating in the head is inexplicable? Not at all; it is, rather, to suggest that the request for an explanation *thus construed* takes what is in effect a conceptual confusion as the locus of an explanandum calling out for an empirical explanation. One can, of course, investigate the psychological and neurophysiological prerequisites or concomitants of doing calculations in one's head, but the only explanation of what calculating in the head is consists of a *grammatical* explanation, a description of the circumstances in which this expression is to be used. To be sure, if we were to discover such-and-such neural concomitants of calculating in the head, we would be able to infer from the fact that we had just done a mental calculation that such-and-such a neural process had just occurred (PI p. 220).

§364(b) raises a consequent, natural worry. Is W. suggesting that calculating in one's head is in some sense less real than calculating on paper? The question is confused: really calculating in one's head is real calculating-in-one's-head, in contrast with pretending to calculate in one's head and blurting out any old number, just as real calculating on paper may be contrasted with pretending to do a calculation on paper. But it makes no sense to ask whether mental calculation is more or less real than calculating aloud or on paper (cf. Exg. §366). The interlocutor attempts one further gambit: is calculating in the head *like* calculating on paper? For it is obviously tempting to think that we call *this* 'calculating in the head' *because* it is an inner process resembling an outer one. W. replies with an analogy: is a drawing of a person, a piece of paper with lines on it, *like* a human body? One might say that a dog is much more *like* a human being than any drawing could be! But one also says that this drawing is a good likeness! Calculating in the head is like calculating on paper in so far as one gets such-and-such a result in both cases, that, if interrupted, one can say how far one has got, etc. And it is also wholly unlike calculating on paper in as much as there is no paper, one writes nothing down, etc. One might say that calculating in the head is much more like humming a tune in one's head than it is like calculating on paper!

1   (i) 'That it has, say, just "come" to him . . . ': that, of course, W. does not want to say. It is characteristic of calculating in the head that if interrupted, one can say how far one has got ('I've added the first two columns, but not yet subtracted the sub-total'), that one can explain the steps of the calculation. If, however, someone can always produce the right answer spontaneously, but cannot say how it is arrived at ('It just comes to me'), we might, at least in some cases, *not* say that he calculates in the head, does mental arithmetic (cf. PI §236), but rather that he can just tell you the answer without doing any calculation.

(ii) 'But what if I said: "*It strikes him as if* he had calculated" ': he can tell us steps of the calculation, even though he does not make any perceptible calculations, and he can tell us the result of the sum, just as if he *had* calculated. So it is almost as if he had calculated somewhere, somehow, and told us about it. Moreover, he is inclined to say 'I did it in my head'. But, of course, his utterance is not a report of a process visible only to him, and what he is inclined to say does not have to be (although it has been) adopted as a model for a form of expression in our language (RPP I §657).

2   MS. 124, 247ff. elaborates at greater length. Three further points are noteworthy. (a) The phrase 'there must have been a calculation going on' means something like: there surely must be a calculating-machine at work there, otherwise getting the result would not be intelligible. That is indeed how we are disposed to view things. W.'s response is ironic: if it is not intelligible, what difference does it make (i.e. would we cease calling this 'calculation in the head' if it turns out that there is no 'calculating-machine' in the head?)? (b) W. tries another gambit: instead of 'explaining' that the person got the right result by reference to the inner process of calculating, tacitly conceived of as an inner calculating-machine, why not turn things upside down and say that it is because the result is the same as that obtained by calculating that we say that he calculated *in his head*? A later addition cancelled this: one could rather say this in cases in which we calculate 'unconsciously'. The point is further clarified by PI p. 220 (see below). (c) W. adds a methodological

suggestion: instead of hypostatizing mysterious inner processes, clarify the inclination to indulge in such hypostatization and then explain the *inclination*!

PI p. 220 elaborates the tie-up between 'saying' and 'saying to oneself', and by implication 'calculating' and 'calculating in the head'. One can tell another what one has said to oneself or calculated inwardly, and one can accompany one's inward speech or calculation with overt actions (e.g. jotting down the number to be 'carried' in adding or ticking off columns of figures), just as one may beat time with one's hand as one sings inwardly.

A further point is added: we are tempted to insist that, nevertheless, calculating inwardly is surely a certain activity which one has to learn! All right, W. concedes, but what is 'doing' and what is 'learning' here? 'Doing something in one's head' and 'learning to do something in one's head' are as different from doing and learning to do something overtly as calculating in one's head is different from calculating.

RPP I §655 illuminates further: one need not look at calculating in the head under the aspect of *calculating*, although it has (as clarified above) an essential tie-up with calculating. Indeed, one need not even conceive of it under the aspect of doing, for doing is something one can show or demonstrate (*vormachen*) to another.

SECTION 365

1   An aside on the peculiar context-dependence of 'real'. Adelheid and the Bishop are, of course, playing a real game of chess, not just pretending to play a game of chess *in the play*. Similarly, calculating in the head is doing a real calculation-in-the-head.

1.1   'Adelheid and the Bishop': in Goethe's *Götz von Berlichingen*, Act II, scene 1, in which the scene opens towards the end of the game (which does not mean that the game had no beginning!). In MS. 129, 75 W. contemplated a different dramatic example, viz. the game of chess in *Nathan the Wise*.

2   MS. 166, 51ff. has a long discussion of 'real' and 'pretend' as used in discourse about a drama apropos the question of whether when one imagines something, one has a real image before one's mind. The criteria for someone dying in a play (e.g. Lear) differ from the criteria for someone dying. But that is no reason for denying that Lear really dies at the end of the play. Similarly, the criteria for someone having a vivid mental picture (image) differ from the criteria for someone seeing a

picture, but that is no reason for denying that someone may really have a vivid mental image of something.

Section 366

1   This continues the theme of §364(b): one is inclined to think that the mental, or 'subjective', is less real than the physical, or 'objective' (since one cannot *touch* it !): but it is noteworthy that in the appropriate idealist or phenomenalist frame of mind, one can talk oneself into the opposite point of view. Both conceptions, MS. 179, 55 comments, signify just as little! For both rest on a mistaken apprehension of the function of language and of its relation to a reality that corresponds to it (MS. 124, 250, interposed between §366(a) and (b)).

   If one is beset by the idea that multiplying 24 by 16 in one's head is less real than doing the calculation on paper, one should reflect on the fact that if a competent calculator says 'I have multiplied 24 by 16 in my head, and the answer is 384', one does not doubt his word. Is this really a multiplication, without writing anything down? To be sure; it is not merely *a* multiplication, but this very one – although in the head, not on paper. Convinced by this point, however, one is inclined to think that if it is a genuine multiplication, then multiplying in the head must be a mental process corresponding to multiplying on paper. It must have the same logical multiplicity as the written calculation and corresponding mental constituents, just as multiplying on paper and multiplying on an abacus might be said to have the same logical multiplicity and corresponding constituents. But this is incoherent, for it presupposes the intelligibility of a method of projection (a rule) which determines the mental image of a sign (e.g. the image of '2' or of '+') as a representation of the sign itself. And that is precisely the presupposition underlying the idea of a private language (MS. 124, 250). For it involves the notion of a private experience (having a mental image of '2') and of our words having a private meaning ('The mental image of '2' is *this*'). And that in turn drags in its wake all the confusions raked over hitherto; for it would be intelligible to wonder which *is* the mental image of '2' or how I know that *this* image I now have is a mental image of '2', etc. But these questions make no sense.

1.1   'it would then make sense . . . ': the objection applies equally to the conception of the psychical constituents of a *Gedanke* implicit in the *Tractatus* (see R 37).

2   MS. 124, 251 continues with a remark on the 'reality' of the subjective and the objective. The idea that one is more or less real than the other is

absurd. We represent *both* in our language, and our ordinary discourse about the subjective is perfectly in order as it is, and no more needs correction by philosophers than our talk about chairs and tables. But one point must be stressed, viz. that the *grammar* of propositions about subjective things is not the same as that of propositions about objective ones; i.e. the language-games are different.

Section 367

1   A difficult remark, rendered even more difficult in translation. At first blush, it seems in flagrant conflict with §301: 'An image [*Eine Vorstellung*] is not a picture, but a picture can correspond to it.'

The conception of calculating in the head that is under attack in §366 is that of a mental process that corresponds to doing a calculation on paper. So what corresponds to a sign on paper, say '2', is a mental image or picture of the sign (cf. MS. 124, 249). We are prone to think of a mental image of an object as a representation of the object in the manner in which a literal image (a picture) of an object is a representation of it. Of course, in the case of such a genuine representation, it *does* make sense to talk of a method of projection according to which the picture is a representation of that of which it is a picture.

A *mental* image (*Eine Vorstellung*) or picture (*Vorstellungsbild*) however, is *not* a representation, and there can be no method of projection determining it as a representation of what it is an image of. It is the imaginer's *avowal* that determines it as an image of this or that, and *that* is not based on his observation of his image or on a method of projection, since it is not based on anything (cf. PI §377). One does not determine what object one is imagining by reference to a resemblance between it and the mental image, as one may sometimes determine what a picture (portrait) is a picture of (Z §621). One cannot compare one's mental image with what it is an image of in the way in which one can, e.g., compare a portrait with its subject for verisimilitude. It makes no sense to talk of *knowing* or of being *mistaken* about what one's mental images are images of, whereas one may well know, be ignorant, or be mistaken about what a picture is a picture of. In short, 'The image [*die Vorstellung*] is not a picture [*ist nicht ein Bild*], nor is the visual impression one. Neither "image" nor "impression" is the concept of a picture [*ist ein Bildbegriff*], although in both cases there is a tie-up with a picture, and a different one in either case!' (Z §638).

The grammatical observation being made here (PI §367) is that to describe my mental image of . . . *is* to describe what I imagine. The words with which I describe what I imagine can typically also be used to describe what a picture is a picture of. Indeed, one can often, given the appropriate facility, paint what one imagines. In such a case, the verbal description of what one imagines and the verbal description of the picture one has painted may well be identical. So one might say that what one's mental image is an image of is what the picture one has painted is a picture of. Hence a description of what one imagines is also a description of a possible picture which would represent what one imagines. But one must not confuse the description of a possible picture with the description of a private, mental picture which only the owner can see. For the mental image is not a picture, its owner cannot see it, and his description of what he imagines is not the description of a private object. (See LSD 136f.)

.1   (i) 'Vorstellungsbild': the English cannot capture the multivalence of the German. 'Vorstellungsbild' is *mental image*, but also *mental picture* in the sense in which we say 'I have a vivid picture of that long-gone scene in my mind's eye', and further intimates an *imagined picture*.

(ii) 'Wenn Einer seine Vorstellung beschreibt': it is important for this remark that is is *not* phrased 'Wenn Einer beschreibt was er sich vorstellt', although, of course, the whole thrust of the remark *is* that to describe one's mental image just is to describe what one imagines.

2   Vol. XII, 207 has this scrawled in the top margin, not as a constituent part of an argument, but as an epitome of the long discussion (pp. 206 – 8) of the misleading picture (conception) we have of a private object which only its owner can see. It is important, W. stresses, to realize that this is just a simile (*Gleichnis*). It is of the nature of this conception that we can make further assumptions about this inner object and about what a person does with it; for we cannot merely say that he has a private something and does something with it. But if we conceive of someone's mental image as something which only he can see, if we say gravely that we cannot really know what his (mental) picture looks like, then we strip any assumptions about this 'object' of their sense.

MS. 164, 164ff. has a parallel discussion. We may say of someone that he has played chess with another in his imagination. But how does he know that it was chess? Has he learnt chess-in-the-imagination? We could point at a real game of chess and ask him whether *that* was what he imagined, and if he agrees, say that he did indeed have a mental picture (*Vorstellungsbild*) of a game of chess. But what kind of picture is that? What kind of projection of a game of chess is it? There is no answer to this, and it is not a significant question, for a mental image (*eine Vorstellung*) is not a picture (*ist eben kein Bild*). If one compares it with a picture, it would have to be a picture which no one, not even its owner, knows what it looks like! For in answer to the question of what I am imagining, I too, even for myself, can point only to objects perceptible to others. For me to imagine further a pointing finger within my mental image would be a redundant farce, and merely concentrating my attention is not a kind of pointing for me. The mental picture, W. concludes punningly, is the picture which corresponds to my image ('Das Vorstellungsbild ist das Bild, das meiner Vorstellung entspricht'.)

MS. 124, 282 notes that one says that one imagines, e.g., a tree falling, that one sees it clearly before one. One has a clear picture before one's mind's eye. But why a picture? And if a picture, why not a tree?

SECTION 368

1   This provides a·parallel or analogy for the relation between the mental image and the picture which is described when someone describes his image (*seine Vorstellung beschreibt*). The relation is not determined by a method of projection. If it were, it would make sense to say that a person's sincere description of his image (i.e. of what he imagines) is mistaken. That makes no sense, for the criterion for what image someone else has is what he says and does (cf. §377(b)).

Suppose I describe a room to someone with the intention of conveying the impression which the room makes, e.g. that it is eery or sinister. I then get him to paint an *impressionistic* picture from this description to show whether he has understood the description and grasped the impression, the 'atmosphere', of the room. He now paints the room, transposing colours dramatically (one might think of Van Gogh's painting of the café at night in Arles). This is the impression he got of the room from my description. Now what determines whether he has correctly represented the impression of the room (which he has never seen), understood my description of its atmosphere? It is not that he has used a method of projection of green onto dark red and yellow onto blue. It is *my avowal* that that is indeed what it looks like, that that is how it impresses one. (Note that my utterance 'Yes, that is what it looks like' does not rest on comparing my 'private impression' with the picture that he has painted (cf. PI §280). The criterion for whether I have conveyed to him (and he has understood) the impression which the room makes is not whether his painting matches 'my private impression' which 'only I can see', but whether I *react* to his painting with such an avowal.)

2   The sole source for this obscure remark is MS. 162(b), 96 – 9. Since the above interpretation may be thought debatable, and since the role of the remark in the argument of PI is unclear, the complete context is given below:

'Beschreiben' heisst ein Beschreibungsspiel spielen. – Wie sieht so ein Spiel aus? Wir geben dem Andern eine Beschreibung, und er soll irgendwie nach ihr Handeln;

und dadurch zeigen, dass er die Beschreibung verstanden hat. – Da gibt es sehr verschiedene Fälle! Beschreibungen einer Anordnung von Körpern, Beschreibungen von Farben, Beschreibungen von Körperempfindungen, von Stimmungen, etc.

'Beschreibe Deine Empfindungen bei der Zeile: "In allen Wipfeln . . . !".' Ist es klar, was hier gemeint ist? Was hier als Kriterium dafür gilt, dass der Andere es aufgefasst hat?

('To describe' means to play a describing game. – What does such a game look like? We give someone a description and he must act on it in some way, and thereby show that he has understood the description. – There are many different cases! Descriptions of an arrangement of bodies, descriptions of colours, descriptions of bodily sensations, of moods, etc.

'Describe your impressions of the line [of the poem]. "In all the treetops . . . !"[1] Is it clear what is meant here? What counts here as a criterion that someone has understood?)

Then follows a draft of PI §368 which is virtually identical with the printed version. The discussion continues as follows:

'Aber kannst Du die Atmosphäre beschreiben die diese Farbe (diese Zeile) umgibt?' – Warum soll ich nicht die Atmosphäre zur Farbe rechnen und sagen: Wenn ich die Farbe beschreibe, beschreibe ich damit was Du diese 'Atmosphäre' nennst. Will ich sie 'ohne diese Atmosphäre' beschreiben, *dann* muss ich der Beschreibung etwas hinzufügen.

Aber die Frage ist: In welchem Falle sage ich, ich *habe* die Atmosphäre *vermittelt*, und in welchem Falle, ich habe nur die Worte (Farbe), aber nicht ihre Atmosphäre vermittelt? Ich meine: in welchem Fall sage ich, die Vermittlung sei // ist // gelungen? Oder: Wie unterscheiden sich die Fälle, in denen das eine und in denen das andere (ich sage nicht: '*nur* das andre') vermittelt wurde?

('But can you describe the atmosphere that envelopes this colour (this line)?' – Why shouldn't I count the atmosphere as part of the colour and say: if I describe the colours, I thereby describe what you call this 'atmosphere'. If I want to describe them 'without this atmosphere', *then* I must add something to the description.

But the question is: in which case do I say: I *have conveyed* the atmosphere, and in which case: I have communicated only the words (colour) but not their atmosphere? I mean: in which case do I say that I have conveyed this successfully? Or: what distinguishes the cases in which the one and those in which the other (I don't say: '*only* the other') is conveyed?

[1] This is the third line of Goethe's poem 'Wandrers Nachtlied II':

Über allen Gipfeln
Ist Ruh,
In allen Wipfeln
Spürest du
Kaum einen Hauch;
Die Vögelein schweigen im Walde.
Warte nur, balde
Ruhest du auch.

(Over all the hill tops it is still, in all the treetops you can hardly feel a breath stirring. The little birds are silent in the forest. Wait! Soon you too will be still.) Prose translation by David Luke in Goethe, *Selected Verse* (Penguin Books, Harmondsworth, 1964).

SECTION 369

1   This picks up the unfinished business of §363. We have a picture of imagining or calculating in the head as an inner process analogous to an outer one, in which certain things happen which are then described when one describes what one imagined or how one calculated. To understand what 'calculating in the head' means, one should observe what happens when one does a sum in one's head. Then one can give oneself a correct ostensive definition (§362)!

W. concedes that *in a particular case* the answer to the question 'What goes on when you calculate that sum in your head?' might be 'First I add 17 and 18, then I subtract 39 . . .'. But that kind of answer does not explain what calculating in the head means; it presupposes it. If there is unclarity about the general concept of calculating in the head, it will not be eliminated by invoking the concept of doing a specific calculation in the head. For in response to the answer given, we will now ask 'What on earth is it to add 17 and 18 *in the head*?' Moreover, the answer 'First I add 17 and 18, then . . .' can be given in response to the question 'What is it like — what happens when one does a calculation on paper?' So this description cannot characterize the difference between calculating in the head and calculating on paper, any more than the description of what one imagines can serve to differentiate between a picture before one's mind's eye and a picture before one's eyes.

1.1   'In a particular case': it is not a general feature of calculating in the head that each step be thus gone through (cf. Z §89, quoted in Exg. §363, 1).

SECTION 370

1   This methodological remark elaborates, for the special case of imagining, the point already made about thinking in §316 and about sensation in §314. 'What are images?' and 'What happens when one imagines anything?' are questions about the nature or essence of the imagination, and it seems that they are to be answered by careful introspective scrutiny of the phenomena. But a question about the nature of imagination (or thinking, sensation, etc.) is a question about a concept, and concepts are clarified by describing the use of words. Hence the examination of the use of the words 'to imagine' and 'imagination' is not a study of 'mere words' *as opposed* to an investigation into the nature of the imagination; it *is* a study of its nature. (Indeed, this investigation, unlike a lexicographical one, will not confine itself to words, but will also examine the human behaviour, reactions, and responses associated

with imagining which, in appropriate circumstances, constitute criteria for saying that a person imagines this or that.)

The question 'What are images?' appears to invite us to 'look and see'. If we carefully observe what happens when we imagine things, then we will apprehend the nature of images and of the imagination! But, contrary to the empiricist and phenomenological traditions,[2] the question of the nature of the imagination (like the question of the nature of thinking previously examined) cannot be resolved by ostension, let alone by 'private' ostensive definition, or by describing what happens when one imagines anything.

.1   (i) 'dem Wesen der Vorstellung': 'the essence of imagination' would be preferable in order to preserve continuity with §371.

(ii) 'zu erklären ist': 'to be explained'.

(iii) 'nor yet by a description of any process': the failure of answers to the question of what happens when . . . to shed light on the nature of what is signified by a psychological expression is elaborated in numerous other remarks, e.g. §§34 – 5, 661, 675 (for meaning and interpreting), §§139, 152 – 5 (for understanding), §§305f. (for remembering), §§316, 321f., 327, 332, 339, 361, 427 (for thinking), §§392, 394 (for imagining), §§417f. (for consciousness), §545 (for hoping), §§591 – 2, 659 (for intending).

2   BB 24 has a parallel remark about knowing. 'What is it like to know?' is misleading in as much as it invites a description of a process, whereas the point of the question (in a philosophical context) is to clarify the grammar of the verb 'to know'. The question is: what do we *call* 'getting to know'?

SECTION 371

1   An investigation into the essence or nature of the imagination *is* an investigation into the use of the word 'imagination', for *essence is expressed by grammar*. Given that W. clearly does not think that 'imagination' is definable by an analytic (*Merkmal*) definition, how can he suggest that imagination has an essence or nature? There is, in fact, no conflict here, as is evident from PI §92 (cf. Exg. §92, 1.1(i)). The nature of imagination is clarified by a surview of the grammar of 'imagination'.

This brief remark crystallizes a *leitmotif* of W.'s later philosophy.

---

[2] Hume, *Treatise of Human Nature*, Bk. I, Pt i, Sect. 1 and Bk. I, Pt i, Sect. 3; James, *Principles of Psychology*, Vol. II, 46; Russell, AM 144ff.; Husserl, *Logical Investigations* (Routledge and Kegan Paul, London, 1970), Essays 1, 5, and 6.

Superficially it applies to the philosophy of the *Tractatus*, for there the logical syntax of empirical propositions *shows* the essence of things. An immediate difference, however, consists in the fact that according to the *Tractatus* one can only speak about objects, one *cannot express* their essential nature, for propositions can only say how things are, not what they are ('Ich kann nur *von* ihnen sprechen, *sie aussprechen kann ich nicht*' (TLP 3.221)). This difference, one might claim, merely reflects the narrowness of the *Tractatus* conception of a proposition, since what W. later calls 'grammatical propositions' do *not* count as genuine propositions in the *Tractatus*. And since, in the later philosophy, grammatical propositions are said to be expressions of *rules* (and hence fundamentally unlike empirical propositions with a sense), the shift in view might (wrongly) appear to be minor. A more fundamental difference, however, is the fact that in an important sense the *Tractatus* held logical syntax to be responsible to the language-independent essences of things since it *mirrors* the logical form of reality (TLP 4.121). The internal properties of things cannot be described in genuine propositions, but are *shown*. Even in the *Philosophical Remarks* W. still cleaved to this conception in a modified form: 'the essence of language is a picture of the essence of the world; and philosophy as custodian of grammar can in fact grasp the essence of the world, only not in the propositions of language, but in rules for this language which exclude nonsensical combinations of signs' (PR 85). By the time he wrote the 'Big Typescript', however, W. had freed himself from this misconception. According to the later philosophy, grammar is autonomous. Far from grammar reflecting the nature of things, what we conceive to be natures or essences are merely the shadows cast by grammar. This conception is diametrically opposed to that of the *Tractatus*.

2   This remark should be related to the observation 'Like everyhing metaphysical the harmony between language and reality is to be found in the grammar of the language' (PG 162 = Z §55). The *Tractatus*, a culmination of the high metaphysical tradition, explained this harmony in terms of the necessary relations between language and the world. That misconception, resting upon a confused view about the essential nature of a symbolism, projected an intra-grammatical articulation onto an imaginary, essential, extra-grammatical one.

LSD 20 distinguishes two ways of talking about 'the nature' of an object: (a) by specifying its properties which are *not* defining criteria of the object, (b) by specifying its defining criteria. In the latter case, the differences in the 'nature' of different things, e.g. space and colour, are not determined by the properties which we can attribute to them truly as opposed to those we cannot, but rather by the grammar of the words that signify them. The grammar of '1 foot' does not differ from the grammar of 'green' *because* the nature of a one-foot length differs from the nature of the colour green; rather the difference in their nature *is* the difference in the grammars of the respective expressions.

RFM 63 – 5 elaborates critically upon Platonist conceptions of necessity. Geometrical propositions about shapes seem to articulate the essence of such forms; but, W. responds:

> I say, however: if you talk about *essence*, you are merely noting a convention. But here one would like to retort: there is no greater difference than that between a proposition about the depth of the essence and one about – a mere convention. But what if I reply: to the *depth* that we see in the essence there corresponds the *deep* need for the convention. (RFM 65)

Section 372

1   The quoted sentence to be considered appears to allude in a generalized way to the position delineated in the *Tractatus*. At that stage, W. firmly believed that there *are* intrinsic necessities. The possible occurrences of objects in states of affairs 'must be part of the nature of the object' (TLP 2.0123), determined by the internal properties of objects that conjunctively constitute their logical forms (TLP 2.0141). However, it is impossible to describe in genuine propositions the existence of internal properties and relations (TLP 3.221, 4.122, 4.124); rather, they are manifest in empirical propositions that are concerned with such objects occurring in (contingent) states of affairs.

What, then, is the correlate in language to such intrinsic necessities? In one sense, it is the logical form of the symbols that symbolize the relevant objects, the variable for which names sharing certain features are substitution instances. But what is shown by the forms of names, of course, is not something that can be expressed in any proposition, not even a meta-linguistic one. In another sense, to which W. is apparently alluding here, it is the arbitrary grammatical rules for the use of signs. For while the ordinary grammatical rules for the combinations of signs are indeed arbitrary and the correlations of signs with their meanings are arbitrary, the *form* of the resultant proposition is not arbitrary, but corresponds to a logical form (TLP 3.315). '*When* we have determined one thing arbitrarily, something else is necessarily the case. (This derives from the *essence* of notation.)' (TLP 3.342).

If this *is* what W. is here alluding to, then obviously we are being invited to consider the quoted remark by way of *contrast* with the conception of necessity or essence that characterizes W.'s later philosophy. Grammatical rules are indeed, in one sense, arbitrary. They are not accountable to any reality (PG 184), and the propositions constructed in accord with grammatical rules do not *mirror* the objective, language-independent, logical forms of things, as the *Tractatus* supposed (TLP 4.121). On the contrary, what appear to be intrinsic necessities are themselves merely illusory reflections of grammar. 'It is not the property of an object that is ever "essential", but rather the mark of a concept' (RFM 64); for all our talk of *essence* merely notes conventions (RFM 65). Far from the common rules that govern the construction of 'p', '$\sim\sim p$', '$\sim p \lor \sim p$', '$\sim p \,.\, \sim p$' *mirroring* negation (TLP 5.512), they *constitute* it.

For a discussion of W.'s later account of necessity, see Volume 2, 'Grammar and necessity', pp. 262 – 347.

1.1   (i) 'naturnotwendigkeit': a necessity in the nature of a thing, i.e. an intrinsic necessity, not a natural, causal necessity.

(ii) 'abziehen': better 'derive', to preserve continuity with §374, or (excessively literally) in both remarks 'pull off' (as one pulls off a proof in printing) or 'take an offprint'!

2   This derives from Vol. VI, 144, where it occurs in the context of a discussion of negation, viz. that it lies in the nature of negation that double negation cancels out. It reappears in Vol. X, 157 without the prefix 'Überlege' but in quotes. An added note in square brackets says 'Perhaps apropos of the paradox that mathematics consists of rules'. Its context here is as in PG 184 (= BT 235). It was typed into the 'Big Typescript' without prefix or quotes, but these were added in pencil, together with a note on p. 234v. 'Bezieht sich auf Sätze wie $\sim\sim p = p$' ('Relates to propositions such as $\sim\sim p = p$').

The context in the 'Big Typescript' (= PG 184) is significant. It seems as if an ostensive definition could come into conflict with other rules for the use of a word. (This illusion is exacerbated if one thinks of syntactical, combinatorial rules as antecedent to an ostensive definition which gives content to the form determined by syntax. For then it appears as if one might erroneously try to 'inject' the wrong content into that predetermined form!) But this is mistaken, for grammatical rules cannot collide, unless they contradict each other. They are not answerable to a meaning (a content, such as a *Tractatus* 'object' in the world); they *determine* a meaning (which is not an object, but the use of a word). In that sense, grammatical rules are arbitrary; they are not accountable to any reality. There can be no question as to whether these or other rules are the correct rules for negation, i.e. whether they accord with the meaning of 'not'. For without the rules, the word has no meaning; and if we change the rules, the word will have a different meaning, and we might just as well change the word too (PI p. 147, note (b)). Then occurs PI §372, followed by an explanation of the arbitrariness of rules of grammar (like the rules of chess), which are constitutive, in contrast with the non-arbitrariness of rules of cooking, which specify means to a logically independent goal.

Section 373

1   The nature or essence of anything is given by rules of grammar which determine the application of an expression, for they fix the concept in question.

1.1   '(Theology as grammar)': an allusion to a remark W. attributes to Luther, that theology is the grammar of the word 'God'. AWL 32 interprets this to mean that an investigation of the word would be a grammatical one, clarifying what it makes sense to say about God. What counts as ridiculous or blasphemous here would also show the grammar of the word.

2   The contention that grammar tells us what kind of object anything is is heir to PR 54: 'Grammar is a "theory of logical types" '; i.e. what a theory of logical types endeavoured futilely to do is already done in, laid down by, the grammar of a language.

2.1   (i) 'kind of object': PG 463f. warns against two different uses of 'kind'. We say that infinite numbers are a distinct kind of number from finite ones, and assimilate that remark to such a claim as 'Coxes are a different kind of apple from Bramleys'. But whereas in the latter case we distinguish objects (apples) by their properties, in the former we distinguish different logical forms. BB 19 amplifies: distinctions between kinds of numbers, kinds of propositions, kinds of proofs, are distinctions between different *grammatical structures*.

(ii) '(Theology as grammar)': Z §717 gives an example: 'You can't hear God speak to someone else, you can hear him only if you are being addressed.' That is a *grammatical* remark.

Section 374

1   After the three remarks about natures or essences, W. reverts to the main theme, viz. the characterization of a mental image (or of calculating in the head). The picture that we have here is of a 'private object', something which only its owner can see, but which he cannot show to others. It seems that one derives ('abziehen' as in §372) a description, takes an offprint, from this object when one describes one's mental image.

One is almost irresistibly tempted to represent the matter as if there were something one *couldn't* do – as if one were prevented from showing other people one's mental image and so had to make do with a second-best, viz. giving them a description taken from the object which they cannot see. One way to combat this misleading picture is to yield to it and to investigate the incoherences that follow from trying to apply it. This task is undertaken in the next sequence of remarks.

2   This derives from Vol. XVI, 134, from which it was copied, with modifications, into Vol. XII, 243f. The context in both sources is the remark 'I can't *know* whether he says the ABC to himself in his mind'. But, W. replies, does *he* know? What if we were to say: he can't know either, he can only *say* so? One might say that he can no more check whether what he has is what is called 'pain' than I can, for there is no check. The language-game begins with his *saying* that he has pain, not with his *knowing* (Vol. XII, 243 modifies this: he can no more check whether what he imagines is really the sound we call 'a' than I can. But, of course, it would be equally wrong to say that he does *not* know whether he imagines the sound 'a', for that would mean that he was uncertain whether it was 'a' that he imagined. It would be more correct to say that there is here neither knowledge nor doubt. The language-game begins with his *saying* that he imagines . . .) So the language-game begins, as it were, with a description that does not correspond to a descriptum (though this grammatical remark, Vol. XII adds, could also be completely misleading). Then follows a draft of PI §374. In Vol. XVI, instead of the last sentence, we have:

Als finge das Sprachspiel also in Wirklichkeit *nicht* mit der *Äusserung* // dem Ausdruck // an, sondern mit dem 'privaten Gegenstand', nur könne ich diese Wurzel meines Ausdrucks nicht vorzeigen.

(As if the language-game did not really begin with the utterance // expression //, but with the 'private object', only I could not display this root of my expression.)

In both manuscripts the sequel applies these reflections to the conception of remembering as an inner process. All that really means, Vol. XVI, 134 notes, is that the language-game begins with the expression of remembering.

Z §134 (see Exg. §248) pursues a different strategy. Rather than yielding to the temptation to use the picture of a private object, with its corollary that one cannot do something here (viz. one cannot show it to anyone), W. insists that we should not say 'one cannot', but 'it does not exist in this game' or 'there is no such thing here'. One must not confuse the bounds of sense with limitations or constraints. It only makes sense to talk of being prevented from doing something or being unable to do something (constrained not to do it) if something *counts* as doing it. Otherwise the 'can't' merely registers a grammatical convention (cf. BB 54, 56).

3   A perfect target for this remark is given in Frege's 'Thoughts', which W. read:

> it is impossible to compare my sense-impression with someone else's. For that, it would be necessary to bring together in one consciousness a sense-impression belonging to one consciousness and a sense-impression belonging to another consciousness. Now even if it were possible to make an idea disappear from one consciousness and at the same time make an idea appear in another consciousness, the question whether it is the same idea would still remain unanswerable. It is so much of the essence of any one of my ideas to be a content of my consciousness, that any idea someone else has, is, just as such, different from mine.[3]

Here we have, with a vengeance, the picture of the private object which no one else can see and off which I read its description. How then does one compare images, in Frege's view? Very poorly – 'If two persons picture the same thing, each still has his own idea. It is indeed sometimes possible to establish differences in the ideas, or even in the sensations, of different men; but an exact comparison is not possible, because we cannot have both ideas together in the same consciousness.'[4]

SECTION 375

1   This opens the investigation of the application of the picture of the mental object accessible only to oneself, off which one reads a description which communicates to another what one imagined, said to oneself, or calculated in one's head. How does one teach anyone to read to himself? *Not* by inducing in him an inner process called 'reading to oneself' and bringing him 'to the point of giving himself a correct ostensive definition' (PI §362). One does not teach someone what 'reading to oneself' means by telling him 'what takes place' when one reads to oneself (cf. PI §361). One teaches a person to read to himself only after he *can read*, just as one can learn to calculate in one's head only if one can already calculate (PI p. 220; Exg. §364, 1). Moreover, one cannot intelligibly teach a person (who has just learnt to read aloud) how to read to himself by telling him to do just the same as he does when he reads aloud, only without making a sound. But one might say, 'Now look at what is written here without reading it aloud, close the book, and tell me what it says!' If he does so, however, he does not derive a description of what he has read to himself from scrutiny of a 'private process' of reading to himself, but from looking at the written words without reading out loud! How does one know if he can read to himself? By his reports of what he has read, by whether he is 'afterwards able to repeat the sentence

---

[3] G. Frege, 'Thoughts', in *Collected Papers on Mathematics, Logic and Philosophy*, p. 361.
[4] G. Frege, 'On Sense and Meaning', in ibid., p. 160.

word for word or nearly so' (PI §156). But, to be sure, this is not a report of an inner process which only he can see. How does he know that what he is doing is reading to himself? Here too (cf. Exg. §374, 2; Vol. XVI, 134) one might say: he does not *know*, he can only *say* that he has read the passage to himself. There is no question of either knowing or being uncertain, for 'I think I am reading to myself, but I'm not sure' is senseless.

SECTION 376

1   One cannot explain what it is to calculate in the head, read to oneself, or say something to oneself in terms of the idea that what one does is just the same as what one does when one calculates, reads, or speaks aloud, only in the head. *That* explanation by means of identity does not work here (cf. PI §350), although, of course, if A calculates 17^3 on paper and B calculates 17^3 in his head, then one may say that B did in his head the same calculation as A did on paper. But that *presupposes* and does not give a criterion of identity for calculations in the head. Pursuing further the application of the misbegotten picture of the 'private object' which I cannot show to anyone but from which I derive a description, W. now examines the question of the criterion of identity of images, silent sayings, etc. Since they cannot be shown to another, they must, it seems, be identified 'indirectly'.

What is the criterion for two different people *doing the same* 'in their heads' (e.g. reciting the alphabet)? W. addresses in the first instance the Watsonian behaviourist position, and only obliquely the view, more popular today, that the same neurological processes must be going on in the brains of the two people. Watson wrote: 'I should throw out imagery altogether and attempt to show that all natural thought goes on in terms of sensory-motor processes in the larynx.'[5] It is *possible* W. concedes, that identical laryngal physiological processes go on in two people who are saying the ABC to themselves or thinking or wishing the same thing. But we do not teach the use of 'saying . . . to oneself' by reference to the identification of such a laryngal process, *nor by reference to any brain-process.* The occurrence of any such process is therefore only inductively correlated with inward sayings, calculatings, etc., and hence the inductive correlation (if one is found) *presupposes* a distinct criterion for identifying silent speech or calculation. And, of course, it is perfectly possible, even if there are such correlated processes, that my imagining (saying to myself) the sound 'a' when reciting the alphabet in my mind

[5] Quoted by Russell, AM 153, from J. B. Watson, 'Image and Affection in Behaviour', *Journal of Philosophy, Psychology and Scientific Methods*, 10 (July 1913).

and someone else's doing so correspond to *different* processes in each of us. And that shows that the *concepts* of identity or difference of mental images cannot be determined by reference to physiological processes.

2.1   (i) 'a process in the larynx or the brain': PI p. 212 observes with respect to aspect-seeing that the psychological concept hangs out of reach of any physiological explanation. *Mutatis mutandis*, this remark applies to imagining, saying to oneself, etc. (cf. PI p. 220).

Z §§608ff. remarks that no supposition is more natural than that there should be *no* process in the brain correlated with thinking, so that it would be *impossible* to read off thought-processes from brain-processes. We are inclined to think that there *must* be a corresponding process, but that merely indicates that we are in the grip of a picture. For why the 'must'? – Otherwise, we might reply, one could not *explain* thinking; it would be utterly mysterious! – Not at all. We could not explain thinking *in that way*, but who says that it must be explicable thus? And if there were such a psycho-physical parallelism, would that be any *less* mysterious than its absence?

SECTION 377

1   The 'logician' in (a) echoes the view criticized in §350 ('It is 5 o'clock on the sun' means simply that it is just the same time there as it is here when it is 5 o'clock). But that manoeuvre has been shown to be futile. It is a mistake to think that the concept of X is given independently of the criteria of identity for X's. What counts as the same X or a different X is a contribution to the grammar of the expression 'X', not a further (epistemological) question that can be subsequently settled once the concept of X is determined (cf. PI §353). An analogous absurdity to severing a concept from the criteria of identity for things falling under it is the idea that the concept of being high is determined independently of the manner in which we establish that a building is high on the one hand or that a musical note is high on the other – as if this were merely an extraneous psychological or epistemological question and not part of the grammar of 'high building' or 'high note'.

(b) follows §350 in taking the criterion of sameness of two images (parallel to the identity of time here and on the sun) as parasitic upon the criterion for an image being an image of such-and-such, e.g. red. (In §350, of course, there *is* no criterion for its being 5 o'clock on the sun, and *therefore* no criterion for its being the same time on the sun as it is here.) In the third-person case, the criterion for the redness of his image is that he says, e.g., 'I am imagining the colour red' or points at a poppy and says 'That is the colour I imagined'. But in my own case, *I have no criterion*. I do not say 'I am imagining red' on the grounds of my behaviour, any more than I say 'I am in pain' on the basis of my behaviour. So too, if someone says how he imagined the colour of the wall to be (e.g. that ↗ colour), and I respond that I imagined it the same, I employ no criterion of identity.

Does this finally explode the idea that I 'derive the description' of what I imagine from a private object, read it off the facts which are accessible only to me? No, not yet. For the wayward philosopher may try yet another avenue, viz. that in one's own case one *recognizes* one's mental image as an image of, say, red. One might then rightly say that the description is read off the facts. This is explored in the next remarks.

1.1   'wie ein Mensch sich von der Gleichheit überzeugt': 'how a person satisfies himself of identity'.

2   LPE 281 raises with respect to mental images a question parallel to PI §253 on sensations: viz. *can* two different people have the same mental image? Here too we are tempted to argue that I cannot have your image, therefore I cannot have the same image as you, but only one exactly similar. But for precisely the same reasons as in §253, this is confused. If A and B have an image of X characterized in the same way, then they have the same image.

2.1   (i) 'For myself, when it is my own image, none': MS. 166, 29f. observes that in such cases we are misguidedly tempted to transpose the grammar of physical objects to the mental domain. But

> we can't apply any such criteria in our own case, and that's what we mean by talking of the privacy of the objects. Privacy here really means the absence of means of comparison. Only we mix up the states of affairs when we are prevented from comparing the objects with that of not having fixed a method of comparison. And in the moment we would fix such a way of comparing we would no longer talk of 'sensations'. (In English)

Of course, one is inclined to object that in one's own case too, one distinguishes between pretending to have . . . and really having . . .; for 'surely I must make this distinction on some grounds! Oddly enough – no! – I do distinguish, but not on any *grounds*!' (MS. 166, 44).

(ii) 'And what goes for "red" also goes for "same" ': MS. 180(a), 60f. explains – when two impressions (or images) are like *this* ↗ (and I can *show* you in the course of explaining what it means to be the same), then we call them the same. I don't recognize that they are the same in any different way than that they are red. For I say that my image is red, i.e. an image of something red, if it is this ↗ colour; and I say that my image is the same as the one I had yesterday if both were images of this ↗.

3   It is tempting to think that distinguishing between sameness and difference (independently of the concept of what it is that is identical or different) is the most fundamental and simple of the mind's operations. This was nicely articulated by James:

> *the mind can always intend, and know when it intends to think of the same.*
> This sense of sameness is the very keel and backbone of our thinking.[6]

and subsequently:

> Any fact, be it thing, event or quality, may be conceived sufficiently for purposes of identification, if only it be singled out and marked so as to separate it from other things. Simply calling it 'This' or 'That' will suffice.[7]

SECTION 378

1   In response to §377, the interlocutor shifts to a judgement of identity of two mental images in one's own case, e.g. saying that I now have the same image as I had yesterday. Surely, before I can rightly say this, I must *recognize* them as the same, just as before I can rightly say that *this* is the same letter as the one I saw yesterday, I must recognize it as the same. Similarly, one is inclined to think that if I conjure up an image of A and an image of B, then *before* I can say that I imagine them as being the same colour, I must *recognize* the two images as being of the same colour.

The claim is confused. If recognizing were a mental event or process that occurs prior to saying that the two images are the same, then how is one to know that once this has occurred, the word 'same' describes one's recognition; i.e. how is one to know that this event is 'recognizing them as the same'? Does one also have to recognize the recognition? That is evidently absurd. But if I say 'I imagine A (or: My image of A is) *this* ↗ colour' (pointing to a red apple) and then add 'And I imagine B (or: My image of B is) *this* ↗ colour' (pointing again to the apple), then someone could indeed say, 'So you imagine them as being the same colour' or 'So your mental images of A and B are of the same colour'. In this case, one might say, 'I express my recognition in some other way', viz. by pointing at a sample (cf. Exg. §379).

Justification, it has already been argued (PI §265), consists in appealing to something independent (the measure, as it were, must not shrink or expand at the whim of what is measured). Now, in conformity with the previous discussion of rules, W. stresses that a justification must be (potentially) public. For just as there can be no 'private' (i.e. unshareable) rule, so too there can be no 'private' justification, otherwise there will be

---

[6] James, *Principles of Psychology*, Vol. I, p. 459.
[7] Ibid., p. 462.

no distinction between being justified and thinking that one is justified.
So if I need a justification for using a word, it must also be one for
someone else. (A rule which I can follow must be one which it *makes
sense* for another person to follow.) But my characterization of my
mental image as being red or as being the same as the one I had yesterday
neither needs nor admits of justification. It is neither justified *nor*
unjustified; but, of course, 'to use a word without a justification does
not mean to use it wrongfully' (PI §289).

1.1   'dass das Wort "gleich" meine Erkenntnis beschreibt?': should this be
translated 'that the word "same" describes what I recognize (or am aware
of)' or 'that the word "same" describes my recognition (awareness)'? It
might be said that it makes no difference, since 'to describe my
recognition', if it means anything in this case, means to describe what I
recognize. But perhaps the more cumbersome version, as well as being a
more literal translation, also captures better the philosophical bafflement.
(Cf. 'eine Vorstellung beschreiben' in §367.) Note that 'recognize' does
not distinguish 'erkennen' from 'wiedererkennen'.

2   This derives from MS. 180(a), 65f., which is part of an extended
discussion of recognition of mental images (pp. 57 – 72). W. explores,
and rejects a variety of avenues:
    (i) What does one call 'comparing one's own images'? Well, I say, e.g.,
that I have the same image of red as previously. So how do I compare
them? One is inclined to say that one directs one's attention to whether
they are the same or different. But how do I do that? Isn't it just twaddle?
Isn't it rather that if asked in appropriate circumstances whether they are
the same (and it is that which is the directing of attention), I react with
words?
    (ii) How does one compare heights? – with the unaided eye or with
the aid of a theodolite, etc. How then does one compare two sense-
impressions in the course of comparing heights with a theodolite? There
seems to be no 'how' about it. One wants to say 'I look', 'I direct my
attention', etc. And when that happens? Then I simply see that they are
the same or not the same.
    (iii) So should one say that I 'see immediately' that the impressions are
the same? That too would be nonsense. MS. 180(b), 2 elaborates this: it
only makes sense to talk of immediate recognition (or of discerning
immediately) if it also makes sense to talk of mediate recognition (or of
discerning mediately). There are language-games with this contrast: e.g.,
I can recognize or discern immediately that this is N's handwriting; I
don't need M's testimony. But this possibility of contrast does not apply
here.

LSD 110ff. focuses more sharply on the fact that it makes sense to talk of recognizing only where it also makes sense to talk of misrecognizing. We can speak of recognition only where we can also talk of correct and incorrect. But if there is no criterion of recognizing something correctly or incorrectly, then there is no room for talk of recognition at all. We say: It is the same *and* he recognized it; but if the criterion of its being the same is that he 'recognized it', then, again, we do not have a case of recognition at all. If the criterion for having the sensation or image is that one sincerely says so, that means that there is no such thing as misrecognizing it. And that means that there is no such thing as recognizing it either.

3   That recognition lies at the heart of first-person discourse about, e.g., memory and imagination is a fundamental tenet of empiricism, clearly articulated in Hume's explanations of the relations between impressions and ideas. Russell was heir to that tradition: 'It is this fact, that images resemble antecedent sensations, which enables us to call them images "of" this or that. For the understanding of memory, and of knowledge generally, the recognizable resemblance of images and sensations is of fundamental importance' (AM 155).

Section 379

1   In §378 the interlocutor supposed a process of recognition to mediate between having a mental image and describing it, e.g., as the same as an image one had yesterday. W.'s response was: once the recognition has occurred, how is one to know which word applies? Now he probes further. One wants to say 'I recognize it as *this*, and then I remember what it is called'. This makes sense only if *it* and *this* are distinct and, moreover, only if I can point to *this* (cf. §378: 'Only if I can express my recognition in some other way'). In a psychological experiment, for example, I may recognize the picture on the screen as a picture of *this* geometrical figure on the table. Then I may remember that this figure is called 'an icosahedron'. But in the case of a mental image, neither of these two conditions is satisfied. (Of course, I might say 'I had a vivid mental image of that curious figure on the table – what is it called?')

1   'Ich erkenne es . . . ': to preserve uniformity with §§378, 380 – 1, better 'I recognize it'.

2   This derives from the long discussion in MS. 180(a); see Exg. §§201, 2(i), and 202, 2(i).

SECTION 380

1   'How do I recognize that this is red?' The question is an expression of
succumbing to the temptation to interpose an act or process of recognition between seeing and saying 'This is red'.[8] Note that W. has
broadened the scope of the discussion; for now, it seems, he is no longer
concerned only with characterizing one's mental image as an image of
red, but also with characterizing a colour one sees as red (cf. MS. 180(a),
61ff.). For in respect of the confusion that is here in question, viz. of the
interposition of a *private* transition from what is seen to saying what is
seen, seeing red and imagining red are similar.

      If we suppose that when I see something red I recognize that it is red,
and if we think that recognizing that it is red is an event or process
antecedent to saying that it is red, what should we say that we see *before*
we 'recognize' that what we see is red (MS. 180(a), 61)? The interlocutor
is tempted to say 'I see that it is *this*' and then he remembers what 'this' is
called. But what is the 'this' that he sees it to be? Of course, he could say
that he sees that the object is this colour, pointing to something *else*,
which functions as a sample. That is correct, but now we note that he
must see that the object before him *is* the colour of the sample. Does he
also *recognize* the identity of the colour of the sample and the colour of
the object before him? And does he now need a sample for this identity,
and so on *ad infinitum*?

      Evidently that is not the trap into which he has fallen. Rather, in seeing
that the object is *this*, he wants to point to the object itself, in fact to its
colour! Or, more accurately, to his impression of its colour. And he
wants to point with his attention! This is spelled out in BB 175: one
wants to let what one sees speak for itself, as if the colour seen were its
own description. In fact, W. argues, one is merely going through the
motions of attending to a sample, although there is no sample. For an
object cannot be a sample of itself, and an ostensive definition says
nothing about the object which is functioning as a sample. One seems to
be pointing out to oneself what colour one sees, whereas all one is doing
is staring at a coloured object, as it were contemplating a possible sample
which is not used as a sample but seems to be its own description.

      Why does W. contend that the interlocutor is steering towards the idea
of a private ostensive definition? One reason is this: one wants to say 'I
see *this*, and then I know what it is called'. But what is 'knowing what it

---

[8] This is parallel to the thoughts that I must understand an order *before* I can obey it, know
where my pain is before I can point to it, etc. 'We are treating here of cases in
which . . . the grammar of a word seems to suggest the "necessity" of a certain
intermediary step, although in fact the word is used in cases in which there is no such
intermediary step' (BB 130).

is called'? Well, I must be able to justify saying that it is red. An ostensive definition, a rule for the use of 'red', is a justification (LSD 16). But I do not employ a public sample here. I recognize that what I see is red; I remember that that is what it is called. And now it must seem as if

> recognizing always consisted in comparing two impressions with one another. It is as if I carried a picture of an object with me and used it to perform an identification of any object as the one represented by the picture. Our memory seems to us to be the agent of such a comparison, by preserving a picture of what has been seen before, or by allowing us to look into the past (as if down a spy-glass). (PI §604 = PG 167 = Vol. XI, 7)

But an *impression* is not a rule (LSD 17), and there is no such thing as a private sample.

§380(c) clarifies: one wants to invoke a rule to justify the transition from 'I see *this*' (which really amounts to 'I see what I see', i.e. it amounts to nothing at all) to 'I see red'. But no rule can justify the *private* transition from seeing to words, i.e. to giving expression to what I see. One has to *do* something, viz. *say* 'This is red'. In the first place, even where there *is* a genuine rule, it has to be *applied*. And although there can be rules for the application of rules, explanations come to an end, and then a rule must be applied, without *further* guidance. In the second place, a 'private ostensive definition' is not a rule. The very idea of a rule mediating between a subjective impression (seeing *this*, for example) and words is incoherent, for there can be no technique of application here, no institution of use of a rule; there would be no objective regularity in the use of this putative rule and hence no distinction between applying it correctly and thinking that one is applying it correctly. (Cf. Vol. 2, 'Following rules, mastery of techniques and practices', pp. 178 – 9; Exg. §§201 – 2).

2   This derives from MS. 180(a), 67 – 74. It is noteworthy that this discussion of recognition led up to a draft of what is now PI §§201 – 2 (cf. Exg.). A more polished, re-ordered version occurs in MS. 129, 116ff., and a more compressed re-drafting of that, approximating to the final draft, occurs later in the same MS. at p. 182 (see Vol. 2, p. 148).

W. discussed recognition extensively. A number of further points bear on the remark here. The concept of recognition is far more specialized, variegated, and context-sensitive than one supposes. It would be quite wrong to say that I recognize familiar objects in my room everyday when I see them or familiar faces of my friends whom I see daily. One context in which we speak of recognizing something or someone *as* such-and-such is if we initially do not know, or do not realize, that it is such-and-such (MS. 180(a), 62). But if a philosopher were to ask whether we recognized the furniture in our room this morning, we would probably say 'Yes'. If so, we mean no more than that on seeing it, we did *not* ask ourselves what it was. Here we conflate absence of lack of recognition with presence of recognition (cf. LSD 17f.; PG 165ff.) Only in very special circumstances does it make sense to talk of recognizing a colour (e.g. 'That brilliant yellow reminds me of something . . . Ah, yes – it is the colour Turner used in his painting of . . . '). But when I look at the sky and see that it is blue, I cannot be said to go through a process of recognizing the colour (cf. MS. 180(a), 61 – 3). Of course, I may look at a coloured object and see its colour, but not remember what it is called. But then I can tell someone later and point at a sample, saying 'It was this ↗ colour', and he may say 'Ah, yes – that's eau-de-Nil'. It does not follow that when I look at a red poppy and say that it is red, I first recognize that it is red and then remember what that colour is called.

SECTION 381

1   The interlocutor persists: if I do not recognize that the colour of this tomato is red by first seeing *this* and then knowing what it is called, how *do* I recognize it? The question is misleading, but one might answer 'I have learnt English'. Of course, that is not a *way* of recognizing, nor is it a justification for saying 'This is red'. It merely reminds us that 'knowing' here consists in mastery of a technique of the use of a word. Someone who knows what 'red' means can *say* when confronted with a red object in daylight that it is red. But nothing mediates between his seeing and saying.

1.1   'Wie erkenne': to preserve uniformity with §§378 – 80, better 'How do I recognize?'

2   This derives from MS. 180(a), 68, where it is followed by:

Wie weisst Du, dass diese Worte hier passen? – Nun, ich habe sie gelernt. Und wie weiss ich, wie ich diese Lehren hier anzuwenden habe?
   'Die Lehren lassen mich im Stich; ich muss jetzt einen Sprung machen' heisst: Ein 'Sehen, dass dies rot ist' nützt mich nichts, wenn ich doch erst noch Worte finden muss // zu den Worten oder Handlungen übergehen //, die der Situation // Lage // passen.

(How do you know that these words fit here? – Well, I have learnt them. And how do I know how I am to apply this teaching here?
   'The teaching leaves me in the lurch; I must now make a leap' means: A 'seeing that this is red' does not avail if I must still find words // make the transition to words or deeds // which fit the situation // circumstances. (MS. 180(a), 68 – 9)

That is to say, mastery of the technique of using 'red' cannot intelligibly be thought to fall short of being able to apply it. The use of a word is guided by a rule, but *given the rule*, one must *apply* it.

BB 148f. observes that the temptation to say that something *happened*, e.g. an act of recognition, between seeing and saying that such-and-such is red, something which makes one say 'That is red', stems from the fact that one can look at an object and say a word, viz. 'red', and still not be naming the colour. But, by implication, knowing what 'red' means is not something that happens. Nothing *makes* me call what I see 'red'; rather, I exercise my capacity to name colours.

It is noteworthy that throughout the numerous discussions of colour-recognition there is a perhaps unavoidable equivocation on 'justification'. On the one hand, W. insists, one may say that there is *no* justification, no *reason* for saying that something one sees is red (LSD 126; RFM 406). One has no *ground* or *criterion* for an ordinary, immediate colour-judgement. On the other hand, he insists, an ostensive definition, which is a rule for the use of a word, *is* a justification (LSD 17). Though confusing, there is no inconsistency here. An ostensive definition is not an evidential or criterial justification. Moreover, our ordinary colour-judgements are typically made in the absence of any sample (although they make sense only because they belong to a language-game which is essentially played with samples). But one may point to a sample to determine agreement in definitions, and that one points to a correct sample is a criterion of one's understanding of the colour-name in question. One may also justify one's calling A 'red' by pointing to a sample of red and saying 'That↗ colour is red, and A *is* that colour'. This justifies one's application of the word to A; i.e. it vindicates one's use of the word, but not by way of evidence or justifying grounds of judgement. Moreover, it does not answer the question of how one *knows* that what one sees (viz. A) is red. For there is no answer to that question save 'I know what "red" means, I have learnt English'. Finally, though appeal to a sample can, *in this sense*, justify the application of a word, the agreement of the colour with the sample cannot be further justified – that, in the practice of the language-game with colours, is what is called 'being red' (cf. RFM 406).

SECTION 382

1   After generalizing the problem of recognizing the colour of one's mental image to recognizing a colour *per se*, W. now reverts to the mental image. The picture that is being explored is of a 'private object' from which one derives a description (PI §374). Part of the conception is

the idea that understanding a word is associating it with a mental image, and also that uttering a word and meaning it is having a mental image and, as it were, transcribing it into words. It is these ramifications of the primitive picture that are now under attack.

Suppose I hear the word 'blue' and an image comes to mind. How can I *justify* this occurrence? For if I cannot justify it, it is mere coincidence and belongs to the natural history of the use of the word. *That* I associate the word with a mental image does not determine correct from incorrect uses of the word, for I must associate it with the *right* mental image. Whether it is right is determined by the rule for the use of 'blue', and that is not, and does not involve, a mental image. But if so, then the mental image, even if it is 'right', is irrelevant to whether I understand the word.

Of course, I was taught how to use the word 'blue', but not by being shown a mental image of blue (LSD 39f.). Rather, I was shown samples and told that *that* ↗ colour is blue. But a mental image is not a sample. One cannot point at a mental image, even in one's own case; and the phrase '*This* mental image' has no ostensive, but only anaphoric, use.

2   Vol. XII, 120 has a draft of this in the context of a long discussion of knowing what the word 'blue' means. The salient points are: (a) I cannot test whether I understand what 'blue' means by calling a blue mental image to mind. For how can the word 'blue' show me which colour I should select from my mental colour-box, and how can the colour which I imagine show me that *it* is the right one? Do I *choose* which image fits the word 'blue'? And can't the *wrong* one come (p. 114)? (b) The criterion for whether I understand the word is the agreement of others to my applications of it (i.e. that this is what is called 'blue'), not the image of a colour that comes into my mind (p. 115). (c) It is tempting here to try to distinguish between objective and subjective understanding. One might conceive of my subjective understanding as a matter of associating an image with a word heard or read (as if one turned a knob and a little card with a picture on it pops up). So subjectively understanding a word would mean associating it with a picture; objectively understanding it would mean associating it with the *right* picture. One might then say that a language, in so far as it is understood only subjectively, is not a means of communication with others, but a tool-box for one's own private use. But the question is whether this is still to be called a language. It is to be so called only if one plays language-games with oneself; and that is indeed possible, as in Robinson Crusoe's case. Yet what he does counts as a language-game only in so far as it displays an appropriate regularity of behaviour. If someone makes noises, yet displays no such regularities, we could not say 'Perhaps he is speaking a purely private language in which he associates each noise with the same mental image' (pp. 116 – 8).

On p. 120 is a draft of PI §382(a) – (b), followed by

Was heisst denn hier: '*diese* Vorstellung'? Kann ich denn auf sie zeigen? Kann ich etwa *in mir* auf sie zeigen, wenn sie *meine* Vorstellung ist? Wenn ich mir einen blauen Kreis und einen Pfeil vorstelle, der auf ihn zeigt – zeigt der Pfeil auf meine Vorstellung? Könnte ich mir auf diese Weise private hinweisende Definitionen geben? (Denke immer an den *Gebrauch* der Zeichen!)

(Yet what is here called '*This* image'? Can I point at it? Can I perhaps point at it *in myself*, if it is *my* image? If I imagine a blue circle and an arrow which points at it – does the arrow point at my image? Could I give myself private ostensive definitions in this way? (Think always of the *use* of signs!))

To imagine an arrow pointing at a blue circle is not to point, nor to imagine anything pointing at an image of a blue circle, any more than to imagine something rotating is to rotate a mental image!

SECTION 383

1   Having provided an antidote to the temptations of the private object off which one reads its description, W. reverts to the methodological point raised in §370: one ought to ask not what images are or what happens when one imagines something, but how the word 'imagination' is used. This makes it appear as if we are interested only in words, not in the nature of imagination; but that, W. urged, is an illusion. Now he examines a further source of confusion. To be sure, we are not analysing a phenomenon, i.e. describing what happens when, e.g., we think (understand, imagine), but a concept, e.g. the concept of thinking (understanding, imagining). We are indeed concerned with describing the use of a word. But now this may appear like a commitment to a form of nominalism. Nominalists repudiate the Platonists' idea that words stand for universals, abstract essences in reality, and insist that there are only words. (Similarly, the formalists in mathematics deny that numbers are abstract objects and insist that there are only numerals.) But this crude dichotomy is misleading. One is led to impale oneself on the horns of this dilemma through a misguided commitment to the Augustinian picture of language, according to which all words are names, which either name something or name nothing. The nominalist is right to think that there are no *entities* corresponding to abstract nouns, adjectives of quality, or numerals. The Platonist is right to insist that qualities or numbers are not just words. The dilemma is avoidable once the idea that all words are names which stand for some entity is abandoned. The description of the *use* of words will clarify the concepts that bewilder us, illuminate the difference between numerals and numbers, bring to light the nature or essence of thinking (cf. PI §§370 – 3). The essence of

thought is not to be found by analysis of the phenomena of thinking, but by clarification of the use of the words 'think' and 'thought'.

Section 384

1   This emphasizes the general point of §383. It is a fundamental misunderstanding to think that I must study the headache I now have (the phenomenon) in order to clarify philosophical problems about pain (cf. PI §314). But it is no less misleading to suppose that clarifying the use of a word falls short of analysing, rendering perspicuous, the concept it expresses. When one learns the correct use of the word 'pain', one learns the *concept* of pain. Hence, if an investigation into the essence of thinking is a conceptual investigation, it is to be pursued by describing the use of the relevant words.

Section 385

1   After the lengthy detour, W. now picks up the thread of §369. The concept of calculating in the head is parasitic on the concept of calculating. Does it follow that being able to calculate in the head is parasitic on *having done* calculations out loud or on paper? W. does not answer the question here, but only raises the further question: what would be the criterion here for being able to calculate in the head? Is the implied conclusion that it is *not* imaginable for someone to learn to calculate in his head unless he does calculations aloud or on paper?
    MS. 124, 252 suggests that that would be wrong.

> Wäre es denkbar, dass Einer im Kopfe rechnen lernte, ohne je schriftlich, oder mündlich zu rechnen? Nun warum nicht. 'Es lernen', heisst nur, dazu gebracht werden, dass man's kann. Aber könnte man dazu *abgerichtet* werden? – Es könnte uns Einer Rechnungen schriftlich vormachen, wir würden nie welche schreiben, oder aussprechen; aber nach und nach kämen wir dahin, das Resultat ohne Fehler hinzuschreiben.

> (Would it be conceivable for someone to learn to calculate in the head without ever calculating on paper or aloud? Well, why not? 'Learning it' means only: being brought to the point of being able to. But could one be *trained* to do it? – Someone might demonstrate written calculations to us, although we would never write any down or say them aloud; but by and by we would come to the point of writing down the result without mistakes.)

What would be the criterion here for being able to calculate in the head? Well, giving the correct answer and giving the right justification for it when challenged, as well as indicating how far one had got if interrupted, etc. – in short, the same criteria as in ordinary cases.

So far, so good. But is it also conceivable that a whole society might be acquainted only with calculating in the head? That is obviously more doubtful. What would the teaching and the training look like? The criteria for calculating in the head would not interlock, as they do in the previous case, with calculating aloud or on paper. It would make no sense for someone to say 'Wait, I've added the first two columns, but not the third', for the concept of a *column* of figures is parasitic on written notation. And so on. One might conceive of such beings asking one of their kind to multiply 123 by 794, and him then answering '97,662'. The others might pause a moment and then say 'Yes, that's right'; and so on. But is this *calculating in the head*? For remember, they *have no concept of calculating* (unlike the previous case). One might, given further details, conceive of this as a limiting (degenerate) case (as a point is a limiting case of a conic section). But equally, one might deny that the concept of *calculating* had any role to play here at all. Instead, one might say of these beings that they know the answers to sums, *without calculating*. (Would that be 'intolerably mysterious'? No more so than knowing the answer by doing a calculation in the head! (cf. §364))

1   'gravitate towards another paradigm': viz. that of the mathematical prodigy who can answer without calculating.

2   In MS. 124, 247ff. this occurs in a consecutive sequence of remarks incorporating PI §364 and §366, all on mental arithmetic.

It might seem at first blush that the above interpretation conflicts with the later remarks 'Only if you have learnt to calculate – on paper or out loud – can you be made to grasp, by means of this concept, what calculating in the head is' (PI p. 216) and 'You can only learn what "calculating in the head" is by learning what "calculating" is; you can only learn to calculate in your head by learning to calculate' (PI p. 220). There is no conflict, however, for in the envisaged scenario (MS. 124, 252) the learner *is* taught what calculating is; it is demonstrated to him. True enough, he *does* no calculation aloud or on paper, but one may presume that he corrects the overt miscalculations of others, checks his calculations in the head against his teacher's written calculations. Here one might well say that he *can* calculate on paper, but does not. Not so, however, in the 'limiting case' of a tribe who 'calculate only in the head'.

SECTION 386

1   W.'s investigations into the concept of calculating in the head look like qualms about whether he really calculates in his head. (In §364 the interlocutor interpreted W. as suggesting that doing a sum in one's head

is not really calculating; to which the reply was 'It is real calculating-in-the-head!') Hence the interlocutor says, quite rightly, that if one knows what it is to calculate, then if one says that one has calculated something in one's head, one will have done so. For if one had not so calculated, one would not have said that one had. And, by parity of reasoning, if one says one has a red mental image, then one's mental image is red. And so on.

This is all true, but it mislocates W.'s qualms, which are not qualms over whether he may not be *mistaken* in saying that he has calculated in the head or over whether his mental image might be not red but some other colour. For, to be sure, it makes *no sense* to suppose that one might make such a mistake. And here is the nub: for how is it *possible* that all doubts and uncertainties are excluded? The interlocutor supposes that the inward calculation and the mental image of red are private processes or objects from which one derives their description (cf. PI §374). Hence his exclamation 'You always know well enough what it is to calculate' and 'You know what "red" is elsewhere'; if one knows when to call an apple 'red', surely one can be confident about calling one's mental image 'red'!

But that is precisely mistaken. However good my eyesight, it makes *sense* for me to make a mistake about the colour of an object in view (the light may be poor; the object may be in the shade or in the vicinity of other objects whose colours induce a deceptive appearance; or I may have been looking at very bright objects whose effect is to distort my perception for the moment). But does my confidence that I have imagined *this* colour stem from my knowledge that my mind's eye is not bedazzled or from the fact that the light of the mind casts no distorting shadows? If my assertion that my mental image was *this* ↗ colour were read off a 'private object', then it might be supposed that I *look* at my mental image and look at this patch of cloth and see that they are the same colour. But that makes no sense. There is no such thing as *looking* at my mental image (it does not matter, e.g., whether the light is poor), and my mental image cannot be said to *look like* the colour of the cloth. The representation of the image in reality, by, for example, painting a patch and saying '*That* is the colour I imagined' is not done by comparing the image with reality (the patch) for match in the manner in which a representation of the colour of the curtains in a painting is done by collating.

The interlocutor objects that one can recognize a man from a drawing straight off, so why not a colour one has imagined from a splash of paint? Well, one can – one can say: that is the brilliant yellow I imagined. But in the case of the subject of a portrait, I can say what he looks like (youthful, with humorous eyes, unruly hair, etc.) and can say that he looks as the drawing represents him as being. But if I represent my mental image by a patch of paint, I cannot say that the coloured patch tells you what my image *looks like* or say what my image *must look like* if it is to be an image of this colour. There is no such thing as *teaching* someone to have a mental image of precisely this colour, although he may indeed have one and say so.

1   (i) 'das Abbilden der Vorstellung in die Wirklichkeit': 'representing the image in reality'.

(ii) 'Sehen sie sich denn zum Verwechseln ähnlich?': 'Do they look so alike that one might mix them up?'

(iii) 'I cannot accept his testimony . . .': the interlocutor is inclined to say that he *knows* that his mental image is red. If asked how he knows, he will insist that he can see the colour before his mind. Asked whether he is certain that it is precisely this shade of red, he will reply that he is quite certain, that he has no doubts. Does this not refute W.'s case? Does it not show that the mental image is a private object off which one reads a description? No, not at all. For this is not *testimony*. It is not a *report*, which is very probably true. Rather, it is an expression of the pictures we use in this domain. It shows what we are inclined to say, what figures of speech come naturally to us when we talk about the imagination. (But it does not show that they are only figures of speech. And it does not reveal the peculiar application of these turns of phrase; *that* requires the philosophical skill in noting grammatical differences which W. is trying to teach us.) Cf. PI §594(c).

(iv) 'what he is *inclined* to say': and what he is inclined to say is, of course, not philosophy or a theory, but the raw material for philosophy, something for philosophical treatment (cf. PI §254).

2   MS. 124, 274 follows this with a draft of PI §316. What goes hand in hand with this misconception of imagining is the idea that the concepts of the 'inner', e.g. thinking, can be clarified by 'introspective observation', by noting 'what happens' when we are thinking.

'But it is *this*: that we should be able . . .': MS. 124, 73f. is more explicit:

Sondern dies: Gefragt, welche Farbe ich mir vorgestellt habe, zeige ich auf sie, oder beschreibe sie; aber wie kommt es, dass ich das ohne weiteres tun kann; dass mir das Abbilden der Vorstellung in die Wirklichkeit so wenig Schwierigkeit macht? Sehen sich denn Vorstellung und Wirklichkeit zum Verwechseln ähnlich?

(But it is this: if asked what colour I imagined, I point at it or describe it; but how is it that I can do this without more ado; that representing the image in reality gives me so little difficulty? Do image and reality look as alike as two peas?)

1   What then is the 'deep aspect' of the matter? It is, presumably, the
logical character of avowals of the inner, that something which has the
form of a description of an object visible only to its owner is not one, that
two language-games should be homologous, yet so utterly different.
And further, that a mental image, which seems a picture *par excellence*, a
'super-likeness' of that of which it is an image (PI §389), is not a likeness
at all and is not a picture.

1   We can, without more ado, point out or describe the colour we have
imagined (§386). We can also, without more ado, say that we can show
someone what colour violet, for example, is. In the former case we are
tempted to give a pseudo-explanation of how it is possible that we
should be able to do this, viz. that we *copy* our mental image (when we
paint what colours we imagined) or read off its description by observing
it. A parallel illusion besets the latter case, for we are inclined to think
that our confidence that we can show someone what violet is (i.e. that we
know that we can show it) rests on the fact that we conjure up a mental
image of violet. If we can do *that*, we think, then we can surely show
someone what violet is: if we are given a paintbox, we simply point at
the pigment which is the same colour as our violet mental image!
    Both pictures are misconceived. That I am able to show (or say) what
colour I imagine is not a capacity distinct from – logically independent
of – being able to imagine a certain colour; for showing (or saying) what
colour I imagined is a *criterion* for having imagined that colour. And
conversely, an inability to show (or say) what colour one is imagining
(given, e.g., a comprehensive colour-chart) is a criterion for not, or not
clearly, imagining a specific colour at all.
    Similarly, knowing that I can tell you what colour violet is does not
rest on conjuring up a mental image of violet (although one may do so).
For, (a) one would then ask how one knows that the mental image one
has conjured up is a mental image of violet rather than of some other
colour. One cannot say that one 'recognizes' it (PI §378), and if one falls
back on the simple assertion that one can conjure up an image of violet at
will, one might as well simply insist (probably rightly) that one can pick
out violet on sight. (b) If one can conjure up a mental image of violet,
how will that enable one to identify the violet paint in the paintbox?
There is, after all, no technique of laying an image alongside reality as a
measure. A mental image is not a sample and cannot be compared with

reality; i.e. there is no such thing as comparing my mental image with a coloured object to see if they are the same colour. For a mental image of violet does not *look like* the pigment in the paintbox, and no one, myself included, can *look at it* (cf. Exg. §386).

How then *do* I know that I shall be able to do something? W. reduces the question to its right, farcical proportions: how do I know that the state I am in is that of being able to do that thing? But against *this* muddle we have been forewarned: being able to do something is not a mental state, as being excited, depressed, or (perhaps) being in pain are (Exg. PI p. 59n.; BB 117f.), and an avowal of ability is not an avowal of being in such a state. (And if it were, should one argue: I am in such-and-such a state now, and in the past I have always found that when I am in such a state, I subsequently succeed in doing so-and-so?) So do I *know* that I can show you what violet is? Of course, just as I know that I can recite the ABC. How do I know? Well, I might say again, 'I have learnt English', I know what 'violet' means (and a criterion for my knowing that is precisely that I do pick out violet on sight). But what justifies my claim to know this? One might reply 'I have used this word correctly countless times in the past', but also 'that we don't need any grounds for *this* certainty either. What could justify the certainty *better* than success?' (PI §324).

2   These reflections originate in PR 57f. My assertion that I can point out a certain colour may express the expectation that I shall recognize it on sight in the same sense that I expect a headache if I am hit on the head. This is an expectation that 'belongs to physics', i.e. has inductive grounds. Or it may not have such grounds and, W. here suggests, would not be falsified if I fail to recognize the colour. 'Instead, it is as if the proposition is saying that I possess a paradigm that I could at any time compare the colour with.' But both interpretations, he continues, are suspect. For, regarding the first, if I do give a sign of recognition when I look at a colour, how do I know it is the colour I *meant*?[9] And with regard to the second, 'we are still forced to say that the image of the colour isn't the same as the colour that is really seen, and in that case, how can one compare these two?' Nevertheless, W. concludes, 'the naive theory of *forming-an-image* can't be utterly wrong.'

His position at this stage was clearly unstable. The seeds of suspicion grew; the 'naive theory' *is* utterly wrong. In the sense in which a mental image has a colour (is an image of a colour) it *is* the same colour as the object one points at when one says 'That ↗ is the colour I imagined'; but, of course, the image is not a sample, and the criterion for its being

---

[9] Well, I said I can pick out *violet*, and *this* is what is called 'violet'. So my characterization of my image presupposes my mastery of the use of the word.

such-and-such a colour is not its *match* with a public sample, but the
speaker's avowal, which rests on no criteria at all (PI §377).

Section 389

1   W. concludes this part of the discussion by pin-pointing one deep
aspect of the illusions that beset us here. We think of our mental images
as pictures which only we can see, in fact as 'super-pictures' which
cannot be misinterpreted. For an ordinary picture, though it is a picture
of X, may look like (and be wrongly taken to be) a picture of Y. But it is
essential to a mental image of X that it is of X and nothing else. So it
comes to seem like a super-likeness. Yet this is confused, for that the
mental image of X *is* an image of X is not determined by its likeness to
X. We are prone to think that it is a picture which needs no interpretation, so closely does it resemble what it is a picture of. It is true that it
needs no interpretation and also that it makes no sense to suppose that I
might be mistaken in my characterization of my mental image. But that
is not because it looks more like its object than any picture. It is rather
that it neither looks like nor fails to look like its object. It is not a picture
at all. How does one *know* that one's image is of X and not Y (which
looks like X)? One does not *know*, nor can one be mistaken. One *says so*,
without grounds, as one says what one means or what one thinks.

2   The relation between an image and what it is an image of is
comparable not to the relation between a portrait and its subject (where
the portrait may resemble someone or something else), but to the
relation between an expectation and what fulfils it (BB 36), a thought (or
proposition) and what makes it true (PG 161), or a possibility and what it
is a possibility of (PI §194). It is not an image *of* X in virtue of a method
of projection or in virtue of a similarity, let alone a 'super-likeness'. (Cf.
LA 67.)

Section 390

1   This opens a fresh sequence of remarks on the imagination which are
concerned with the relation between imaginability and the bounds of
sense. §281 and §284 gave ample reasons for dismissing as irrelevant
image-mongery anyone's insistence that they *can* imagine a stone's being
conscious.

1.1   'And if anyone can do so': since W. clearly holds that there is no such
thing as a stone's having consciousness or being conscious, how should

this be understood? Not – that perhaps someone really can imagine this, but it is of no interest. For 'a stone's being conscious' is a senseless concatenation of words, and there is here nothing *to* imagine. So either (a) someone can conjure up a certain mental image in connection with these words, but that is just irrelevant image-mongery; or (b) someone *says* he can imagine it, but that is of no interest (cf. MS. 179, 58, quoted below).

2   This originates in MS. 165, 59. Its context is an exploration of the different language-games with 'image', which illustrates the categorial diversity of the use of distinct psychological verbs, a diversity that necessitates the careful investigation of particular cases. After a fragmentary draft of PI §§391, 393 – 4, W. observes that here, as always, the first mistake we make in a philosophical investigation is the question itself. Then

> Aber hat nicht Spinoza gesagt, wenn ein Stein Bewusstsein hätte, würde er glauben, er fiele zur Erde weil er fallen will? Das ist die Art von Fiktion die in einer Fabel am Platz sein kann, aber in der Philosophie gar nichts leistet. Erstens: Wie haben wir uns das vorzustellen dass ein Stein Bewusstsein hat? Zweitens: Welchen Grund haben wir zur Annahme, ein Stein, wenn er etwas glauben könnte, würde eher das als das glauben? Drittens: Wenn wir, die wir doch Bewusstsein haben, von einer Höhe herabstürzen, sind wir der Meinung wir fallen, weil wir fallen *wollen*?[10]

> (But didn't Spinoza say, that if a stone were conscious, it would believe that it falls to the earth because it wants to fall? This is the sort of fiction which has a place in a fable, but in philosophy achieves nothing. First: how are we supposed to imagine a stone's being conscious? Secondly: what reason do we have for the supposition that a stone, if it could believe something, would believe this rather than that? Thirdly: when we, who are conscious, fall from a height, are we of the opinion that we fall because we *want* to fall?)

Then, one remark later, occurs a draft of PI §418(b), followed by §390.

In a fairy-tale, we can talk of pots and pans seeing and hearing (PI §282), but this is a special game with language that we play, a kind of nonsense. If someone says that he can imagine a conscious stone, this is a similar nonsense, an idle play of the imagination that traverses the bounds of sense to no purpose.

MS. 179, 58 supposes someone saying 'I'm not sure whether I can't imagine that this chair is in pain'. So what! In what way is that of any interest? What connection does it have with our ordinary life? This remark is followed by a draft of PI §391.

---

[10] There are three different drafts of this remark, of which this is the most polished.

SECTION 391

1   Someone who insists that he can imagine a stone's being conscious is
indulging in mere image-mongery. Unlike the narrator of a fairy-tale or
fable, his putative imagining has no consequences, save to stir up
philosophical clouds of dust. What does his imagining amount to, save
mere words which lead nowhere? By contrast, one might actually
imagine that the people in the street are in frightful pain, but are artfully
concealing it. But if this is really to be a case of imagining, I must not
merely say to myself 'His soul (mind) is in pain, but what has that to do
with his body?' for that would again be mere image-mongery (*Vorstelle-
rei*), motivated by confused philosophy. Rather, I must suppose *artful*
concealment, strength of will not to show the pain. I might even imagine
sympathizing with them, but not showing my sympathy out of respect
for their insistent self-control. And so on. Here, unlike the example of
§390, I can really be said to be imagining and not just idly playing with
words.

1.1   (i) 'I as it were play a part': analogously to the actor in §393 below.
         (ii) 'Wenn ich das tue, sagt man etwa . . .': 'When I do this one might
say . . .' Note the connection drawn here being imagining and action
(see §393).

SECTION 392

1   So I can imagine people in the street being in frightful pain, but
concealing it. On the other hand, to say that I can imagine a stone's being
conscious is merely idle words. Is the difference, then, a matter of what
goes on in me when I am asked to imagine the one or the other? Does
imagining so-and-so consist in such-and-such going on in my mind
when I imagine it? But then someone might reply, 'I can imagine it too,
but *without* such-and-such going on.' For example (cf. §391), he might
insist that he can imagine one of the people in the street being in frightful
pain yet artfully concealing it, but *without* saying to himself 'It must be
difficult to laugh when one is in such pain'.
      However, whether one can or cannot imagine something is not
determined by what goes on in one's mind when one tries to imagine it.
A report of what *went on* when one imagined . . . is 'natural science',
whereas to say *what one imagined* when one imagined . . . is a criterion
for having imagined it. But these may appear similar, and then the
analysis fluctuates misleading between empirical correlation and grammatical description of what counts as 'imagining such-and-such'.

Section 393

1   The interlocutor still insists that a *picture* of pain or a paradigm of pain must be involved in imagining someone who is laughing to be in pain (cf. PI §300). For, obviously, I do not imagine any pain-behaviour, I imagine pain – which he has. But that route has been blocked, since imagining pain is not picturing pain (ibid.). So what do I imagine when I imagine someone who is laughing to be in pain? Well, just that! But then, what is the process of imagining? Why should imagining be a *process*?

W. endeavours to relieve the philosophical pressure by reminding us of a context outside philosophy, i.e. a context in which language is *not* idling, in which we tell someone to imagine something. Thus we might tell an actor to imagine that one of the other characters is in pain and concealing it, but we do not tell him what he must do. (Nor do we describe to him what must 'go on in his mind'.) We tell him what he is to imagine and then see how he now interprets the role. Outside philosophy, imagining something interlocks with *action* (cf. §391).

.1   (i) 'And I do not necessarily imagine *my* being in pain': of course, one might, for one might say to oneself 'If I were in such dreadful pain, I should find it fearfully difficult to laugh like that; it would need great self-control'.

(ii) 'For this reason the suggested analysis is not to the point': the analysis of imagining so-and-so in terms of a 'process' of imagining. The addition of the word 'either' in the translation is both unnecessary and misleading.

2   Vol. XII, 146 makes clear what primitive picture stands in the way of a perspicuous representation of the concept of imagining. We conceive of someone imagining a red circle in terms of a picture of the person with a red circle floating, as it were, in a cloud above his head, just as artists represent a person dreaming by painting him lying asleep with a cloud hovering over him in which the 'dream picture' is painted, or again, as films represent recollections by a round image surrounded by darkness and blurred at the border. Is that what a memory 'looks like'? And yet everyone understands what this image signifies. Here one sees the primitive pictures of processes in another person's mind that correspond to forms of expression in our language.

Section 394

1   Having reminded us of the kind of context in which we say 'I imagine that . . . ' or tell someone to imagine something, and hence having

clarified the irrelevance of 'inner processes', W. now reminds us of the contexts in which one might ask someone what actually went on when he imagined something. These are, for example, the contexts of empirical investigations into accompaniments of imagining or into the heuristics of the imagination. And the answer we would expect would not be a description of *what was imagined*. ('When I imagine someone in frightful pain but not showing it, I always think of a scream cut off suddenly.')

SECTION 395

1   This draws what is, by now, an obvious conclusion. We are inclined to think of imaginability as a criterion of sense, but *many* unclarities surround that thought. There is unclarity over what *counts* as imagining, e.g. whether someone who says that he can imagine a stone's being conscious has actually imagined any such thing (although clearly, if we say that he has, it is no criterion of sense). There is unclarity over the role of mental imagery in imagining: does the absence of any mental image imply unimaginability? Moreover, does the presence of mental imagery guarantee sense? And does its absence imply lack of sense? Finally, in cases where one *can* imagine such-and-such, where 'such-and-such' makes good sense, does the fact that one can imagine it *explain* what the expression means? The answer to all these questions is 'No'.

2   MS. 129, 16ff. follows this with a long remark enumerating a variety of unclarities. 'I can imagine someone in frightful pain, but not showing it' would be followed by a description of *how* one imagines this (e.g. 'It must be difficult to laugh, . . . etc.'(PI §391)). 'I can imagine a society in which it is indecent to calculate except to pass the time'; here 'I can imagine' means roughly 'I can elaborate this picture'. 'I can imagine an endless row of trees' means, more or less, that I can associate a picture with this phrase. But it does not give an explanation of the infinite. And so on.

SECTION 396

1   If imaginability is not a criterion of sense, is not imagining something in association with a sentence a criterion of understanding? Not at all; the criteria of understanding lie in behaviour, in explanations, and in the use one makes of a word or sentence, not in accompanying mental imagery (PG 73; cf. PI §449).

Section 397

1   It is a crucial feature of the imagination that one can say or otherwise exhibit (e.g. by a drawing) what one imagined and how one imagined it. For the criterion for someone's imagining something is that he says or portrays what he imagined. Hence the question of whether imaginability ensures sense (§395) amounts to the question of whether representability by those means of representation by which one describes what one imagined ensures sense. One can, for example, draw what one imagines, and this *may* illuminate the use of a sentence and clarify its sense. But in other cases, e.g. those of imagining another person dreaming (Exg. §393, 2), a wholly misleading picture may obtrude itself.

1.1   'Mittel der Darstellung': 'means of representation'.

CHAPTER 4

The self and self-reference
(§§398 – 411)

INTRODUCTION

This sequence of fourteen remarks deals with the self or, more perspicuously, with aspects of the use of the word 'I' and 'my' which generate certain kinds of philosophical confusion. It is linked to the antecedent discussion of the imagination in as much as the example with which scrutiny of the concept of 'the visual room' ('the subjective world') begins is that of imagining. This, however, is incidental, for 'the visual room' just is personal experience in general.

Part A (§§398 – 403) opens with the interlocutor's exclamation 'Only I have got THIS', apropos his imagining or seeing something. But this is illusion, since one cannot see one's mental images or visual impressions, one does not 'have' something that one's neighbours may not equally have, and the experience upon which one concentrates incorporates no owner and no object to which 'I' might refer. But when one's gaze is idling, when immersed in philosophical reflection, it is easy to generate such representational idealist, and ultimately solipsist, illusions. The 'visual room', W. emphasizes, has no owner in the sense in which the material room has.

§399 embroiders on the absence of any 'owner' of 'the visual room'. §§400 – 1 ward off misunderstandings. The absence of an 'owner' (a 'visual owner' of the 'visual room') is not a physical discovery or a phenomenological one, but a feature of the grammar of descriptions of what is seen or imagined, etc. So too, the 'visual room' itself is not a discovery but a new grammatical articulation making possible new kinds of descriptions (of how things strike one perceptually), new ways of looking at things.

§§402 – 3 elaborate the absence of any role for 'I have . . .' in the description of *what* I imagine or how I see what I see ('I have the impression that . . .'). Rather, this phrase pin-points *for others* the grammatical character of the ensuing description. Once this feature is noticed, one is tempted to accuse ordinary language of misrepresenting the facts; but this temptation stems from our failure to apprehend the different *uses* which expressions of similar *form* have, viz. 'I have . . .' and 'He has . . .'. For a form cannot be false to the facts. This confusion lies at the root of metaphysical disputes, in which a *representational form* is attacked (by solipsists or idealists) for misdescribing the facts and defended (by realists) as if it correctly described the facts.

The structure of Part A:

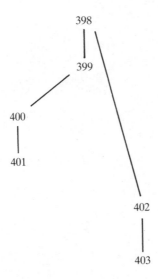

Part B (§§404 – 11) focuses on the use of the first-person pronoun and possessive pronoun. §404 reminds us that in saying 'I am in pain' I neither name nor point to a particular person, any more than when I groan. Indeed, in a sense, I do not *know* who is in pain. I do not find out *who* is in pain by identifying a person, viz. myself, and attributing pain to the person thus identified. Rather, in giving verbal expression to my pain, I draw attention to myself (§405). §406 examines a natural objection: granted that in drawing attention to myself I do not *name* myself, surely when I say 'I am in pain', I want to *distinguish* between myself and others. This, too, subtly distorts the role of 'I have . . .'. §407 further explores the kinship between a groan and an avowal of pain. It is *saying* 'I have a pain' which is a criterion for who is in pain (like groaning), but *what is said* does not identify who is in pain. §§408 – 9 examine a final objection designed to save something of the apparent referential role of 'I'. Surely when I say 'I am in pain' I have no doubt about *who* is in pain, i.e. I *know* that *I* am. But this is nonsense (cf. PI §246). An analogy illuminates the absence of any function for 'Now I know who is in pain – I am'. §410 summarizes the source of the confusions. It lies in misconstruing the role of the first-person pronoun and in distorting its peculiar relation to names. §411 notes differences in the use of the first-person possessive pronoun.

The structure of Part B:

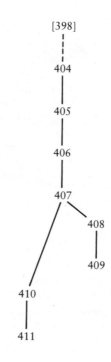

Correlations

PI§[1]	Vol. XII	Vol. XVI
398	211–13	62–7
399	221	88
400	221	91
401	222	92–3
402	213	68^2; 78–80^3
403	154	
404	155–6	
405	157	
406	158	171
407	165	174
408	169	
409	169–70	162–3, 230^4
410	332–3	
411	183	174–5, 223, 242–3

[1] Note that this sequence of remarks, unlike some of the subsequent ones, did *not* occur in the Intermediate Version. The decision to interpose this brief discussion of the first-person pronoun was therefore taken only while compiling the final draft.

[2] First six lines only.

[3] Remainder of PI §402.

[4] An early draft of the last six lines, together with a note 'For p. 169' which refers to Vol. XII.

I AND MY SELF

1. *Historical antecedents*

Contemporary debates about the role of the first-person pronoun transpose onto a linguistic plane the discussion of the essential nature of a human being that stems, in modern times, from Cartesian metaphysics. Descartes took it for granted that there can be 'no act or accident without a substance for it to belong to',[1] and concluded correctly that a thought cannot exist without a thinking thing, a substance in which to inhere. Awareness of his own thoughts, he argued, 'proved' his existence as a substance named or signified by the word 'I'. But 'what this "I" is' must be investigated, since 'I must be on my guard against carelessly taking something else to be this "I" and so making a mistake in the very item of knowledge that I maintain is the most certain and evident of all.'[2] The *sum res cogitans* argument convinced him that 'this "I" – that is the soul by which I am what I am – is entirely distinct from the body',[3] and is an *immaterial substance*. Not being extended in space, it is indivisible and hence simple. Being simple, he thought it to be an indestructible, immortal substance[4] numerically identical through time.

Given the supposition that the word 'I' signifies a substance, it is perhaps understandable that Descartes had no qualms in using the expression 'this "I" '. But such a use of the indexical 'this' is as illegitimate as 'this "that" ', 'this "he" ', or 'this "now" '. It is not merely ungrammatical; if it is unclear which object one is speaking of in saying 'that↗ ' or 'he↗ ' (accompanied by an ostensive gesture), then adding 'this↗ that↗' can no more clarify things than pointing with one's left hand can clarify what one is pointing at with one's right hand. Moreover, in the special case of the word 'I' (whether accompanied by a reflexive gesture or not) there is no more *room* for disambiguating of whom I am speaking than there is room for disambiguating of what time I am speaking in saying 'Now . . .' – although, of course, I may still have to say who I am or what time it is.

---

[1] Descartes, 'Reply to the Third Set of Objections', AT VII, 175f.

[2] Descartes, 'Second Meditation', AT VII, 25.

[3] Descartes, *Discourse on Method*, AT VI, 33. To be accurate, the 'sum res cogitans' argument alone does not purport to prove this, but needs the additional argument of the 'Sixth Meditation'.

[4] There is an important equivocation on 'substance', signifying indestructible 'stuff' (material or immaterial) and also persistent particular.

Locke gave prominence to the perceptual model of inner sense, arguing that it is 'impossible for anyone to perceive without perceiving that he does perceive. When we see, hear, smell, taste, feel, meditate or will anything, we know that we do so . . . by this everyone is to himself that which he calls *self*.'[5] It is our consciousness of our experiences that 'makes everyone to be what he calls *self*; and thereby distinguishes himself from all other thinking things';[6] indeed, 'it is by the consciousness it has of its present Thoughts and Actions, that it is *self* to it *self* now, and so will be the same *self* as far as the same consciousness can extend to Actions past or to come.'[7] It is noteworthy that this use of 'self' as an apparent sortal noun was an innovation, and arguably an aberration. Unlike Descartes, Locke did not think that a 'self' is a thinking *substance*, but only that it is 'annexed' to a substance, which may change without the self changing. For if I 'have the same consciousness' that I did such-and-such in the past as that I am writing now,

I could no more doubt that I . . . was the same self, place that *self* in what Substance you please, than that I that write this am the same *my self* now whilst I write (whether I consist of all the same Substance, material or immaterial, or no) that I was Yesterday. For as to this point of being the same *self*, it matters not whether this present *self* be made up of the same or other Substances.[8]

Linguistically tortured and philosophically confused as this passage is, one correct point shines through: to be in a position to say that I, who am writing this now, experienced this or that in the past, I do not first have to ensure that I am (or, perhaps better, my body is) made of the same stuff as he who had those previous experiences. But Locke sowed further seeds of confusion in suggesting that 'I' signifies a self, a thing distinct from the substance to which it is 'annexed', which is the 'bearer' of that consciousness 'which makes every one to be what he calls *self*'.

Hume sank deeper into this quagmire. He denied that we are 'every moment intimately conscious of what we call our SELF', i.e. a simple (indecomposable) continuant. The only object which would satisfy that specification would be a constant, invariable *impression*, which would give rise to the *idea of the self*. But, Hume observed, there is no such constant impression. Employing Locke's perceptual model of 'inner sense', he contended that 'when I enter most intimately into what I call *myself*, I always stumble on some particular perception or other . . . I never can catch *myself* at any time without a perception, and can never observe anything but the perception.'[9] Hence he concluded that what is

---

[5] Locke, *Essay Concerning Human Understanding*, Bk II, Ch. xxvii, Sect. 9.
[6] Ibid.
[7] Ibid., Bk. II, Ch. xxvii, Sect. 10.
[8] Ibid., Bk. II, Ch. xxvii, Sect. 16.
[9] Hume, *Treatise of Human Nature*, Bk. I, Pt. iv, Sect. 6.

called 'the self' is 'nothing but a bundle or collection of different perceptions which succeed each other with an inconceivable rapidity, and are in a perpetual flux and movement.' Hume's twentieth-century heirs would argue that the self (my self, the I) is a logical construction out of perceptions, and that these expressions are only apparent names, not real, logically proper names.

However, having abandoned the model of a subject of experience, Hume was faced with the problem of discovering a principle of unity that determines a series of experiences *as* the experiences that are *his*. Causal connectedness and resemblance seemed the only glue available to bind together the bundle of experiences; but such principles can be thought to unify a manifold only if it makes sense for the constituents of that very manifold *not* to be thus united. Causation and resemblance, in Hume's jargon, can provide no *real connection* among distinct existences; but that the 'perceptions' I have are *mine* is a 'real' (logical) connection, not an empirical one. For it makes no sense to query whether the perception I am now enjoying is really mine or perhaps someone else's, *a fortiori* to *find out* whether it is mine by detecting whether it stands in relations of causation and resemblance to my previous experiences. Hence Hume's confession of failure in the Appendix to the *Treatise*.[10]

Hume's account earmarks the stalemate between rationalism and empiricism, as is evident in Reid's objection to the 'bundle theory': 'Whatever this self may be, it is something which thinks, and deliberates, and resolves, and acts and suffers. I am not thought, I am not action, I am not feeling; I am something that thinks, and acts, and suffers.'[11] But, constrained by the misconceived framework of the debate, his objections falter, for the only alternative to Hume's subjectless associationism seemed to be a lapse back into a vague Cartesianism: 'My thoughts, and actions, and feelings, change every moment – they have no continued, but a successive existence; but that *self* or *I*, to which they belong is permanent, and has the same relation to all the succeeding thoughts, actions, and feelings, which I call mine.'[12] The bankruptcy of empiricism was definitive, and is evident a century later in Mill.[13]

An obscure alternative to the hopeless dichotomy emerged with Kant. His criticism of Cartesianism went deeper than Hume's, and he grasped some of the flaws in Hume's account. Rationalist psychology, he argued, confused the unity of experience with the experience of a unity, i.e. of a

---

[10] 'All my hopes vanish, when I come to explain the principles, that unite our successive perceptions in our thought or consciousness. I cannot discover any theory which gives me satisfaction on this head.'

[11] T. Reid, *Essays on the Intellectual Powers of Man*, Essay III, Ch. iv.

[12] Ibid.

[13] See J. S. Mill, *An Examination of Sir William Hamilton's Philosophy*, in *Collected Works*, Vol. IX, pp. 207f.

soul-substance. This illusory substance appears simple (and hence inde-structible) because the rationalist confuses the absence of reference to a complex object, a 'manifold' subsumable under the category of substance, for a reference to a simple object. Kant did not abandon the perceptual model of 'inner sense', but saw that within these constraints the self-ascribability of experiences is a purely formal feature of concep-tualized experience. It makes no sense to *look*, as Hume purported to do, for a subject of experience in 'inner sense'. Rather, any 'experience' of which I am 'aware in inner sense' must be such as I can attribute to myself – the 'I think' must (analytically) be capable of accompanying all my representations:

> The renowned psychological proof [of the rationalist doctrine of the soul] is founded merely on the indivisible unity of a representation, which governs only the verb in its relation to a person. It is obvious that in attaching 'I' to our thoughts we designate the subject of inherence only transcendentally, without noting in it any quality whatever – in fact without knowing anything of it either by direct acquaintance or otherwise . . . . The simplicity of the representation of a subject is not *eo ipso* knowledge of the simplicity of the subject itself, for we abstract altogether from its properties when we designate it solely by the entirely empty expression 'I'.[14]

Kant pin-pointed the source of error as the confusing of the purely formal character of 'transcendental self-consciousness' with conscious-ness of a pure soul-substance. Awareness of the necessary self-ascribability of experience, 'the "I think" that must be capable of accompanying all my representations', is not an awareness of a Cartesian self. He did not, however, deny that there is such a thing as empirical self-consciousness yielding self-knowledge. His account is obscure and is rendered incoherent by the demands of his transcendental idealism. The first-person pronoun in psychological statements seemingly refers to an empirical subject of experiences; but Kant fails to clarify what this empirical subject, which is an object of possible experience, might be. This empirical 'self' is indeed aware of fleeting experiences and conscious of itself as so aware. Being an object with an autobiography, a history, it must be part of the temporal, phenomenal world. Hence the 'self' that appears to itself is itself mere appearance. So the 'self' as it is in itself, the 'noumenal self', must underlie it, as noumena underpin phenomena. This entity must be both unknowable and also the known subject of the moral law. For the moral 'self' must be free, subject to the laws of practical reason, rather than to the constraints of causality. So it must be super-sensible and atemporal and must also have a moral history, being the subject of temporal moral judgements. 'I have an obligation to . . .' seemingly refers to the ethical subject, the bearer of good and evil; but

---

[14] Kant, *Critique of Pure Reason*, A 355.

how, within the bizarre framework of transcendental idealism, that is possible is never made clear.

Substantialism, associationism, and transcendentalism, as William James classified them,[15] constituted the primary apparent alternatives for philosophical analysis of the nature of the 'self'. As James remarked, 'Terribly, therefore, do the sour grapes which those fathers of philosophy have eaten set our teeth on edge.'[16]

2. 'The I, the I is what is deeply mysterious'

Wittgenstein's first attempt to grapple with the philosophical problems which cluster around the use of the first-person pronoun and which have bred such questionable expressions as 'the self' or 'the ego' (which, being Latin, sounds less offensive than 'the I') are to be found in the *Notebooks 1914 – 16*. A small selection of these reflections were incorporated in the *Tractatus* 5.6ff. Wittgenstein's familiarity with the history of philosophy was slight, and the tradition sketched above was transmitted to him primarily, if not exclusively, through Schopenhauer's *The World as Will and Representation* (which he had read as a teenager, and was perhaps re-reading during June and July 1916[17]) and through Russell.

Schopenhauer's philosophy was a version of transcendental idealism. Like Kant, he was critical of the Cartesian conceptions of 'the knowing subject' as a self-subsistent immaterial substance and of 'the external world' consisting of material substance set over against the subject as object of possible knowledge. The knowing subject properly conceived is indeed 'the supporter of the world, the universal condition of all that appears',[18] a presupposition of the possibility of experience and knowledge. But as such it cannot be a constituent of the world as we experience it – the world as representation. Rather, it is transcendental, and its relation to the phenomenal world is comparable to the relation of the eye to the visual field – for the 'eye sees everything except itself'.[19] Equally, the world as we experience it is not independent of our experience of it; it is, as Kant had argued, phenomenally real, but transcendentally ideal. The world as representation, is ordered in space and time, which are the forms of sensible intuition, and is subject to causality – the Principle of Sufficient Reason, which is the sole category of the understanding. The perceiving subject is as much a part of the

---

[15] James, *Principles of Psychology* Vol. I, p. 371.

[16] Ibid., p. 366.

[17] The evidence for this consists in the Schopenhauerian tenor (including metaphors and turns of phrase, as well as specific references) of the notebook entries for this period (cf. NB 72 – 91 and earlier remarks under 23 May 1915).

[18] A. Schopenhauer, *The World as Will and Representation*, tr. E. F. J. Payne (Dover, New York, 1966), Vol. I, p. 5.

phenomenal world as are the objects it perceives. But the noumenal subject, the thing-in-itself, which is the correlate of the world-as-representation, is not, as Kant had claimed, unknowable. For we have access in inner consciousness to 'the single narrow door to the truth': viz. the Will. Our subjective awareness of intentional action is an awareness of the objectified Will. The Will thus conceived is the noumenal reality underlying the phenomenal world. It is not to be viewed as one will among many, but rather as the metaphysical or World Will. It is unique, although it manifests or objectifies itself in the strivings and impulses of phenomenal particulars, inorganic and organic alike. In this (obscure) sense, individuality and plurality are illusory (phenomenal). Philosophical insight can penetrate the veil of Maya to apprehend that the plurality of individuals is merely the spatio-temporal objectification of the one, unique World Will.

Russell transmitted to Wittgenstein the predicament of classical empiricism. In *The Problems of Philosophy* (1912) he conceded to Hume that 'acquaintance with the contents of our minds', which, in accord with tradition, he termed 'self-consciousness', is not consciousness of a self, but only consciousness of particular thoughts and feelings. Nevertheless, he claimed, it is *probable* 'that we are acquainted with the "I" '. His argument was that

All acquaintance . . . seems obviously a relation between the person acquainted and the object with which the person is acquainted. When a case of acquaintance is one with which I can be acquainted . . . it is plain that the person acquainted is myself. Thus, when I am acquainted with my seeing the sun, the whole fact with which I am acquainted is 'Self-acquainted-with-sense-datum'.[20]

Consequently, the word 'I' is a logically proper name of this self with which one is aquainted. But, contrary to the rationalist tradition and to Reid's philosophy of common sense alike, 'it does not seem necessary to suppose that we are acquainted with a more or less permanent person, the same today as yesterday.'

The self thus conceived seems to be no more than a bare subject of predication demanded by the grammar of psychological verbs. It is not surprising, therefore, to find that in the manuscript *Theory of Knowledge* (1913) Russell shifted ground uncomfortably:

Hume's inability to perceive himself was not peculiar, and I think most unprejudiced observers would agree with him. Even if by great exertion some rare person could catch a glimpse of himself, this would not suffice; for 'I' is a term we all know, and which must therefore have some easily accessible meaning. It follows that the word 'I', as commonly employed, must stand for a description; it cannot be a true proper

---

[19] Ibid., Vol. II, p. 491.
[20] Russell, *The Problems of Philosophy* (Oxford University Press, London, 1967), pp. 27f.

name in the logical sense, since true proper names can only be conferred on objects with which we are acquainted . . . We may define 'I' as the subject of present experience.[21]

So the first-person pronoun is not really the name of an object given in experience, but rather does service for a definite description. What a 'subject' of experience might be is left obscure, and whether Russell really thought that one might 'catch a glimpse' of one's self is left equally opaque.

Wittgenstein approached the problems of the logical analysis of first-person propositions through an investigation of the very specific issue of belief-sentences. In 'A believes that p' and 'I believe that p', one proposition, namely 'p', apparently occurs non-truth-functionally within another, contrary to the thesis of extensionality. It looks as if such propositions describe a relation between an object and a proposition, and indeed Russell had construed them thus in his three articles 'Meinong's Theory of Complexes and Assumptions' in *Mind*, 13 (1906). In 'On the Nature of Truth and Falsity' of 1910,[22] Russell repudiated this dual-relation analysis in favour of a *multiple*-relation theory of belief (judgement or thought) on the grounds of ontological parsimony. For the dual-relation analysis committed him either to the existence of propositions in addition to facts or to the impossibility of false beliefs. For 'A believes that p' may be true even though it is not a fact that p, so 'p' must (apparently) exist if false judgements or beliefs are to be possible. But Russell denied that over and above facts there exists propositions. Hence, he argued,

If I judge that A loves B, that is not a relation of me to A's love for B, but a relation between me and A and love and B. If it were a relation of me to 'A's love for B' it would be impossible unless there were such a thing as 'A's love for B', i.e. unless A loved B, i.e. unless the judgement were true; but in fact false judgements are possible. When the judgement is taken as a relation between me and A and love and B, the mere fact that the judgement occurs does not involve any relation between its objects A and love and B; thus the possibility of false judgements is fully allowed for.[23]

Wittgenstein agreed with the repudiation of the dual-relation analysis (cf. TLP 5.541), but held the multiple-relation analysis to be likewise incoherent. For it does not ensure the preservation of sense; it does not suffice to mention just the constituents, or even the constituents and the form (unless in the proper order). For that will not exclude the possibility of, e.g., 'A believes that the table penholders the book' – i.e. the

[21] Russell, *Theory of Knowledge, the 1913 Manuscript* (Allen and Unwin, London, 1984), pp. 36f.

[22] Russell, 'On the Nature of Truth and Falsehood', in *Philosophical Essays* (Longmans, Green and Co. London, 1910), pp. 170 – 85.

[23] Ibid., p. 180.

possibility of believing nonsense (NB 96f.). This shows that the propositional form must occur in belief-propositions. In the 'Notes Dictated to
G. E. Moore' of April 1914, the analysis focused on the first-person
pronoun, and proposed a resolution that subsequently occurs in the
Tractatus: 'The relation of "I believe *p*" to "*p*" can be compared to the
relation of " '*p*' says *p*" to "*p*": it is just as impossible that *I* should be a
simple as that "*p*" should be ' (NB 118).

This is partially clarified in the *Tractatus*. Propositions with two verbs,
as Russell called them (i.e. A believes (judges, thinks, says) that *p*) are of
the form ' "*p*" says *p*'. This does not correlate a fact with an object A (or
I), but rather correlates facts by means of the correlation of their objects
(TLP 5.542). More explicitly, Wittgenstein's idea seems to have been
that such propositions correlate the fact that constitutes a proposition (a
symbolizing fact, which may be a propositional sign in its projective
relation or a *thought* consisting of physical constituents (R 37)) with the
fact, or rather the state of affairs (possible fact) it depicts, by correlating
the constituents of each. This shows, he held, 'that there is no such thing
as the soul – the subject, etc. – as it is conceived in the superficial
psychology of the present day. Indeed a composite soul would no longer
be a soul' (TLP 5.5421). 'I' in 'I believe that *p*' is not a logically proper
name signifying a simple object, an empirical soul or substance. There
are indeed psychic facts, some of which constitute representations of
how things are in the world; they have psychic constituents, but there is
no soul-substance or simple object that 'owns' these psychic elements.

This neo-Humean strategy was subsequently synthesized with the
reflections on solipsism and the self of 1915 – 16 in *Tractatus* 5.63ff.
'There is no such thing as the subject that thinks or entertains ideas,'
Wittgenstein declared, for a description of 'the world as I found it' would
include my body, which parts of it are subordinate to my will, etc., *but
not the subject*. Thus far Hume was moving on the right lines – although
he was wrong to think that it was a matter of fact that he could not
encounter 'the self' in experience. For the *philosophical self*, which is the
concern of philosophy (TLP 5.641) is the *metaphysical subject*, not an
empirical object that could be given in experience (e.g. the body or the
psyche studied by empirical psychology), but a 'limit of the world' (TLP
5.632; NB 79), 'not a part of the world but a presupposition of its
existence' (NB 79). This Schopenhauerian thought[24] Wittgenstein tried
to clarify by means of a Schopenhauerian simile: the relation of the
metaphysical self to experience, to the world, is comparable to the
relation of the eye to the visual field (TLP 5.633f.). For, on the one hand,
'you really do *not* see the eye' (or, as Schopenhauer put it, 'the eye sees

---

[24] Schopenhauer, *World as Will and Representation*, Vol. I, p. 5.; Vol. II, p. 15.

everything except itself'[25]), and on the other hand, it is irresistibly tempting to argue that in some sense 'I also always find myself at a particular point of my visual space' (NB 86), even though the *I* is not an object I can confront (NB 80). The fact that the eye is not a constituent of the visual field (and, by implication, that the I is not given in experience) Wittgenstein connected with the fact that no part of our experience is at the same time *a priori* (TLP 5.634; NB 80) – whatever we see or experience could be otherwise. But, by implication, that *this* experience is *my* experience is no more a contingent fact than that *this* visual field is *my* visual field.[26]

With studied obscurity, Wittgenstein concluded that this shows 'that solipsism, when its implications are followed out strictly, coincides with pure realism. The self of solipsism shrinks to a point without extension, and there remains the reality co-ordinated with it' (TLP 5.64). Whether this is a repudiation of solipsism or a refinement and affirmation of *empirical realism and transcendental solipsism* is unclear. What is clear is that Wittgenstein thought that some aspect of solipsism is both true and metaphysically necessary (and hence ineffable): 'What the solipsist *means* is quite correct; only it cannot be *said*, but makes itself manifest' (TLP 5.62). And it is also perspicuous that Wittgenstein's Schopenhauerian reflections of 1916 reveal a commitment to the transcendental reality of the metaphysical self, which is identical with the willing self, the bearer of good and evil. On 5 August 1916, Wittgenstein wrote:

> The thinking subject is surely mere illusion. But the willing subject exists.
> If the will did not exist, neither would there be that centre of the world, which we call the I, and which is the bearer of good and evil.
> What is good and evil is essentially the I, not the world. The I, the I is what is deeply mysterious. (NB 82)

This mysterious metaphysical, willing self is not a human being, nor is it even a particular among others. Rather, as Wittgenstein put it in Schopenhauerian language: 'As my idea is the world, in the same way my will is the world-will' (NB 85).[27]

As far as the *Tractatus* programme of logico-linguistic analysis is concerned, it seems that Wittgenstein held that the first-person pronoun is not a 'name', but would disappear on analysis. In some cases, one might suppose, it would be replaced by body-referring expressions, themselves subject to further analysis. In other cases it would be

---

[25] Ibid., Vol. II, p. 491.

[26] The same point can be expressed by means of one of Wittgenstein's later metaphors, viz. that it is not a fact of experience that *this* visual field is seen by the 'geometrical eye'. The underlying idea, as he subsequently realized, is incoherent.

[27] For a more detailed examination of these obscurities, see P. M. S. Hacker, *Insight and Illusion*, rev. edn (Clarendon Press, Oxford, 1986), Ch. IV.

swallowed up in some detailed description of a field of psychic constituents, a Humean bundle, although again, this is not the final level of
analysis.

It is obscure what strategy he would have adopted with respect to
propositions about mental states of other people.[28] It is possible that he
thought that such references to other people would be analysable into
propositions about their behaviour, which in turn would decompose into
propositions about one's own current experiences. This would marry a
form of analytical methodological solipsism with ineffable transcendental solipsism. The truth that lies at the heart of solipsism, the centrality
of the metaphysical self, the bearer of good and evil, will ineffably be
shown by the *constant form* of all fully analysed sentences.

3. *The eliminability of the word 'I'*

When Wittgenstein resumed philosophical work in 1929, he jettisoned
the Schopenhauerian transcendentalism – no more is heard of 'the self of
philosophy' or of the metaphysical or willing self. Indeed, the aberrant
philosophical usage, 'the I' and 'the self', likewise disappears, except in
criticisms of misconceptions. Two important points, however, were
retained for a while. First, he continued to think that there is some
non-trivial sense in which the word 'I' can be eliminated from a language
without loss (WWK 49). He quoted, with approval, Lichtenberg's
contention that instead of 'I think' we ought to say 'It thinks', on the
model of 'It is raining' (M 309). This analytical claim, now severed from
the logical atomist doctrines of the *Tractatus* and embedded in the
methodological solipsism of the *Philosophical Remarks* (and the conversations with Waismann), can be seen as a logico–linguistic residue of his
earlier Schopenhauerian criticism of the Cartesian doctrine of the soul.
Secondly, Wittgenstein argued that first-person experiential propositions
– and their analogues in a language without a first-person pronoun –
have a special adequacy. They constitute 'primary language'. Indeed, it is
their special status which is reflected grotesquely in the distorting
mirrors of rational psychology, transcendentalism, and solipsism (cf. M
311).

The opening sentence of his reflections on the subject in the *Philosophical Remarks* earmarks the beginning of a change in method and
perspective: 'One of the most misleading representational techniques in
our language is the use of the word "I", particularly when it is used in
representing immediate experience' (PR 88). Traditional puzzlement
about the nature of 'the self' is to be resolved not by introspection,
metaphysical insight, or logical analysis into indefinables, but by scru-

---

[28] NB 49 is relevant, but opaque.

tiny of a representational technique. We must investigate the role of the first-person pronoun.

It is, he argued, an eliminable expression (WWK 49), and its role can be clarified by imagining how a language without this word might fulfil the same representational function. One can imagine a language of an oriental despot in which the despot himself is, as it were, at the centre of the language. When he has a toothache, he (and everyone else) says: 'There is toothache'. But when someone else, N.N., has a toothache, one says: 'N.N. is behaving as the Centre behaves when there is toothache.' This form of representation, Wittgenstein urged, is just as intelligible and unambiguous as ours. Indeed, given the form of analysis to which he now cleaved, it must have seemed *more perspicuous* than our language, for 'it would serve to show clearly what was logically essential in the representation' (PR 88). For it not only brings out the essentially 'subjectless' character of first-person experiential propositions, it also makes clear the logical character of 'hypotheses' about other people's experiences.

A mono-centred language can have anyone as its centre; but, Wittgenstein insisted, a language with *me* as its centre is privileged. However, its special adequacy cannot be stated. 'For, if I do it in the language with me as its centre, then the exceptional status of the description of this language in its own terms is nothing very remarkable, and in terms of another language, my language occupies no privileged status whatever. – The privileged status lies in the application' (PR 89). In conversation with Waismann he explained that a language of which I am the centre is one 'in which I can as it were say that I feel *real* pain' (WWK 50). The point where the particular status of these different languages comes to light is that when I say 'There is toothache' in the language of which I am the centre, what I say is *compared directly with reality* (cf. WWK 50, n.1).

This, as he later realized, is confused. But it is true that 'N.N. is behaving as the Centre behaves when there is pain' is no substitute, *as far as N.N. is concerned*, for *his* saying, in a language of which *he* is the Centre, 'There is pain' or, as we would say in our grammar, 'I have a pain'. One wants to be able to complain about one's pains even though one has *not* manifested them in behaviour and so cannot truly say 'N.N. is behaving as the Centre . . .'. A truthful avowal of pain ('There is pain' as said by the Centre) does not require the speaker to check *his behaviour* before he speaks to ensure that he speaks truly; but speakers other than the Centre can (in his language) only say 'N.N. is behaving as . . .', which will be false if N.N. is not behaving thus. Unlike the Centre's avowal of pain, in these cases there is room for error. Finally, in a language of which I am *not* the Centre, I cannot, as it were, say that I am in pain without saying who I am.

It is obvious that a mono-centred language is unsatisfactory for speakers other than the Centre. It lacks some of the articulations of our language. This is only to be expected, since it was designed expressly to highlight the first/third-person asymmetry *in our language*, and Wittgenstein's suggestion was that in effect *each of us* speaks, and is the centre of, such a (tacitly) mono-centred language. So the *explicit* asymmetry of the invented language allegedly makes clear something that is evident only in the application of ordinary language.

But is it obvious that, *for the Centre*, such a Lichtenbergian language *is* adequate? This question has two aspects. First, is it true that in *my* language alone 'I can as it were say that I feel *real* pain'? In a sense that is so, since *ex hypothesi* in another's language I, N.N., must say 'N.N. behaves as the Centre behaves when there is pain'. But the construction rests four-square upon the supposition that 'pain' in 'I have pain' (or 'There is pain' said by me in *my* language) is defined by reference to a private sensation and is privately verified by my having a pain. And it is equally supposed that 'pain' in 'He has pain' does *not* have the same meaning as in 'I have a pain'. So in attributing pain to others, one is, in some ineffable sense, *not* attributing *real* pain to them. From this bizarre perspective, a mono-centred language of which I am the Centre will obviously appear especially adequate. But the adequacy rests on an illusion.

Secondly, does this language, as Wittgenstein supposed, have the same logical multiplicity as the application of the appropriate first-person fragment of ordinary language by a particular person? Is it true that although it would not 'be in any sense more correct than the old one, . . . it would serve to show more clearly what was logically essential in the representation' (PR 88)? This seems more problematic than Wittgenstein envisaged in 1929. For 'I' has a use not only in 'experiential propositions', but also in sentences such as 'I am sunburnt all over' or 'I am *n* years old' or, even more significantly, in introductions ('I am N.N.'), in reports of one's activities ('I am writing a letter', 'I have read your essay'), in expressions of intention ('I'll go to London tomorrow'), and in the large and diverse class of performative utterances ('I promise . . .', 'I declare . . .').

It is *probable* that to the extent that Wittgenstein then reflected on this question, he thought that where 'I' was not eliminable in favour of a subjectless form, it can be replaced by 'this body'. In *Philosophical Remarks*, cheek by jowl with the claim that 'I' is eliminable, he wrote ' "I" clearly refers to my body, for *I* am in this room; and "I" is essentially something that is in a place, and in a place belonging to the same space as the one the other bodies are in too' (PR 86). In his lectures of 1932/3 (after he had abandoned his distinctive form of methodological solipsism), he argued that 'I' is used in 'two utterly different ways', one in which it is 'on a level with other people' and one in which it is not. Where 'I' is replaceable by 'this body', there 'I' and 'he' are 'on the same grammatical level'. The sentence 'I've got a matchbox' and 'I've got a bad tooth' are 'on a level' with 'Skinner has a matchbox' and 'Skinner has a bad tooth'. In these cases 'I have . . .' and 'Skinner has . . .' are both values of the same propositional function, and 'I' and 'Skinner' both denote 'possessors'. But in such sentences as 'I have a toothache' the word 'I' does not 'denote a possessor' and is not 'on the same level' as 'he' (M 308ff.).

The suggestion of a sharp dichotomy in the use of the first-person pronoun persisted, in transmuted form, in the *Blue Book*. There Wittgenstein distinguished between 'the use of "I" as subject' and its use 'as object'. Where 'I' is used as subject, as in 'I see so-and-so', 'I try to lift my arm', 'I think it will rain', 'I have a toothache', there is no recognition of a person, and there is no possibility of misidentification of a person, i.e. of mistaking another person for myself. But in such sentences as 'I have grown six inches', 'I have a bump on my forehead', 'My arm is broken', there is a recognition of a particular person, and the possibility of error has been provided for (BB 66f.)

It is significant that these claims sink from sight. It was plausible, within the phenomenalist framework of methodological solipsism, to suppose that there is a simple dichotomy between 'primary experience' (expressed in 'genuine propositions') and 'hypotheses'. Given that conception, 'I have a pain' will naturally be allocated to the former category, and 'I am six foot tall', like 'N.N. is six foot tall', will be allocated to the latter. But the idea that all first-person sentences are either concerned with 'the primary', which is logically independent of the body, or are about one's body (picked out as '*this↗* body') is a contaminated residue of Cartesian dualism. It presupposes the analysability of first-person action-sentences such as 'I am writing a letter' into 'This body is . . .' and 'There is a willing . . .', together, perhaps, with a causal rider. Similarly, expressions of intention such as 'I'll go to London today' must be decomposed into a *prediction* about my body and a *statement* about my will. But this is patently misconceived, as Wittgenstein later realized.[29] For statements about *behaviour* are not statements about bare bodily movements (see 'Behaviour and behaviourism', §4), and our concepts of intention and purpose are not of cogs that mediate between ethereal drive-shafts and physical axles. Not only is the analysis impossible, it wholly misconstrues the distinctive uses of such sentences. It is true that there are *some* first-person sentences which can be replaced by sentences

---

[29] This criticism of Cartesianism was independently elaborated by Ryle in *The Concept of Mind*.

about the body, e.g. 'I am sun-tanned all over' and 'My body is sun-tanned all over'. But it does not follow that the word 'I' sometimes means the same as 'this body' and sometimes does not – that would be highly misleading, suggesting an ambiguity where there is none. It would be more illuminating to say that 'I' and 'this body', for a short range of their use, run on parallel tracks.

The *Blue Book*'s attempt to salvage something from the flawed dichotomy of *Philosophical Remarks* is likewise erroneous. It is true that in the use of 'I have a pain' no room has been provided for misidentification of the subject, for there is here, as Wittgenstein later elaborated, *no* identification of a subject. But it is by no means clear that in such sentences as 'I have grown six inches', 'I have a bump on my forehead', or 'I have broken my arm' there is a *recognition* of a person (myself),[30] or that the possibility of misidentification has been provided for in the sense in which it has in 'N.N. has broken his arm'. I may be mistaken about whether my arm or your arm is broken or, in exceptional circumstances, whether *this* arm is mine or yours. But in such cases, when I mistakenly say 'I have broken my arm', for example, I do not *misidentify* myself or *mistake* myself for you; rather, I mistake my arm for yours, mistakenly attribute to myself something correctly attributable to you.

It is perhaps an awareness of these and similar points that partially explains why the idea of an essential duality in the use of 'I' lapses after the *Blue Book*, although, of course, that is not to say that the differences between 'I have a pain' and 'I am six foot tall' are not fundamental. Rather than a duality of essentially redundant uses of 'I' and essentially body-referring uses, as earlier envisaged, it would be better to think of a whole spectrum of sentences in the first person, ranging from avowals, through first-person reports, self-identifications ('I am N.N.', 'I am the so-and-so'), and first-person action-sentences, to a large variety of logically different kinds of description of oneself (including descriptions of one's mental state) and sentences which run parallel to bodily descriptions (e.g. 'I am six foot tall'). Similarly, the endorsement of a Lichtenbergian language as a more perspicuous representation of the logic of a sub-class of first-person sentences is dropped, although, of course, such a language may still be invoked as an illuminating object for comparison. To make clear how the use of 'I' differs from the use of proper names, descriptions, other personal pronouns, and demonstratives, it is not necessary to argue for its essential dispensability – although it is true that instead of saying 'I have a pain', one may say 'It hurts', whereas one cannot similarly replace 'N.N. has a pain' by such a sentence with a dummy pronoun and no person-referring expression. Nor need one argue that the 'special adequacy' of the first-person

[30] Unless, perhaps, I say this on looking at a photograph of myself.

experiential proposition is ineffably manifest in the application of a mono-centred language in order to clarify the special role of such propositions as *expressions* or *manifestations* of the inner, by contrast with their third-person counterparts, which are descriptions. But it was true to say that the logical peculiarities of such sentences are manifest in their *use*, as *Äusserungen* which are criteria for corresponding third-person assertions. And this, Wittgenstein noted in his lectures in 1946/7, would be visible even in a language with *no* personal pronouns, in which N.N. said not 'I am in pain', but 'N.N. is in pain'. For this, in his mouth, would be an utterance (*Äusserung*) of pain, not a description (LPP 49).

4. ' "I" does not refer to a person'

Throughout the 1930s, Wittgenstein persisted in his efforts to clarify the philosophical problems about the nature of 'the self'. These problems seem to limit us to a choice between three alternative types of solution: (i) Cartesian doctrines of the mind or soul – a substance, connected to the body, to which we refer by using the word 'I'; (ii) Humean theories according to which there is only a *fiction* of such an 'inner self' to which we *seem* to refer; (iii) Kantian accounts according to which 'I' on the one hand signifies the form of all experience, and on the other mysteriously refers to a noumenal object, the moral self. Wittgenstein came to think that these options, including their more recent derivatives such as his own transcendentalism in the *Notebooks 1914 – 16* and his 'no-ownership' conception in *Philosophical Remarks*, are all symptoms of grammatical misunderstandings. In his lecture notes in the mid-thirties, he wrote: 'I am trying to bring the whole problem down to our not understanding the function of the word "I" and "this ↗ " ' (LPE 308).

He agreed with Cartesians that 'I' is not used 'because we recognize a particular person by his bodily characteristics' (BB 69), a feature particularly obvious in first-person experiential propositions. When I say 'I am thinking of such-and-such', the word 'I' does not refer to my body. But that 'I' is used differently from 'my body' does not imply that some new entity besides my body, viz. the ego, has been discovered (AWL 60). And it is an illusion to suppose that since in using 'I' we do not refer to our bodies, therefore we must be using it 'to refer to something bodiless, which, however, has its seat in our body' (BB 69). In an argument reminiscent of Kant's third paralogism, Wittgenstein observed that 'It seems that I can *trace* my identity, quite independent of the identity of my body. And the idea is suggested that I trace the identity of something dwelling in my body, the identity of my mind' (LPE 308). This idea arises from the fact that when I say that I did such-and-such in the past, I do not employ any criteria of subject identity; I do not check to see whether, as it were, I still have the same body. But that is not because I check on the continued identity of something other than my body. For suppose that 'I constantly change and my surrounding does: is there still some continuity, namely, by it being *me* and *my surrounding* that change?' (LPE 300).

But the neo-Humean reaction to Cartesianism that is evident in Russell is equally confused. For ' "Is my person (or a person) a constituent of the fact that I see, or not?" expresses a question about symbolism in the form of a question about nature' (LPE 282). Both Hume and Russell had pretended to look for their 'selves' in introspection, Hume supposing that if he found a persistent impression, it might be his self, and Russell thinking it possible that one might occasionally catch a glimpse of one's self, and that it is probable that one is acquainted with it. The *Tractatus* too erred in conceiving it to be a super-empirical fact or a truth of metaphysics that 'nothing *in the visual field* allows you to infer that it is seen by an eye' (cf. Exg. §402, 2.1). But to claim that one has looked for a self and not found it or to insist that such a search *must* be in vain presupposes the intelligibility of such searching. But the search is unintelligible – like 'looking for the East Pole', not like looking for the source of the Nile or even for Eldorado. It is not that one *cannot* find it, but that nothing *would count* as finding it.

The word 'I' is one symbol among others with a practical use, and it has that use in the context of pervasive, and therefore unremarked, facts about us. Although 'I' does not mean the same as '*this* body', it 'only has meaning with reference to a body' (AWL 62). If, when people spoke, all the sounds they made came from the same loudspeaker in the same voice, the word 'I' would have no use (AWL 24). The use of 'I' depends on the correlation between the mouth which says 'I' and the body from whose mouth the word 'I' is emitted. This is evident, for example, in avowals of pain; for a criterion for A's having a pain when *his* hand is pinched is that the *Äusserung* 'I am in pain' (or, what comes to the same thing, 'That hurt *me*') comes from *his* mouth (AWL 62).

It is immensely tempting to claim that the solution to these traditional puzzles is embarrassingly simple, viz. that although 'I' refers neither to a body nor to a self, it refers to a *person*, as 'he' and 'you' do. This Wittgenstein sometimes flatly denied: 'It is correct, although paradoxical,' he wrote (Vol. XII, 215); 'to say: "I" does not refer to [designate, *bezeichnet*] a person.' This contention undoubtedly goes against the grain and needs careful examination in order to discern what he was driving at. A simile Wittgenstein used with respect to the word 'today' may put one on the right trail: 'I' does not differ from person-referring expressions (e.g. 'N.N.', 'The so-and-so,' 'he') as a hammer from a mallet, but as a hammer from a nail (cf. BB 108). What must be done is to compare the use of the first-person pronoun with the uses of person-referring expressions to see whether the differences justify Wittgenstein's paradoxical claim.

The key to his conception lies in his often reiterated and *prima-facie* bewildering remark that *I don't choose the mouth which says 'I . . .'* (Vol. XVI, 25). When I express my pain in an avowal, I do not do so by choosing *this* mouth rather than another, any more than when I manifest pain by groaning I choose the mouth from which I groan. When I use the first-person pronoun, I employ no principle of differentiation to select one person from among others. Hence too, 'It has no sense to ask "How do you know it's *you* who sees . . . ?", for I don't *know* that it is this person and not another one which sees before I point. – This is what I meant by saying that I don't choose the mouth which says "I have toothache" ' (LPE 311).

That I do not *name* anyone when I say that it is I who . . . is obvious enough. 'I see X' does not mean the same as 'The person so-and-so sees X' (LPE 298), even though if I say 'I see X', *someone else* can on the grounds of this say 'The person so-and-so sees X'. But to grant that 'I' is not a name is still a long way from conceding that it does not refer to a person. 'He' is not a name either, but in saying 'He sees X', one is surely referring to a person.

It is tempting to claim that not only is 'I' a referring expression, it is a super-referring expression, for it is guaranteed success, being immune both to reference-*failure* and to referential *error* or *misidentification*. And if one so thinks, a simple explanation for these features is at hand; for, one will argue, the rule for the reference of the word 'I' is that it refers to whoever uses it. But one might be suspicious here; for is this not like arguing that an arrow stuck in the wall, around which one draws a bull's eye, has hit the target? Wittgenstein certainly was suspicious (and in the following passage expressed himself more cautiously than in Vol. XII, 215 (above)):

' "Ich" in meinem Munde bezeichnet *mich*.' Bezeichnet den dieses Wort in *meinem* Munde etwas besonderes? Ich wollte wohl sagen: ' "Ich" bezeichnet immer den Mensch der es ausspricht.' Aber was heisst das, es bezeichne ihn? Gibt es denn da nur *eine* Möglichkeit? (Vol. XVI, 230)

(' "I" in my mouth refers to [designates] *me*.' Does this word in *my* mouth refer to anything particular? I really wanted to say: ' "I" always refers to the person who utters it.' But what does it mean, it refers to him? Is there only *one* possibility?)

This suggests a more flexible way of challenging the idea that 'I' refers to a person in the sense in which 'you' and 'he' do, i.e. that the use of 'I' runs parallel to the use of 'you' or 'he'. Wittgenstein did not explicitly say what 'possibilities' he had in mind, and his point must be gleaned from his practice. 'Reference' is not a 'meta-logical' expression (in Wittgenstein's special sense of this term) with a sharply circumscribed use and strict *Merkmal*-definition. It is natural (although perhaps not to philosophers) and correct to explain it by reference to a range of simple paradigms which overlap but are not uniform. In this respect 'reference' is like 'name' or 'proposition'. And Wittgenstein's practice, in his extensive reflections on the first-person pronoun, was to compare its use with that of a central range, and a range of features, of expressions that are employed to refer to something.

One paradigm of reference is the use of an appropriate expression such as 'this', 'there', or 'he' in a sentence, accompanied by a deictic gesture. In such cases we typically refer to *this↗* thing, *that↗* place, or '*this↗* person'. A sentence such as 'He has . . .', used on a particular occasion, has no sense unless it is related to a name, description, or ostensive gesture (Vol. XVI, 170). For an explanation of what was meant will specify by these means *who* was meant. And in the absence of such an explicit or implicit relation one will not understand, or fully understand, what was meant. In this sense, an ostensive gesture (name or description) belongs with 'he . . .' (Vol. XVI, 35). But do I, when I say 'I have . . .' *point at myself* (BB 67)? Do I even point figuratively, as it were? The mouth which says 'I' does not thereby point to anything (BB 68). It is not as if the very same pointer, so to speak, points now to him, now to me; 'I' and 'he' have very different functions in language (Vol. XVI, 171). Saying 'I . . .' is more like raising my hand to draw attention to myself than it is like pointing to someone. And when I raise my hand to do so, I do not thereby point to myself, any more than when I point to the sun, for example, I point to two things, viz. the sun and myself, just because it is I who am pointing (BB 67). And so too, when I say 'I meant him ↗ ', I am not *also* pointing to myself, although I am also drawing attention to myself. One might say that 'I' is the point of origin on the co-ordinate system of deixis, but not a point on the deictic graph (cf. BT 523); or that it is the centre of deictic reference and therefore not on its circumference. (One might say that all we are doing here is pointing out the difference between (○) and (◁) .) An ostensive gesture does not, in this sense, belong with 'I'; and if I say to you 'I am tired', you will not fail to understand what I mean *because* I have not pointed to myself. In this respect the use of 'I' does not converge on this paradigm of reference.

It may be objected that one *does* sometimes point at oneself when one says 'I . . .'. But if I point at myself, I do not use the same gesture as in pointing to *him* ↗ , and my gesture does not have the same function. For it does not serve, as does the gesture accompanying 'he', to avert misidentification. Rather it *draws attention* to myself, like raising my hand or clearing my throat loudly before I speak (BB 67). I can *point him out* by pointing at him, but I do not *point myself out* when I point at myself. I do not *thereby* pick myself out from among others (except when I point at a photograph of myself in a group); and what looks like immunity from misidentification or reference-failure is in fact the absence of any reference at all. If, in saying 'I . . .' I do point at myself, I am, of course, modelling my use of 'I' on that of 'he ↗ ' or 'this ↗ person'. But, Wittgenstein notes, this makes 'I' similar to 'he' only in the way a degenerate identity-statement is similar to a genuine one. In proving that

the sum of the angles of a triangle is 180°, we draw a diagram

and say that α = α', β = β', and γ = γ (BB 68). In this way 'I' is referentially similar to 'he'. So one might say, although Wittgenstein does not, that the use of 'I', when accompanied by a reflexive gesture, is a case of *degenerate* reference, in the sense in which a point is a degenerate case of a conic section or a tautology a degenerate case of a proposition with sense.

A different line of attack seems equally plausible: one can surely say that the word 'I', in the mouth of a particular person N.N, refers to that person. For if N.N. says truly 'I ϕ', then others can say 'N.N. ϕ s'. And equally, N.N.'s utterance 'I ϕ', if a candidate for truth at all, will be true if and only if that person, N.N., is ϕing. Hence, one might conclude, it is difficult to see how 'I' can be failing to refer if that is how it helps to determine the truth or falsity of the first-person utterance. Wittgenstein addressed the first limb of this objection. One can indeed say that in the mouth of a particular person 'I' refers to that person *in the sense that* if he rightly says 'I ϕ', then others can say truly 'N.N. ϕs'. But this transformation from first to third person is, so to speak, *for others*. For me, 'the word "I" is not a signal calling attention to . . . a person' (LPE 307). And one cannot significantly say that 'I' in my mouth refers to *me* (cf. Vol. XVI, 43), any more than one can significantly say that 'this' in my mouth refers to that (without pointing).

With respect to the second limb of the objection, different cases should be distinguished. Avowals (*Äusserungen*), at least at the most expressive end of the spectrum, are perhaps dubious candidates for truth, but for argument's sake we may disregard this. The utterance of 'I have a pain' is itself a criterion for the truth of 'He has a pain' said of the speaker. It is the fact that the utterance comes *from his mouth* that constitutes the ground for saying of him 'He is in pain'. But that no more shows that N.N.'s utterance 'I have a pain' *refers* to N.N. than the fact that his groan of pain comes from his mouth, and is likewise a criterion of his being in pain, shows that the groan *refers* to him. His saying sincerely 'I have a pain' does not rest on the criterion that *he* says this or on any other criterion, and he does not identify a person *for himself* when he avows his pain. Rather, he draws attention to himself, and *we* identify who is in pain.[31]

In other cases, where the utterance is not itself a criterion for the corresponding third-person assertion, e.g. 'I am seated' or 'I am locked out', the first-person assertion is, of course, true if and only if the corresponding third-person assertion is true. And if one wishes to call that a case of referring, one may do so. But one should still note, first, that 'what determines the truth' of what I say when I say 'I am locked out' is the fact that I am *locked out* (i.e. to verify it, I do not identify a subject), and second, that the fact that I used the word 'I' in saying what I said does *not* 'help to determine the truth or falsity of the *first-person* utterance'.

One might plausibly object that when one uses an expression to refer to a particular person, one distinguishes or intends to distinguish between that person and others. The role of the referring expression is to specify *which* person one is talking about. And surely, when I say 'I ϕ' ('am in pain' or 'am seated') I do just that! Wittgenstein again invites us to note *differences*. First, when I groan 'I am in pain' or exclaim 'I *am* tired', I am not distinguishing between myself and others by *identifying* a particular person. I am not selecting or picking out one person among others; and I am not saying that *this* person is in pain or tired, only that *I* am (cf. Vol. XII, 158). Rather, what I say *enables my hearers* to identify who is in pain.

Even in cases where, in using a first-person sentence, I do want to distinguish between myself and others, the use of 'I' is still subtly different from the use of 'he' or 'N.N.'. If I am among a group of people, and I, as opposed to others, volunteer for something or confess that I, and no one else, did something awry or announce that I alone know something, I am surely distinguishing between myself and others. But it does not follow that I do so by identifying myself as *this person*, N.N., who I am (cf. PI §406). For in numerous such cases I want to distinguish myself from others not by picking myself out from among them, but by obtruding myself upon them. And here, one might prefer to say, I draw attention to myself, but do not refer to myself. But if, while I was talking I said ' . . . the ϕ er . . .', believing myself to be the ϕer, I might later explain that I was, of course, referring to myself.

Proper names of people are one typical paradigm of referring expression, and it is instructive to recollect how differently the use of 'I' and the referential use of proper names is learnt. For the different mode of learning reflects the fact that one is learning to use very different

---

[31] Similar considerations apply to performatives. 'I promise . . .' does not say who promises; it is used by a speaker to *make* a promise. But 'I, N.N., promise . . .' *also* identifies me, says who I am.

instruments of language. One learns a proper name by being told 'He ↗ is N.N.', and one might be taught how to use a proper name to refer to a person by being told 'when *this person* ↗ has pains, you say "N.N. has pains" '. But does one learn how to use the word 'I' by being told '*This person* ↗ is I'? And is one taught the use of 'I' in the sentence 'I have a pain' by being told 'When *this person* ↗ has a pain, you say "I have a pain" ' (Vol. XVI, 153)? Similarly, if someone says 'He has a pain', one will not know what he meant unless one knows to whom he referred, viz. to N.N. or to *that person* ↗ . So one will ask 'Who do you mean?' But if someone says 'I have a pain', can one still ask 'Who do you mean?' In short, one does not learn the use of the word 'I' in the way one learns the use of paradigms of referring expressions. 'I' is more like 'now' than it is like 'N.N.' 'the so-and-so', or 'he', and it shares some of its anomalous features relative to those paradigms. Failures of understanding, misunderstandings and misidentifications of reference that arise with respect to typical referring expressions, cannot arise in that way with 'I' (or 'now').

Even more marked differences come to light when one examines the sub-class of first-person sentences uses of which constitute *Äusserungen*. When I exclaim 'I have a pain' or 'I think that such-and-such', when I announce 'I say, . . .' or 'I'm going now', I am not *stating* that a certain person has a pain, thinks such-and-such, is speaking, or is about to go, I am manifesting my pain, giving my opinion, drawing attention to myself, or expressing my intention. I do so by using the first-person pronoun, but in so using it I do not pick out one person from among others. One might object that just as when I assert 'He is in pain' or 'N.N. thinks such-and-such', so here too I *know* or believe *of* a certain person that things are thus-and-so with him. But, as has been argued previously, this is misconceived. I do not *know* that I am in pain – although that is not because my evidence is slender. And I do not know, by being in pain, that someone else does not have the same pain (cf. PI §408; Vol. XVI, 43f.). 'I know' prefixed to an avowal, unlike 'I know' prefixed to a corresponding third-person sentence, does not signify an item of knowledge. Furthermore, a whole battery of epistemic terms – e.g. 'I doubt', 'I wonder', 'I suspect', 'I guess' – either cannot intelligibly be prefixed to first-person present-tense psychological sentences or, if they can, they function quite differently from cases where they are prefixed to third-person sentences. These differences too earmark the distinctive role of the first-person pronoun over this part of its range of use, a role which makes it fundamentally misleading to treat it as being on the same level as person-referring expressions.

Teaching differences was Wittgenstein's method for dissolving philosophical problems. For these problems typically arise through assimilating one type of expression to another which it superficially resembles or through taking one simple paradigm to determine a certain kind of speech-function where a whole family of distinct but overlapping paradigms is more appropriate. The history of philosophical reflections on 'the self' exemplifies the nature of these tangled knots in our understanding. One thread that runs through these numerous knots is the conviction that the word 'I' names, designates, or refers to something, a mental substance, a thinking thing associated with a substance, a bundle of perceptions, or a transcendental subject. This century has continued to dance to these classical tunes, but in the modern, jazzed-up syncopation of logico-linguistic analysis. 'The self' has variously been conceived of as an object of acquaintance or a logical construction, and, more recently, the first-person pronoun has been thought to be a super-referring expression guaranteed against reference-failure or mis-identification, like a magic arrow that always hits the bull's-eye. Wittgenstein's endeavour was to draw our attention to differences between the word 'I' and proper names, descriptions, and other personal pronouns, differences in function, in identification of the bearer, in grammatical combination with other expressions, in verification, etc. These differences are compelling, and they led Wittgenstein to deny – paradoxically, as he admitted – that the word 'I' is a referring expression at all. But, as he remarked in a different context, 'When white changes to black some people say, "It is essentially still the same". And others, when the colour darkens the slightest bit, say, "It has changed completely".' (See Exg. of p. 46n.) What matters crucially is that one be aware of the differences; and if thereafter, one still wants to say that 'I' is nevertheless a kind of referring expression or, better perhaps, a degenerate referring expression, nothing need hang on that preference as long as one does not assimilate the function of the word 'I' to an inappropriate paradigm of reference.

1   W. here reverts to the theme of §253, viz. the illusion of unique possession of experience that is rooted in the fact that we employ the representational form of ownership when we talk of experiences. We say that we *have* mental images, *have* pains, and *have* visual (or other perceptual) impressions. In the grip of this illusion one is inclined to think that another cannot *have* what one has, and one is then disposed to employ the indexical expression 'this' to emphasize what it is that another cannot have; for one will insist 'At any rate only I have got THIS' or (as in §253) 'But surely another person can't have THIS pain'. But one forgets that there can be no deictic use of 'this' in respect of one's experiences, but only anaphoric or cataphoric reference. 'Only I have THIS' serves no purpose, for one cannot point, either for others or for oneself, at the mental image or visual impression one has. To be sure, one can *say* what one has, e.g. a vivid image of such-and-such or a splitting headache. But, of course, someone else may have that too.

What one *has* when one imagines something or when one sees something is not something which others, by contrast with oneself, cannot see. For one does not see one's mental images or visual impressions. We do indeed speak of *having*, but this having is not a kind of *possessing* at all; and in having a certain image one does not possess something that others cannot possess, since one does not *possess* it oneself. (That of which one cannot be dispossessed, one cannot possess either.) Furthermore, if one excludes others from having what one has, e.g. a vivid image of such-and-such, then one thereby renders it senseless to talk of *having* in one's own case. It makes sense to talk of oneself as having a visual impression or mental image only if it also makes sense to talk of someone else having the same impression or image (cf. BB 55).

If the interlocutor's insistent remarks make no sense, how can W. say that he understands them, that he knows what the interlocutor means? It is not that he understands their sense, but rather that he is familiar with the circumstances in which the temptation to say such things becomes irresistible (cf. Exg. §275 and 'The world of consciousness', §1) and has anatomized the phenomenology of philosophical illusion in such cases, e.g. how one thinks to point at the 'private object' *with one's attention* (§§274f.), how one *immerses* oneself in a colour-impression that seems to belong to oneself alone (§277), and how one stares motionless at what one sees (BB 66). So what is the interlocutor speaking of? W. clarifies: he is speaking of personal experience, of the perceptual impression an object gives one. If the interlocutor is sitting in a room, one might say that he is speaking of 'the visual room'. But he projects upon his discourse about his visual impressions the grammar of the actual visible objects he sees, and it is precisely here that he goes wrong. One can walk about, look at, point at the actual room; it may belong to one, to someone else, or to no one. But one cannot walk about, look at, or point at one's visual impression of the room; there is no such thing. We do indeed use the same form of expression in characterizing our visual impressions as in describing what they are visual impressions of, but the visible room and the 'visual room' are categorially distinct. The visible room may contain its owner, may have or lack an owner. But the grammar of our discourse about the 'visual room' excludes any *owner*. *I* do not enter into the characterization of how what I see strikes me, any more than the eye is part of the visual field. And my 'ownership' of the visual impression is not a *feature* of the impression, but consists in *my* giving expression to how the visible room struck me.

§398(c) gives a parallel case of a shift in the grammar of 'ownership'. The grammar of the visual room is as different from the grammar of the visible room as the grammar for characterizing a picture of an imaginary landscape is from the grammar of descriptions of a landscape. (One can say 'The farmer is just about to enter the house', but one cannot add 'Wait a moment and you'll see'! What it makes sense to say of what is depicted does not always make sense to say of the depiction.)

.1   (i) 'Was ist dann das, wovon du redest?': 'But what then are you talking about?' W. is not suggesting that he is familiar with this private object (*diesen Gegenstand*), but rather with the confusion that leads to such ideas.

(ii) 'Es gehört insofern nicht mir an . . .': better 'In so far as it cannot belong to anyone else, it doesn't belong to me either!' or, 'in so far as I want to apply the same form of expression to it as to the material room in which I sit, it does not belong to me.' For in the sense in which the visible room may be mine, the 'visual room' is not.

2   This derives from Vol. XVI, 62 – 7, preceded by a remark connecting it with the subject of PI §253, for the idea that another cannot have the mental image before his eyes which I have before my eyes is parallel to the idea that another cannot have the same pain as I have. It is only a metaphor to say that one 'sees' it 'before one', a simile of inner sight. And, of course, another can imagine what I imagine and can have the same mental image as I do.

Then follows a draft of PI §398. In the sequel, W. explores at length the confusion of genuine ownership with the representational form of ownership. In the former case, but not the latter, it makes sense to ask 'Does it really belong to you; doesn't it perhaps belong to someone else?' (Vol. XVI, 70). When I say that I have a certain mental image, I don't have to know *who* has it! Indeed, it makes no sense to say 'I *know* that I have this (or, a certain) mental image'. Does it mean that I know that I have *this* one rather than some other one? Or that I know that *I* have it? Both are senseless. What would it be like if I had a different mental image, which I mistook for this one, or none at all, but just fancied that I did? What would it be like if someone else had this mental image, viz. a mental image of X? That, of course, is possible. One wants to say, not 'This, which I describe thus-and-so', but rather, 'This, which I see before me' or just 'This' (pp. 71f.). But there is no deictic use of 'this' in respect of one's sense-impressions or mental images.

2.1   (i) 'the "visual room" ': the 'visual room', as is evident from the previous quotation, is a particular case of the 'room' of personal experience. LPE 296f. talks here of *the world* (of experiences) that lies behind words ('the world as representation', *Die Welt als Vorstellung*, as Schopenhauer called it); but, W. stresses, 'if the *world* is idea, it isn't any person's idea. (Solipsism stops short of saying this and says it is my idea). But then how could I say what the world is if the realm of ideas has no neighbour?' (This harks back to the Schopenhauerian ideas of W.'s youth (NB 72 – 91).)

(ii) 'I can as little own it as I can . . . point to it': BB 71f. remarks, 'If, however, I believe that by pointing to that which in my grammar has no neighbour I can convey something to myself (if not to others), I make a mistake similar to that of thinking that the sentence "I am here" makes sense to me (and, by the way, is always true) under conditions different from those very special conditions under which it does make sense.'

(iii) 'But then he cannot for example enter his house': Vol. XVI, 62 has instead, 'Aber hier hat "gehören" eine andre Grammatik als gewöhnlich, denn der Bauer kann z.B. sein Haus nicht benutzen' ('But here "belonging" has a different grammar than ordinarily, for the farmer cannot, e.g., make use of his house'). The picture is a picture of the owner sitting before his house, but the painted house does not belong to the painted owner.

SECTION 399

1   This explores further the picture of the 'visual room', the 'world as idea' (cf. LPE 297). If the 'visual room' had an owner, the owner would

have to be a possible constituent of the 'visual room', an object of 'visual experience'. But one cannot locate oneself in one's visual field, and the 'visual room' is not *a part* of a larger space wherein its owner might be located. I can stand in front of the stove I see, but I cannot stand in front of my visual impression of the stove (Vol. XVI, 89f.). The first-person pronoun in 'I have a visual impression of the room' or 'I imagine the room thus: . . .' does not designate anything I see or imagine. (Of course, I might imagine myself looking at the stove, but my 'visual body' cannot see (Vol. XVI, 90).) Philosophers who find themselves in these dire straits have argued that 'the I', or 'the self', is therefore merely a bundle of perceptions (as it were, a collection of visual furniture) or a logical construction out of sense-data or a transcendental subject or, as W. himself argued, the limit of the world (TLP 5.641). But this is merely to compound confusion with mystification.

1.1   'There is no outside': visual space has no limits, for it is not *part* of a space. That is why it is absurd to try, as psychologists have done, to *draw* a visual image or visual field (in this peculiar sense of the term). Cf. PR 267. And it is not a part of space, for whereas one can ask where in one's visual field the stove is located, one cannot ask where one's visual field is located (BB 8).

2   This derives from Vol. XVI, 88, which further comments on the quite different use of spatial expressions in the domain of mental and visual images, by contrast with physical space. One speaks of having a visual image, mental image, or after-image *before* one, but not *behind* one. One cannot see *another part* of one's visual space. And so on. These remarks are not phenomenology, however, but grammar.

SECTION 400

1   Our discourse about visual impressions and mental images sounds like the description of a discovery, as if introduction of these forms of expression were in response to finding that apart from the physical world there is also the world of imagination and of subjective experience. But this is illusory. To talk of things being blurred at the edge of one's visual field (unlike talk of images on a photograph being blurred), of conjuring up an image of something revolving (which is not to revolve an image!), is to introduce a new way of speaking. We thereby add new articulations to our language (Z §425) which make possible not descriptions of new objects (objects in the world of sense-data), but new descriptions of, or descriptions essentially related to, familiar objects (e.g. descriptions of

how objects strike one, impress one), new language-games (e.g. of describing how one imagines things).

1.1   (i) 'a new comparison': we compare our visual impressions to objects of vision and use the language of visible objects to describe our visual impressions of objects.

(ii) 'a new sensation': Why so? Because the substratum of such visual experiences is mastery of a technique (cf. PI p. 208), the *concept* of seeing is modified here, as it is in the case of aspect-seeing (PI p. 209). Hence the introduction of new forms of description itself modifies our visual experiences – we can see things in a sense in which, in the absence of these conceptual techniques, we could not (cf. §401). The term 'sensation', however, jars here.

2   BB 57f. compares the confused disagreement between realists, idealists, and solipsists with the confusions over unconscious thoughts and feelings. Psychoanalysts 'were misled by their own way of expression into thinking that they had done more than discover new psychological reactions; that they had, in a sense, discovered conscious thoughts which were unconscious'. But in fact what they had done was primarily to introduce a new grammatical movement, a new way of speaking.

SECTION 401

1   This amplifies §400: we think of the introduction of a new articulation in grammar as heralding the discovery of new objects, as if 'There are sense-data' were on the same level as 'Material objects consist of electrons' (cf. BB 46f., 64, 70).

§401(b) suggests that saying that one has *merely* made a grammatical movement is misleading, for this grammatical articulation makes it possible to describe what previously was not describable, viz. how things appear to us to be (even though they are not so). So we have a new way of looking at things (*eine neue Auffassung*) and can record not only how they are, but how they strike us as being, how they impress us. One might compare this to the introduction of an impressionistic style of painting, as opposed to a purely naturalistic one.

It is unclear what W. means by a mere new grammatical movement which does *not* introduce a new way of looking at things.

1.1   'Du deutest die neue Auffassung . . .': 'You interpret the new way of looking at things as . . .'.

SECTION 402

1   The 'visual room' has no owner, and it is readily viewed (wrongly) as a discovery. Now W. warns against a further misinterpretation. It is indeed true that the words 'I have' in 'Now I have such-and-such an image' are merely a sign to someone else. They do not signify anything in the image that I entertain. In this respect they function rather like prefacing one's remarks by 'I say!' (or by loudly clearing one's throat). The utterance 'I say! Such-and-such is the case' does not *tell* one's hearer who is saying something, but rather draws the hearer's attention to oneself (Vol. XII, 171).

One may recognize this feature and misinterpret it. For one is now inclined to say that ordinary language is here defective, that it *misdescribes the facts*. One might then entertain the thought of a more accurate language in which one did *not* say 'I have such-and-such an image', but rather made a special sign with one's hand and merely gave a description of the image. So too Lichtenberg suggested that instead of saying 'I think', we should say 'It thinks', as we say 'It rains'[1] (M 309). Similarly, the author of the *Tractatus* proclaimed as a metaphysical insight that 'there is no such thing as the subject that thinks or entertains ideas' (TLP 5.631; see Exg. §402, 2.1, below). But this is immensely misleading. Such philosophers achieve a partial insight into the different *uses* of expressions with grammatically similar *form*, but misconstrue it. 'I have such-and-such an image' performs its role perfectly satisfactorily; it is used to tell another what I am imagining.[2] It has the same grammatical form as 'John has such-and-such an image', but a very different use. The latter is asserted on the basis of behavioural criteria, whereas the former is groundlessly avowed. The latter involves reference to a person and the possibility (intelligibility) of misidentification of the person, as well as mistaken description of what he is imagining, whereas the former does not. They can both be said to be descriptions; but if so, then descriptions of logically different types.

Philosophers who criticize the first-person mode of expression have a picture, viz. a picture of 'unowned data', which conflicts with the *picture* of our ordinary mode of expression, viz. the subject as owner of the image. But they fail to notice that the conflict is one of *form*. Noting correctly that 'I have' is not here fulfilling the same role as 'He has', they infer that 'I have such-and-such an image' misdescribes the facts. But that

---

[1] Of course, this is confused; for 'thinks' is not a feature-placing predicate. Moreover, Lichtenberg never clarified what, if anything, we should say instead of 'He thinks'.

[2] Although, of course, this language-game of telling is altogether different from telling someone what happened in Parliament yesterday (cf. Exg. §363).

is quite wrong. The role of 'I have such-and-such an image', unlike that of 'N has such-and-such an image', is not to identify a person who has a certain image, but to describe what image *I* have. (Those who hear what I say will identify who is imagining without more ado.) And what expression could *more correctly* describe what images I am entertaining than 'I have such-and-such an image'? The philosophers' complaint is one about the misleading similarity of form between sentences which fulfil very different functions; but they misconstrue their grievance. For the *form* of an expression cannot say something false; it is what the expression *says* which is true or false. I would indeed be misrepresenting things if I said 'I have such-and-such an image' when I have a different image or when I am not actually imagining anything at all. But the form of an expression cannot say something false when what the expression says is true; the only way for 'He has pains' to be false is for him *not* to have pains. (Does 'It is raining' misrepresent the facts because one cannot ask 'What is raining?'?)

The confusion is instructive and of quite general import, for meta-physical disputes are typically enmeshed in this very confusion. Idealists and solipsists attack the normal form of expression as if the mere form stated how things are; whereas the only cogent case that can be made out in their favour is a recommendation to adopt a different form in which the very same facts are represented in different guise (see Exg. §403). For when the idealist tells us that material objects are *really* only collections of ideas, he does not mean that one will not hurt oneself if one scrapes one's shins against a table; and when the solipsist argues that only the present is real, he does not mean that he did not have breakfast this morning. Rather, they misconstrue what they are doing, conflate different forms of representation, and think they have achieved an insight into the true nature of things. Similar confusion is evident in those realists who in effect defend our normal form of expression against idealism and solipsism, but do so by stating facts we all know, as Dr Johnson did in 'refuting' Berkeley by kicking a stone, or (less crudely) G. E. Moore did in 'proving the existence of the external world' by demonstrating that he had two hands.

1.1   (i) 'Vorstellungswelt': 'world of representation', though quasi-technical, might better capture the Schopenhauerian picture involved here, as well as implying greater generality than 'the imagined world'.

(ii) 'ist wie ein "Jetzt Achtung" ': 'is like an "Attention now!" '; i.e. it is like the heralding of an announcement the function of which is to draw attention.

(iii) 'As if, for example the proposition "he has pains" . . .': why the shift from 'I have an image'? Perhaps because it is potentially misleading to talk of avowals as false, rather than as untruthful or insincere. But then why not 'He has an image'?

2   Vol. XII, 213ff. adds further points:

(i) One wants to say that when one has pains, there are just pains, and there is no question of a person entering into the experience. So wouldn't simply 'Pains!' describe the whole fact of the matter? But, first, is that a description? And secondly, what purpose does it serve? One misguidedly compares the situation with one in which a description is to be given. So one thinks of the imagination (or the domain of experience) as a *world* that is to be described, as a geography book describes the earth. But how far is the expression of pain the description of a world, and what is it for? The contrast is comparable to the difference between (a) 'At such-and-such a place there is a house which has such-and-such features . . .' and (b) 'Once upon a time there was a wealthy man who lived in a house which . . .' (or 'Imagine a house which . . .'). The application of these 'descriptions' in the various cases is altogether different.

(ii) In saying that 'I have . . .' is only for others and not for myself when I describe my images, one may still be misled. Is it only for others because I *know* that the image is mine?

(iii) One is inclined to say 'What more can he know than how things are? And he comes to know that by means of the description of the image.' Here one does indeed conceive of the description as a description of 'a world'. But this obscures what such a description is for, what one does with it.

By implication we are invited to reflect on the language-games with 'I imagined things thus', on the contexts in which one tells someone how one imagines something, and the consequences in the language-game of giving such a description. Here too, one might emphasize, the language-game *begins* with the description of what one imagines.

One might compare the 'I have . . .' to the direction-arrow on a map. It too belongs to the map, only not to the map as a picture. (Rather, it shows what one can do with the picture.)

2.1   (i) 'the description of the image is a *complete* account of the imagined world': this was the view taken in TLP 5.63 – 5.634, esp. 5.633.

> Where *in* the world is a metaphysical subject to be found?
> You will say that this is exactly like the case of the eye and the visual field. But really you do *not* see the eye.
> And nothing *in the visual field* allows you to infer that it is seen by an eye.

Vol. XII, 235 (mis)quotes the final remarks:

'Nichts im Gesichtsfeld deutet darauf hin etc.' (Log. Phil. Abh.). Das heisst sozusagen: Du wirst vergebens im Gesichtsraum nach dem *Seher* ausschauen. Es ist nirgends im Gesichtsraum zu finden. – Aber die Wahrheit ist: Du *tust* nur, als suchtest Du nach einem Etwas, nach einer Person im Gesichtsraum, die nicht da ist.

('Nothing in the visual field indicates, etc.' (Tract. Log. Phil.). That means, as it were: you will look in vain in visual space for the *viewer*. The viewer is not to be found in visual space. – But the truth is: you only *pretend* to be looking for a something, for a person, in visual space, who is not there.)

The Kantian (Schopenhauerian) observation of the *Tractatus* presented an insight into the bounds of sense as a metaphysical discovery. But the truth is that there is no space *in grammar* for an owner in the visual field, not no space in the visual field. And confusion over this point leads naturally to the further two ideas, first, that the description of the *Vorstellung* (image or representation) is a complete account of the *Vorstellungswelt* (world of representation) and second, that ordinary grammar misrepresents the facts. But what seems like a description of a private world is not a description of a *world*, but of what one imagines (or of how what one perceives strikes one) – a description which has various uses, all of which are *unlike* descriptions of the world.

(ii) 'the words "I am having" are like "I say! . . ." ': as noted above, this is an inaccurate translation, although it does make the right point. Coincidentally, W. did comment on this use of 'I say!' Vol. XII, 170 observes that if one prefaced every sentence with 'I say!', the role of which was to attract attention (like clearing one's throat), it would be absurd to claim that every sentence says who is talking. Applying this reasoning to 'I have . . .', it would be absurd to interpret a person's description of his images as saying whose they are. Their role is to introduce a description of what one imagines.

(iii) 'we are tempted to say that our way of speaking does not describe the facts as they really are': BB 69 compares our confusion here with one which might arise among philosophers in whose language, instead of saying 'I found nobody in the room', one said 'I found Mr Nobody in the room'. They would probably find the similarity between 'Mr Smith' and 'Mr Nobody' disturbing and might wish to abolish it, as philosophers have recommended abolishing the 'I' in 'I have a pain'. But, W. stresses, 'We are inclined to forget that it is the particular use of a word only which gives the word its meaning'. '*Mr* Nobody' is misleading, since 'Mr' is standardly used to introduce a singular referring expression. But, of course, 'Mr Nobody' is *not* used like a singular referring expression. One cannot ask where Mr Nobody is, and there is no Mrs Nobody. The sentence 'Mr Nobody is in the room' in the envisaged language no more misdescribes (falsifies) the facts than Alice's 'I see nobody on the road'.

3   Many empiricists from Hume onwards fit the bill of this remark. Russell may serve to exemplify the style of thought:

It is supposed that thoughts cannot just come and go, but need a person to think them. Now, of course it is true that thoughts can be collected into bundles, so that one bundle is my thoughts, another is your thoughts, and a third is the thoughts of Mr. Jones. But I think the person is not an ingredient in the single thought: he is rather constituted by relations of the thoughts to each other and to the body . . . It would be better to say 'it thinks in me', like 'it rains'; or better still 'there is a thought in me'.[3] (AM 18)

SECTION 403

1   This amplifies §402. W. once envisaged a language of an oriental despot in which, instead of saying 'I have a pain', the despot said 'There is pain', and instead of saying 'N.N. has a pain', he said 'N.N. is behaving as the Centre [the despot] behaves when there is pain' (cf. WWK 49; PR 88f.). Of course, this would not imply that the facts of the matter were being overlooked or distorted. If N.N. behaved as the Centre behaves when there is a toothache, the dentist would treat him, etc. Equally, the *concepts* differ, so the objection to this mode of expression that other people have the same as the Centre is incorrect; for no one *has* anything (in this form of representation). But, of course, people with serious injuries and diseases behave in the same way, viz. as the Centre does when there is pain.

So this new mode of representation does not describe or misdescribe the facts 'as they really are' (§402), for a grammar can neither conflict with nor conform to the facts. It is the application of a grammar in statements that is answerable to the facts. So nothing would be gained by adopting this novel notation. But equally, the solipsist (coherently construed) was not suggesting that only he should be treated at the hospital. Rather, he was under the *illusion* that an alternative notation would describe the facts better (as if 'There is pain' would be more accurate than 'I have a pain'). Whereas all he has really noted is that the use of 'I have a pain' is very unlike that of 'He has a pain'.

1.1   (i) 'Art der Darstellung': 'mode of representation'.
(ii) 'As long as a notation were provided . . .': we would have to distinguish between being in pain and pretending to be in pain, for example. This could be done thus: 'N.N. is behaving as the Centre does when there is pain' = 'N.N. is in pain', and 'N.N. is behaving as the

---

[3] To which one wants to reply 'Who's me?'

Centre does when it looks as if there is pain, although actually there is not' = 'N.N. is pretending to be in pain'. Other moves can be imagined for concealing pain, having pain but not showing it, etc.

(iii) 'Other people have just the same as you': this would be no objection, since the envisaged grammar would make no room for this grammatical articulation. But again, analogues for sameness of pain can be envisaged in terms of relations between patterns of behaviour.

2   Vol. XI, 154 has this preceded by one of the very few remarks in which W. reflects on the fact that our language *does* provide an alternative form of expression to that of ownership. What is it, he queries, that rebels against the form of expression 'I have . . .' here? Well, there is available a different form of expression in which the question of 'mine' does not arise – indeed, is quite senseless. We would simply say 'It hurts now'. But it is remarkable, he adds, that in such a discussion we are inclined to say of our ordinary mode of expression: 'Really what this means is . . .' (as if the form of an expression were *wrong*). It is noteworthy that we do *not* ordinarily rebel against the form of an expression, but only when doing philosophy.

2.1   'neither does the solipsist *want* any practical advantage': BB 58f. explores this at length. One cannot reply to the solipsist by appeal to common sense (e.g. 'Why do you tell us this if you don't believe that we really hear you?'). Rather one must remove the temptation to attack common sense. The source of the solipsist's puzzlement is dissatisfaction *with a notation*, which presents itself in the guise of an insight into the nature of things. Three points must be borne in mind, however: (a) The new notation (e.g. that resembling the oriental despot's above) is not justified by the facts. The rationale for the solipsist's notation is not that *his* body is the 'seat of all life'. (b) By a new notation no facts are changed (cf. BB 57). One symbolism is as good as another and no one symbolism is necessary (AWL 22). (c) The solipsist does not actually go through with the shift of notation, but mixes up the new notation with the old one (AWL 23). He generates incoherence by proclaiming 'Only *my* pain is *real*' for 'my pain' belongs to the same system as '*his* pain', and 'real pain' to the same system as 'pretended pain'.

SECTION 404

1   Having clarified the nature of the 'visual room', W. now turns to the 'owner'. We naturally conceive of the first-person pronoun as fulfilling a similar role to the third-person pronoun. So 'I' seems to signify the

owner of the visual room, the *res cogitans*. This idea, however, rests on a confusion of form and function.

§404(a) opens with the paradoxical remark 'When I say "I am in pain", I do not point to a person, since in a certain sense I have no idea *who* is'. Despite its air of paradox, W. insists that it can be justified (cf. PI p. 195(f)). Of course, it does not mean that I do not know who I am, know that my name is N.N., etc. (although that too is possible in cases of amnesia). But does it follow from the fact that I know that I am N.N., and the fact that I have pains that I know who has pains? After all, 'I, who am N.N., know I am in pain' makes no more sense than 'I know I am in pain' (PI §246).

W. does not focus on this point here (see §408), although it partly explains the phrase '*in a certain sense* I have no idea *who* is' (my emphasis). Rather, he concentrates on 'the main point', viz. that in saying 'I am . . .' I do not point to, pick out, or identifyingly refer to a person. I do not name a person, as I do when I say 'N.N. is in pain', but others can discern who is in pain from my utterance, as indeed they can from my groans of pain. One might say that the difference between 'He is . . .' and 'I am . . .' here corresponds to the difference between pointing and raising one's hand.

§404(b) explains one aspect of the difference in role between 'I am . . .' and 'He is . . .'. To know who is in pain is to know that a certain person satisfying a certain description or specifiable by ostension fulfils the criteria for being in pain. One may specify very many criteria identifying a person, but in saying '*I* am in pain', one invokes no criteria, for one does not *identify* a particular person as he who is in pain, nor does one *point at* a particular person, as one does with 'He is in pain'.

1.1   'Personal "*identity*" '/'my saying that "I" am in pain?': the rationale for *both* scare-quotes *and* italics is not clear. It is evident that W.'s concern here is not with the link between the notion of identification and the criteria of sameness and difference of persons, but with the fact that in saying 'I am in pain' one does *not* identifyingly refer to a person. (For discussion of personal identity, see BB 61f.; AWL 60 – 3; PLP 214 – 16.)

2   Vol. XII, 155f. has this followed by a remark which throws light on the independence of 'I have a pain' from criteria of identification of a person. For 'I have a pain' is not replaceable by 'L.W. has a pain' if, for example, a radical change of bodies occurs (cf. LPE 308). The function of 'I have . . .' is altogether unlike that of 'L.W. has . . .' as this expression is used by others.

2.1   'someone else sees who is in pain from the groaning': Vol. XVI, 25 elaborates. I experience pain, but not that *I* have it. For myself, I groan with pain; for others, I say 'I am in pain'. The groan corresponds to 'pain', perhaps, but not to 'I'; rather, my groan shows another that I am in pain in as much as *I* groan. But when I groan with pain, it is not as if I choose *this* mouth in order to express the fact that it is *I* and not someone else who is in pain (cf. BB 68). Later (Vol. XVI, 170) W. remarks that to say 'I have a pain' is *to complain*. He who thus complains is said to *have* a pain. Hence one can't call the complaint the *statement* that so-and-so has a pain.

SECTION 405

1   Granted that the role of 'I' in 'I have a pain' is very different from that of 'N.N.' in 'N.N. has a pain', and granted that by using it I attract the hearer's *attention* to myself, then surely when one uses it, one wants to draw his attention to *a particular person*? Of course, I am a particular person, say N.N., and not someone else. And when I groan 'I am in pain' I do draw the attention of others to a particular person. But does it follow that I use 'I am in pain' because I want to draw attention to a particular person, namely N.N.? No, that may still be misleading, distorting the distinctive role of the first-person pronoun here. I need not mean *any* person when I groan 'I am in pain', any more than when I just groan. (But when I say 'He is in pain' I mean *him* ↗.) I do not *single out* a particular person from among others by any referential device (I do not choose the mouth that says 'I am in pain'); I get *others* to single out *me*. (Who is me? No matter, let them find that out, as long as they help me!) And when they single me out, they do not do so in the way in which I have, since I have not done so at all. Their identification does not rest on a proper name, definite description, or ostension that I have supplied, but on a signal I have evinced.

Note that 'I say!' similarly functions to draw the attention of others to myself, without singling me out in any particular way. Pointing serves to draw attention to a particular person, namely . . . (and here one gives an identifying description), but raising one's hand draws attention to oneself (and there is no 'namely' about it, any more than when one groans). If the teacher asks 'Who knows . . .?', and I raise my hand, *he* can supply an identifying description if he pleases.

1.1   'The answer might be': presumably because it is not *incorrect*, but potentially misleading with respect to the distinctive role of 'I'.

SECTION 406

1   The interlocutor grants that when I say 'I am in pain' I want to draw
attention not to a particular person satisfying some description, but to
myself. Nevertheless, he now objects, with 'I have . . .' I surely want to
distinguish between myself and other people! Clearly this is sometimes
true, e.g. when the teacher asks 'Who can . . .?' or 'Who knows . . .?'
But equally obviously it is not so when I merely groan with pain; rather,
I just manifest my suffering. And does that not apply also when 'Oh! Oh!
I've hurt myself!' is wrenched from my lips? Nevertheless, even in those
cases where it might be said that I do want to distinguish between myself
and others, does it follow that I want to distinguish between myself
characterized by name and others similarly characterized?

2   Vol. XVI, 171 has:

  'Aber Du gebrauchst doch "ich" im Gegensatz zu "er". Also, unterscheidest Du
doch dadurch zwischen Personen.'
    . . . Aber es ist nicht, als zeigte jetzt gleichsam derselbe Zeiger auf mich. 'Ich' and
'er' haben eben (*ganz*) verschiedene Funktionen in der Sprache.

  ('But you do use "I" in contrast to "he". So you do distinguish thereby between
persons.'·
    . . . But it is not as if the same pointer, as it were, is now pointing at me. 'I' and 'he'
have after all (*wholly*) different functions in language.)

  Vol. XII, 158 has the first sentence of §406, followed by the explanation:

  – Das heisst also: ich will nicht sagen, der Andre habe Schmerzen, *sondern ich*. – Ich
will die Worte sagen, die ich sage, und nicht andere. Aber das Wort 'ich', obgleich es
an derselben Stelle im Satz steht, wie 'er', funktioniert anders. Weiss ich denn, wer
redet, wenn ich weiss, dass ich rede?

  (– That means: I don't want to say that the other person has pain, *but that I have*. – I
want to utter the words I utter and not others. But the word 'I', even though it stands
in the same position in the sentence as 'He', functions differently. Do I then know
who is speaking when I know that I am speaking?)

  Six pages later W. reworks the material from Vol. XVI, 171[4]:

  'Aber Du gebrauchst doch "ich" im Gegensatz zu "er". Also unterscheidest Du doch
zwischen Personen.' Nun, ich sage in diesem Fall 'ich', und sage nicht 'er'. Und 'ich'
steht allerdings an der gleichen Stelle im Satze, an der in andern Fällen 'er' steht. Aber

----

  [4] For the complex dating of Vol. XII and its parts, see G. H. von Wright, 'The
Wittgenstein Papers', in his *Wittgenstein* (Blackwell, Oxford, 1982), pp. 50f., and S. Hilmy,
The Later Wittgenstein (Blackwell, Oxford and New York, 1987), Ch. 1.

es ist nicht, als zeigte *der* Zeiger jetzt auf *mich* (d.h. hier: auf meinen Körper), der sonst auf einen Andern zeigt. (Denn nicht darin besteht es, dass *ich* Schmerzen habe: dass sie jetzt in *meinem* Körper sind.) Denn ich bin ja eben versucht zu sagen: vom Andern wisse ich, dass er Schmerzen habe, weil ich sein <u>Benehmen</u> // ihre Wirkung // <u>beobachtete</u>, von mir – weil ich sie *fühle*. Aber das ist eben sinnlos, weil 'ich fühle Schmerzen' dasselbe heisst, wie 'ich habe Schmerzen'. Es scheint hier so, als hülfe mir in einem Fall der *eine* Sinn, im andern Fall der andre, den Besitzer des Schmerzes finden, wie ich etwa einen Gegenstand einmal mit den Augen suche, einmal mit den Ohren. Und man kann wohl sagen, dass mich in einem Fall der Gesichtssinn zum *Ort* der Schmerzen leitet, im andern Fall der Sinn des Schmerzgefühls; aber mein Schmerzgefühl leitet mich nicht zum *Besitzer* des Schmerzes.

Wenn jeder dieser Leute 'weiss', dass er Schmerzen hat – weiss denn jeder etwas anderes? Weiss nicht jeder dasselbe, nämlich: '*ich habe* Schmerzen'? – Anders aber, wenn es heisst: 'er hat Schmerzen' – denn 'er' bezieht sich auf einen Namen, eine Beschreibung, oder (<u>ei</u>ne) hindweisende Gebärde; ohne eine solche Beziehung ist der Ausdruck ohne Sinn.

'Ich' und 'er' dienen // haben eben // in unserer Sprache nicht gleichartigen Zwecken // gleichartige Funktionen //. (Vol. XII, 164f.)

('But you do use "I" in contrast to "he". So you do distinguish between persons.' Well, in this case I say 'I' and don't say 'he'. And, to be sure, 'I' stands in the same place in the sentence where, in other cases, 'he' stands. But it is not as if *the* pointer, which otherwise points at others, is now pointing at me (that means here: at my body). (For that *I* have pains does not consist in this: that they are now in *my* body.) For I am indeed inclined to say: I know that another has pains because I <u>observe his</u> <u>behaviour</u> // their effect //, that I have pains – because I *feel* them. But that is actually senseless, for 'I feel pains' means the same as 'I have pains'. It seems here as if now one sense, now another, assists me in finding the owner of the pain, as if, for example, I look for an object now with my eyes and now with my ears. And one can indeed say that in the one case I am led to the location of the pain by the sense of sight, in the other case by the sense of feeling (-pain);[5] but my feeling of pain does not lead me to the *owner* of the pain.

If each of these people 'knows' that he has pains, does each one know something different? Doesn't each one know the same, namely: '*I have* pains'? – But it is different in the case of 'He has pains' – for 'he' is connected with a name, a description, or <u>an</u> ostensive gesture: without such a connection the expression is without sense.

'I' and 'he' do not serve // have // the same purpose // function // in our language.)

SECTION 407

1   It is the *expression* of suffering (the *Äusserung*) that identifies the sufferer, not a self-reference or self-identification. One might imagine

---

[5] This seems a wholly mistaken assimilation of sensation to perception. I do not *find out* where my pain is by feeling it in my arm, as I find out where a pin is by feeling it in the armchair. However, this does not affect the point W. is making. W. rectifies it some pages later in Vol. XII; cf. Exg. §408, 2.

the heroic officer referring the stretcher-bearers to someone else screaming in pain further down the trench. He says, through clenched teeth and
with a groan, 'Someone is in pain – I don't know who.' So the
stretcher-bearers help him too, for he is clearly in pain himself.

2   It is unclear from the MS. sources (Vol. XII, 165; Vol. XVI, 174)
whether this is what W. had in mind here. Other, more far-fetched
possibilities are (a) an amnesiac (but then the phrasing is very poor and
misleading); (b) a different form of representation, in which 'someone',
which is obviously not a referring expression, does service for 'I'. This is
illuminating, but then 'I don't know who' is wrong, and misplaced.

SECTION 408

1   The interlocutor tries one last move to preserve his picture of the
functioning of the first-person pronoun in avowals. Surely 'I' *is*
employed to distinguish between myself and others. For do I not know
something to be true of myself and not of others when I say 'I am in
pain'? I am not, after all, in danger of making a mistake through
ignorance of who is in pain? So when I am in pain I surely know *who* is in
pain (contrary to §404).

This is to no avail. A constituent of 'I don't know whether I or
someone else is in pain' is 'I don't know whether I am in pain' (the 'or
not' is redundant), and that, as argued (cf. §246), is not a significant
proposition.

2   Vol. XII, 169 has this, preceded by the observation that 'I know that *I*
have pains because I feel them' seems like 'I know that *I* have the
"Plumpsack" because I feel it' (as opposed to seeing it). W. is referring
here to a children's game of this name. The 'Plumpsack' is a knotted
handkerchief and also the player who holds it. The children stand in a
circle, facing inwards, while the player holding the 'Plumpsack' moves
around behind them until he touches one of them with it, drops it and
runs round the circle, chased by the person he has touched, trying to
obtain the vacated place without being hit with the 'Plumpsack'.

'Du weisst doch insofern, wer den Schmerz hat, als Du weisst, dass *Du* ihn
hast' – scheint etwa zu sagen: 'Du weisst doch jedenfalls, dass der Schmerz jetzt bei
Dir ist' – so wie man sagt: 'Ich weiss jetzt, wo der Plumpsack ist, – weil nämlich *ich*
ihn habe.' Das heisst aber *doch*: 'Jetzt bin ich nicht mehr im zweifel darüber, wer ihn
hat, – weil ich ihn nämlich habe.' Aber kann man auch sagen: 'Jetzt bin ich nicht mehr
im Zweifel darüber, wer Schmerzen hat, weil ich sie habe'? Bin ich über die Andern
jetzt weniger im Zweifel, und war ich über mich vorher im Zweifel?

('You do know who has the pain in so far as you know that *you* have it' perhaps seems to say: 'At any rate you do know that the pain is with you' – as one says 'Now I know where the *Plumpsack* is – because *I* have it.' But that *actually* means 'Now I am no longer in any doubt about who has it – because I have it.' But can one also say: 'Now I am no longer in any doubt about who has pains, because I have them'? Am I in any less doubt about the others, and was I previously in any doubt about myself?).

Section 409

1   This gives an analogy to illuminate the point made in §408 and especially in Vol. XII, 169 (just quoted). In the game with the electrical shocks, it would indeed be odd to say 'Now I know who is feeling the shocks, it's me' – odd, but not, in this context, unintelligible, since it just amounts to 'I am the one who is being electrified'. If I feel a shock, at any rate I know that no one else is being electrified (*ex hypothesi*). But now suppose that I can feel the shock even when someone else is electrified. In this case 'Now I know who . . .' drops out of the game, for it *draws no distinction*. Pain is akin to this latter case. (The former is more akin to the game with 'Who has the "Plumpsack"?', wherein I can see whether others have it and feel on my back if I do.) Obviously I can feel pain whether or not another is in pain (pain is unlike the 'Plumpsack'). So the fact that I have a pain tells me nothing about whether others do or do not have a pain too. And equally, that I have a pain now gives no quietus to any doubts I might have as to whether I have a pain, since doubts are senseless.

Section 410

1   The indexicals 'I', 'here', and 'this' are not names (although Russell notoriously thought that each individual use of 'this' was a paradigmatic case of using a pure name, and W. once seems to have thought that 'this' incorporated the general form of a name as such (cf. NB 61)). But these indexicals are connected with names, and that in *various* ways. The peculiarities of the word 'I' that have been discussed in the previous six remarks are facets of the special use of this expression (and something different would have to be said of 'here' and 'this', not to mention 'now'). One feature common to these indexicals is that although they are *not* names, nevertheless they are used to explain names (that is one of their connections with names). If asked who N.N. is, I may, if I am N.N., answer 'I am N.N.'. I may explain what a colour-word means by pointing at a sample and saying 'This is red'. And I may, while showing visitors around Oxford, stop before the Sheldonian and say with a gesture '*Here* is the Sheldonian'.

.1   'dass die Physik charakterisiert ist': i.e. it is a defining feature
(*Merkmal*) of this science – the propositions of physics are *impersonal*,
ahistorical, and typically *context-free*. Hence indexicals are excluded, like
route maps in an astronomical atlas as opposed to a road atlas.

3   James argued that despite interruptions of consciousness by sleep, 'the
consciousness' remains sensibly continuous and one. What now is the
common whole? The natural name for it is *myself, I*, or *me*.[6] Russell
characterized the first-person pronoun in a preliminary way as an
'ambiguous proper name' (LK 164). 'The word "this" ', he wrote, 'is
always a proper name' (LK 167). Further 'there is such a relation as
"attention", and . . . there is always a subject attending to the object
called "this". The subject attending to "this" is called "I", and the time of
the things which have to "I" the relation of presence is called the present
time' (LK 168).

SECTION 411

1   This concludes the discussion of the words 'I' and '*my* experience' by
noting the diversity of uses of 'my'. In particular W. is concerned with
the distinction between what he called the 'reflexive' and 'possessive' *my*
(Vol. XVI, 174).

In the case of 'Are these books *my* books?' we have an example of
property ownership. An ostensive gesture can pick out which books are
mine, viz. *these* ↗. That they are mine is determined by the fact that they
are in my possession, that I purchased them, or was given them. (Of
course, lawyers will distinguish possession from ownership and real
property from, e.g., copyright.) Ownership of books is alienable, and
there may be books that belong to no one.

Having limbs is different. It is not legal institutions or social conventions that make *this* foot *my* foot. Which foot is *my* foot? Well, I can point
to it and say '*That* ↗ is my foot'. But note that the ostensive gesture here,
unlike that with 'These books ↗ are my books', is *reflexive*. Can there be
any doubt for me? Yes, in cases of paralysis or loss of sensation. For *my*
foot is the foot that moves when I wiggle my toes; it hurts me when I hit
my toe, but I don't feel a thing when I hit yours, etc. But in cases of
paralysis or anaesthesia these criteria are of no use, and we obviously fall
back on the co-ordinate criterion that my foot is the foot attached to my
leg. Note that 'ownership' of limbs is in principle, and of organs is (now)
in practice, transferable.

Having a body is different again. 'Which is my body?' can intelligibly
be asked of mirror-images (perhaps in a Hall of Mirrors at a fairground)

---

[6] James, *Principles of Psychology*, Vol. 1, p. 238.

or of photographs. In these cases one can point at the image, ask whether *that* ↗ is me, whether *that* is what I looked like as a baby. But if one says '*This* is my body' with a *reflexive* gesture, this is only an *explanation* of the use of 'my body'. Hence, too, the only *practical* application of the quesion 'Is this body my body?', where it involves a reflexive gesture, is in teaching a child how to use 'my body' and 'his body' (Vol. XVI, 223). For it makes no sense for me to be mistaken over which body is mine (save in the case of mirror-images or pictures). I do not own my body as I own my books; if I sell myself into slavery, it is not 'just my body' that I sell, and I am not left bodiless. 'Does my body look like that?' means the same as 'Do I look like that?' (although, of course, 'I' does *not* mean the same as 'my body').

What, finally, of 'Is this sensation my sensation?' What practical application does W. have in mind? He gives no clue, save to note that an ostensive use of the demonstrative pronoun is here excluded, as is the pseudo-ostention of directing one's attention. Possibly what he has in mind is an anaphoric reference to a description of a sensation, perhaps when one is reading a medical book and trying to identify one's own illness from the description of the symptoms.

1.1   'Under certain circumstances, however, one might touch a body': it is unclear what W. is thinking of. One possibility is a rhetorical question accompanied by tapping oneself on the chest: 'Is this body my body?' one might exclaim, 'Then I am at liberty to abuse it as I please!' Another possibility is as an exclamation of delight as one looks in the mirror after a prolonged effort to lose weight; here one touches one's body, pats one's flat stomach, etc.

2.1   (i) '*my* books . . .*my* foot . . . *my* body . . .': Vol. XII, 183 notes that 'my' can be defined as *possessive* or as *reflexive*.
(ii) 'mine': Vol XII, 185 remarks that 'mine' is what I *have*. If you want to find out what is mine, look to see who owns it, e.g. who bought this house, who dwells in it, etc. But what if one asks 'Look to see whether this is *my* face'? (Of course, this too has a use if I refer you to a photograph of my class at school thirty years ago.)
(iii) 'Does my body look like that?': Vol. XVI, 242 notes that this is equivalent to 'Do I look like that?' Further, in saying 'This is my body' and 'This is me' ('Das bin ich'), one makes the same indicative gesture, but of course 'me' ('ich') does not mean the same as 'my body'. One must beware, however, of the idea that the two expressions 'I' and 'my body' signify different things, for that idea tempts us to give our form of speech the primitive interpretation that 'I' dwell in my body.

CHAPTER 5

Consciousness

(§§412 – 27)

INTRODUCTION

Part A of this 'chapter' runs from §412 to §421. It consists of a brief discussion of a limited range of questions about the nature of consciousness. W. does not attempt here to survey the grammar of this expression, but only to relate it to the antecedent preoccupations of the book. Some confusions and bogus mysteries surrounding the concept of consciousness exemplify philosophical diseases hitherto diagnosed, and these can be dispelled by therapies that have already been explained.

§412 opens the discussion by noting the feeling of an unbridgeable gulf between consciousness and brain-processes. The illusion of a mystery, of a gulf between wholly disparate, unconnectable phenomena, is a projection of a categorial distinction, of a difference in the grammatical character of certain expressions. The sense of mystery afflicts us only in philosophical reflection, when language is idling.

§413 draws attention to one source of our confusion, viz. the idea that we can examine the nature of consciousness by introspection. But the attempt to do so, like James's attempt to investigate the 'central nucleus of the Self' by introspection, reveals only the state of the philosopher's attention when, in such circumstances, he thinks of consciousness and tries to analyse the meaning of the word. §414 gives an analogy for the vacuousness of seeking to uncover the nature of consciousness thus, and §415 is a general methodological remark.

§§416 – 21 focus on a pair of suppositions implicit in the illusion of a mysterious gulf between brain-processes and consciousness. When we thus project a category distinction in grammar onto reality, we think that consciousness is an object of experience, that we are witnesses in our own case to the fact that we are conscious. Hence we imagine that the proposition 'I am conscious' is used to record an item of indubitable Cartesian knowledge. But that is not the role of this sentence (§416). One does not, as the Cartesian supposes, observe or perceive one's own consciousness, and the experience which occasions one's saying 'I am conscious' is not an experience of being conscious (§417). The idea that we are witnesses to our own consciousness conceives of our consciousness as a fact of experience, something we witness in our own case and report for the benefit of others. But this leads to a peculiar incoherence (§418). For consciousness is then conceived to be a curious, perhaps indescribable, experience that contingently accompanies human activities, but not those of trees. If so, it would have to be possible to describe the lives of human beings (including myself) who lacked this peculiar experience of consciousness. But this makes no sense.

That human beings are conscious (or unconscious), whereas trees and stones are not, is a grammatical remark, not an empirical observation. This point is ironically highlighted in §419. §420 explores the supposition that other human beings, though behaving as normal, nevertheless lack consciousness. The supposition is meaningless, although it may produce an uncanny feeling as when one views something (the cross-pieces of a window) as a limiting case of another (a swastika). §421 concludes this part of the discussion by endeavouring to dispel the feeling of paradox that may beset us when philosophizing about states of consciousness.

The structure of Part A:

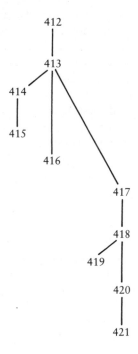

§§422 – 7 explore the status of pictures that are embodied in our forms of representation. We have a picture of the soul (as in ethereal being within the body) or blindness (as a darkness in the head) or a benzene molecule (as a hexagonal ring). In all these cases the picture is prominent in the expressions we use. It is important not to dispute the correctness or validity of these pictures (§§422 – 4), but equally important not to be misled by the pictures into thinking that they represent the facts as if they were proto-theories. What must be investigated is the *application* of these pictures, the uses of these expressions in human life. For whereas pictures, literal or verbal, are typically surveyable at a glance, have an immediately obvious application, and hence fulfil a useful role in guiding us in the application of an expression, in the philosophically bewildering cases this is not so. In the domain of the mental, for example, pictures force themselves upon us, for they are built into our forms of representation; but their application is unclear and difficult to survey, and they exacerbate our conceptual confusions when philosophizing (§425). Indeed, the picture associated with mental concepts (like those associated with certain concepts in set-theory) suggests an ideal use for a god, which we cannot achieve (§426). But this is an illusion. When we say that we would like to know what is going on in someone's head, this typically means that we would like to know what he is thinking; and the way to find out what he is thinking, even for a god, is not 'seeing into his consciousness' (§427).

The structure of Part B is linear.

Correlations

PI§	PPI(I)§	MS. 129	MS. 124	MS. 165	Vol. XII	Others
412	294	81–3	263–6			
413	295	84–5	266			
414				221		Vol.XVI,88
415						MS. 157(b), 80; Vol. XV, 1
416	296	84	275			MS. 179, 48–9
417	297	85	275–6			MS. 179, 50–1
418	298	86	277			MS. 179, 53
419		126	238			
420	299	86	277–8			MS. 179, 53–4[1]
421	300[2]	87	285			MS. 165, 158–9
422				282		
423				324		
424				325		
425				159		
426				162		Vol. XVI, 29f.
427				340		

[1] PI §420(a) only.
[2] This is the final remark of PPI(I).

THE WORLD OF CONSCIOUSNESS

1. *The world as consciousness*

In his lectures during the May Term of 1932 Wittgenstein said that he himself had often been tempted to say 'All that is real is the experience of the present moment' or 'All that is certain is the experience of the present moment'. Anyone who is at all tempted to embrace idealism or solipsism, he added, knows the temptation to say 'The only reality is the present experience' or 'The only reality is *my* present experience' (M 311). Were the *Notebooks 1914 – 16* not available, one might have supposed these remarks to be a generous concession that it is intelligible how one can edge oneself into a solipsist or idealist frame of mind. But the Schopenhauerian passages in the *Notebooks* written between June and November 1916 suggest that Wittgenstein had indeed been tempted, and had succumbed to the temptation. In a strikingly sybilline passage, he wrote:

> What do I know about God and the purpose of life?
> I know that this world exists.
> That I am placed in it like my eye in its visual field.
> That something about it is problematic, which we call its meaning.
> That this meaning does not lie in it but outside it.
> That life is the world. (NB 73)

Some days later he elaborated:

> The World and Life are one.
> Physiological life is of course not 'Life'. And neither is psychological life. Life is the world. (NB 77)

And subsequently he added the Schopenhauerian thought that

> Only from the consciousness of the *uniqueness of my life* arises religion – science – and art.
> And this consciousness is life itself. (NB 79)

The equation of the world with 'life' and 'life' with consciousness ramified into the mysterious account Wittgenstein gave of the 'philosophical self' (see 'I and my self', §2). 'The philosophical I is not the human being, not the human body or the human soul [mind] with the psychological properties, but the metaphysical subject, the boundary (not a part) of the world' (NB 82). But, again echoing Schopenhauer, the philosophical self is stripped of all individuality, for 'I am my world'

(NB 84), and 'As my idea is the world, in the same way my will is the world-will' (NB 85).

The transcendental idealist (Schopenhauerian) drift is further evident in the claim that 'it is equally possible to take the bare present image as the worthless momentary picture in the whole temporal world, and as the true world among shadows' (NB 83), and in the contention that in death 'the world does not change but stops existing' (NB 73). What exactly Wittgenstein made of these apocalyptic pronouncements is very unclear, and likely to remain so. But there can be little doubt that they originate in Schopenhauer's *The World as Will and Representation*. There Schopenhauer adumbrated a strange, mesmerizing picture of consciousness. The concept of consciousness, he argued, 'coincides with that of representation in general'.[1] That the world is my representation is 'like the Axioms of Euclid, a proposition which everyone must recognize as true as soon as he understands it'.[2] The deep insight achieved by modern philosophy, according to Schopenhauer, is:

that the *objective existence* of things is conditioned by a representer of them, and that consequently the objective world exists only as *representation* . . . The objective as such, always and essentially has its existence in the consciousness of a subject; it is therefore the representation of this subject, and consequently is conditioned by the subject, and moreover by the subject's forms of representation . . .[3]

Actual or phenomenal individuality, according to Schopenhauer, is unreal; it is an aspect of our enslavement to the blind forces of the will. But in aesthetic experience and in contemplation of the sublime, we can free ourselves from our bondage and transcend our own particularity. Here one achieves 'pure contemplation, absorption in perception, being lost in the object, forgetting all individuality'.[4] Thus liberated, 'We are no longer the individual; that is forgotten . . . we are only that *one* eye of the world which looks out from all knowing creatures.'[5]

It is doubtful whether one can make sense of these dark sayings, and it is not to our present purposes even to explain why they might seem to make sense. What is important for the discussion of Wittgenstein's later reflections on the concept of consciousness is that he evidently sympathized with at least some aspects of this poetic metaphysics and had once been caught in this web of illusion. He had indeed experienced the seductive power of a certain form of solipsism ('What has history to do with me? Mine is the first and only world!' (NB 82)). It was surely with his own experience in view that, in response to his imaginary inter-

---

[1] Schopenhauer, *World as Will and Representation*, Vol. I, p. 51.
[2] Ibid., Vol. II, p. 13.
[3] Ibid., Vol. II, p. 5.
[4] Ibid., Vol. I, pp. 196f.
[5] Ibid., Vol. I, pp. 197f.

locutor's conception of the world as representation ('the visual room'),
he later wrote:

'It is true I said that I know within myself what you meant. But that meant that I
knew how one thinks to conceive this object, to see it, to make one's looking and
pointing mean it. I know how one stares ahead and looks about one in this case – and
the rest. (PI §398)

It is interesting that in his lectures in the early 1930s, Wittgenstein
picked up the theme of consciousness as conceived by the metaphysician.
Moore reports him as saying:

'In one sense "I" and "conscious" are equivalent, but not in another', and he compared
this difference to the difference between what can be said of the pictures on a film in a
magic lantern and of the picture on the screen; saying that the pictures in the lantern
are all 'on the same level' but that the picture which is at any given time on the screen
is not 'on the same level' with any of them, and that if we were to use 'conscious' to
say of one of the pictures in the lantern that it was at that time being thrown on the
screen, it would be meaningless to say of the picture on the screen that it was
'conscious'. The pictures on the film, he said, 'have neighbours', whereas that on the
screen has none. (M 310)

It is doubtful whether he would later have said that there is a use of
'conscious' in which it is equivalent to 'I'.[6] But the principle of contrast
which he invoked here by means of the phrase 'having neighbours'
recurs both in the 'Lectures on "Private Experience" and "Sense Data" '
and in the brief, oblique riposte to solipsism and idealism in *Investigations*
§§398 – 402.[7]
    One is tempted, in moments of philosophical intoxication, to insist
that 'Surely, if I'm to be quite frank I must say that I have something
which nobody has' (LPE 283) – viz. my personal experience. This is
surely unique – it has no neighbour! But, Wittgenstein replies, this
'uniqueness' is not the uniqueness of a single exemplar of something; it is
rather the uniqueness of a *special position in grammar*. And in *that* sense,
what is unique *has no owner*. One wants to say 'At any rate only I have
got THIS'; but in reply one should ask

In what sense have you *got* what you are talking about and saying that only you have
got it? Do you possess it? You do not even *see* it. Must you not really say that no one
has got it? And this too is clear: if as a matter of logic you exclude other people's
having something, it loses its sense to say that you have it. (PI §398)

Idealism leads solipsism, for if the *world* is idea, it is not anyone *else's*
idea. But solipsism errs in thinking that the world thus conceived is *my*

---

[6] But he might have said that the misuse of 'consciousness' is akin to the metaphysician's misuse of 'I' as the name of a *res cogitans*. Equally, the illusory 'experience of
consciousness' is similar to the illusory 'experience of the self'.
    [7] Cf. also WWK 50; PR 85f.

idea, for *I* do not enter 'the world as idea'. In this sense 'the visual room' (PI §398), the 'world of private experience', has no owner.

Nevertheless, 'consciousness in general' (as Kant might put it) may still seem equivalent to the world experienced, the world as representation. And when Wittgenstein insists on the unintelligibility of private ostensive definition, on the incoherence of private ownership of experience, on the confusions surrounding epistemic privacy of experience, and when he denies that 'toothache' means *this* or 'fear' means *that*, it can readily seem as if he is neglecting the essence of the matter: ' "the experience or whatever you might call it? – Almost the *world* behind the mere words?" ' (LPE 296). In words reminiscent of his own reflections of 1916, Wittgenstein concedes that it *seems* that he neglects life, 'But not life physiologically understood but life as consciousness. And consciousness not physiologically understood, or understood from the outside, but consciousness as the very essence of experience, the appearance of the world, the world' (LPE 297).

What leads us into this strange illusion? After all, Wittgenstein distinguishes, as we all do, between saying 'I have a toothache' when one has a toothache and saying it without having a toothache, and so forth. So in what sense is he 'neglecting' something? 'Isn't what you reproach me of', he adds ironically, 'as though you said: "In your language you're only *speaking*!" ' (LPE 297). Does the illusion not stem from the idea of 'the world of consciousness' as the gold backing for our verbal currency? We conceive of this 'world' as a space peopled with experiences, sense-impressions, feelings, etc., which we *name* by private ostensive definition and observe *in foro interno*, describe in words for the benefit of others, etc. For we are indeed tempted to talk of the *content* of experience thus, to insist that:

I know what toothaches are like, I am acquainted with them, I know what it's like to see red, green, blue, yellow, I know what it's like to feel sorrow, hope, fear, joy, affection, to wish to do something, to remember having done something, to intend doing something . . . . I know, too, what it means to parade these experiences before one's mind. When I do that, I don't parade kinds of behaviour or situations before my mind. (RPP I §91)

Furthermore, one would like to say:

'I see red *thus*', 'I hear the note that you strike *thus*', 'I feel sorrow *thus*', or even '*This* is what one feels when one is sad, *this* when one is glad', etc. One would like to people a world, analogous to the physical one, with these *thus*es and *this*es. (RPP I §896)

Such are the temptations. But enough has been clarified in previous essays for it to be obvious that they must be resisted. The concept of the content of experience thus invoked is no more than that of the 'private object', the sense-datum, the 'object' one grasps immediately in 'introspection' (RPP I §109). Do I really know what it means to parade these experiences before one's mind? Can I *explain* it, to others or to myself (RPP I §91)? The whole battery of arguments against the intelligibility of a private language demonstrates the vanity of this idea. One can only, as it were, 'people a world' with *this*es and *thus*es where there is a picture of *what is experienced* to which one can *point* as one gives such explanations (RPP I §896). But that is not intelligible here, in the '*world of consciousness*'.

The 'world of consciousness' does not belong uniquely to me, since it 'belongs' to no one. 'I can as little own it as I can walk about it, or look at it, or point to it' (PI §398). The 'contents' of this 'world' cannot be seen by others; but then neither can they be *seen* by me. To conceive of experience as 'a world', to think that it is in fact *the* world, is to construe a grammatical articulation as a quasi-physical phenomenon that one observes (PI §401). One can describe what one perceives, and also report the fact that one is perceiving what one thus perceives. But such a report is not a description of a unique, private, immaterial 'world of consciousness'.

2. *The gulf between consciousness and body*

If one is captivated by the picture of two 'worlds', the world of physical things, events, and processes and the world of consciousness peopled with mental objects, events, and processes (see 'Privacy', §1), then the nature of consciousness and states of consciousness is bound to seem mysterious. For these two worlds seem to be constituted of different *materials*, made of different kinds of substance. The physical world, as Descartes argued, is made of material substance, and the mental world 'is liable to be imagined as gaseous, or rather, aethereal' (BB 47). The latter evidently does not consist of material substance, so we are prone to think of it as consisting of immaterial substance. (Similarly, when we insist on the distinctness of numbers from numerals, we point out that numbers are not concrete objects, and are inclined to think of them as abstract objects.) But when asked to explain what this immaterial substance is, we falter. To say that its essence is thinking, as Descartes did, merely compounds the confusion – for the Cartesian concept of thinking is not coherent.[8] So we are inclined to insist that although we cannot point at this ethereal substance for others, each of us can, as it were, point at it *in foro interno* for himself. For surely we are, each of us, witnesses to our own consciousness (PI §416)? All *this*, we feel, is the world of my consciousness – it is indeed *my* world, and sometimes it seems to be *the* world.

[8] See A. J. P. Kenny, *Descartes* (Random House, New York, 1968), pp. 68 – 78.

Conceiving of consciousness as a private realm populated by private experiences, one is bound to be puzzled at its evolutionary emergence. Here we adopt a particular picture: 'The evolution of the higher animals and of man, and the awakening of consciousness at a particular level. The picture is something like this: Though the ether is filled with vibrations the world is dark. But one day man opens his seeing eye, and there is light' (PI p. 184). It seems, quite rightly, that consciousness, experience, emerges when phenomena in the physical world have evolved a certain degree of complexity (BB 47). For, to be sure, we do not attribute consciousness to plants or experience to an amoeba. A very complex biological substratum, a highly evolved nervous system, is a character-istic feature of conscious creatures. But here our picture of consciousness as an inner world, as light within the soul, leads us into confusion. For now the 'evolutionary emergence of consciousness' suddenly seems utterly mysterious. How could something so different from material things and their properties *emerge* from what is, after all, merely a more complex arrangement of matter? Could this whole, extraordinary world of consciousness spring into being through nothing more than an increase in the complexity of neural organization?

On the one hand, there seems to be 'an unbridgeable gulf between consciousness and brain-process' (PI §412). For how could *this*, my current experience, my present state of consciousness, be produced by a process in the brain? How could the ethereal emerge from the material? It is hardly surprising that a nineteenth-century scientist, Tyndall, should write:

The passage from the physics of the brain to the corresponding facts of consciousness is unthinkable. Granted that a definite thought and a definite molecular action in the brain occur simultaneously, we do not possess the intellectual organ, nor apparently any rudiment of the organ, which would enable us to pass, by a process of reasoning, from one to the other.[9]

And it is equally unsurprising that contemporary scientists and psycho-logists should concur, finding consciousness 'a great mystery',[10] and confessing that 'no one knows what consciousness is, or whether it serves any purpose.'[11]

On the other hand, it can seem equally baffling that we can attribute consciousness and states of consciousness to material things at all. For are living beings, animals and humans, not physical objects? And how can a

[9] Tyndall, *Fragments of Science*, 5th edn, p. 420; quoted by James, *Principles of Psychology*, Vol. I, p. 147.
[10] J. P. Frisby, *Seeing: Illusion, Brain, and Mind* (Oxford University Press, Oxford, 1980), p. 11.
[11] P. N. Johnson-Laird, *The Computer and the Mind* (Fontana, London, 1988), p. 353.

mere physical object be conscious (cf. PI §283)? I *experience* my own consciousness, one is inclined to say, but how can I transfer this idea to objects outside myself? How can physical bodies in the physical world have something as alien to physical phenomena as consciousness? And if one thinks, as many philosophers and psychologists do, that it is the *brain* that is conscious, this exacerbates the mystery. For how can the mere matter inside the skull be conscious? Of course, when one attributes consciousness to things other than oneself, one does not attribute it to stones or plants. And if one is loath to attribute consciousness to a body as such, one is inclined to think that one must therefore attribute it to the mind or soul that certain bodies, e.g. human ones, have. For surely 'one has to say it of a body, or, if you like, of a soul [mind] which some body *has*' (PI §283)! But if we are puzzled at the idea that a body, a mere physical thing, could be conscious, we should surely be no less puzzled at the idea that *a body* might have a mind or soul.

These apparent mysteries reflect our mystification. We project our own misunderstandings of the conceptual or grammatical articulations of our language onto reality, and rightly find reality thus conceived to be unintelligible. When we insist upon the mysterious gulf between physical phenomena and facts of consciousness, when we hold with Tyndall that 'we try to soar in a vacuum the moment we seek to comprehend the connection between them', we in effect confuse the shadows of different grammatical rules for a cleft in reality.

The first step towards clarity is to remind ourselves that it is only of a living human being and what resembles (behaves like) a living human being that one can say that it is conscious or unconscious (PI §281). We do not attribute consciousness or lack of consciousness to stones, trees, or machines – not because they are insufficiently complex in structure or physical constitution, but because they are not living creatures that behave like us in circumstances in which we attribute consciousness to each other. We do not say of a tree that it is unconscious, for nothing would count as a conscious tree, and we do not say of a machine which is switched off that it will regain consciousness when it is switched on again.

Consequently, bafflement at the idea that the brain of a human being is conscious is misconceived. For the brain is no more a conscious being than a tree is. When a person who has been under an anaesthetic stirs, groans, and opens his eyes, we say that he has regained consciousness, that he is awake. But we do not say that his brain is awake. For it is not his brain that sits up in bed and asks for a drink, looks around, and gets out of bed. The brain, to be sure, is a highly complex organ – but it is not an organism. Consciousness is attributable to an organism as a whole, not to its parts, no matter how complex. And it is attributable to the organism on the grounds of its behaviour, its exercise of its perceptual faculties, its susceptibility to sensation, and its voluntary action (see 'Men, minds, and machines', §1).

One might object that surely the brain is the organ of consciousness. One can be completely paralysed, yet conscious for all that; but one could not be conscious without the brain. So must it not have some properties that confer consciousness upon it? This is confused. First, even if the brain were the organ of consciousness, it would not follow that the brain is conscious. For the eyes are our organs of vision and the ears our organs of hearing, but metonymy apart, our eyes do not see or our ears hear; rather, *we* see with our eyes and hear with our ears. Secondly, our brains are not organs of consciousness in the sense in which our perceptual organs are organs of perception. For we are not conscious, i.e. awake, *with* our brain. Nor does it make sense to talk of being conscious *of* something, e.g. the ticking of a clock or the disorder in a room, with our brain. The brain, unlike the eyes, is not an organ the movements of which we can voluntarily control or which we *use* as we use our sense-organs to perceive, since it does not move and we cannot control it. Nor is it the organ of consciousness in the sense in which the stomach, the functioning of which is likewise beyond our voluntary control, is the organ of digestion. For while digestion is a process that takes place in the stomach, being conscious is not a process, and it does not 'take place' in the brain. Although one can be paralysed yet still conscious, neither being conscious (as opposed to being unconscious) nor being conscious of something (i.e. having one's attention caught and held by something) are acts or activities of any bodily organ, since they are not acts or activities at all. It is true, of course, that unless the brain were functioning normally in certain respects, one would not be conscious, nor would one be enjoying states of consciousness, since one would be unconscious. But equally, unless the brain were functioning normally, one would not be able to talk; yet no one would say that the brain is the organ of speech.

To say that only living creatures which behave in certain respects like human beings can be said to be conscious or unconscious is to make a grammatical statement. But does this really solve our predicament? For are living creatures not *things*, physical objects? And how can a mere physical object be conscious? The question is misleading. For although it is true that human beings have bodies, they are not identical with their bodies (see 'Behaviour and behaviourism', §4). In the ordinary use of the terms 'thing', 'object', 'physical (or material) object', not only does one not say that human beings are things or physical objects – one *contrasts* them with objects or things. If asked to explain what the expression 'a physical object' means, no one would point at a human being and say 'That is a physical object'. And if someone were to over-value his chattels, giving preference to them at the expense of people, one would remind him that they are only things, mere physical objects. Used thus, the expressions 'thing', 'object', and 'physical object' are, as it were, demoting or derogatory terms.

If, when philosophizing, someone insists that human beings are physical objects, he is evidently diverging from this common use, and we should press him to explain what he means. If he means that human beings are not minds or souls causally linked to bodies, we should agree. A person, though not identical with his body, is not some other substance over and above his body. If he means that there are many properties (e.g. being sunburnt all over) with respect to which it is indifferent whether they are ascribed to the person or to his body, we should likewise agree. Human beings have physical dimensions, location, take up space, move or stay still, etc. As has been stressed, for part of their use, 'N.N.' and 'N.N.'s body' run along parallel tracks, *but only for a small part*. For even predicates of movement are not univocally attributable to a person and his body alike, and many (e.g. walks, runs) are indeed not licitly attributable to the body at all. To that extent it is both ill-advised and unnecessary to claim that human beings are physical objects; for the modest truths that are thereby intimated can be stated, as above, without this misleading form of words.

If the philosopher insists that at any rate a person's body is a physical object, we might go along with that. A corpse, the remains of a human being, can be said to be a physical object (although it is to be treated with a dignity which we do not generally accord to mere physical things). And we may concede that in certain respects a living human being is no different from a corpse: thus, if a corpse falls from a high cliff and a human being falls from a high cliff, the laws of physics will not discriminate between the two – the trajectory and the acceleration of both is described by reference to the laws of free fall. But a corpse is not a human being:

> Our attitude to what is alive and to what is dead is not the same. All our reactions are different. – If anyone says: 'That cannot simply come from the fact that the living move about in such-and-such a way and the dead do not', then I want to intimate to him that this is a case of transition 'from quantity to quality'. (PI §284)

The categorial difference between what is alive and what is not, in particular between what is sentient and what is insensate, is marked in countless ways in our language, and is manifest in countless ways in our reactions and attitudes. One way in which it is marked is, as noted, in the peculiar locution of 'having a body'. We say that a person has a body, and speak of the body metonymically as 'a living body', as opposed to a corpse. A person's body, like all physical objects, consists of such-and-such quantities of chemicals; but one cannot say that a person consists of quantities of chemicals. ('He is flesh and blood' is no more a statement of what a person consists of than 'War is war' is an instance of the law of identity.) But it is the person, the living human being, that is said to be conscious. And no one would say 'My body is a human being'! So the very question of how a mere physical object like a human being can be conscious leads us astray from the start. A human being is not a mere physical object, but a living creature that acts and behaves, has goals and purposes of its own, perceives its environment, and responds in endlessly variegated ways to what it perceives.

We attribute consciousness to a creature on the grounds of its behaviour in the circumstances of its life, not on the grounds of its neural organization and complexity. There is no deep mystery about how a living creature can possibly be conscious; after all, the alternative, for a sentient animal, to being conscious is being asleep or unconscious. And there is nothing mystifying about the fact that the living are awake for most of the day. Consciousness does not 'emerge', like an ethereal halo or 'astral body', from inanimate matter. Rather, the biological constitution of living creatures becomes more complex as one ascends the evolutionary scale, and more forms of response and reaction to the environment are made possible. When these are manifest in certain forms of behaviour, the concepts of consciousness and states of consciousness get a grip; but these are not concepts of an inner realm. What particular neural structures make possible these forms of sentient and conative behaviour that manifest consciousness is a matter for empirical investigation – but no metaphysical mystery is involved.

That human beings and higher animals are conscious creatures is not an empirical truth, but a grammatical one. For just as one does not know what it would be for a stone or a tree to be conscious, so too one cannot picture what it would be like for human beings to lack consciousness (PI §418). Of course, one can, up to a point, imagine what it would be like if human beings were zombies; one can tell science-fiction tales about people walking mechanically, eyes glazed, speaking in a monotone. But this is not to the point; for what we are required to imagine is that human beings, behaving just as they normally do, are really not conscious at all, but mere automatons. This is not intelligible (PI §420). One cannot even entertain the thought, as one can in the case of being in pain, that these people might be pretending. For while one can pretend to be unconscious, as one can pretend to be in pain, there is no such thing as pretending to be conscious (Z §395). The assertion that human beings are conscious, like the assertion that human beings see, feel, and hear, only has a use as a grammatical proposition. It might be employed as part of an explanation of what the expression 'human being' or 'conscious' means.

What now remains of the 'unbridgeable gulf between consciousness and brain-process' (PI §412)? This is an illusion induced during philosophical reflection. For, after all, when we are told that A, who drank a bottle of whisky, lost consciousness, we do not feel that something strange and miraculous has occurred. It does not strike us that the influence of alcohol involves crossing an unbridgeable gulf. That illusion arises only when we think in terms of 'a realm of consciousness', of a ethereal world populated with psychological objects. For then one is prone to think that each of us has privileged access to this special domain, that each of us is witness to the fact that we are conscious, as if being conscious were a phenomenon that we experience. In the grip of this picture, Wittgenstein suggests,[12] we are inclined to try to turn our attention on to our own consciousness and to wonder how *this* could be produced by a process in the brain. Part of what is awry about this thought is the very notion of 'turning one's attention upon one's own consciousness'. One is said to be conscious of something, e.g. the ticking of a clock or a pain in one's back, when one's attention is caught and held by that thing. But there is no such thing as being conscious of one's consciousness, for being conscious is neither an experience nor an object of experience. Rather, to have any experience at all, to enjoy any 'states of consciousness' whatever, one must be conscious. Similarly, one can attend to all manner of things, both perceptibilia and one's sensations, moods, and feelings; but consciousness itself (unlike one's states of consciousness) is not an object of attention or experience. So what does one actually *do* when one thinks that one is 'turning one's attention on to one's own consciousness'? Wittgenstein sketches one plausible possibility: one stares fixedly in front of one, with eyes wide open but a vacant gaze. For one is not gazing at or attending to anything in particular, since it is one's consciousness itself that one wishes to attend to, not something else of which one might be conscious. But then 'turning one's attention on to one's own consciousness' will not show one what consciousness is or what the word 'consciousness' means, but only the very peculiar state of one's attention when one says to oneself 'I am attending to my own consciousness' (PI §413). And that state of attention is, to be sure, very queer, since it involves, as it were, setting oneself to attend to something, but not actually attending to anything!

Once one realizes that this curious illusion stems from a misuse of words and misdirected attention (akin to trying to discover, as James tried,[13] what the experience of the self is like), is it really mysterious that specific brain-events should produce curious 'facts of consciousness'? In an appropriate setting there is a perfectly decent, unparadoxical use for the sentence 'This is produced by a brain-process'. In an experiment in which part of the brain is stimulated by micro-electrodes, the patient might report that a flashing of light on the periphery of his visual field

---

[12] This, of course, is not the only way in which we can engender this confusion.
[13] James, *Principles of Psychology*, Vol. I, p. 301; cf. Exg. §413.

resulted from the electrical stimulation (PI §412). And this is no more mystifying than the fact that certain pressure on the eyeball produces double vision. There may well be empirical ignorance about specific neural processes here, but no metaphysical mysteries.

3. *The certainty of consciousness*

A venerable tradition going back at least as far as Descartes conceived of consciousness as the immovable rock against which the waves of scepticism break. The fact of our own consciousness seems to be the one *indubitabile* that can never be shaken. Indeed, it was upon this foundation that Descartes endeavoured to construct the edifice of human knowledge. I cannot doubt that I am conscious, for in order to doubt anything at all, I must be conscious. So it seemed to Descartes that I must *know*, indubitably, that I am conscious; or, what for Descartes comes to much the same thing,[14] that I am thinking. And if I cannot fail to know this – if error here is impossible – then surely I have an indubitable foundation from which to infer my existence, and later my essential nature, and all the rest.

What Descartes failed to see is that here (as in the case of avowals (*Äusserungen*) of experience too) doubt is excluded by grammar, not by conclusive evidence. Far from each person being witness to his own consciousness, there is no such thing as observing or perceiving one's own consciousness (cf. PI §§416f.). One has, and can have, no grounds or evidence for claiming to be conscious. Indeed, one cannot *claim* to be conscious. For one cannot say 'He claims that he is conscious, but he is mistaken'.

> Imagine an unconscious man (anaesthetized, say) were to say 'I am conscious' – should we say 'He ought to know'?
>
> And if someone talked in his sleep and said 'I am asleep' – should we say 'He's quite right'?
>
> Is someone speaking untruth if he says to me 'I am not conscious'? (And truth, if he says it while unconscious?) And suppose a parrot says 'I don't understand a word', or a gramophone: 'I am only a machine'? (Z §396)

It is not intelligible for it to *seem* to one that one is conscious, for 'It seems to him that he is conscious but he is mistaken' is nonsense. One can dream that one is asleep or dream that one is awake or conscious, but to dream that one is conscious is not to be conscious, nor is it to seem to oneself to be conscious. Descartes' Archimedean point is located beyond the bounds of sense:

---

[14] Descartes, *Principles of Philosophy*, Pt. I, Sect. 9: 'Hence thinking is to be identified here not merely with understanding, willing, and imagining, but also with consciousness.'

' "I am conscious" – that is a statement about which no doubt is possible.' Why should that not say the same as: ' "I am conscious" is not a proposition'?

It might also be said: What's the harm if someone says that 'I am conscious' is a statement admitting of no doubt? How do I come into conflict with him? Suppose someone were to say this to me – why shouldn't I get used to making no answer to him instead of starting an argument? Why shouldn't I treat his words like his whistling or humming?

'Nothing is so certain as that I possess consciousness.' In that case, why shouldn't I let the matter rest? This certainty is like a mighty force whose point of application does not move, and so no work is accomplished by it. (Z §§401f.)

'I am conscious' looks like, and is intended by the Cartesian-minded philosopher to be, an empirical proposition. But it has no intelligible negation; it admits of no doubt, and consequently actually precludes certainty too; it does not express something of which one might be ignorant, but, by the same token, it does not say anything which one can be said to know. In this sense it can be said not to be a proposition at all, or to be a degenerate proposition. There is indeed *a* use for the sentence 'I am conscious', but this is not to make an epistemic claim, let alone to express an item of indubitable knowledge. Nor is it to convey to others my private observations or to report my current experience. It is rather akin to a signal. If, as I recover consciousness after an anaesthetic, I say to the nurse, whom I notice walking about the room, 'I am conscious again', I am giving her a signal. I do not say this after 'observing my own consciousness', but after observing the fact that she thinks I am still unconscious. I might just as well say 'Hello' (PI §416).

The Cartesian distortion of the use of 'I am conscious' is co-ordinate with an equally misguided distortion of attribution of consciousness and states of consciousness to others. Mesmerized by the inner/outer picture of the mind, we are inclined to think that we come to 'recognize' consciousness in ourselves and then 'transfer' the idea to others (cf. PI §283). Reflecting thus, it can readily seem as if what we observe is mere behaviour, and that we infer that there is, as it were, a consciousness behind it (cf. 'Behaviour and behaviourism', §4). What licenses this inference? Is it that when one is conscious and in a given state of consciousness, one notices the muscular movements of one's face, which one also sees in the faces of others? No; this is absurd. It is a piece of theorizing, an explanation, which is out of place when what is needed is a description of the use and circumstances of use of words:

Consciousness in another's face. Look into someone else's face, and see the consciousness in it, and a particular shade of consciousness. You see on it, in it, joy, indifference, interest, excitement, torpor, and so on. The light in other people's faces.

Do you look into *yourself* in order to recognize the fury in *his* face? It is there as clearly as in your own breast. (Z §220)

We *see* a human being giving angry, proud, ironical looks. We perceive the glimmer of amusement, the flash of anger, or the dull grief in a person's eye. This is how we speak and how we characterize what we see in another's face. To acknowledge this plain fact is not to make concessions to a behaviourist theory; nor is it to admit that one sees the glance in 'just the way' that one sees the shape or colour of the eye (Z §223). On the contrary, the shape or colour of an eye can be seen in an autopsy room – but the passionate look or loving gaze can be seen only in the face (Z §224) and in a context.

We do not see facial contortions and make inferences from them (like a doctor framing a diagnosis) to joy, grief, boredom. We describe a face immediately as sad, radiant, bored, even when we are unable to give any other description of the features. – Grief, one would like to say, is personified in the face.

  This belongs to the concept of emotion. (Z §225)

The countenance, Cicero remarked, is the portrait of the mind, the eyes are its informers.[15] Apropos Rembrandt's portrait of his friend, the poet Jeremias de Decker, Jan van Petersons wrote: 'O Rembrandt, you paint de Decker so that his soul shines through his face.'

  Of course, states of consciousness are not facial expressions, and consciousness is not behaviour. But they are exhibited, manifest, in behaviour, mien, and facial expression. We can see that a person is conscious, what he is conscious of, and often what state of consciousness he is in. We do not infer it 'problematically' from mere facial contortions and 'bare bodily movements'; although it is true and important that we can veil our eyes, conceal our feelings, pretend, and dissimulate. It is an absurdity, foisted on us by our own misconceptions and misconceived pictures, to think that we might be wrong in supposing other humans to be conscious beings. It is no more a *supposition* than it is a supposition that *I* am conscious (RPP I §930). The only kind of case in which one might be wrong about another person being conscious is when one sees an unconscious person stir and wrongly supposes that he has regained consciousness.

---

[15] Cicero, *De Oratore*, Bk. III, §59: 'Imago animi vultus est, indices oculi.'

SECTION 412

1   The idea that there is an unbridgeable gulf between something as *material* as a brain-process and something as immaterial, *as diaphanous*, as consciousness comes naturally to the mind of a philosopher or a psychologist, or indeed of anyone caught in the trammels of the abstract noun 'consciousness'. Brain-processes can be observed in laboratories, monitored by inserting electrodes in the brain, traced through complex neural networks in the cerebral cortex. How can these result in something so categorially different as *consciousness*? At what point in the innumerable electro-chemical interactions in the brain does consciousness arise? Indeed, how could something like consciousness arise from the firing of nerve-cells? The questions induce vertigo.

W. begins with the phenomenology of this particular bafflement. First, he draws our attention to the fact that this bemusement does not arise in the ordinary stream of life. Secondly, he notes that this sense of vertigo is characteristic of logical legerdemain. We have a similar feeling when we are told that one infinite set is *larger* than another, that there are *more* reals than rationals. Thirdly, what produces this feeling in the present case is the illusion of 'turning my attention on to my consciousness'. It is noteworthy that this phrase has *no* use in ordinary life. But when reflecting on the nature of consciousness, instead of examining the way the words 'consciousness' and 'conscious' are *used*, we think to investigate the phenomenon by, as it were, watching ourselves while we are conscious (cf. PI §316). And since we are attempting to isolate 'consciousness itself', not consciousness *of* what we see, hear, or feel, we are prone to 'concentrate' on vacant staring or gazing, which seems to give us the pure consciousness uncontaminated by particular objects of which we might be conscious. It is not surprising, then, that the phenomenon should appear singularly elusive.

§412(b) is a reminder for the particular purpose at hand (PI §127), bringing words back from their metaphysical to their everyday use (PI §116). For one might indeed say 'This is produced by a brain-process' in a neuropsychological experiment in which electrodes are being inserted in one's brain. 'This *what*?' – 'This flashing of lights that I am now experiencing at the periphery of my visual field.'

1.1   'Was ich so nannte . . .': the translation has omitted the parenthesis
'(for these words are after all not used in ordinary life)', 'these words'
being 'turning my attention on to my own consciousness'.

2.1   (i) 'an unbridgeable gulf between consciousness and brain-process':
MS. 124, 263 remarks that the strongest expression of this idea is the
thought that both are different aspects of the same thing. This is
exemplified by the claim, remarked on elsewhere (MS. 165, 145), that
states of consciousness are neural processes 'seen from the inside' (cf.
Exg. §270, 2). James quotes C. Mercier, *The Nervous System and the Mind*
(1888), p. 9.:

> Having thoroughly recognized the fathomless abyss that separates mind from matter,
> and having so blended the very notion into his very nature . . . the student of
> psychology has next to appreciate the association between these two orders of
> phenomena. . . . They are associated in a manner so intimate that some of the
> greatest thinkers consider them different aspects of the same process.[1]

(ii) '(The same giddiness attacks us)': MS. 129, 81 remarks instead that
this feeling, as in set-theory, is a sign of confusion, not of the *difficulty* of
the object.
(iii) 'which I uttered as a paradox': Vol. XII, 325 remarks on Pascal's
characterization of man as a weak, thinking reed. If one said that man
was a talking reed, the remark would resonate quite differently. But
'thinking' here should mean *being conscious*. The tone suggests the
paradox that a piece of matter should be conscious. And yet, of course,
there is no paradox here at all. As W. observes elsewhere (TS. 229, §735),
'Only when we disregard its use is a proposition paradoxical.'

3   James wrote:

> Mental and physical events, are on all hands, admitted to present the strongest
> contrast in the entire field of being. The chasm which yawns between them is less
> easily bridged over by the mind than any interval we know. Why, then, not call it an
> absolute chasm, and say not only that the two worlds are different, but that they are
> independent?[2]

SECTION 413

1   The attempt to discover the nature of consciousness by introspection,
by 'turning my attention on to my own consciousness', is quite futile.

[1] James, *Principles of Psychology*, Vol. I, pp. 135f.
[2] Ibid., p. 134.

For the question as to the nature of consciousness, like the question as to the nature of imagination (PI §370), is to be answered by examining the use of a word. For we are not analysing a phenomenon, but a concept (PI §383). W. has already shown (PI §§316ff.) that observing what goes on in one's own mind while one is thinking will not clarify what thinking is, but only what goes on while one is thinking. Here the introspectionist commits an even more grievous error. For while one can attend to what goes on in one's own mind when one is thinking, there really is nothing to attend to when one purports to 'turn one's attention on to one's own consciousness'. Here one has a case of introspection akin to James's endeavour to discern the character of 'the self'. What he discovered was not a peculiar inner object which is 'the self' or 'the Self of Selves', but rather the state of his own attention when he says 'self' to himself. In both cases one is searching for a pseudo-object.

1.1   (i) 'William James': James's announced goal was to settle for himself 'how this central nucleus of the self may *feel*'.[3] He concluded:

> the *'Self of Selves', when carefully examined, is found to consist mainly of the collection of these peculiar motions in the head or between the head and throat*. I do not for a moment say that this is *all* it consists of, for I fully realize how desperately hard is introspection in this field. But I feel quite sure that these cephalic motions are the portions of my innermost activity of which I am *most distinctly aware*.[4]

(ii) 'so far as it means': the qualification is necessary, of course, because the truncated reflexive pronoun is itself the source of conceptual illusions concerning the nature of a person or human being.
(iii) '(And a good deal could be learned from this)': e.g. about the phenomenology of philosophical illusion (cf. PI §§274 – 7).

SECTION 414

1   An analogy for such cases of introspection: the loom is one's mind; going through the motion of weaving is attending to it; and the weaving of a piece of cloth is clarifying the nature of consciousness or 'the self'. The emptiness of the loom corresponds to the absence of any inner object of awareness called 'consciousness' or 'the self'.

[3] Ibid., p. 298.
[4] Ibid., p. 301.

SECTION 415

1   A methodological remark (associated with PI p. 56n.). It is not obvious why W. located it here. Its MS. context is not this (see also RFM 92).

What are the 'remarks on the natural history of human beings' which we do not notice because they are omnipresent? Presumably such elemental facts as that we cry out in pain when we stub our toes, flinch when another person near us hurts himself, that a mother nurses a child who cries in pain and does not think that maybe the child is pretending; and more generally that our own attitude towards others (whom we recognize as human beings) is an attitude towards a person, and that this attitude does not rest on an inference from observations of their behaviour (cf. PI p. 178). And why are these (and many other) remarks pertinent to philosophy? Because in countless ways the facts to which they draw attention condition our language-games.

Some commentators have seen in this remark (and in its consequences in W.'s philosophy) an affinity with Humean naturalism. But this can be misleading. Hume invoked general facts of nature to disarm sceptical qualms of any practical consequences. In his view the voice of Reason deprives us of any *grounds* for repudiating scepticism about the 'existence of the external world', the 'unity of the self', etc., but Nature comes to our aid:

> If belief, therefore, were a simple act of thought without any peculiar manner of conception, or the addition of a force and vivacity, it must infallibly destroy itself and in every case terminate in a total suspense of judgement. But as experience will sufficiently convince anyone who thinks it worthwhile to try, that though he can find no error in the foregoing arguments, yet he continues to believe and think and reason as usual, he may safely conclude that his reasoning and belief is some sensation or peculiar manner of conception which 'tis impossible for mere ideas and reflections to destroy.[5]

All rational argument speaks in favour of sceptical conclusions. They not only *make sense*, but are supported by justifying reasons. Mercifully, however, Nature has not left the matter to Reason, but 'has doubtless esteem'd it an affair of too great importance to be trusted to our uncertain reasonings and speculations'.[6]

But this is far removed from W.'s strategy and argument. He invokes facts of natural history to remind us of the context in which our

[5] Hume, *Treatise of Human Nature*, Bk. I, Pt. iv, Sect. 1.
[6] Ibid., Bk. I, Pt. iv, Sect. 2.

language-games are played; he draws our attention to the backdrop of regularities of human behaviour which give point to the grammatical structures we employ. Those sceptical doubts which Hume conceived of as well supported are vacuous, not because we cannot bring ourselves to believe them to be justified, but because they are *senseless*. What look like good reasons supporting such doubts involve subtle violations of the bounds of sense, and they are repudiated neither because we cannot, as a matter of fact, believe them, nor because they are false, but because they make no sense.

Hume and W. concur in the idea that there is a dramatic gulf between philosophical theory and human, natural practice. Hume, however, holds that gulf to be harmless because of our inability to give credence to philosophical theory even though it is true. W., on the other hand, argues that the philosophical theory is nonsense, that the doubts can be stated only by violating the rules of grammar that give the constituent expressions their meaning. They are *idle* doubts, not because of natural inability to hold them to be true, but rather because they are mere houses of cards, illusions generated by grammatical confusion.

SECTION 416

1   In philosophical reflection it can readily seem as if the fact that human beings are conscious is the one indubitable fact before which scepticism must come to a halt. We surely agree that we enjoy perceptual experiences, and in as much as we are in a position to do so, are we not witnesses to our own consciousness? But, W. objects, we misconstrue here the possible role of 'I am conscious'. Saying this to myself is vacuous; saying it to another, if it is conceived as registering a piece of Cartesian knowledge (something known to myself alone by the mere 'experience' of being conscious), would not be understood. For so conceived, 'consciousness' would have to signify *this*, which I have. And that, as has been shown, is not intelligible. But, of course, propositions such as 'I see', 'I hear', 'I am conscious' do have their uses, only not as reports of Cartesian *indubitabilia*.[7]

1.1   'sie haben *Bewusstsein*', 'Ich habe Bewusstsein': 'they are *conscious*', 'I am conscious' – and so too in §§418, 419.

---

[7] For the Cartesian, of course, it is not 'I see' or 'I hear' that registers an item of indubitable knowledge, but 'I seem to see' or 'I seem to hear'. 'I am conscious', however, is viewed by the Cartesian as equivalent to 'I think' as he conceives of thinking.

2   In MS. 179, 48 and MS. 124, 275, which is derived from it, this passage is preceded by a draft of PI §316. This makes it clear that the interlocutor here imagines that to get clear about the nature of consciousness we must observe ourselves while we are conscious, and that what we thus observe will be what the word 'conscious' means.

Z §§401f. elaborates the thought in a more explicitly Cartesian direction (see 'The world of consciousness', §3).

Section 417

1   The interlocutor, who thinks that we are witnesses to the fact that we are conscious, conceives of consciousness as an object of introspective observation in which one *perceives* one's consciousness. But, W. responds, there is no room for *observation* here. (Could I *fail* to discern my consciousness? Could I *make a mistake* in my observation? Could I keep a record of my consciousness? Well, I might keep a diary when in hospital, and write 'Today I recovered consciousness after being in a coma for a week'. But is that a record of *an observation*?)

Similarly, there is no question of *perception* here. For I do not see, hear, etc. my consciousness. One is tempted to say that 'perceive' here signifies the fact that I am attending to (or even, am aware of) my consciousness. W. does not repeat the objection, canvassed in §412, that 'attending to my consciousness' is a form of words with no ordinary use at all. Instead he raises a fresh one, viz. that the interlocutor wanted to report an indubitable fact, viz. that he is conscious, but now finds himself reporting a quite different one, viz. that he is in a state of attending to something. Is this meant to be equally fundamental and indubitable? And is it independent of being conscious?

It is clear enough why the interlocutor wishes to insist on such inner perception or attention. For he thinks of consciousness as an *experience*, hence something to which one may attend. But that is a mistake. To have *any* experience, one must be conscious; i.e. if X is unconscious (or asleep), we do not say 'X is having such-and-such an experience'. (Note that dreaming is not an experience!) It is not *an experience* of being conscious that occasions my saying 'I am conscious again', but rather the experience of noticing someone tiptoeing around my bedroom in the evident belief that I am asleep.

2.1   (i) 'but that my attention is disposed in such-and-such a way': MS. 179, 51 has 'sondern, dass ich mich in einem bestimmten seelischen Zustand befinde, wie wenn ich sage "Ich bin aufgeregt".' ('but that I find myself in a certain mental state, as when I say "I am excited".')

(ii) '*What* experience?': MS. 179, 51 and MS. 124, 276 move in a slightly different direction. This question must be answered, W. emphasizes, and in a way that will be intelligible to others (i.e. not by reference to a mythical inner object known only to myself). For I learnt the language from others, and what they cannot understand, I cannot either.

SECTION 418

1   The Cartesian interlocutor takes the fact that he is conscious to be a fact of experience. Of course, it is an empirical fact that he is now conscious, yet might have been unconscious if the anaesthetic had not worn off. But that is not what he means. His conception is that a particular inner experience occasions (§417) and makes true his statement 'I am conscious', and further, that the inner experience is what 'consciousness' means. As he sees things, human beings are their own witnesses that they are conscious; this is a fact that they experience, each for himself, and can then convey to others. This, W. implies, is to confuse a grammatical remark with an empirical observation. We say of human beings and of what behaves like human beings that they are conscious or unconscious (PI §281), but we apply neither concept to trees and stones. This is a rule of grammar, which determines what it makes sense to say, not an empirical observation.

The interlocutor, who conceives of the proposition that human beings are conscious creatures as an empirical fact, must be able to give an account of what it would be like if they were not. Of course, he does not mean that all human beings might fall asleep (as in *Sleeping Beauty*). So his supposition that other human beings might lack consciousness does not mean that they would, in the ordinary sense of the term, be *unconscious*. No – they would *behave* just as they normally do; for, after all, behaviour is not consciousness! But they would 'really' be automatons – a point explored in §420. Hence the supposition that others might lack consciousness would make no *perceptible* difference. But what about oneself? Here one is forced to say that one would not be conscious – there would be, as it were, no light in one's soul. One would not have all *this*, which is now before one's mind's eye! And yet one's behaviour and speech would not differ one jot! One imagines that one would be, as it were, an empty shell, but one that was nevertheless exactly like a full one, except from the inside. But here one is trying to imagine a coin with only one side!

2   MS. 179, 53 has this, preceded by a further pair of remarks that follow the draft of PI §417. The interlocutor exclaims 'But I am conscious!' and

W. replies ironically: 'How curious that I know that this is called "consciousness".' The obvious implication is that on the interlocutor's conception 'consciousness' is the name of a 'private experience'.

3   Russell articulates (without fully subscribing to) the empiricist confusion upon which W.'s remarks is targeted:

> If there is one thing that may be said in the popular estimation to characterize mind, that one thing is 'consciousness'. We say that we are 'conscious' of what we see and hear, of what we remember, and of our own thoughts and feelings. Most of us believe that tables and chairs are not 'conscious'. We think that when we sit in a chair, we are aware of sitting in it, but it is not aware of being sat in. It cannot for a moment be doubted that we are right in believing that there is *some* difference between us and the chair in this respect: so much may be taken as fact, and as datum for our inquiry. (AM 11).

SECTION 419

1   An ironic remark apropos §418. There are circumstances in which it is correct to say that a certain tribe has a chief, but are there any circumstances in which one might add 'and the chief is conscious'? Is there any such thing as fulfilling this social role and *not* being conscious? Clearly 'The chief must surely be conscious' is not an empirical observation resting on the fact that one has never come across chiefs who run the affairs of a tribe but who lack consciousness.

2   Z §394 pursues the same point more explicitly:

> What would it mean for me to be wrong about his having a mind, being conscious? And what would it mean for me to be wrong about *myself* and not have any? What would it mean to say 'I am not conscious'? – But don't I know that there is consciousness in me? – Do I know it then, and yet the statement that it is so has no purpose?
>
> And how remarkable that one can learn to make oneself understood to others in these matters!

These remarks exemplify one aspect of the dependence of sense upon the context of use. 'I am conscious' does have a use – in very special circumstances. But it has none to register an item of indubitable Cartesian knowledge.

SECTION 420

1   This explores the thought introduced in §418, viz. what it would be like if (other) human beings lacked consciousness, where being conscious

is conceived as an 'inner experience'. Can't one imagine it? Here we have a case of a picture obtruding itself upon us and yet being of no use at all (PI §397). We can entertain the idea when alone; we then imagine people as automatons, hence going about their business with a vacant stare as in a trance. Whether this picture can be filled in intelligibly is debatable; but the idea that they are automatons is doing *some* work in so far as they differ from normal human beings in their gaze. (Nothing, as it were, lies behind their eyes.) But, in contrast with the case of imagining that the people one sees in the street are in frightful pain but artfully concealing it (PI §391), to imagine that those very people one sees behaving normally are mere automatons runs up against the limits of sense (see 'Behaviour and behaviourism', §4). For after all, neither an automaton nor a human being can pretend to be conscious (Z §395). At most, one can induce in oneself a strange feeling of alienation in this case.

1.1   'seeing one figure as a limiting case . . .': and by so doing we can alter the impression it makes on us (cf. MS. 179, 55).

2   Vol. XII, 234 (= Z §251) explores a similar line of thought. One is inclined to think that the supposition that this person, who behaves quite normally, is nevertheless blind makes sense. 'After all', one wants to say, 'I picture it.' But the picture here does no work; it is all there is to the bogus assumption.

PI p. 178 examines a related thought. It is just as misguided to suppose that we *believe* that others are *not* automatons (or indeed that we are *certain* that they are not).

SECTION 421

1   This identifies one source of our confusions when we drift into the Cartesian seas of doubt. We think of the physical as material, extended in space, public, and tangible. The mental seems to belong to a different domain, a different 'order of being'. It is private, accessible directly only to its owner, intangible, even ethereal; it is the 'inner', hidden from the sight of others, correlated only causally with the physical behaviour of bodies. When in the grip of this picture, innumerable mundane sentences suddenly seem paradoxical, mixing up two different ontological realms in a way that appears to distort the facts of the matter. We say 'He suffered great torments and tossed about restlessly', but can that which suffers torments be the same as the body which tosses about? Isn't it the mind or soul that suffers torments and the body that tosses about? Is there not an unbridgeable gulf between states of consciousness and physical states? Would a better language not *analyse* such sentences on

this model: instead of saying 'He embraced her joyfully' should we not say that his body embraced her and his soul was joyful?

W. tries to defuse the bogus paradox by drawing our attention to an analogous case of 'mixing the tangible and the intangible' which does not induce in us any sense of paradox. *The number three* and *stability* are not tangible either; but no one feels any logical impropriety in the sentence 'These three struts give the building stability'. Once we notice this, our intellectual unease may be lessened. Then we may be able to see the sources of our confusion, which are manifold.

W. does not here identify them, but merely gives us a methodological reminder, steering us away from the Augustinian picture (which is one root of our troubles). Instead of thinking of the sentence as a description (and of its constituents as names of entities, tangible or intangible), we should conceive of the sentence as an instrument for certain purposes and of its sense as its employment. By implication, we should not conceive of 'He suffered great torments . . .' as naming three objects (viz. a mind, suffering, and torment) which must be 'ontologically homogeneous', and he 'He tossed about restlessly' as naming another three objects which, by contrast, must 'belong to a different domain'. Rather, we should think of the circumstances in which it is appropriate to use such a sentence, e.g. a nurse's report to a doctor on how a patient fared in the course of the night, and of the purposes it serves, its possible roles in a language-game.

2   This was the concluding remark of the intermediate version of PI, completed in late 1944 or early 1945. If W. thought of this, for a short while, as a finished work, then §421 must presumably be viewed as concluding the series of remarks on consciousness, and the final sentence as epitomizing a methodological *leitmotif* of the book.

2.1   'But does it worry you if I say . . .?': the method exemplified here is analogous to that described in PG 212: 'we must describe a language-game related to our own. . . ., Such a contrast destroys grammatical prejudices and makes it possible for us to see the use of a word as it really is . . .'

Section 422

1   This and the following five remarks explore the fact that we have, laid up in the forms of our languages and in the metaphors and similes we use as a matter of course, a *picture* of the mental and of its relation to the physical, of the soul and of its relation to the body. It is one of the great strengths of W.'s approach that he does not dismiss these pictures as false

proto-theories. Philosophical theories grow out of these pictures, but only through their misinterpretation. The pictures themselves are, as it were, emblematic illustrations of concepts, iconographic representations of grammatical structures (cf. PI §295). And just as we should look at the sentence as an instrument and at its sense as its employment, so too we should view these word-pictures as illustrations and learn their point by examining their applications.

To believe that men have souls or minds is not *per se* to believe in a Cartesian dualist metaphysics. Rather it is to cleave to a certain form of representation of human experience, human relations, and human values. This readily seems mysterious, even mystery-mongering. Hence W. appositely invokes a scientific picture to place beside it. For when we are taught about carbon rings, we do not typically feel metaphysical qualms; nor do we think that we are being hoodwinked. But this involves a picture too, and its sense is difficult to discern. In both cases we need to examine the application of the picture.

1.1   (i) 'What am I believing in when I believe that men have souls?': not, to be sure, that somewhere within the body there is an ethereal object called 'the soul'. PI p. 178· discusses the religious doctrine that the soul continues to exist after the disintegration of the body:

> Now do I understand this teaching? – Of course I understand it – I can imagine plenty of things in connection with it. And haven't pictures of these things been painted? And why should such a picture be only an imperfect rendering of the spoken doctrine? Why should it not do the *same* service as the words? And it is the service which is the point.

Here the picture, e.g. of the soul (represented by a homunculus) leaving the body, is on the same level as the words. In such cases, understanding consists in noting the role which words and picture play in a form of life.

(ii) 'this substance contains two carbon rings': PI p. 184 remarks of the proposition 'The carbon atoms in benzene seem to lie at the corners of a hexagon' that 'this is not something that seems to be so; it is a picture'. To unpack this picture, to survey its application, involves extensive explanations of chemical theory.

2   Something similar can be said of certain literal pictures, e.g. Michelangelo's depiction of God creating Adam in the Sistine chapel (LA 63). A picture of a plant in a botanical handbook is a picture by similarity. Its role is to enable us to identify the plant; it tells us what the plant looks like. This sort of picture therefore has a familiar, straightforward application and a readily understood technique of comparison. Not so the depiction of God: it does not purport to tell us what God *looked like* when he created Adam, and it would be absurd here to say 'Of course, I

can't show you the real thing, only the picture' (as one might say of a historical painting). The role of such a picture is of a totally different kind, and to describe its application is a far more difficult and subtle matter than in the case of the picture of a plant; and so too with our word-pictures of the soul.

SECTION 423

1   It is unclear what the expression 'these things' refers to here. Presumably W. is alluding to such psychological turns of phrase as 'A thought flashed through his head', 'He said in his heart . . .', 'In my mind I saw . . .'. In such cases we use expressions into which a certain picture (not a theory) is built. It is not in dispute that these things happen, that thoughts flash through people's minds, that they see things before their mind's eye. These are the pictures we use, and their validity is not in question. But when doing philosophy, it is important that the applications of these pictures be clarified, lest we be misled by the pictures into constructing philosophical theories or, worse, into criticizing our ordinary ways of expressing ourselves as embodying false theories.

2   Vol. XII, 324 has this in a different context. W. discusses the remark 'It is fate'. What information does one convey to another by saying this? None at all, and yet it is not empty chatter. It gives a picture, a comparison; and it would be wrong to suppose that it is replaceable by a literal interpretation. For only by means of *that* simile and no other can one articulate, give expression to, one's response or attitude. PI §423 follows this remark, and is followed by

Denk wir drückten die Absicht eines Menschen (immer) so aus, indem wir sagen: 'Er sagte gleichsam zu sich selbst: Ich will . . .' Das ist das Bild. Und nun will ich wissen: wie verwendet man den Ausdruck 'etwas gleichsam zu sich selbst sagen'. Denn es heisst nicht: etwas zu sich selbst sagen.

(Imagine that we (always) expressed a person's intention by saying: 'He as it were said to himself: I want . . .' This is the picture. And now I want to know how one applies the expression: 'As it were saying something to oneself'. For it does not mean: saying something to oneself.)

This is then followed by a draft of PI §424.

SECTION 424

1   This repeats the point of §423 and adds an illustrative example. There is nothing wrong with the picture of blindness as darkness in the soul or

in the head of the blind man. One can represent blindness thus: ,

as opposed to (⊛) ; but this picture does not dictate its own applica-

tion, any more than does the explanation 'He is blind who cannot see'.
The question is, what are the criteria for saying of a person that he is
blind? And similarly, when do we say of a person that *this* is how it is in
his head (cf. Vol. XII, 232).

2   RFM 142 observes: 'You cannot survey the justification of an expression unless you survey its employment; which you cannot do by looking
at some facet of its employment, say a picture attaching to it.'

SECTION 425

1   Typically pictures, both literal and verbal, can illuminate the use of an
expression in as much as we find the application of the picture obvious
and unproblematic. An example is given in §425(b): the picture does not
explain, but its application is perspicuous, surveyable at a glance. (And
this, indeed, is characteristic of illustrative diagrams in mechanics or
instruction manuals.) So the picture can illustrate the application of an
expression.
     However, in the case of the pictures we have of the mental, things are
quite different. The pictures are readily available; indeed, they force
themselves upon us. We think of sensations as especially private property, something which we *have* and which we are intimately *acquainted*
with (like a beetle in a box that no one else can see). We conceive of
imagining as akin to sitting in on a private viewing, that we 'see' our
own mental images, which our neighbour cannot see (cf. PI §398). We
are captivated by the idea that thinking is a mental activity, just like a
physical activity, only mental! In all these cases the picture not only does
not help us out of the difficulties we have *when philosophizing*; it
exacerbates our difficulties and is often one of their causes. For *these*
pictures, typically derived from the physical domain, are *not* applied in
the way which we naturally anticipate; i.e. they are not applied as the
corresponding pictures of physical objects, processes, and activities are.

SECTION 426

1   The picture we have, e.g., of pain, the picture that forces itself upon us
at every turn because it is built into our form of representation, seems

utterly perspicuous. I have a pain; you have a pain; i.e. you have exactly the same as I have when I have a pain. What could be clearer? But when we compare the actual use of 'He has a pain' with that suggested by the picture of *having an object*, it seems muddied, a kind of second best. If only, as Hume put it, 'we could see clearly into the breast of another, and observe that succession of perceptions, which constitutes his mind'![8]

Here, in the philosophy of psychology, we have a predicament analogous to something we find in set-theory, viz. a form of expression which seems to be designed for a god who can see, for example, the whole of each of the infinite series of natural numbers, rationals, reals, etc. and see that the set of reals is greater than the set of natural numbers. Hence too, it seems that, while we cannot 'see clearly into the breast of another' but must make do with an indirect route, a superior being would be able to 'see into human consciousness'.

We cannot do what this superior being can, for we lack his cognitive powers. So when *we* use these expressions, our technique of application, relative to that suggested by the picture embodied in their *form*, is a detour, an indirect route. The form of our expressions suggests a straight highway (viz. peering into the mind of another person, correlating the members of one infinite set with another, just as we correlate cups and saucers, etc). But that highway is closed off to us.

Of course, there *is* no such highway, only the picture of one. And it is permanently closed to us only in the sense in which we cannot walk down the painted highway in a picture. For the bounds of sense do not prevent us from venturing into territory in which someone *can* walk; they fence us off only from the void of nonsense.

2   Vol. XII, 162 has this in the context of a discussion of 'ownership' of experience and of the transition from 'I have . . .' to 'He has . . .'. The difficulties we encounter here stem from the fact that we have a picture which makes us expect an application of our expression which is quite different from its actual one.

2.1   'designed for a god': cf. PI §352, where it is said that God can *see* whether there are four consecutive sevens in the expansion of π, whereas we cannot. In PG 484, W. pin-points the incoherence: if we say that we cannot, but that a 'higher intellect' can, grasp an irregular infinite decimal, then we must describe the *grammar* of the expression 'higher intellect'. We must specify what it can grasp (what can intelligibly be specified as being so grasped) and what it cannot; and further, in what circumstances it is correct to say 'It has grasped . . .'. But then it will emerge that describing grasping here *is* itself grasping. And in the only sense in which a higher intellect can grasp, so too can we!

[8] Hume, *Treatise of Human Nature*, Bk. I, Pt. iv, Sect. 6.

Section 427

1   This concluding remark makes clear the sense in which the picture associated with thinking is in order, but does not have a straightforward application. When we wonder what is going on in someone's head, we are expressing not our ignorance of neurophysiology, but our ignorance of what someone is thinking. The picture of an inner process in the cranium is, of course, misleading when doing philosophy; for the use of the phrase 'He is thinking of . . .' is not to describe any such process. But in ordinary discourse this very picture *is* applied unproblematically, only not in the way in which we apply 'I wonder what is going on in his stomach'. Moreover, even if a god could 'peer into' the consciousness of another, he could not see there, for example, what that person was intending (cf. PI p. 217) or indeed thinking, but only what goes on when someone intends to do such-and-such or is thinking of so-and-so.

2.1   'going on in his head': LW §978 remarks that one does not *have* to see the external as a façade behind which mental powers are at work. And when someone talks about himself quite sincerely, one is not tempted by that picture.

———————

CRITERIA

1. *Symptoms and hypotheses*

From 1932/3 the term 'criterion' crops up with moderate frequency in Wittgenstein's writings and lectures. It occurs in the course of reflections on logic (e.g. in emphasizing the differences between various criteria for the truth of general statements (LFM 270), which show that the grammars of 'All men', 'All the colours of the rainbow', 'All cardinal numbers', etc. are quite different). It crops up in discussions of mathematics (e.g. in examining the relation of proof to truth or in arguing that equinumerosity of finite sets and equinumerosity of infinite sets involve distinct concepts). It plays a prominent role in the elucidations of powers and abilities and also in Wittgenstein's investigations into meaning and understanding. And, most obviously, it occupies a salient position in his philosophical psychology.

Nevertheless, Wittgenstein's explicit explanations of what he meant by 'a criterion' are few and brief. Indeed, the main explanation in the *Blue Book* seems inadequate and ill fitted to his later use of the term. It is clear enough that he is concerned with a logical or grammatical relation which, at least in some forms, has gone unrecognized by philosophers and logicians. Certainly the formalization of logic that has flourished during the last century has made no room for a relation of presumptive implication or defeasible support; and to the extent that Wittgenstein's use of the term 'criterion' signifies such a relation, to that extent it falls outside the received scope of reflection on logical relations.

It is hardly surprising, therefore, that it should have given rise to controversy, bewilderment, and misinterpretation. It has been argued that it is a pivotal notion in Wittgenstein's later theory of meaning or semantics. Elaborating further, it has been suggested that it is embedded in an assertion-conditions or assertability-conditions theory of meaning which stands in contrast to Wittgenstein's earlier truth-conditional semantics. And this in turn is held to be an aspect of Wittgenstein's shift from a realist to an anti-realist theory of meaning and metaphysics.

If the discussions and arguments of this Analytical Commentary approximate to Wittgenstein's intentions even remotely, it is clear that such interpretations are wildly off course. Wittgenstein was not rejecting the philosophy of the *Tractatus* in order to replace it with an alternative metaphysics, and he was not engaged upon the construction of anything that could be called a theory of meaning, for he would have viewed any such enterprise as chimerical. It is doubtful whether there is any deep sense in which the *Tractatus* can be called 'realist' (save by contrast with nominalist), and it is evident that there is no significant sense in which the later philosophy can be viewed as anti-realist. Wittgenstein was not taking sides in the muddled controversies of the 1970s and 1980s, and his reflections cannot be fitted into the misconceived pigeon-holes currently in vogue. The premises upon which these latter-day controversies stand would all be rejected by him as dogmas, absurdities, and misunderstandings.

If we are to obtain a clear picture of his use of the term 'criterion', we must eschew theory and engage in patient description. It is far from obvious that it is a technical term or term of art. As we shall see, it converges substantially, though not uniformly, with the ordinary use of the word. It is not part of a *theory* of meaning, but a modest instrument in the description of the ways in which words are used. As we should expect if we have followed Wittgenstein thus far, it plays a significant role in his philosophy, but not by way of a premise in an argument, nor by way of a theory. 'An "inner process" stands in need of outward criteria' (PI §580) is not a thesis from which philosophical propositions are proved. It is a synopsis of grammatical rules that determine what we call 'the inner'.

Although it is not a theoretical term in Wittgenstein's philosophy, the word 'criterion' was the heir to an expression which could, with some justice, be called 'theoretical', one which was embedded in a philosophical account which might be viewed as a theory (even though its author did not see it thus). For part of the role fulfilled by the symptoms/hypothesis relation in Wittgenstein's brief 'phenomenalist' or, as he called it, 'phenomenological' phase in 1929/30 was taken over by the concept of a criterion. However, in the process all the theoretical baggage was shed, and at the same time the later conception of philosophy as descriptive in method and therapeutic in goal rapidly evolved (see esp. 'The Big Typescript', pp. 406 – 36).

It is illuminating to view the role of the concept of 'criteria' in Wittgenstein's later philosophy against the background of his earlier conception of symptoms and hypothesis. This serves to highlight similarities and differences. The notion of a hypothesis, as used in the *Philosophical Remarks*, is itself a remote heir to an undeveloped idea already present in the *Tractatus*. Hence it is from the latter work that the story must begin.

Elementary propositions, as conceived in the *Tractatus*, are essentially bipolar. They determine a logical space, which reality either occupies or leaves empty. If things are as an elementary proposition describes them as being, then the proposition is true; otherwise it is false. The fit between description and reality is sharp; there is no such thing as a vague elementary proposition which is neither clearly true nor clearly false.

Molecular propositions may indeed be vague; they may give reality a certain latitude as it were, but the vagueness must be determinate. For the freedom left to reality is a reflection of the fact that the relevant molecular proposition is disjunctive, leaving open various possibilities. But *which* possibilities are thus left open must be perfectly determinate. Whereas elementary propositions were held to be independent, molecular propositions enjoyed relations of implication, incompatibility, etc. All such logical relations between propositions were conceived as consequences of the combinatorial complexity of the molecular propositions.

Relatively little was said in the *Tractatus* about scientific propositions, and what was said was exceedingly obscure. What Kantian philosophy conceived of as metaphysical principles of nature, e.g. the principle of sufficient reason, the law of conservation, the laws of continuity and of least effort in nature (TLP 6.321, 6.34), are expressions of *a priori* insights concerning the forms in which the propositions of science can be cast. Such principles are not genuine propositions describing reality, but normative principles determining the general forms of laws. A particular scientific theory, such as Newtonian mechanics, 'determines one form of description of the world by saying that all propositions used in the description of the world must be obtained in a given way from a given set of propositions – the axioms of mechanics. It thus supplies the bricks for building the edifice of science, and it says, "Any building that you want to erect, whatever it may be, must somehow be constructed with these bricks, and with these alone" ' (TLP 6.341). Whereas the metaphysical principles of nature merely determine forms of laws, the so-called laws of nature are concerned, albeit indirectly, with the objects of the world (TLP 6.3431). They *construct*, according to a single plan (i.e. a chosen system of forms of laws, such as Newtonian mechanics), the true propositions that we need for the description of the world (TLP 6.343). These laws are not themselves descriptions of necessities in the world, however, for the only necessity is logical necessity (TLP 6.37). Nor are they explanations of why things happen as they do (TLP 6.371). Rather, in formulating natural laws within the constraints of a chosen physical theory, we are guided by the principle of induction, according to which we opt for the *simplest* law that can be reconciled with our experience (TLP 6.363). The law is then employed as a basis for predictions, on the *assumption* (which has no *logical* justification) of simplicity and uniformity. Hence, it seems, laws of nature are best viewed as rules for the derivation of predictions.

When Wittgenstein resumed philosophical work in 1929, he turned his attention to what in the *Tractatus* he had conceived of as 'the application of logic'. It is evident both from the 1929 manuscripts and from the lecture 'Remarks on Logical Form' that he did not see himself, initially at least, as overturning his first philosophy. The project of cooperating with Waismann on the production of *Logik, Sprache, Philosophie*, intended as the first volume of the Vienna Circle's *Schriften zur wissenschaftlichen Weltauffassung*, was advertised in the Manifesto of the Circle in 1929 and again in *Erkenntniss* (1930/31) as being 'in essentials a representation of the ideas of Wittgenstein's *Tractatus*. What is new in it and what essentially distinguishes it is the logical ordering and articulation of these thoughts.'[1] It seems, then, that his first efforts were conceived as further elaborations of the fundamental ideas of the *Tractatus*, together with what may initially have appeared to be modifications and improvements. What collapsed immediately was the logical atomism. The colour-exclusion problem led to the idea of a *Satzsystem*, and the independence of the elementary proposition was accordingly relinquished. Among these early modifications, which ultimately led to the disintegration of the philosophy of the *Tractatus*, was the introduction of the distinction between genuine propositions and hypotheses.

Genuine propositions are descriptions of what is immediately given (WWK 97). They are phenomenological statements (WWK 101) or judgements about sense-data (LWL 66) or 'primary experience'. Hence typical examples of genuine propositions are 'I have a pain' (or 'It hurts', 'There is a pain') or 'It seems as if there is a sphere in front of me'. Genuine propositions are conclusively verified or falsified by being compared with reality, i.e. immediate experience. They are either true or false, but not probable. Indeed, it is senseless to say 'There probably appears to me to be a sphere in front of me' (PG 222). Here there is no gap between appearance and reality, between seeming and being; for it makes no sense to say 'It looks as if there seems to be a sphere here' (PG 221).

Hypotheses, however, have a quite different grammar and constitute an altogether different kind of grammatical structure (WWK 210). They are not genuine propositions at all (or, one might say, they are propositions in a different sense), but rather, are laws for constructing genuine propositions (WWK 97, 210; PR 285). Propositions about material objects, about the experiences of other people, as well as laws of nature are hypotheses (PR 94f., 286; WWK 100f.). They stand in a different relationship to reality from genuine propositions, for they can be neither conclusively verified nor conclusively falsified (WWK 100). They are not true or false at all (PR 283), or not true or false in the same sense (PR 285), but only more or less probable. Nothing forces us to adopt a given hypothesis; but considerations of simplicity, con-

---

[1] *Wissenschaftliche Weltauffassung der Wiener Kreis*, published by Ernst Mach Society (Artur Wolf Verlag, Wien, 1929), p. 47.

venience, and predictive power constitute good grounds for accepting a hypothesis.

Wittgenstein used various metaphors and similes to illuminate the relationship between genuine propositions and hypotheses. One can conceive of genuine propositions as sectional cross-cuts through the connected structure of a hypothesis (WWK 100). They stand to a hypothesis as determinate points on a graph to the straight line that connects them (PR 285) or as the different views or aspects of a material object to the material object *per se* (PG 220). Indeed, the latter comparison is not merely a simile, but an instance of the relationship. For the very notion of an object involves a hypothesis connecting the multiple phenomenal aspects which we experience. The descriptions of our immediate perceptual experiences are determinately true or false, directly verifiable by comparison with the given; but a hypothesis enables the prediction of future experiences. The genuine propositions that give evidential support to a hypothesis Wittgenstein sometimes called 'symptoms' (WWK 159; M 266f.).[2] Symptoms are grammatically related to the hypothesis which they support. They render it probable or plausible, but never certain; for there is no such thing as complete or conclusive confirmation of a hypothesis (PR 285). The probability of a hypothesis is measured by the amount of evidence needed to make it reasonable to relinquish the hypothesis (PR 286). But just as there is no conclusive verification of a hypothesis, so too there is no conclusive falsification; for disconfirmatory evidence can always be accommodated by auxiliary hypotheses (WWK 255).

A hypothesis can be viewed as a law unifying actual and possible experiences (LWL 16; PR 285). Unlike a genuine proposition, a hypothesis permits predictions. Thus, for example, the hypothesis that there is such-and-such an object here connects the perceived aspects of an object in a law-governed manner and licenses predictions about subsequent experiences (WWK 256).

It is plausible to suppose that when Wittgenstein introduced the distinction between genuine propositions and hypotheses he was generalizing his remarks about natural laws in the *Tractatus* while liberalizing the rigid, sharply defined conception of a proposition in that book. The bulk of our everyday propositions seemed clearly to be hypotheses, since the concept of an object inevitably involves the notion of a hypothesis to order, systematize, and simplify the description of the flux of experience.

---

[2] See also F. Waismann, 'Hypotheses', in his *Philosophical Papers*, ed. B. McGuinness (Reidel, Dordrecht, 1977), pp. 38 – 59. This essay was intended as a chapter for *Logik, Sprache, Philosophie* and is derived from Wittgenstein's notes and dictations. The full German version is printed as an appendix to the German edition of *Logik, Sprache, Philosophie*, ed. G. P. Baker and B. McGuinness (Reclam, Stuttgart, 1976).

These propositions are not analysable into truth-functional combinations of elementary propositions or of sense-datum statements. But the relation between symptom and hypothesis is a grammatical, not an empirical, one. That such-and-such symptoms render a hypothesis probable is determined *a priori*, and is not a consequence of experienced (inductive) correlation. The support which a symptom or set of symptoms gives to a hypothesis always falls short of entailment, and a hypothesis can, in principle, always be overturned by subsequent experience. In this sense the evidential support is defeasible; although it would appear that whether defeating evidence suffices to undermine a hypothesis is conceived to be a matter of choice turning largely on considerations of simplicity and convenience. It is important to note that in the *Tractatus*, apart from the brief, undeveloped remarks on natural laws, there was no room for such a logico-grammatical relationship. The official doctrine there was that all logical relations are a matter of entailment, i.e. the inclusion (or exclusion) of the sense of one proposition in (or from) the sense of another.

2. *Symptoms and criteria*

Wittgenstein did not cleave for long to the conception of the relationship between evidential symptoms and hypotheses. Various considerations led to his abandoning it. The most important was his realization that what he had conceived of as genuine propositions describing immediate experience and conclusively verifiable or falsifiable by comparison with reality have a completely different role and status from that which he had supposed. They are not descriptions, but expressions, of experiences; they do not get compared with reality at all, and are not verified or falsified. For here truthfulness coincides with truth, and the truthfulness of an avowal does not turn on a comparison of a proposition with reality. Secondly, the claim that hypotheses are more or less probable, but can never be conclusively confirmed or rendered certain, has to be rejected on the ground that such a proposition can be said to be merely probable only if it at least makes *sense* for it to be certain. For 'probable' and 'certain' are correlative terms within the language-game of describing features of the world, and if there is no such thing as certainty, then 'probable' cannot have its ordinary sense. To be sure, this was implicitly recognized in the account of hypotheses, since they were not conceived to be descriptions, but rather rules for the construction of descriptions. But with the abandonment of the idea that first-person present-tense perception- and sensation-sentences are the genuine propositions, this conception of hypotheses inevitably collapsed. The assimilation of mundane material-object statements and statements about other people's states of mind to statements of laws in the natural sciences is fundamentally misleading, rendering such humdrum propositions as 'The curtains are red' or 'John has a toothache' hypotheses. Yet these are paradigms of ordinary descriptive, non-theoretical propositions that are verified or falsified by reference to experience.

The relation between a hypothesis and its evidential symptoms was displaced by that between a proposition and its criteria. The concept of a criterion is prominent in the 1932/3 lectures (AWL 17 – 19, 28 – 9, 31, 34 – 5, 59, 62) and is introduced with explicit explanation in the *Blue Book* (BB 24 – 5, 51ff.). Thereafter it occurs fairly regularly, both in Wittgenstein's philosophical psychology and in his philosophy of mathematics. Like symptoms in Wittgenstein's earlier writings, criteria are (a) fixed by grammar and (b) grounds or evidence for a proposition. In a shift of terminology, Wittgenstein now introduced the notion of a symptom as a foil for that of a criterion. Whereas a criterial relation is an *a priori* grammatical one, a symptom is a piece of inductive evidence discovered in experience. That p is a symptom for q presupposes the possibility of an independent identification of q, since the empirical determination of p as symptomatic evidence requires the inductive correlation of two distinct, externally related phenomena (AWL 34f.).

To specify the criteria for the truth of a proposition is to characterize ways of verifying the proposition (AWL 17, 19). It is one way of answering the question 'How do you know that p?' (AWL 18f.; BB 24). What distinguishes a criterion from a symptom in the new sense of the latter term is that criteria are fixed by grammar (PI §322), are laid down in language, in rules, charts, etc. (LPE 293), and in that sense are a matter of *convention* (BB 24, 57; AWL 28). These observations may mislead, and may have misled, philosophers. For the notion of a social convention comes to mind here, and with it the suggestion of choice, and often of relative unimportance ('a mere convention') and arbitrariness. With these associations in mind one may wonder how Wittgenstein can claim that the criteria for someone's being in pain are a matter of convention. For, to be sure, no committee resolved to *adopt* these criteria as conventions. That pain-behaviour is a criterion for a person's being in pain is not a matter of arbitrary decision which could just as well have been utterly different, like conventions of dress.

The objection is misplaced, however. Of course, in certain cases, e.g. in introducing new terminology in the course of constructing a theory about a certain phenomenon, one may stipulate criteria, lay down what evidential grounds are to justify the application of a new term (AWL 18). The stipulation of the criteria determines the grammar of the new expression in as much as it determines its use. But clearly these are not the cases Wittgenstein typically has in mind. His claim that the criteria for propositions about the inner or about powers and capacities are a matter of convention is intended to draw a contrast between what is normative and what is empirical discovery. To explain the criteria for toothache, for joy or grief, intending, thinking, or understanding is not to describe an empirical correlation that has been found to hold. For criteria, unlike symptoms (inductive correlations), determine the meanings of expressions for which they are criteria. To explain the criteria for the application of an expression 'W' is to give a grammatical explanation of 'W'. It explains what we *call* 'W', and so explains a facet of the use of the word (AWL 17 – 19). To say that q is a criterion for W is to give a partial explanation of the meaning of 'W', and in that sense to give a rule for its correct use.[3] The fact that the criterial relation between q and W may be neither arbitrary (in one sense at least) nor stipulated, that in innumerable cases we could not resolve to abandon this normative relationship without a change in our form of life, and in many cases could not abandon it at all, does not imply that it is empirical, let alone that it is a matter of *Wesensschau*. We may concede that certain concepts are deeply embedded in our lives, occupy a pivotal role in our thought and experience, yet still insist that their use is rule-governed, a matter of *nomos* rather than *phusis*.

Like the earlier symptoms/hypothesis relation, the criterial relation provides grammatically determined grounds for a proposition. If a criterion for p's being the case is exemplified in appropriate circumstances, then there are good grounds for judging p to be the case. This much, to be sure, is a feature of the ordinary use of the term 'criterion'. Wittgenstein's new use of 'symptom', however, is much wider than we would ordinarily countenance, since any inductive evidence for something counts as a symptom. Where the criterial relation *differs* from the earlier symptoms/hypothesis relation is in its connection with truth, verification, and knowledge. Hypotheses, Wittgenstein had earlier argued, are not true or false, or not true or false in the same sense as genuine propositions. They can neither be conclusively verified nor conclusively falsified. *A fortiori* they cannot be known to be true. Hypotheses are convenient, plausible, or probable, but they cannot, logically, be certain. Criteria, however, are said to be given in answer to the question 'How do you know?' (AWL 17 – 19, 28; BB 24f.), with the proviso that inductive grounds are symptoms, rather than criteria. Propositions the sense of which is partially determined by criteria, e.g. propositions about capacities or the experiences, thoughts, or intentions of other people, are true or false. Criteria constitute justifying grounds for their assertion, and hence are ways of telling whether they are true (BB 57; LPE 293; PI §182), reasons for judging things to be thus-and-so. The criteria for something's being the case, *at least in some instances*,

---

[3] Of course, that is not to say that any rule for the use of an expression is a criterion-specifying rule. Nor is it to say that every expression is used on criterial grounds.

establish decisively, with certainty, that that is how things are. This point will be examined further below.

It was an essential feature of the symptoms/hypothesis relation that there are multiple symptoms for any given hypothesis, just as there are multiple points on a line or multiple cuts through a geometrical structure. A criterion for a given proposition may, in certain cases, be unique. Wittgenstein's explanation of the distinction between criteria and symptoms in the *Blue Book* invokes an example of a concept, viz. angina (tonsilitis), which is defined by a single criterion (BB 25). The criterion for the truth of a mathematical proposition is its proof (LFM 131), and there is nothing unintelligible about uniqueness of proof. Nevertheless, in many cases (including mathematics) criteria are manifold; there may be multiple defining criteria (LSD 20); there are two different criteria for a method of projection coming before one's mind (PI §141); giving correct explanations and using an expression correctly are criteria for knowing what a word means (AWL 48ff.; LFM 20ff.; PI §75); and in different circumstances we employ different criteria for a person's reading (PI §164).

Characteristic of the symptoms/hypothesis relation is the fact that the evidential support which a symptom or set of symptoms gives to a hypothesis can be undermined by further evidence. This feature importantly distinguishes a symptom from a sufficient condition, and allocates to a grammatical (conceptual) relationship a property usually associated only with empirical (inductive) evidence. If p logically implies q, then no matter what other propositions are true, it still implies q. In this sense it is indefeasible. Inductive evidence is different, for however good the correlation between p and q may have been discovered to be (e.g. 99 per cent of X's are men), an additional piece of evidence may undermine the support p gives to q (e.g. this X is a member of the YWCA). Wittgenstein did not, of course, use the (legal) term 'defeasible', but it seems apt to describe a feature of the symptoms/hypothesis relation. Similarly, defeasibility seems to characterize *some* domains in which Wittgenstein employed the term 'criterion'. This is evident in the case of psychological concepts. First, the circumstance-dependence of criteria implies that although p may give criterial support to q in certain circumstances, it will not do so in other circumstances. If someone hits his finger with a hammer and screams, assuages his finger, etc., that establishes that he has hurt himself. However, if all this takes place in a play, then this behaviour counts as acting as if he had so hurt himself. But the defeating evidence is itself defeasible (cf. RPP I §137); for if the actor leaves the stage with a bleeding finger, groaning, etc., then he has obviously accidentally hurt himself. Secondly, the multiplicity of criteria suggests, at least in some cases, the possibility of conflict of criteria. Using an expression correctly and giving a correct explanation of an expression are both criteria for knowing what the expression means. In most circumstances either criterion is a good reason for attributing understanding. But if someone uses an expression correctly, yet cannot explain what it means, or conversely, if he offers an adequate explanation, but misuses the expression, we would not say that he understands the word in question. Indeed, in some cases of conflict of criteria, we would not know what to say. Thirdly, in many circumstances the behavioural criteria for being pleased, annoyed, etc. may be manifest, only subsequently to be undermined by instantiation of the criteria for pretending. Though defeasibility seems to characterize Wittgenstein's construal of psychological concepts and their behavioural criteria, this feature is absent from his explicit explanation of the term 'criterion' in the *Blue Book* pp. 24 – 5 (although present in the subsequent discussion of perception (BB 57)) and from his use of the term in his mathematical writings (see below).

Though the distinction between a criterion and a symptom (inductive evidence) is as sharp as that between a rule and a fact, it is important to note that there is commonly, especially in science, a fluctuation between criteria and symptoms (PI §79). In the *Blue Book* Wittgenstein points out that where a variety of phenomena are found to go together in association with, e.g., a particular disease, it may be impossible in practice to say which phenomenon is the defining criterion of the illness and which phenomena are symptoms, except by making an arbitrary, *ad hoc* decision (BB 25). For most practical purposes it may be unnecessary to make such a decision, and indeed, doctors often use the names of diseases without ever doing so. This need not (though it may) signify a deplorable laxity, precisely because the various phenomena in question regularly coincide. We do not use language according to *strict* rules, and in many such cases it may matter little which phenomenon is taken as definitive and which as symptomatic, or indeed whether the matter is left undecided. Nevertheless, confusions sometimes result from this fluctuation. First, it may seem as if there were nothing at all but symptoms (PI §354). But this would be to confuse an indeterminacy in the rules for the use of an expression with lack of any rules for its use. The fluctuation between symptoms and criteria signifies an indeterminacy in the use, and hence the meaning, of the expression. What even one person takes as symptom and what as criterion will vary from case to case, and in particular philosophical or theoretical arguments concerning a given theory, what counts as criterion and what as symptom will have to be determined by examining or eliciting the manner in which a protagonist uses the relevant correlation on that occasion, viz. as definitive or as empirical. So too, for example, in an argument over the theoretical structure of, say, some part of Newtonian physics, it may well be impossible to determine once and for all what is a symptom and what is a criterion for a given phenomenon. Rather, in the context of that particular argument, it may be determined that if *this* is taken as a criterion for such-and-such, then *that* may be viewed as a symptom, and if that correlation is viewed as inductive, then *this* one should be seen as grammatical. Secondly, the regular coincidence of a variety of pieces of evidence and the absence of any explicit determination of what counts as criterion and what as symptom may in practice lead to confusions due to equivocation and lack of consensus. This may be a consequence of a fluctuation between symptoms and criteria in each person's usage of a term from occasion to occasion. But it may also result from different people using a different element out of a concomitant cluster of phenomena as the defining criterion. Either way, confusions may be engendered. This is nicely exemplified in medical debates over the concept of shock, an issue in which Wittgenstein himself was involved in the Second World War. Depending on how the concept is defined, i.e. what are determined as criteria and what as symptoms, a statement about shock may make good sense or be nonsense. Equally, diagnosis will vary according to the interpretation assigned by different doctors, precisely because the defining criteria vary from one authority to another (equivocation) and from occasion to occasion (fluctuation). Research will be hampered through lack of clear specification of defining criteria acceptable by all, especially in cases in which one is dealing with a set of overlapping but distinct syndromes.[4]

3. *Further problems about criteria*

The survey of the similarities and differences between the symptoms/ hypothesis relation and criterial relations and of the distinction between criteria and symptoms (in the new sense of the term) has established the rough outlines of Wittgenstein's use of the term 'criterion'. To summarize: (a) criteria belong to, or are aspects of, the grammar of the expressions for the use of which they are criteria. Hence (b) they are aspects of, or partial determinants of, the meanings of such expressions; and (c) they are grounds for asserting a proposition, providing justifications for judgements, and hence connected with proof, verification, and knowledge. (d) In some cases at least, there are multiple criteria. (e) In some cases, criteria are defeasible. To sharpen the picture, more light needs to be thrown on the relation between criteria for the application of an expression (or, correspondingly, criteria for the truth of a judgement)

---

[4] See R. T. Grant and E. B. Reeve, *Observations on the General Effects of Injury in Man with Special Reference to Wound Shock*, Medical Research Council Special Report Series, No. 277 (HMSO, London, 1951). This was the project in which Wittgenstein participated at the Royal Victoria Infirmary, Newcastle, during the war. Although not mentioned by name, his hand is evident in the general discussion on the concept of shock.

and the meaning of the expression. That in turn will lead to further elucidations.

Wittgenstein often spoke of criteria as defining expressions. In the *Blue Book* example of angina, the presence of a certain bacillus is said to *define* what it is to have angina (BB 24). In his later lectures on sense-data and private experience he spoke of the defining criteria of something as constituting the nature of the thing (LSD 20). The criterion for carrying out a certain mathematical operation (e.g. adding two integers) defines what it is to perform that operation by reference to the result of the operation (RFM 319). In science we often choose phenomena that admit of exact measurement as the defining criteria for an expression (Z §438). More generally, the criteria for someone's being of an opinion, hoping for something, knowing something, being able to do something, determine what is to be *called* 'being of the opinion', 'hoping', 'knowing', etc. (cf. PI §§572f.).

Similarly, he held that the sense of, e.g., 'A has a toothache' is given by the criterion for its truth, for 'a statement gets its sense from its verification' (AWL 17). Its meaning is given it by the criterion (AWL 18). For 'Asking whether and how a proposition can be verified is only a particular way of asking "How d'you mean?" The answer is a contribution to the grammar of the proposition' (PI §353; see Exg.). To explain one's criterion for someone's having a toothache is to give a grammatical explanation about the word 'toothache' and, in this sense, an explanation of the meaning of the word (BB 24). It is these common criteria which give words their common meanings (BB 57).

A frequent manoeuvre in Wittgenstein's arguments is to show that the presuppositions of his adversary sever the connection between a certain concept and its criteria. When we reflect on visual experience, we are inclined to think that behaviour is no more than a fallible symptom of seeing, for the experience itself is private, and one can see something and not show it. So it seems that only the subject can really know whether he sees or is blind! This is wrong. 'It is clear that we in our language use the words "seeing red" in such a way that we can say "A sees red but doesn't show it"; on the other hand it is easy to see that we should have no use for these words if their application was severed from the criteria of behaviour' (LPE 286). Similarly, it is a crucial feature of the idea of a private language that it severs the concept of pain from the behavioural manifestations of pain that constitute criteria for third-person pain-ascriptions. The language-game with 'pain' involves the criterionless avowal of pain in one's own case, but that presupposes the criteria for third-person ascriptions. These include both natural pain-behaviour and the learnt linguistic extensions of natural behaviour, e.g. the verbal avowal of pain, which is itself a criterion of pain. Our concepts here are erected upon the *normality* of a web of connections, viz. between injury, reactive behaviour, avowal, and subsequent behaviour. The web is not seamless; but were it to unravel, the very concept of pain would blur (as it does in reported cases of lobotomy, where the patient insists that it hurts just as much as before, but that he doesn't mind) and ultimately disintegrate. Again, the sceptical supposition that all behaviour might be pretence severs pretending from its behavioural criteria, and that would make the concept of pretending unusable (Z §571).

These considerations make it clear that the criteria for the use of an expression are bound up with its meaning. Is the meaning of an expression *given* by specifying its criteria? Not necessarily. In some cases in which Wittgenstein employed the term 'criterion' it seems that one *can* say this, e.g. in specifying the criteria for being a triangle (LFM 164) or for having angina (BB 25). In others, he explicitly differentiated *giving* the meaning from *determining* or *helping to determine* the meaning of an expression (AWL 28f.). Screaming in circumstances of injury, assuaging one's limb after having hit it, etc. are criteria for being in pain; but 'to have a pain' does not mean the same as 'screaming and assuaging one's limb in such-and-such circumstances'. Rather, one crucial facet of the use of 'pain' is determined by the fact that this behaviour in these circumstances constitutes a justification for saying 'He is in pain'. Someone who has failed to grasp this does not understand what 'pain' means and does not know how to use it correctly. To specify the verifying criteria for someone's being in pain is to specify *a* rule for the use of 'pain', and in that sense, *part* of its grammar. But it is no less crucial an aspect of the grammar of 'pain' that 'I am in pain' is rightly uttered without grounds, that 'I doubt whether I am in pain' and 'I wonder whether I am in pain' make no sense, and so on.

In as much as the criteria for the use of an expression are in this sense determinants or partial determinants of its meaning, it is not surprising to find Wittgenstein explaining that a change in the criteria involves a change in meaning. For addition (or subtraction) of a criterion forges a new (or severs an old) grammatical link. When scientists find that a certain phenomenon belonging to a cluster of phenomena associated with something admits of precise measurement, they are prone to make it into the defining criterion. Here 'a measurable phenomenon occupies the place previously occupied by a non-measurable one. Then the word designating this place changes its meaning, and its old meaning has become more or less obsolete' (Z §438). Similarly, suppose that we accept a diagram as a proof that a pentagram has as many points as fingers on a hand (LFM 71 – 3). 'This means that we accept a new way of finding out that two things [viz. this hand and that pentagram] have the same number [of fingers and points]. We don't co-ordinate things one with the other now; we just look at this figure. I have now changed the meaning of the phrase "having the same number" – because I now accept an entirely new criterion for it' (LFM 73). Indeed, one of the functions of mathematical proofs is precisely to give us new criteria for equinumerosity or for equality of shape, area, volume, etc. A proof forges a new connection in grammar, and so licenses transformations of empirical propositions which could not antecedently be thus transformed. So too, introduction of new criteria for thinking, desiring, or having motives typically signals a conceptual change. Psychoanalysts erred in thinking that they had *discovered* new kinds of thoughts, desires, and motives, which are just like familiar ones only unconscious. In fact what they had done was to note an array of psychological reactions (e.g. patterns of behaviour and response characteristic of the Oedipal complex) which they brought within the ambit of the concepts of thinking, desiring, or having a motive by introducing a new convention or a new notation. For unconscious thoughts, etc. are not related to (conscious) thoughts as a newly discovered kind of apple is related to Coxes, Bramleys, etc. Rather, a conceptual shift has been stipulated (BB 22f., 57f.). A concept is determined by the rules for the use of an expression, and a change in the rules involves a modification of the concept. Whether we should say that such a change introduces a new concept or merely constitutes a novel extension of an existing one is to some extent a matter of choice, dependent upon what is at stake (BB 58). Failure to notice such conceptual shifts, e.g. in transposing the concept of 1:1 correlation from finite sets to infinite sets, can lead to disastrous confusions.

Criteria are determinants of meaning. They are grammatical or logical grounds for the truth of a proposition. But the kind of logical relation which is involved here is unclear and has been much disputed. Is a criterion a logically sufficient condition or a necessary condition or a necessary and sufficient condition? Or is it decisive for things being thus-and-so *without* amounting to entailment? And how could that be? Or are criteria kinds of evidence which, like empirical evidence, do not amount to entailment, but, like entailment, are determined in grammar? Is that intelligible, i.e. could there be any such thing as necessarily good evidence for something? And if so, could it be decisive?

If we survey Wittgenstein's use of the term 'criterion', we find *prima facie* conflicting accounts. In some cases it seems a criterion is a logically sufficient condition, or even a necessary and sufficient condition for something's being so. In the angina example in the *Blue Book* the presence of a particular bacillus in the blood is said to be *the defining criterion* of angina. 'A man has angina if this bacillus is found in him' is a tautology or a loose way of defining 'angina' (BB 25). In his lectures on the philosophy of mathematics, Wittgenstein spoke of the number of sides of a figure (viz. a closed rectilinear figure in a plane) as a criterion for its being a triangle, and conversely of a figure's being a triangle as a criterion for its having three sides (LFM 164). Similarly, he talked of the

criterion of equinumerosity of sets (LFM 163) and of the proof of a
mathematical proposition as being a criterion for its truth (LFM 131).
These examples suggest that a criterion is a sufficient or necessary and
sufficient condition.

On the other hand, in the subsequent employment of the term
'criterion' in the *Blue Book*, it is clear that it is so used that a criterion is
non-inductive evidence distinct from entailment. One's tactile and
kinaesthetic sensations are said to be criteria for one's finger moving
from one's tooth to one's eye. Here, experiential or perceptual evidence
is a criterion for a proposition about a physical object:

> The grammar of propositions which we call propositions about physical objects
> admits of a variety of evidences for every such proposition. It characterizes the
> grammar of the proposition 'my finger moves, etc.' that I regard the propositions 'I
> see it move', 'I feel it move', 'He sees it move', 'He tells me that it moves', etc. as
> evidences for it. (BB 51)

But, Wittgenstein insists, it is possible for it to *feel as if* my finger were
moving from my tooth to my eye without my finger moving from my
tooth to my eye. The former proposition might be true *without* that for
which it is a criterion being the case. Indeed, we can imagine the visual
criteria (e.g. when I look in the mirror) conflicting with the tactile and
kinaesthetic criteria. If that were so, one might deny that one's finger had
moved thus, even though it felt as if it had. Here it seems that criteria are
conceived to be logical or grammatical grounds or evidence that are
distinct from entailment. They seem to constitute presumptive evidence
which is defeasible by countervailing evidence.

It is significant that this kind of example does not recur in later
writings, with the possible exception of *Investigations* §354 (see Exg.). It
arguably belongs to an earlier phase in his thought, the last remnant of
his 'phenomenological' analysis, which subsequently disappears. This
suspicion is strengthened by the fact that in the context in the *Blue Book*
he still talked, as he later did not, of being 'handicapped in ordinary
language by having to describe, say, a tactile sensation by means of terms
for physical objects such as the word "eye", "finger", etc. We have to use
a roundabout description of our sensations' (BB 52). It is true that in
Investigations, Part 2, he compares the relation of behaviour to inner state
with the relation of sense-impressions to physical object (PI p. 180); but
the point of the comparison is not that in both cases we are dealing with
criteria, but rather that in both cases there is a *complicated* relation which is
distorted by any attempt to reduce it to a simple formula.

However, if we look at Wittgenstein's later use of 'criterion',
especially in the context of his philosophy of mind, it is clear enough that
there is generally a crucial point of continuity with the above passage in
the *Blue Book*. The criteria for 'inner states' or 'inner processes' (PI §580)

are behavioural, but one can behave in such-and-such ways and yet not be in the inner state, and conversely one may be in pain, for example, and yet not manifest it in one's behaviour. Hence the behavioural criteria for being in pain are neither necessary nor sufficient conditions for being in pain. Moreover, criteria are typically multiple, and conflicts of criteria can sometimes occur, typically leading one to withhold judgement. Finally, criteria are circumstance-dependent (Z §492). Hence the criterial support which p gives to q may be defeated. Evidence which in one context suffices to establish that q may fail to do so in another context. Or a subsequent event may defeat the support p gives to q.

How could Wittgenstein fail to notice this equivocation? It seems unlikely that he sometimes employed the notion of a criterion to signify a logically sufficient condition and sometimes to signify logically good evidence. To preserve consistency and to avoid the bewildering notion of *a priori* yet defeasible evidence, it is tempting to argue that one should view a criterion as a necessary constituent of a sufficient condition. For if p is said to be a criterion of q in circumstances C_1, but not C_2, etc., then the conjunction of p with a description of the appropriate circumstances and of the negation of the defeating circumstances would surely amount to a sufficient condition for q.

It is clear that Wittgenstein rejected this move. Two reasons seem to have weighed with him. First, such a manoeuvre presupposes that there is a definitely circumscribable list of conditions (both positive and negative) which is such that if it is satisfied, then it *must* be the case that the person is, say, in pain, sad, thinking, or whatever. But the range of defeating conditions is arguably indefinite, and the defeating conditions themselves are defeasible. Secondly, faithful to the methodological principle that the method of philosophy is purely *descriptive*, that we must look and see how expressions are used, and not construct *theories* about their use, Wittgenstein noted that expressions such as 'to think' are taught under certain circumstances, which the learner does not need to be able to describe. What he must learn is to recognize deviant circumstances as such, and realize that they constitute a reason for withholding a description. But any attempt to characterize the use, the grammar, of an expression by reference to features that have no normative functions in the practice of using that expression will inevitably distort it. Hence his observation

One learns the word 'think', i.e. its use, under certain circumstances, which, however, one does not learn to describe.

But I *can teach* a person the use of the word! For a description of those circumstances is not needed for that.

I just teach him the word *under particular circumstances*.

. . . I cannot enumerate the conditions under which the word 'to think' is to be used – but if a circumstance makes the use doubtful, I can say so, and also *how* the situation is deviant from the usual ones. (Z §§114ff.)

Our grasp of the meaning of psychological verbs, our mastery of their technique of application, is manifest in our using them on the basis of their defining criteria in appropriate circumstances, as well as in the manner in which we teach and explain their use. But a correct explanation of the meanings of these expressions does not require a description of the circumstances in which they are to be used. The complex normative practices that are constitutive of a language-game do not amount to calculi of rules, for 'in general we don't use language according to strict rules – it hasn't been taught us by means of strict rules either' (BB 25). Our explanations of the use of the verb 'to think' do not fall short of what it really means merely because we fail to give an enumeration of all the circumstances in which its use is justified by such-and-such behaviour; indeed, it is doubtful whether there is any such sharply determinate totality. On the other hand, our understanding is defective if, in particular cases, we cannot say or discriminate in what circumstances the expression is to be withheld, e.g. on grounds of pretence, play-acting, parrotting, etc.

If this correctly captures Wittgenstein's thought, then it is not possible to give a uniform account of his notion of a criterion. In some contexts a criterion amounts to a sufficient condition, whereas in others it constitutes grammatically determined presumptive grounds. But it is only if one is misguided enough to think that his conception of a grammatical criterion is part of a novel theory of meaning (perhaps an 'anti-realist' semantics as opposed to a 'realist' or 'truth-conditional' semantics) that one need find any incoherence here. What is constant in his use of this term is that criteria are laid down in grammar (in contrast with symptoms, which are discovered in experience), that they determine or partially determine the meaning, the use, of expressions, and that they are grounds for assertion, justifications for judgements, and answers to the question 'How do you know?' Given that constancy, the further grammatical features of criteria vary from one kind of language-game to another. It should not be expected that what counts as a criterion for the truth of a mathematical proposition should share all the logico-grammatical features of criteria for the truth of psychological propositions. For what it means to say that a mathematical proposition is true is quite different from what it means to say that an empirical proposition is true. The first signifies that a formula belongs to our system of mathematics, that it is a norm of representation integrated by a proof into the vast network of the grammar of number, etc.; whereas the second signifies how things happen to be in the world. There is no temporal dimension to mathematical propositions, hence no circumstance-dependent defeasibility. The contrast with the logical character of, and criteria for, psychological statements could not be greater and should not be at all surprising. These kinds of concepts belong to quite different language-games, and they fulfil very different roles and occupy very different positions in our lives.

Wittgenstein employed the notion of criteria in four distinct domains: (a) in his philosophy of mathematics, (b) in his brief allusions to the fluctuation between criteria and symptoms in science, (c) in his discussions of potentialities, powers, and abilities, both animate and inanimate, and (d) in his philosophy of psychology. There is a parallel between (c) and (d), since many crucial psychological expressions signify capacities rather than states, processes, or experiences. It is in these two domains that Wittgenstein used the term 'criterion' to signify grammatical grounds for a proposition which are distinct from entailment, yet in many cases justify a knowledge-claim. The remainder of our discussion will be concerned exclusively with this notion.

4. Evidence, knowledge, and certainty

It is noteworthy that in the discussion of the grounds for judging something to be possible, to have a power or capacity, as well as in discussing the outer criteria for the 'inner', one seems to be concerned with 'cross-categorial' support. Occurrent properties or past, present, and often subsequent performances are the criteria for potentialities and abilities; similarly, past, present, and subsequent behaviour – the 'outer' – constitutes the criteria for the 'inner'.[5] In both kinds of case it seems, when doing philosophy, as if there were a gulf between two different domains, between actuality and potentiality and between behaviour and the mental. Confused by this misconceived picture, philosophers have been tempted to reify powers on the one hand (and to conceive of them as occult causes of their exercise) and mental phenomena on the other (conceiving of sensations or sense-impressions as 'inner objects', these likewise being cast in the role of causes of their behavioural expression). When the *grammatical* differences between powers and their actualization and between the mental and the behavioural are construed as *reflections* of ontological realities, then the apparent gulf between distinct 'ontological realms' also seems to be reflected in a gap in our reasoning about powers or about the 'inner'. For our judgements rest on grounds which do not *entail* the existence of powers or experiences. We often judge a person to have the ability to ϕ, e.g., on the basis of his past performances. But one

---

[5] Whether someone had the ability to ϕ at time t is often manifest in what he does at time t_1, and what someone meant is frequently exhibited by what he later says.

cannot say that having ϕd n times in the past *entails* that the person has the ability to ϕ. We justify the judgement that a person is in pain by reference to his current behaviour. But one cannot say that this behaviour *entails* that he is in pain. Consequently, scepticism breaks out, and it seems that we can never really know whether a person is able to ϕ or is in pain, that our judgements are at best probable and never certain, for our evidential grounds are never really adequate.[6]

It was Wittgenstein's aim to cure philosophy of these diseases of the intellect. Ontology is only a shadow in the Platonic cave, a projection of grammatical structures. To resolve our philosophical difficulties, we must turn away from these shadows and examine the distinctive grammars of the problematic expressions, describe the language-games in which they occur. In both domains Wittgenstein employed the notion of a criterion, not as a technical term within a novel theory, but as a humdrum expression useful in the description of linguistic practice. His main discussion of powers and abilities is in the *Brown Book* (see Volume 1, 'Undersanding and ability', esp. §7). This will not be further examined here, save *en passant*.

Ascription of psychological predicates rests on behaviour in appropriate circumstances. It is what people do and say, how they act and react in certain contexts, that constitutes the justifying grounds for whether they are in pain, perceive things, are cheerful or depressed, are thinking or imagining, etc. The behavioural grounds for such judgements are evidently distinct from entailment. Equally clearly they are not symptoms. It is not an empirical discovery that people scream when they are in severe pain, that they avoid obstacles in their path which they see, and laugh when they are amused. These forms of behaviour, in context, constitute *logical* criteria (Z §466). Wittgenstein frequently explained that such behavioural criteria are *evidence* for sensations, experiences, emotions, or moods, for thinking, remembering, or imagining, and so forth. The use of the term 'evidence' here (e.g. BB 51; PI §641, p. 228; Z §439) is potentially misleading, for the concept of evidence is strongly associated with inductive support, i.e. symptoms. If p is inductive evidence for q, then it makes sense to identify q independently of p. To observe that p falls short of observing that q, as when one observes footprints or fingerprints. In judging that q on the basis of the evidence that p, one is typically inferring from the observed to the unobserved. Philosophical scepticism about other minds is rooted in the insight that the relation between behaviour and inner state cannot conform to the model of

---

[6] The next move on the philosophical treadmill is to espouse one form or another of reductionism, e.g. the reduction of powers to their exercise or to their vehicle or its structure (see Volume 1, 'Understanding and ability', §7) or the reduction of the mental to behaviour (see 'Behaviour and behaviourism').

inductive evidence for a phenomenon. It might be supposed that when Wittgenstein introduced the notion of criterial evidence for the inner as a novel logical relation, viz. as necessarily good evidence for something, he was stipulating or moulding a theoretical concept. The point of this theoretical innovation might then appear to be to demonstrate how one can, *pace* the sceptic, bridge the ontological gulf between the outer and the inner and close the gap in the problematic inference from behaviour to the mental.

This misconstrues Wittgenstein's intentions. There is no 'gulf' between the outer and the inner, any more than there is a 'gulf' between what one has previously done and what one is able to do. The wince of pain, the shriek of agony, the careful nursing of the injured limb are, of course, not themselves sensations. But they are not 'mere' behaviour either, but *pain*-behaviour, logically or grammatically bound up with the concept of pain. There is no 'gap' between criterial grounds for inner states and the propositions about inner states which they support. Hence it is neither necessary nor indeed possible to concoct new logical forms or relations to fill it. Rather, there is a distinctive language-game, which needs to be described in order to curb our tendency to confuse it with a different one and hence to view it as defective by reference to a wrong paradigm. The criterial evidence for the inner falls short of what it is evidence for only in the sense that it does not *entail* it, but not in the sense of falling short of direct observation. Hence 'I observed his behaviour but not his pain' is not like 'I observed the breadcrumbs left on the table, but not the loaf of bread'. If one denies that one can observe another's pain, this is at best like denying that one can checkmate in draughts and not like denying that one can checkmate Fischer. One might, perhaps, deny that one can observe the pains of another person; this is tantamount to emphasizing the grammatical proposition that pains are not visibilia, but are felt or had, not seen. But one cannot deny that one can observe *that* someone is in pain. Granted that pain-behaviour is not itself pain (behaviour is not a sensation!), to observe pain-behaviour is, *ceteris paribus*, to observe that a person is in pain.

We are tempted to think otherwise because we invoke the picture of direct, as opposed to indirect, knowledge and then contrast our judgement that another person is in pain with his avowal of pain, conceiving of the latter as an expression of direct knowledge. But this is misconceived (see 'The inner and the outer', §2). The behavioural criteria for pain are the best possible grounds for judging someone to be in pain; this is precisely how such judgements are justified. But it is misleading to suggest that, as with empirical evidence, i.e. symptoms, they are grounds from which one draws an inference or derives a conclusion. One does not say 'I saw him break his leg and scream, so I concluded that he was probably in pain' or '. . . so I inferred that he was in pain'. Rather, if asked how I knew he was in pain, I might say 'I heard him scream and saw him writhing in pain'. The pain is not identical with its behavioural expression, but it is not hidden behind it either.

As we have seen, our concepts of the inner do not bring behaviour, circumstances, and experience into necessary connection (MS. 169, 68f.). Similarly, our concepts of capacities do not bring past performances and current state, circumstances, and capacity into necessary connection. In both kinds of case we operate with flexible concepts. To imagine what it would be like to operate here with more rigid concepts, we would have to envisage a far greater degree of uniformity and predictability in respect of human behaviour. It is important that when human beings injure themselves and scream, etc., then normally they subsequently behave in such-and-such ways. Similarly, it is important that when people have previously behaved thus-and-so, have been taught in such-and-such ways, and now say 'Yes, I can . . .' or 'Now I understand', then they normally go on to do this or that. These normal regularities of phenomena are, as it were, the gravitational force that holds our language-games stable. Were these regularities in human life different, our language-games would lose their point. Nevertheless, the regularity is not mechanical, nor is it perfectly predictable. And our concepts reflect the irregularity in this pattern no less than the non-uniformity in our reactions to exemplifications of the pattern (see 'The inner and the outer', §3). For inflexible, rigid concepts to be appropriate, we would have to imagine human beings to be much more machine-like, akin to automatons. But they are not, and for that very reason, we would not know where to begin with analogous concepts which did involve necessary connection.[7]

In this area, criterial support is defeasible. But to insist on defeasibility is not to deny the legitimacy of knowledge-claims justified by criteria, let alone to open the door to philosophical scepticism. First, a claim to know that another person is in pain (or is sad or joyful, understands something, is able to read or multiply, etc.) cannot be undermined by the fact that the grounds supporting the claim are defeasible, but only by adducing countervailing grounds that defeat them. If the ordinary criteria for someone's being in pain are exemplified in an appropriate context, then the onus of disproof lies with the sceptic, and the logical possibility of defeat is not a defeating condition. Secondly, admitting the possibility of

[7] It is ironic that some contemporary philosophers and scientists yearn for a scientific millennium in which the 'unscientific', supposedly inadequate psychological concepts of ordinary discourse (absurdly referred to as 'folk psychology') will be replaced by allegedly more appropriate concepts devised by cognitive science. These concepts, derived from computer science, will have none of the elasticity, let alone constitutional uncertainty, of ours. They will be appropriate for the description of machines; and it is no coincidence that such philosophers and scientists talk incoherently of the 'mind/brain' and refer to the brain as the 'mind-machine'.

defeating conditions does not mean denying that there are any grammatical limits to defeasibility. In a particular case it may well be that sceptical qualms can be rejected as unintelligible. If someone is thrown into the flames, etc., it makes no sense to say 'Maybe he is not in pain, but just pretending'. There are circumstances in which one may say that there is no such thing as pretending. More generally, in certain circumstances, nothing *counts* as a defeating condition. Hence we do, very often, know when other people are in pain (PI §246); the truth of a confession is *guaranteed* by the special criteria for truthfulness (PI p. 222); the criteria for a capacity *demonstrate* (*beweisen*) that a person has a capacity (PI p. 181). Here and in numerous other passages Wittgenstein suggested that the criteria for the truth of a proposition justify a knowledge-claim. Similarly, he insisted that propositions such as 'He is in pain' may be as certain as '2 × 2 = 4' (PI p. 224). To be sure, there are logical differences between the certainty of mathematical propositions and the certainty of judgements about the inner, but not differences in the degree of certainty. For 'I can be as *certain* of someone else's sensations as of any fact' (PI p. 224). It seems, both from Wittgenstein's writings in the 1930s and from the *Investigations*, that he conceived of criterial support as decisive, conferring certainty, *ceteris paribus*, and as justifying a knowledge-claim.

It is therefore interesting to discover that in his very last writings, when he discussed the 'constitutional uncertainty' of the inner and the role of 'imponderable evidence' (see 'The inner and the outer', §3), he explicitly introduced the notion of uncertain criteria (*unsicheres Kriterien*). His thoughts here were arguably fragmentary; different inclinations jostle and conflict; and he did not live long enough to revise and polish these final remarks.

Four related features were clearly uppermost in hs mind: (a) the relative unpredictability of human behaviour, the fact that what follows from a sincere manifestation of an inner state or experience is, to a degree, indeterminate; (b) the absence of agreement in our *reactions* to other people's manifestations of the inner, something which stands in marked contrast with our widespread agreement over mathematical calculations on the one hand and perceptual judgements (e.g. about the colours of things) on the other; (c) the cultural relativity of many of the criteria for the inner (viz. not being able to 'find one's way around' with members of an alien culture) and the individualized character of many such judgements (e.g. if I know a person well, I may be absolutely certain that things are thus-and-so with him, yet be unable to convince another, even though I *can* cite the grounds that convince me (PI p. 227); (d) the imponderability of much of the evidence for the inner, especially in matters of subtle nuances of emotional response (thus I, who know the person well, may be quite certain that he is sad or upset, but I may not be able to cite *any* convincing grounds (cf. PI p. 228).

It is the latter three points that disrupt the picture previously delineated. For it is they that are reflected in the fact that in certain circumstances the grounds of judgement for the inner are not decisive, or that they are decisive for me, but not for others who share the same concept. I may be certain that my friend is upset, yet another person may not be, and neither of us is being irrational. How can this be? Criteria are laid down in grammar and are constitutive of the concepts for which they are criteria, yet disagreement in certain cases, 'constitutional uncertainty', is possible! If the grounds of judgement for someone's inner state sometimes turn on intimate acquaintance with the particular person, on cultural differences, or even on imponderable evidence, it is not obvious in what sense they are laid down in grammar or in what sense they partly determine the meaning of the relevant expression. This can seem puzzling, but it is not really so. The grammar of the 'inner' is distinctive and must be described as it is, rather than measured against the yardstick of other, quite different language-games. What is laid down in the grammar of these concepts, in the 'rules of evidence' for the 'inner', is precisely this form of elasticity in application. The grammar here reflects the irregularities in the complex pattern of the outer and the non-uniformity in our reactions to other people's expressive behaviour. Our concepts are so moulded as to tolerate imponderable evidence (although, to be sure, that presupposes ponderable evidence), cultural differences, and better or worse judgement about, and insight into, human beings and their natures.

It was such factors which led Wittgenstein to point out that there can be complete certainty, yet no certain criteria (*kein sicheres Kriterium* (MS. 174, 22)). So too, there is constitutional uncertainty in the language-game. The uncertainty, for example, in recognizing someone's annoyance is not simply an uncertainty about his future behaviour, but 'lies much more in the concept of an uncertainty of criteria' (MS. 173, 92). To be sure, we say of an expression of feeling that 'it appears to be genuine'. But this only makes sense if there is such a thing as 'That is genuine', and if so, there must be a criterion for it. But does it follow that the criterion is certain (MS. 174, 21)? Of course, one may still *be* quite certain about the other person's feelings, yet be unable to cite anything that would justify one's certainty. Nevertheless, there is nothing irrational here. If one knows a person well, this is how one reacts. And although one cannot say what in his behaviour convinces one, one's certainty is taken seriously. For one's description of another person's psychological state, and the conviction with which one gives it, is itself a criterion for one's own response, for one's sensitivity, perceptiveness, and sincerity. One's response is not only or even typically a mere *opinion*, but a sincere (or insincere) reaction. Differences in the patterns of interpersonal reaction are part of the fabric of human life, and it is only to be expected that they should be reflected in our concepts.

The idea that in some cases there are no certain criteria did not, of course, lead Wittgenstein to espouse any form of scepticism. In so far as the concept of a criterion for the inner plays a role in his demonstration of the incoherence of scepticism, it is not because criteria are uniformly decisive. Rather, one salient flaw in the sceptical argument is that concepts of the inner are there severed from *any* criteria, whether they are, in this sense, certain or not. And Wittgenstein's last writings on philosophical psychology do not suggest that there are *never* certain criteria. Introduction of the notion of a penumbra of 'constitutional uncertainty' of the inner manifests his recognition of features in the grammar of the mental which are (at best) distorted and misrepresented in philosophical scepticism. In contrast to the sceptic, Wittgenstein wrote, 'I do not say that the evidence makes what goes on within us *only* probable. For as far as I am concerned, there is nothing missing from the language-game' (MS. 169, 131). The sceptic mistakes the limits of a language-game for shortcomings in the playing of the game. Wittgenstein's concern was to describe the rules of the game, with all their indeterminacy. Recognition of the fact that there can be criteria which are not certain earmarks a further elasticity in our concepts of the mental and characterizes an important facet of our language-game, and hence too of our lives.

INDEX

INDEX

(Since the exegetical part of this book corresponds exactly to PI, this index should be used in conjunction with the original text and its index.)